THE THREAT OF LOVE

In Abby's heart, Alexander was not a Yankee, not the enemy who threatened to destroy all she knew and loved. And as his gentle hand reached out to caress her cheek, she was taken in by his tender ways. But when his hand moved further down—to her slender neck—her mind begged him to stop. Distraught, she turned to leave.... Suddenly, his hand took hold of hers, pulling her into his arms. And before she could protest, his mouth came down for a lingering kiss. Unprepared for the consuming fire that burst within her—an onslaught to her senses—she clung to him, responding to his kiss with a vibrant fire of her own....

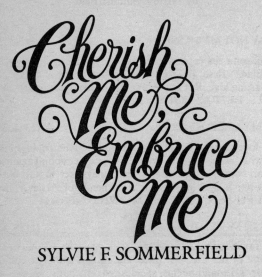

Cherish Me, Embrace Me

SYLVIE F. SOMMERFIELD

ZEBRA BOOKS
KENSINGTON PUBLISHING CORP.

ZEBRA BOOKS

are published by

KENSINGTON PUBLISHING CORP.
475 Park Avenue South
New York, N.Y. 10016

Third printing: November 1984

Printed in the United States of America

To Leslie Gelbman, whose name should have been patience—for all the support and the gentle nudge that kept me going . . .

Prologue

Paris, 1851, Midnight

The closed carriage rattled through the streets of Paris. Dimly lit streets, wet with a steady falling rain. Jules Dubonne sat back against the velvet seat of the rich carriage. His brows were furrowed with deep thought and some painful memories.

The conditions in France after the overthrow of Napoleon was miserable beyond anything which the experiences of Europe presented. Although the defeat of Waterloo visibly ended the war and left France without means of further resistance, armies continued their advance, and aimed to humiliate the unhappy people from whose merciless hand they had endured injuries so deep.

The miseries of the fallen nation were deep, abject and unutterable. The French could not forget the fact that the presence of the Bourbons on the throne was a symbol of humiliation and disgrace.

Jules thought of the new king, Charles X who had succeeded his brother Louis XVIII. Charles remembered well the ruination of his brother and his death, brought about by the revolution.

Jules himself could feel the crisis that was building. It

was the first time in his life he had ever felt fear. The fear was not for himself; it was for his wife and three children. It was also for the first time in his life he had ever considered leaving his beloved France.

He was on his way, at that moment, to a meeting of men who would be considered traitors to the crown. He did not know for sure but he felt a revolution was being planned. He did not know what he would do when the plans were revealed to him, but an idea had already begun to take shape. His thoughts came to a halt the same moment the carriage did. The door was opened for him and he stepped out.

He walked up the steps to the door and rapped twice, a prearranged signal. The door opened and the man who appeared in the doorway to welcome him was one who had been his friend and companion over many years. They had grown up together, received their education together, and fought in the grim and bitter battles of the Napoleonic wars together. Now they were to face the most difficult battle of their lives, and make a decision that would affect them for the balance of their days.

"Jules," he said quietly, the sound of relief in his voice.

"I am sorry to be late, Emil."

"It's all right Jules as long as you're here."

"You sound upset, Emil, what has gone wrong?"

"These ... these imbeciles. They are talking revolution."

"Again?" Jules said bitterly. "Have not enough young Frenchmen shed their blood? Do they want more slaughter? We are exhausted."

"You come and speak Jules. Your voice is heard above mine. You come and tell them that this is insanity."

Jules nodded and followed Emil who moved rapidly ahead of him toward a lighted study.

Several men sat about the comfortable room. Men who were his friends, men he had fought and shed blood with. Men whose course of action he was going to try desperately to change.

He greeted each man and was greeted warmly in return. After he was made comfortable with a drink and a good cigar, the conversation began to flow about him. As the midnight hour stretched into early morning, Jules realized that his arguments were falling on deaf ears. He also began to realize that he could not again fight in an unwinnable revolution. Another dim thought began to flicker in the recesses of his mind. The small germ of an idea began to take hold and grow. The meeting ended unresolved and other meetings were planned. As Jules reentered his carriage and sat back in the seat he opened his mind. His mind drifted to a conversation he had overheard. He had been out one evening with some of his and Marie's friends. They had gone to the theatre, then on to dinner. After dinner, the men had taken a few moments to have a drink together.

Jules could not help overhearing the conversation between two men who sat near him. They spoke of a country on the other side of the ocean. A country that had fought for its freedom and won it. Fought against unbelieved odds, fought a country that had been a dominant power in the world.

"America," he mused. As he listened he began to wonder what this new country was like. He rose and went to their table.

"Gentlemen," he smiled. "I could not help overhearing your conversation. I must say that what I heard intrigues me. Would it offend you if I were to join you and ask a few questions?''

Both men rose and extended their hands. ''Not at all, sir,'' one smiled. ''It will be a pleasure to share a drink and answer any questions you might have.''

''I am Jules Dubonne.''

''Yes, I know,'' the second man chuckled. ''In fact there is not a man in this room who does not know you, sir. Your reputation precedes you.''

''I am Carl Rossman.''

''Ah, yes, Monsieur Rossman,'' Jules replied. ''I too, have heard of you. The stability of your bank is well known.''

''Thank you. This is my colleague, Monsieur James Galbreath, a friend from the country of which we were speaking.''

''What you have been saying interests me a great deal. Do you mind if I ask a few questions?''

''By all means, sir, please join us.''

Jules did, for a very lengthy and a very enlightening evening.

Now his thoughts returned to the present. To Marie, his wife, to Alexander and Dante, his young sons, and to Celeste his daughter ... to escape, and to a new and different future for his family. A safe future, free of war, of hatred and of bloodshed ... somewhere in a new place where freedom dwelt.

One

The sun had barely crested the horizon, its tentative rays leaping from shadow to shadow spreading its golden light. Marie Louise lay wide awake and listening intently as she had been most of the long night.

She listened for the approach of the carriage that would bring her husband home from the strange nocturnal visits he had made so often in the past few weeks.

Fear held her, fear that drew her back in time. Back to the days when she had just met Jules Dubonne. Handsome, gallant, Jules Dubonne, who was an officer in the army of the brilliant general Napoleon Bonaparte. Marie was the only child of a prosperous innkeeper. She had been a happy girl, quick to laugh, with sparkling eyes and a sweet disposition. She had served often in the inn for dinner customers, but her parents would not allow her into the tavern when the nighttime customers became a little more rowdy and sometimes intoxicated.

Her life had been a happy one until her father had become ill. The illness had gradually worsened, and with it the inn began to deteriorate. It was too much for her mother whose strength too began to fade.

Then Marie was stunned by the death, first of her father, then, four weeks later, her mother. She was left with an inn that had acquired a large debt.

Grimly determined not to lose what little she had, Marie had worked long intense hours both in the dining room with three other girls she had hired, and in the tavern at night.

But trying to run the business herself was more than she could handle. Merchants who sensed her insecurity because she was a woman, took shameless advantage of her.

Slowly her debts mounted, and slowly she became more tired and discouraged and very much afraid. The inn was slowly slipping through her fingers. Her greatest fear was for the dark future she seemed to be gazing into.

Then, when she was in her most desperate and blackest moment, Jules appeared. She could not believe he really was so attracted to her, yet he returned again and again. Then he had asked her to join him for dinner. After that Jules put forth a campaign of courtship that swept a breathless Marie off her feet and into his warm and waiting arms.

Their courtship had been a whirlwind affair, and before she knew what had happened, Jules had carried her over the threshold of marriage.

She had been so proud of Jules in his uniform with his sun gold hair and smiling green eyes. She had never lost that pride, and her love had grown in the twelve years they had been married. Twelve years, and they had shared the birth of two sons and a daughter.

Then had come the battles. One after another, and for a while the army of Napoleon seemed to rule the world.

She was the only one who knew that Jules had come to hate the deaths of the young men in his command, and the pain and despair their deaths brought.

Marie rose from the bed in which she could find no peace or rest until Jules shared it with her. Slowly she walked to the window and looked out.

Marie was a slim delicate woman. The morning sun glistened on her pale gold hair and its glow was reflected in her purple blue eyes. She turned from the window when she heard the footsteps outside her door. The door opened and Jules was there. She ran across the room and threw herself into his arms. His arms crushed her to him and his lips sought hers in what seemed to her like a kiss of desperation.

"Jules . . . Jules," she whispered.

"Such a reception," he chuckled. "You have not slept since I left, have you, my sweet?"

"How can I sleep when you are not here?"

"Ah, ma petite, what about the nights I was away with the army?"

"Do you think I slept then? And I see the same look in your eyes tonight that I did then. What is happening Jules? You must tell me."

"Yes, you are right, cherie, I must tell you. I have been turning thoughts over and over in my mind until I am dizzy with them."

"Come sit down, tell me of these thoughts. Maybe if you speak of them, the answers will be clearer in your mind."

In another bedroom, not far from theirs, Alexander Dubonne stirred awake when a small insistent hand shook his shoulder.

"Alexi . . . Alexi . . ." came a tiny whispering voice.

13

"Huh," he groaned and rolled over. He opened his eyes reluctantly, for his dreams had been most pleasant. "Celeste," he whispered, "what are you doing here? Where is Madame Clarey?"

Alexander, at the age of eleven, had shed the aura of babyhood by being moved from the nursery and given his own room. Celeste, at eight, was still under the watchful eye of Madame Clarey, a strict and ever watchful governess. It surprised Alexander that Celeste had been able to slip away without Madame Clarey noticing.

"She thought I was asleep as she went down to talk to Monsieur Ormond."

"Why?"

"I don't know, she talks to him a lot, and sometimes they go to his room and drink tea together."

Alexander was dubious about whether it was tea they drank together, but he said nothing.

Ormond was the teacher for Alexander and his younger brother.

Alexander sat up and braced the pillows behind his head. "Why are you up so early anyway?"

"It . . . it's still dark there, and I'm afraid . . . and I'm cold. Can I stay with you for a little while Alexi . . . Please?"

"Of course you can, come along and get under the covers before you freeze."

He shoved the blankets aside so she could get in and she scrambled under immediately drawing as close to him as she could get.

"What woke you up, Celeste?"

"Papa just came home. I heard his carriage."

"Just came home? You mean now, just now?"

"Yes, just now. I was going to Mama but she and

Papa are talking."

"Oh."

"Alexi," she said in a conspiratorily soft voice, "Papa is not going to go away again, is he?"

"Why do you ask?"

"They're saying that word again."

"What word?"

"The one that always makes Mama cry."

"What are they talking about?"

"About wars and battles and Papa fighting. What's a war, Alexi, and what's a battle?"

Alexander, whose respect and admiration for his father and for his military position was unbounded, had played at war constantly with models his father had given him. It had brought about more than one serious discussion between father and son in which Jules had tried to explain to Alexander the side of war that was not so romantic or rewarding.

"A war is when two countries gather up all their men and fight against each other and try to kill each other. A battle is what they call it when the two armies meet each other."

"Kill each other," she said in a shocked voice. "Why do people want to kill each other?"

"I don't know, Celeste."

"Did ... did Papa ever kill anybody?"

"I suppose he did, after all he fought with the Emperor Napoleon for years."

"Oh, Alexi, I hope Papa does not go away again. I don't want him to ever kill anybody again," she said, tears thick in her voice.

"There's no war now. Maybe Papa was talking about something else."

This silenced her for a moment, then she turned to him, her purple blue eyes wide with fear. "Alexi . . . you won't ever fight in a war, will you?"

"I'm too young," he laughed.

"But, when you grow up, you won't go away, you won't ever kill anybody?" Now her eyes threatened to flood with tears.

To stem the flood of expected tears, he smiled. "No Celeste, I'll never go away and I'll never kill anyone. Don't worry."

"And . . . and you won't let Dante go either will you?"

"I can't exactly tell Dante what to do."

She smiled. "Of course, you can, Alexi. Dante would always do what you wanted him to do. Tell him . . . tell him not to ever go to war or to ever kill anybody."

Sighing with exasperation, yet pleased that Celeste admired him so, he replied. "Celeste, if you'll be good and let me go back to sleep, I'll tell Dante not to ever go to war and not ever kill anybody, all right?"

She nodded and snuggled down into the bed. Alexander closed his eyes with a half smile on his face, but the smile was soon to disappear as he again heard the click of his door.

"Alexi?" came another whisper, "are you awake?"

"Between you and Celeste, I've got no choice. Come on in, Dante."

The boy who crossed the room was very nearly a copy of the boy in the bed. They had the same clear steady green eyes and the same mass of thick burnished gold hair. The second boy, two years younger than the first, crossed the room quickly and bounced upon the bed.

"Alexi," he said. "Today is the day . . . you promised."

16

"Promised?" Alexi questioned, "promised what?"

"Your pony, remember, you said today you'd let me ride. Maybe if Papa could see that I could ride him, he would let me have a pony of my own and Monsieur Ormond could teach me to ride and jump like he did you."

"I know I promised, Dante, but did I say anything about riding before the sun is even up?"

"But Alexi," Dante pleaded, "I want to be able to ask Papa at dinner, and how can I ask him for a pony of my own if I can't tell him I can ride."

Alexander sat up now, giving up all hope of getting any more sleep. He laughed. "Do you expect to learn to ride in one morning?"

"No," the younger boy chuckled. "But I would not be lying to Papa if I told him I had ridden before."

"All right, Dante, you go and get dressed. Celeste, you scamper back to the nursery before Madame Clarey comes for you. I'll get dressed and meet you at the stables."

Dante leaped from the bed and ran to the door, Celeste rose a little more reluctantly. Going back to the quiet nursery was not much to her liking.

Alexander smiled. He knew how hard it was for her. He and Dante had much more freedom and being boys spent more time in the company of their beloved father. He also knew that Celeste harbored a taste for the freedom her brothers shared, and that she was guarded well by the watchful Madame Clarey against such things.

"If you could slip into some clothes quickly, Celeste, I'll take you to the stables with us and maybe give you a ride on my pony."

Her eyes widened in delight. Outside of her parents,

who dwelt in a special place outside of any other relationship, Alexander and Dante filled her entire world. For either of them she would have laid down her life.

"Really, Alexi! Really! You'll let me ride your pony?"

"No, not let you ride alone, Father would skin me, but I'll lead you around. Only if you hurry. Five minutes."

With a small cry of delight, she was gone and Alexander felt it was finally safe to arise and get dressed.

Alexander looked at himself in the mirror as he finished dressing. Clear green eyes met his in the mirror. He was, at this point in his life, probably the happiest boy in the whole of France. Within a month he would celebrate his twelfth birthday. He was tall for his age and showed signs already of being broad of shoulder and strongly built. He was also pleased that he was the son of Jules Dubonne and Marie Louise who held such a position in society. They were wealthy, but beyond that, Alexander admired them both.

His father was a hero, not only in the eyes of France but in the eyes of his family, and it was Alexander's desire to be as much like him as he possibly could.

Their family had always been a close one, and Alexander enjoyed his position as elder brother, and the responsibility it carried with it. There was a camaraderie between him and Dante and they mutually shared a gentle guardianship of Celeste. He just finished the last of his preparations when Celeste returned. She was breathless and her cheeks were pink signalling the haste with which she had dressed.

"I'm ready Alexi."

"Good, let's go before anyone else is up."

They left his room and were met in the hall by Dante. Together the three of them made haste to the stables.

Alexander had been gifted with a pony for his expected twelfth birthday. He took great pride in it and under his father's watchful eye had learned to ride it exceedingly well and exceedingly quickly.

He put a bridle on the pony and led him from his stall, then he set about saddling him while he gave move by move instructions to a very attentive Dante and a wide eyed Celeste. When he turned to them, after the saddling was finished, he smiled.

"Who's to be first?"

Although Dante would have given his life to be first to mount, the sense of gallantry handed down from father to son would not allow this.

"Let Celeste go first. I'll wait."

"Lift her, Dante, I'll hold the pony."

Celeste uttered a giggle of sheer delight as Dante lifted her into the saddle. She grasped the pommel in both hands as Alexander began to walk slowly leading the pony along.

After they had made their way twice about the confines of the paddock, Alexander lifted Celeste down and solemnly handed the reins to Dante who valiantly tried to control his excitement.

Dante's excited laughter floated behind him as he galloped the pony about the track.

Jules and Marie stood at the window of their bedroom and watched the antics of their three children. Jules chuckled at Dante's enthusiastic joy, and the obvious pleasure of the two who were urging him on.

"Look at them, cherie," Jules said softly, as he slid

his arms about her and held her close to him. "They are rare gems, these children you have given me. Do I have the right to sacrifice them all in the name of glory?"

"Are you so sure, Jules?"

"Sure?"

"That what you suspect will really occur?"

"Ah, cherie," he sighed. "I wish I were not so sure. I served too long under Napoleon Bonaparte not to know how all the males in his family tend to think. There will be more war, more bloodshed. It will not be long in coming. Maybe," he added quietly, "just long enough for young Alexi to become old enough to fight."

He saw the fear leap into her eyes.

"Alexander! No Jules, I could not bear it. To see him ride away as you did so often, to know he might be wounded ... killed, no Jules, we cannot let that happen."

"Do not get upset, Marie. It is a long time yet, plans have not been completed. It will give me time."

"Time for what?"

"We must be cautious, Marie. I shall continue to go to the meetings ... but I shall continue to make my plans." He turned her to face him and took hold of her shoulders. Looking down intently into her eyes he said softly. "You trust me, Marie?"

She smiled a slight half smile that held such memories for him. "Have I not always trusted you, my beloved?"

"Then do as I tell you for now, and I will begin arrangements for us to defend ourselves and our children against the inevitable chaos that will occur."

"What do you want me to do, Jules?"

"Be discreet, but find a tutor for our children."

"But they have a tutor."

"One who speaks English."

"English ... why?"

"Because I intend to take you and the children to America. Slowly, I have been sending money there to a friend of mine. He will buy us a home and help us to adjust. It would be better if the children could learn to speak the language before we go."

"America ... leave France?" Blindly she thought of the security this place had brought her after the terrible insecurity she had had after the deaths of her parents.

The house was a beautiful reflection of herself. Its walls cool soft colors. Furniture that had been slowly selected piece by piece until she had created an atmosphere of comfort and serenity.

She thought of her children, happy and well adjusted, absolutely safe in their own minds. What would uprooting them do to them?

She thought also of all the friends she had taken the time and care to cultivate. It would mean leaving everyone and everything she knew and loved.

"I do not like to leave my home any more than you do, Marie, but when I think of my children, then I realize nothing is too much of a sacrifice. You and the children are my world. If we are together then nothing else matters." His eyes held hers. "Will you find it too difficult, my dear?"

Her arms came about his waist and she lay her head against his chest. Closing her eyes she felt the security of his strong arms about her.

"No, Jules, no. You know I would go with you to the ends of the earth if you asked me. Now that the future of our children is at stake there is no more to be said. I shall see to a tutor immediately."

He chuckled and with one arm still holding her close he tipped up her chin and brushed her lips with his.

"You are a woman of great courage, my heart, and I believe I love you more today than I did the first day I met you. As the years go on, you seem to grow more beautiful and more desirable each day."

" 'Tis love that begets love, my beloved husband, and I am grateful *le bon dieu* sent you to me."

Again Jules chuckled as his lips found hers in a kiss that, as always, could take away her breath and any other thoughts but him. Shrill excited laughter interrupted them and they both turned to look again toward the children.

Alexander was shouting encouragement and Celeste was literally bouncing up and down in her excitement. Dante had the pony in a full run and was headed toward a low fence. In a moment it was obvious to both parents he fully intended to jump it.

"Mother of God!" Marie exclaimed. "He has never ridden before! Jules, stop him!"

Jules' hand tightened on hers, but his glowing green eyes held steady on the young boy astride the pony.

Dante's intent gaze held the barrier as the pony grew nearer and nearer. He could hear, in a remote way, his brother's shouted words of encouragement. The pony reached the fence, gracefully she lifted from the grass. Up ... and over with a deliriously happy boy still clinging to her back.

"Bravo, Dante," Jules said softly. "Bravo, my son."

Marie breathed a sigh of relief and sagged against him weakly.

Dante slid from the pony's back and turned to meet

his brother and sister.

"Dante, that was beautiful," Alexander laughed. "But I wouldn't advise you to tell Papa you jumped the fence the first time you rode. First he might not believe you and second he might whip you for doing it."

"But I did it Alexi!" Dante fairly shouted. "I did it!"

"You surely did. I couldn't do that the first time I rode. You're going to be a great rider."

"Will you help me convince Papa at dinner in case he says no?"

"Yes, I will."

"I will too," Celeste said quickly. "I saw you jump the fence. I'll tell Papa you should have a pony of your own. You should have the best pony in the whole stable . . . except for Alexi's."

Both boys laughed at her obvious near worship of her brothers.

The balance of the day followed a repetitive pattern. Lessons for the boys in the small room adjoining the instructors quarters. Lessons that included mathematics, literature, history, Latin and a smattering of geography.

For Celeste, there was time spent with her mother, a late morning outing with Madame Clarey and a short nap in the early afternoon. Usually she would have her dinner early and be in bed before the family had dinner at eight. It was only recently that Dante had been considered old enough to join them and Celeste could barely wait until she were old enough too. Tonight she especially wanted to be there just to be able to add her voice to her brothers and to support Dante in his quest for a pony of his own.

Her mother sat quietly sewing when Celeste tentatively approached her. "Maman."

"Yes, Celeste."

"I have tried to be a very good girl today."

Marie looked up quickly, then a half amused smile touched her lips as she again bent her head over her sewing.

"Yes, Madame Clarey says you are on your best behavior. I am quite pleased. I'm sure Papa will be also."

A moment of silence followed while Marie waited for what she knew was coming.

"I will take my nap early."

"Very good."

"Maman."

"Yes."

"If Alexi and Dante are good they always get some kind of gift or something."

"And you believe you deserve some kind of reward just for being obedient?"

"Oh, Maman ... could I just have dinner with you and Papa instead of in the nursery with Madame Clarey. Please, Maman, I shall be good, and I promise not to spill and I shall be very quiet ... please, Maman."

Marie smiled down into Celeste's pleading eyes. "Well, I see no harm in it. Yes, Celeste, since you have been such a good girl, you may join us for dinner. Have Madame Clarey bring you down just before eight."

Celeste threw herself into her mother's lap and hugged her fiercely, placing a kiss after kiss on her cheek as she chattered happily, "Oh, thank you, Maman, thank you!"

"You had best run along and have your nap or you will surely fall asleep before dinner," Marie laughed.

"Yes, Maman," Celeste kissed her once again before

she left and Marie watched her leave. She felt again the same feeling she had when Jules had told her of their future plans. A strange sense of an impending presence sent a shiver of icy fear through her.

As quickly as it came, it was gone when her usual good sense argued with her vague fear and won. What could happen when Jules was guiding them?

She had just left her room and walked to the head of the stairs, prepared to start down to dinner when the sound of conspiratorial voices came to her. Looking over the edge of the banister she saw Dante and Alexander seated on the bottom step. She would not have continued to listen had not the next words held her in silence.

"You must be direct and honest, Dante. Papa would see right through you if you did anything else. Papa has a way of just looking at you and knowing if you're trying to fool him."

"Then what should I tell him, Alexi?"

"Tell him the truth. That you rode my pony today, that you took the jump easily, and that you really want a pony of your own."

"He might punish me for making that jump without permission."

"If Papa decides that then you must take your punishment like a man. But you can still ask him for a pony."

"All right, Alexi," Dante sighed. "I just hope Papa is in a good mood tonight and doesn't decide punishment is necessary after all."

"Papa's always fair, Dante, you'll see."

They rose and walked into the huge dining room while Marie walked down the stairs with a pleased smile on her face. Again she felt the power of Jules' love and influence surround her. It had guided her sons in such a way that she could still feel the love and respect in their words as they had talked about him.

She had just reached the bottom of the stairs when she heard the clatter of running feet behind her. She turned to see Celeste coming down the stairs as fast as her little feet could carry her.

"Celeste," she laughed, "the first thing you must learn is that a lady never runs into the dining room."

Celeste stopped and gathered herself together controlling her rapid breathing. "Yes, Maman."

"Come," Marie motioned her to walk beside her. "If you are going to be joining us for dinner from now on, let me see what kind of lady you can be."

"Yes, Maman," Celeste said quietly. Marie smiled again as she watched Celeste inhale, lift her chin and suddenly acquire such a dignified look that Marie nearly laughed. When they walked into the room, Jules was seated at the head of the table and Alexander and Dante on each side of him. All three rose when they walked in. Alexander leaped to his feet to assist his mother with her chair while Dante went to help Celeste with hers.

Jules' eyes met Marie's across the table glowing with love and pride in the three children who sat with them.

They waited quietly while the meal was served. When the servants were gone, they began to eat. It was then that Marie surreptitiously watched Alexander nod to Dante, saw Dante gulp, grip his fork a little tighter and turn toward his father who looked to him at the moment as the largest most formidable human in the world.

"Papa," Dante said hesitantly.

"Yes, Dante?"

"May I . . . may I tell you something I have done? I think you will be pleased."

"Of course. Tell me, is it about your ride on Alexander's pony today, or is it about the jump you so rashly took?"

"You saw me?" Dante gasped. Even Alexander looked dismayed while Celeste's eyes began to glitter in rebellion.

"Yes, I saw you. I have only one thing to say."

"Yes, Papa," Dante said glumly, sure the hard hand of discipline was about to fall.

"That I think it was an obvious feat of great courage to take that jump at your age and since you had never ridden before, both your mother and I watched and were very proud of you."

Dante's eyes glowed as he gazed from one parent to the other, then crossed the table to his brother who was smiling broadly.

"I told you Dante, Papa is always fair."

"Do not be too hasty, Alexander," Jules said firmly. "I am proud of what Dante has done, but that does not excuse the fact that he did it without either your mother's or my permission."

Both smiles faded as they watched Jules face.

"Dante, you have proven you can ride and ride well, for that reason, I intend to get you a pony of your own."

"Yes, Papa," Dante choked, knowing more was coming.

"You will groom the pony, walk him, feed and water him."

"Yes, Papa."

"But you will not ride him for two months. It will teach you to curb your impatience and receive permission from either your mother or I before you plan any-more escapades. Is this satisfactory, Dante?"

"Yes, Papa."

"Good, now I suggest you both eat and retire early for we shall go to town tomorrow and purchase your pony."

The children's heads bent over their plates and Jules eyes again met Marie's across the table accepting her slight nod and pleased smile at the way he had cared for Dante's pride and emotions at the same time.

Later that night, they sat before a low burning fire. His arms about her, Marie lay her head against Jules broad chest. "I love you so very much my dear Jules," she said softly. "And I will tell you that your children feel the same. I overheard them talking."

"All the more reason that I take them away soon, Marie, mon amour we will go where we can share the rest of our lives with them, watch them grow without being afraid of such terror and war as we have known."

"Yes, love, yes," she whispered as she willingly lifted her lips to meet his in a fierce demanding kiss that ignited their blinding love as it always could from the first moment they had met and would until the last breath of their lives.

Two

The English tutor's name was Francis Gilbert. He was a highly educated man who had received his education in the best schools England had to offer, but to the distress of his parents he had chosen to try adventuring before he had accepted a post at an English school which he had considered rather staid and extremely dull. He had found himself by an act of strange misfortune, or good fortune, in France when Napoleon had searched the zenith of his career. Caught in the magic of it, he found himself, several years later, without funds and his desire to go home dominant. He appreciated the opportunity when Marie interviewed him for the position as English teacher and promised to pay his passage home along with a sizable remuneration for his efforts.

He accepted the position quickly, and took an instant to form a liking for the three Dubonne children.

For Dante, the language seemed to come easily, but for Alexander and Celeste, it was much more difficult. It was the only field in which Dante could surpass Alexander and, though it surprised him, he enjoyed the temporary reversal of their roles. As for riding, Dante knew immediately that he would never be able to touch Alexander's expertise.

A few months after Francis came, Jules decided that Alexander was old enough to begin his lessons in weapons. Dante never missed one of these lessons and watched in wide-eyed wonder as Alexander was taught the art.

Alexander excelled quickly in this field and Dante found he could barely wait until he was old enough to join him.

While he was racing against time in the training he felt his children would need, Jules was trying in vain to hold back the dam of revolution he knew was brewing.

Again, under the protection of night, he went to meet the men he knew were conspiring. He went again, to try to stop them even though he knew it was useless.

Again his carriage drove through the darkened streets of Paris, again the familiar house and a repetition of the coded knock. As it had been before, the door was opened by Emil Martinique. Emil had, as usual, given all his servants a night off so there would be no unwelcome ears and no one to carry tales of the men who met here.

"Emil, mon ami," Jules said as he entered the house and removed his coat. "You do not look well, my friend."

"I am not well. I have tried, over all these months I have tried, and still it goes on and on, this talk of revolution. I am tired, Jules, tired of war, tired of bloodshed, tired of trying to make them understand. It is all for nothing as your words were, all for nothing."

"They have decided? It is final?"

"I believe so, but Jules . . ."

"Yes, Emil."

"If the final decision is made . . . I shall not remain in Paris. I want no more part of this, I have seen and lived through enough."

Jules agreed with him but remained silent. He too was through with all thoughts of war and revolution. He too, had decided not to remain in Paris, yet his plans carried further. He would not just leave Paris . . . he would leave France forever.

The majority of his plans were already made. His children had enough command of the English language to pass and he intended to ask their English tutor to join them and continue his children's education.

Most of his negotiable wealth already rested in a bank in Philadelphia. A house had already been purchased, and tentative feelers had been reached out for businesses in which Jules could invest.

He had come here one last time to try and dissuade these formidable warriors against revolution. He had reservations about his ability to do so, yet he loved these men like brothers, and he did not want to see them caught up in what he felt would be a tragedy.

Inside the room, he stood and surveyed the four men who awaited him.

Phillipe Poincare rose to meet Jules, his hand extended in friendship. Phillipe was, of all four, one of the closest to Jules. They had shared much together including the drastic and deadly retreat from the steppes of Russia. It was Jules who had literally dragged Phillipe along when the intense cold and starvation tried to claim both of their lives.

Their hands clasped, then they gripped each other in a warm embrace.

"Phillipe, my friend. It is good to see you."

"Even under these circumstances?" Phillipe smiled.

"Under any circumstances," Jules replied.

Another man rose to join them. George Valois. He too extended his hand. It was George, Jules felt, who was the continual drive behind this decision. It was George who would never accept the descent of the Napoleonic star.

The third man, Henri Gautier, had become a friend of Jules in another campaign.

Pierre Taboret was the fourth man, and the one of which Jules knew the least for he was more a friend of Phillipe's and he and Jules friendship had been most recent.

"Gentlemen," Jules said.

"Please Jules," Phillipe smiled, "sit down and have a glass of wine."

"Thank you," Jules laughed, realizing his mood had been less friendly and more tense and worried.

He sat down, accepted the glass of wine Phillipe handed him, sipped, then relaxed in his chair. Emil sat down beside him and for a few minutes, the room was silent. It was Phillipe who spoke first.

"Jules, decisions have been solidified, plans are made."

"I see," Jules replied sadly. "Then it is of no use for me to continue to argue with you?"

"I do not understand," George replied. "It would seem to me that you, of all people, should be the most enthusiastic. It was you who fought nearly to the death for Napoleon. Why, now, do you withhold yourself from us. We need your help, Jules. Your help and your influence. You know you have the power to draw many to us if you would only speak out."

"Yes," Pierre replied. "You agree with us, do you not, that Louis would be good for France. He would be as strong a leader as his uncle was."

"Louis Bonaparte has many good ideas," Jules replied honestly, "but he has more desire to be emperor as his uncle was. Sometimes it seems the desire outweighs the good ideas."

"People will rally to him. They need him now. They need to push the Bourbons from the throne permanently," Pierre replied.

"France cannot stand more bloodshed now," Jules said. "Her young men have been depleted at a horrifying rate. People are hungry, and everything is in disarray. We need more time to rebuild, to regain our strength. I, for one, am both mentally and emotionally exhausted. We also have weakened ourselves in the eyes of other countries and you and I know the strong will always prey on the weak. We must be prepared for others to attack instead of stirring up inner conflicts."

"With Louis in command," George said, "there will be no question of other countries attacking. We will reach out and crush them first."

Jules eyes glittered dangerously. "And do we have another emperor who wants to rule the world instead of worrying about his hungry people at home?"

"He would make France the strongest nation in the world."

"Not by depleting her wealth and her young hearts in war after war. We need a time of peace. Then we need a man who wants to rebuild. Our strength will come from within, not from how many other countries we can defeat."

George rose and walked to the window. He stood

looking out with unseeing eyes until he could control some of the anger that shook him.

"Jules," Henri said gently, "many of the military would follow you, you know that."

"Yes, I do," Jules replied. "It is why I will not lead them down the path to more destruction and bloodshed. Do you think it is only of them that I fear. I myself find it very difficult to be responsible for any more death."

"You know all of our plans," George spoke, his stiff back still toward them. Jules tried his best to control his fury.

"Do you believe I would betray you?" he asked in a calm deceptive voice.

"Good God!" Phillipe said angrily. "No man in this room would think such a thought. Your courage and loyalty are well known."

Jules eyes were still riveted on George's back. George turned slowly. He could see the dangerous glitter in Jules eyes. He also knew that Jules could not be surpassed with pistol or saber in a duel.

"I had no intention of implying any such thing. I only mentioned the fact. No, I would not imply that you or any in this room would betray us. I apologize if you misconstrued my words."

Relief was on the faces of all present. The last thing they wanted was a duel between two of their own for fear the cause of it might bring to light their activities.

"Can I not prevail upon your sanity to stop this thing before it gets started?" Jules said.

"It is too late, Jules." Phillipe said, "All is arranged. We only hoped to add your name."

"There will be bloodshed in the streets, Phillipe," Jules said softly. "Are you prepared to accept the useless waste that will occur?"

"Jules my friend, both of us must stand by our convictions. You must go your way and I mine. That is the only thing I will regret about this, that for the first time in many years, we will not be at each other's side to protect each other. I shall miss you, but I respect your thoughts as always."

"I wish you well my friend," Jules replied quietly.

Again they embraced, knowing it might be the final time they would ever see each other. Jules shook hands with each of the others, then, without another word, he picked up his cloak and left, not wanting to look back into the faces of the friends he knew were lost to him forever.

Jules rode home, his mind deep in memories. Memories of the friends he had just left, memories that would be all he had left of days past. The time was short, and he was afraid of only one thing. That the insurrection would begin before he could get his family safely away, that it would surround them and absorb them as just another number in the list of fatalities.

He slept restlessly that night, and Marie, who lay beside him unable to sleep at all, listened to his muttered words, felt his tension and knew something was about to happen to her family that had disastrous possibilities.

It was in the wee hours of the morning when Marie could tell by the ceasing of Jules thrashing about and the quietness of his breathing that he too was awake. He lay still for he did not want to waken her.

"Jules," she whispered softly.

"You are awake my love?" came his answering whisper. "I'm sorry, I didn't mean to disturb your sleep."

The rustle of the bedclothes sounded in the dark quiet room as she turned to him. He put his arm about her and held her close. With a sigh she rested her head on his broad chest and her arm lay across his waist.

"You have something to tell me, Jules. Why do you let it worry you so?"

"You know me so well," Jules chuckled.

"I have not shared this bed with you all these years without knowing when something troubles you."

She could hear the rumble of silent laughter deep in his chest and her mouth quirked in a half smile.

"Yes, Marie, I have something to tell you."

"What is it?"

"It is time for us to leave. In fact, I am afraid if we do not hurry we might not succeed."

"What must I do?"

"You are not frightened?"

"Yes ... yes I am frightened, but not of anything outside. I am only frightened that somehow, some way, we might be separated. That is the only thing I could not bear. Anything else I can cope with. You and the children are all that matters, my love. If it will keep us together, keep us safe and well, I am prepared to do whatever you say."

"Have you prepared the children?"

"I have tried. Their English is atrocious, but they can make themselves understood. I'm sure they will get by, and they will learn more after we become settled."

"Excellent."

"How soon, Jules?" she said quietly.

"We begin to pack tomorrow."

"Tomorrow! So soon?"

"Marie, we must leave many things behind. Take only

what is most valuable. In three days, I hope to be ready to leave. After that I do not know for sure if we can safely get away."

"The house . . .?"

"We must forget it, it is lost to us."

"Very well, Jules. We will be ready to go in less than three days."

He drew her tight against him his lips brushing a kiss against her hair.

"Marie, my sweet Marie. I love you so very much. You are my world, Marie, you and our children. It is for their sake that we must do this. I would not ask you to sacrifice all for anything less."

She rose on one elbow and looked down into his face. It was shadowed, but the moonlight touched the fiery glow of his green eyes. Slowly, she bent and brushed his lips with hers. "I love you, Jules, you and the children. There is nothing you could ask that I would consider too great a sacrifice. I love you."

She sensed his pleasure as he lifted both hands, tangled them in the mass of her pale gold hair and drew her head to his. Her lips accepted his willingly.

Their years of happy marriage had so attuned them to each other that no words were necessary now for them to understand the flame of desire that blossomed between them now as it always had in the past. The love between them had grown from a fiery sexual thing to a gentle sharing of each other. It was a mutual giving that touched the center of their worlds and strengthened the love that was to carry them through great disasters and great success and joy.

The next day saw the beginning of turmoil in the house as Marie began giving orders for the packing of

37

what they would need for this journey. Sweet gentle Marie ran her house like a commanding officer. Servants jumped and ran to follow her orders. The children, aware that some great event was about to take place in their lives tried to do what their mother wanted in hopes of finding out soon what was happening.

Jules and Marie had agreed upon one thing; she would be the one to tell Celeste and he would explain to Alexander and Dante.

For Celeste, the explanation was a very frightening thing, and she spent most of her time clinging to one member of the family or other as if afraid they would disappear. For Alexander and Dante, it was the most exciting thing that had ever happened in their lives. As Jules explained the best he could considering their ages, they stared at him with wide absorbing eyes.

"Papa," Dante questioned, "you mean we have to go away from here forever, that we'll never come back?"

"Yes, Dante, that is so."

"Couldn't we just go visit Aunt Hortense, then when it's all over we can come home."

"It's not that simple, son. You cannot understand now, but when you are older, you will see why this was necessary."

Alexander had remained silent, and for the first time in his life, Jules could not read the thoughts behind his shuttered eyes. It was later that night when he sat in his study, when the entire house was asleep, when he was trying to sort his own thoughts in his mind, that he heard the gentle rap on his study door. He knew before he spoke that it was Alexander who waited for admittance. Silently, he prayed he would have the answers for this quiet intelligent boy.

"Come in," he called.

The door opened a few inches and Alexander's head appeared around it. "Can I talk to you, Father?"

Jules caught the dropping of the childish Papa and the usage of the more adult Father.

"Of course, Alexander, come in."

Alexander came in and closed the door quietly behind him. He walked across the room and sat in the chair opposite his father. For several minutes, he remained silent.

"There's something on your mind, Alexander?"

"Yes, Father."

"Something worries you?"

"Yes, Father."

"Don't you think you'll feel better if we talk about it?"

Alexander nodded, but Jules could see he was searching for words.

"Is it something about our leaving, Alexander?"

The questioning eyes lifted to meet his, there was no fear within them, only a vague look of doubt. "Father," he began hesitantly, "if we leave France now, it ... it won't be because we're afraid will it, I mean ... nobody will consider us cowards, as if we're running away, will they?"

Jules could sense that this question had torn deeply into this pride-filled lad, and that he had to be careful not to do more damage with a careless answer.

"Alexander," he said quietly, "I have tried always to support and fight for what I knew was right, and I have tried to teach you to do the same.

"Yes, Father."

"You would not consider me a coward would you, my son?"

"Oh, no, Father! I didn't mean . . ."

"Sometimes, Alexander it takes more courage to go against public opinion and do what you feel is the right thing to do for the others you love." He sighed deeply, then continued, aware that Alexander was absorbing and weighing each word.

"Alexander, I have fought in a terrible bloody war, fought because I thought it was right and because of the pride in myself, my family, my country. Under these circumstances, I would fight again. But this is not the same. This is a revolution that will make the streets run red with blood, the blood of people I have fought with and fought for. I feel it is wrong, and I will not turn my weapons against my own people, and I do not want to see my sons do so. To stay here, we must either take part in it or die. I love you all too much to see your lives cut short. I feel it is wrong Alexander, and I must have the courage and so must you, to stand for what we believe and to defend those we love. Do you understand a little better?"

"Yes, Father," Alexander said softly. "One must have the courage to do what every one else thinks is wrong if he feels it is right."

"You have summed it up well. Remember it, Alexander. You will face many times in your life when you will have to choose to do what is right in your own heart no matter who tells you differently."

Alexander's shoulders straightened perceptibly, and Jules smiled down into intelligent eyes that reflected the pride and determination he felt.

"Come let us share a glass of wine together. It is not often men understand each other so well. I hope it is always this way between us, Alexander. I may not always have the right answers, but I will always try my best to help you find them."

Alexander's eyes glowed with pleasure. To be able to share wine with his father like a man grown was almost more than he could bear.

Jules rose and walked to a table where he poured himself a liberal amount of wine, then a small amount of wine in another to which he added water. He handed it to Alexander who took it with trembling fingers. Lightly Jules touched his glass to Alexander's. "To the family," he said softly.

"Yes, sir," came the whispered reply. "To the family ... and to you, sir."

"Thank you, Alexander," Jules said solemnly. They both drank.

"Now I suggest that you get to bed. Your mother would be quite upset to find you up at this hour ... and," he laughed, "drinking wine with me. Suppose we keep it a secret for now?"

"Yes, sir," Alexander grinned.

Jules chuckled when he saw the new stature to which his older son had grown. "Good night, Alexander."

"Good night," Alexander replied, and he walked across the room and opened the huge oak door. Then he turned and looked at his father. "Thank you, Father," he said softly, and then he was gone and the door closed softly behind him.

"You're welcome, my son," Jules whispered. "You're very very welcome."

Jules picked up his glass and drained it, then he went back to his chair before the fireplace and picked up the book he had been reading. He had only turned a page when again he heard the door open. He thought it might

41

be Alexander returning so he placed the book aside and turned to face the door.

The door opened further, and the rustle of silk skirts against the floor told him who was making a silent nocturnal visit. "Marie," he said softly, "I thought you were asleep."

He could hear her light chuckle as she moved across the floor to his side, then sat down on his lap and put her arms about his neck and proceeded to kiss him several times.

"I'm not complaining, my dear," he laughed as he tightened his arms about her, "but I'd like to know what I've done to receive such a magnanimous reward. I'd like to be able to do it again and again."

"I love you Jules, and I am so grateful I was wise enough to choose you for the father of my children."

"If that is what I have done to receive such treatment," he replied a wicked glitter in his eyes. "I should be very pleased to repeat it."

"Less than an hour ago, I went into the children's rooms to see that all was well. Celeste was asleep, as was Dante. I was surprised to find Alexander's bed empty."

"Yes?"

"I came down to tell you."

"And you found him here."

"Yes," she said softly, "I did not mean to eavesdrop, Jules, but I am glad that I did. He will be a credit to the Dubonne name one day."

Jules held her close, and she lay her head against his chest.

"If we succeed in our escape," he said quietly.

She lifted her head and looked at him closely. She could see the worry in his eyes. "Do you think we won't?"

"Marie, it has already begun. In small towns and villages near here. Soon, like a plague, it will sweep through Paris. I have tried to devise a logical path of escape that will keep us away from danger. My name is irrevocably linked with the others. If this plot fails, and I am sure it will, they will be searching for me."

"Jules, you frighten me."

"I'm sorry, but you must know the truth in case . . ."

"In case! . . . What?"

"In case you must take the children and go on alone."

Marie sat up, her eyes glowing and her voice firm. "Jules Dubonne, listen to me carefully. I will not leave this country . . . this city . . . no, even this house unless you are with me. You must understand this, for on this subject I shall brook no argument. Either we go together . . . or we do not go."

"The Valois were always an obstinate family," Jules smiled.

"And I was the most obstinate of them all. Did I not insist on marrying you even though I was only sixteen."

He laughed and pulled her down into his arms again kissing her firmly and expertly with a kiss that would always have the ability to erase everything from her mind and her heart but him.

"You are a brave and beautiful woman, my sweet Marie," he murmured as his lips drifted down the soft slender column of her throat and burned across the gentle rise of her breasts. "We shall go together, for I could not bear your loss."

He rose from the chair, lifting her slender body with him. Slowly he stood her on her feet, then hand in hand they walked up the stairs to the bedroom they had shared so long and with such deep love.

The door closed behind them, and again they shared the bed to which he had brought her as a bride and in which all three of her children had been born.

The house was dark now, and quiet, as was all the streets about them. Quiet, with a strange dark tense quiet that always heralded the severest of storms.

The storm would break soon, and when it did, it would come very near destroying the family that slept safe and warm within the walls of the Dubonne home.

Three

The family slept while the flame of revolution burst into life. The well laid plans began to move. It started in small towns surrounding Paris and like a deadly flood, it rolled in an unstoppable force toward the city. People, unhappy, hungry and frightened, followed the skilled people who were placed among them to incite their passions and stimulate their anger to an irrational point. They were no longer fighting for one man, or against one king, but against the spectre of insecurity and fear. They rose like a ravenous animal, an animal whose taste for blood was insatiable . . . any blood . . . all blood.

Jules was wakened abruptly by the sound of shouting in the streets, and the reverberating echo of someone pounding on his bedroom door. Pale rays of early dawn touched the room with a shadowed gray light.

Marie sat up abruptly and found her husband already half dressed and cursing as he strode toward the door.

He jerked the door open to find a rather frightened and very pale butler. "Joseph," he said sharply.

"Monsieur Dubonne, it is a riot, sir. They are threatening to burst in at any moment. What shall we do, sir?"

"Have the children dressed and brought to their mother, then I want you and the rest of the servants to find safety among your families and friends."

"But what about you, sir ... you and the family ... they might ..."

"I'll be taking my family out of here, now. Go, Joseph. I want you and the rest of my people safe. Do you have a safe place to go? Do the others?"

"Yes, sir, but ..."

"No buts, Joseph. Bring the children and then get yourself and the others to safety."

"Yes, sir."

Joseph left reluctantly. Marie was already beginning to dress.

"Dress warmly, Marie, and see that the children are the same. We have a long and dangerous trip ahead of us."

"Yes, Jules," she said quietly.

He smiled as he noticed the absence of tears or any other sign of feminine vapors. He knew, by the pallor of her face, that she was frightened just as he knew she would not surrender to it.

Within moments the children were brought to them by Joseph and Madame Clarey. They too were extremely frightened. Alexander and Dante were doing their best to keep their fear under control. Celeste was crying in fright and Marie took her in her arms to comfort her.

"Thank you, Joseph," Jules said. "Please see that Madame Clarey gets to safety. Have all the others gone?"

"Yes, sir, the others are gone," Joseph replied. "Madame Clarey and I have discussed it, we do not wish to leave either you or your family, sir. We have been

46

with you many years. We choose to be with you for the balance of our lives."

"I have taken the liberty to pack some warm clothes for the children," Madame Clarey said firmly, "we are ready to leave whenever you and Madame Dubonne are."

"I cannot let you do this," Jules protested. "If they catch us it will not go well for you."

Madame Clarey lifted her chin in defiance. "I have cared for Madame and the children since their birth. No rabble is going to frighten me so much that I will leave my poor darlings in a time of need."

"I, too, sir," Joseph said stubbornly, "have been with the Dubonne family for twenty years. I should like to stay, sir."

Jules knew that argument was useless and there was not much time left.

"See that everyone has a warm cloak. Bring some blankets and what food you can get quickly, then harness the horses to the sturdiest carriage. I will join you in the stable within minutes."

"Yes, sir," Joseph said. He beckoned to Madame Clarey who followed him quickly from the room.

Jules turned to Marie who already had the children and herself bundled well and stood wide-eyed, frightened, but prepared to do whatever else Jules told her to do. He went to her and gently took her in his arms. "We must not let the children see that we are frightened, my love," he whispered against her hair. "It is a long and difficult journey we have ahead of us and we are the only source of courage they have at the moment."

He felt her trembling body grow still in his arms, felt

her clinging arms relax their holds on him. She looked up into his eyes and slowly gathered strength from their love-filled gaze.

"I'm all right, Jules," she said quietly. "What do you want me to do?"

The roar of the crowd in the streets grew louder, then suddenly, with a shattering crash that brought a scream from Marie, a rock crashed through the bedroom window spraying glass about the room.

"Extinguish the candles, quickly," Jules said. Both Alexander and Marie ran to the candles and blew them out, casting the room into darkness. Quickly Jules called them to him and they left the room. Jules noticed with approval that Joseph had extinguished all the other candles in the house.

"Alexander, take Celeste's hand. Marie, keep Dante beside you. We know this house without need of light. We will make our way to the stables as quickly as possible."

Struggling to keep their fear under control, they worked their way down the darkened halls. They could hear the gates give way and strong fists battering on the front door.

"Quickly!" Jules said. "Down the back stairs to the servants quarters. We will leave through the lower level."

Their heels clicked rapidly on the smooth hard floors as they sped up their steps. The servants area of the house was much darker than the upper, so Jules had them form a chain with himself in the lead. Slowly they moved ahead until Jules stopped.

"Here is the outer door. I see no one between here and the stables, but there might be. We must make a dash. Run as fast as you can."

He heard Celeste's whimper and Marie's choked sob and he realized their fear was rapidly overcoming them.

He took his pistol which he had loaded and thrust in his belt. He could not give them too much time to think for their fear would paralyze them to the point that they would not move at all.

"Marie, give Celeste to me."

Marie handed Celeste into his arms. He held her snugly against him and felt her tiny arms clasp his neck his terror. She buried her head against his shoulder.

"Shhh," he comforted. "Do not cry, my little one. Papa will let nothing happen to you." It helped to stop some of her tears but she did not lift her head nor did her arms lessen their grip.

"Alexander?"

"Yes, sir," came a firm answer.

"You and Dante on each side of your mother, when I give the word, run!"

"Yes, sir."

Jules smiled to himself. Alexander would do well. Slowly, he opened the door and looked about. The area seemed safe, but there was too much cover for anyone who intended to surprise them. He pushed the door completely open. In the distance he could see the carriage and horses. Joseph and Madame Clarey would be waiting. Taking a deep breath and grasping Celeste tightly in one arm and gripping the pistol in preparation he spoke to Alexander.

"Run Alexander! Run Dante!"

The words had barely left his lips when Alexander and Dante dashed for the carriage. He was behind them immediately. They were three quarters of the way to the carriage when the sound he had dreaded and had listened for came to him. The mob had begun to circle the house. Several men in front of the others had spotted them. With a shout they began running toward them. To keep more distance between Marie and the mob, he spun on his heels, took deliberate aim and shot the first man around the house. It effectively made the others stop. It would only be a minute, but it was all the time he would need.

Marie and the boys had already tumbled inside the carriage. In a moment Jules was behind them. He slammed the door shut and the horses, under Joseph's whip, leaped ahead.

Now the mob was dashing across the lawn toward the carriage. Jules knew they had to reach the outer gate before them. Quickly, he thrust Celeste into Alexander's arms. Then he reloaded his pistol. He opened the window of the carriage and looked out.

Between the carriage and the outer gate, several men ran. Both Jules and Joseph knew if the carriage was ever stopped it would be the end for all of them. Madame Clarey and Marie both screamed as Joseph put the whip to the horses and again they gave a nervous leap, and acquired a little more speed. Suddenly the men were around the carriage. To the passengers, it seemed like a witch's cauldron. There was a surging sea of faces, a cacaphony of voices, an occasional scream and ugly words shouted. One man clung to the door and despite Jules efforts to make him release his hold, he clung as if desperate, his leering face gazing at the women. Then deliberately, Jules lifted his pistol and shot him. Blood covered the door as the man's face first registered surprise, then fear ... then death as his hands slowly released their hold and he fell.

They had clattered past the broken gates now and slowly they could hear the roaring of the mob fade behind them. Jules sat back in his seat and Marie collapsed against his shoulder in tears. Celeste had been put on Alexander's lap and he held her tight. His eyes met Jules over her head. Again Jules was surprised that no fear seemed to linger there.

Alexander was remembering Celeste's words, "I don't want Papa to ever kill anyone again ... you won't ever kill anyone will you Alexi? ... Grimly, he tightened his lips for he knew if he had been in his father's place he would have wanted to do the same.

The carriage rattled at breakneck speed through the dark side streets. Joseph was doing his best to skirt the main area of the city where, from the sight of smoke and flames touching the early morning sky and the roaring sound of aroused citizenry, the worst of the riots were taking place.

The carriage careened along tossing the occupants from side to side. None of them complained for they knew what might be following behind them.

It was not until they left the outskirts of the city of Paris and found themselves on a quiet dirt road that Joseph pulled the lathered horses to a stop. When he came to the door of the carriage, Jules had already opened it and was helping Marie and Madame Clarey out. Everyone was shaken and pale. They stood about for a few minutes stretching their sore and aching bodies, while Joseph rubbed the tired horses and he and Jules discussed the best way they could travel to remain free.

"What is the best way to go, sir? We must surely stick

to the back roads, the least traveled roads."

"Yes, we must remain unseen," Jules replied.

"You, sir, if I might say, will find it very difficult to remain unseen. And your oh, so beautiful wife, her beauty is well known and well remembered."

"Again, Joseph, I am afraid you are right. We," he chuckled, "are going to do some foraging in the next small town we find. We must take away the aura of wealth and become just a poor merchant traveling with his family."

"It will be very dangerous."

"Yes, but our ship is due to sail from Le Havre in a few days and we *must* sail with it."

"We are not far from my village. If you would honor me, sir, you could come to my house until we could get you and your family some suitable clothes."

Again Jules laughed. "It was a great day of wisdom that led me to hire you Joseph."

"Thank you, sir," Joseph's usually well controlled face broke into a grin. "By the way, sir ... we must walk."

"Walk!" Jules said thoughtfully. "I'm afraid my wife and children, not to mention Madame Clarey, would not be able to make that distance on foot."

"If you would consider my advice, sir?"

"Joseph," Jules smiled, "I would listen to any advice you might have. At this moment, I have nothing but respect for your every thought."

"Hide the carriage, sir, and we will ride the horses to the outskirts of my village. There we will hide the horses. When we have gotten you and your family the right apparel, then we need only to take the horses back to the carriage and be on our way."

"Good man. We will do so immediately."

Between Jules and Joseph they managed to hide the carriage. Then they took the four horses. Alexander and Dante were each mounted on one, and Jules put Celeste in front of Alexander with a word of caution that he was to hold her tightly and only walk the horse. He and Joseph mounted the other two with Madame Clarey a reluctant passenger behind Joseph and Marie clinging to Jules. It was a most uncomfortable trip and to Marie, it seemed to last for hours.

Everyone was in a state of exhaustion when they finally came to the outskirts of Joseph's village. They hobbled the horses in a patch of grass well secluded in a stand of huge thick branched trees. Jules carried Celeste as they followed Joseph to the home of his birth.

The only people in residence in the small five room house was Joseph's elderly mother and a widowed sister a year or two older than Joseph. Joseph's sister Emilie was a quiet woman who made Joseph's guests as welcome as she could with the limited things they had. After a meal of sliced mutton, cheese and dark bread which they washed down with a little wine, Celeste was put down for a nap. Marie sat in quiet conversation with Emilie while Joseph and Jules sat over a map and decided what they would do and how they would do it.

"We will of course borrow some clothes from your mother and sister for my wife and maybe some from you that might help change my looks."

Joseph laughed. "I'm sure all of mine will be entirely too small for you, sir, but Emilie still has some of her husband's. She will also have some for your children."

"The children ... how?" Then Jules stopped. "She had children of her own?" he questioned softly.

"Yes, they died of the plague with her husband."

"My God, I'm sorry."

"It has left Emilie . . . changed," Joseph said. "I'm sure she will be happy to let you use the clothes to keep your children safe."

"I can never repay her, Joseph."

"Yes, sir, there is a way to repay her."

"How? Tell me how and I will do it gladly."

"If I can save enough money for my sister to come to us, will you agree to give her service in your home?"

"Most definitely, Joseph. I would be delighted to give her a position. It would be the least I could do to show my gratitude both to her and to your loyalty. If we get safely away."

Emile did as Joseph said she would do. She opened a chest of clothes that had been packed away for a long time. The clothes of her husband's, although they fit Jules reasonably well, were a little snug and brought a mischievous twinkle to Marie's eyes.

Jules smiled when his peasant wife stood before him in a dark wool dress fitting her lovely figure to perfection.

"I always thought, my love," he chuckled, "that you would look well in anything. You have just proven I was right."

The children dressed in the rough clothes looked like any other farmer's children except for their attitudes. Born to wealth, they could not control the way they had been taught. Alexander still bore his good manners and pride that bordered on arrogance. But Jules knew it was the best he could expect for now. At least it gave them a chance for survival.

After a late supper, the children were made pallets on

54

the floor close to the fire and were soon asleep. Joseph's sister shared her mother's bed and gave hers to Jules and Marie. Joseph slept on a couch in the same room as the children. Madame Clarey insisted on sleeping near the children also.

Neither Jules or Marie could sleep well after their harrowing escape, and knowing that there was a long dangerous trip still ahead.

"Jules?" Marie whispered.

"Yes, love?"

"Will the ship wait for us if . . . if we are late?"

Jules remained silent for a long time and she knew, with a sinking heart, what his answer would be. "No, love, it cannot wait for a few people whose fate is so uncertain. If we are not there on time, the captain will be forced to sail without us."

"What will we do? It is so long a trip. Can we make it Jules?"

"We will make it," Jules said determinedly. "I will not allow you or my children to fall into the hands of this . . . rabble. No, we will make it."

They spoke no more. Jules held her close and after silently praying for their escape, she fell into a restless slumber. Jules lay awake for a long time, making plans for their flight. The first gray light of dawn found him still awake.

Joseph came, rapping gently on the door, before the sun was up. Jules slid from the bed quietly, dressed and then woke Marie. "Come love, we must wake the children. It is time for us to leave."

It was a very quiet group of children who stood before them.

"I have been thinking, Joseph," Jules said. "The

carriage is entirely too rich for us to be travelling in. It will be stopped immediately, and they will wonder how a poor farmer came to have such a luxury."

"Yes, sir, I've had the same thought. That is why I have taken the liberty to harness two of the horses to our old farm wagon. I thought it would be more appropriate even if it is more uncomfortable."

"We cannot worry about comfort now. We have to worry about safety."

"Yes, sir. And you have decided on the safest route?"

"From here, Poissy, then on to Veron. If we make it safely that far, we shall go on to Caudebec, then Elbeuf. From then to Harfleur, then, if God is willing, all is well, on to LeHavre.

"Very good, sir."

"The most direct route, probably the most heavily guarded and most dangerous, but we do not have the time to go any other way."

By the time the sun crested the horizon, the wagon and passengers were well on their way. As Joseph had said, the wagon had seen better days. It was an uncomfortable, jolting ride. Marie padded the bottom of the wagon with the blankets they had, which alleviated some of the discomfort, but by the time they stopped, late in the afternoon, all were physically exhausted.

They ate a short, cold meal, and long before any of them were ready, Jules announced that they again must be on their way.

It was late that night that they neared the town of Poissy. Joseph found a secluded place for them, then while he went to the town to forage both for food and for news, Jules built a fire and Marie made the children as comfortable as she could with her limited resources.

By the time Joseph returned and the food was eaten, the children were already half asleep. It pleased Jules to see Alexander cover Celeste with a blanket and see she was safe before he and Dante curled up together. It took them only moments to fall asleep and Jules, Marie, Joseph and Madame Clarey sat about talking for a short time before they too sought the negligible comfort of the blanket by the low burning fire.

The journey to Veron was uneventful, but even now more uncomfortable. Stiff bodies, unused to sleeping on the hard ground complained painfully at every bump of the wagon. By the time they reached Caudebec safely, Jules' outlook became more optimistic.

"We can make it Joseph," Jules said. "We shall reach Elbeuf and be able to circle around it and be on our way to Harfleur by tomorrow morning. From Harfleur it is only a short way to the port and our ship. We shall make it Joseph."

"Yes, sir, I believe we shall."

"If we do," Marie said firmly, "I shall never ride in a wagon again. In fact I do not think I shall have the stomach or the constitution to ever ride in a carriage for quite some time."

"I quite agree with you, madame," Madame Clarey said, "I myself intend to do quite a bit of walking."

Again they were seated around a low burning campfire. Marie, seated in front of Jules who sat behind her on a piece of log. His hands rested on her shoulders rubbing rhythmically to ease the stiffened muscles. The children were already asleep. After a few more minutes, Joseph and Madame Clarey both went to sleep.

Marie closed her eyes and enjoyed the strength of her husband's hands slowly working away some of the tensions of the day. Gently, he bent forward. Brushing her hair aside, he kissed the nape of her neck.

"My dear, I must tell you again how very proud I am of you. You are a most courageous lady, and I love you more every moment I am with you."

Marie smiled as his arms closed about her and she lay against him enjoying this moment of quiet and peace.

"If it were not for you, my love, I would not be courageous at all. I'm really quite a coward you know, and I am still terrified that we will be caught."

His arms crossed before her holding her tight against him.

"I will have no one, not even you, refer to yourself as a coward. How many other women would face such danger as bravely and calmly as you have."

"Oh, Jules," she said softly, "You are my strength, you are my courage, you and the children. Do you really believe I would have been able to do this had I not your strength to lean on? No, my love, you are my strength."

"It's time we slept love, morning will come much too soon. We have to arise early if we are going to make our ship on time."

"Jules ... what if we are late?"

"Don't think of it, Marie. We cannot be late. If we are, it will take a long time to find another ship ... maybe there would not even be another. It would be disaster. Come, let's go to sleep, I refuse to let my mind dwell on it."

She sighed deeply as they lay on their blanket. He drew another over them, and soon they too slept.

A cool drizzle of rain wakened them the next morning. Jules did not want to say anything to Marie, but he knew it would slow them down. He only wondered if it would slow them down enough that the ship would sail without them.

They traveled slowly as the rain turned the road into mud. The children, with Marie and Madame Clarey huddled in the bottom of the wagon and Jules covered them with the blankets. Still they were wet, cold and quite miserable when they reached the outskirts of Harfleur.

It was a cheerless silent group that curled under the wagon to sleep that night.

The next morning was gray and cheerless, but the rain had subsided. Time was growing short. Jules was filled with a deep sense of dread. They had to make the harbor at LeHavre before the morning tide the next day, or the ship would depart without them.

He looked at Marie, disheveled, wet and dirty, a Marie he had never seen before, for despite it all, she smiled reassuringly at him and he reached for her hand.

"Marie," he said, "this will be the longest hardest stretch of all. We cannot sleep for the balance of the day or tonight, except to rest the horses. You must be prepared, and keep everyone as comfortable as you can. There is little bread and cheese left. You must ration it out over the day. No matter what, we cannot stop. Do you understand?"

"Yes, Jules do not worry. We have made it this far. We must not fail now."

"Good girl," he said gently, "now hurry, we must get loaded and start."

Marie nodded. Quickly, she and Madame Clarey gathered the children and explained as best they could what had to be done.

"Don't worry, Mother," Alexander smiled at her with

tense lips and determined eyes. "Dante and I shall take care of Celeste. She will be all right. If Father says we must make it, then we must."

Marie's eyes glistened with tears to see how much more stature Alexander had acquired through these difficult days. Celeste clung to Alexander's hand and Dante stood stubbornly beside him.

"We'll be all right, Mother. We had best be going. We do not want to waste any valuable time."

"Yes, Dante," she said softly, "come, we must go."

Joseph set the horses to the best pace he could get without exhausting them too soon. To Marie, it seemed as if every rut in the road was found by the wagon's wheels. Her body ached with fatigue.

During the day, she rationed what little food there was left, and by the time the sun had set, the food and water were gone. Now they had to face the long grueling night with the fear eternally in their minds that they might yet be too late.

Occasionally, Joseph stopped to let the horses rest. While it was still day, Jules forced them all to get out of the wagon and stretch their cramped muscles. When night fell and the children finally slept, he did not disturb them.

Despite the agony of their mad dash for freedom, the sun was already rising before they reached the outskirts of LeHavre. Marie watched its bright rays crest the horizon and for the first time since their exodus, she felt the touch of failure and despair.

"Jules," she said softly.

Jules did not answer. He too felt the bitter taste of defeat. Joseph urged the horses into a bone-jolting run. This was their last chance, their only escape was minutes away. Was the ship still there or not?

They skirted the city and finally rolled to a halt at the docks.

Both of them breathed an audible sigh of relief when they saw the tall masted ship that rocked gently at the dock.

Four

Marie and Jules stood at the ship's rail and watched the coast of France fade into the distance. Both were silent, for they were leaving all that they had known and loved for a future that was uncertain.

"We are safe now, Jules, they cannot stop us now, can they?"

"No, love, we are safe. We are on our way to a land whose whole philosophy is based on freedom. There will be no more problems, and no more revolutions or wars in the lives of the Dubonnes."

They stood together, lost in their dream, while fate would spin a web that would entangle their lives and toss them in a stormy sea. It would come very near destroying them, nearer than anything else in their past had ever done.

Once on the high seas, both Jules and Marie relaxed. The release of tension was felt by the children who took immediate advantage.

Alexander became the captain's shadow, hanging on every word he said and bombarding him with question after question.

Dante, slipping from his role of the gentleman's son,

discarding his shoes and stockings, climbed the rigging like a monkey. Marie gasped at her first sight of him seated in the crows nest engaged in questioning the young sailor on watch who answered with amused tolerance. Jules had to calm Marie, but he refused to force Dante down.

"Let him alone, Marie. He is a very brave boy and he's enjoying himself."

"But he'll fall."

"No, I doubt if he will."

Marie said no more, but she chose not to look when Dante was climbing about on the spars and trying to learn not only the routines of the sailors but their own special language.

If the children were pleased at their circumstances, Marie and Jules were even more so, for they found each other in a way that seemed more rewarding than any other time in their lives.

The captain had provided a small area they could share alone and a separate one for the children to share. Usually by the end of the day the three of them were so exhausted they would fall into their beds and be asleep by the time their heads hit the pillow. They grew brown and healthy in the bright sun, their hair turning to pale gold. Even Celeste, who was under more strict care, seemed to bubble over with health and happiness.

Francis insisted the boys resume some education. He erected a canvas canopy on the deck and there he instructed the boys two hours during the day and another hour after supper.

No clouds touched the blue sky. No harsh breezes ruffled the ocean. To the people aboard ship, it seemed like a fairyland voyage. All was going well ... too well.

It was over six weeks later, Jules and Captain Caulder stood together.

"We'll be nearing land soon?" Jules questioned.

"You are anxious to get your feet on solid land again, Monsieur Dubonne?" the captain laughed.

"Well," Jules replied. "I cannot say I have not enjoyed the voyage but I am more a soldier than a sailor."

"By tomorrow morning, we should be nearing the coast of the Carolinas. After we pass that I'll be relieved for it will be a short trip to our destination."

"Relieved? Should we face a problem when we reach the coast of these Carolinas of which you speak?"

"Aye, we could. It's probably the most dangerous place we will find in the whole journey."

"Well, I shall pray we pass this place in safety, for I am most anxious to reach land and get my family settled again."

"Speaking of your family, sir, I must compliment you on yours. Your wife is a lovely woman and your children are rare fine ones."

"Thank you, sir. I shall tell Marie, it will please her. She has a great admiration for you and the way you handle your ship. As for my children, it is needless for me to tell you how much they have enjoyed this voyage. It has added a whole new dimension to their education and their lives."

"Will you and your family join me for dinner this evening? I have a small gift for each of the children if you do not mind."

"We will be delighted."

As Jules finished speaking the captain's gaze left his and drifted beyond Jules' shoulder. From the admiring glow in his eyes, Jules could tell it was Marie. She stopped beside Jules and slipped her hand under his arm and she smiled up at the captain.

"Good afternoon, Madame Dubonne," he smiled, "the sea air is good for you. You're fairly blooming."

"Thank you captain, I have enjoyed this trip very much."

"I have just invited your whole family for dinner tonight and your husband has accepted."

"I shall look forward to it," Marie smiled.

"Good, now if you will excuse me, I have some work to take care of; enjoy this beautiful sunshine."

Marie and Jules watched him walk away. They did enjoy the sunshine and the soft breeze, but only for a few minutes, then the children exploded onto the deck and the rest of the day was spent with Marie holding her breath at their antics and Jules laughter encouraging them.

Marie was glad when the time came for them to go below and prepare for dinner. She admonished them about their manners and what was expected of them.

Despite her admonitions, the boys stormed the captain for memories of his past adventures. He seemed to enjoy telling them tales, some of which Jules thought, were elaborated upon by the captain for the benefit of his young audience.

When the meal was over, the captain stood and raised his glass. "May I propose a toast, Monsieur Dubonne. To you and your family. May you find all you expect in America."

They drank, then the captain picked up a small box he had lying beside his plate. "I have something here for each of the children. With your permission,

Monsieur, Madame?"

"Of course, Captain," Jules replied.

He opened the larger box and took three smaller boxes from inside.

"I have here something very special for each of you. On one of my trips, I went to the south sea islands. There I was fortunate enough to pick up something very rare. On this island, they had produced a small supply of gold and an immense supply of pearls. These three small medallions were made up for me by the island's chief. I have kept them for a long time, but now I think I have found the perfect people to give them to."

From one of the boxes, he lifted out a medallion on a slim gold chain. It was the size of a small coin. A flat piece of pure gold, very slim. The rare thing was that it had three small pearls imbedded in it as if they were emerging from a gold bed pure, white, and very beautiful.

He motioned Celeste forward, and when she stood beside him, he dropped the chain over her head.

"I hope it brings each of you the luck and good wishes with which it was intended."

"Thank you, sir," Celeste said quietly, and she returned to her mother's side. Dante and Alexander were very impressed with the gift and they vowed they would never remove the medallions from their necks again as long as they lived.

Long into the night, Alexander and Dante whispered together about how they would like to sail also to the island from which the beautiful medallions had come, and about how they would always wear them and hand them down in their family for all the future Dubonnes to enjoy.

They finally slept, as all the people on the ship did, except the men who were posted on watch for the night.

They were nearing a very treacherous area and the captain had cautioned them to keep an exceptionally close watch. Sudden storms had tossed more than one ship upon the rocky shores of the Carolinas. More ships had been unable to find safety and had sunk near the area known as Nag's Head.

They had watched the weather, for it was the most dangerous threat. Wild storms would appear suddenly and a ship would stand small chance of escape.

It was nearing three in the morning when the man who stood at the wheel felt the touch of the increasing breeze between his shoulders. He gazed upward, watching the intensity with which the wind filled the ship's sails and carried it forward at a greater and greater speed.

"Liam," he said to the man who stood beside him. "Go below and tell the captain to come on deck. He wanted us to tell him if the wind lifted."

"Aye," Liam replied. He made his way toward the companionway, completely unaware of the young boy who sat in the shadows and watched the full sails in rapt fascination.

Dante and Alexander had spent some time after dinner whispering together, too excited to sleep and too thrilled with the remarkable gift the captain gave them. Their heads were filled with the enchantment of far away places. They had vowed to each other in childish enthusiasm that they would never part with the amazing gift, that it would be part of the Dubonne heritage.

After Alexander slept, Dante still remained awake. This voyage had been the most exciting thing in his life and he hated for it to end. He knew they were nearing their destination and he was unsure of how this new land and new life would be. He stirred restlessly in the narrow bed. The cabin was warm and he thought of the enticing cool breeze that could be found on deck. Dante was never one to think of something and let it slip by. Quietly, he slipped from his bed and donned his clothes. The nights were breezy, but still warm so he left his heavy coat behind and put on a light jacket. He did not want to disturb Alexander or Celeste, mostly because he knew Alexander would not let him disobey his father by going on deck, and if Dante insisted Alexander would have gone with him knowing the punishment if they were found, would fall on him.

He tiptoed across the dark cabin and opened the door and slipped out, closing it quietly.

He didn't want anyone to see him for the report would immediately be given to his father. Jules anger was one thing he could not bear. It crushed Dante if his father sent a frown in his direction.

He made his way on deck and found a dark shadowed corner where he could not be seen. He lay back and folded his hands behind his head and gazed up at the starlit sky. He wondered why the stars seemed so much closer here than they did on land.

The sails were full and the steady rise and fall of the ship lulled him. He enjoyed the sound of the waves as the ship's bow cut through them. A feeling of lassitude crept through him and slowly he drifted into sleep.

The ship began to rise and fall more rapidly, then suddenly the storm broke about it with a crash that wakened Jules and Marie with a start.

It seemed to explode about them with the fury of the

wrath of God. Fear paralyzed Marie momentarily, but Jules leaped from the bed and grabbed for his clothes to be abruptly thrown from his feet by the violent toss of the ship.

"The children!" Marie screamed.

"Put some clothes on, Marie," Jules ordered crisply, "I shall go for them."

Her face was white and fear held her immobile. Jules went to her and gripped her shoulders firmly, giving her a shake. "Marie! Get hold of yourself. The children will need us, we must be calm."

She nodded and he watched her heroically grip her terror. Even though her face remained stark with fear, she climbed from the bed and began to dress.

Seeing she was temporarily under control, he flung open the door and ran across the narrow passageway to the children's cabin.

He opened the door to find a hysterical Celeste being comforted as best he could by a very frightened Alexander. He was sitting on the edge of Celeste's bed holding her. Her arms were wrapped about him so tightly he could not move.

"Don't cry, Celeste," he was repeating. "It's nothing but a storm. We've had storms at home before and you weren't afraid."

Her teeth chattered in fear and she was visibly trembling. Jules could see the intense relief in Alexander's eyes as he walked across the floor and lifted Celeste up into his arms. She clung desperately to his neck as the ship lurched again almost throwing Jules from his feet.

"Waken Dante and come to our cabin, Alexander," he commanded in a firm voice and Alexander turned to obey, only to find Dante's bed already empty.

"Dante's not here, Father," he shouted above the noise of the storm.

"Good God," Jules muttered, as thoughts filled his mind as to where Dante might be. He handed Celeste back to Alexander. "Take her to your mother, see they stay in the cabin. I will go and find Dante."

He put his hand on Alexander's shoulder and their eyes met. "Keep calm son, and keep your mother and Celeste calm. Everything will be all right."

"Yes, Father," Alexander answered, and again he struggled to control the deep fear that twisted within him.

When he entered his parent's cabin, Marie, frantic now with worry, took Celeste in her arms. Between soothing words for the child she questioned Alexander.

"Where is your father?"

"He went to look for Dante, Mother."

"Dante!" her alarm sounded in her voice. "What happened to Dante, where is he?"

"I don't know, Mother. When the storm woke us, Dante was already gone. Father has gone to find him. He said for us to keep calm, the storm will pass soon."

Marie sat down, holding Celeste close to her, her face pale.

At that moment, a ripping sound from the hull of the ship reverberated through the cabin. Marie nearly screamed with alarm, but held it for fear she would terrorize Celeste even more than she was.

Alexander could barely stand the strain. He was afraid, and that alone shook him to the core. Worse, he could see visions of his father and brother in the grip of the storm, maybe dying.

Unable to cope a moment longer he jumped to his feet and ran to the door. "Alexander! No!" his mother called, but it was already too late. The door swung back and forth—Alexander was gone. Marie closed her eyes, held Celeste close and began to pray.

He was nearly tossed from his feet several times, but Alexander made his way up the steps to the companion-way.

The scene that met his eyes was one that would linger in his memory the rest of his life. It was one of unnamable pain and terror.

Jules had made his way to the deck. Sailors were moving about rapidly trying to lower the sails and get them laced to the spars before the intense wind whipped them to shreds. Black rolling clouds darkened the world while streaks of lightning ripped the night sky. Waves crashed over the rails of the ship threatening to wash away anything or anyone in their way.

Jules stood with his back to Alexander his eyes searching desperately for any sign of his son.

The rising wind tore at him, and he had to cling to the rail for support. At one moment a huge wave crashed on him and Alexander watched him slide half way across the deck before he found another hold. When he regained his feet, his eyes were still searching for Dante.

They must have both seen him at the same moment. Dante was trying his best to work his way toward the safety of his father's strong arm. His slender body was no match for the huge waves that crashed about him. He was nearly drowning in them and he could only manage to move inch by inch.

Jules called his name and began to move toward him. "Hold on, Dante," he shouted. "Don't try to come to me, just hold on."

But his words were lost in the rain swept gale.

"Dante, Dante," Alexander prayed to himself, "please hold on ... hold on."

For a moment it seemed as if Jules was going to succeed in getting to Dante in time. Then tragedy struck. To Alexander's horrified eyes, the scene before him seemed to happen slowly. He could see clearly Dante's frightened face. He could hear his father's anguished cry. Then a loud tearing roar as a top part of the mast split. Streamers of rope, like the arms of an octopus, waved in the gale. It dropped toward the deck below so violently that it bounced.

As it bounced close to Dante who froze in fright, the wildly flying ropes entangled themselves about the boy. Broken spar, ropes, and boy were lifted with the bounce of the spar and in the glaring flash of lightning, they disappeared over the side into the black swirling maelstrom below.

"Dante!" Jules agonized scream could be heard above the roar, echoed by the sheer anguish of Alexander's cry. Jules ran toward the rail, intending to go over the side after his son. Even though the pain of it touched them all, Captain Caulder shouted for him to be stopped. It took five men to capture and hold Jules.

Alexander too attempted to go to his brother's aid. His eyes blinded by tears, he did not even realize he was screaming his brother's name over and over.

He was lifted in strong arms and held. It was a long time before he realized it was his father who held him. His world was a dark aching place and he could not restrain his tears. He clung to his father and dimly realized his tears were being echoed. Then, mercifully, his world darkened and he was given the momentary escape and peace of unconsciousness.

He lay very still, for with the return of consciousness came the unbearable pain. "Dante," he murmured. But Dante was gone, swallowed by the dark cold angry sea.

He could hear someone crying, and realized the rumble of thunder was still echoing about the ship. He didn't want to open his eyes, not now, not ever again. The ship still rolled with the force of the storm, but the storm that lived within was more destructive and more painful. He would carry it within him for a long long time.

Someone came and sat on the edge of his bed. He reluctantly cracked his tired and burning eyes open. His father sat beside him. Jules face was ravaged with misery.

Alexander reached for him and Jules took his hand.

"Father," he whispered. "Dante . . . ?"

"He's gone, Alexander," Jules replied in a voice deep and broken with pain."

"Mother?"

"I have told her what happened . . . how it happened. Alexander, do you know why Dante was on deck?"

"No Father . . . I . . . I know I should have cared for him more. I'm sorry."

"Alexander," his father said firmly. "I will not have you blaming yourself in any way. No one is responsible. It is a tragic accident. We . . . you and I . . . we must make it as easy for your mother and sister as we can. Celeste too is grief-stricken. We must help them."

He stared at his father, realizing again the strength of the man who gazed back at him from red-rimmed eyes.

"Do you understand son?" he said softly.

Alexander knew his father was sharing his strength with him, giving him a reason to hold himself together and in the process telling him that he need not hold any guilt in his mind. At that moment, he loved his father more than at any other time in his life.

"Yes, Father," he replied.

"Good," his father nodded. For a moment, he gazed at Alexander, then he bent and lifted him against him. He crushed him to him as if it could ease the grief that threatened to destroy him. Alexander, too, clung to his father as fresh hot tears stung his eyes.

"Try to get some sleep son. Tomorrow will be a very difficult day. Do you want me to get you anything, something to drink?"

"No, Father."

Again Jules smiled reassuringly and then Alexander was alone. The grief suddenly bombarded his mind and he turned his face to the wall and held the pillow to his face to muffle his agonized tears.

Jules stood for a moment over Celeste's bed. She slept from exhaustion but even in her sleep, she whimpered softly.

When Jules returned to his cabin, the ship's rolling and heaving was already beginning to lessen. He had given Marie some brandy and forced her to lie down, but when he came into the cabin, he found her seated on the edge of her bed staring blankly into space. The shock was almost too much for her mind. He went to her, sat down beside her and drew her into his arms. She sobbed once, a dry sob filled with more pain than he had ever heard before.

"I cannot bear it Jules, I cannot," her voice whispered.

"I felt I could not bear it either, my love. In fact I almost leaped after him. But then I realized that we are all that Celeste and Alexander have. They need us."

"So black ... so cold," her voice had a far away sound that frightened Jules. He had to reach for some way to draw her back from the brink of the abyss over which she hovered.

"Marie, we must help Alexander. He needs our help."

For a moment he thought she might not have heard him, then her voice came again in a desperate agonized whisper.

"Alexander?" she repeated as if reaching for the words he had said.

"He desperately needs our help."

"He's hurt?" she said in alarm. "What has happened to him?"

"He ... he blames himself for Dante's ... death." The word came hard for him, for it forced him to accept the finality of it.

"Blames himself? But that is impossible. In God's name, why?"

"I imagine some of it is my fault," Jules said in a resigned unhappy voice. "I have always placed Alexander in a position of being an example, a leader for Dante. It seems he's taken that so seriously that he believes if he had been watching over Dante, he would never have left the cabin and all this would not have happened."

"Oh, Jules, my poor child," she cried.

"Marie, will you listen to me? Can you try to understand what I'm saying."

"Yes ... yes, Jules."

"Alexander cannot live with this. We have lost Dante.

75

No matter the pain, we must not let Alexander carry a load of guilt that will ruin the balance of his life. It is a thing that will go from him to Celeste who worships him. One day it could destroy them."

Now he felt Marie was listening. "What must we do Jules?"

Jules began to explain what he thought Alexander's emotions were, and what the two of them could do to help him. For hours they sat and talked, remembering Dante and his short years with them. As the words began to flow, the tensions were slightly relieved.

Exhausted, Marie finally slept. They passed the Carolina coast safely, but the loss of Dante made the balance of the voyage a solemn quiet affair.

Jules spent hours with Alexander, talking, trying to explain a thing he felt he could barely understand himself—the death of someone beloved. By the end of the voyage, he knew he was only partially effective. Alexander would need a lot of time to erase the sight of his brother being swept into the darkness of a stormy sea from his memory.

They were met at the docks three days later by Jules friend, Monsieur Eugene Claret. He escorted them to the home he had purchased for them.

It was a lovely house, but the glow of homecoming was dimmed by the void left by the absence of Dante.

Alexander kept much to his room for the first few weeks they were there. Eventually, it was Celeste who retrieved him from his deep depression and drew him back into her world by her love and her dependence on him. Yet it was a long time before Marie and Jules heard him laugh again or watched him enjoy any of his past pleasures such as riding.

Alexander found it difficult to ride the pony his father gave him for a long time.

Slowly time began to close the wound, but the scar would always remain. Alexander never told his parents of the nightmares that kept him from sleeping, of seeing the scene over and over again. Dante's fear-filled face, the almost lazy lifting of the broken spar as it drew him to his death.

He would waken from sleep bathed in sweat and crying.

For Jules, the nightmare was also repeated. In his mind the thing that had driven him from France was responsible for his son's death. He promised himself he would never again condone any form of revolution or war.

It was a promise he would not be able to keep, for the day was coming. A day that would bathe his adopted country in blood. A day that would threaten to take away from him the son he loved.

It was a time the family would face unbelievable trials and tremendous upheaval. Yet it would be a time when the temper of men was forged into iron and the Dubonne family would sink their roots deeply into American soil and begin to grow with the nation they had made their own.

Five

Terror filled Dante's mind until he screamed with it as he felt the tangled ropes twine about him and lift him from the deck. He saw clearly the horror on his father's face for a heart stopping second, then he tumbled over the rail and hit the dark waters below.

He sank below the turbulent waters, the spar dropping and pulling him with it. His lungs fought for air, and he swallowed salty tasting water. There was a harsh buzzing in his ears as his brain demanded air for his laboring lungs. He flung his arms about frantically trying to free himself from the entangling ropes. It was useless. He was going to die and he was afraid. That was the thought in his mind as consciousness began to ebb.

The spar, completing its downward plunge bobbed to the surface. Dante's head broke the surface and he gasped great gulps of air. Gratefully, he clung to the spar.

He was alone, drifting in the troughs of waves that towered over his head. There was no sign of the ship. He felt lost and unbearably afraid. There was nothing he could do but cling desperately to the spar and pray.

He tried to remember all the prayers he had ever

known. The storm tossed the boy and spar as if they were toothpicks. It took every ounce of concentration Dante possessed just to keep his hold. Numb fingers gripped the spar for he knew if he surrendered, he would be totally lost.

He had no idea of time that passed as he hovered on the edge of consciousness. He never realized when the storm ceased for his tangled mind could only contain one thought, to cling to the spar that was the one thing that stood between him and the depths of the ocean.

The ropes that were tangled about his body helped to hold him firmly even when consciousness finally lapsed. The last thing he remembered was bright sunshine. Slowly, it and the deep blue of the sea faded from his vision. All grew dark as he slipped into oblivion.

The wagon creaked along the dry dusty road. Its driver held the reins and urged the horses on. He was in a hurry to carry his baggage to its final destination. He was a very large man, his hair straw blond and his blue eyes faded and narrow from squinting endless days into the hot sun. He was broad of shoulder, yet his physical appearance was beginning to deteriorate. He had been at one time a handsome man, but signs of dissipation showed plainly in the puffy eyes and sagging chin. Closer scrutiny would show the telltale signs of mixed blood. Caleb Mackin was the grandson of Ezra Mackin and a black slave he had owned at the time. His father, born of this union, found life difficult. He was stranded between two societies which would not accept him. He eventually married a slatternly girl, the daughter of a small dirt farmer. It was a hard life and his wife Martha gave it up after the birth of Caleb. She died, leaving Caleb with a father who found his only solace in a bottle. Caleb's young life embittered him against both societies. He drank too much, fought too much and hated too much.

Eventually he lost the remnants of the farm his father had left him. Good fortune touched him only once in the form of Gregory Wakefield who gave him a position of overseer on his plantation. On the stipulation that Caleb was to stay sober, refrain from gambling and do his job to Gregory's satisfaction. This Caleb did for he realized what his situation would be if Gregory threw him out. He would be destitute.

Despite his hatred of them, Caleb took a wife who was a slave. She was as light of color as he. Lizell loved him, for she alone knew the pain unacceptance had brought him. It surprised him when he found that he had begun to love her also. Despite this, he insisted they would have no children. He was determined that he would bring no more children like himself into the world that had no future for them.

He was returning from a slave selling trip and carried a considerable amount of money with him. No one bothered Caleb, for his reputation with the long knife he carried preceded him.

Now he was hot, tired and thirsty, and very anxious to get home. Gregory had provided him a small home which Lizell had made into a haven where he could shut out the rest of his world.

He clicked the reins against the horses' rumps to move them along a little faster. Settled into a more rapid gait, Caleb let his gaze roam about him.

The road on which they travelled could barely be

called that. It was hard-packed dirt, deeply rutted. There was a much easier road to travel on, but Caleb preferred this one for two reasons. It kept him from meeting too many people, and it wound down the coast. He could hear the brush of the sea against the sand, and, as always, it soothed him.

He let his gaze wander out to sea, sensing a feeling for freedom there he had never known.

He must have been gazing at the object on the sand long before his mind registered what it could be.

He pulled the wagon to a halt and sat looking at it for a few minutes. At first he thought it was a piece of driftwood. Then slowly he began to see a form.

"Mind's playin' tricks on me," he muttered. He was about to urge the horse into motion, but curiosity got hold of him and refused to let go.

"Damn," he said, angry with himself. If he climbed down the rocks to the beach it would be another extra hour before he got home.

He jumped down from the wagon. After he tied the horses, he went over the edge of the cliff and climbed down the rocks to the beach.

As he walked closer he could see that his first thoughts had been right. It was a person.

"Dead," he murmured. He stopped beside the body and looked down. "A child," he said. "How the hell did a boy get here?"

He knelt beside Dante, and could see no sign of life. The boy's face was white and there was no perceptible sign of breathing. He bent forward and lay his hand against Dante's chest. The skin was cold and clammy. His lips were blue as were his extremities. He held the pressure of his hand for a long time before he felt a slight flutter from within. The fluttering heart was giving up the fight.

Quickly, he began to undo the ropes that held the boy to the piece of wood. When he had him free, he took off his coat and wrapped him in it.

It took quite a bit of maneuvering but he got back up the cliff to the wagon. He deposited the boy in the back of the wagon making sure he was wrapped securely.

Climbing back up on the wagon, he slapped the reins and urged the horses into the fastest gait they could maintain for the balance of the journey to the Wakefield plantation, High Oaks.

Gregory Wakefield stood at the window of his study gazing out over the side lawn of his plantation. He had a cigar gripped between his teeth and a glass of brandy in his hand, the other held the curtain aside so he could get an unobstructed view.

He was proud of all he had built, for with his own sheer energy, he had taken a rundown farm, which he had bought with the last dime he had, and had built it into one of the most impressive profit making plantations in the area.

All in all, he was satisfied with his life. Gregory was a tall slim man, wiry of muscle and lean, for he worked as hard himself as he worked the men under him. He had dark brown hair just beginning to gray at the temples. A short beard and moustache to match beneath piercing dark eyes. His skin was bronzed from the hours he spent in the sun.

He sipped the brandy thoughtfully. He was awaiting Caleb's return with the money from the sale of three slaves. He did not like to sell what he referred to as 'his people', yet he had been forced. Reluctantly, his mind slipped to the reason behind it.

He thought of Virginia, his wife, the love of his life. A fragile auburn haired woman he had fallen in love with the moment they met.

She had been the daughter of a very wealthy family, and they had looked down their aristocratic noses at the poor farmer who had wanted to wed their daughter. They had refused, but he and Virginia had loved each other too much to let their refusal stand in their way. They had run away and married. He was overjoyed at the way she stood beside him and worked, giving him more incentive to build. He knew it was she who made it all possible, and there was nothing he would not do to help her through the painful time she was experiencing. It meant more money, more doctors, yet he could not find it in his heart to refuse her for it was the desperate attempt to give him an heir that had put her health in such a delicate balance.

He thought of the four children who lay in the family cemetery, and the way his wife weakened and seemed to lose some of her life and vitality after each one.

Now she had heard of another doctor who might be able to help her carry a child to its full term. In desperation, she had begged him to let her go, and there was nothing he would not do to see her happy. The sad look that always lingered in her eyes hurt him. He sold the three slaves, knowing the money might be for nothing. What worried him the most was the way her mind seemed to slip a little after the death of each child. He wanted a son, but not at the expense of Virginia's life.

He was surprised to see the wagon turn up the long shaded drive at such a rate of speed. He knew Caleb would not press the horses unless it was important. He dropped the curtain, set the glass of brandy down and started across the room. Before he could get to the door, Caleb was already knocking upon it. He opened it quickly.

"Caleb, what's wrong."

"You'd best come with me, sir. There's something in the wagon you should see."

Gregory followed Caleb out. When they stood by the wagon, Gregory looked down on the unconscious boy who lay so white and helpless within.

"Who is he?"

"I don't know, sir. I only know he's not from any family hereabouts. I found him on the beach. Seems he must have been washed overboard from some ship."

"Poor child," Gregory said. Gently, he lifted Dante in his arms and carried him in the house.

"Virginia!" he called as he began to mount the wide staircase.

He heard the rustle of her skirts as she ran down the hall. Gregory had never shouted before so she knew it had to be a drastic situation.

She was at the top of the steps when she stopped. She watched him carry his burden up.

"Who ... Gregory ... who ... ?"

"I don't know, my dear. Caleb found him on the beach. He looks more dead than alive. Send someone for Doctor Wagner."

She gave the orders, then returned to the bedroom to watch Gregory lay Dante gently on the bed. He seemed so small and defenseless that her heart went out to him.

She sat down on the edge of the bed and took his cold hand in hers. "We must get several blankets. Cover him and keep him warm until the doctor gets here," she said.

Gregory went to the cupboard and took out several blankets. These they wrapped Dante in.

Gregory watched fascinated at the new glow that appeared in Virginia's eyes as she held the unknown child's hand in hers. He knew she was thinking of the children lost to her. For a moment, he was afraid.

"Caleb says he must have been washed overboard from some ship. He ... he belongs to someone Virginia," he said softly so the words would not hurt.

"I know," she whispered, but she clung to Dante's hand. "He is so small ... so helpless ... like the others."

Gregory could not bear the pain in her voice, and the echo of desperate longing. He knew he would have to find the family to which the boy belonged and return their son to them. But first they would have to help him survive, and from the way he looked, Gregory was doubtful if they could succeed.

Virginia held Dante's hand until the doctor arrived. Gregory had to almost force her from the room while the doctor examined him. They stood in the hallway silent, yet Gregory could physically feel where Virginia's mind was. It seemed forever until the doctor rejoined them.

"Doctor!" Virginia said urgently. "How is he? Will he live, he must live!"

"What he has been through is a drastic shock; I have no way of knowing how long he has been in the water. I fear fever and pneumonia. It will take a great deal to save his life."

"Tell me what I must do doctor," Virginia said determindedly, "I will care for him personally. I will see he has all he needs. We will keep him alive, you'll see, we will keep him alive."

Gregory and the doctor exchanged glances, worried about the strain of this situation on Virginia's already fragile condition. Virginia sensed their feelings.

"I will care for him," she said firmly, "I will keep him alive."

"To return him to his parents if he gets well," Gregory added softly. He and Virginia's eyes met and held.

"Yes, to return him to his family."

The doctor sighed and began to give her minute instructions for Dante's care. She listened intently, nodding now and then when he finished, she thanked him, went back inside the bedroom and closed the door behind her.

"Gregory," the doctor said in a worried voice, "you must not let her push herself, her health is too delicate now since . . ."

"Since we buried Parker. I know she hasn't been the same since he died. It's as if she is losing hold on everything. I will take care of her, doctor. Maybe she needs something or someone to care for now. I will see there's plenty of help and that she does not tire herself too much."

The doctor nodded and walked away. Gregory watched after him wondering if he would be able to do what he said. He had seen Virginia's face, he had known that mentally, she was reaching out of the dark, maybe for the final time and he wondered just what would happen when he had to take the boy away.

Virginia stayed by Dante's bed day and night, but

instead of growing tired or becoming ill, she seemed to grow stronger and stronger. Gregory was amazed at the metamorphosis and held on to it for as long as he could.

Dante seemed to slip deeper and deeper into the fever. His breathing was labored as his lungs fought for air.

Virginia, who sat at his side through the dark hours heard his mumbled words, listened to his tangled memories until she could nearly put a story together about his past.

It was five days later, late in the evening, that Gregory reentered the bedroom. He stood beside the bed and rested his hand on Virginia's shoulder. Absently, she reached up and patted his hand, but her attention was on Dante. It was then, to his relief he could see that the boy seemed to be in a natural sleep.

"The fever has broken?" he questioned softly.

"Yes, just an hour or so ago. He will probably sleep now for several hours."

"Good," he said firmly as he reached down to grasp her hand and pull her to her feet. "Now it is time you get some rest."

"But I cannot. He will need me when he wakens. Gregory, he will be in a strange environment, among strange people. He will be frightened. I must be here when he wakens."

"And you shall, my love. Beulah will sit with him while he sleeps and I shall personally give her orders to come waken you at the first blink of an eyelash."

"But Gregory . . ." she protested.

In one swift move, he bent and lifted her into his arms. He walked across the hall to their room ignoring any further protest she might make.

Inside their bedroom, he stood her on the floor by the bed. Slowly and deliberately, he began to undress her. He slipped a nightgown over her head, then began to loosen the pins in her hair letting its soft auburn strands drift through his fingers. Her thick glossy hair was one of the things he loved most about her. It had always been a source of never ending pleasure for him. Gently, he cupped her face in his hands and kissed her. "I love you so much Virginia. I will not have you doing yourself any harm, not for any reason in the world. My life and all I have are useless without you."

He watched her eyes fill with tears as her lips curved in a tremulous smile.

"But Gregory, he is so lost, so helpless."

"And so would I be without you. He is safe for tonight. Will you spend some of your love and care on me. I need you as badly as he does ... no, maybe more. He has many things in his future. I have and need you ... only you."

Her arms came about his waist and she lay her head against his chest. He sighed, closed his eyes, and savored the pleasure he always felt when he held her in his arms.

"I do love you, Gregory," she whispered. "I'm sorry if I ever made you worry for a minute. It's just that ..."

"I know. Don't you think I know how you feel. Don't you think I know the pain you carry. Don't you think I feel it too."

"Is it my fault Gregory," her voice was so quiet he barely heard the words.

"Good God, no! It's no one's fault. It is God's will."

"Then maybe ... maybe this could be God's will too," she looked up into his face. "Maybe the ship went down, maybe he is the sole survivor. That could be, couldn't it. It is possible."

"Well, yes, it is possible."

"Gregory, when he regains consciousness and can tell us what happened ... if the ship has gone down, if he has no one couldn't we ..."

"Keep him!"

She nodded, her eyes glowing with a bright flame of hope.

"My dear, even if the ship went down, even if he is the sole survivor, surely the boy has some relatives somewhere. It is our duty to help him find them if it is possible."

She sighed and he tightened his arms about her. "I know how difficult it has been for you, Virginia. When you are feeling better, we will see what can be done about adopting a child."

He knew she was silently crying. They both where well aware of how difficult if not impossible this would be.

Again he bent and lifted her in his arms, and lay her against the pillows. Then he sat beside her. He had not touched her since their last child had been born and had died. It had been months. That he wanted her, had wanted her every waking moment since, they both knew that he would not touch her unless he was invited.

She lifted both arms and put them about his neck. She smiled through her tears. This man had done his best to give her the best life had to offer. At first, it had been hard, but the past few years had been ones of luxury. The only thing wrong in their own private heaven was the inability to keep the children they had conceived together.

"I would be able to sleep much better if you share my

bed. It is so much warmer with you beside me. You have been gone too long, husband."

This was the Virginia he had loved and married. He knew it was finding the boy that had renewed the life within her. At this moment, he did not care for the reasons, he only knew he had his wife back, a wife he had missed for many long dark nights.

He bent forward and brushed her soft lips with his feeling the flame of it lick through him. God how much he wanted her.

Gently he lifted her against him feeling her soft pliant body mold itself against his. She was again the sweet giving woman. Their love making was a poignant, gentle thing. He feared to hurt her and so restrained himself until she urged him, murmuring words of encouragement and surrender.

Afterward, they lay together, his arms about her. This time had always been their sharing time, their time to discuss their thoughts and feelings. The fact that she clung to him but remained silent told him that her thoughts were still on the boy who slept in the next room.

"Virginia?"

"Yes, Gregory."

"You do understand?"

"Understand?"

"Why I must find the boy's family."

"Of course, I understand that. His parents must think him dead. They must be grieving ... if they are still alive."

"You still think they might be dead also?"

"You said it was a possibility the ship might have gone down."

"Yes, but I also said there was a possibility of other relatives."

"Yes," she replied quietly. "I will think of them as monsters, evil monsters who do not want him. I can picture his life a misery. Being shoved from relative to relative because no one loves him."

Gregory chuckled. "You do have quite an imagination. I swear if I find no relatives who want him, I'll keep him myself rather than put him through such an ordeal."

She sat up immediately. "Will you promise me that Gregory?"

His smiled faded. "You trapped me, woman."

"Is it so very difficult to think of him as ours?" she said quietly.

"No, that's the problem. It's not difficult at all."

"Then if you find his parents are dead, if you find no relatives or unbearable ones, will you ask him if it would please him to stay with us?"

"But Virginia, it just isn't right."

"What's wrong with it? Would you want to be the one to push an orphan child out into the cold cruel world with no one to protect him?"

Now they both laughed as he squeezed her in a ferocious embrace.

"No, my love, I will not cast the boy out into the storm of life with no one to protect him."

They laughed together and made love again like two exuberant children. They slept holding one another.

It was long after Gregory slept that Virginia wakened. She lay in the silent darkness of her room, enjoying the feel of Gregory as he lay beside her. One of his arms lay possessively about her. She remembered all their lives together. Gregory had always done everything in his power to make her happy.

It crushed her to think of the way Gregory tried to keep his desire for a son from her. She knew he loved her and did not want her to think of herself as a failure. Painfully, she remembered the children she had buried. Somehow she was sure that she would never be able to give her husband the son he so desperately wanted.

She thought of Dante again. Silently, she prayed that there was no one out there to whom he might belong.

"Dear God, I know it's wrong, and if there is to be punishment for it I know I am condemned. But please, give me this child ... please."

She curled against Gregory and slept peacefully for the first time in a long time.

She was content for the moment, but the man who lay beside her, feigning sleep, had heard the prayer. It disturbed him more than anything had ever done in his life before. He was afraid of what the future might do to her and to their love.

Six

Dante's mind struggled up from the blackness that had enveloped him. He was warm. The last thing he had remembered was the intense bone-chilling cold. He was weary. Too weary to move, even to breathe, and he did not have the strength to open his eyes. There was no feeling of time and he did not know how often he had slipped in and out of consciousness.

Gentle hands touched him accompanied by a soft voice. "Mother," he thought with pleasure. Occasionally a masculine voice came to him and his thoughts reached for his father. Of course, he thought, his father had leaped into the waves, braved the horrible storm to save him. He was safe. Again he drifted into a deep contented sleep.

He wakened, but he did not possess the energy to open his eyes. He lay still, savoring the warmth and comfort of the bed. Household sounds came vaguely. He sensed that someone was seated near his bed for he could hear the rocker creak as it moved back and forth, and someone hummed lightly in a soothing voice.

He gathered all the strength he had to lift his eyelids and look about him. At this first sign of wakening the rocker stopped. So did the humming cease. He heard the person rise and walk rapidly across the room. In another moment, the door closed behind her.

He wondered how long he had been sick to make him so weak and to have enough time to have arrived in their new country.

He found he was exhausted just thinking about where and why he was here. He closed his eyes again and nearly fell back to sleep when the door opened and two complete strangers came in. They stood for a moment gazing at him and he returned their gaze with just as much curiosity.

Dante was the first to speak. Forgetting that he would be in a strange country, a country in whose language he had only a tentative grasp, he retreated to his own native tongue.

"Bonjour, je m'appelle Dante Dubonne. S'il vous plait, pouvez vous me dire si ma mere et mon pere vont bien? Et, s'il vous plait, pouvez vous me dire ou je suis."

Virginia had received an extensive education for a girl. She had several years of French lessons. She replied immediately, overjoyed that they could communicate.

"Je m'appelle Virginia Wakefield. C'est Gregory Wakefield. Vous etes dans notre maison et vous etes en surete. Pouvez vous parle anglais?"

"Yes, Madame," Dante replied hesitantly. "But I do not speak it very good ... well. You will understand I hope. Are my mother and father here. I ... I would like to see them, to know they are well."

Gregory and Virginia sat, one on each side of his bed. Virginia took his hand in hers and he could clearly see the pity in her eyes. A searing pain struck him breathless.

Quietly, in a sensitive gentle voice, Virginia explained to him how they had found him, brought him to High Oaks and nursed him back to health. He had been very ill for a very long time and they had been afraid he might die. They did not know if his family were still alive, or for that matter where he had come from.

"We have prayed for you," she concluded. "Prayed you would survive, then you could tell us where you came from."

Dante gulped back hot tears that threatened to embarrass him. He said in a thick choked voice. "How long have I been here?"

"Almost two weeks."

"Two weeks!" he said. "And there has been no word about a shipwreck."

"Not here. Not along our part of the coast," Gregory said. "Now that you are on the mend I shall personally check the entire area and see if there is any word. I will send out word also to see if your ship the ... ?"

"*The Blue Gull.*"

"I shall do what I can to find your family, or word of your family. You must eat, sleep and regain your strength."

"I would be so grateful, sir. I shall do what you say, but ... how soon can you find word of my family. They must be certain I am dead. My mother will be hurt so badly. I must let them know I am alive."

"Dante," Virginia said softly, "you must understand. If the ship went down ... well ... it's possible your family is gone."

Now he could barely control the pain and the tears.

"No, Madame, no! Please don't say that. They must be alive! They must! What will I do without them. I will be alone. No! They must be alive."

"Virginia!" Gregory said, "that was unnecessary at this moment. The boy has been through enough. Let him at least have hope."

"He must also accept what might be," Virginia replied. "Dante, we are your friends. You are welcome to stay here for as long as you like."

"I ... I know you have saved my life but ... I ... I want to go to my family. I know they must be alive, I know it. You will try to find them, Monsieur?"

"Yes, Dante, I'll try to find them."

"You must get some rest. I shall go down and have a breakfast prepared." Virginia said. "If you intend to regain your strength, if you are going to find your ... family. You must get your health back. We will talk again later."

"Yes, Madame."

Virginia patted his hand. She rose and went to the door.

"I shall return with breakfast. We will begin to put some meat on those bones. You are much too thin."

She left, closing the door quietly behind her. Dante and Gregory sat in silence for a moment, then Dante spoke in a restrained voice.

"Do ... do you think the ship went down sir? Do you think they are ... gone, all of them?"

"Dante, I'm sorry to say this, but there is a possibility. This area and north of us is a very bad stretch of ocean, it has claimed more than one ship."

Dante was too weak to hide his fear. He trembled with it and the tears fell from exhausted pain filled eyes.

Gregory lifted him against him and felt the slender arms cling. It roused an emotion he had not surrendered to in a long time, an aching need to hold a child in his arms.

"It is best to cry," he said softly and held Dante close to him while he sobbed out his fear.

When he could cry no more, Gregory laid him back against the pillows. Dante seemed to be relapsing into a state of shock and Gregory knew he had to help draw him out of it.

"You must tell me something Dante."

"Tell you," Dante murmured listlessly, "tell you what, sir?"

"About you and your family. How you came to be coming to our country. All that happened. I would like to know about them and about you. I would like to be a friend."

"What do you want to know, sir?"

"How many in your family?"

"My father, Jules Dubonne, was a soldier under Napoleon, sir, a very brave one. He has medals and . . . and a very handsome uniform. He let me hold his sword one day but I was too little to carry it."

"I see, and your mother?"

"Oh, sir, she is the most beautiful lady in France. Father has seen a lot of people and he said so, mother was the prettiest of all."

"I take it you agree," Gregory smiled.

"Oh, yes, sir."

"You were their only child?"

"No, sir. I have an older brother, Alexander. He's two years older than me, and a sister Celeste, she's the baby."

"I see. Why did your family leave France?"

"I don't exactly know, sir. Father said we had to go away before someone got us."

"He was afraid of being captured by someone," Gregory mused. He must have been a supporter of Louis Bonaparte.

Dante caught only one word—afraid. "My father has never been afraid of anything in his whole life," he said belligerently.

"I didn't mean it like it sounded," Gregory apologized quickly. "I meant he was afraid someone would hurt his family so he decided to take you all to safety. Do you know what his destination was?"

"I think he said something about a place called Phila ... Phila ..."

"Philadelphia?"

"Yes, sir, I think that was it."

"I'll tell you what I will do, Dante."

"What sir?"

"I shall take a trip to Philadelphia and see if the *Blue Gull* arrived safely. If it did, I shall tell your family where you are. They can come and pay us a visit and take you home with them."

"Oh, sir, I would be so grateful. I just have a feeling they're alive."

"Well, you eat well, and get well, and I shall find out everything I can."

"Thank you, sir, thank you."

Virginia returned with a tray laden with food which Dante tried to eat, but his neglected stomach would not take so much so quickly.

For the next few days, Dante tried to do everything he could to regain his health and Virginia lived in a state of euphoria. Gregory had to admit he had never been happier. The presence of a child had suddenly changed a large elaborate house into a comfortable happy home.

Virginia blossomed, and he heard the return of laughter he thought had been permanently stilled.

He began preparations for his trip north and knew Virginia was silent on the subject because she refused to face the fact that Dante might soon be taken from her.

Dante was carried down and sat in a chair on the sunny veranda the day that Gregory had chosen to leave. Gregory stood with him while his horse was brought. Virginia also stood in silence. She said nothing, but he could not miss the agonized pleading in her eyes. He could not find the words to console her so he kissed her goodbye, mounted and rode away.

The trip from High Oaks, Georgia to Philadelphia would take him quite some time. He could only take the trip in short stages. He rose early in the mornings and rode until noon, resting his horse occasionally. He would stop at least an hour for lunch, he would find an inn or lodge for the night. Sometimes, he slept under the stars. It gave him a lot of time to think, more time than he wanted. He had never faced himself more honestly than now. He wanted Dante for a son, he wanted to see his wife's face happy, he wanted someone to leave High Oaks to. He wanted that link that formed the chain between man and immortality . . . a son. He wanted . . . but he did not have the right. It was wrong to even think of severing a family, of taking from them the joy of having a son such as Dante promised to be. He agonized over his thoughts night after night, day after day and hour after hour. Yet when he reached the outskirts of Philadelphia, he still had not taken the final step in resolving the problem.

* * *

Virginia had already put the future from her mind. She had Dante here for the moment and she was going to enjoy it for as long as it lasted. She wanted him to fall in love with High Oaks. If fate were to grant her what she wanted so desperately it would be a way to ease Dante's pain a little. She thought of all they had to offer Dante.

High Oaks Plantation was 10,000 acres of lush land. The main house was a large two story building with a porch that extended across the front and on both sides. Huge white pillars supported a veranda that extended about the entire house. The house contained twenty-one rooms. The main door opened into a black and white marble entrance way with a huge black and white marble circular stairway. A huge crystal chandelier hung directly over the center of the marble entrance way.

Downstairs, there was a large dining area with pale gold walls and all matching decor done in shades of gold from deep rich gold to the palest soft shades. There was a ballroom finished in shades of red, a library with a cut stone fireplace, polished wood floors and bookshelves from floor to ceiling. A large sitting room with another large fireplace and equipped with soft comfortable chairs and couches. Another room filled with beautiful green plants and flowers and white benches and chairs at strategic and comfortable places. An office designed for a man, a man of definite appetite and excellent taste. Huge chairs, large comfortable couches and an immense desk that was definitely put there for a useful purpose.

Another room that had been built for no other purpose than to hang the huge portraits of all the family ancestors. Another room was set aside for the mistress's daytime activities and entertainments. There was also another smaller dining room for the family's quieter meals.

The master study and the music room stood next to the school room. There were fifteen bedrooms upstairs, five of which had accompanying sitting rooms. The mansion was a magnificent edifice that was a monument to the culture and the man who had built it.

She thought again of the man who had created this wonder from nothing. It would be a magnificent legacy to give a son.

She spent most of her waking hours with Dante, entertaining him by reading to him, playing games and sometimes just talking. She watched him smile with pleasure when she appeared and it made her heart swell with longing.

They had long conversations, sometimes in French. They had begun to be able to laugh together he, over her atrocious French and she over what she delightfully countered as his atrocious English.

Each day found him a little stronger, and each day she let him do a little more. First it was getting up and dressing himself, then she let him come down for meals. Then they began to take short walks which developed into longer ones. He was thrilled with the stables that housed so many beautiful horses, and extremely thrilled when she offered him a pony.

"I would be pleased to be able to ride it while I'm here, Madame," he said so formally she very nearly laughed. "But my parents would never allow me to take such an expensive gift."

"Then let me give it to you and you can leave it here for all the times you might come to visit. Wouldn't it be nice to come and spend some time with us occasionally."

"Oh, yes, Madame, I should love to."

"Then it is settled. The pony is yours. But first you must be a lot better before you can ride. Are you taking your tonic regularly as Beulah told you?"

"Oh, yes, Madame, I am quite well, really I am."

"Then maybe if you eat a good supper, get another good night's rest, I will let you take a short ride tomorrow."

His eyes sparkled in delight and he nodded his head rapidly.

"I shall, Madame, I promise."

"Dante?"

"Yes, Madame?"

"Must you call me Madame?"

He looked at her blankly for a few moments. "But ... what shall I call you, Madame. Father would be very upset with me if I were disrespectful."

"I see ... well, let me see. Can I not be your honorary aunt? That way, you could call me Auntie Virginia."

He pondered this for a moment, then replied. "I think that would be fine. I have never had an honor ... honor ... honorary. Yes, I've never had an aunt like that before."

"Do you have many aunts?"

"I don't have any."

"Oh ... what about your grandparents?"

"They are dead. I never knew them."

"I see. Then you have no other relatives than your family."

"No, no one."

"Well you can consider Gregory and I as honorary

aunt and uncle. Now, you must name your pony if you are going to own him."

He thought about this for some time. "I shall name him Storm."

"Good heavens, what a name," she laughed.

"If it had not been for a storm, I would not have him."

"Very well, Storm it is. Now let us walk back to the house. Remember, a good supper and a good night's rest."

"Yes, Auntie Virginia."

He kept his word, but was up the next morning as soon as the sun rose. Virginia was surprised when she heard the timid rap on her door.

"Come in," she called.

Dante stepped inside. He was fully dressed and she knew immediately why. "Go down and tell cook to give you something to eat. I shall dress and be right down. We will go for a short ride this morning."

He was gone in a blink of an eye and she rose from the bed laughing. She sang as she dressed and many ears about the main house were pleased with the sound of it.

She herself suddenly realized she was singing and stopped for a moment as the realization struck her that she never had been happier in her life than she was at that moment.

They had her horse and his pony saddled and she gave him a short tour of the property that belonged to High Oaks. He was amazed for it was even more than his parents had owned and he had thought them extremely rich.

"But you own so much land. It is like . . . like a whole country."

"Yes," she mused. "You might say it is a little country."

"A lot of people must build their houses on your land to help you take care of it."

"No, we have slaves for that."

"Slaves?"

"Yes, the blacks. They belong to us. They are here to follow our orders. We own them."

"Own," he smiled. "You are teasing me, Aunt Virginia. Nobody can own somebody."

"Yes, dear, we bought them, like we bought everything else in our home."

"You mean you buy people?" he said in a shocked voice. He was even more shocked at her reply.

"They are not people, my dear. They are slaves. Slaves are not quite as intelligent as other people. They need someone to tell them what to do. We buy them and train them. They have a good home here. We treat them well. They're only beaten if they do something seriously wrong. Don't worry, my dear, you will get used to giving them orders and used to them obeying you. Gregory will explain when he returns."

Dante had doubts about this situation but he said nothing. Surely he had misunderstood her. He would wait for Gregory to return and explain it to him again. Possibly his English was faulty. They rode daily and afterwards would have a quiet breakfast together. Later she would give him some lessons in English and history.

Occasionally, she would play the piano for him, or have him read to her as a method of improving his understanding of the language.

Always she came to tuck him in at night and talk for a few minutes before she blew out the candle and he slept.

Virginia rose very early one morning several weeks after Gregory had gone. For some unaccountable reason, she had not been able to sleep. She walked out on the veranda and sat watching the first gray light of dawn touch the night sky.

She could see for miles down the road that led to High Oaks. After a few minutes, she saw a lone rider coming in her direction. It was Gregory, she could tell by the expert way he rode.

Quickly she rose and went downstairs. Out the front door and down the long drive. She wanted to talk to Gregory alone before Dante knew he was there. She had to know first if she had to give up what little happiness she had found or if she could keep Dante at High Oaks forever.

Seven

Gregory saw Virginia waiting for him beneath the shade of one of the huge oaks that lined the drive. When he reached her, he dismounted, tied his horse to a low hanging branch and walked to her side. She was trying to read his face and could not. He took her in his arms and held her close. He did not want her looking at him for a few minutes. He spoke the words that might damn him forever.

"The ship went down, Virginia. Everyone aboard went down with her. The boy's family was completely wiped out."

"Oh, my God, poor Dante," she cried. "This will be such a terrible thing to tell him."

"I will tell him myself. It's best that way."

He did not want Virginia to be in any way responsible for the terrible lie he was about to tell.

They sat beneath the shade of the tree while she told him how well Dante was doing. She told him how much she had enjoyed him all those weeks and how Dante had begun to improve both physically and mentally.

"I know, outside of worrying about his family, he has been happy here, Gregory. He will need someone now.

Can we not beg him to stay with us. We could be some source of help to him during this tragedy?"

"I was already thinking of that, my dear. When the shock of this is over, I shall talk to him about staying with us. Maybe, eventually, if he wants us as much as we want him, he would even consider letting us adopt him. Since he has no family left, we can offer our support and urge him to let us help fill the void."

"Oh, Gregory," she cried, as she threw her arms about his neck and kissed him passionately. "I love you so very much. There never has been a man as kind and understanding as you are. If he agrees, I shall try to be the best mother in the world. I shall try to fill the black emptiness in his life with love and laughter until we can teach him to love again."

"I know you will, love, and I . . . I shall try to make a good father . . . I shall try to make up for all that he has . . . lost."

"Come, let us go into the house. The sooner we tell him, the sooner he can begin to rebuild his life again."

They rose and walked side by side leading the horse behind. At the front door, he handed the horse's reins to a groom. He gazed at the stairway, reluctant to walk up and face the boy. Slowly, he walked up and Virginia watched from below.

She sorrowed for the grief Dante would feel, yet she felt a surge of intense joy. The possibility that he could one day be hers washed almost every thought from her mind.

Gregory stood in front of Dante's door several minutes before he knocked. He heard a stir within, then the door opened and a fully dressed Dante appeared. He looked frightened.

"I saw you come, sir ... did ... did you find any news about my family?"

"I have Dante," Gregory said softly. "May I come in. We must talk."

"Yes sir," Dante stepped back and Gregory came in closing the door behind him. Dante's face was stark and drained of life. He knew without asking, yet the words had to be said. He felt as if he could not breathe and an almost unbearable pain enveloped and threatened to overwhelm him. He said the next few words in a hoarse whisper.

"They're dead?"

"Yes, Dante. I'm sorry. The *Gull* went down with everyone aboard. They are all lost." He had tried to soften his words yet they came out sounding severe and outright.

He watched Dante's face go even paler, and tears form that he tried his best to contain. He reached out and clasped the boy's shoulder in a strong grip.

"Sometimes life gives us more than we feel we can bear, yet God always gives us the strength to bear it. It is a tragic thing but you have friends here. Friends who would like to help you through this dark time and show you that you have a good future ahead of you. Your family would want you to go on and to be strong."

"I know sir," Dante whispered. "But ... Mother, Celeste ... I can't believe."

"You must remember only the good things and try to keep from thinking of anything else. It is difficult I know, but not impossible. You'll find as time passes you will become stronger and stronger with each day."

"Yes, sir ... can ... can I be alone for a while?"

"Of course," Gregory replied gently. He gave Dante's

shoulder another reassuring squeeze then left. When the door closed behind him Dante ran across the room and threw himself down on the bed. He tried to muffle his excruciating tears with his pillow.

He cried until his eyes burned and no more tears would come. It took him several days of concentrated thought to sort out exactly how he felt. He would mourn his parents for the rest of his life. He would remember them always, but he knew he had to go on living. He wondered what his father would expect him to do.

Slowly, he tried to place his situation in perspective. He would stay at High Oaks until he was old enough to take care of himself. He had no place else to go and he knew the Wakefields wanted him to stay.

He was made more than welcome at High Oaks and as the days began to drift along, he fell into a pattern of living. They offered him warmth, friendship and a life that promised to be fulfilling and good. He would be able to get a good education and could some day look forward to being able to travel and to own a place like High Oaks himself.

At this point, he did not know that the Wakefields looked forward to the time when he would be so at home at High Oaks that he would consider becoming an adopted son.

Gently, Gregory began to take him under his wing. The constant guilt he felt at what he had done remained now and would always remain. If he ever considered telling the truth he had only to look into Virginia's face, and see the happiness that Dante had brought. That was enough to bury the guilt deeply.

Even though Dante and Virginia spoke French often, the language began to slip. His French accented English became tinged with a Southern drawl that was at once both amusing and yet strikingly interesting. He began to make friends with the children who lived on neighboring plantations. Some would remain his friends for the rest of his life.

Slowly the days turned into weeks, then to months, then to years. As the time began to flow by, friends, neighbors and even the Wakefields themselves, began to drop the French accented Dante, and before he was twelve he was the only one who remembered that he was anyone but the Wakefield boy ... Dan.

It was only when he reached his fourteenth birthday that he and Gregory had the talk of which Gregory had looked forward to for so long. A time when he thought Dante was old enough to understand all he would say.

They had celebrated his birthday with a small gathering of friends, and afterwards had presented him with a gift of a new saddle for his horse and new riding boots.

When the evening was over, Gregory and Dante walked along the long darkened porch of High Oaks. For a time they were both silent, held by the beauty and serenity there.

Gregory knew Dante had begun to love both High Oaks and he and Virginia.

"Dan, I've something to talk over with you."

"Me, sir?"

"Yes. Have you been happy here at High Oaks?"

For a few minutes Dante was silent and Gregory knew his mind reached backwards. He was remembering again all that had been so brutally taken from him. Again Gregory's conscience chafed under the strain of knowing that all he had to do was to tell Dante his family still lived. Tell him and Dante would be overjoyed . . . but he would be gone. He knew, much as he loved Dante now, that Virginia had made him the most important part of her life. He could not, would not, allow her to receive the final hurt that might destroy her forever.

"I suppose so, sir," came the hesitant reply. "You and Mrs. Wakefield have been awfully good to me. I don't know what I would have done or where I would have gone if you hadn't taken me in and cared for me like you did."

"Dan, you know Virginia and I both love you very much and we want you to be very happy and at home here. In fact, I have something very serious I would like to talk over with you. Will you hear me out completely before you say anything. I would not want you to agree or refuse without a great deal of thought."

"Yes, sir."

"Dan . . . High Oaks is very dear to me. I built it with all the love and energy I possess. You have visited the cemetery with Virginia so you know of the children God has seen fit to take from us."

"Yes, sir, I know," Dante replied softly. He remembered the tears in Virginia's eyes and the pain he could see there.

"I have reached all my goals in life but one. I have everything I shall ever need. But a man needs someone . . . someone to follow after him, someone who could share the same love of the land. Dante, I would not ask you to forget those you loved. I would not ask you to deny your name, of which you are extremely proud," he smiled, "even though most people refer to you as Dan Wakefield."

Dante smiled. "I've gotten tired of telling everyone different, sir. I don't mind."

"I know, it's why I felt it was a good time to ask you. Dante, I would like to have you as my heir. I would like you to inherit High Oaks when I die."

Dante was stunned. "Sir ... you want to give High Oaks to me? But sir ... maybe ... maybe one day you will have ..."

"More children of my own? No, Dan, no. It will never be. I should hate to see High Oaks go to ruin when I'm gone. I should like to see it go to a capable man, and that is what I think you are rapidly on the way to becoming."

Dante was silent for a moment then he looked at Gregory with wide honest eyes. "There's something more, isn't there, sir?"

"Yes, Dan, there is. To make everything legal, it would have to be an official adoption. I wouldn't want some long lost relative I never knew to be able to cause any problems."

"Official ... you mean I would have to change my name?"

"No, you wouldn't. You will always be Dante Dubonne ... but why can you not be Dante Dubonne Wakefield?"

"Dante Dubonne Wakefield," Dante whispered.

"I know it's a shock, but Dan, I'm not asking you to give up anything. High Oaks will assure your future. The two of you together will be a power in this state one day. I want to know that I have done all I can to help you replace what you have lost, and I want to have the peace of mind knowing High Oaks will be in safe hands when I'm gone. Will you think about this for a while?"

"How long can I think about it?"

"As long as you like," Gregory smiled as he rested his hand on Dante's shoulder. "There is no pressure on you. But think about this. You have no living relatives. When you marry, you will be Dante Dubonne and continue your family's line. You will also be a Wakefield and continue my line. In fact, you are the last hope of both names."

Gregory gave his shoulder a gentle shake then turned and walked away leaving Dante to think over what he had said.

It was the only thing that was to occupy Dante's mind for the next few months. He thought of his parents with an intense ache. He thought of Celeste and Alexander. He realized the truth of Gregory's words. He was the last of the Dubonnes and he was their only future. Could he find a future on his own, with no money, no family, no one to stand with him? He knew it would be nearly impossible. To make his future as a Dubonne, he also had to make his future as a Wakefield.

Neither Gregory or Virginia said anything else to influence him. He sensed the urgency and the need within them. He also sensed that everyone on the plantation seemed to know what had transpired between he and the Wakefields and were waiting to see what he would do.

It was a load for a young boy to carry, and it kept him awake at nights, wandering about the plantation aimlessly during the day. That was the way he ran across Jessie.

He rode Storm across the fields and through a tree shaded area until both boy and horse were tired. Then he dismounted and walked Storm to cool him off. His mind, deeply involved in future thoughts was so pre-occupied he did not see anyone approaching him until he was only a few feet away. Then he looked up suddenly and was startled by the immense size of the man who was walking toward him carrying a fishing pole over his shoulder.

Dante was sure he had never seen a man as big or as dark in his life. He stopped in his tracks, fascinated by his appearance.

"Mornin', " the man said in a low rumbling voice that seemed to come from somewhere deep within him. "You be da boy of da Wakefield's?"

"Yes, I'm Dante. Who are you?"

"I'se Jessie."

"Jessie, who?"

"Jus Jessie."

"Do you belong to the Wakefields, Jessie?"

"I doan belong to nobody but Jessie, boy, I'se a free man. Yo' step-pappy wuz de one what set me free."

"Oh," Dante replied, but he would have given his life to question Jessie more closely.

Jessie's eyes twinkled in amusement as he read the boy accurately.

"I be goin fishin. Yo wan to come along?"

"I've never been fishing. I don't even have a pole," Dante replied, disappointment in his voice.

"Ah can cut yo one in no time. My place is jus' over dat hill. Come on, we fix yo up a pole."

Dante walked along beside Jessie until they crested the next hill. In a small shaded valley below was a small cabin. Once they reached it, Jessie told Dante to tether his horse after he unsaddled it.

"Ya won't be needin' him fo' a while."

Jessie cut a long straight pole from a nearby tree and fashioned Dante a rough pole.

"Come on boy," he grinned, "them fish is bitin' and I sho am hungry fo' a mess of 'em for suppa."

Dante laughed. He felt exuberant. He had not felt so excited about anything since he had come to High Oaks.

He and Jessie started out on foot. After they had walked a little less than an hour, Dante could hear the murmuring sound of a stream. It was not long until they found it. Laboriously and patiently Jessie taught Dante the fine art of fishing. They had caught several while Dante was struggling in his mind to find a way to get himself invited for supper.

Jessie's sparkling eyes rarely left the boy, and he sensed both loneliness and a distressed mind. He knew such emotions probably more than anyone else in the area.

"Yo' be hungry, boy?" he questioned gently.

"Oh, yes, sir, I'm starved."

"Come along. We'll fry up these fish then I'll ride back home with you."

Dante had never enjoyed a meal more than this one, and he was pleased that when Jessie rode with him back to High Oaks he extended an invitation for Dante to come again and visit.

It began a relationship rare and beautiful ... true friendship, yet it was some time before Dante could bring himself to ask all the questions that crowded his mind.

They were seated beneath the shade of a huge tree. Their poles braced against the ground, they watched the slow moving water in a state of contented lethargy.

"Jessie?"

"Uh huh."

"Can I ask you something?"

"Sho, boy, ask."

Dante knew that everyone including Jessie knew of the proposed adoption. "What would you do if you were me?"

"Nobody can tell you that, boy, everybody's different and does things fo' different reasons."

"Do . . . do you think I'm betraying my father if I do?"

Jessie was quiet for a moment. Then he began to speak softly, as if his mind had reverted to a different time and place.

"Lemme tell you a little story boy. Seems like a long time ago, I wasn't no bigger 'n yo'. My life was good. I lived with my family a long long way from here. Then one day, the slave traders came. They caught the whole bunch of us. They put us on board a ship . . . a hell ship, to bring us here. On the way, a whole passel of 'em died . . . including my mother, father and my sister. I thought my life was over, that I could not live with the hurtin'. I was a scared boy and I began to grow into a scared man. Then one day, I realized I was so scared and hurt by the past I wasn't livin' no life at all. That's when I learned that every man has to live out the life God gave him no matter how much hurtin' there is in it. No matter what you get or lose, it's still the only life you've got."

"You were a slave, Jessie? How did you get to be free?"

Jessie chuckled. "Makin' a long story short, I jumped in the river and saved Mr. Wakefield from drownin'. He said he'd give me anything I wanted . . . I wanted my freedom. He gave it to me." He turned and looked at

116

Dante, his dark eyes steady. "The only person yo' can betray in this life is yo self boy. Yo' be a good straight honest man and no matter what name they call you, your daddy would be proud of you."

"It . . . it's hard, Jessie."

"I know. But they aren't nuthin' easy in this life. Still you got to keep goin' and you got to make somethin' out of what you got. Pears to me you got a lot of good things goin' for you. You got rememberin' a good people that had you and started you off, and you got good people who want to pick you up and help you keep goin' along. Yup, pears to me you got a chance for the best, and that would just be what your parents would have wanted for you. Keep your memories, but live the rest of your life."

Dante was quiet, and Jessie let him have the time to think. It was a quiet, thoughtful boy who helped Jessie clean and eat the fish they had caught. Then Jessie stood at his cabin door and watched him ride slowly away.

"Yo' a good boy, chile," he murmured. "Yo' gonna be all right once yo get your feet under you."

At breakfast the next morning, after a long and sleepless night, Dante informed Gregory and Virginia that he agreed to the adoption.

Dante's decision changed everyone's life. It brought a happiness to High Oaks that had never existed there before. Gregory filled Dante's days with knowledge of the plantation and how it was run. He was beginning his training as lord of the manor . . . and slowly he began to like it. Virginia made sure his social life brought him in contact with all the best families.

He grew in the shadow of High Oaks, steeped in the tradition and beauty of the South. He grew tall and handsome. His world began to consist of honor, pride and love of his adopted home and family.

The gold medal he always wore about his neck was the one link with the past he clung to. He held his memories close to him, Celeste, Alexander, his parents would always be part of him. But he knew now that he had to separate the past from the future, and the future was for Dan Wakefield, heir to High Oaks.

High Oaks became the center of the county's society. Virginia Wakefield glowed as the mistress of the mansion. She was happy as was Gregory as they watched Dante become all they had ever hoped for in a son.

If all at High Oaks loved him, so did many on other plantations in the area. Women found his golden good looks nearly irresistible and his humorous drawl sprinkled with French drew them to him like bees to a honey pot.

It was a gay colorful world he was to inherit, but the gaiety and color were to die, and again his whole world would be faced with change.

But before the holocaust, before the trial began, he was to meet the two women who were to influence the rest of his life in a way he could not even imagine.

One was to guide him to the future and the other would guide him to the past.

Eight

Carriages lined the drive of High Oaks. There was to be a happy celebration this bright summer day. Dan Wakefield was home from college and his parents had arranged a homecoming celebration. Abby Southerland sat in the carriage with her two cousins, Catherine Markland and Christina Clayton, and gazed up at the beautiful home. She had been hearing so many stories about High Oaks and Dan Wakefield that her curiosity had been aroused. It amused her that her two cousins were so smitten with Dan Wakefield that they could barely talk of anyone else.

She had been visiting the Marklands when the invitation came and they had insisted she come along. The Southerlands, wealthy planters from across the state had given their one and only daughter a very rare thing for the times, an extensive education. To all outward appearances, she was a quiet, gentle spoken, well bred woman. Few people saw the inner core that contained a will of iron and a determination that would have astounded them.

Her father, a self-made millionaire, had recognized the keen intelligent mind beneath the pretty exterior and had encouraged it. She had received some of her education in America and some in Europe which had also allowed her to travel extensively.

Her mind, quick, assured and self-contained, was matched by an extraordinary beauty. She was slender and slightly taller than what was considered stylish. Her hair was thick and a deep vibrant auburn. Her skin, a smooth creamy ivory brought to startling contrast her wide sea blue eyes. She was quick to smile and laugh. The smile, broad and open, quickly disarmed everyone she turned it upon.

She had been listening with interest to the situation that was brewing in her country, and despite what her logic told her about the South's vulnerability, she was intensely, even fiercely, loyal to it.

Her thoughts were drawn back to the two women who accompanied her when their laughter interrupted her reverie.

"Oh, Abby, wait until you meet him," bubbled Christina, the more excitable of the two. "He is absolutely beautiful. Isn't he Catherine?"

Catherine Markland always reminded Abby of a tiny Dresden doll. She seemed so fragile, as if a strong wind would easily blow her away. Her eyes, wide and crystal blue, were fringed with thick long lashes. Her hair was a pale gold and tumbled in a mass of curls that were constantly becoming wayward and had to be restrained with much effort on Catherine's part. Abby watched her blue eyes darken at Christina's words and realized immediately that Catherine was very much in love with the young man of whom she spoke.

"Men aren't beautiful," Catherine answered firmly. "They are handsome. Dan is handsome."

Abby smiled. "I can't wait to meet this paragon of masculine virtue. He sounds like Adonis and Samson rolled into one."

As their buggy arrived at the door each was helped down by Catherine's quiet brother who was amused by Christina's enthusiasm. Richard and Dan Wakefield were friends and he wondered what Dan would say if he knew how Catherine and Christina felt about him. He also wondered what effect the blue eyed beauty sitting across from him would have on Dan, who, in Richard's estimation, had a very discriminating eye for beautiful women.

The sound of music drifted through the open windows. A slim black boy opened the door for them and they entered to be greeted by Virginia and Gregory. After she had greeted the others enthusiastically, she turned to Abby.

"This is our cousin from Georgia, Mrs. Wakefield. She has been visiting with us for a few weeks and we insisted she come with us to meet you all and see the most beautiful home in the state," Richard said.

"Why, thank you, Richard," Virginia smiled at Abby. "And welcome to our home, Miss Southerland. We are more than pleased to have you here."

"Thank you Mrs. Wakefield. Please call me Abby."

"Come Abby," Virginia smiled. "Please let me introduce you to the rest of our friends."

She took Abby's hand and tucked it through her arm and led her into the huge dining room where a long buffet had been set.

Abby, as Richard thought she would, caused quite a stir, and many eyes followed her progress about the room mentally trying out compliments and flowery words that might capture her attention at the dance that would follow later in the evening.

Abby smiled at each, but was wondering where the much talked about Dan Wakefield was.

Dan was at that moment in his bedroom throwing off sweaty wrinkled clothes as rapidly as he could while an amused valet was laying out his fresh clothes. The tub of steaming hot water felt good to Dan's tired muscles as he climbed into it. But there was not much time to enjoy it, he was already over an hour late for his own party.

"Yo mammy sho gonna be upset with yo iffen yo' doan get down pretty soon."

"I know," Dan replied as he scrubbed rapidly and fairly leaped from the tub reaching for a towel. "She hasn't sent anyone up for me, has she? She'd skin me if she knew I've been in the stables with a new foal all morning."

"No, suh, she ain't sent no one, and no one goin' to tell her. Dat new foal finally come?"

"Yes," Dan grinned. "She's a beauty, a trim little filly that will grow into a racer if I've got an eye for it."

"Yo' sho enough do, sah, ain't yo' always ridin' the winner in all the races."

Dan grunted as he pulled on his shoes and grabbed for his jacket. He shrugged it over his broad muscular shoulders. "Just lucky," he said as he went to a mirror and tried to tame his thick mass of wayward golden hair.

"No suh!" the valet said firmly, "tain't luck. Yo' rides a horse like yo' was born on one."

Dan laughed. He looked at himself in the mirror. He was tanned a deep golden brown that told of innumerable hours in the sun. It highlighted his mass of golden hair and the white sparkle of his square even teeth.

His crystal green eyes sparkled with health and enthusiasm. They were intelligent and filled with the challenging glitter of amusement. His body was tall, lean and gracefully muscled.

He turned to face the smiling valet. "Look all right?"

"Yassah, but looks ain't going to count iffen yo' doan get down there pretty quick."

"Right," Dan chuckled. He went rapidly to the door and left. He half-ran, half-walked to the top of the huge stairway. There, he stopped and looked down to see if angry parents were in view. No one was about so he descended as rapidly as possible and walked into the huge dining room, where he was soon surrounded by delighted guests. He was congratulated, fussed over, complimented and flirted shamelessly with while he slowly made his way about the room in a search for his mother so he could, first find out if she were upset with him, and second to apologize for being late. Then he stopped in his tracks. He had found his mother, but she stood with what he thought was the most beautiful woman he had ever seen.

Dan had never been fainthearted when it came to the fair sex; he had a charm that had successfully won him favors. Now he made his way to his mother's side, his eyes held by the dark haired beauty next to her. He put his arms about his mother's waist and kissed her lightly on the cheek.

"Dan," she exclaimed, "where in heaven's name have you been?"

"Sorry mother, I didn't mean to be late," his eyes were holding Abby's, aware of the amusement and a fleeting thing that lingered in their depths that intrigued him.

"Dan, this is Abby Southerland, she's Catherine and Richard's cousin from Georgia."

"Ah," he said softly as he took Abby's hand and kissed it lightly. "The men in Georgia must be desolate at the loss of the fairest vision in their world."

"Why thank you, Mr. Wakefield," Abby replied.

"Oh, please, not Mr. Wakefield, Dan ... all my friends call me Dan, and I do hope we are going to be good friends."

"Yes ... Dan," she answered.

"And I shall call you Abby. Do you like to ride, Abby?"

"Why, yes ... I do, why?"

"I knew it," he laughed.

"Dan has an affinity for horses and a great deal of admiration for anyone who rides," Virginia replied. "Sometimes, I think he would sell his soul for a fast race horse."

"Now, mother," he chided, "not my soul ... but then," he shrugged and both Virginia and Abby had to respond to his laughter.

"Abby," Dan said quickly while the humor still lingered, "will you share the first dance with me tonight? To help me celebrate my homecoming."

Taken unprepared, Abby agreed, but before Dan could speak again, several of his friends surrounded them and he was drawn away.

"He is quite ... quite ..." Abby began.

"Intense," Virginia replied with a smile. "Dan has always been like that, rather quick to reach out for everything."

Abby watched Dan in the circle of his friends laughing and enjoying the best of his life. She agreed silently with Christina's words, he was beautiful. She thought again of the look in her cousin Catherine's eyes and vowed she would not get caught in Dan's charm for she knew what Catherine felt for Dan was more than just a fleeting enjoyment of his charm. She loved him and Abby would not interfere with them. She also felt her future was going to contain more than being wed to a wealthy man whose main thought would always be horses and his own pride.

Later in the afternoon, Abby found herself alone for a few minutes on the wide stone patio of High Oaks. She looked out over the beautiful well laid rose gardens. She stood, mesmerized by the still peace and contentment that seemed to lie over the land. Her reverie was interrupted by the sound of voices in the garden just below her. She walked to the edge and looked over. Below her three men stood in conversation.

"I'm telling you that now that man is elected it will mean secession."

"Did you hear what he said when he was elected?"

"What?"

" 'The power confided in me will be used to hold, occupy and possess the property and places belonging to the government' that's what he said."

"Possess hell! He'll never cross onto Southern soil. None of us would allow it!"

"I've heard they've occupied Fort Sumter. That looks enough like aggression to me."

"Well, his aggression will be answered. We will rise up and prove to him he cannot dictate to us."

Their voices faded as the three men began to walk away from her, but her stunned mind was recording only one thought over and over . . . war! . . . what these men said meant war!

She was startled by a voice at her elbow. "Abby?"

"Oh, Catherine!"

"I'm sorry if I startled you. The ladies are going upstairs to freshen up for tonight."

"I'm coming. Catherine, I overheard some men talking below. They are talking of secession ... of ..."

"War," Catherine replied quietly. "Yes, I know. I've heard nothing else for the past few weeks. All the young men are excited about it as if it were a game of some sort. My God," her voice died to a whisper. "Don't they know war means dying ... dying."

Abby watched her, realizing Catherine was not the fragile child woman she looked to be. Their eyes met and without another word, they turned and walked inside.

There was the sound of music, laughter and voices in friendly animated conversation that greeted Abby and Catherine when they came down the stairs later in the evening.

Dan who stood in a group of his friends, had kept one eye on the stairs, He was the first to see Abby and Catherine descend them. He watched for a moment, aware of what a beautiful contradiction they made. Abby, dark, tall and mysterious, Catherine small, light and sensitive.

He and Catherine had known each other for a number of years, almost from the time the Wakefields had found him. He had seen her so often that it was hard for him to realize he had never really known her at all. Yet he was spellbound by the mystery in Abby's blue eyes. Both women were a challenge and he was always prepared for just such a challenge.

With a swift word to the friends he was talking to, he left them and walked to the bottom of the stairs. He smiled up at them and had no realization of the different points of view of the two women who walked toward him.

Abby smiled, seeing a tall handsome young man who was the composite of all the ways and beliefs of the South. He was gallant, charming and sure of himself. She knew she could enjoy him and the fun they could have together, yet she felt there was a stronger, greater need within her that could not be found here.

Catherine smiled at him, seeing only with her heart the man she had loved for a long time, and the only one she would ever belong to. She knew that, no matter how sweet Dan was, he saw her as a friend and she prayed constantly for the day that he would look at her with awareness and love in his eyes.

"Now how lucky can one man get, to escort the two most beautiful women here. Can I count on my luck to claim the first two dances. I believe," his eyes sparkled at Abby, "you did promise."

She smiled her agreement and he extended an arm to both of them and they walked into the ballroom. It was only a few moments later that Catherine's first dance partner came to claim her. Dan smiled and asked for the next dance to which she quickly agreed.

Dan turned to Abby. "I believe this is our dance?"

She smiled and he escorted her to the floor and took her in his arms. They swirled about the floor to the smooth strains of the waltz.

"So you are Catherine's cousin. It's funny I've never seen you before."

"I've not visited Catherine often, and I imagine you

were away when I was here. But I have heard quite a bit about you."

"Oh," he cocked an eyebrow and looked very serious. "Something good I hope?"

"I wouldn't want to swell your head," she laughed. "But there are many in this room who would swoon over you."

"You don't strike me as the type to do that."

"Hardly."

"Well," he grinned. "I shall have to polish up my charm. It seems to have failed where you're concerned."

"You are quite charming, and interesting, but my family and I shall be returning to Georgia in a few days so you will be polishing for nothing."

"A few days, then you might be interested in seeing our new foal tomorrow. She's a pretty thing, just born today."

"Oh, yes, I'd love to."

"She's unnamed so far. Would you like to name her?"

"How very nice!" she exclaimed.

"Then I shall come over and ride back with you tomorrow, say about two?"

"Two would be fine," she smiled up at him realizing suddenly that her promise to stay away from him had been for nothing. She wondered suddenly what Catherine would think when Dan came for her the next day.

"Dan?"

"Yes?"

"Would you mind very much if Catherine came also? Like you, horses seem to be one of her main interests in life."

"I didn't know Catherine felt that way but she's welcome if she wants to come."

Feeling pleased with herself for her maneuvering, Abby relaxed and enjoyed the balance of the dance. It was a pleasure, for Dan Wakefield danced with effortless grace and she did enjoy his expertise and the feel of the hard muscular arm that held her.

The balance of the evening was filled with laughter and dancing. It seemed as if a brilliant glow of grace and beauty touched the mansion and enveloped all the people in it, and it was in the wee hours of the morning that the last carriage rolled down the driveway.

Virginia was exhausted but exuberantly happy. She had her son home to stay and nothing in her life pleased her more than that. Gregory and Dan enjoyed a last brandy together before going to bed and Virginia sat with them silently enjoying their conversation and watching the two men who made up her entire world.

Gregory lifted his glass and smiled at Dan. "Welcome home, Dan. This house has been dismally empty without you. I'm sure I speak for your mother too when I tell you how glad we are to have you home."

"Thank you, Father. I'm glad to be back. Going to school is the best way to learn to appreciate all I have here. There is no place in the world like High Oaks."

"Well, I cannot say I'm not glad to have you home. This scare talk about war has sent the price of cotton skyrocketing. I'm going to put every inch of ground into cotton this year. We'll make a killing," Gregory said enthusiastically.

Dan looked uncomfortable for a moment, then he reached out and gently set his glass on a table.

"Father, can I tell you something, something you

won't like, but something I firmly believe?"

"Of course you can."

"I ... I don't think the talk about war is scare talk anymore. I've been talking to a lot of people. My professors and a lot of other people who've been watching the situation closely ... well, they think we will be at war soon. If we're smart, we'll plant in staple, staples that can keep High Oaks independent and able to survive in case ..."

"In case?"

"In case we have, hah ... unforeseen difficulties."

"Just what does that mean?"

"Father," he said softly, "you know I love High Oaks and you two, more than anything else in the world. You know I'll fight, I'll do anything to defend you."

"Dan!" Virginia said in alarm.

"What you are trying to tell us, Dan?" Gregory said.

"That I want High Oaks to survive," he replied quietly. "That I'm afraid. There are too many who speak with courage without thought. Wild enthusiasm is not enough. We don't have the resources to win. What if ... what if they block up our harbors and keep us from shipping our cotton, then where do we go?"

"Dan, we must not panic. This cloud might just pass away. We've heard such militant words before, cool heads that lead us will surely know if we're prepared or not."

Dan could see his father held no doubts the South would take no precipitous action, and he didn't want to argue with him on his first night at home.

"Of course," he shrugged with a laugh, "maybe I'm just seeing dark shadows where there aren't any. But could we at least keep a few fields for food instead of cotton ... just to humor me?"

"Why not?" Gregory smiled. "Suppose we ride out tomorrow and decide just how, what and where we'll plant this year."

"Good, I'd like that. I haven't ridden over High Oaks for a long time."

"Then suppose we get some sleep or we'll be too tired to ride anywhere."

The three of them felt guilty over the same cause. They refused to see the brewing tragedy that stood before them.

Catherine, Abby and Dan were a threesome for the entire two weeks of Abby's stay. Abby enjoyed every moment of it with exception of two things. She realized that Dan thought he was in love with her, and she realized that Catherine loved him with her entire soul.

Abby and her family were to return to Mississippi shortly. The day before she was to go was the first time she and Dan had been alone. It had taken quite a bit of maneuvering on Dan's part, but he wanted to talk to her without others about.

They rode for a while enjoying the rare green beauty of High Oaks, then they tied their horses beneath the shade of a tree and sat talking.

"You're going home tomorrow," he said.

"Yes," she replied.

"We will miss you ... I will miss you. Why is there such a hurry for your family to return."

"I don't know really," she answered. "My father seems to be alarmed about something and he can't wait to go home."

"Alarmed?"

She turned to look into his eyes. "Dan, my father is sure there is going to be a war. He wants us to be home if anything happens. What do you think?"

The last thing Dan wanted was to talk about the political situation. He shrugged. "I don't know, Abby, of course, I have heard all the shouting and anger. A lot of hotheads are shouting secession, but there must be some level heads on both sides to keep control."

"We have family in the North," she said softly. "I cannot see us lifting a gun to fight them, yet where else could we stand but for our own home if something did happen?"

"I should hate to think of it, I would pray for leaders with cool heads and steady hands. All the family I have is here, I should hate to see our country split, yet I would die for High Oaks and the people who have loved and cared for me and given me so much."

"I too," she said softly "would give my life for those I love and the home that nurtured me."

He was caught by the quiet firmness of her voice, then he laughed shakily. "And why are we talking about such things on a day as beautiful as this. I brought you here so I could tell you something."

She knew almost exactly what he was going to say, and it hurt her not to be able to return the love he thought he felt for her. Maybe, she thought, if she just let their future separation cool his emotions, she could give him time. Time for him to discover the truth in what Catherine felt for him. His thoughts were so involved in her he could not see the depth of love that had always been there waiting for his discovery.

"Abby," he began, "I can't tell you how much sharing

these past few weeks has meant to me. I've never enjoyed myself with anyone so much.''

''I've enjoyed my stay here also.''

''I would like your permission to come occasionally and call on you.''

''I should be very pleased,'' she replied, knowing he wanted more, more she could not give. She had always felt that when the man came along that would hold her love, she would know. There would be no hesitation, no way to deny what she felt. And he would be the same, reaching for her with the inner knowledge that she was meant to be his. It was not what she felt for Dan, and deep inside she knew that Dan was infatuated with her and fooling himself into believing it could be more. His next words convinced her she was right. He lifted her hand and pressed a gentle kiss against the smooth skin.

''You are very beautiful Abby, and you are so different from anyone else I've ever met.''

Abby smiled to herself. Imbued in the suave gallantry of the day, Dan would perceive that a courtship had to be proper and that she would be the shy genteel young lady who would blushingly encourage him until he attained enough courage to reach for what he wanted.

Within she knew two things for certain. One, that she liked Dan Wakefield very much but did not love him. Love to her meant an emotion that did not need sweet words and patience. He would sweep her from her feet and command her surrender with a passion she could not withstand or would want to. Two, that if Dan had really loved her, he would be the one to do just that. If aroused to the depths of passion, Dan would not wait for propriety to lead him.

''Thank you, Dan,'' she said softly, and rose before he

could speak again. "I should be very pleased if you would visit, and I'm sure my parents would be glad to see you and your family. Speaking of my family, I must get back. They are preparing to leave and I'm sure they will be wondering where I am."

When she began to move toward the horses a reluctant and somewhat surprised Dan could do nothing but follow.

They rode back to the house slowly, he, wondering what opportunity he could find that could take him to Fernhill, the Southerland plantation in Mississippi, and she with her mind turned toward tomorrow and the adventure that might be waiting in the future.

They arrived at the stables, dismounted and turned their horses over to the groom. They were laughing and talking over some frivolous nonsense as they started toward the house. Then Dan stopped when he noticed that several buggies were sitting in the curved drive.

"You having unexpected visitors?" Abby said.

"Unexpected, but certainly not strangers. Some old friends of father's. I imagine they're getting him upset with this talk of war."

"Who is it?"

"Mr. Priam and that militant minded son of his."

"Have I met them?"

"I think so. At the Ferrigut Ball. The tall white haired man and the son that runs about extolling his dueling abilities and running off at the mouth about making ready for war."

"Oh, yes," Abby laughed, "I do remember the man . . . and his son."

Again they were laughing together as he held open the door for her. They walked into the sitting room to find a very quiet and solemn group.

"Good afternoon everyone," Dan said as he bent and brushed a light kiss on his mother's cheek. "Everyone looks so serious. What has happened?"

"Dan," Gregory said softly and Dan was held in startled silence by the shock and pain he heard in his voice. "Yesterday morning, at four thirty . . . we fired on Major Anderson at Fort Sumter. I am afraid such an action can only result in one thing . . . we are at war."

Nine

Jules Dubonne and Marie settled comfortably in Philadelphia. They found the people receptive to them and in no time established a wide circle of friends.

Jules' money had been well invested by Eugene Claret, a Frenchman who had preceded them by many years. He had found them a large, well placed home that suited Marie very much. He and his wife introduced them by way of parties, picnics and other social gatherings.

At first, Alexander refused to attend these functions. He took solitary rides, walked, often alone, and began to frequent his father's library. There he immersed himself in books. It was a source of escape, escape from the nightmares and the feeling of guilt that kept him awake more nights than he would ever tell his parents about.

Jules cautioned Marie to leave him alone. "He will find himself. The boy is searching for the man ... he will find him."

"Are you so sure Jules? He seems so alone. Since Dante ... was lost to us. He misses him so much."

"Yes, Marie, I'm sure. I feel I know him, and I know he's going through a crisis. Time, love and understanding. That's all he needs to see him through."

It was the finding of his first real friend in America that did much to help Alexander. George Brinton McClellan, Jr. was the son of a military family. He was bragging about it when he and Alexander met ... or collided.

Marie and Jules had finally convinced Alexander to come to a picnic with them. He went reluctantly and only to satisfy Celeste who begged him to come with her.

Several sons of prominent families were seated together beneath the shade of a tree talking. Among them William Hyde, Thomas Kane, Harry Russell and George. George was standing forth on life in the military with enthusiasm. He was eloquent in his descriptions of the glories of war. Most of which he had read about or imagined.

George was tall for his age and very slim. He had a broad engaging smile, a shock of blue-black hair and the most startling blue eyes that seemed to pierce within anyone they fell on.

"I'm telling you," he was saying, "in a couple more years, I'm going to the Military Academy. By the time I'm out there'll sure be a war somewhere. My father says there always is. I'm going to make me a name and cover myself with glory."

Alexander, who had been drifting about, came within hearing distance at that moment. He froze in his tracks and stood listening while George continued his praise of military life, war, bloodshed and everything else connected with it.

Alexander's mind rolled backwards to what his father had told him about war and the battles he had been in. It also struck a very vulnerable place in him. War had forced them to run from France. War had taken Dante from them.

"What do you know about war?" he said.

All heads turned toward him in surprise.

"What?" George said.

"I said what do you know about war? You think it's all flag waving and glory. People have to die in a war. Have you ever seen a man die?"

"Who are you?" George asked. He was angry that attention had so quickly been taken from him. It was a thing George was not accustomed to.

"That's the French boy," Harry Russell offered. "They just moved here. Maybe," he added with a laugh, "he'd be afraid to fight. I heard all French boys were sissies."

"Dubonne," George said. "Your name's Dubonne, isn't it?"

"That's right."

"Well," George smiled his best smile as he rose to his feet. Aware now that all eyes were again on him. Alexander watched him. He saw the smile, he also saw the angry gleam in George's eyes. "You sound like some expert. You ever fought in a war, Frenchie? How many men have you killed?"

"You don't have to have been in a war to know killing someone is wrong. I guess all you have to have is a conscience."

George's smile faded and his eyes glistened dangerously. "You suggesting I don't have one?"

"I'm not suggesting anything. I'm just trying to tell you that seeing a man die is not fun and glory. It's ugly ... very ugly."

"The old warrior talking," George scoffed. "You

sound like you've seen a man die."

"I have," Alexander said softly.

There was a silence so deep that even their breathing seemed to be hushed. In a quiet voice Alexander told them of their fear filled escape from France and the face of the man his father had shot. Then in a voice deadened by anger at fate he told them how they had been forced from the country. "War was the cause of it all, and war took my brother's life. You can shout glory and honor until the end of the world, but that's a lie . . . it's all a lie."

Alexander's eyes were glittering with angry tears, and he turned and walked away leaving the others looking after him dumbfounded.

George was the first to regain his equilibrium. Quickly he ran and caught up with Alexander, who did his best to ignore him. Somehow the words he had spoken seemed to release the tension that had been bottled up within him so long. Now he had begun to blame war instead of himself for Dante's death.

"I . . . I'm sorry," George said hesitantly.

"It's all right."

"No, it isn't. I don't usually act so stupid. I didn't mean to say what I said."

"And I guess I never meant to say what I did," Alexander stopped and turned to George. "But it made me feel better."

George smiled and Alexander responded as most people did, with an answering smile.

A friendship had begun which would carry them through an eventful and sometimes dangerous future.

It pleased his parents that Alexander seemed to have gotten control of himself. It also pleased them that he had found a friend.

Alexander and George discovered that they had many likes and dislikes in common. For the balance of that summer they shared the warm days. George admired Alexander's ability to ride, so Alexander began to teach him. George returned the favor by making sure Alexander was included in everything the young people of the area did.

Slowly, Alexander began to confide in someone. A thing he had not been able to do before. He opened his past to George, telling him about Dante and their lives before the fateful trip to America. He told him the story of the gift the captain had given each of them. George admired the strange looking object.

"He gave one to each of us, me—Dante and Celeste."

"It's a beautiful thing," George replied. "Don't you ever take if off?"

"No, I never will. I don't know if you understand, George, but it's kind of a link with Dante. That sounds silly, doesn't it?"

"No, I can understand that. It's a way of keeping your brother close. I imagine Celeste feels the same way."

"I suppose so. I know she won't take hers off either."

"Alexander," George said quietly, "I know how you feel about war, how you blame it for everything it's cost you, but, well, you're a part of this country now. You'd defend it, wouldn't you?"

Alexander thought about this for a while, for his anger against war had eliminated such thoughts before.

"I ... I guess, I would, but I would probably hate every moment of it. Why?"

"Well, I'm still going to go to the Academy when I'm

old enough. I wouldn't want my being an officer destroying our friendship."

"George, everybody has to do what he feels is right. The first thing I would defend would be every man's right to do as he felt was just. It has nothing to do with our friendship as long as you don't feel I should be doing the same as you."

"My father and some friends were talking the other day, your father came up in the discussion."

"My father, why?"

"They were talking about defense. You know my father's been a career officer, just like my grandfather, all his life. They said your father was an officer in Napoleon's army."

"He was."

"They're going to approach him to take sort of an inactive command in the army. Good men are needed if we ever want a well trained army."

"He'll refuse."

"How do you know?"

"That's the reason we came here. Father could not be part of it anymore. He began to hate the command that cost so many lives. He was sick of war. It would take some catastrophic event to make him agree."

"Well, I know they're going to ask him anyway." Alexander shrugged and the subject was changed.

Later that afternoon, they went riding, stopping to swim in a secluded area near the river well shaded with trees.

When Alexander returned home, he was not surprised to see two carriages in front of the house. He knew who the visitors must be and the reason they were there. It was not in Alexander's mind to eavesdrop but as he passed the study door the first words he heard held him as he waited for his father's reply.

"This country needs a strong army for its protection. We may one day face a war."

"You have been listening to rumors," came Jules amused voice. "Fanatics shouting into the wind. Must we be led by them."

"Fanatics! You have not seen the condition of the slaves in the South as I have."

"Slavery will kill itself. Even if it does not, economics will make it unrewarding to keep them," Jules replied.

"You're wrong. The Southerners consider slavery a religious, moral and social blessing. They feel the slave system of the South is superior to the industrial system of England, France and the North."

"I do not think the men in the south are fools," Jules replied. "The North, by far, outnumbers them and contains much greater sources of reserves. No, sir, they are not fools. They would never do anything so rash as to split this country in two. It might mean the entire country's destruction."

The reply was spoken softly and as if the man was in sorrow, "You are the fool if you believe that. Maybe, you should take a little journey through the South. Have a look for yourself."

"If I am a fool, I am a fool who does not believe the only way to change a country's situation is war," Jules replied in a voice equally soft. "I have seen revolution my friend, I have fought in such a war. It would take a great deal to make me do so again."

Alexander left the door at that moment. He felt his father had spoken eloquently with the same emotions he felt. It would be a long time, and take a shocking episode to change his feelings. He felt at that moment a oneness with his father and a renewal of what he felt was right ... there was no cause for war.

Life took on a bright glow for Alexander and the others in his family. They were pleased to see Alexander regain his footing and begin to respond more fully to life.

George affirmed that his plans to enter the Military Academy when he was old enough remained unchanged. Alexander stood on his beliefs. After a time, they mutually and silently agreed that this subject was never to come up between them again.

Most things in their lives became a humorous contest, their competition held in a fun loving vein. It began with games when they were thirteen and ran the gamut from then on with mock duels, riding contests, and any other field they could find. By the time they were fifteen their eyes began to turn toward the fair sex.

Now a whole new competition began, and they wholeheartedly threw themselves into it. George drew on his magnetic smile and charm to capture hearts while Alexander took advantage of his French and the mystique of his European background to do the same.

Girls found his strategic use of the French language hard to resist. Combined with his golden hair and tall lean body, Alexander captured their undivided attention.

As friends, George and Alexander were sure there was nothing that could bring them any closer. There was, and it was an incident that very nearly cost them both of their lives.

Alexander was seventeen, a vibrant handsome and self assured seventeen. The family had been invited to a huge picnic and he was looking forward to it with enthusiasm. The enthusiasm included a blue eyed beauty that had his interest at the moment.

He stood before the tall mirror in his room examining himself carefully.

At seventeen, he had reached his full height, three inches over his father's six feet. His shoulders, broad and strong, strained against the fabric of his rust colored jacket. Fawn colored trousers hugged his slim hips and long legs. His hair, brightened to burnished gold from the sun, was a perfect foil for his tanned skin and green eyes. He smiled, his teeth, white and square, sparkled in pleasure at his anticipation of what his care for his lengthy preparations might reward him with.

A rap on the door drew his attention, and at his call, Celeste's head appeared around the door.

"The carriage will be ready in a few minutes, Alexi," she said. "Mama says to hurry up, you know how upset Papa gets when we keep him waiting."

"I'm ready," Alexander replied.

Celeste's eyes glittered with mischief. She was thirteen, and had been terribly pampered by her parents and her older brother whom she adored. She had just discovered that she could get away with more with Alexander than anyone else could.

"My goodness," she laughed. "Dianna Greenwood will surely be impressed with how beautiful you look. She might even give you the kiss you were trying so hard to get at the Mayerlind's party."

Alexander glared at her in mock anger. "One of these days, Celeste, I'm going to catch you eavesdropping on private conversations. When I do, you won't be able to sit down for a week."

Her eyes widened in innocence. "But Alexi ... there wasn't any conversation. You were too busy keeping her from talking."

Even he had to chuckle at the devilment in her eyes and the way she had eluded any thought of wrongdoing.

"Come along," he said. "Let's not keep Father waiting any longer."

The two of them left his room and joined their parents who were already boarding the carriage.

The winding road that led from the Dubonne home to the Greenwood estate was shaded by huge oak trees. On a bright sunlit summer day, it was a joy to ride leisurely along.

There seemed to be an extraordinary glow to the day. The whole family sensed it. It was as if this was a day meant to be pressed between the pages of memories.

Less than three miles from the Greenwood mansion, they were momentarily startled by loud shouts.

"Good heavens!" Marie exclaimed.

Alexander laughed. It was the Greenwood boys, Russell and Harry and another of his friends Wesley Rainey. The three of them had decided to ride out and escort the Dubonnes to the party.

They rode alongside the carriage shouting happily to Alexander who waved in return. As they galloped in a display of exhibitionism, Alexander's attention was drawn to the face of his sister. At a little over thirteen, he thought of her as a child, yet her sparkling eyes never left one rider.

"My God," he thought in amusement, "she's got a crush on old Wesley." He reminded himself to return some of her tormenting later.

Wesley Dylan Rainey was a year younger than

Alexander. A tall slim boy, forever laughing. His eyes were a deep blue which hovered near purple. His deep auburn hair was thick and willful and he was continually trying to tame it. He had an exuberant sense of humor, and Alexander was sure the idea for this reception was Wesley's. At sixteen, thirteen year old girls were far beneath his dignity so it never occurred to him to look at Celeste in any other way but sisterly, which had ruined many parties for her.

They were escorted through the front gates and welcomed when they arrived at the front door by Mr. and Mrs. Greenwood.

As usual, there was a separation of adults from young people as rapidly as possible. Alexander joined his friends whose first thought was eating. Then, when stomachs were comfortably full, they gathered beneath the shade of a huge tree to discuss one of their main interests in life—racing their thoroughbred horses.

Celeste too, gravitated toward friends her own age, yet she seemed to find a way to keep Wesley Rainey in her sights. Her crush on Wesley had begun the very first day he had walked into their home. He had smiled at her as one would smile at a baby sister. From then on, pats on the head or an amused word now and then was all she received, and only as a passing thought. It may have been a passing thought to Wesley, but Celeste's grim determination grew each time she saw him. Sometimes painfully, sometimes angrily, but all times with her mind on one thought and one thought only ... she and Wesley Rainey would some day share a common destiny. At this age, she wasn't sure what or even how, yet she believed it completely.

It did not take the young men long before their

discussion about horses went from bragging to challenging. Before too long, a race was instituted.

Alexander rode as if he and the horse were one, and the contest usually ended up between him and the rest. George looked forward to the day when fate would let him beat Alexander. It was not a case of jealousy, for he admired Alexander's skill, yet he had the urgent desire to beat him even if it only happened once in his life.

If George's desire to beat Alexander was strong, it was nothing compared to some of the others such as Wesley, Harry and Russell. The area of the race was one that had been used for the same purpose many times before. It was two hundred yards long oval shaped with an expanse of green lawn bordered by a track of smooth dirt.

They positioned their restless high spirited horses in as straight a line as possible. Then a shot was fired by one of their friends who had decided to remain a spectator.

The horses leaped ahead. Amid encouraging shouts from the onlookers they raced down the dirt track.

Alexander bent low over his horse's neck softly urging him to greater and greater speed.

George was beside himself with excitement. For the first time in his life, he found himself slightly ahead of Alexander. It was less than a few inches, but he was ahead, and he fully intended to remain so. He grinned as he heard Alexander's happy laughter behind him.

They took the first turn, George and Alexander almost side by side. The others, in somewhat of a pack were slowly but perceptibly falling behind.

Very slowly, George began to pull ahead of Alexander . . . inch by inch.

Around the second turn and into the long straight stretch toward the finish line. George now in the lead by more than a length, Alexander behind, and several lengths behind them the entire pack of thundering horses.

George's exuberance was to be shortlived. Alexander watched with shocked eyes as the saddle girth on George's saddle snapped and he began to slip sideways. He clung desperately to the neck of his now uncontrollable horse. Fear lent him strength as he realized that if he fell, he would be trampled to death by the pack behind him that would be unable to stop.

He heard Alexander shout, but could not make out what he was shouting. Slowly, Alexander drew his horse up beside George's.

"George!" he shouted.

George turned his head to look and saw Alexander's outstretched arm.

"Jump! Take my arm and jump. My horse will hold us both!"

Perspiration on George's brow and his wide eyes denoted his fear, yet grimly, he slowly released his hold on the horse's neck. In one quick move he reached and jumped at the same time.

The saddle of his horse fell to the ground as he felt the strength of Alexander's arm draw him safely up behind him. He clung to Alexander as they dashed across the finish line and stopped.

George was pale and trembling as he faced an Alexander who was just as pale and shaken.

The rest of them stopped their horses and surrounded them.

"My God George," Russell said. "That was a mighty

close call."

"Yes, you came damn near getting killed. We'd never have been able to stop before it was too late," Harry said anxiously.

"It's a good thing Alexander was that close," Wesley said. "None of the rest of us would have been able to get to you in time."

"Yes," George replied in a shaky voice as he held out his hand to Alexander who took it in a firm grip. "I owe you my life, Alexander. I'll never forget this. It is a debt I'll never be able to repay."

"It was nothing you would not have done for me, besides," Alexander grinned now, "It was the only way I could keep you from beating me. You see, my horse came across the finish line first."

Everyone laughed, both in relief and joy at the touching friendship they were witnessing.

"I'm sorry, Alexander," George replied with a chuckle. "But I'm afraid I'll have to argue with you on that point."

"What?"

"Now I ask you all for an unbiased opinion," George laughed as he waved his arm to include them all. "Did we or did we not cross the finish line together, and, if that is so, then I declare the race a tie."

There was hilarity among them all as they agreed there was no doubt George and Alexander had crossed the finish line together and the race indeed had to be called a tie.

"That," George declared happily as he flung his arm about Alexander's shoulder, "is about as close as I shall ever come to beating you. Now, come, and let me toast you and give you thanks for saving my life."

Alexander laughed and threw his arm about George's shoulder, they walked to the house together.

The picnic turned into a rousing celebration for all of them. In fact, both George and Alexander drank more than they were used to.

Alexander was taken home by an amused father, a somewhat upset mother, and a gleeful sister who could not wait to tactfully remind him of his escapade.

Ten

Dark storm clouds began to gather on a very distant horizon. They remained unnoticed by Alexander and his friends whose lives were filled with good things. Alexander enjoyed his life to the fullest. He felt there was nothing more he could enjoy. By the time he was nineteen, he had tentatively tasted the shy gentle kisses and a few stolen caresses from many of the girls in his circle of friends. Then, into his life, came Belle Thompson.

Belle's family were poor dirt farmers who lived quite some distance from Alexander's. Their paths would most likely never have crossed except that fate seemed to have willed it so. Belle would be an experience Alexander was quite unprepared for.

Belle was seventeen, but a seventeen with the experience of thirty. She liked men, all men.

Her raising had been haphazard, by parents who did not really care what became of her at all. Her father farmed as carelessly as he did everything else. Consequently, there was usually barely enough food for the family to survive on. Belle learned, by the time she was fifteen, that she was very pretty and that her prettiness could be traded for favors that would make her hard life a little easier.

Still, she chose carefully who she would bestow favors upon. Her discriminating taste depended not on the ones who could give her most, but the ones she could respond to and who were kind and gentle with her. Also she chose ones who knew the value of silence. It might have been the reason that Alexander had never known her name or anything else about her.

Belle gave the lie to her background, by her exceptional beauty. Her parents, both quite unremarkable, had given birth to a slim delicate child who had grown prettier every day.

Her hair was the color of corn silk, and her eyes, a deep lustrous blue, were wide and clear. Her skin, a translucent gold, was smooth and soft. Her body was slim yet rounded and very obviously woman.

She wakened and stirred restlessly on her uncomfortable corn husk cot. The sun was already up and her small room was already warm.

She knew it would be some time yet that her parents would laze abed. Quietly, she rose and slipped her thin cotton dress over her head. She had slept naked as she had in the summer months since she was a baby. She drew her hair over her shoulder, braided it, tying the end with a small strip of cotton cloth. Slipping into her worn shoes, she silently left the house.

She wandered along a heavily wooded path that led to the river where she had swum many times before. The sharp trill of early morning birds was the only sound and the rays of the sun were beginning to warm the air already.

A squirrel dashed madly from her path and scurried

up a tree where he sat and chattered belligerently at her for disturbing his foraging for food.

At the river's edge, she reached for the hem of her dress and drew it over her head. She dove neatly into the water.

Swimming was one thing she thoroughly enjoyed. She dove down as far as her lungs would allow her, then sought the surface. She floated on her back and gazed at the blue cloud-free sky.

She thought of her life and realized again, as she had many times before, that she hated it. She hated the dirt farm to which she was chained by poverty. She hated the defeating way she had of acquiring the few small things she possessed. Again an urge possessed her as it had many times before. A way to escape this dull and life sucking existence.

She swam until she was tired, then she left the water. She patted herself dry with her dress then slipped it on again. She walked to the shade of a tree and sat beneath it, resting her back against the rough bark.

She closed her eyes and began to absorb the sounds about her. Slowly, she drifted into a light sleep.

She was startled awake by a sound, and it was a few minutes before she realized what it was. Someone else had found what she considered a secret place of her own. Someone else had just dove into the water and was swimming.

She rose and walked within a few feet of the bank, then a soft amused smile crossed her face and she stood, hands on hips, and watched a man she knew quite well walk naked and unaware of her from the water.

Alexander had drunk too much—entirely too much. The party, held at the town house of a friend, had been

153

somewhat wild. They had gathered to wish his friend a bon voyage for he was about to leave on a long cruise.

Much laughter and camaraderie had led to one drink after another. He did not even know when he began to lose track. He only knew that when he wakened his head thumped furiously and his queazy stomach threatened to become violent at any moment, and he still had to face the long ride home.

He mounted his horse with a groan of agony and urged him to walk ... slowly, so the pounding beat in his head in his head would not increase.

If he thought his misery would ease as he rode along, he was sadly mistaken. The bright morning sun seemed to him like a hot knife that pierced his skull and played havoc with the mind within until all he could think of was cool water to ease his pain. Desperately he thought of some way to ease the pain, then he thought of a quiet spot along the river where the trees shaded it and the current was slow. He headed the horse in that direction.

When he reached the river, he tied his horse under a tree and walked to the river's edge. It took a great deal of energy to get off his boots. Then his clothes followed as fast as he could get them off. The cool inviting water beckoned him. Instead of wading out slowly, he dove in.

The cool water was a shock at first, then he could feel the cobwebs fade from his mind along with the pain.

He swam easily, rolling in the water, and floating then diving below the surface to come up gasping for air.

Finally, though he felt much better, his tired muscles shouted enough. He swam toward shore until his feet could touch bottom. Then he stood and waded into the shallows shaking the water from his thick golden hair. He had not quite reached the shore when he heard a deep amused throaty chuckle. He looked up and shocked filled his eyes as they met Belle's.

Momentarily stunned, he stood stock still, forgetting for a moment that he did not have a stitch on ... then she laughed. He could feel his cheeks get hot with embarrassment and he stepped back until he felt the water cover him.

"I'm ... I'm afraid you have me at a little disadvantage," he smiled the best smile he could muster under the circumstances. "I didn't know anyone else was here."

"This is kinda my private place," she replied, her eyes still roaming over him.

"I didn't mean to trespass. If you'll turn your back, I'll dress and be on my way."

Slowly, with a provocative sway of her hips, she began to wade into the water. "I didn't zackly mean you couldn't share it with me."

He opened his mouth, but for the life of him, no words would come. Instead, he found his eyes captured by the half wet dress that molded itself against her and the stirring in his loins as he recognized the admiring invitation in her eyes.

The rising water circled about her waist. Then rose to touch more enticing curves. Her smile grew wider as she read his face. He could not move, nor could he stop the sudden blaze of desire that leaped within him.

She stood a few inches away and looked up into his eyes. Slowly, she reached out and drew one finger gently down his chest. "You're Alexander Dubonne," she said.

He heard the velvet in her voice without hearing the mispronunciation of his name.

"I've never seen you around before," he said.

"Well," she laughed again, and he found he liked the open free sound of her laughter. "I don't zackly fit in the same circles as you do. But I'm sure glad I met you." Again her fingers trailed across his chest. "I have a feeling you and I could be ... friends."

"What's your name?" he asked and she heard the sound she was waiting for. The return of the firm masculine tenor of his voice.

"Belle."

"Where do you come from, Belle?"

She motioned behind her. "My folks have a farm over there."

"There ... the Thompson place ... I ..."

He stopped, realizing that somehow he had hurt her. She turned from him and he reached out and grasped her arm, turning her again to face him.

"I'm sorry, Belle, if I said anything to hurt you, I didn't mean it."

"Don't bother, Mr. Rich Dubonne. You don't have to say trash to look it."

"Don't be stupid," he snapped. "No one is trash unless they let themselves be."

She stopped, then turned to look at him her eyes wide and searching, then he smiled again. "You mean that, don't you?" she said softly.

"Yes, I mean that?" he replied. Then he laughed again. "Besides I'm in no position to fight with you or anyone else."

The sparkle of her laughter blended with his again. She reached down and took the hem of her dress. Pulling it over her head, she tossed it near his clothes on the shore. "Now, we're both in the same position."

Alexander's circle of women friends had never

included a pagan goddess like this, but he had no intention of letting her get away from him.

He reached out and encircled her waist in his hands, surprised at its slimness and the velvety smooth texture of her skin. She moved against him so easily that for a moment he was not sure who had moved first.

Then slowly he bent his head and touched her lips with his. Her lips parted when they met, and suddenly he felt as if he had been immersed in a cauldron of flame. When he lifted his head, she smiled, then she took his hand and led the way to the grass covered shade of the trees. Without a word, she drew him down with her to the soft grass.

Alexander's urgency was expertly controlled and he found himself blindly obeying commands. Commands that set the fire coursing through his veins. She was a need that filled him, and he felt a joyous giving in her that he had never felt before.

For her, it was different also. It was the first time she had ever felt such sheer pleasure. Alexander's hard lean body possessed her completely. She promised herself that this first time would not be the last.

They lay apart for a moment, both too sated to speak. Then something happened to Belle that had never happened with any other man. Alexander began to talk to her, to ask her questions about herself, and to listen with interest to what she said.

She spoke to him, telling him things she had never told anyone before. Her desires and dreams . . . and her fears.

"Don't be afraid of life, Belle. You can make something of it if you really want to."

"Aw . . . don't talk like that. I can't even read or

write, and I don't know nothing."

"I could teach you to read and to write."

"You ... you could? You would?"

"Yes, I would."

She sat up, her face lighted with pleasure. "We could meet here once a week or so. I'd be a good student really," she said with vibrant enthusiasm. "I'd study so hard."

"Then it's a bargain?" he said.

For a moment she was silent then she said, "A bargain has two sides. I won't take from you without givin' you somethin' in return."

"You've given me more than anything I could have ever thought of before."

"But I won't take from you any free gifts. We will make a bargain," she replied. "I will teach you love, and you will give me my future."

Her voice was so firm and final that he knew she thoroughly meant every word she said.

"Then, it's a bargain I get the best of," he said.

"I think it's fair," she replied.

"I think it's a blessing no one would ever believe if they knew. But it's one I'll be grateful for the rest of my life."

"Funny," she said as she bent toward him. "I have the feeling it's me that's going to be grateful."

He had no reply, his mind, hands and body were too much involved at the moment.

It proved to be an enlightening and instructive summer for both of them. Alexander was amazed by her insatiable desire to learn, and it was not too long that she was following words in books with her finger, pronouncing them slowly then questioning him on their meaning. It was a joyous summer in which he would not let any outside influence intrude. He ignored the angry muttering about slave holders and all the other outrageous stories he heard about the wealthy plantation owners and their abuse of their slaves. He listened to his father's words that spoke of the real violence and bloodshed of war and joined his father in speaking against violent reaction that his father suspected came from fanatics who sought to rouse the people to action.

The fall leaves sent a blaze of color over the countryside. Alexander and Belle sat under a tree discussing the last book he had given her to read.

Alexander had been trying to find a way they could meet during the winter months. He talked more than she without realizing she was strangely quiet.

It was quite a while before he ceased to talk and become aware that she was seeking words to tell him something.

"Belle ... what is it? What's wrong? Don't you want to see me any more?"

"Alexander, you know that isn't true. You know I care for you more than anyone else, but ..."

"But what?"

She had been gazing away from him, and now she turned to face him. Her eyes met his directly and honestly and held.

"Alexander, do you want to marry me?" she said softly.

The answer was immediately written on his face and in his eyes. A fleeting look he tried to hide, but her astute gaze caught it, she smiled, and said the next words as gently as she could. It was the first time she realized he could be hurt by the bonds of society as much as she.

"It's all right, Alexander. That can't hurt me any more. I know you can't ... that you never could, no matter what. It's why I'm going away."

"Where, Belle, how?"

"You've given me a lot of nice things. I have everything you've ever given me, even the money for new clothes you wanted me to have. I'll use all them so that I can make use of the greatest gift you gave me," she pressed the book close to her. "I'm going to make a new life for myself, Alexander, and to do that, I have to say goodbye to all the past."

"Even me?"

"Especially you. If I don't I'll be locked into this world the rest of my life. One day you would hate me and I would hate myself."

He knew she was right. If she wanted to make a new life, it had to be. Yet he was surprised at the knot of pain that nearly choked the breath from him. She could feel his misery and his search for words.

"You've spoken to me so often, Alexander, of honor, independence and the way each person should have control over his own destiny. I've had a good teacher. Tell me you are proud of me, and that you wish me luck and happiness. It would mean a lot to me."

"I am proud of you, Belle, and I do wish you all the good luck in the world. I guess I'm being selfish ... I'm going to miss you."

"Would you believe me, Alexander, that you are the only thing that I shall miss? You are the only thing I shall remember with pleasure. Maybe, one day, we will meet again."

He took the book from her hands and laid it aside.

Then he took her in his arms and kissed her, knowing it was for the last time.

He sat beneath the tree a long time thinking how easy it was for life to snatch from one the things he loved the most. Dante came into his mind from the shadowed place where he always remained. He relived Dante's death as if it were yesterday. A vow formed in his mind and he allowed it to possess him. One day he would find the one who would spend the rest of his life with him, and he would allow no trick of fate to take her away. He would hold and keep what he wanted no matter what threatened them. He had no realization that a cold and bloody war would one day do that. That it would threaten to take away from him the only real love he would ever know.

He rose, then noticed the book that Belle had left behind. It lay on the ground. He lifted it, brushed off the dirt and slipped the book into his pocket.

Mounting his horse, he rode home in less than an amiable mood.

When he arrived he had hardly dismounted before he heard his name shouted. He turned to see George riding up the drive.

He stood, watching George's rapid approach, knowing that some special thing had happened. When George dismounted beside him, his face was flushed and his eyes sparkled.

"You look excited, something happen?"

"I should say," George laughed.

"Well, don't keep me in suspense, tell me what it is."

"I've been accepted at West Point."

"The military academy?"

"Right!"

"Congratulations, George." Alexander smiled as he extended his hand. "I know it's what you've always wanted. I wish you the best of luck. Come on in and have a drink with me."

George laughed, and after they had given the horses over to the stable boy, he threw his arm about Alexander's shoulder and they walked into the house.

Inside Alexander poured two drinks. He handed George one and they touched their glasses together.

"Here's to military life. I hope you find it all you hoped for."

"Thanks, Alexander, I wish you were going with me. But I know how you feel about war so I won't ask again."

"When do you leave?"

"First of next month."

"Good, you'll still be here for Celeste's party. She'd be upset if you didn't come."

"I don't think it's me she'd miss so much as old Wesley. She certainly has eyes for him or hadn't you noticed?"

"She's only sixteen," Alexander laughed. "I don't think Wes has even looked in her direction. She's still a baby."

"A baby!" George laughed. "You haven't really looked at her lately have you? She's one of the prettiest girls in the state and if you haven't noticed a lot of other boys in the area sure have."

For a moment, Alexander was quiet. It was true, he hadn't really paid much attention to Celeste this summer. In fact, he had been too involved with Belle to think about any of his family.

As if in answer to his thoughts, he heard laughter and

light footsteps descending the stairs, then Celeste swept into the room like a fresh summer breeze.

It startled him to realize that sometime in the past few months, Celeste had grown up. Grown into a lovely young woman.

"Hello, George," she said, but her eyes swung back to Alexander who was looking at her in what she considered a very strange way.

"Celeste," George laughed. "It's good to see your pretty face. I will tell you my good news, your brother doesn't seem to be too enthused."

"What good news?"

"I've been accepted at West Point. I leave next month. In four years, I'll be a lieutenant in the U.S. Army."

"Oh, I am happy for you," she smiled. "You were certainly meant to be in the Army. You look so ... commanding."

George flushed in pleasure and Alexander laughed to himself. Celeste had not only grown up she had turned into a little flirt.

"I only hope the war waits for me," he replied.

Celeste's face paled. "War? What war?"

"George is under the impression that the slavery situation could make the South secede from the Union," Alexander stated. "It's all talk Celeste. No one believes it will happen in the first place, and the South is wise enough to know they don't have enough factories or ships to win such a war." He gazed angrily at George who suddenly realized Alexander was annoyed with the way such talk seemed to upset Celeste. He immediately changed the subject. Soon, they were on safer ground discussing Celeste's sixteenth birthday party as she laughingly tried to guess what he had bought her.

By the time George left Alexander believed Celeste's mind had been taken off all other thoughts but her party. He was wrong. She had barely heard the door click behind George then she turned to face Alexander.

"Alexi . . . I've heard a lot of people talking. There's more to this talk of war than you are admitting, isn't there?"

"Celeste we can't let ourselves be swayed by a lot of rabble rousers. There's a lot of that on both sides. Father says he doesn't believe the government would let such a thing happen. They'll find some way to ease the strain and keep this country in one piece. It would be disaster if he couldn't."

"But . . . if he didn't . . . if he couldn't. What would happen, Alexi? You . . . you would have to fight, maybe Papa . . . maybe," she was trembling.

"Maybe Wesley?" he questioned softly.

She went to his side and looked up into his eyes. "Remember, when I was a little girl, I asked you once about war. You said . . ."

"I said not to worry, Celeste. I don't want to fight in a war and nothing has happened to change my mind. Now, let's stop this foolish talk and forget about it. Would you like me to give you your birthday present now?" he smiled to keep the sternness from his voice.

"No, I'll wait until my party. I want this party to be so special. Mama has bought me a stunning new gown."

"You'll be beautiful. I expect you'll turn a lot of heads that night. From the way you were fluttering your eyes and flirting with George, you should have all the boys in the area eating out of your hands."

She laughed gaily. "I intend to have fun, lots of fun. I

164

intend to dance every dance, to laugh and enjoy myself."

"Well, don't break too many hearts, little flirt. One of these days, you'll have to pick out a husband."

"Don't worry, Alexi ... I'll be careful."

"Well, I'm going up and change. Father wants me to bring the buggy to pick him up. I'll see you at dinner, Celeste."

She watched him walk from the room. Then the smile on her lips and the brightness in her eyes faded. She walked to a window and looked out on a bright red and gold day.

"Oh, Wesley, why don't you even look at me. Can't you feel how much I love you?" she whispered to herself. She bent her head forward and rested it on the cool glass.

"Maybe ... maybe he'll notice me at the party. Maybe he'll realize how much I care. Maybe ..." her thoughts went on into a dream she had dreamed so many times. A dream that found her in Wesley's arms, a dream in which she saw his eyes light with love and felt the strength of his arms about her.

Eleven

The Dubonne mansion glittered with the light of a million candles. One carriage after another rolled up the curved drive to deposit guests at the front door. The sound of music floated on the warm summer breeze amid the sound of laughter and conversation.

Jules and Marie greeted their guests. Tonight was one of the happiest nights of their lives, for tonight would announce the coming of age of Celeste Dubonne. They were proud, and they wanted it to be the highlight of Celeste's life, and a fond memory for the future.

The Raineys arrived, and as Wesley aided his mother from the carriage, he was wondering just how he would manage an extra dance or two with a girl named Patricia Longly. She was a dark haired beauty who had caught his eyes a few weeks before. They had shared a stolen kiss or two at other parties and tonight he was hopeful that his luck might carry him a little bit further.

As soon as they entered the ballroom and greeted the Dubonnes he began to circulate among the other young men to see if he could make a bargain to trade dances. It was an unspoken agreement among gentlemen at such parties that each would dance twice with the girl who was the reigning debutante.

With much coaxing, Wesley managed to trade his two dances with Celeste with two of Patricia's. It meant he would not dance with Celeste all evening, but since he thought of her as a baby sister, it really seemed no loss to him at the moment.

Alexander walked down the hallway from his room to Celeste's. There he knocked on her door. He heard her call and opened the door. Inside he looked across the room at one of the most remarkable transformations in the world. He whistled softly.

"Celeste, you really look like a grown up young lady, and quite beautiful if I may add. You should take the whole room by storm."

Celeste looked grateful. She turned from the mirror in which she had been examining herself. The pale gold hair had been coiled atop her head with fringers of soft curls on her forehead and slim neck. Her wide purple blue eyes reflected the sea blue color of her gown. Marie had taken a great deal of time in shopping with Celeste for just the right gown. From Alexander's point of view, they had been quite successful. It was cut a bit lower than Marie had wanted, but Celeste looked so beautiful in it she could not refuse.

From the soft drape of material that caught the curve of her shoulders and curved across the soft rise of her breasts, it was cut plainly and very nearly severely. But from the waist it cascaded out in layer upon layer of lace with small flowers of orchid and white caught here and there.

She wore no jewelry except the thin gold chain that matched the one Alexander wore. The gold medal with the three pearls lay in the valley between her breasts.

She turned about slowly and Alexander nodded his approval. Then she went to him and kissed his cheek lightly. He could smell the soft sweet scent of her.

"Thank you, Alexi," she said softly.

"For what?" he laughed.

"For the way you started my evening."

"I've come to escort the lady of the evening down to meet her court."

His eyes caught the medal and his smile faded. He lifted it gently in his hand and their minds were both caught in memories. "He would be eighteen now," she said quietly. "It's at times like these when we are so close and share so much that I miss him so."

"Yes, especially the good times. He was so full of laughter and fun. Funny how close he seems to be sometimes ... like it never happened. I'm glad you always wear it, Celeste."

"I always shall. Somehow, it seems to keep him close to me ... to us, for I'm sure you feel the same as I."

"Yes, I guess I'll never shake it. To me, it's as if he is still alive. But," he smiled. "tonight is your night. Are you ready?"

"Yes, I am," she laughed as she tucked her arm in his and they left the room. They stood at the top of the stairs and watched the swirl of color below them for a few moments. Then they looked at each other, and started slowly down.

As she neared the bottom of the stairs, heads began to turn toward her. Many of the local men who knew her as a pretty child stood stunned as a graceful goddess appeared before them, and one by one they began to count their blessings that each of them would have at least two opportunities to dance with her ... except

Wesley Rainey.

Wesley stood with disbelieving eyes as Alexander led Celeste across the floor to stand by her parents, then for a moment he closed his eyes with a quiet groan.

It was soon obvious to him that none of the men he had traded with would even consider changing the extra dance they had with Celeste.

As the night proceeded, Celeste began to wonder why Wesley kept his distance, even though she immensely enjoyed the new and flattering attention she was receiving. She could see he was watching her closely, for each time she looked at him, she found his eyes on her.

It was Alexander who finally heard what Wesley had done. He laughed, yet he sympathized with Wesley when word of it reached Celeste's ears. It was less than half way through the evening that disaster struck for Wesley.

Celeste had been dancing and laughing and thoroughly enjoying herself for two hours, but now she felt the need for a moment's rest and some cool air.

She made her way to a balcony where she stood for a moment in the shadows and enjoyed the cool breeze.

Two men walked out on the balcony, they were speaking to each other so she felt it best she stay where she was. They would be gone soon and at the moment she was too tired and too involved with thoughts of Wesley to want to talk to them. Then her interest became more intense when she heard Wesley's name mentioned. The intense interest turned to disbelief, then to anger and beyond to absolute fury at their words.

"Has old Wesley asked you to return the dance with Celeste he traded with you?" one asked.

"Fat chance," the second laughed. "She's the sweetest, prettiest thing I've seen in years. I've danced once with her and I'll damn well have the second. Maybe I could even convince her to walk in the garden with me."

"You'd best not let Clara see you. Didn't you get engaged to her? Besides, I wouldn't make her brother angry. He seems a rather formidable foe I wouldn't want to tangle with."

"Well," the second man chuckled, "a little kiss in a dark garden shouldn't upset anyone, especially if they don't know anything about it."

"God, did you see old Wesley's face when he saw her? He nearly swallowed his tongue. I'm safe in saying he regrets giving away his chance."

They laughed heartily then walked back into the ballroom.

Celeste stood frozen, slowly absorbing the import of the words she had just heard. Wesley didn't want to dance with her, he gave the dances away as if she were nothing. Slowly, her blazing anger simmered, and slowly she regained control of herself. With a soft deceiving smile she reentered the ballroom.

Alexander stood talking with some friends of his. He was a little surprised when Celeste came up beside him.

"Alexander, come dance with me. I'd like to talk to you."

Covering his surprise, he led her to the floor, anxious to see what was wrong. "What's the matter Celeste?"

"Alexi, do you remember the last dance here, you and George kept switching partners?"

"Yes, why?"

"I want you to switch partners now." He looked at her for a moment then he laughed.

"Can I guess who your unsuspecting partner is going to be?"

"I'll bet you could," she smiled up at him and he could see the reflection of his own laughter in her eyes. He looked about until he spotted Wesley and his partner, then he moved in their direction.

To say that Wesley was surprised was an understatement, to say he was not pleased was even more so, for in a few minutes, he held a smiling beautiful Celeste in his arms.

"Celeste," he said, as his eyes held hers, "I've been trying to dance with you all evening. It's hard to get close to the prettiest girl in the room."

"Thank you Wesley, I'm glad to hear you feel that way. I thought maybe you didn't want to dance with me."

"Didn't want ... Celeste when I saw you tonight, I thought you were the most beautiful woman I've ever seen."

"But you couldn't ask me to dance?" she persisted enjoying his discomfort.

"I tried, but you've been surrounded all evening."

"Faint heart never won fair lady, Wesley," she said in a cool amused voice.

The dance ended and they stood together. "Now," she said softly, the sweet smile still on her face, "Suppose I tell you why. Suppose I tell you that you traded away your dance with me to dance with someone else. Suppose I tell you, Wesley Rainey, that I never want to speak to you again as long as I live."

Without a moment's slip of her smile, she turned and walked away from him, leaving him stunned for a moment. It would have been better for him if he had understood a woman's mind a little better. Instead of leaving the ballroom and going upstairs she walked across the room and out onto the semi-dark balcony. There, smile intact, she waited for Wesley.

Once the shock had left him, Wesley was overcome with shame at what she had said and the way she must feel about him. As quickly as he could move he crossed the room and stepped out on the balcony. For a moment he could not see her, then looking over the balcony he saw her standing in the garden below.

Quickly he went down the steps and very nearly ran to her side.

"Celeste," he said gently "Let me talk to you, at least let me explain."

"I really don't see what there is to explain," she said, her voice dripping frost. "It must be all over the ballroom. I'm so ashamed. To think that I am so distasteful to dance with that someone would actually trade away a dance just to get away from me."

"Celeste . . . I . . . I'm sorry. I'm truly sorry. Before God, I never meant to hurt you."

She turned to face him. "Hurt me," she repeated softly, seeing the misery on his face. Her eyes softened. "I think you did yourself much more harm than you have me. I'm sure all your other girlfriends would be quite upset to find out how deceivingly you operate."

"I don't care what anyone else thinks. I just want you to forgive me for being so stupid. It's just that . . ."

"That what?"

"That I've never really seen you before. I know you're angry, but try to understand. I always thought of you as Alexander's baby sister. I . . . I just never saw you as a woman. I didn't think you'd care one way or the other if I danced with you or not."

For a moment she was silent, then she decided to let

172

him know how she really felt. Very quietly she spoke. "But I do care, Wesley, I guess I always have."

He couldn't quite believe his ears. This beauty before him was actually telling him she cared for him, maybe had for a long time. He was completely shaken and did not quite know how to handle it, which was a surprise in itself.

"Celeste ..." he said, "you ... you're not getting revenge for what I did? I mean ... it's true, really true?"

Her eyes twinkled in mischievous devilment. "Maybe ... maybe I'll let you guess about that for a while."

He chuckled. "In the meantime, can I have one of the dances I so foolishly lost?"

"I'm afraid sir," she said, "that if we return to the ballroom, I shall be honor bound to dance with others."

"Well," he said softly, "why can't we dance here?"

"Here?"

"The moonlight's bright, the music is clear and I have the prettiest girl in the ball here. I can't think of a better place to be."

Without another word, she raised her arms. His arm slid about her waist and they began to sway slowly to the soft beat of the music.

For Celeste it was the brightest moment of the night. For Wesley it was the dawn of a whole new experience. The slim girl he held in his arms awakened an emotion he had never felt before. He wanted to draw her closer and closer but rigid rules bound him. The soft scent she wore filled his senses, as did the emerald eyes that smiled up at him.

The music stopped a full two minutes before either of them realized it. They were held in a magic moment.

Their eyes held, and Wesley could resist no longer. Slowly he drew her closer and bent his head to lightly touch her lips with his.

Celeste had shared familial kisses with her parents and her brother, but she was completely unprepared for the warm flush of pleasure that coursed through her at the gentle touch of Wesley's lips on hers.

That she had never been kissed before he knew immediately, and all his breeding told him to stop, but his disobedient heart refused to listen. He tightened his arms about her and claimed her mouth in a kiss that was rapidly slipping beyond both of their control.

It was only rigid self-control that forced him to hold her a little away from him. They looked at each other in wonder at this blinding new emotion.

"Celeste, do you think your parents would allow me to call on you, I mean ... if you want me to?"

"I want you to, Wesley, but we must ask my father. He might think I'm still too young to have beaus call on me yet."

"Beaus," he exclaimed happily, "if I have my way, there will be no other beau. Can we talk to your parents tonight?"

"I think not, but maybe if you come to dinner tomorrow night you can talk to Father afterwards."

"I'll be there."

The music started again. Wesley would have taken her back into his arms but reluctantly she backed away.

"People might be whispering if we stay out here any longer. If Father heard he might be angry with you. I ... I should die if he were angry with you."

"No, the last thing I want is your family upset with me."

Knowing there was nothing else he could do, he took her elbow and led her back into the ballroom where she was immediately surrounded by other young men and swept away from him.

The balance of the night, he watched her laugh and dance and enjoy herself, but a grim solid determination began to grow in him. One day, he promised himself, Celeste Dubonne would belong to him—forever.

Celeste informed her parents of her invitation to Wesley for the next evening. They agreed, but shared a glance between each other that went unnoticed by both Celeste and Alexander. Their baby was growing up and neither of them were quite sure it pleased them.

Alexander took the opportunity to tease Celeste a little, but ceased when he finally realized that this was not a game, but a very serious thing for her. He knew, of course, that Celeste had had a crush on Wesley since she was twelve, but he had not realized that it had begun to develop into a much stronger and more lasting emotion.

The night of the dinner, Celeste was nearly in tears for nothing seemed to satisfy her. Her hair was wrong, the dress she wore was wrong and she definitely felt like an insecure child. She stood at her mirror fussing, with frustrated tears in her eyes, when she heard the rap on her door. Her mother entered before she could even answer.

"Celeste, Wesley is here. We've been waiting for you for quite some time. It's certainly not polite to keep that young man waiting so long."

"Oh, Mother," she cried mournfully, "I look terrible. I look like a little girl in my mother's party dress. My hair is awful, he won't want to look at me!"

Marie smiled and went to her side. She took Celeste's fluttering hands in hers.

"Celeste, listen to me. Stop trying to be something you are not. Brush out your hair and tie it with a ribbon. Your dress is very pretty. Wesley will not be looking at either. He will be too busy looking into your pretty eyes. I'm sure if he cares for you then what you wear will be of no importance to him at all. After all, child, he is not here to judge you, he is simply here to enjoy your company. If that were not so, I'm sure he would not have bothered to call at all."

"Do you really think so, Mother?"

"Yes, I do. We've been talking while we were waiting for you and even though he is a gentleman, you can see his impatience for your presence. He watches the stairs as if his life depended upon it."

"Does he really!" Her eyes began to glitter with bright happiness.

Quickly she undid her hair she had so elaborately twisted atop her head. She brushed it to a mass of pale gold curls and bound it with a green velvet ribbon. The dress she wore was white with tiny green flowers in it. When she turned to face her mother again, Marie smiled and nodded. "You are you," she laughed, "Beauty does not need too much adornment, Celeste."

Celeste ran to her mother and kissed her enthusiastically on both cheeks.

"I love you Maman," she whispered.

"You have not called me that in a long time, not since you were a baby. Now you are a woman grown." There was a note of almost sadness in Marie's voice.

"Nothing changes my love for you, Maman."

Marie smiled, hugged her daughter close, trying to

fight the happy tears in her eyes.

"Now come, let's not keep that young man waiting any longer. He was nearly beside himself when I came up. Remember he is sitting under the relentless gaze of your father and your brother."

"I once accused him of having a faint heart," Celeste laughed. "If he survives that I will know he is a man of extreme courage."

They laughed together as they left the room and started down the stairs. When Celeste reached the bottom of the stairs and entered the huge sitting room, Wesley leaped to his feet, a smile on his face. Both Jules and Marie struggled to keep their faces straight at his obvious relief when Wesley saw Celeste.

"Good evening, Wesley," Celeste said with such a regal air that even Alexander found it difficult to believe that this was the same Celeste who had been in such an extreme nervous condition all day.

"Evening, Celeste," Wesley said. His eyes absorbed everything about her. "You surely do look pretty tonight."

"Thank you," Celeste replied softly and her cheeks pinkened under his steady warm gaze.

To Wesley it was as if the others were not present and the rest of the world faded away. She looked so delicate and fragile that it caught his breath.

"Celeste," Jules said, and she started a little at the sound that interrupted the pink cloud on which she had existed for the past few moments.

"Yes, Father?"

"Young Wesley has asked my permission to call on you from time to time."

Celeste was breathless. "Yes, Father," she said softly.

"You are quite young yet, Celeste," her heart fell to her feet as did Wesley's, "but I see no harm in his coming here occasionally as long as you both understand that it will be quite some time before you can make any serious plans."

"Mr. Dubonne," Wesley said firmly, "I understand. If Celeste will agree . . . well, I would like to come under any rules you care to make . . . Is it all right with you, Celeste?" he added softly.

Her cheeks grew rosier, but her crystal green eyes held his. "Yes, Wesley, yes, I would like you to come . . . under any circumstances."

She watched his eyes dance with pleasure. "Well," Alexander said as he rubbed his hands together, "now that is settled could we please eat? I'm starved."

"You are always starved," his mother replied. Jules extended his arm to Marie who took it.

"Then come, my dear, let us feed him before he expires from hunger."

Wesley took Celeste's hand and tucked it under his arm and the five of them went to the elaborately set and well laden table.

The dinner was excellent and there was much laughter and shared pleasure. After the meal was over, Wesley, with Jules' permission, took Celeste for a stroll in the garden.

The soft scent of magnolias filled the air and the trill of chickadees made a rhythmic kind of music. It was a magic time, a time of gentle beauty, and a time they would one day recall with painfully sweet memory. It was a gallant time, a time of knights on shining horses, a time of chivalry and Wesley Rainey was the finest example of the youth of the day. His pride and honor meant more to him than anything else except the woman in his life. To him, she was all things. Fine, gentle and pure. To him, she was the one thing he would lay down his life for. "I'm glad your father gave his permission, Celeste. I don't know what I would have done if he had refused."

She smiled up at him, her eyes sparkling with laughter; it made him laugh.

"You know I would have tried to see you anyway. I probably would have had your father and your brother driving me off with pistols."

"Father is not an unreasonable man. It's no secret in this family that I have had a terrible crush on you since I was a child."

He stopped and looked down into her eyes, his face lit with shy pleasure. "Have you? Really?"

"Yes, I've been teased about it often enough. That and the fact that you couldn't see me at all."

"Every man is entitled to one stupid mistake in his life; that was mine. But I certainly don't intend to repeat it. From this moment on, I intend to take advantage of every moment of your time you will permit. I intend," he added softly, "to try to convince you to love me as much as I do you, and one day to be my wife."

Celeste felt the warmth of him and it sent a shiver of expectant pleasure through her. She remained still and quiet as slowly he put his arms about her and drew her close. She sighed contentedly as she put her arms about his neck and lifted her lips for his kiss.

Inside the house Marie sat with her embroidery and watched her husband and Alexander challenging each other over a game of chess. Alexander was winning, which was a rare thing, and Marie smiled to herself knowing Jules' mind was outside in the garden with a young woman he still considered his baby.

The silence in the room was interrupted by the appearance of the butler who announced the presence of George McClellan.

"Show him in, Maxwell," Jules said. He rose, "Shall we finish this game later?"

His eyes twinkled. "The most strategic way to get out of admitting defeat."

Alexander laughed. "You've probably plenty of tricks up your sleeve yet and you plan to think them out and whip the pants off me later."

They were laughing when George walked in the door. But his appearance sobered them for he stood in the cadet's uniform from the military academy of West Point.

"George," Alexander said. "Come in."

George strode toward them purposefully, proud of his new uniform and the things to which he had so recently dedicated himself.

"You look so handsome in your uniform, George," Marie said.

"Thank you Mrs. Dubonne."

"Can I get you a drink?" Alexander questioned.

"No," George laughed. "We've been celebrating enough. I want to get home sober enough to see my parents' reaction."

"Your father will be pleased," Jules said.

"Yes, sir," George flushed with pleasure. "I know he will, it's ... it's my mother I'm worried about. I know she's never said it, but I think she feels one military man in the family is enough. Especially now."

"Especially now?" Marie questioned. "Why now?"

There was a silence that lasted just a moment too long as the men exchanged glances. One of embarrassment by George, of annoyance by Jules, and displeasure by Alexander.

"Are one of you going to explain to me or should I guess," Marie said calmly. "I imagine this disgusting talk of war has excited all the young men. Why is it men must resort to killing each other to settle their disagreements?"

"If it came to that," George replied, "we have to defend the Union. We cannot let those slave killers control the United States. We must defend the right."

"The right," Jules said, his gaze holding George's. "George, I've fought in many battles, all for what I thought was right. Do you know what I've discovered is always true?"

"No, sir."

"That the results of war never approximate the supposedly noble objectives for which such conflicts are fought. War is abnormal and peace is normal; war can be equated with pathological emotionalism and irrationalism."

He stopped, realizing that George would never be so impolite as to argue with him in his own home and in front of Marie. George's eyes were shuttered so his emotions would not show, but his face was flushed and his hand involuntarily clenched.

"I'm sorry, George," Jules said quickly. "I did not mean to insult a most welcome guest. Please forgive me."

"It's quite all right, sir. Knowing all your experience I understand how you feel. But this situation is different, sir."

"Of course," Jules replied softly, but Alexander knew this was not what he felt.

Before anyone could speak again, Celeste and Wesley returned. It brightened the atmosphere immediately for the two of them radiated happiness. Even George could sense the warmth despite his controlled anger.

Although they wanted him to stay for a while, George insisted he had to get home. He was anxious to see his parents' reaction to his finery and to talk with his father whose military influence would reassure the young man of his ambitions.

Wesley left a short time later and as soon as he was gone, Celeste excused herself so that she could go to bed and dream of her knight and the love they shared.

Alexander and Jules returned to their game of chess, where to Alexander's laughing dismay, in a few short moves, his father trounced him unmercifully.

"I knew it," Alexander groaned when his father made the last strategic move. "All I had to do was give you a moment to concentrate and it would cost me the game."

"Would you like to try another?" his father asked.

"Good God, no!" Alexander exclaimed. "You have beaten me for the last five games. I believe I'll try someone a little less practiced than you a while longer before I ever challenge you again."

Both Jules and Marie laughed.

"I'm going to bed," he announced as he stood and stretched. He kissed his mother and they heard him whistling as he took the steps two at a time. Then they heard the closing of his door.

As always, as Marie's eyes followed his tall form, she thought of the boy they had lost and the still empty feeling within her. Jules, who could read her thoughts, went to her and sat beside her, taking her hand in his.

"He has grown into a good strong young man, Marie. A man of which I am very proud. We," he added softly, "should thank God for him and Celeste."

"I do, Jules, I do. I do not know what we would have done without them. I love them both and I am so very proud of them. Still ... I miss him. I suppose I always shall."

"Yes, we always will. But we must hold Alexander and Celeste a little closer because of his loss, for they miss him too. We must fill that empty spot within each other to be able to stand the pain."

"Yes, love," she sighed as he drew her into his arms and held her.

Twelve

True to Alexander's prediction, Celeste captured the hearts of most of the young swains in the area. Although he and Celeste were the only ones who knew the truth about her feelings, Alexander watched as Wesley, time and time again, had to do battle for her attentions.

Jules and Marie agreed immediately that Celeste was entirely too young to even consider becoming engaged to anyone, and no matter how much they liked and even favored Wesley, they said nothing else.

The days and nights sparkled in a never ending stream of activity. Both Alexander and Celeste in the mainstream of society enjoyed all the pleasures it had to offer.

George, when he did have time free from the academy, joined them.

Days tumbled carelessly by and the laughter drowned out the low rumble of war. Alexander listened to the talk, but deliberately held away from joining in the fever that began slowly to embroil the multitudes. He wanted desperately to believe that the strong authority and cool head of Abraham Lincoln would control the situation and keep them from beginning what he thought would be a wasteful holocaust.

Secretly he worried over and over about what he would do if it came to a conflict. War was a distasteful thing to him, yet deep in his heart he held a powerful love for his adopted country. The thought of killing his own countrymen was repugnant to him. He knew, if pressed to a choice, he, like George, would defend the union against secession for he realized that to split the country in two was to weaken it and make it an easy conquest for other more militant countries.

George had been home for a short week's vacation. His return to the academy would mark the beginning of his third year. He and Alexander had taken an opportunity to go for a ride. It was one of the few times they had been able to talk alone.

They walked along together, resting their horses, and talking.

"There's no way out of it, Alexander," George said firmly, "you're deliberately blinding yourself if you believe war can be prevented."

"You still say that word so easily, George. I think it means something different to you than it does to me."

"I don't think so, Alexander, before maybe I thought it was more glory than anything else. Studying under some of the men at the academy that I have, maybe I look at it more realistically. But we cannot allow this country to be made into two. There is no way we'll survive that. I don't take the word easily, but at least I face it."

"And I don't?"

"To be honest, I don't think so. Believe me Alexander, you're going to be faced with a choice. Tell me, what will you do?"

Alexander walked in silence for a moment and George remained silent, waiting.

"I'd wear the uniform, I'd fight ... but I would hate it and pray it would end quickly."

"Amen," George said softly. "Don't you think we all feel the same?"

"God," Alexander said, "to turn on each other, it seems ... impossible."

George was about to speak when they saw another rider approaching. He was riding at top speed, pushing his horse. Alexander and George exchanged looks. No one would pressure a valuable horse like that unless something drastic had happened.

When the rider drew up alongside them they recognized a young stable boy.

"Mr. Alexander!" the boy said breathlessly.

"What is it?"

"You're wanted at the main house. Your father says for you and," he looked at George, not quite sure by what title he should address him.

"Lieutenant," George said helpfully, smothering a smile.

"Yes, sir, he wants you both quickly. As quick as you can get there he said."

The three of them rode as rapidly as possible. Leaving their horses at the stable, George and Alexander ran across the green lawn. They entered the main house to find confusion.

Marie and Celeste were trying not to weep. Jules face was pale and Wesley Rainey stood by Celeste's chair, his face pale but trying to remain calm though his eyes glittered with excitement.

"Father! What is it? What's wrong?"

"Word has been sent for George. He's been called back to the academy immediately."

Now Alexander could feel a premonitional tremor. "Father?"

Jules held himself erect and through stiff lips said the words Alexander had dreaded hearing.

"They fired on Fort Sumter yesterday morning. We ... we are at war."

For a moment there was complete and absolute silence. Then George turned to Alexander.

"This is one time when I hate to say I told you so. What will you do?"

Alexander looked about the room at his tearful mother and sister and his father. Resignedly he said in a firm voice, "I'll ride with you."

The final decision made, he seemed to be relieved as if the inevitable had been faced and now no spectre hung over his shoulder.

Abby Southerland looked at her father with disbelieving eyes. Her cheeks were flushed with anger.

"Why! Why must I stay here!"

"Because," he replied, his face just as angry as hers, "crossing the lines to carry messages during a war is a thing punishable by death. You are not, I repeat, not permitted to go with me."

"Father," she said in a more reasonable voice, "you would certainly be more suspicious traveling alone. A Southerner crossing and recrossing lines. Father, if I went with you they might believe you were taking me to visit relatives."

"That's poppycock!" he shouted, "and I will not

permit it, so do not speak of it again. I am leaving tomorrow. You are not! That is final!''

Abby clamped her mouth shut, glared at her father with virulent anger sparkling in her eyes. Then she spun about and left the room slamming the door solidly behind her.

In her room, watched by the wide dark eyes of her maid, she paced the floor. Her eyes were a crystal blue, frigid with her anger.

''Damn, damn!'' she muttered, and the young maid gasped. It certainly was not an expression a lady used even in the confines of her own room.

''He can't do this to me, Loel,'' she said. ''Just because I'm a woman he thinks I can't do anything to contribute. Why is it men think they're so .. so ... all powerful.''

''Yessum,'' the maid said in a soft voice filled with fear.

''I'm not going to let him get away with this, Loel.''

''What you gonna do, Miss Abby?'' the maid questioned as the fear began to build in her. She had been maid to Abby too long not to know that Abby usually did exactly what she planned to do.

''I'm not sure yet,'' Abby said, ''but don't worry, Loel,'' she smiled, ''I'll think of something. This is my country too, and I intend to do what I can to help.''

The young maid sighed. There was no stopping Miss Abby when she aimed to do something. Loel was afraid of only one thing. Abby might choose to take her along. She reflected back on what had started the argument between Abby and her father.

The news of war had been a shattering thing. Abby's father, having relatives in the North, had been requested to desert his Southern sympathy and go North. There he would work as an agent and send news of the Union Army's movements South. Abby had been excited. She had not thought her father intended she should stay home. She had used every argument including begging and tears but none of them had any effect on her father, who wisely worried more about her safety.

Loel stood beside Abby as her father rode away the next day. Loel was more worried now than she ever had been for Abby stood, smiling gently and speaking softly to her father. She wished him a fond and affectionate farewell.

The carriage had barely left the driveway when Abby turned to Loel. "Now," she smiled and Loel's heart sank, "come along with me, Loel. We have some packing to do."

"Packing! Oh, Miss Abby, what you gonna do? Yo ain't gwine up dere. Yo pappy will sho be angry with you."

"Maybe, but once I'm there, then there's not much he can do about it now is there?"

Abby walked back into the house with a distressed Loel at her heels.

Rodger Southerland arrived at the train station in Philadelphia. His second cousin, Paul Drake, met him at the station. Paul, though his home had been Philadelphia for some years, had been born and raised not too far from Atlanta. His sympathies lay with the South. He shook Rodger's hand and escorted him to a carriage he had waiting.

"Did you have any difficulties?" Paul asked.

"No, no problems. I don't think this is the kind of thing they've taken into consideration so soon. It will give us time to get organized. We must set up some kind of organization so that when we learn anything word can be sent immediately."

"I've already begun to do that. The only problem, is . . . just how do we get this information. We need to find a way to make our home a place where the Yankees would like to gather. A place where they would feel free to talk."

"Well, we'll think of something. For now, let's just get settled so I can look around the city and find a place to begin."

Paul grunted in agreement and they remained silent on the ride to Paul's home.

Four days later, Rodger and Paul were seated in the parlor of Paul's home. They were drinking brandy and smoking. They were still trying to figure out just how they could get access to the military personnel in the city. Relaxed access that would put them in contact with loose tongues. Loose tongues that would speak of troop movements, supply routes and future battles.

"There has to be a way," Paul said angrily. "If only I were not a widower and had myself a beautiful wife I could have parties. That would bring 'em. Nothing loosens a tongue like a whiskey and a beautiful woman."

They laughed together, then the closing of the door made them both turn around. Abby stood inside the room smiling. "Well," she said softly, "when do we have the first party? The Confederacy is on the march. I think it is time we all began to work together."

"Abby! Confound it girl! Can you never be obedient?

Didn't I tell you to stay home?"

Rodger's face was mottled with anger, and Abby's nonchalant smile did nothing to lessen it.

"You will go back home immediately," he fairly shouted. But Abby smiled a cool self-possessed smile as she walked across the room and stood beside them.

"You may shout and bluster all you please, Father," she said, "but I am here and I am staying. The South needs all her patriots now, and I am as much a patriot as you are."

Paul smiled and extended his hand to Abby. She gave him hers and he kissed it gently. His eyes twinkled at her in silent amusement.

"Rodger," he said gently, "you have just given us the way to open our home. My sweet beautiful cousin, visiting here will be a lovely attraction for any red-blooded Union officer in existence."

Rodger's face became pale and his hand trembled as he reached out to touch Abby. "It is too dangerous. If they caught us they would hang us. Abby, they would have no mercy on a woman in time of war. They would hang you also."

"Father," she replied, her voice gentle and her blue eyes warm with affection, "we need the courage of every loyal Southerner. Do you limit courage to men alone? Do I not have the right to defend all that you have taught me to believe in?"

Rodger was defeated and he knew it. He had instilled all these qualities in Abby, and he had been proud of her abilities and her quick intelligence ... now he had to prove it. His shoulders sagged, and in sympathy, she reached up and kissed his cheek. Then she turned to face Paul. "When do we begin?" she said softly.

It was done so quietly and so subtly that no one really noticed. If asked no one would have been able to say when Paul Drake's home became the center of social activity. All they would have simultaneously claimed would have been that Abby Southerland, Paul's cousin, was the loveliest woman in Philadelphia. She was a sparkling, vivacious woman and a genuinely intelligent person whom a man could talk to.

No one would have known of the information that moved from the Drake home to Brigadier General Joseph E. Johnston and brought about a Confederate evacuation of Harper's Ferry and a defeat of the Union army at First Manassas.

The Union forces gathered there initially to defend Washington and gradually grew in strength until this became their main camp. Facing it at Manassas was the camp of the Confederates with General P. T. Beauregard in command.

This battle was a rousing defeat of the Union forces and sent them fleeing toward Washington.

Alexander had the benefit of his father's military mind and training all his life. This and the wealth of his father had, as was the custom of the time, allowed him to buy a commission. Even though he had done so, he wanted to be able to lead them properly so he had put himself through the same training as his men. He had studied strategies and maps with his father until his mind was numb with them. Continually in the back of his mind, was the fear that he would not be able to fight, not be able to kill. The battle of First Manassas was a defeat that stung bitterly. He blamed it on many things, but deep inside it shattered some of his poise and self esteem.

He had been granted a short leave, and he went home. He wanted to discuss with his father what had gone wrong. He could not believe a Union force which completely outnumbered the opposition could have been routed so.

He arrived home just after the dinner hour to find that his father and mother were not home.

"Where have they gone?"

"To a dinner party, sir."

"Where?"

"At the home of a Mr. Paul Drake, sir."

"Have someone lay out my dress uniform and get me a bath while I shave."

"Yes, sir."

"Oh, and have a carriage brought around, I want to talk to my father tonight and I feel the need of something strong to drink."

"Yes, sir."

Alexander went to his room and immediately poured himself a stiff drink. He downed it quickly and poured another. This he sipped while he removed his clothes. When the bath water was brought, he sank into it with a grateful sigh. He relaxed long enough to finish his second drink then he left the tub and began to dress.

The dark blue uniform was complimentary to his tall lean form. The already broad shoulders seemed broader while the already slim muscular body seemed even slimmer. The gold hair was brought into stark contrast and combined with the deep tanned skin, his green eyes sparkled.

Satisfied, he pulled on his boots and went down to the carriage that waited for him. Less than an hour later, he disembarked before a huge gaily lit mansion.

Paul Drake's house was set up so that he could entertain guests on the main floor for dinners and then take them up the huge winding staircase to an immense ballroom on the second floor.

Paul's servants were well trained, for Alexander had barely raised his hand to knock than the door was opened and he was graciously ushered inside. Paul had chosen his servants well. All were friends of his, and all shared his faith and love of the Confederacy. Anyone in Union uniform especially one of rank, was immediately given all the hospitality they could want.

"Good evening, Lieutenant."

"Good evening. I'm Lieutenant Dubonne. I believe my family is here?"

"Oh, yes, sir. They have just finished dinner sir. The gentlemen are in the library having cigars and the ladies have gone upstairs."

"Good, I could use another drink."

"Come this way, sir."

Alexander followed him across the wide entrance hall and down a narrow hall to the library door. There he knocked discreetly, then opened the door to usher Alexander in.

"Alexander!" Jules said as he left the group of men he had been standing with and came to Alexander's side.

"You know almost everybody here except for Mr. Drake and Mr. Southerland. Paul, this is my son, Alexander."

Alexander extended his hand to Paul who took it in a

firm grip.

"How do you do Alexander, I have been hearing quite a bit about you."

"Me, sir?" Alexander lifted a quizzical eyebrow.

"Some of your officers have a very high regard for your potential."

"I'm afraid, sir," Alexander laughed, "it's a secret they've kept well guarded from me."

Paul laughed. "Come and sit down, can I get you something to drink?"

"Yes, please."

"Whiskey, brandy?"

"Whiskey will be fine, thank you."

Jules cast Alexander a surprised look, but remained silent. The conversation began again and Alexander found a comfortable seat where he could let it flow about him.

Eventually, as it did in all gatherings, the conversation touched upon the battle. Many opinions were given, and Paul remained silent, listening. Then his eyes fell on a contemplative Alexander.

"What do you think caused the rout?" he directed the question at Alexander who looked at him first in surprise, then in serious thought.

"We outpositioned them, and we outnumbered them," he said quietly.

"Then why did we evacuate? Why did they win?"

Alexander's eyes lifted to his and Paul felt the first tingle of warning that this man could be dangerous.

"It may sound foolish to you."

"Say what you think," Paul smiled.

Alexander replied, "I think they knew our plans before we did."

There was a moment of silence as they all digested this.

"Good heavens man, do you know what you are saying? You are accusing one of our officers of being a traitor? Do you suspect someone in particular?" Rodger asked.

"No, Mr. Southerland," Alexander shrugged, as if he already regretted what he had said. "I'm tired, and my ego has been rather bruised by this confrontation. It's just a feeling," he laughed, "I suppose every defeated warrior needs someone to blame."

Everyone laughed as Paul did, but his eyes did not miss the fact that even though he had made a joke of it, Alexander had been quite serious. He had a slight sense that something was wrong and Paul did not want it to go any further. He needed Abby's help to take Alexander's mind off sensitive ideas . . . like spies.

"Well gentlemen, shall we join the ladies upstairs for some dancing?"

They agreed and set aside their empty glasses. Paul escorted them all to the ballroom, then he slipped away after the music had started and walked down the hall to Abby's door and knocked.

"Come in," she called.

Paul walked in and closed the door behind him. Then he stood in profound admiration at the woman who stood across the room from him. He thought without a doubt she was the most beautiful creature he had ever seen.

Abby's brilliant auburn hair had been drawn up from each side of her face and held in a mass of curls that fell to her waist. The dress she had chosen was of sea blue that matched her eyes and cut so daringly low that he half expected her every breath to be the one that released her slim body from all confinement.

"Abby my dear, you are enough to take a man's breath away."

"Thank you, Paul," she laughed. "I hope it can keep their minds on me and not on what they are saying. Is there anyone in particular that might have any information?"

Quickly Paul explained about the arrival of Alexander and what he had said.

"It would be best, Abby, if you could find out just how suspicious he is. He's a good future prospect. I've talked to others about him. He has a brilliant military future. He also might just be in a position one day to have access to a lot of information."

"Lieutenant Alexander Dubonne," she repeated. "Would he be any chance the son of Marie and Jules Dubonne?"

"Yes, he is."

"I've heard his name mentioned before. Well, shall we go?"

They walked down the hall slowly and stood in the doorway watching the dancers for a moment and smiling at people they knew.

Alexander, who was already well into his fourth whiskey, had been standing with his back to the door. He turned when the man he had been talking to gazed over his shoulder with admiring eyes. Following his gaze Alexander was momentarily stunned. His eyes drank in her rare beauty like a man dying of thirst. He could feel his blood warm and his pulses pound. He had seen beautiful women before but this one was different than any other.

"Who is that?" he whispered.

"Abby Southerland, our hostess," the man beside him said.

"My God, she's the loveliest creature I've ever seen."

"Even from this distance," the man laughed. "Wait until you are closer."

Alexander decided immediately that he had to get closer. He began to walk toward them edging between people. Paul saw him coming. Still smiling, he said quietly, "Lieutenant Dubonne is headed this way."

Abby looked toward the direction Paul was coming. She was prepared for many things but not to look up into the face ... of Dan Wakefield.

Thirteen

Abby quickly regained control of her reactions. She smiled as Alexander was introduced.

"How do you do, Lieutenant Dubonne," she said softly.

Alexander had not missed the moment of shock that had registered on Abby's face before she composed herself. He wondered what it was about him that had shaken her for a moment. She was entirely too beautiful and too self contained a woman to have been impressed by a handsome face and a uniform! he thought, yet something about him had definitely startled her for a moment.

"I am utterly amazed," he said.

"I don't understand, Lieutenant, amazed at what?" she replied, answering his smile.

"That someone as lovely as you could live in this city and my luck could be so bad that I've not met you before this."

He watched her eyes sparkle with laughter and found he wanted to hear her laugh, and to again see the glitter of humor in her astonishing blue eyes.

"And," she teased, "you have met every beautiful

girl in Philadelphia?"

"No, but now that I've met you there is really no need of searching any longer. The best cannot be surpassed."

She laughed, a soft throaty sound that sent an expectant tingle down his spine.

"Thank you Lieutenant Dubonne. A man with a silver tongue such as yours must not have too much difficulty finding beauty wherever he might search."

Paul had strategically moved away, and left the two together. If anyone could get any information from someone he was assured it was Abby. He watched Abby and Alexander laugh together and he smiled to himself. At least if Alexander had a suspicion of anyone in particular Abby would know by the end of the evening.

Alexander was feeling a double source of intoxication. He had drunk four whiskeys on an empty stomach, and he was slowly drowning in a pair of sea blue eyes.

His arm about her waist and her hand in his, they whirled about the floor to the strains of a Strauss waltz.

Their eyes seemed to be only for each other, and many in the room watched the couple. His gold head bent above her dark one, they gave all about them the feeling that these two matched each other completely.

Less than half an hour later, Abby allowed herself to be maneuvered into a walk in the garden with Alexander. They went down the wide stairway and out into the moonlit garden.

As they strolled along, Alexander took her hand and tucked it under his arm. They walked for a few minutes in silence.

"You don't come from Philadelphia," he stated.

"Oh," she smiled "and where do I come from?"

"I don't know exactly. I detect an accent you have

learned to disguise. I would say you were educated in Europe right?"

"That's right," she replied. Then she launched into a well rehearsed story of her past. "I was born in Kentucky," she said this for Kentucky was the only neutral state at the time. "My father has done business with Paul for some time. Since the war has broken out, Father thought it would be better for business if he moved closer to Paul."

"You'll be living here permanently?" he questioned hopefully.

"At least for the duration of the war," she answered honestly.

He stopped and looked down into her eyes. The moonlight washed over her, bathing her in its pale golden glow. His eyes became serious and intent.

"I'm glad," he said softly.

She stood very still, her eyes held by his, and suddenly a feeling of warmth enclosed her. It was as if something from deep within him reached out and enfolded her. Something from the depths of her stirred, then burst into life. The intense shock of it caused her to tremble. This was something she had not planned on, yet she could not seem to find the words to break the spell he seemed to be weaving about her.

He stood close to her and every sense in her felt his overpowering size and masculinity. She liked the clean scent of him and the subtle feeling of strength that called to some strange need within her. Desperately, she fought the urge to sway toward him and have those strong arms close about her. Hold her and protect her from the dark unpredictable future.

She inhaled deeply and gripped her wayward emotions.

"And why are you glad?"

He smiled. "Because Abby," he said, "you and I both know I want to see you again." He paused, then a warm chuckle followed, "and again and again and again."

She laughed, grateful that humor had helped her release herself from the magnetic hold he seemed to have over her.

"I have a feeling we will see you again. You strike me as a very determined man."

"When I see something worth being determined about."

Again she tucked her hand under his arm and they continued to walk.

"Tell me about yourself, Alexander Dubonne."

"First you tell me something."

"What?"

"When Paul Drake first introduced us, you acted as if you had seen a ghost. Do I remind you of a long lost beau or something?"

He was so accurate that again she was shocked and he felt it.

"I do, don't I? . . . remind you of someone."

"Yes, you do. In fact he looks so much like you that you could be brothers. It is remarkable. The same hair, same eyes, same features, less than an inch or so difference in height. Built the same. It is really remarkable."

"Who is he?" Alexander asked softly. He was looking straight ahead, but she sensed he was listening intently for her answer.

"Part of my past and no one you would know. He's someone from home."

"Abby . . . ?"

"No, no more about me, Alexander. I want to know about you."

"What do you want to know?"

She shrugged, which caused Alexander to hold his breath to keep from gasping at the effect she created.

"I was born in France, raised here in Philadelphia," now he chuckled devilishly. "I'm handsome, good humored and a fine catch for a beautiful woman looking for a husband."

She had to laugh with him, then she became serious.

"This is no time for anyone to think of anything except what is happening to our country. You should know. I understand you were at Manassas a few days ago."

"Yes, I was."

"The battle was bad?" she said softly.

"All battles are bad," he replied firmly. "Any time one man aims a gun at another it is bad."

"The Confederacy won," she reminded.

"It was only a battle, Abby, not a war, and I've a suspicion someone sent ahead some information. I wish I could figure out who or how."

Abby's heart thudded heavily. "Are you suggesting there are Northern people who would actually sell plans to the South?"

He stopped and looked at her as if a thought had just occurred to him. "Or a Southerner masquerading as a Northerner and sending information that way."

"Spies," she whispered.

He was aware he was talking too much about suspicions that he could not prove.

"Abby," he said gently, "I did not bring a beautiful woman into this garden to talk about spies."

She was aware that they were well away from the house in a shadowed corner of the garden. She was also aware that Alexander Dubonne was much more dangerous than she had first thought. Dangerous to her cause ... and to her.

"Alexander ..." she began, planning on suggesting they go back to the house. Gentle fingers touched her lips and stopped her from speaking. She closed her eyes as his fingers brushed her lips then across her cheek to slip gently down her throat.

"I'm glad I came here tonight, Abby Southerland," he said gently, "I'm glad I met you now, tonight. You are very beautiful and I want to know you better. Will you see me again?"

He waited quietly while she drew a shattered breath.

"Is this the time and place?"

"For us? Yes. There is a terrible time coming Abby. Sometimes it is good to have someone to reach for when the world turns dark."

Her mind screamed at her to stop him. To keep him from saying anything else for he was the enemy. Only her heart refused to think of him as enemy. She had to get away from him, to gather herself together to remember that this man was a Yankee. The force that threatened to destroy all she knew and loved.

Firmly and very deliberately she gathered herself together. Forcefully she pushed all other thoughts from her mind except one. He was a Yankee and she was a Confederate spy. If she let him too close to her, in honor, he would have to see her hang for what she was doing.

Her cause forced her to use him to find out all she could and send that information on. It was the only way she could stand for what she knew and believed in. She would not let this Yankee overwhelm her. Her strength and determination returned. For tonight she had found out all she needed to know. Close to Alexander she would find out more. There was no other way. Maybe, when this was over, he would find a way to forgive her. For now, she had her duty, and she had the strength to perform it.

"I would like to see you again, Alexander. I would like for us to be friends."

"Friends," he said softly, "I warn you, Abby, I intend for us to be much more than friends."

"We shall see what the future holds. For now, we had best return to the house before we are missed."

She turned to walk away and suddenly his hand was on her arm. He spun her about and pulled her into his arms. Before she could speak his mouth came crashing down upon hers.

She was not prepared for the consuming fire that burst within her, or for the onslaught to her senses that left her clinging to him and responding to his kiss with a vibrant fire of her own.

As quickly as it happened it was over. She stepped back from him. The challenge had been given and accepted. The war had begun. His eyes followed her as she walked away from him. If she had turned around she would have seen the awakening fierce hunger that showed plainly in his eyes. A hunger that would not be eased until he possessed this cool dark haired goddess who had just invaded his life.

By the time they reached the ballroom she had mastered her thoughts. Though they danced together several more times, Alexander was aware she had built some sort of defense between them. It did nothing except create a deeper desire within him. She could see it in his eyes. The game they were about to play was extremely dangerous ... and her life could hang in the balance.

Alexander did call on her the very next day. She agreed to accompany him and they went for a ride. It was interesting, and for several days she enjoyed his company as he enjoyed hers, yet he was frustratingly aware that a barrier stood between them. He did not know what it was, but he was grimly determined to find out and destroy it.

Alexander's leave was over and he had received orders to report back to duty. The first person he wanted to see was Abby. He wanted to know that he would be welcome when he returned. He did not realize that what he told Abby was immediately put on paper in code and carried to Southern forces.

When decoded the message warned that a Union force was about to attempt to cross the Potomac at the place called Ball's Bluff, two miles east of Leesburg.

Alexander was with the force which attempted the crossing. They were severely and brutally defeated and had to face an ignominious retreat.

As he lay in his bedroll two days later, Alexander's mind was most thoroughly occupied with one thought. Again he felt the Southern forces had been prewarned. They had been ready and waiting for them. Mentally he went over the names who would know what they were attempting. None of them could be put in the position of traitors.

Angrily, he pushed the thoughts aside for they twisted within him until he felt, with black frustration, that he was working about in circles and missing something that should have been obvious.

He welcomed thoughts of returning to Philadelphia to see Abby again, but it was over three months before he was granted a leave and enough time to return home.

Fourteen

Word of the battle of Ball's Bluff reached Paul, who was content with the outcome. He and Abby had done their job well. The Confederacy had won again and it did much to bolster morale.

He and Abby were standing in his library where he had just told her.

"The Confederacy is proud of you, Abby. You have done much for morale to bring about another victory. Each one will be a step toward the final one."

Words Alexander had said came back to her, 'It is a battle, Abby, not the war.'

"Paul?"

"Yes, my dear."

"Have . . . have you heard any word about Alexander Dubonne? Do you know if he . . . if . . ."

"If he survived?" Paul said softly. "Yes, Abby, I've heard. In fact I've taken the pains to find out. He is well . . . embarrassed and angry, but well. Ball's Bluff had been an embarrassment to the whole Union force. Abby," he seemed for a moment to be searching for words, "you are quite fond of Alexander."

"I . . . I like him."

"Like?"

She remained silent for a moment and he could see the emotions in her eyes.

"He's the enemy, Abby," he added softly.

"I know," she said quietly, "I know."

"You must be objective. One cannot love the enemy."

"Paul, maybe it would be better . . . maybe I would be more effective if I worked from another base. You know he will come here."

"Listen to me, Abby, we all have to undergo some test of our strength. We all have to face the things that must inevitably be done. Alexander is no fool. You run, and it will take him no time at all to figure out just what has happened. He is a source of information . . . and you will do what must be done or the defeat of what we stand for and believe in will weigh heavily on your shoulders."

"I cannot see him."

"You can, you must. I know he will be on leave soon. He will come to you, and you will see him. You will watch and listen."

He went to her and took hold of her shoulders. "You came to us, Abby, filled with fire and enthusiasm. We need that now. The battles have just begun. Will you allow this to defeat you or will you give us the help we need. Are you a patriot, Abby?" he added softly, "or were all your words a foolish woman's lies?"

He released her and turned away, crossing the room, he left, closing the door softly behind him. Abby buried her face in her hands and wept.

She stood for some time in the silent room, then, her decision made she left the room. She ordered a carriage and when it was ready she left to visit Jules and Marie

Dubonne ... to ask about the health and welfare of Alexander.

When Alexander arrived home, weeks later, he was delighted to find that Abby had been worried enough to come and see his family and to ask about him regularly.

His impatience caused him to brush aside all propriety. Despite the fact that it was late at night he rode to the Drake house.

The surprised butler informed him that both Mr. Drake and Mr. Southerland were out for the evening. He was even more surprised when Alexander asked if Miss Southerland was still awake.

He made Alexander wait while he went up to inform Abby that he was there. His surprise was even greater when Abby told him to go and tell Alexander that she would dress and be down to see him in a few minutes.

Alexander stood by the remains of a low burning fire. The soft click of the door caused him to turn and he and Abby faced each other across the dimly lit room.

"I thought my memory lied to me. It didn't," he said quietly, "you are the most beautiful woman I have ever seen."

She smiled and slowly walked toward him. She wore a blue velvet dressing gown and her hair had been brushed until it shone and left free to fall about her. When she stood close to him, he could smell the subtle touch of her perfume.

He reached out and touched her hair gently as his eyes told her of the tumultuous emotions that swirled within him. She watched the warmth in his eyes build until it reached out and touched her. His gentleness reached within her and touched an emotion she was trying desperately to control. Over and over she kept saying to herself that this was her enemy, yet she could not control the wild beating of her heart or the urgent need to be held in the strength of his arms.

Slowly she reached out and lay her hand against his chest.

"Welcome, home, Alexander," she whispered. "I have missed you."

He smiled. "For weeks I have planned all I would say to you. Words filled my mind then. Funny, they're all gone. Just a few remain . . . God, I have missed you, and . . . I love you Abby."

No matter how she had prepared herself for such words they struck her so deeply she almost cried out. She closed her eyes as he slowly drew her into his arms. With a deep surrendering sigh she let herself be caught by the magic of him as he crushed her to him. He held her in a fierce embrace for a moment, then gently he cupped her face in his hands and touched his lips to hers.

First, it was a gentle brush of his lips across hers, then he kissed her forehead, her closed eyes, her cheeks, then his mouth returned to hers, this time to drink deeply of the sweetness he had dreamed of for so long.

The dam within her burst and released the floodgates of desire that flowed through her like molten lava. Slowly her lips parted under his searching mouth as his tongue explored the sweet recesses within. She responded with a heated need that blinded her senses to everything but Alexander.

When he released the ties of her robe, she did not know, nor did she care, for his lips were branding the soft curves of her breasts. The robe fell away from her and all that was between them was the thin gown she wore beneath.

She moaned softly as he slid it down from her shoulders.

"Abby, Abby," he murmured against her throat as his hands caressed her and drew her even closer.

Hardened passion-filled nipples tingled at the touch of his lips, and a flame licked through her as his hands sought to explore.

Slowly, they dropped together to the rug-covered floor and the breadth of his shoulders blotted everything from her vision as he looked down into her eyes.

"I need you, Abby, as I have never needed anyone before," he whispered. She lifted her arms about his neck as his mouth again claimed hers in a kiss that rocked the foundations of her world and left her spinning beyond control.

He left her only for minutes to discard the jacket and shirt he wore. She watched the red embered firelight gleam across his muscular body and she reached for him as he discarded the last piece of inhibiting clothing and returned for her.

He knelt beside her for a moment, his eyes forming a picture his memory would carry for a long time. Against the dark rug her body gleamed pale and shimmering in the half light. The nightgown, tangled about her hips increased her sensuality, revealing yet concealing.

He slid his hand up her slim waist to gently cup one breast. "What a magic creature you are my love," he said softly, "I cannot believe I have existed until this moment."

He was beside her then, gathering her into his arms,

claiming her forever his. They blended together as if they had been made thus.

Blind to everything but the need for each other they moved together. The negligible interference of the nightgown took only a moment to do away with. Now his gentle hands sought more intimately as his lips created a song of love against hers.

He sought to raise her passions with his, to fling into the cauldron of burning desire with him. He tormented her passion with searing lips and gentle searching hands until she moaned with the intense flaming need, an all-consuming need.

He was filled with intense joy when he heard her murmured words of love and of need, and felt her body search for his and to ease the wanting that blossomed within her.

With a groan of beautiful agony, he could not restrain he pressed himself deeply within her. He felt her hands grip him and heard the love murmured cry and held himself immobile for a moment until the first touch of pain had gone and a spreading warmth replaced it. Then he began to move slowly and surely, filling her and branding her his forever.

They moved together now with an urgent passion. She clung to him and closed her eyes, letting him fill her entire world.

They reached a fiery completion and tumbled together over the brink of the flame-kissed void. It left them gasping and weakly clinging to one another.

He rolled his weight away from her and lay on his side braced on his elbow he looked down into her eyes. Gently, he brushed away wayward strands of hair from her moist brow. He bent forward and lightly touched her lips with his as he drew her against him.

"I had not imagined anything as perfect and beautiful as this," he murmured against her hair. "I love you, Abby."

She clung to him, her eyes closed, listening to the steady beat of his heart.

"If I could just stop time now, keep this moment forever," she said softly. "I would feel so safe and secure."

"You are safe," he said. "I'll never let you go, Abby." He tightened his arms about her possessively. "I want you for always, not for just this moment."

She knew what he was going to say before he said it and she knew what her answer must be, yet she did not know what words she could say to make him understand.

"I have three weeks leave, Abby. I know it's fast but I can't stand the thought of letting you go even for a minute. Will you marry me quickly?"

"Alexander . . ." she began, "I . . . we must talk."

There was a moment of complete and utter silence, for he had read the emotions in her voice accurately. He held her a little away from him and looked deeply into her eyes.

"You don't want to marry me?" he said and even though his voice was firm she could feel the doubt and hurt he felt.

"I didn't say that, Alexander. Don't doubt that I love you, I could not bear it. Try to understand what I'm going to say."

"I can only hear you say I love you Alexander. Why should we wait? Why can we not share all the days we can get?"

"I . . . I can't Alexander, I just can't. I cannot marry

you until all this terrible thing is over."

"Why, Abby, why?" he said, desperation cutting through his voice.

"Alexander, one day soon, Kentucky will go with the South. My father plans on returning home then. We ... we might be enemies."

"We will never be enemies, you and I. How could we fight one another. I love you too much to consider such a thing. Let your father go home. Stay with me, Abby, I need you."

How she wanted to cry out for him to hold her, keep her safe within his arms forever.

"I cannot, Alexander," she said softly and finally. "It would create terrible problems for you, for us. We will wait. I promise you one thing. If you still want me when this war is over, then all you have to do is send for me and I will come. Until then all I can give you, Alexander, is all my heart and love for as long as I live."

Her words sounded so final, yet he forced himself to believe he could change her mind. They had some time to share together and he would convince her some way, somehow that she belonged only with him.

"I won't let you go," he whispered as his arms enclosed her. "You belong to me. Somehow, some way, I'll prove to you that nothing should stand in our way. Especially this cursed conflict."

"Alexander ..." she began to protest, but warm seeking lips stopped her words.

The searing need, and his overwhelming hunger for her ended all resistance as again she was lifted with him by their mutual desire.

The opponents had faced each other, a tentative battle had been fought. Now the real battle was about to begin.

Despite her love for him, Abby's loyalty to her home and her cause was a thing she clung to with tenacity. She knew Alexander would never forsake his loyalties no matter how much he hated war, and she prayed silently that one day he would understand that her loyalties demanded as much of her.

It was in Alexander's company for the next three weeks that Abby found herself in a position to see and hear much. At social gatherings people of influence, and position spoke casually and openly of things which they would never have spoken had she not been with Alexander.

She listened carefully and transferred bits of information to Paul. It was his job to piece together all the information and build it into plans. Then to send those plans along to other sources who would make use of them.

But it was Alexander who often filled in small pieces of information she would not otherwise have gotten.

They were together every moment Alexander could find, for he could not seem to get enough of her. The continual battle reigned. Each time they were together he tore at her resistance, each time he pleaded with her to marry him.

He came very near success the last time they were together before he was to return to duty.

They had gone to a party with Alexander's family, Paul and Abby's father. Once there, Abby and Alexander had slipped away to return to the Drake house and spend his last night at home the way they both wanted it. In each other's arms.

They lay on a blanket in front of the fireplace, his lean body holding hers protectively against him. They watched the fire, savoring this time of beauty. She lay with her back to him while his body molded against hers and his arm lay possessively across her hip. Occasionally, he would brush a gentle kiss on a soft rounded shoulder.

Their love-making had been all possessive yet gentle in a way it had never been before.

He was leaving, she did not know the destination or for how long he would be gone. She did not want to know for she knew when the information was hers, Paul would find a way to get it to the right people. This time she was more frightened for Alexander's life. This time she loved him too much to take the chance. She would go on with her duties, but she would not jeopardize Alexander's life, there was too much fear from the battles alone without her knowing that she had been the one to tip the scales.

"Abby," he whispered gently his lips nuzzling her ear.

"What?"

"Where are you? You have been dreaming again, your mind was so far away."

She turned in his arms and looked up into his eyes. He smiled for her eyes were warm and filled with love. Maybe, he thought, his perseverance would be repaid. Maybe she was ready to put aside all the reasons in her mind that stood in the way of their marriage.

She placed her hand against his cheek and he turned his head and kissed her palm.

"Oh, Alexander, I do love you so. Believe that, no matter what, if we're separated for a while think only of that. You have your duty to do and I . . . I have mine."

"You say you love me, Abby," he said softly as his lips touched gently a delicate ear and slid down her throat. "Don't you have a duty to me . . . to us? Abby, marry me now, tonight."

"Don't Alexander . . . don't please. You know I cannot."

"Cannot . . . or won't?"

"Oh, Alexander," she sobbed as she drew his mouth to hers. "Please don't ever doubt that I love you . . . I love you." Her voice died to a whisper as she tried to convince him with her kiss the depth of her love.

She felt the hunger and need within him as his mouth searched hers with hot searing kisses. As if he would be able to brand her his forever.

He gathered her into his arms, pressing her close to him, savoring the soft breasts that were crushed against him. Gentle hands caressed her smooth skin seeking to lift her passion to match his own.

She clung to him with a desperation born of fear. An aching need within her responded to his every touch, every kiss, until she was lost to everything but him. Uncontrolled passion possessed her, uncontrolled need made her seek his love with an abandon that sent his senses soaring.

He was lost in the depths of her love, lost to the magic of her slim silken body. He wanted to absorb everything about her and hold it within him for the long sleepless nights he would be without her.

Within her, he found the fulfillment of love and he sought to return what he found.

Strong arms lifted her, a lean hard body pressed against hers, demanding and vibrant. Liquid flame coursed through her, blinding her to anything but the need for him. She called out to him in love and passion and clung to him as they soared beyond anything they had ever shared before. The shattering climax left them breathless and clinging to one another.

"Oh, Abby," he whispered against her hair. "The days will be so black without you."

She sighed, resting her head against his shoulder. He cradled her in his arms gently and held her until their thudding hearts returned to normal. Reluctantly he spoke quietly.

"You know we have to go now?"

"Yes ... Alexander, when do you leave?"

"Six in the morning. I ... I don't want you to be there. I want to say goodbye to you tonight and hold the memory of you like this. I want to carry you with me like this until I get back. Then we will continue this argument about marriage. One day, I will win. I'm not a man who takes no easily."

"When this is over," she replied, "there will not be any no's. I will never let you go away from me again. If ... if you still want me."

"If! Woman, how can you say such a thing? Have I not literally begged you to marry me? Abby, nothing in this world could make me stop loving or wanting you."

He had meant his word to be amusing, and was surprised to see the glint of tears in her eyes.

"Abby, why do you cry? I'm sorry if I said anything to upset you." He kissed her tear-wet cheeks. "Please hold your love for me safe until I get back. We will save the rest of our words for then."

They dressed, and Abby walked with him to the door. There, he turned to her. He took her into his arms, the last time for a long time.

"Keep safe, Alexander," she cried, "don't let anything happen to you. I should die if anything happened to you."

"Don't worry my love, I'll be all right. I am not a hero and I've too much to come home to, to do anything foolish. I'll be back soon."

"I love you Alexander ... please, please always remember that."

"I will," he whispered. She closed her eyes as his lips touched hers and did not open them until she heard the door click shut behind him.

Then she pressed herself against the door and cried for the despair she faced knowing his love would one day turn to hate when he knew what she was.

Fifteen

Dan sat before a low burning campfire. He was tired, utterly and completely tired. He had never remembered being so tired even when he had worked so hard at High Oaks or labored all night over the birth of a foal or the illness of one of his beloved horses.

He sat with half closed eyes and listened to the far away sound of someone lightly strumming a guitar and singing in a soft voice.

> As the blackbird in the spring
> 　'Neath the willow tree
> Trilled his song I heard him sing
> 　Singing Aura Lee
> Aura Lee, Aura Lee
> 　Maid with golden hair
> Sunshine come along with thee,
> 　And swallows in the air

A half smile formed on his lips when he heard the words. "Maid with golden hair." His mind slid slowly back to that day at High Oaks when they had first heard official word of the start of the war. He and Abby both had been stunned at the grim words. It was only a day later that Abby and her father left for home.

Virginia had watched Dan with wide-eyed fear, a more bitter fear than she had ever known before. Her previous children were ghosts she had never known, but Dan was her life. She cried when he came home a few days later dressed in the gold and gray of the Confederacy. He thought her tears were of pride in him. He did not know she cursed the war for she had sensed that one way or another, it was going to take her son from her.

A vibrant enthusiasm ripped through the South, catching the sense of chivalry and devotion in her youth. Dan was caught up in it and marched away as self-assured and arrogant as the rest. None of them had ever lifted arms toward their fellow man before and the battle of First Manassas, though a victory for the South, did much to shatter dreams.

Dan had been afraid. A thing he could admit to no one else, in fact he found it a difficult thought to face alone. He had been so afraid in the heat of the battle that he had cried, he could feel the hot tears on his cheeks and taste their salt on his lips. It took every ounce of strength he had not to turn and run. Afterward he had gone off alone and tried to look within himself. Abby had said she would be willing to die for her home, he remembered. But was death so easy to face he thought. It frightened him more that in the next battle, because of what he remembered, he might turn and run. That was a more frightening thing than anything he had ever faced before.

Endless days of tramping through a sea of mud after heavy rains had left all the men exhausted. Now they found themselves camped near a place called Shiloh in a dense forest.

He had slept fitfully part of the night, then could not sleep any more. He sat by the fire and listened to the strains of music. Catherine's small face wavered before him. Maybe it was the reference to golden hair in the song that made him think of her, or maybe it was because he remembered the last few days he was home.

There seemed to be an atmosphere of strained happiness. It was as if the whole South stood on the edge of a precipice, knew it, and had decided to laugh in the face of impending disaster.

Dan walked alone across the stone patio and down the steps into the garden. He could hear the strains of music and laughter from the house but felt a need of solitude. He wanted to absorb the beauty of High Oaks, and tonight it seemed to be at its best.

The perfume of magnolias hung in the air and he could hear the sighing whisper of the breeze through the trees. He walked slowly, enjoying the moment when a movement beneath one of the trees near the small pond caught his eye. Something white shimmered for a moment in the darkness and he realized a woman stood alone watching the moonlight on the water. He wondered, as he walked toward her, who would be out here alone. Then, when he was close enough he realized it was Catherine and she seemed to be lost in some dream.

He didn't want to frighten her so before he got to her he called out softly, "Catherine?"

She stood still for a moment, but the stillness about

her told him she was aware of who called her. Then slowly she turned to face him. The moonlight touched her pale gold hair and glistened against her skin.

"Dan," she answered softly.

"What are you doing out here alone?" he questioned as he came to stand beside her.

"I might ask you the same thing," she smiled. "I thought you would be among the celebrating gladiators." Her smile eased the words but still they startled him.

"Gladiators," he said and was aware his voice sounded stiff.

"I'm sorry ... I didn't mean to say that. It's just that ..."

"That the thought of war and battles upsets you," he finished gently. "You're not alone Catherine. Very few men know what a battle is about, and the few that do don't enjoy it."

She was silent, then she walked to him and put her hand on his arm. For the first time he became totally aware of Catherine. The scent of her perfume touching him, a soft fragrance that matched her. She was so small that she had to tip her face up to look at him and when she did the moonlight touched it. He was shaken by the look in her eyes. He did not understand it, but to him it seemed as if she were in intense pain.

"You have changed since you came back from Manassas. What happened Dan?" Her voice was so gentle, and they had been friends for so long that he wondered if she would understand. Again he looked down into her eyes ... then, haltingly, he tried to explain what had happened to him. When he stopped talking there was silence again, then he said, "You think

I'm a coward, Catherine?"

Now she gripped his arm with both hands and gave him an angry shake. "A coward! You? Oh, Dan, you are as far from a coward as you can get. A man who knows no fear is not courageous. It is the man who knows and understands fear and faces it who has the real courage. I will not have you calling yourself a coward! I will not!"

Her last words ended on a sob and he was surprised and somewhat shaken. It had never occurred to him that Catherine felt this way about him. She had always been a childhood friend. Now, for the first time he really looked at her, and saw a beauty that shocked him deeply. What shocked him even more was the sudden glimpse of truth. Catherine was in love with him.

Their eyes met and held, his asking and hers answering with open and sincere honesty. She watched the realization dawn in his eyes and she remained silent, breathlessly waiting. There was no denial in her. She loved him, had loved him for as long as she could remember. Now she could not speak, she waited for him to turn away . . . or to reach for her.

Abby had been right about Dan. He had admired her, but, once roused by a deep emotion, he was not the kind of man to let it slip away from him. He reached out and gently drew Catherine to him. Enclosing her in his arms he felt her tremble as he held her for a moment in silence.

Catherine wanted both to weep at his gentleness and to cry out in her joy of him. She rested her head against his broad chest and slid her arms about his waist. She felt him brush a light kiss against her hair, then he said quietly, "How long have I been such a damn fool not to see what beauty there was here in my own garden." He whispered.

Then he tipped up her chin and smiled down into her eyes. "I've been a blind fool."

She could not help the tears that escaped to slide down her cheeks, for he was saying what had existed only in her dreams for so many years.

Gently he brushed the tears from her cheek, then slid his hand to the back of her head and drew her to him. He bent his head and touched her lips with his. He felt her lips, moist with her tears, tremble then part beneath his.

Her body, pressed against him, though tiny, was rounded and soft. He felt flame leap through his veins as her arms encircled his neck. Now his arms surrounded and held her in a fierce embrace as his mouth claimed hers in a kiss that shattered her thoughts to a million fragmented pieces.

Nothing existed in her careening world except Dan. He crushed her to him in strong arms that took away her breath and his mouth ravaged hers with searing kisses that found only willing surrender in hers.

He drew her with him to a bench that stood at the base of the tree. There he drew her down on his lap, his arms encircling her waist he buried his face in the soft curve of her throat. She slid her hands into his thick hair and held his head close to her. With closed eyes she savored the joy she felt as she heard him whisper her name softly.

He knew he had to control this consuming thing for her good and for his. This was not the time or the place.

He held her close to him, her head lay on his shoulder and they were content to be so for some time.

"Tell me Catherine?"

"What?"

"When you knew."

She laughed softly. "Remember when you first came to High Oaks? You were nine and I was seven. My parents brought me over to meet you. You were so frightened, so upset that you barely spoke. I could feel how hurt you were and I think you sensed it and didn't understand. You thought it was pity. I remember you ran out of the room and refused to come back. I think I have loved you from that moment."

"And it took me all this time," he chuckled. "What in heaven's name is the matter with me?"

"You just looked at me so often that you never saw me."

He tipped her head up and kissed her again hungrily. She responded in a way that sent his spirits soaring. She would always be there to give him love. This tiny wisp of a girl seemed to possess all he would ever need to sustain him for a lifetime.

He remembered now how they had strolled through the gardens, reluctant to go inside and share their new found happiness with anyone else.

The singing had stopped and the camp was slowly wakening.

They were preparing for a battle. The Union force was less than five miles away, yet neither army knew of the presence of the other.

Dan thought of what Catherine had said about courage. He smiled. There was no doubt, he thought, that he was frightened as all hell. He wanted nothing more than for this war to be over and to go home to Catherine, marry, and fill High Oaks with the laughter of children.

It was a bright clear Sunday morning and the Confederate camp was prepared to move when a scouting party from the camped Union forces accidentally ran across it.

The small incident served as some warning to the Union camp but not enough. The charging Confederates burst upon the Union soldiers only partially formed and partially ready. Breakfast was forgotten as men dashed out to fight. To make matters worse, the Union army found itself fighting in a three-sided box. On the right was a swampy stream, on the left was another stream and another to its rear. Through the only entrance to this box the Confederates poured in an irresistible avalanche.

The shock of the battle was too much for raw Union recruits to bear; they broke and fell back.

Alexander tried to rally the men about him; he shouted and cursed, unaware that Dan, riding through with the advancing Confederates was aiming his gun at him. He fired, but a sudden jarring of his horse, threw his bullet out of line and it neatly grazed Alexander's cheek, who again cursed violently. The battle of Shiloh would be well remembered by both Alexander and Dan, but a long time would pass before brother would know he had fought against brother.

From Shiloh, Alexander again was called to Philadelphia, but this time for a reason he couldn't believe.

Dan, with a slight wound of the left arm was allowed to return home a few days to recuperate. He arrived at High Oaks prepared to convince Catherine to marry him and that the wound in no way hampered his activities.

When he did arrive home, it was already after supper and the sun was setting complacently on the horizon.

Virginia had immediately had a tray of food prepared for Dan who ate with a great deal of pleasure. Army food was not exactly a pleasure for him who was accustomed to the finest cooking.

He shared a quiet evening with Virginia and Gregory who had no idea of his urgent need to go to Catherine as soon as he could. It would be the next day before he could go, for propriety would not allow a visitor after sunset for a young girl.

Dan lay awake on his bed, his brain twisting in circles. The more he thought of Catherine the more he wanted to see her even if it was only for a moment.

Finally he could stand it no longer. Vibrant dreams of Catherine had been in his mind too long and the grim realization of battle told him that time and life could both be very short.

He walked across the lawn to the stables. There without waking the stable boy, he saddled a horse. In a moment he was mounted and on his way to Catherine.

Catherine lay awake also. Word had come that Dan was home, yet she knew he would not come to her tonight. It was the first time she hated the rules and regulations that governed their lives. She wanted to see him, to have him hold her and tell her all the things she had longed to hear for so many years.

The night was warm and the french doors to her bedroom stood open so she could get what little breeze there was. She lay on her bed thinking of Dan, knowing sleep would be a long time coming.

Dan tied his horse under the trees and walked across the garden. From all the times he had visited here, he knew exactly where everyone's room was. Soon, he stood below the balcony outside Catherine's window. The room was dark and he wondered if she slept so soundly that she could not hear.

He bent down and gathered a few pebbles in his hand. Accurately, he threw one that tinkled against the window frame. He waited, then he threw another. Again he waited then threw the third.

Catherine had heard the first one and had sat up on her bed watching the window. The second one told her she was not imagining things. When the third one struck, she was already crossing the room.

She walked out on the balcony and smiled down at the shadowed form below. Even in the dark, she knew him.

"Catherine," he whispered.

"Dan, if someone finds you here there will be gossip."

"Come down for a minute," he replied. She thought of having to slip through the dark house without waking anyone and she was shaken with uncertainty.

"I can't."

"Why?"

"I just can't. I'll waken someone."

He smiled as he called back words that frightened her more. "If you don't come down, I'll come up. I have to talk to you."

She knew he meant exactly what he said. "Wait," she called hastily "wait, I'll be down in a minute."

Swiftly, she slid into her slippers and grabbed up her robe as she ran to her bedroom door. She opened it quietly and went out into the dark hall and drew the door closed behind her.

She crept down the hall and to the top of the stairs. Quickly she ran down, her feet silent on the carpeted steps. She reached the bottom and turned down the short hall that led to the garden door.

She opened it and went out. For a minute she could not see him, then she sighed deeply as she saw his tall form walking toward her. She could contain her joy at seeing him again no longer so she ran to his waiting arms. He caught her against him, ignoring the small twinge of pain for it could not compete with the sense of elation as he held her.

They laughed softly together, happy to hold each other in the midst of the insanity of war.

His mouth sought hers, soft and sweet and eager to share. He crushed her against him as if he could hold her within and never let her go. His mouth seared her with blinding hot kisses that touched her cheeks, eyes, mouth then roved down her throat to the valley between her breasts. She whispered his name softly as she clung to him feeling the urgent need building within her for more and more of this sweet agony.

It was with the greatest reluctance that he slowly slid her to her feet and released her. Again, as it had before, she felt a cold sense of loss when his arms released her. She knew at that moment there was no going back. He was hers, to love and to share her life with. He needed her, especially now when the threat of separation—even death—faced him.

"I'm so happy you came, Dan. I knew you were home. I prayed for the hours to pass so you would come."

"But you didn't expect me tonight," he said and she could see his white smile in the moonlight.

"No, I didn't . . . but I hoped."

"Catherine you are so beautiful," he said softly. He reached out and lay his large hand against his face.

"No more tears?" he questioned gently.

"No more tears, no more doubts," she answered as her eyes held his.

"Catherine ..." he began, and she could feel the deep need in him.

"Dan, do you know something awful?"

"Awful ... what?"

"You have never once yet said I love you to me."

"Said ... haven't I tried to show you, can you not feel the magic when we are together?"

"But," she smiled, "I want to hear you say it. You will not know how many times I've wanted to hear you say it."

He drew her back into his arms and held her tight against him while his cheek brushed her hair.

"Little idiot," he whispered, "I love you. I'll say it again and again for all the times I was stupid enough not to see love."

He bent and caught her mouth with his, sliding his hands into her hair to hold her while his mouth played an urgent song of love on hers. When he released her, she was breathless and dizzy from the searing touch of flames.

"Does that tell you?" he whispered gently.

"Oh, Dan," she whispered softly as she moved closer and raised her hand to touch his face. "I want you to tell me more, so much more. I want you to tell me tonight and every night for the rest of our lives."

He understood her need, for it matched his, yet he was shaken by the depths of her giving love. Gently, he held her. "Are you sure, Catherine ... very sure?"

"I have never been more sure of anything in my life. I want to be with you."

Sixteen

Dan would have given his soul to have been anywhere else with Catherine except a dark garden. He could not see himself making love to Catherine on the ground like an animal in heat.

He held her, cursing his misery, and wanting her more than he had ever wanted a woman in his life before. What was even worse was knowing that she wanted him as badly as he wanted her.

"Dan," she said softly, and for a moment he could have sworn there was a hint of laughter in her voice.

"What?"

"If we walk across the garden we would run right into the gardener's cottage."

"The gardener's cottage," he repeated, then his heart leaped only to still quickly. Where there was a gardener's cottage, there usually was a gardener. Now he was sure he heard a muffled laugh and made their ridiculous position even worse on his emotions.

"You wouldn't be laughing at me in my darkest hour now would you, woman?"

She laughed and tightened her arms about his waist.

"A gardener's cottage," he said miserably, "usually

comes equipped with a gardener."

"Not this one," she whispered.

"Oh?" he said hopefully.

"Mr. Girard has gone for a week to visit his daughter."

"Bless Mr. Girard," he chuckled, "and his daughter."

He slid his arm about her waist and slowly walked across the garden to the small cottage that sat in the dark corner of it. At the door, Dan stopped. He put both arms about her and whispered softly, "This could be our honeymoon cottage. I may ask your father to sell it to me so we could come here once a year as an anniversay celebration."

"For a honeymoon," she replied, "you need a bride."

"I've got one."

"Not yet. You haven't gotten around to asking me to marry you."

He took her shoulders and held her a little away from him. In the moonlight, he could see the laughter in her eyes.

"Marry me, Catherine," he said gently, his eyes intent, "now, tonight."

He saw the laughter fade and a deep look of love replace it. With a quick laugh he took his hand from her shoulders. He removed a gold ring from his finger that had been a gift from Virginia on his birthday. He took Catherine's hand in his and slid the ring on her finger.

"I love you Catherine," he said seriously. "I want you to marry me more than I have ever wanted anything. This ring is all I have at the moment to seal our promise. Will you wear it? Will you marry me?"

The ring was entirely too big for her finger, but she closed her hand to keep it from falling off and pressed her hand between her breasts. "Oh, Dan, of course I will marry you. It has been my one dream since the first moment I met you."

"Then this is all the ceremony we need between us, your promise and mine."

In one move he bent and lifted her in his arms. Her arms encircled his neck and she brushed her lips against his cheek. He pushed the door open with his shoulder and stepped into the dark cottage, then he kicked the door shut behind him. For a moment he stood, holding her and moving his lips against the curve of her throat.

"Dan ... oh, Dan," she whispered. "I love you so much I feel I cannot contain it."

He stood her on her feet, but held her close to him. Again his mouth sought to renew the flame that had brightened between them. It sprang to new and vibrant life as it always would.

He stepped back from her for a moment and she could hear him fumble about the room. She stood still, wondering what he was doing. Then suddenly a candle glow illuminated his face as he smiled at her over its glow, and for a moment, she felt unsure and a little afraid. He saw the look and walked back to her side. He took her face between his hands and held her eyes with his.

"Don't be frightened of me, my darling, never of me. That I love you and want you is true, but I can wait. I want you to be assured that what I feel for you is so real, so good, that it will last no matter what. I'll be happy just knowing you love me as I love you."

What he said was perfect, because it washed away all

her fears and doubts. "I'm not afraid, Dan," she whispered, "and I want to belong to you. I want you to carry my love with you whenever you go. I want it to keep you safe and well and bring you back to me."

"Catherine," he whispered as his lips touched hers. It began with the gentlest of touches, again and again he kissed the corners of her mouth, her cheeks and slowly, slowly he began to stir the flames of passion. She clung to him, her eyes closed and her warm moist lips slowly parted to accept his. She felt her senses spiral upward as the warmth of his love inflamed her. When his lips left hers, she stood for a moment with her eyes closed, then she felt his hands slide from her shoulders and a gentle tug on the belt of her robe. Her eyes opened and met his. He stood motionless waiting to see if there was any fear or doubt in her eyes. But nothing was there but warm loving acceptance.

He untied the robe and pushed it from her shoulders, and it slid to the floor in a forgotten heap. The nightgown she wore was thin and the neckline low and loose. He gently drew it down from her shoulders and let it follow the robe in a heap at her feet.

He gazed at her in profound admiration, miniature perfection, her slim body was ivory and gold, kissed by the pale glow of the candle. Her hair glimmered in the half light like fine spun gold.

"God," he said in breathless wonder, "you are all the beauty I've ever dreamed of."

She smiled, then she took the two steps that separated them. With no hesitation, she lifted her hands and began to unbutton his jacket.

It took him only a moment to rid himself of the material obstruction that stood between them. Now it was her time to admire.

He was broad shouldered and hard muscled. The mat of hair on his chest was as gold as his hair. Slim of hip and long lean muscles ridged his taunt stomach and long legs. He was well endowed by nature and for a moment it shocked her ... but only for a moment.

He drew her soft cool body close to him and tingled with the shock of her soft curves leaning against him. Her slim arms came about him and for a long moment they simply held each other. Then he tipped her head up and took vibrant possession of her mouth. This time there was no restraint, her complete surrender to him told of her urgency to possess him.

His hands slid down the smooth curve of her slim back to her hips to press her more firmly against him, while his lips traced a heated path down her slender throat to the soft curve of her shoulder.

The need of her was nearly an unbearable agony that cursed through him as her slim fingers caressed him and drew him even closer to her. He could bear no more. Swiftly, he lifted her into his arms and crossed the room to the bed that stood in the corner. He put one knee on the bed then felt, turning his back so that he dropped against the bed drawing her with him. She gasped at the suddenness of it, but the sound was silenced as he turned her to lie beneath him and sought her mouth again in wild abandonment.

She moaned softly yet clung to him as he caressed her hardened nipples with seeking fingers. They were joined by lips that lit them with flame and caused her to writhe in his arms and call his name.

There was nothing solid in her world but Dan as he bent above her filling her world, her heart and her body with the blinding intense heat of his love.

She whimpered softly at the first invasion of her womanhood, but the pain soon turned to an intense spreading warmth that lifted her beyond all she had ever known.

They soared together to the high pinnacle of ecstasy and tumbled helplessly into the cauldron of molten desire that consumed them.

She could hear his harsh breath and the heavy thudding of his heart that matched the wild pounding of hers.

She must have cried out in the depths of her passion, but a hard hungry mouth brought silence.

Deep all consuming fulfillment left them clinging weakly to each other as the world righted itself and reality regained control. He held her in silence, their sweat slicked bodies quivering with remembrance.

He shifted his weight from her and drew her against him. They lay in silence as he slowly caressed her hair that fell across his body. There was no need for words for each sensed the others feelings to perfection.

"Catherine?"

"Yes?"

"How long did you say the gardener would be gone?"

"For a week."

"I've still three nights at home. Catherine ..."

"Yes, Dan, yes. We will share this place for as long as we have. When you come home ... when this war is over, we'll build a place of our own."

"I've never hated anything so much as the thought of leaving you. I may be gone for a long time this time. The war is building. I don't even know where you can write to me, but I'll let you know as soon as I get there. You will write often?"

"Every day," she said softly.

"I want to come over and talk to your parents tomorrow. I want to ask for you and maybe beg them to let us marry soon."

"Mother will be scandalized if we try to rush into a wedding. I'm her only little girl," she laughed, "she will want to see it all properly done."

He turned on his side and she could see the emerald glint of laughter in his eyes. "Oh Catherine," he chuckled, "I do believe it has been most properly done. You are my wife and nothing or no one is going to take you from me."

She blushed, but could not help but laugh with him.

"Yes, my dear love," she replied as she quickly kissed him several light kisses. "It has been most properly done. Now you are stuck with me, sir and for years and years to come."

"I shall try," he said in mock seriousness, "to do my best to tolerate your presence in my life."

"Oh, Dan!"

"What?"

"What if they refuse," she said her voice filled with alarm. "I am not of age, and they might not want us to marry until this war is over."

He wrapped his arms about her to still her alarm. "Catherine, do you think I will let anything or anyone come between us now. You have said you will marry me. You have told me in the most beautiful way that you love me. Now you are mine and no power on earth will take you from me. Tell me something?"

She gazed at him with curiosity, and he kissed her several times, savoring her response, before he continued.

"If worse comes to worse, would you marry me and come to High Oaks anyway. If we were forced to, we could tell them that we consummated the marriage just a little before the vows were said. Would you sacrifice yourself that for me?"

"Dan there is no sacrifice too great if it will give me you."

She watched as pleasure danced in his eyes and sighed deeply as he tightened his arms about her possessively. But after a few minutes, he groaned with misery. He sat up and looked down at her, molding a picture to carry in his mind all the days and nights he would be without her.

"I hate to let you go, but I've got to get you back to the house before dawn. We would have some time explaining if they sent a search party looking for you."

He was about to move away again when she reached out and held him. He looked at her for a moment in surprise then his eyes grew warm.

"It is still some time before dawn," she whispered. "Don't leave me now, Dan. Now that you have wakened me I feel the need for you stronger than ever. Will it always be so with us? Will we always be able to find this joy in each other. I would die if it were ever to fade away and you no longer needed me."

"Yes love," he said gently as he gathered her to him. "It will always be this way for us. We will never let it change."

Again his mouth descended to possess hers, and again he was lifted beyond the realms of reality and into the bright glowing fire of her love.

The first gray touch of dawn was on the horizon when they walked back across the garden. At the door he held her for one last possessive moment, then the door closed between them.

Catherine went to her room and crawled under the covers. She lay back and gave her thoughts over to the night and the tender memories of Dan.

Dan strode easily across the expanse of tall trees until he found his horse. He patted its neck gently and with affection and the horse nuzzled him in delight at his attention.

"Come on old fellow, we'd best get home. It will be full day anyway before we get there. I'll have to start thinking up some answers to questions. Maybe I'll say I felt in need of a drink, after all," he laughed happily. "I'm drunk enough right now to have been imbibing all night." He talked to the horse all the way home, too excited and pleased with his world to remain silent.

"She's so perfect, so beautiful, and she's mine, Appollo, all mine. I don't know how I could have been such a fool, not seeing her before. Anyway, it's not too late."

When he did arrive home it was just in time to meet Virginia and Gregory coming down to breakfast.

"Dan!" Virginia said in surprise.

"Are you just getting home?" Gregory asked, for he was just as surprised as Virginia. "Where in heaven's name have you been all night?"

"Well," he lied happily, "I started out to get a drink, met some friends and we played cards. I guess I just lost track of time. Are you two going anywhere today?"

"No, I've nothing planned," Virginia replied as she turned to Gregory. "Have you dear?"

"No, nothing important, why?"

"Well, I plan on having a guest for dinner."

"That's fine dear, who?" Virginia replied.

"I'd like to have the Marklands over, Mother. There's some things I'd like to talk to Mr. Markland about."

"Of course, I'll send a message over immediately," Virginia replied and went back to her room to see to the writing and sending of the note immediately. Gregory chuckled as she walked away.

"What's so amusing," Dan asked.

"If you had said you wanted a dinner for forty guests instead of four she would have taken it the same way. I would say the woman is quite fond of you, Dan."

"She's wonderful, both of you are. How many people would have picked up a waterlogged stray like me and given him the whole world. Nothing I could do could come near showing the appreciation I have for all you have done for me."

"Believe me, Dan," Gregory said as he clapped his hand on Dan's shoulder, "you have given us as much as we've given you. Now what is this thing you have to talk to Mr. Markland about?"

"Well, Father," Dan began, "if you don't mind I'd rather save it for tonight. It's a thing I'd rather you all heard at the same time."

"All right," Gregory laughed, "keep your secret. Come on in and have some coffee with me. Then you'd best get some sleep or you won't be able to stay awake to talk to anyone tonight."

Catherine was silent when she was told that they had been invited to the Wakefields, but all the way to the dinner she trembled both with fear and excitement.

She sat across the table from Dan and could not keep her eyes from his. She felt a deep sense of security when she saw the warm glow of love in his eyes.

Though Gregory and Mr. Markland missed the warm looks across the table, it did not pass the astute gaze of Viginia or Catherine's mother. They exchanged knowing smiles and waited patiently for the lovers to speak of it.

When they were all seated comfortably in the drawing room, Dan rose from his seat and went to Catherine. He reached his hand down to her. With a smile she placed hers in it and he drew her gently to her feet to stand beside him. Together they turned to face their parents. "Catherine and I," he began in a steady strong voice, "would like to have your permission to get married. We love each other very much and if we could we would like to have the wedding right away."

He was surprised at the fact that no one seemed to be at all surprised.

"I ... I hope this doesn't cause any problems," he said, "but no matter what Catherine and I will be married."

Dan said the words firmly and only Catherine knew of his unsteadiness as he nearly crushed her hand in his.

Catherine's father rose and Dan was prepared for just about anything except what he heard.

"Well," he smiled, "so my baby has finally captured you Dan, my boy. It has been no secret she's had her eyes set on you for years. We've listened to enough tears to know."

"Father!" Catherine said half in anger and half in amusement.

"Well if I have my way there will be no more tears for Catherine. Do we have your permission to get married soon?"

"If her mother agrees and she can make all the arrangements between now and then you can get married the next time you are home on leave."

Dan reached out his hand to Mr. Markland. "You won't regret this decision sir. I'll do my best to make her happy."

"I can tell that by the look in her eyes right now young man."

The evening ended with much laughter and discussions on how plans would be made.

Dan and Catherine looked at each other in silent promise.

It was very late that night that the lovers again crossed the garden hand in hand to their small cottage. There they lay together after a wild and tumultuous love making that had left them fulfilled and satisfied. They lay and discussed their lives together, making each other the sweet and loving promises all lovers make.

When Dan left High Oaks a few days later he said a fond farewell to his parents. He held Catherine close to him and kissed her hungrily.

"Don't worry, love," he whispered, "I'll be home soon. Then we can begin our lives together."

She smiled, kissed him and held him close, and only after he rode away did she let the tears escape.

Some strange touch of fate gave her the feeling that something terrible was going to happen before she held Dan again. She was afraid and she didn't know of what. All she prayed for was Dan's safe return and the end of a conflict that might, one day, rob her world of his beloved smile.

Seventeen

Through the beginning battles of the war, the Confederate Army was heavily outnumbered yet managed to win every battle but the first. It was safe to say most of the Union force was astounded at this. A few, like Alexander, knew it was only the beginning, that the Union force was entirely too strong, too well equipped to lose.

The South had laughed at what they called President Lincoln's "paper blockade." They spoke about it scornfully and doubted it would ever become a threat to the Confederacy.

Gradually, more and more warships were collecting outside the main Confederate ports. Blockade runners were growing cautious and Abby and Paul found it becoming more and more difficult to get messages across the lines.

They sat now in Paul's comfortable living room.

"Have you heard from Alexander lately, Abby?"

"Yes," she replied gently.

"You're ot going to tell me anything about where he is or what he's doing are you?"

"No."

"I could find out myself, Abby," he said in a quiet voice.

"Don't Paul ... please." Her eyes raised to his and he could see they contained fear and determination. "If you do anything to harm Alexander I shall go home. You will have a hard time keeping all the contacts I've made. Some of them you don't even know."

"You'd give up all we've done, the fine network we've got? Alexander takes his chances in this war same as any other soldier. The same as you do. Only if they catch you, you'll be hung. Matter of fact, I think Alexander has a better chance than you do."

"Paul!"

"All right, Abby, all right. I'll not try to find out anything about Alexander's outfit or where they are. But, it won't change things, Abby. I mean the way he'll feel about you when he finds out what you are and the fact that what we've done has cost much for the Union Army."

"I know," she whispered softly. "But, I have him now. I'll take one day at a time. I love him, Paul, I can't help it. I'll hold him for as long as I can then I'll pray one day he'll be able to forgive me."

"Do you think he will?" Paul said, sympathy deep in his voice.

"I don't know, I can only hope," she said. "But, no matter what I won't put him in any more danger than he is."

Paul sighed and sipped his brandy in meditative silence. After a few minutes, Abby rose and walked to the door. There she turned and looked back at Paul and she smiled.

"Thank you, Paul," she said quietly. His eyes rose to

meet hers, then he lifted his glass in silent salute. Then she left the room, closing the door softly behind her.

He watched the closed door for a minute thinking about the knowledge that lay in his pocket. The location of Alexander and his men was already known to him. And he knew this one time he would not use it.

Abby walked up the stairs to her room. She felt so tired. They had entertained a group of men with a small dinner party. Men who laughed and drank and whose wives said too much. Paul and the information she had heard gave her a headache and a deep burning need to see Alexander again.

She went to a small desk and took a letter from the top drawer. It was the last one Alexander had sent her over a month before. She had read and re-read it, yet, she sat down to read it again for it seemed to bring him closer to her. For a moment the words blurred. Hastily, she brushed the tears from her eyes and read.

My Dearest Abby,

We have had days and days of rain but I don't mind. It has mired us so deeply in mud that we cannot move so I have a lot of time to think. In fact, I have been lying here thinking of you. God, how much I miss you! I love you, Abby, and all I can keep in my mind any length of time is coming home to you when this insanity is over.

War has always been a thing I have hated the thought of, and the only reason I fight is to keep our country from being severed in two. If we do not remain united we will become prey for any other militant country that would take the time to pluck us like a ripe grape.

But, I did not write to speak to you of war but of love. I have found if I close my eyes that I can conjure up the most beautiful fantasies, all of you and all of the beautiful love we share. In my dream I can feel you next to me, feel your softness in my arms and taste again the sweet lips that drive me to madness.

No matter how much I try, I cannot understand why you won't marry me, but, I warn you, when I come home we will face this again. I need you, Abby. I need to know you will always be there, always be my anchor amid all this blackness and death. You are my strength. All the hopes and dreams I have of a future depend on you.

With the Confederates being squeezed by the blockade, the course of the war is slowly shifting. They have won some battles, but the war will inevitably be ours. I pray it's over soon and we can put this behind us and begin a new and promising life together. Think about it, Abby. Brighten my life and make me a happy man when I come home by saying you'll marry me. You will never regret it for I give you my heart, my soul and my promise that I will do everything in my power to make you happy.

Don't try to answer this letter now for we are about to move out. We're outside a town called Kernstown. If all goes well we will meet the Confederate Army there sometime next week. We will defeat them, I hope, for it will be one more step toward home and you.

I will write again as soon as I can. I'm thinking

of you always.

All my love,
Alexander

She held the letter close to her and closed her eyes. They already knew that the South had been defeated at Kernstown. There had been a tremendous number of casualties. It had been over a month and there had been no word from or about Alexander. Her heart was frozen in fear. She dreamed horrible nightmares of him lying dead on some battlefield.

She could not sleep, there was no use in trying. She folded the letter and put it with the others Alexander had written her. If the day came that she no longer had him, she would have the letters to keep her memories alive.

She took down her hair from its intricate coiffure and brushed it and was about to undress when she heard the light rap on the door. She knew all the servants were long in bed and the only person in the house now was Paul for her father had taken some messages to their contact and would not return until the next day. She walked to the door and opened it.

"What is it, Paul? Is something wrong? Father?"

"No, no, Abby. Don't get frightened." Paul smiled. "We have a late visitor and he would like to talk to you."

"Oh, Paul, I'm so tired, can't you do this?"

"Afraid not, my dear. This one is all yours."

She sighed and went out into the hall pulling the door shut behind her.

"Oh, by the way, Abby, I have to go out," he said blandly. "I'll most probably be gone all night."

"Paul, I don't like being left alone with any of those men. You promised me that."

"Now, Abby, would I leave you alone with anyone I considered a danger to you? You will have no trouble with this one."

They had reached the bottom of the stairs where Paul had left his coat on a table. He picked it up and shrugged into it.

"He's in the library, Abby. I gave him a drink and told him you would be right in."

Before Abby could answer, Paul was walking across the floor and out the door.

For a moment she was angry. Angry with Paul for leaving her and angry with the men who would sell their loyalties. At that moment her loyalty to her cause strengthened her. "Yes, Alexander," she thought, "maybe this will help to end this conflict sooner." She walked with resolution to the library door and pushed it open. She gazed in breathless shock at the man who stood across the room from her.

"Alexander!" she cried. She ran across the room and in a moment she was in his arms. She felt them close about her with a sense of homecoming and intense joy. Then hard strength crushed her to him while a hard hungry mouth ravaged hers. She clung to him, weak with pleasure and returned his kiss with a wild and passionate surrender.

They laughed and cried, kissing each other again and again, delirious with the joy of holding each other again.

He held her a little away from him to look at her.

"Fantasies are nothing like the real thing," he laughed. "I have held you in dreams for weeks, but, it never felt as good as this. Come here, woman, let me kiss you again just to prove this is not a dream."

He drew her back into his arms again and kissed her fiercely until she gasped for breath.

"Alexander, please, let me catch my breath," she laughed. "Let me look at you. It seems so long since I've seen you."

But, when she did get a good look at him she realized he must have been traveling for hours. He looked tired and a stubble of beard told her he had not taken time to shave. It was the first time she had not seen Alexander at his immaculate best and her eyes must have registered her surprise.

"You will have to forgive me, darling," he said. His eyes sparkled with tender amusement. "But, seeing you was entirely too important to consider anything else. I stopped at home to say 'hello, goodbye' and took another horse and came right here. Do you mind?"

Tears sprang to her eyes and she reached out to gently touch his face. He watched her eyes deepen to warm enclosing passion.

"Oh, my darling," she whispered. "No, I don't mind. Hold me, Alexander. I have missed you so desperately."

He held her close, his lips brushing her hair and for some time it was enough just to hold each other.

"I never thought I could find such peace until you," he said gently. "You are the only sweet sane thing in this world. God, I hate this separation from you."

"How ... how long do you have?"

"Forty-eight hours."

"Forty ... Oh, Alexander, so little time!"

"But, I had to see you, even if it is only for an hour—for a minute. Abby, do you understand?"

"Yes, Alexander, I do."

"I . . . I have a friend who has a small cottage not far from here. He's given me the key. Abby, come with me."

"Yes," she said softly and without hesitation. "We will send the rest of the world away. At least we will have forty-eight hours that are ours alone."

He smiled and she felt a sense of loving elation as his emerald eyes seemed to touch her with warmth.

"I love you, Abby, and I'm grateful for finding you."

"I'll leave a note for Paul and my father. We'll leave now," she said softly. "I don't want to waste a moment we can share."

They used a carriage of Paul's and rode together in silence to the cottage. They went inside and closed the cottage door between them and the rest of the world.

Alexander sat in the tub of luxuriously hot water with a contented smile on his face. Across the room Abby sat on the edge of the bed and watched him, laughing at his pleasure.

"You laugh, woman, but you have no idea how a bath feels when you haven't had one for days."

He had shaved before his bath and now felt the best he had in weeks. Abby watched rivulets of water on his broad shoulders and chest and an intense desire to reach out and touch him caused her to shiver in expectation.

"Are you never coming out of that water? You shall turn into a fish in another minute."

He grinned devilishly, "Why don't you join me?"

She shook her head negatively. Slowly she stood up and with trembling fingers she began to loosen the buttons on the front of her dress. She shrugged it from her shoulders and watched him as the smile faded and a glow of pleasure touched his eyes. He waited motionless as one piece of clothing slowly followed another and she stood before him.

He gazed at her, spellbound with the rare and unbelievable picture she made.

She walked to within a foot of him and reached out to run her fingers lightly up his arm and shoulder, then touched his cheek lightly.

"Why don't you join me?" she said as an answer to his challenge. She turned away to walk slowly toward the bed, giving him a warming view of slender legs and soft curves as she did. Before she reached the bed, she laughed again as she heard the quick splash of water and heard him step quickly from the tub and follow her. She felt his arms close about her and heard his rough laugh in her ear.

"You witch," he chuckled. "You are a beauty that could make Neptune rise from the sea."

She was swung up and into strong arms and felt his lips against the curve of her throat.

They tumbled on the bed together and she lay across his chest, her long hair surrounding him. Her lips sought his in an urgent blinding need.

His hands slid down her slim back to softly rounded hips to press her close to him.

Senses spiraled upward to be lost in a whirlwind of passion. They sought each other; touching, tasting and sharing an emotion that knew no bounds.

He drew her beneath him and their eyes met and held.

He gently brushed strands of hair from her face then bent his head to taste again the warm giving lips. Gently his lips traced a path down smooth heated skin.

"Abby, my dear beloved Abby, have you any idea of how much I love you, how much I've missed you?"

"As I have missed you, Alexander, with my whole heart and soul," she replied softly.

Her eyes closed in passion as his hands gently touched, caressed and renewed the heat of their love.

Her arms slid up and encircled his neck drawing him even closer. Their bodies blended in a white hot joy and she could feel the need in him enclose her, hold her and fill her, giving her a sense of completion that caused her to cry out.

Wild abandon made them blind to anything in their world but each other and this small part of Eden they had created for such a short time.

They clung to each other in a desperate need born of fear, fear that this rare and beautiful thing would be taken from them.

Slowly their turbulent world righted itself and they lay together. A silent moment that spoke volumes of words.

"It seems," he said in painful anger, "that I am always saying goodbye to you."

"Shhh, my love. We have tomorrow and another night. Let us take what we have and make it our time to remember. One day there will be no more goodbyes."

"Yes," he said softly as his hand caressed her hair. "We have tomorrow so we will just think of that. No goodbyes today."

She smiled. Rising onto her elbow, she smiled down into his eyes.

"Hello, Alexander," she whispered.

"Hello, Abby," he replied gently. He reached for her, to hold her and block out the tomorrows.

They spent the next day in quiet solitude. They

walked together in the woods, hand in hand, and spoke in whispers as lovers do, afraid the world would intrude into their privacy.

That night they lay before a low burning fire. It had been some time since either of them had spoken.

"Abby," he began quietly. "Will you listen to me?"

She trembled with the knowledge of what he was going to say. What he wanted was impossible. It was too late for either of them to turn from the course they had chosen to follow.

"I always listen to you," she laughed, trying to bring humor into what she knew to them both was deadly serious.

"You listen but, sometimes I think you don't hear me. Things are going to begin changing in a short time. The feelings toward Southern born people is going to shift from tolerance to outright attack. You and your father are not safe here."

"What do you suggest we do?"

"Come home with me. Marry me, Abby, and I'll at least be able to keep you and your father safe. The war doesn't have to touch you."

"Oh, Alexander, you are wrong. The war has already touched us both. There is no way for either side to turn back now. We must all follow whatever course we have chosen. You are a Union officer. Do you think you can marry a Southern girl and not have it affect you and your family?"

"I don't give a damn about others!"

"But, I do. I love you, Alexander, with every breath I take I love you more. I understand what you are saying but, I will not let you sacrifice your beliefs nor will I let you jeopardize your family for me. I ... I believe my father plans on leaving here soon.''

"And you think I'll just let you walk away from me, not knowing if I'll ever see you again?''

"I'll go with my father for as long as he needs me. When this is over, when we can marry without it harming the lives of others. . . . If you still want me, I will come to you. But, we cannot, we will not marry until the war is done.''

"You keep saying, 'If I still want you' as if you expect something to change my mind. Nothing outside of death could ever change my love for you.''

"Then our love is to be put to the test. If you love me as you say, time can do nothing to harm us, no matter how many miles separate us. We'll have our time, Alexander, but until then we must accept the conditions. The war stands between us. Marriage now cannot change that. When, if I take marriage vows, I want to be able to do it with no reservations or fear. They will mean my life to me. Until then we will share what ever time we can find together.''

He knew his battle was lost, yet he felt there was something more that stood between them. He could not think of what it might be and soon soft caresses and warm waiting lips erased all other thoughts from his mind except that he had her here and now. He vowed to continue his battle, just as he vowed that one day Abby would be his wife and they would share the balance of their lives together.

Their forty-eight hours were over and they left their private place and returned to Paul Drake's home.

Alexander left Abby at the door for he had to retrieve his things from his parents' home and return to duty in less than six hours.

Abby stepped inside the house and closed the door behind her. When she turned around she saw Paul coming down the stairs. His face was gray with fatigue and fear.

"Abby, thank God you're here!"

"Paul, what's wrong," she said, alarmed at his appearance.

"Your father, he's been shot."

"Shot! Where is he?"

"Upstairs."

Abby flew up the stairs and to her father's room. She knelt by her father's bed. He lay so still that she was frightened. She looked up at Paul.

"What happened?"

"It seems someone is wise to us. When your father tried to make contact, they were waiting for him. I've taken the ball from his shoulder. Abby, I have to get him away from here."

"Will he be all right?"

"Providing he doesn't get caught and hung."

"What do you want me to do, Paul?"

"There are all the papers on my desk in the library. They have to be destroyed. I will take your father to McGraths; you burn the papers and join us there."

She stood up, prepared to do what he said when he took hold of her arm.

"What about Alexander?" he said softly. Her heart twisted within her but she returned his gaze levelly.

"I . . . I guess fate has chosen for Alexander and me. I love him, Paul, I always shall. But, I will do what has to be done and pray that God gives us another chance sometime, somewhere in a peaceful future."

"You are a very courageous woman, Abby."

She smiled then turned from him so he would not see the tears that blurred her eyes.

She helped Paul get her father safely in the buggy. Soon it disappeared from sight. Then she returned to the house.

Along with Paul's papers there was some incriminating evidence in her personal papers. She went to her room and went through the papers one by one, gathering the ones the enemy could use. She took these down to the library where she deposited them in front of the fireplace. Then she took the time to sort through Paul's. When she had everything, she knelt in front of the fireplace and built a fire.

When the fire crackled crisply, she began to feed the papers into it one at a time, making sure each one was thoroughly burned.

She went back upstairs and changed into riding clothes then returned to the library. Taking the poker, she pushed the ashes about making absolutely certain.

She was satisfied and was about to turn and leave when she froze at the click of the door. Then a voice came that stilled her blood and filled her with deep anguish.

"Well, Abby. It seems your little game is over. It seems your fool has finally learned the truth. I must compliment you, love," the voice said bitterly. "You used me well."

She turned about and her eyes raised to Alexander's cold emerald gaze. They stood looking at each other across a void that felt to her to be a million miles wide.

Eighteen

Alexander rode home, his mind involved only with thoughts of Abby and their future. Somehow and some way he would get through that stubborn streak. He didn't see how her birthplace could make a difference. Once she was his wife, no one would question where her loyalties lay.

He was tired and had decided he would take the last five hours he had left to get some sleep before he made the long ride back to camp. But he had barely closed the front door when he heard rapidly approaching footsteps and then saw his father approaching him.

"Alexander, for God's sake come in quickly. I must tell you something."

"You're excited. What happened?"

"I've just had a late visitor who has told me an astounding story. We only have a matter of a few hours before the military goes to the Drake house. It seems Paul Drake and Mr. Southerland are Confederate spies."

Alexander stood motionless. He couldn't believe what he was hearing.

"Abby," he said quietly.

"Now, nothing says Abby is mixed up in this. Maybe she didn't know what they were doing."

But the words Abby had said to him tumbled neatly into place. His world suddenly seemed to shatter like fragile glass. At first, anger flooded him. He had been used ruthlessly to give informtion to the enemy. If it had been another man he would have returned to the Drake house and shot him. But this was Abby, sweet, beautiful, loving Abby who had made his world a bearable place in which to live.

"Father, I've got to go to her. I have to know the truth."

"You haven't much time. Alexander, do you want me to go along with you? Maybe I have enough influence to help."

"No, Father, if you want to help me, get me a few more days' leave. I have to have some time."

"Yes, go, I'll get you the time if I have to threaten General Macon personally with some information I have."

Alexander left, forgetting how tired he was. Knowing only that he had to face Abby to find out if all her words of love had been a lie. She couldn't be a spy! he thought in agony, she couldn't!

The Drake house sat on a very quiet street. It sat back from the road a considerable distance and the boundaries were a high iron fence. Alexander found the side gate open and rode through. The drive was long and passed in front of the house and disappeared around the side. He knew it led to a side entrance.

On the side of the driveway opposite the house were several trees. He tied his horse under one and was about to walk to the side door when he saw a small buggy being driven up. The driver halted the buggy by the door and waited. Alexander stood in the concealing shadows of the trees and watched.

He was soon rewarded for his patience when Paul Drake emerged, said a few words to the driver who jumped down to assist him. In a moment he could see what they were doing. Paul, Abby and the driver were on each side of Abby's father who looked as though he were nearly unconscious. They put him in the buggy and Paul joined him while the driver again climbed atop and quickly urged the buggy into motion.

Without doubt they were escaping something and because Abby was not going with them his heart leaped with the idea that she was innocent of what they were about.

He watched the buggy disappear, then walked across the drive to the side door that still stood ajar. He pushed it open and went inside. He stood in a long dark hallway and could see the glow of light at the other end. His footsteps were muffled on soft carpet as he walked the hall. Before he could step out into the light he saw Abby coming down the steps with a load of papers in her arms.

He watched her cross the foyer and go into the library. He walked to the library door in time to see her, on her knees, feeding the papers into the fireplace. She was extremely careful to see that each one was burned thoroughly. And he knew why. There was no longer room for much doubt in his mind. He stepped back into the shadows as she rose and left the room. She ran upstairs and for a minute, he was going to follow her.

Instead, he waited. She came back down dressed for riding. The deep blue outfit molded to her tall slim frame and her dark hair had been twisted into a knot atop her head.

To him she was still the most beautiful, most desirable woman he had ever seen. He could not help the need and love that blossomed within him but, he did not intend to let her use him again. He would not lie to himself, nothing in the world could change the fact that he loved her, yet the pain of her lies and callous using of him was a harsh reality he had to accept.

He walked to the library door and saw her on her knees before the fireplace with a poker in her hand making sure the damning evidence was completely destroyed.

When he spoke, the sound of his voice echoed in the silent room and he heard her gasp, then saw her startled blue eyes turn to him.

"Alexander!"

"Surprised to see me?" he asked coldly. "Did you think I was on my way to gather more information for you?"

"Alexander," she said gently and one hand reached toward him. He ignored it and continued to watch her, for a plan had, at that moment, come into his mind.

"Let me explain," she said.

"Oh, come now, Abby," he laughed. "Do I look so stupid to you? I know all I need to know. My father told me the news when I got home. They'll be coming here searching for your father soon. Where has Paul taken him, Abby?"

Her hand dropped limply to her side but, her eyes met his fearlessly. Despite his emotions he had to admire her courage knowing what she might face.

"He's wounded, Alexander," she said softly.

"He's a spy," he snapped.

"So am I," she whispered.

Anguish cut through him like a knife. "No!" he wanted to shout, "you're my love and I cannot let you go." Instead he answered quietly.

"I know. Do you have any idea what they do to spies, Abby?"

She turned her back to him so he could not see fear in her eyes.

"I am a soldier for my cause the same as you are for yours. I fight for what I love and believe in. I am ready to face the consequences for my actions."

Her back was straight and her words, in spite of the fear he knew she felt, were firm and strong. At that moment he loved her more than he ever had before. And at that moment his plans solidified themselves.

She was not aware he had moved, yet he went to the window and removed a cord that held the drapes.

Silently he moved up behind her, the cord in his hand. When she sensed him close she spun about but, it already was too late to defend herself.

Rough, strong arms grasped her firmly and despite her fierce struggles he soon had her hands firmly bound behind her.

She gazed up at him in shock.

"What are you doing? This is not necessary, Alexander. I was will to go to the authorities."

"That's fine," he grinned, "But, you see, my dear, I'm not willing to give you to them."

"What are you going to do?"

"Well, Abby, I think I read you pretty well. You thought, since you were a woman, they would go easy on you, maybe toss you out of the state. Then you could go to your father and Paul and be about your business of spying again. Well, you can forget it, Abby. First they wouldn't forgive so easily and second, but most important, I'm not going to let you loose on some unsuspecting, trusting man again like I was. No, Abby, your spying days are over."

"You can't just . . ."

"Can't I?" he chuckled. "And who's going to stop me?"

"This is insanity!" she cried, but for the first time her eyes registered some kind of fear. "Where are you taking me?"

He gripped her chin in a firm hand and tipped it so their eyes held.

"I know a cottage, well away from here, where no one goes. It would make an ideal lovers' hideaway. Only this time the couple who are going to share it are enemies, not lovers. I'm not going to let you loose on the unsuspecting Union Army again." He laughed but, his eyes were cold and hard. "And I'm not going to let another fool walk into your sweet scented trap. You are my prisoner, my sweet rebel, and you'll stay my prisoner until this is over."

Now a new kind of fear bubbled within her. He was angry, that she knew by this rough hands and cold, relentless eyes, but, to be his prisoner in a cottage they had shared with so much love made her weak with fear. To hold her, away from everything for God knew how long was something else she could not believe.

"Alexander, let me go! I'll go home, you'll never see me again."

"No."

"You can inform everyone, I would not be useful as a

264

spy again. Let me go home!"

"No!" he said firmly, and held in check the words he wanted to say—I can't let you go out of my life, Abby. I want to know you're safe and can no longer be harmed by this stupid conflict—instead he spoke in cold, hard, clipped words. "One doesn't trust a spy that has already made a fool out of him so often. No, I'll take care of this and no one will be the wiser."

"I'll never forgive you for this," she gasped angrily.

"Who has asked for your forgiveness? You hold yourself too high. I don't need your forgiveness as much as I need to keep you out of circulation. No, I will not trust you again, but, I will put an end to your activities."

"My father, Paul! They'll come searching for me."

"Of course they will," he said and his brows grew together in a fierce scowl. "And when they come to me, I will use you as you used me, as a threat over their heads. Yes, when they come to me, it will effectively put an end to all their activities also."

For the first time tears stung her eyes. Her lips trembled with the pain she was trying so heroically to contain. Desperately he wanted to hold her, comfort her, yet, instead he lashed out again.

"Don't waste your tears on me, love, I have learned my lesson. Save them for some other fool."

She was about to speak when the sound of approaching hoofbeats came. He lifted her easily in his arms and walked down the long dark hall to the side door. Outside, he stood her by his horse. He was about to mount when she spun about to run. Neatly he stuck out his foot and she tripped, sprawling in the grass. With her hands tied behind her, she tasted grass and dirt in her mouth and sputtered angrily. Roughly she was dragged to her feet and pushed toward the horse. He mounted swiftly then reached down and effortlessly drew her up in front of him.

"That was a stupid thing to do," he laughed. "All you have succeeded in doing is getting your face dirty."

He nudged the horse into motion and they circled the back of the house. In a few minutes they were away from the house riding along at a steady even pace that ate up the distance to their destination.

She remained stiff, trying not to brace her body against his. He knew she must be miserable. He held the reins in his right hand and put his other about her, drawing her body firmly against him. It cushioned the ride and eased the discomfort. Neither of them spoke for they both knew words would be without effect. She could not say anything he would believe and he could not tell her what he really felt.

They rode through the woods to the secluded cottage. There he dismounted and lifted her down beside him. They both stood for a moment, each unaware the other was reliving brief, beautiful memories. He pushed her inside and locked her in until he cared for the horse. Then he returned to the cottage.

It was dark inside and he had to fumble about for candles. He remembered where they were and in a few minutes had one lit.

They stood for a minute gazing at each other, caught in the magic of memories. Then he turned his eyes from her. For a moment she saw a gentle look in his eyes, then they hardened as if he were defending himself from some emotional blow.

"Alexander, you cannot just keep me here. One day you will have to go away. What then? Am I to be tied here to starve?"

"Don't worry, I've already thought of that. You had best begin to make yourself comfortable. You are going to be here a long, long time," he replied as he walked to her side and untied the cord that bound her.

They looked at each other across the glow of the candle.

"Why don't you go and lie down, Abby," he said. "You needn't worry. I certainly have no intention of raping you. My tastes have changed. I guess you might say I've been stung once and I've no intention of getting stung again. As far as I'm concerned, you are a rebel spy and I will hold you here as long as necessary to keep you from doing any more harm."

Anger flooded her at her own helplessness and she struck out at him. The slap sounded sharp in the room and livid red marks appeared on his cheek. She watched in fascination as his eyes deepened to an angry sea green. Then he reached out and gripped her shoulders in a fierce grip that made her cry out. She was nearly jerked from her feet and suddenly, she was enclosed in a passionate embrace.

His mouth swept down upon hers, taking possession. It was an angry, punishing kiss meant to crush her and humiliate her yet, slowly it became lost in the warm sweetness of her response. It was the last thing he wanted, yet her warmth seemed to enfold him, to somehow seep within him until he could almost be drawn into the magic of her.

She knew resistance was useless and she wanted to weep with the touch of his lips on hers. They were angry and they punished her mouth, ravaged it in a wild kiss until she moaned softly with the hurt.

As quickly as he had grabbed her he released her. It was so sudden that she stepped back several steps gazing at him in surprise.

"Oh, Alexander," she whispered softly. "Before you hurt us both, let me go. Maybe ... if we don't punish each other now, we will be able to pick up the pieces."

"Too late, Abby," his voice came softly as if from the deepest part of him. "It is much too late."

She closed her eyes with the pain of his voice and the soft, final words.

"Go and get some sleep," he said finally in a voice that was tired and far away.

He went to the fireplace and began to build a small fire. The bed sat in a shadowed corner of the room. She lay on it and watched him as he sat before the small blaze. It was obvious his thoughts were deep ... and bitter.

Hot tears fell silently as she watched him. He sat before the fire and contemplated the flaming warmth without seeing it or feeling it.

In desperation, she knew she either must get away from him or cast aside all she believed in and loved and go to him in complete surrender. This her pride would never let her do. She knew he might take her in anger but, he would not be able to reach out for her in love for a long, long time ... if ever.

He knew she was watching him with accusing eyes from the bed and his deepest desire was to go to her, hold her and let her love ease the pain that lingered somewhere deep within. But, was it love? Had it ever truly been love? He thought of the peace and warmth he had felt in her arms and the pain of it nearly lifted him to go to her.

When she drifted into sleep, she did not know, nor did she know of the moment he had lifted the candle and walked to the bed and stood looking down at her.

He watched her dark hair spread against his pillow, saw the slow rise and fall of her breasts beneath the material of her blouse.

Was it all a lie, Abby? he thought. Was all the beauty just a lie?

He sat on the edge of the bed without disturbing her sleep and gently took one of her hands in his. He could see the angry red marks the cord had made about her wrists and he hated himself for doing it.

She stirred and whispered his name softly, then her hand clung to his as if it had found safety in its strength.

He held her hand for some time then gently, he untangled her fingers from his and placed her arm across her body.

He rose and went back to the now dying fire. He sat, unable to sleep, and made plans for what he would do in the days to come. It was near morning before he dozed fitfully and it was at the break of dawn that he rose and went to the door.

He stood and watched the sun come up, remembering how they had stood, only a few days ago, together and watched an amazing sunrise.

Then he was aware that she was awake and watching him. He turned to face her.

The sun sparkled in his gold hair and he looked so handsome and strong that she wanted to smile and reach for him ... But, she knew she had to rebuild his trust, convince him to let her go home. If she did she would now have to remain there until the war was over and he came for her ... if he wanted to come for her.

She thought she might be able to mend the gap a little by reestablishing some dialogue between them. It was destined for failure.

"Alexander . . ." she began. But the eyes he turned to her were wary and filled with distrust.

"Don't, Abby. This is your prison for the duration of the war. When it is over, I'll let you go home . . . Until then you are here, and here you will stay."

Nineteen

Celeste sat at her darkened window worriedly gnawing her lower lip while her eyes scanned the expanse of lawn that spread between the house and the stables. She was watching again for the figure that she had seen cross the lawn so often lately.

In the wee hours of the morning several weeks before, she had first seen him, and had watched him again a few nights later. Then, she had made it a point to watch him come and go. It was not like Alexander to be sly about anything. She had seen his face daily for the last few days and realized, as only one so close to him could, that something painful was locked away inside him.

He had been ... different lately, and she could not understand why. His mind always seemed to be somewhere else, and that place had seemed to be something that caused him pain for she could see it clearly in his eyes when he thought no one was watching him.

He had been on a three week extended leave and she knew it was nearly over. He would have to leave soon and as that day drew close he seemed to become more and more nervous. What worried her more was that she knew when he did return from his mysterious rendezvous he had not slept but had paced his bedroom floor in restless footsteps . . . and he had begun to drink too much. This was so alien for Alexander that she had become determined to find out just what it was that hurt him so much.

She wondered if it had anything to do with Abby Southerland leaving for home so abruptly. She had sensed, when she had seen them together, that Alexander had felt very deeply for the beautiful Abby. But she knew Alexander. If he really wanted Abby he would fight for her, not drown himself in whiskey or surreptitious visits to other women. No, something was drastically wrong and she loved him too much to let it go any longer. If there was any way to help him, she would find it.

It was not the only reason Celeste sat and waited. She needed to talk to Alexander, to enlist his help. She wanted to marry Wesley on his next leave. She was aware that both of her parents wanted her to wait until the war was over, but she could not. She loved Wesley with her whole being and she was frightened. She wanted to be his wife, to share his time when he was home, to belong to him completely. Each time he left she was afraid something might happen to him, she would never have known him completely, never have belonged to him. She sighed, for she realized Alexander might be her last chance. Could she make him understand that she wanted to marry Wesley now and share each precious minute of his life that she could?

She stirred on the window seat as sleep tried to overcome her. This might be the last chance for her to be able to win Alexander to her side, that she might have for a long time.

It must have been four in the morning and she was beginning to believe he was not coming home at all. She heard a muffled sound from the area of the stables then saw Alexander walking slowly across the lawn toward the house.

She left her window, went hastily across the room and down the darkened hall to the top of the steps. As she started down she heard the library door close and soon a band of light flowed from under the door.

She walked down the stairs and stood by the door for a few moments. She gently opened the door without a sound and swung it open.

Alexander stood across the room with his back to her in the process of pouring a drink. She was surprised to see him down it quickly then pour another. Then he walked to a chair and sat down. He held his glass in both hands, gazing into it as if the answer to his problem was there.

She had never seen him look so dejected and so completely unhappy. His face was still. To her he looked pale and worried.

"Alexi," she said softly but he was so intent on his thoughts he did not even hear her. She walked slowly across the room and stood by his chair. "Alexi," she repeated.

He looked up, startled.

"Celeste," he stood and set the glass of whiskey aside. A mask slipped over his face and he smiled. She was upset because Alexander had never been secretive or devious before, especially with her and she wondered what could have been so terrible to force him into it now. "What in heaven's name has you up at this hour?"

"I might ask you the same question. I've been waiting

for you for hours. Alexi, what's the matter?"

"Matter ... with me? What are you talking about, Celeste? There's nothing the matter with me except the thought of going back to camp."

She didn't believe that for a moment but she was aware that for the first time in his life, Alexander had shut her completely away from him. Maybe, she thought, if I talk about my troubles to him, he'll be able to talk to me.

"Of course, we're all worried about this fight, Alexi ... it's why I wanted to talk to you. I need your help."

"My help? What's the matter, Celeste?"

"Do sit down, Alexi. You pace like a lion in a cage and you're so tall you make me nervous."

He hadn't realized that he was doing exactly what she said—intimidating her with his tension. He went to a chair and sat, waiting expectantly for her to speak again. She went to him and dropped to her knees in front of him. She took both his hands in hers and smiled up at him.

"I guess I have always come to you with my troubles."

Now he smiled in genuine pleasure.

"For us it will always be like this, Celeste. If I can help you with anything, tell me and I'll do my best to do whatever I can."

"Alexi," she began hesitantly. "Mother and Father ... well, they always listen to you. They always take what you say seriously."

"Now, Celeste, I'm sure Mother and Father take you very seriously."

"Not about this."

"This what?"

"Alexi, I'm nearly nineteen. I'm not a child anymore."

"No, you're a beautiful woman."

"Thank you. I'm glad someone sees me as I am."

"Celeste, what are you getting at?"

"Wesley."

"Wesley? What about him?"

"I just received a letter from him and he said in a few weeks he would be home."

"So?"

"Oh, Alexi, this war is so terrible, anything can happen!" Her green eyes pleaded with him to understand. "I want to marry him when he comes home. Every moment is so very precious that I don't want to waste them. I love him, Alexi, and I want to be his wife. I want to be with him and share everything with him. I want to make every precious moment count. If anything, anything should happen to him, I want the memories of our love to keep. Oh, Alexi, please try to understand. Please, help me."

Alexander could feel the deep pain within him. He would have given his soul to hear Abby say those words to him. He understood, maybe even better than Celeste herself, the need to hold someone you loved close to you.

"I wonder," he said gently, "if Wes knows just how very lucky he is?"

"You do understand," she replied and her eyes filled with tears. "Oh, Alexi, you have always understood me. You don't think it's foolish do you?"

"No, Celeste, I don't think it foolish. It's beautiful."

"Then you will help me?"

"What is it you want me to do?"

"When Wesley comes home we're going to ask

Mother and Father if we can marry right away. Will you stand with me?''

''You bet I will. If it means anything, I'm on your side.''

''It means a lot, Alexi,'' she said tenderly. ''It means my whole life to me. Wesley is my life. I love him so much.''

''Be happy, Celeste,'' he whispered as he gripped her hands in his. ''That's important. Be happy and don't let anyone or anything stand in your way. Not Mother and Father, not even the war.''

She raised her arms to embrace him and he held her close for a minute. She knew instinctively that Alexander had been terribly hurt by something. She wanted to ease the pain and didn't know how.

''Now,'' he said as he held her away from him, ''you had best get some sleep. It's nearly morning.''

''Alexi?''

''Now what?'' he laughed. ''Don't tell me I have to convince Wesley too?''

''No,'' she replied but her eyes studied him seriously. She was surprised when his eyes dropped from hers and he rose from the chair. He stood with his back to her unbuttoning his jacket. ''Alexi, let me help you as you have me.''

''Go to bed, Celeste. I don't know what you're talking about and I am very tired.''

''Please, Alexi,'' she whispered. ''Don't shut me out. I love you.''

He turned to face her and his gaze was affectionate and tender.

''Not now, Celeste. I need time to work on this myself first. But when I need someone to talk to, it will be you.

Now, go on to bed. I'll be all right."

She knew he was not going to say any more yet she felt he knew she had reached out to help him and that he would come to her in time if he needed her. She went to him and kissed him.

"Goodnight, Alexi, and thank you."

"Goodnight, Celeste, don't worry. We'll work it out."

She left the room. Alexander looked at the door a long time before he shook the reverie away. He lifted the forgotten glass of whiskey and walked to the window to gaze out at the first rays of dawn. He drank the liquor and realized no matter what he did his mind and heart returned to Abby. God, how vivid her memory was! The past few weeks wavered before his mind.

He had stood by the door saying words he hated and did not feel. He had seen the pain in her eyes, yet he had been too hurt to believe in her again. He knew he might have to find some place else to hold her, someone to help him, just as he knew, despite what she had done, that he loved her completely. If he turned her over to the authorities, they would hang her as a spy. If he let her go she would be out of his life at least until the end of the war, maybe forever. He loved her too much to take a chance on either.

The cottage was well equipped with everything anyone might need for a stay of a month. Alexander knew if he was forced to keep her here, he would have to go for more supplies.

There was a small barn where three to four horses could be kept. He went to it and began to search. Finding what he wanted, he returned to the cottage.

Each of the six windows of the cottage had wooden shutters. With the hammer and nails he found in the barn, he nailed them closed from the outside.

Abby sat within listening, aware that he pounded each nail with furious anger. It closed off most of the light and when he returned he lit two candles. Then he set about preparing them some food. When he was finished, he set the two plates on the table. He went to her.

"Come and eat," he said and there was a gentleness in his voice that he could not control. She knew, if she wanted to be able to talk him out of this insane scheme she would have to comply with whatever he said. She rose obediently and went to the table and began to eat. He sat opposite her but, she observed, he toyed with his food more than he ate.

"Why don't you tell me the truth, Abby? There's no way out of here for you, you might as well tell me. Just who and what are you and where did you really come from?"

"My name is really Abby Southerland," she replied. "I was born in Georgia. My father has a plantation there. When the war broke out, they thought my father, with all his business contacts here, could be useful to the South as a spy."

"And the damn fool brought you along and convinced you to help him," Alexander replied coldly.

"You're wrong," she said gently.

"I am?" he queried, disbelief in his voice.

"Yes," she replied, her own anger rising. "I came here alone. I followed my father without his permission. I did it of my own free will and for loyalty to my home and all that I love. I would do it again if I had the chance. You made your choices . . . I made mine."

"Well, you are not going to have the chance."

"Alexander, why are you doing this to me? You have nothing to gain. Even if you let me go I am useless as a spy again. You need only tell them my name and what I look like and there is nothing more I can do."

His eyes held hers and even though he tried to shutter them against her, she could see an unsure look. It was a thing she would work on.

"Tell me, Abby, the first time I met you, you looked startled. Did I remind you of someone you cared for?" The words were said as an idle question yet he held his breath waiting for her answer.

"Yes," she replied. "He was someone I liked very much."

"Did you love him," his voice softened to almost a whisper.

"No, Alexander. No, I did not love him." I love you, Alexander, her mind cried. Look at me with love again, believe me, Alexander and let me go.

"Who was he?"

"Dan Wakefield. His father owns High Oaks Plantation. One of the most beautiful in the state." Her mind went back to Dan and Alexander watched her eyes soften with remembrance. At that moment he hated Dan Wakefield. "I imagine Dan is somewhere fighting. I hope he survives. He and his family are wonderful people. Maybe ... maybe you will meet someday."

"Maybe."

The candle glow left the room semi-dark, yet he could see the softening of her blue eyes. They gazed across the table at each other. Now the battle was in full force. Each wanted to change the other, yet neither would change. She wanted to convince him to let her go; he wanted to convince her to surrender, to make her understand what he knew to be the truth.

"This war is a tragedy in many ways, Abby."

"I know."

"I don't think you do. Already the course of it has begun to shift. The South cannot win."

"Would you desert all you knew and loved, all your obligations, your beliefs, because the chances of their survival were slim?"

He did not answer but she could read his face too well by now. He wouldn't.

She smiled. "Then how can you expect me to do what you cannot?"

"Can't you understand?"

"I understand that you want me to be a coward. Would you want me that way, Alexander?" She said the words softly. He rose from his chair and walked around the table to stand behind her. She did not move and closed her eyes as she felt his hand gently touch her hair.

"Want you?" he said quietly, "I will never deny that I want you, Abby. I will never deny you are part of my blood I cannot exorcise. No, maybe I don't even want to exorcise you. I guess I will always want you . . . love you. But I cannot let you go, my rebel. I cannot see you caught and hung and I cannot bear the thought of you reaching for someone else. I am caught in a trap I cannot escape. My only consolation is that I shall hold you in the same trap."

"Don't do this, Alexander," she said in a voice so soft he could barely hear. "Let me go."

He stepped beside her and, reaching down, took hold of her wrist. She looked up in surprise. His face brought a small cry of protest to her lips. "Alexander ... Please ... Don't."

"Ask me not to breathe, Abby," he said gently. "Not to hear, taste, touch, but, don't ask me not to love you, to want you. We are enemies, you and I, but, we love and we always will."

Slowly he drew her to her feet and she could feel the iron hard strength of his arm as it encircled her and drew her to him. He was right. She could not fight the truth of what they shared. She gave a soft moaning cry as his mouth claimed hers in a soul shattering kiss.

He held her bound to him while his lips played randomly on hers, touching, tasting and savoring well remembered sweetness. Then he held her away from him for a moment and their eyes touched.

"Do you see that I can't let you go?"

"Do you see that I must?"

"I love you, Abby."

"And I love you."

"Then forget this damn war! Stay with me. Give me your word you'll stay and I'll take you home. We can marry and be happy."

"No, Alexander. I love you. But I would not be happy and eventually you would be miserable too. The only way for us is for you to trust me again and have enough faith in my love for you to let me go."

"I can't let you go, Abby," he groaned as he pulled her again into his arms. "To an uncertain future, to maybe being caught, maybe being in the middle of a holocaust from which there will be no escape. It is safe here, Abby."

"It's a safety in which I would die ... and maybe watch our love die," she whispered.

She wanted to weep for she knew he would not listen to her arguments as long as he thought he was protecting her.

He captured her face between his hands and with infinite tenderness he kissed her. The kiss was a question and she gave him the answer by pressing herself close in his embrace, surrendering completely to his kiss. She wanted him as much as he wanted her and she could not lie about it to him or to herself. She stood immobile as with gentle hands he removed the clothes she wore. His hands caressed her and she trembled beneath the warmth of his touch.

He lifted her in his arms gently, cradling her against him. Her arms about his neck, her head lay on his shoulder.

He sat on the edge of the bed holding her on his lap. His lips pressed against her throat and sent expectant quivers through her and she clung to him.

He fell back across the bed, pulling her with him, rolling to his side drawing her beneath him. She gazed up into his startling green eyes, darkened with the intensity of his love for her.

"You understand, Abby, that I will hold you until this is over even if you hate me for it."

"And you must understand that I will escape if I can."

He laughed. "No, Abby," he whispered as his lips lightly brushed hers. "You will never get away from me. If I have to follow you to the ends of the earth, I will. You belong to me, you're part of me and I'll never let you go."

Before she could speak again his mouth claimed hers in a possessive kiss that pushed every other thought from her mind except Alexander and the hunger for him that raged through her.

With deliberate control he began to lift her senses until they took flight with his, soaring beyond anything she had ever felt before. He left her only for a moment. In the half-light, she watched him discard his inhibiting clothes, admiring the symmetry of his lean, muscled body. Then he was beside her again, his arms gathering her to him and his hungry mouth claiming hers.

Their love was a vibrant, beautiful thing, intensified by the knowledge that each time they were together might be the last.

Each time they were together, the same battle was fought and each little war ended the same way. They put aside their differences and joined in a passionate renewal.

He knew that if he gave her the opportunity she would be gone. He had put that thought aside for awhile but it had to be faced when the time for his return to duty came.

Now he stood at the window and tried again to find a way out of this dilemma. Two more days, he thought tiredly, then he would have to go. Two more days to share pleasure and love with Abby then he would have to leave. He sighed tiredly, facing another long night trying to reach for the elusive answer.

He laughed to himself. Maybe he would ask Celeste to be guardian while he was gone. It was the last desperate grasp for a safe way out, and, for a minute he considered it seriously, but only for a minute. It was too much to ask even of a devoted sister. Besides, he knew Abby too well now. Quick and intelligent as Celeste was she would be no match for Abby. No. He had to find some other way both to protect her and to make sure she was not free.

"Well," he thought as he again sipped from the glass, "I'll find a way tomorrow. There has to be a way."

He watched the first gray light of dawn streak the horizon. He wondered if Abby watched too. He prayed for the day when the ugliness of war would be a forgotten thing and Abby could come to him free and unrestrained. They could marry, build a home and have children. Caught in his fantasy, he watched the sun brighten the new day. He allowed his dream to hold him for some time, then he changed clothes and went downstairs to join his unsuspecting family for breakfast.

Twenty

Dan laid aside his gun and sank to the ground in a state of complete exhaustion. He was dirty, hungry and nearly overcome with the desire to walk away from everything and go home.

"Home," he thought as he folded his hands behind his head and closed his eyes. Home with its wide vistas of green lawn and tall shady trees. Clean sheets on his bed and food, plenty of good warm food.

He could almost feel the breeze in the trees and smell the sweet scent of wild honeysuckle in the air.

Then his mind shifted to the one thing that always was with him. He conjured up visions of Catherine. Catherine with her soft hair falling about her. Catherine laughing with him, walking with him, loving him.

The leaves had already fallen from the trees and a cool nip in the air signaled the beginning of winter.

He was sickened with war. He had faced the "enemy" in four battles since he had left home. Each one had been a Confederate defeat and each time they had fallen back, they had lost so many men that Dan found the carnage hard to believe.

He felt dirty with the blood of men he had killed.

The South, with its supplies cut off, was slowly being strangled by the blockade. Food and medicine were in extremely short supply. The army, with its life's blood being cut off, began to look like the desperate force it had become. Dan was worried about his family and about Catherine. If the army was short of supplies, food and clothing, what were the people at home doing without?

He was so involved he did not hear another man approaching until he sat down beside him. Dan opened his eyes, smiled, then closed them again.

"Hello, Hooker. Where've you been?"

"Out roundin' up sumpthin' to eat, boy," the older man laughed. "Kilt me a rabbit so iffen you get up offen your back and help build a fire, I'll let you help me eat it."

"A rabbit!" Dan said as he jerked to a sitting position. "I didn't know there was a rabbit between here and Atlanta."

"You boys shore are rotten hunters. Now, me, I kin find sumpthin' to shoot anytime. Stick with me, boy, and you won't go hungry."

Dan began to gather twigs to start a fire and his mouth watered at the thought of something besides weevilly biscuits for supper. Hooker skinned the rabbit, skewered it on a stick and braced it over the fire. They sat back to wait.

"Hooker?"

"Yeah?"

"You think we're going to go to winter quarters?"

"Yeah, maybe. Who knows what all them officers is plannin'. More ways to get us killed I expect."

"You heard anything at all?"

"Yeah," Hooker said, disgust in his voice.

"What? Bad news?"

"Boy, they ain't been nothin' but bad news in the past year."

"What did you hear?"

"Heard Gen'l Lee got whipped at Antietam. Union army chased him for a ways but didn't catch up to him. Then, I heard things didn't go so well for us. Been a lot of talk about Fredericksburg, but, I don't know for sure what happened yet. All I know is it's gettin' cold and I ain't had a good meal for too long."

They sat close to the fire and ate the rabbit when Hooker finally claimed it was cooked enough.

They had spent almost three months in this camp. No activity and no word of what was going on elsewhere had drawn all the men's nerves taut with the strain. Coupled with bad food and even poorer clothes with which to face the coming winter was the fact that no mail had come for a long time. Dan had no way of knowing if his parents or Catherine were well.

After they had finished eating they remained quiet for awhile. Hooker absently poked the remains of the fire with a stick.

"Hooker, you ever get scared?" asked Dan.

"Hell yes, every time I pick up that gun I get scared."

"I don't mean that kind of scared, I mean scared that we're going to lose this war. Scared of what might be happening at home. We haven't heard anything we can believe except the Union has crossed into our territory."

"I been thinkin' on that too. When everything got started I kind of had a suspicion we wuz biting off more than we can chew. But even if I wasn't rich I had a good life. I don't want no Yankee comin' here and tellin' me how to live. I guess the thing that scares me most is what might happen if we do lose."

"I wonder what's happening at home?"

"You worried about that pretty little girl of yours?" Hooker teased. "Maybe she's sparkin' somebody else."

Dan grinned. "Catherine isn't that kind of girl. She's sweet and loyal. Only, she's so . . . so delicate, so little. I worry if she's all right."

"Knowin' women she's probably doin' better 'en you. Women has a way of pickin' themselves up and facin' just about anything. Most times better 'en men kin do. She'll probably pick up a gun herself if the Yankees decide to step on your precious High Oaks," Hooker chuckled at Dan's panic-stricken look.

"Hooker! Christ, do you think it might ever come to that!"

"Now don't get excited, boy. I guess if things get that bad we'll be right there beside 'em when the shootin' starts. 'Sides, I thought you got a letter a few weeks ago from your Catherine."

"Over two months ago," Dan said angrily. "She's trying to make everything look fine. I just wish I was there to help them."

"Well, I expect we'll be doin' somethin' one day soon, either movin up or back."

Dan lay back on the ground and watched as the first evening star silently began to glitter in the sky. Even when he had been lost from his family as a child and had felt the misery and pain of separation he had never felt as lonely as he did at this moment. He felt a deep and intense need to walk the rich soil of High Oaks and taste the remembered joys of home. To see Catherine again and hold her close to him. Suddenly, he felt a deeper sense of loss than he had ever felt before.

Hooker rolled himself in his blanket and was soon asleep but sleep was an evasive thing for Dan. He sat up, stirred the embers of the fire and threw another piece of wood on it. He took Catherine's well worn letter from inside his shirt and read it again even though he knew most of the words by heart.

My Dear Dan,

I pray this letter will find you. I have written so often and received no reply. Some of my letters have even been returned to me.

I also pray this letter finds you well. We have heard of the defeats we have suffered and the casualty lists are frightening. I know I should feel guilty about the others but the only thing I can feel is relief that your name is not among them.

When you were home, Dan, I told you I loved you. I did not know the meaning of love, loss or loneliness until you were gone.

Oh, Dan, I wish I had not listened to you. I wish I had married you before you left instead of waiting until you returned.

I have gone to our cottage which is empty now since the old man left after losing his son. I sit there in the dark and feel your presence. Oh, Dan, I miss you so much and want you so much.

When you come back we will fix the cottage up and live in it. It is the most perfect place for us to begin a new life.

Your mother and father are well, but just as frustrated as I with the inability to contact you.

But all of the slaves are gone. Your father

still farms a small plot of land by himself. He has said many times he is grateful to you for insisting he plant some food instead of cotton. It has been a great help not only to us but some of our neighbors. Your mother is so wonderful. She has opened High Oaks to all of the boys who are passing. They can have a hot meal and sometimes a bed in which to sleep. Always, we ask about you and sometimes are fortunate enough to find someone who has crossed your path or, at least, knows of you. She and I devour every word.

We are well, Dan, but, there is a vacancy in all our lives we cannot fill. You are missing and nothing for any of us will be quite the same until you return.

Please keep yourself safe, my darling. I love you, Dan. Hold on to that as I do. It helps me face each day without you. I love you and I want you to come home safe. I want to share the rest of my life with you. More than anything, I want us to start a good life together.

All my prayers and love are with you, Dan. Bring them back to me.

All my love,
Catherine

Absently he refolded the letter and put it back inside his shirt. It was his one strong link to home. He knew he could suffer the loss of anything else he carried but the letter.

He sat, gazing into the reddened embers and envisioned High Oaks as an open house for every soldier who passed by. No words could have described to him better the course of this tragic affair. He felt so disoriented, so lost. What was happening to his world and to all the ones he loved?

It took every once of will power he possessed to push the agonizing thoughts from his mind before they grew to proportions he could not handle.

He rolled himself in his blanket and, with grim determination, sought sleep.

It was a crisp, clear morning, quiet, with only the sound of the birds. Dan didn't want to open his eyes. The sound of the first explosion brought him abruptly awake and groping blindly for his gun.

Hooker had leaped up beside him.

"What in the hell was that?" he shouted over the confusion. But Hooker's answer was drowned in the rapid sound of three more consecutive explosions.

"Yankees!" Hooker shouted as they grabbed their guns and sought more adequate shelter.

The exploding shells made craters and Dan and Hooker jumped into one before the gray mist of the explosion had drifted away. Falling earth still rattled about them.

At that moment charging Union soldiers appeared from a stand of trees less than seven hundred yards away.

Disorganized men were mixed up with the dead and the dying and stumbling aimlessly about or attempting to scramble away.

The shouting, screaming and cheering mingled with the roar of artillery and exploding shells created a perfect pandemonium.

All might have been lost for the Confederates camped in the small valley except the Union did not take into consideration the charismatic leadership of Colonel John Singleton Mosby.

His sheer heroism and leadership re-organized his nearly panicked men to hold off the enemy until late in the day when re-enforcements came to their rescue.

There was sporadic fighting for three days before the Confederates finally beat the Union off and followed a controlled retreat.

Hooker suffered a wound high on his shoulder and Dan had to nurse him as best he could. To make matters worse, it began to rain. The roads slowly turned into a sea of mud through which nothing could move. It forced them into a cold, wet and very miserable camp.

The hasty lean-to Dan had built sheltered him and Hooker inadequately. Rain seemed to find every source of entry. They were cold, wet, hungry, lonely ... and frightened though none of them would admit it.

Now there was nothing to do but sit and wait for the rain to cease and new orders to tell them where they were headed.

Dan did not take the letter from his shirt during this time. He felt the warmth and love of Catherine would call to him too strongly and he might just do as many others were doing. He might just lay down his gun and go home.

Catherine stood on the front porch of High Oaks. She had begun visiting, then, knowing how she worried about Dan, Virginia had asked her to stay until his return.

She stood now watching the two ragged soldiers making their way up the long drive of High Oaks. God, she thought, each time they come they are worse than the ones before. Miserable, wretched men, wounded, hungry, with hardly enough clothes on their backs to keep them from the elements.

"Oh, Dan, where are you? Are you well, or hurt? Are you hungry?" she murmured to herself as the two men reached the steps. Both were the worse for wear yet, one did his best to support the other.

"M'am," the stronger one said. "Is this High Oaks? We was told if we could get this far we could find shelter."

"Yes, this is High Oaks. Come around to the kitchen door. We'll get you some food. You can sleep in the barn tonight with the others." Catherine smiled and came down the steps to lead them.

"You sure are an angel, M'am," he replied. "I don't think Jeb here could have made it much further."

"We've very little medicine but, we'll do the best we can. Where were you?"

"Missionary Ridge, M'am, with Cleborn's outfit."

"Your friend was wounded there?"

"Yes, M'am. I'm takin him home."

"I . . . I know you're not in his outfit, but, would you by any chance know Dan Wakefield?"

"Wakefield?" He pondered, then shook his head negatively. "Who's he with?"

"Colonel Mosby."

"They was hit pretty hard a couple of weeks ago. I heard they got caught asleep. There was an awful lot of casualties and they had to retreat pretty fast. Colonel Mosby is a damn . . . darn good officer, M'am. If anyone can get his boys out safe, he can do it. Sometimes not hearin' is the best news."

"Yes," Catherine replied softly, trying to control the hot tears that threatened. It had been so long since she had heard from Dan. She didn't even know if the letters she wrote every day reached him.

Virginia had turned High Oaks into a place of safety for all passing Confederate soldiers. When the battles had begun to turn against them and all men were needed, Gregory had gone to fight.

They had nearly run through everything edible and all medical supplies, yet they refused to close their doors to the bedraggled warriors who found their way to them.

The barn and stables had been turned into a make-shift hospital with what they considered the very worst supplies possible.

Both Virginia and Catherine, with the three older slaves who had chosen to stay, did their best to ease the plight of the men who came to them.

Some of the men who had found sanctuary here had remained to help with the others. They said nothing to each other of the aura of fear and despair that had begun to settle about them.

Catherine and Virginia worked from sun up to sun down. It never ceased to amaze the men with whom Catherine worked that this slim, golden girl could do so much. To them she was the Southern dream and they never failed to be gallant and admiring. All of them by now felt they were nearly brothers of Dan Wakefield and all of them prayed silently that her dreams would be answered and he would come home safe.

It was dusk and the whole world seemed to be touched by a gray half-light. Catherine sat on the front porch, her back resting against the cool pillar that supported the roof. She looked out across the neglected lawns of

High Oaks. From a distance she could hear the stirring of people but she pushed the knowledge of their existence away and let her mind have the relaxing luxury of reliving the days she and Dan had shared in the beauty of High Oaks' past.

"We will rebuild it," she thought. "When this terrible war is over and Dan comes home, we will make it like it was." She closed her eyes and let the welcome dream claim her.

She was startled to awareness by the drum of hoof-beats on the drive. Someone was pushing a horse to urgent speed. She stood and watched the rider approach. It was one of the young soldiers that had been sheltered here until his wounds had healed. They had all taken turns in keeping watch for invaders. Now he skittered his horse to a stop and leaped from its back, running up the steps to stand beside her.

"Yankees," he gasped. "They's camped about eight or nine miles from here. Come morning they'll be here. We got to get everybody away."

"Yankees," she repeated. "Here, on High Oaks?"

"Yes, M'am, Miss Catherine. We have to hurry. We got to get everyone away from here."

"Yes ... yes," she replied, her frightened mind slowly regaining control. "Go and tell Mrs. Wakefield. Have all the wounded taken to those old slave cabins on the Ridgeland property. The house is gone and it's over-grown. They'll find some safety there. Go! Hurry!"

"Yes, M'am." He dashed away. Catherine stood for a minute looking in the direction the Yankees were camped. Her chin lifted stubbornly and her eyes grew cold. This was High Oaks. It was Dan's. It was his life and she would protect it as best she could, even from the dreaded Yankees.

Before dawn the last trace of the wounded had been done away with. Virginia and Catherine stood with the last remaining two who were doing their best to argue about the women's decision to remain.

"We can't leave you here unprotected, M'am," one of them said firmly. "There's no telling what those bloodthirsty Yankees might do."

"You go with your men," Virginia said firmly. "If you are caught, there's no way to help you. We're much safer than you. This appears to be a well led group not a group of leaderless scavengers. We must stay to see that High Oaks is not burned as I hear some others have been. Please, go. Your men need to be cared for. We will be all right. As soon as they leave, we will come for you."

"I don't like this ... running," the other answered stiffly. "And leavin' women behind."

"If you remain," Catherine said gently, "we might pay a greater price for having you here. They might think they have to use force on men. With women it might be different. Please, please go."

Reluctantly, the men agreed that she might be right. They mounted, then one of them smiled at Catherine.

"If I ever run across that man of yours, I'll have to tell him what a courageous and beautiful woman he's been lucky enough to get."

"Thank you, Sergeant Mayer. Good luck."

"We'll see you soon." The men rode away.

A deep, heavy silence fell over High Oaks as Virginia and Catherine stood on the porch and awaited the Yankees.

It was not long before they could see the long line of

blue turn up the drive. It was led by a tall, handsome young lieutenant who stopped his horse at the foot of the steps. He dismounted, handed his reins to a sergeant, then walked up the steps. He removed his hat and smiled pleasantly at the two women.

"I'm afraid, ladies, that I must commandeer this house for a few days. We're awaiting a change of orders and it would be much better to await them with a little more comfortable shelter than the elements provide. May I ask the name of this place?"

"High Oaks," Virginia replied proudly. "It is my home. My name is Mrs. Virginia Wakefield."

"It must have been very beautiful."

"It was," Virginia replied coldly. "Before the Yankees invaded us. You have been quite destructive, Lieutenant. You must enjoy war."

He flushed as if the remark touched a sensitive spot.

"No, M'am. I . . . I've learned a lot of lessons in this war. No, M'am, I don't like destruction but, it is here and we must finish it."

"What's your name, Lieutenant?" Catherine asked.

"McClellan, M'am, Lt. George McClellan."

Twenty-one

George rose early six days later and, after he dressed, walked down the long, empty halls of High Oaks to go down to breakfast. His men supplied much of the fare they ate because there was very little left there from past times.

It had not taken him long to realize that men had been cared for in this house, as close a time as hours before they had come. He also felt both these women knew where the group of Confederates were at this moment. Yet, he also knew they would not tell him. What surprised him was his reluctance to question them. He had fought many battles in this war and had tasted, first hand, the reality of the pain and bloodshed. A lot of his dreams had been brutally shattered.

He admired Virginia's cool acceptance of their presence and the way she seemed to hold a command over herself that so disarmed any man in her presence. He automatically treated her like the lady of the manor even though she was dressed in plain cotton and the manor was a vacant shell of a once beautiful home.

He knew something else that had shaken him severely. His admiration of Virginia was great ... but he was completely, desperately falling in love with the tiny, beautiful Catherine Markland. It angered him, yet there was nothing he could seem to do about it. Each day he was in her presence, he felt lost to the stormy emotion that controlled him.

Subtle questions had led him to understand that High Oaks was not Catherine's home. It took considerable questioning to bring to light the situation that kept her here. When he had finally put the pieces of the puzzle into place, it began to build the flames of jealousy and envy for Dan Wakefield.

Catherine wore the ring Dan had given her on a thin chain about her neck for it was entirely too large for her. When Dan returned, he would have it cut to size. She wanted it as her wedding ring for it held such beautiful memories.

The day he discovered why she wore the ring was the day he discovered that this slim girl had awakened something in him that once awakened began to devour not only his heart, but the ideals with which he had fought. He could no longer give the enemy the appearance of faceless evil. The enemy became people, people who loved and hated as he did. He was completely unsettled by the changes Catherine was bringing about.

He remembered well the day she had finally told him about Dan. It was the fourth day they had been camped at High Oaks and he had just finished the early evening rounds among his men as he always did. He was crossing the lawn of High Oaks when he saw her walking slowly down the path that led to a small cottage. He quickened his pace and in a few minutes he was close enough to call to her.

"Miss Markland!"

She turned about quickly and he could see a moment of fear on her face at being caught so far away from the house, alone and with night coming. He was quite pleased when he saw the fear fade and a quick smile replace it. He strode rapidly to her side.

"You shouldn't be out at night," he warned. "My men are only human and it has been a long time since they've been home. You could easily be taken for a remembered girl back home."

"I'm sorry ... I didn't think ..."

"You were going to that cottage over there?"

"Yes."

"I'll walk you over. That way I can see you get back to the house safely." He smiled to soften the thoughts behind his words and took her arm. They walked toward the cottage in silence.

The inside of the cottage was dark and he heard Catherine fumble about, but only for a moment, before she found a candle. In a few moments, pale light bathed the room. At that instant he knew that this place was visited often, most likely by the girl who stood beside him. He knew nothing about large plantations for he had always been city bred, yet, he knew, because of its unassuming comfortable air, that it must be servants quarters or the home of a caretaker.

"Charming," he said quietly. "It's very comfortable."

"Yes," she replied quietly. He watched her as her gaze moved about the room. It was as if the place were a beloved home to her. He sensed that it held something very special to her.

"You come here often?"

"Yes . . . every day if I can."

"Why, Miss Markland? I mean, with that beautiful mansion at your disposal, why would you have such an attachment to this place?"

"My name is Catherine," she smiled. "All my friends call me so."

"And . . . you consider letting a Yankee be your friend?"

She sighed then turned to look at him, the candle glow reflected in her eyes.

"I have a choice between enemy and friend. I am so tired of the hatred and the war. Could we not just consider ourselves friends while you are here?" She smiled again. "I promise not to raise arms against you if you will say the same. We could have a temporary truce."

"I should like that," he said gently, realizing he meant it completely. "Now, Catherine, tell me why you like this place so well."

"It . . . It is our place . . . Dan's and mine. One day we will live in it. It was here that Dan gave me this." She touched the ring gently. "It will be my wedding ring."

"He's a lucky man," George replied. "You were childhood sweethearts, I take it?"

"Hardly," she laughed. "Dan and I were friends for a long, long time. I loved him when I first met him, but he hardly noticed me."

"Not a very discerning man."

"He was nine and I was seven."

"Oh, I see."

"Dan was so frightened. After all, he was a stranger here. He was an orphan and the Wakefields took care of him. They didn't adopt him until he was quite a bit

301

older and could choose for himself."

"Not a very difficult decision, all that wealth."

Her eyes flashed angrily at him. "Dan is not that kind of man. He loves his foster parents and he loves High Oaks."

"I did not mean to start the war again. Forgive me. Tell me more of Dan Wakefield, or whatever his name is."

"You know, I hardly remember what it was, that was so long ago. It was French though."

"I see."

"I think," she said quietly, "you and Dan could be friends if you could just lay down your guns and resolve your differences."

"Don't dream, Catherine. What is begun has to be finished. The South is on her knees already. It will not be long before her death knell is sounded."

He watched her eyes lift to his in defiant pride. At that moment he wanted to reach out and take her in his arms and hold her. She too could read his face.

"We will not let this die, Dan and I. When he comes back we will marry and rebuild High Oaks. We are one, Dan, me and High Oaks. Here we gather our strength. This soil gives us life. Together we will never be beaten ... We will never surrender."

He watched her, knowing he could never reach her and he felt the agonizing touch of something sweet and gentle that lingered just beyond his reach.

"I'd best see you back to the house now," he said, "It's late."

"Yes," she replied. She blew out the candle and walked ahead of him to the door.

It had been six days now and he still awaited further

orders. He had watched Catherine's early evening visits to the cottage but never interrupted them again. If he did, he was afraid he would say words that couldn't be recalled and he knew the tentative peace they had would be forever broken.

Catherine was aware that he purposely stayed away. A few nights later she was grateful for this. She walked down the familiar path to the cottage door. She opened it and went inside. She stood in the dark room for a minute to adjust her eyes, then she walked across the room and took a candle from the mantel. She never got a chance to light it for a soft voice froze her in her tracks.

"Don't light the candle, love. I don't need it to see your beauty and it's best the Yankees don't know I'm here."

She spun about facing a darker corner of the room from which the voice had come. "It was a dream," she thought. I want him so badly that I think I hear him.

"Dan?" she whispered.

A dark shadow moved slowly toward her and she heard his soft muffled laugh as his arms surrounded her and she was lifted against him. She said nothing else for all words were stopped by the hard, hungry mouth that claimed hers. She clung to him, fearing it was a dream from which she would waken and find him gone.

"Oh, Dan," she gasped when his lips finally released hers. "You are real. You are really here?"

"I'm here, love," he said gently. "I'm here. Let me hold you. You don't know how desperately I've needed to hold you."

Now realization struck her.

"Dan, this is dangerous! There are Yankees in the house!"

303

"I know."

"You know?"

"Sergeant Mayer told me. I ran across them up at Ridgeland. He told me a lot of beautiful stories about you. Called you an angel of mercy. Told me if I didn't appreciate what a rare gem I have, he would be glad to take over for me. I told him I not only knew and appreciated you, but that I'd kill the man who tried to take you, Yankee or Rebel."

"You knew the Yankees were at High Oaks and still you came. Are you crazy? If they catch you they'll kill you!"

"Catherine," he said softly as his lips began to brush gently across hers. "I would have walked through the gates of hell and shook hands with the devil just to hold you for a minute."

Tears blinded her as his kiss became gently insistent. She could not fight the flood of joyous desire that cursed through her. All resistance fled before the warmth of his kiss and the need within him that bound her to him.

"How I've dreamed of holding you," he murmured. "Loving you. It is the only thing that has kept me going all this time. I must be gone before dawn if I'm to get past the sentries. Catherine ..."

Her fingers touched his lips to silence him. Her eyes had become accustomed to the dim light now and she could see him.

"Then do not waste a precious moment of our time," she said softly. "I need you to love me, Dan, to hold me, to tell me that this will all pass and someday we will be together forever."

He reached out a trembling hand and began to

unbutton her dress. She stood still, her eyes half closed, warm pleasure flowing through her at his gentle touch.

He could see the pale shimmer of her body in the dim, gray shadows and he drank in her rare beauty as if he were a man dying of thirst. His hands reached again to caress her with a feather light touch. His fingers touched her lips then drifted down her slender throat to a soft shoulder, down to caress one passion hardened breast then the slim curve of her waist. It rested gently on her hip, then slowly he drew her toward him and again his head bent to taste her upturned mouth.

Tenderly and with exquisite patience he teased her mouth with soft kisses, nibbling gently, touching their sweetness with his tongue as if he were tasting the nectar of the gods. She moaned softly as the flame of need burst within her and sent shivers of ecstatic pleasure to every nerve in her body.

Slowly, his lips traced a flaming path over her skin. He knelt before her pressing his lips to the valley between her breasts then moving slowly from one passion filled peak to the other. His hands slid about her and held her tightly to him as he covered her smooth skin with the flame of his need.

She gasped with the delicious pain as gently he nibbled her sensitive skin and her hands turned in his thick hair to press him closer ... even closer yet.

He heard her muffled sob as the sheer joy of him captured her and her body trembled in expectant agony. She was filled with no other thought but the need of him.

Suddenly, she quivered with the cold as he left her for a moment. She did not open her eyes but listened as he threw aside his clothes. Then he was beside her again to chase away the cold and bring to her the intense heat of his love for her.

Effortlessly, he swung her slim body up into his arms and quickly covered the few steps to the bed.

Dan fought the desire to take her quickly, to ease the painful need, he wanted to savor each touch, each kiss, each exquisite moment. He would have to treasure them for a long, long time.

Patiently he lifted her senses until she existed in a world of need, a world that held only Dan and the flame of their love.

His hands caressed, followed by seeking lips that drove her to a frantic desire. He heard her call out in passion and felt the joy surge through him. It was only when the need drove him to the brink of insanity did he give himself the pleasure of his all consuming desire.

He captured her mouth with his to silence the passionate sounds she was making without realization.

Then he joined them, entering her and filling her with the power of his demanding possession.

She was wild, unleashed passion now and he released all hold on reality and surrendered completely to the fire that branded his soul forever.

They tumbled together into the depths of blazing passion and lost themselves in a completion that left them weak and trembling and clinging to each other as if to hold on to something solid amidst a blinding violent storm.

"Oh, Catherine, my dear, sweet, beloved, Catherine. You are the only bright and beautiful thing in this world and I love you beyond anything any man has ever known."

"And I love you, Dan. Oh, I love you. I cannot bear

this separation. I am so frightened."

"Shhhh, love," he whispered. "Don't be afraid. We'll see this thing through, you and I. One day soon it will be over. We'll start a whole new life. I will never let anything separate us again."

"Promise me, Dan," she pleaded, and he could hear the tears in her voice. "Promise me you'll come back to me safely. My life would end if something happened to you!"

"I promise, my sweet love, I promise," he murmured as he held her close to him and rocked her gently in his arms.

He knew it was time for him to go yet he tempted fate to hold her just a few minutes longer. He knew what was happening in the world around them and he was as frightened as she. He had made her a promise tonight, he thought, but, would he be able to keep it tomorrow?

Twenty-two

Wesley Rainey approached the Dubonne house with anxiety gnawing in his stomach. He was sure the Dubonnes would refuse to let Celeste marry him now, but he was prepared to enjoin in a more difficult battle than he had been in since the war had begun. He did not want to fight her family, but he knew he would. He would fight, beg or do anything else that would make Celeste his.

He turned up the long drive, then reined his horse to a stop and smiled as he saw Celeste running toward him. He dismounted in time to catch a laughing breathless Celeste in his arms. He took immediate advantage of their hidden spot to crush her to him and kiss her most thoroughly. Then he held her from him.

"You look beautiful ... you also look excited. Has something happened?"

"Yes! Oh, yes! I've been waiting for you. Come to the house quickly."

"What's going on, Celeste?"

"Wes, I know I promised to wait until you got home to ask Mother and Father if we could marry, but ... something happened."

"What? Will you stop fluttering and tell me what."

She laughed gaily and told him what had transpired in her house the day before. "I knew Mother and Father might refuse because of the war. I also knew if they would listen to anyone, it would be Alexi . . . so I went to him. I told him how desperately I wanted to marry you now. Oh, Wes! He said he thought I should! He even said he'd talk to Mother and Father with us if we wanted."

"What a piece of good luck for me," he laughed. "But I'm surprised. Alexander has always been so protective of you. It's hard to believe he wouldn't agree with your parents and ask you to wait until the war is over."

Her face became serious for a moment. "I think Alexi is thinking about himself."

"What do you mean?"

"I don't know for sure, but I think Alexi was in love with Abby Southerland. When she and her father left to go home it made him realize how waiting can make things slip away from you. Sometimes he seems so . . . unhappy. Maybe when this dreadful war is over he can go and find her."

"Maybe," Wes said thoughtfully. "He'll be headed that way sooner than he thinks."

"What are you talking about?"

"Celeste, don't say a word about what I'm telling you, but Sherman's gathering strength. They're transferring Hood, his and several other outfits too. I wouldn't be surprised if Alexander was among them. He's going to make one heavy concentrated effort to cut the South in two, maybe to end all this."

Her startled heart heard only one thing. Wes would

be going into battle soon. She looked up into his eyes and tears glistening in hers.

"Oh, Wes," she murmured in a choking voice.

Gently he cupped her face in his hands and kissed the tears away.

"If your parents agree we'll be married right away. But whether or not, we'll make every minute count. I love you, Celeste . . . I love you." His lips touched hers lightly, and she closed her eyes and clung to him.

Reluctantly, he let her go, then he gazed toward the house. He took her hand in his.

"Come, let's go ask them. This is more than any man should be expected to stand."

Jules Dubonne had reluctantly agreed to work as a military advisor, but had refused admantly to don a uniform and lead men into battle again. It was the reason he already knew about Sherman's intended attack.

He watched Celeste and Wesley come into the room where he and Marie were having late morning coffee, and he knew what was on their minds. He knew, if he were Wesley, that he would be feeling the same. He had gone into battle often enough leaving a tearful Marie behind. Always he had been grateful she had been his wife and they had shared rare and beautiful moments for him to carry into battle with him.

Before they had come into the room, Celeste had sent for Alexander. It was only a few minutes before he appeared. This did not pass Jules' attentive eyes either. He smiled to himself, Wesley and Celeste had sent for the strongest reinforcements they could have. He looked at Marie who smiled at him with awareness in her eyes.

"Father, Mother," Celeste began hesitantly. "Wes

and I would like to talk to you about something very important."

Jules' upsetting gaze locked upon Wes who returned it with as much courage as he could muster. Jules had a way of looking at him that could well nigh come near destroying all his reserve. This time it was too important for him to lose his courage at the last moment. He wanted Celeste too badly.

Alexander caught Celeste's eyes and smiled encouragingly at her.

"Sir," Wes began, "Celeste and I ... well, I'll be leaving soon and we want to share as much time as we can together. We'd like your permission to marry ... right away."

Marie closed her eyes for a moment, knowing the pain and heartache her daughter might have to suffer. Hadn't she suffered them herself so long ago? Then she thought of how much joy she and Jules had found in their rare moments together. She knew she would have done nothing different. She remained silent, waiting for Jules to speak. She did not know her astute son had read her face well and knew without a word that Celeste had another ally.

Alexander thought he read refusal in his father's eyes.

"Father, before you decide," he said gently, "consider how it was with you and Mother. I remember stories of how you fought to marry her when everyone else was against it because of another war. Don't Celeste and Wes deserve the same happiness as you and Mother have found? Time is too precious to waste a moment of it."

Jules looked at Alexander. He smiled, but inside he registered the fact that Alexander carried some burden that had hurt him in some way. He promised himself to speak to Alexander about it as soon as possible. It was nearly suicide for a man to go into battle with a mind concentrated on problems elsewhere. For now, there was the problem of Celeste and Wesley. To him, his daughter was still his baby and he was quite reluctant to part with her. His gaze returned to Marie, in whose eyes he saw memories past.

"Why," he said gently, "do I suddenly feel that I'm outnumbered? I feel as if I have been outflanked by superior forces."

Celeste went to him and put her arms about him. "I love you, Father. You and Mother have given me everything all my life. Please try to understand how much I love Wes and want to be with him."

"No matter what happens in the future?" he questioned gently.

"No matter what. We will face the future together as you and Mother did. We will have each other for strength and love, as you and Mother did. If we have children we will try to give them the immense love and happiness you and Mother have always given us."

Jules sighed, knowing he was lost, for his love for Celeste could not refuse her her happiness.

"When do you have to be back, Wesley?" he questioned.

"In three days, sir."

"Three days," he repeated. "Well, if we can get Rev. Willoby to perform the ceremony so quickly . . . then I guess your Mother and I must reluctantly give you away."

"No Father," Celeste smiled as she rose on tiptoe to kiss him, "I will never be gone from you. Always I will love you for your care and understanding. Thank you, Father, thank you."

He held her close to him for a moment, then he reached to shake a happy Wesley's hand.

"I'll take good care of her, sir, I swear." Wes said.

"You'd best," Alexander laughed, "or the war will look like a Sunday afternoon tea party."

They all laughed at this, but Wes had understood Alexander's thinly veiled threat.

Celeste and Wes went for a walk in the garden just for a few minutes to share their happiness alone. Marie found some absolute necessities that had to be cared for before the wedding. Jules and Alexander sat alone.

"How about joining me in a drink, Alexander. We can toast the forthcoming wedding."

"Yes, of course."

"Whiskey?"

"Yes."

Jules poured two drinks then handed one to Alexander.

"To Celeste and Wesley, I hope all goes well in their lives together," Jules said.

"Amen," Alexander echoed quietly.

Jules sat down in a chair opposite Alexander.

"I haven't questioned you before about this," he began. "I heard Paul and the Southerlands got away. It was terrible to find out they were Confederate spies."

"Yes," Alexander said noncommittally. How could he tell his father of the girl he held prisoner. Could he explain to him that it was fear of losing her forever that forced him to hold her. Would his father understand? He realized his father was still talking, and it took a great deal of effort to draw himself back from dreams of

Abby and concentrate on what his father was saying.

"There is a lot of talk among the military heads about Sherman's plans," Jules continued. "It seems rather bloodthirsty, the plans he has made. They will live off the land and destroy everything in their path as they go. I guess it is always the way for military success, but I hate the needless waste of lives and property. Alexander!"

Alexander drew himself away from his dark thoughts. He looked up to see his father's sympathetic gaze on him.

"Did you love her Alexander?" he said quietly.

"I loved her then," Alexander replied, "and I love her now."

"No matter what she has done?"

"I fight with an army, Father. Can I be held personally responsible for the deaths we cause? It is war. She did what she felt she had to do. No, I don't blame her ... yes, I will always love her."

"What are you going to do?"

"Pray that this bloody disaster is over soon. Then I intend to try to make her forget all that is past and start a new life with me."

"Will you know where to find her?"

"Yes," Alexander replied quietly, "I will know exactly where to find her."

Jules was about to question the strangeness of Alexander's reply when a knock sounded on the door.

"Come in," Jules called.

The butler opened the door and stepped inside.

"There is an officer here to see you and Lieutenant Alexander, Mr. Dubonne. He said it is very urgent."

"Tell him to come in."

In a few minutes the butler escorted a young officer into their presence, then left closing the door quietly behind him.

"Good afternoon, Murphy," Jules said.

The young Lieutenant smiled hesitantly and his eyes seemed to be drawn to Alexander.

"You have a message for me?"

"Yes, sir," He cleared his throat and began to speak words that seemed to be drawn reluctantly from him. Many of the young officers knew of the attachment between the Dubonnes and Paul Drake ... and between Alexander Dubonne and the beautiful Abby Southerland.

"I was told to bring the news to you, sir, and I find it quite difficult. I hope I am not the cause of too much unhappiness."

"What is your message, Murphy."

"I've been told to tell you the military post on the border captured the two spies, Mr. Drake and Mr. Southerland six days ago."

Alexander started to speak but Jules interrupted. He did not want Alexander to say anything that might make a bad situation worse.

"There's more isn't there?" he replied.

"Yes, sir ... there is."

"Tell us the rest, Murphy."

Now Murphy's eyes held Alexander's with an unreadable almost pleading look.

"They ... they've been tried, sir ... by a military court ... they've been hung as spies."

Alexander felt as if he had been struck a blow. Jules watched his face grow pale and saw him sit slowly down as if all the strength had been drained from him.

"Thank you, Murphy," Jules smiled at Murphy who watched Alexander, seemingly to want some kind of forgiveness for the news he had brought. No sign came from Alexander. Finally he dropped his eyes, turned and left.

Alexander was stunned. How could he carry such news to Abby . . . how could he not tell her the truth. Would the tenuous hold he had on her love die when he told her. Even if he wanted to let her go now he couldn't. There would be an intense search for her. Every road South would be watched. Now he had to hold her to keep her alive and safe.

He had to go to her, now. He had to tell her the truth. He had to make her understand that she could never hope to reach home safely . . . she had to stay with him.

Abby tried every way possible to escape her comfortable prison, but she could not. The windows had been well secured and Alexander had locked the door but not before he had made a thorough search of the rooms to make sure there was nothing she could use as a weapon or tool to help her.

Once she had exhausted herself she sat and tried to gather her thoughts and her courage together.

It had been two days and one long and lonely night since Alexander had been there. She felt certain Paul would have sent someone to search for her by now. Her nerves were stretched taut with worry about her father's and Paul's safety.

If they had approached Alexander to ask of her or even to trade or beg her safe return would he tell her? Her mind knew he wouldn't.

She understood how Alexander felt, and she could forgive him knowing he loved her and wanted her safety, yet she knew he deliberately refused to understand how she felt. He thought he was doing what was safest for her.

She would try again when he returned, try to make him understand that if they wanted to keep their love, he would have to let her go, for if he continued to hold her, slowly he would destroy what was between them.

She loved him completely, yet the values they held, the loyalties they had, and the obligations they felt to opposing sides made them enemies. Their love could not exist on that plane for she felt smothered, bound helplessly, and she would fight for the freedom to come to him in love and not as a prisoner of his love.

She had not been able to eat much, and had slept restlessly, waking often from dark dreams she could not remember.

Now she paced the floor nervously. Some inner instinct made her shiver with a premonition. She felt a black smothering loneliness. At that moment she would have welcomed any word or sound of human companionship.

The sound of approaching hoof beats stilled her. Was it Alexander or had Paul and her father somehow traced her and come to set her free?

Footsteps sounded on the porch and when the key turned in the lock she knew it was Alexander. She faced the door and watched it swing open. He stood in the late afternoon sunlight.

Again, despite her other emotions, she was forced to admire his tall lean body. His golden hair, touched by the sun.

"Alexander," she said softly.

Silently he closed the door, then she was surprised to see him turn, lock it again and put the key in his pocket. It was the first time he had done so and she wondered if he thought she might be able to escape him. He crossed the room and stood close to her. Then without a word he encircled her slim waist with both hands and drew her to him. His arms bound her close and he took her mouth gently but firmly with his. The kiss was sensitively sweet. It demanded nothing. It spoke only of his deep love and need for her.

He meant to tell her immediately, but her sweet surrender was more than he expected. Her slim arms encircled his neck and her lips gently parted beneath his as she pressed herself closer to the warmth and strength she found in him.

He lost all hope of clinging to reality when he felt her reach for him, cling to him in need.

Slowly the kiss grew warmer, deeper, until the world was lost to them and they reached again for the magic that could always bind them.

"Abby," he whispered against her throat. "I do love you. You are the sweetest dearest part of my life."

"Love me, Alexander," she pleaded in a voice husky with passion. "Hold me."

He knew the treachery with which he held her now, but he could not deny himself what might be the last time she would come to him freely with love not hate in her heart.

His mouth sought hers now with an almost violent demand. His blood heated to a flame coursed through him as he felt her respond with an urgent need that matched his.

Clothes were hastily and carelessly thrown aside, and they tumbled on the bed together. He covered her trembling lips with heated kisses, then let them rove where they would. Her eyes, cheeks, her slender throat, the soft rounded curves of her breast, the soft flat plane of her belly. He tasted each spot and moved to taste another and yet another.

Unleashed passion rose in devouring fury. His senses soared as he felt her wild response. She gave herself more completely than she had ever done before. Nothing was held back as she sought with hands, lips, and slim heated body to possess him as he was possessing her.

He knew her now, knew how to lift her senses, knew how to create a wild abandoned passion, and he used his knowledge. He felt her body quiver beneath his hands. Heard her passionate words call to him and he could have wept with the sheer joy when their bodies blended and moved together with a blinding surge that carried them to a cataclysmic explosion that left them both clinging weakly to one another.

In the midst of passion they had not noticed the dark clouds that had covered the early evening sun. Nor had they heard the low rumbling thunder that had grown about them.

The storm had broken, rising to a thunderous height, but they had not heard it. The storm within stood as a rival to the one without.

As their passions had calmed so had the storm outside. They held each other now in the dim half light and listened to the gentle patter of rain on the roof.

They did not speak for a long time. He held her, he tried to form words in his mind that might ease the pain of the words he had to tell her.

He closed his eyes, feeling her curled warm against his side. He let his hands gently caress her hair and the smooth skin. He wanted nothing more than to hold her like this forever. To erase the pain of the world that hovered outside the door.

He felt her shiver a little and tighten her arm about him.

"Cold?"

"A little."

"Lie still," he chuckled as he kissed her lightly. "I'll build a fire."

He found his way across the half dark room. He knelt and built a small fire in the fireplace.

Abby lay on the bed missing his warmth and the strength of his arms about her. She watched the firelight touch his bronzed lean muscular body and brighten the gold of his hair as he bent to stir it to more life. She shivered again but this time it was with a sense of possessive pleasure. She could feel the touch of him, taste the pleasure of him and knew with finality that no other man would ever be able to reach within her and touch the center of her being as he had done. She loved him completely and without doubts. She had decided then to surrender and stay with him forever.

She felt nothing would change her now. She was wrong. For fickle fate was to snatch their happiness at the peak of its fulfillment.

He was drifting in thought, still contemplating the fire, when she called softly to him.

"Alexander," she said in a throaty whisper. "Come back here."

He stood up and bent to take his pants from the floor

and put them on. Then he came to the side of the bed. He took her hand in his.

"Abby, come sit by the fire with me. I have to talk to you."

She came to him wondering why the rain suddenly sounded cold and lonely and why even by the fire with his arms about her she suddenly felt a shiver now that was not of cold ... it was of fear.

Twenty-three

"Alexander, what is it? What's happened?"

"Abby, I know there's no easy way to tell you this. I love you and I would rather die than to cause you such pain."

"I . . . I don't understand. What are you trying to tell me?"

He took both her hands in his and held them tight. He tried to hold her eyes with his to tell her, even while he spoke such terrible words, that his love was strong.

"It's Paul Drake and your father," he said quietly.

"Father . . . they've been caught."

"Yes, they've been caught."

"Alexander where are they? Let me go to my father. Can't we do something to help? Your father, Alexander, can't he . . ."

"Abby."

She became silent and now her eyes widened with the terrible fear.

"No," she whispered softly. "No, Alexander. They . . . they would have to have a trial."

"They've had a trial . . . by a military court."

"A military . . . Alexander, please . . . no."

He saw the fear blossom in her blue eyes, saw them fill with tears, watched as the tears escaped to slide down her cheeks.

"They're dead, Abby. They were found guilty and hung."

She almost collapsed and he put an arm about her to steady her. She nearly leaped away from him gathering her own strength together.

"Don't," she gasped. "Don't touch me," she sobbed once, an agonizing sound of intense pain. "You . . . you knew when you came here? Why didn't you tell me? Was this a little punishment for your prisoner to prove you are powerful?"

"Abby, you know that isn't true, I love you. I wouldn't hurt you this way. Don't you see, if I had let you go with them that night, they would have caught you too. You would be gone now and I could have done nothing to stop it."

"I should have been with them!"

"Abby, don't say that!"

"Where was I when my father died?" she cried in anguish. "Lying in bed like a traitor with a Yankee."

"Don't think that way!" he said angrily. "There is no Yankee or Confederate with us. We're part of each other, Abby. We're not enemies! We never will be. Listen to me, Abby. They're looking for you. There's no place safe for you . . . except here with me."

"Don't hold me Alexander. I will die! Let me go. How can I live with myself knowing they died for a cause while I did nothing. You have to let me go. I cannot bear the guilt."

"And I cannot bear the thought of letting you go. It would take them no time to find you. Do you think I could bear the pain and guilt if they hung you? Don't I count for anything at all? Does our love mean nothing to you?"

"If you loved me you would let me go," she said quietly.

"If you loved me you would understand and know I can't," he replied. "So where do we stand, Abby, loving and hating, lovers and enemies?"

She buried her face in her hands and cried deep wracking sobs. He put both arms about her and brushed his cheek across her hair. She lay against him and the pain crushed her. She allowed it to wash over her for a few minutes.

It was a few minutes that lowered Alexander's guard. He thought she had finally surrendered, finally acknowledged the fact that there was no safe way he could let her go.

"Abby," he whispered gently, "the South is on her knees. It will not be long until this war is over. If you want to go home then, I'll take you. We'll take your father home. I'll do anything to help you forget the past. We have a beautiful love to share, Abby, and a future together. Let's just hold on to our dreams of tomorrow and try to forget all that's happened before."

"Tomorrow," she murmured softly, "yes, I must think of tomorrow . . . and my father's memory. Here he is a spy . . . hung like a criminal. But at home he will be a hero. He must be taken home and buried beside my mother with the honor and love he deserves."

"We'll do that, Abby. I swear, when this is over we'll do that."

She looked up at him, but this time her eyes were shuttered against him. The rain made a gentle drumming sound on the roof, and the cottage, lit only by the glow of the fire was warm and quiet.

Alexander brushed the tears from her cheeks then touched her moist lips with his.

"Abby, I'd like to take you someplace more comfortable. I'd like to take you home. Celeste is being married soon. I'd like to have you there beside me. Will you come? Will you let me keep you safe until this is over? Once the war is finished and you are my wife no one will cause us any problems."

Her voice was controlled and quiet now and he felt relief that the final battle of their war was over.

"I must dress and make myself more presentable if I'm going to leave this cottage. I could not travel far like this."

He looked down at her and smiled. Her slim body touched by the glow of the fire gleamed like ivory and gold. Her hair tumbled about her in amber profusion.

"I like you like this. I must remember to bring you here more often."

"For now I must dress. Will you put another log on the fire so I can see what I am about?"

"Of course," he replied. He went to the pile of logs and took one. He knelt by the fire and threw the log on, watching it catch. He did not see Abby move quickly to the logs and pick up another sturdy one. He went to turn away from the fire and the log she carried descended. Bright lights exploded in front of his eyes and he murmured her name in surprise as blackness appeared and he slowly tumbled into it. He collapsed at her feet. She knelt beside him to assure herself she had done him no serious injury. She felt the strong solid heart beat.

Quickly she slipped into her clothes and braided her

hair. Then she felt through his pockets for the key. At the door she turned to look at him.

"I'm sorry, Alexander. I love you and I hope someday you can forgive me."

She opened the door and ran out into the steady falling rain. She saddled Alexander's horse, knowing without it, it would take him some time to get home and get another before he could search for her.

Alexander began to stir to slow wakefulness, and the first thing he heard was the drumming of slowly receding hoof beats.

"No, Abby, no," he whispered to himself as he struggled to his feet. He felt his head gingerly where a nice sized lump was forming. A wave of nausea struck him as he weaved his way toward the door.

He moved as rapidly as he could, but there was no sign or sound when he reached the porch. He stepped down, looking down the long path. He stepped down, unaware now of the rain that beat against him mingling with the tears that touched his face.

Abby was an excellent horsewoman, and it was good that she was for Alexander's horse was a huge stallion meant to carry the weight of a man and to be controlled by a stronger heavier hand than hers.

She felt the tremendous strength explode beneath her and bent forward to let him have his head. She cared for nothing but putting a lot of distance between her and Philadelphia. They galloped along throwing up a fine spray behind them.

They left the wooded area and burst upon the dirt road. Mud flew from beneath the hoofs of the huge beast as he thundered down the road.

Time meant nothing as the huge animal covered immense distance with his free stride. Abby began to wonder if she had the strength to bring the huge beast to a stop when the time came.

They were flying down the center of the road. Abby was mud splattered, thoroughly soaked and completely disoriented. She had no idea where they were headed.

She began to pull at the reins to slow the horse, maybe stop him so she could have a chance to look about and find some landmark.

She did not have the strength. The horse had the bit between his teeth and she had lost control over him completely.

Desperately she jerked at the reins, but at the same time a brilliant flash of lightning struck a nearby tree and it dropped nearly upon them.

The horse reared and what control Abby had was lost. The slipperiness of the saddle and the poor hold she had was enough to unseat her. With a sharp scream she was flung to the ground. When her body struck it was with enough force to crush the wind from her. She rolled a few feet, then her head struck a rock and darkness enclosed her. She lay still on the cold wet ground as the rumbling thunder rolled about her and rain washed in rivulets over her quiet pale face.

The storm began to abate, and the heavy rain began to slacken, then turned to a faint misty drizzle. After some time it stopped completely.

The closed carriage rolled along the road. When it crested a small hill the driver reined in sharply and brought the four horses to a halt.

He stared for a moment at the slim body that lay in

the mud alongside the road. Then a voice from inside the carriage called out to him. A soft feminine voice that spoke with a decided French accent.

"George, what ees eet?"

"I don't know, your Grace. It looks as if someone had an accident. Appears dead to me."

The curtain to the window was pulled aside and a woman's face appeared. She gazed at the mud splattered body for a few minutes.

"Eet ees a woman, George. Please to get down and see if she ees living."

"Yes, M'am," the man replied. He tied the reins, climbed down and went to kneel at Abby's side.

"She's alive, your Grace."

"Quickly, George, bring her inside. Good heavens, how did she ever get out here alone?"

The man lifted Abby as the woman swung the carriage door open. He laid her across the seat opposite the woman.

"We must take her home and call a doctor. Hurry, I don't know if she is injured badly."

"Yes, Ma'm," the man replied. He swung up on the seat of the carriage as the woman drew the door shut and soon the carriage rolled away.

Less than an hour later it pulled to a stop in front of a huge mansion a few miles from the city.

Abby still had not regained consciousness. She was carried gently to a beautiful room and laid upon a bed.

The woman snapped crisp precise orders in a voice that seemed well used to obedience. Soon the clothes were removed from Abby's cold body. She was washed, dressed in a warm nightgown and tucked between warmed sheets.

The doctor came, cleansed, stitched, and bandaged the cut on her head.

"Let her get as much rest as possible, Madam," he said. "She will regain consciousness with a severe headache but no other damage has been done."

"Thank you, Doctor," the woman smiled. "I shall see she ees well cared for. It ees to answer my curious nature. I must hear the story of how she came to be there."

When she closed the door behind the doctor, the woman's smile faded. She stood and looked at Abby for some time. Then she rang for her maid. When the young girl appeared she said firmly.

"Go and get both Phillipe and George. I have something I want them to do."

"Yes, Ma'm," the girl bobbed a curtsy then was gone. In a few minutes the two men who had been sent for stood in front of the Countess and listened to the most surprising orders.

Abby woke to bright sunlight that pierced her protective eyelids and caused her head to ache. Slowly she opened her eyes but the pain in her head made her groan and close them again as nausea claimed her and the room momentarily seemed to spin.

Memories came flooding painfully back, and she wondered if Alexander had found her and if this was the Dubonne home.

The door opened and a young maid came partially into the room, saw that she was awake, turned and left before Abby could speak. Abby closed her eyes trying to think of what she would say to Alexander when he came.

Again the door opened. But Abby was to be surprised, for it was not Alexander who came in but a very beautiful woman somewhere near her own age ... and a complete stranger to her.

"Ah, ma chere," she said in a velvety voice. "I see you are finally awake. How are you feeling?"

"Terrible. I have such a headache. Where am I? The last thing I remember was that my horse threw me."

"You have received a terrible blow on your head. My doctor has seen to it. You are quite lucky."

"I'm very grateful. May I ask Madam, where I am and who you are?"

"I am Countess LeClerc and you are in my home. You are quite welcome to stay as long as necessary until your health returns. Is there someone to whom I can send a message ... to inform them where you are. They must be quite worried about you by now."

"No ... please," Abby began. She was searching about for a reasonable excuse for why she had been where she was and why she did not want anyone to know where she was. The last thing of all she wanted was for Alexander to find her now.

The Countess' astute gaze was watching her closely and a small smile played on her full sensuous mouth. For several minutes, she watched Abby search frantically for some logical words the mysterious Countess might accept.

The Countess came and sat on the edge of the bed and took Abby's hand in hers. Abby could smell the exquisite perfume she wore.

She was, Abby thought, an extremely beautiful woman. Obviously one born to wealth. Everything about her spoke of wealth and of excellent taste. Her hair was gold and done in severe yet exceptionally beautiful coiffure. The gown she wore was tastefully plain, yet it spoke of wealth.

"It is so much easier for us both," she smiled to make her words easier, "if you were to tell me the truth ... Abby Southerland."

"You know who I am?" Abby breathed forlornly.

"Oui, I know much about you. I have taken great pains to find out." She watched Abby's eyes closely. "I will not turn you in to the authorities if that is what you think. I am not one to deal randomly with the authorities unless it is of absolute necessity. I find they ask entirely too many questions."

Abby breathed a sigh of relief.

"Now," the Countess repeated with a friendly squeeze of Abby's hand and a warm smile. "Suppose you satisfy my intense curiosity and tell me what you were so desperately fleeing."

Abby began at the beginning, when she had followed her father North and began to work for the Confederacy. The only thing she left out was her personal affair with Alexander. She told the Countess that she had been captured and held prisoner there, she had discovered that her father and Paul Drake had been caught and hung. She had escaped her prison and was fleeing when the horse had thrown her.

"You are a very courageous young woman. For such courage you should be allowed to escape. I will help you. It interests me to do so, I am so very bored and this sounds quite exciting."

Abby laughed, then winced as her head reminded her of her injury.

"You are supposed to get some rest. I shall have

some food sent up to you. After you have eaten, you must sleep, then we shall decide how we can get you across the lines and back to your home.''

''You are very kind to a stranger. Especially one who is being sought as a spy. You could be in a great deal of trouble if you are found aiding me.''

''No, non, non, cherie,'' the Countess laughed. ''I am never in trouble. There is always a greedy man, a hungry man, or an oh so handsome man and I can deal with all three. This shall be an exciting escapade. I shall help you go home, then I shall be your guest for a while and you will show me this magnificent plantation.''

''You would be a most welcome guest. I want to go home so desperately.''

''And your father, Cherie?''

''I shall go to the military once I'm home and ask if they can request the return of my father's body.''

''It should be,'' the Countess said softly, ''you have other family at home?''

''No, my mother died when I was a child. I've no sisters or brothers.''

''You will be alone, with all the terrible things that are happening you will be alone?''

''I'm afraid so.''

''Non! I cannot let that be. I shall be with you. At least until this is over. I am a welcome guest, no?''

''Yes.'' Abby could not help but laugh at the Countess' airy disregard for danger to herself. And her seeming delight at the adventure they were about to be partners in.

''Now, you must get some rest. We will talk tomorrow. We will make plans, and then I shall begin to make arrangements. You will see, cherie, I have many unconventional friends. We will see you safely home."

The Countess rose from the bed and walked lightly to the door. Abby had to admire again her beauty and her obvious breeding, yet the way she seemed excited about dangerous adventure.

When the door closed behind the Countess Abby closed her eyes. She did feel extremely tired and the pain in her head was overpowering. She slept for a while, then was wakened by a maid with a tray of food that emitted an enticing aroma. She realized it had been a long time since she had eaten. She managed to eat everything on the tray and an hour later found her asleep again.

For two more days, Abby, though she resisted, was forced to stay abed. Her headache finally disappeared. She felt well, had a good appetite and all signs of the slight fever she had had was gone.

Finally, the third day, the Countess accompanied the maid in with the breakfast tray. She sat with Abby and chatted happily while Abby ate, occasionally she would break off a piece of toast and nibble while she asked Abby questions.

When Abby was finally considered completely well by the doctor and allowed to rise the Countess knew all about Abby, her past and her present. All except for Alexander Dubonne. A name Abby never mentioned.

"Well, cherie, it seems the doctor thinks you are well enough to be up and about. It is good."

"Yes, thanks to you. I shan't ever forget your kindness."

"Well, now you must get up," the Countess laughed. "I have a closet filled with clothes you can choose from. When you are dressed I shall tell you about all the talk that has gone about. There is quite a search for you. It seems they think you have gotten away with all kinds of plans and ... whatever it is these fighting men hold so dear. Ah! Men must always turn to war must they not?"

"You don't believe in the cause of either side?"

"Causes, my dear, should be one's self and one's happiness. Surely you could be loyal to your cause, surely you could, as your father did, die a hero's death. But is it not better to look for love, for joy, for happiness? Is it not better to live with one another in peace?"

"One must defend one's home and beliefs," Abby said.

"If every man stayed home to defend his home there would be no battles. If every man believed in the value of human life there would be no wars. Wars are fought by greedy men who make a profit. It is better to find someone to love and who loves you and believe in that. But! I shall talk of war no more, nor of beliefs or causes. Now we must get you home. Hurry and get dressed and we shall talk."

The Countess left the room. Abby rose slowly and thoughtfully from the bed. All she had to do was go to Alexander. He would love her and keep her safe.

For a few minutes she was tempted, then her mind turned to her father. She owed him more than to just cast aside all he believed in, all he had died for. No, she would see through to the end what she had started. Maybe, when it was over, Alexander would be able to forgive her. Maybe, one day, they could start a life together.

For now she had to face the world the only way she

knew. With pride and firmness in what she was taught to love and believe in.

She chose a plain green dress from the multitude before her, then, when she was dressed, she left the room and went downstairs. Down to make plans that would carry her farther and farther away from Alexander and any love they might have shared.

Twenty-four

Alexander had walked back into the cabin aware of how empty it felt. He had put the rest of his clothes on rapidly. It would be a long way to travel on foot, but he had to go as rapidly as he could, for fear of what could happen to Abby when she was found turned him cold with terror.

A woman as beautiful and attention gathering as Abby would not be able to hide for long in a city that knew her well. It would only be a matter of hours before someone would recognize her.

When he put on his clothes he gave one last look at the place in which he and Abby had shared so much. Then he closed the door behind him. Somehow he had to find her before anyone else did.

The rain still fell in misty sheets, and he was soaked to the skin within minutes of leaving the porch.

He set off at a slow loping run that he knew he could sustain for a long period of time. He determinedly controlled the panic that battered against him.

Thoughts twisted in his mind and he groaned with the agony as thoughts of what could happen to Abby without his protection filled his mind. He envisioned her held in a dark prison, worse yet, tried and hung. It tore a painful cry from him he could not contain. Tears blurred his eyes, but he continued the distance eating run.

It had been over forty-five minutes. His breath was coming in quick labored gasps and he knew he would have to stop for a few minutes to catch his breath.

He had just reached the muddy road at the edge of the woods. He stopped and leaned for a moment against a tree. It was then he saw a dark form standing more than forty feet down the road.

"Major," he whispered, and a whole new wave of fear washed over him. His horse stood, the reins dragging the ground. Alexander began a stricken search for Abby. The horse had to have thrown her.

Slowly, he approached the huge animal, speaking softly. The horse laid back his ears and his flesh quivered as if he was about to run. Then suddenly it seemed he recognized Alexander's familiar comforting voice. Alexander held out his hand and the horse nickered gently. He caressed the velvety nose and rubbed his hand down the heavy neck. Then for a moment he rested his head against the horse's wet coat.

"Where is she, Major?" he whispered softly. "Where in God's name is she? I've got to find her, I've got to. What use is anything without her?"

He mounted Major and began a slow methodical search for Abby, but no sign of her could be found. After a long hour of searching he knew she was gone. His only wild thought was where and with whom.

He rode back toward home, keeping a close watch for any sign of Abby, but he knew she could not have gotten that far or he would never have found Major.

He arrived home to a darkened house, and he was

grateful. At this moment he did not want to explain his condition, either physical or mental, to anyone.

He sat on the edge of his bed and very slowly began to remove his wet uncomfortable clothes. He cast them aside, dried himself off and put on clean clothes.

He was searching his mind for ways to find traces of Abby. Worst of all, he had to keep his search quiet. What would a Union officer be doing searching for a woman already branded a Confederate spy?

He slipped back out of the house as quietly as he had come and began a search of every place Abby might have gone, and he questioned everyone he thought might have some knowledge. This he had to do in a roundabout way so as not to rouse any suspicion. There was no sign ... no word ... it was as if the world had opened up and swallowed her.

He had not slept all night and he came home late in the afternoon the next day exhausted, yet still unwilling to answer any questions. His family knew him much too well ... they asked him no questions but waited until he felt he could come to talk to them.

He was quiet and withdrawn during the simple ceremony that united a very happy Celeste and a proud Wesley. It was a family affair, with only a few favored guests invited. Mostly close friends of both Wes and Celeste ... and Alexander ... and both Marie and Jules had time to watch Alexander.

He stood and watched the ceremony, his mind and heart reaching for thoughts of Abby. "Let her be safe," he prayed silently, "even if I cannot have her at least let her be safe."

Wesley and Celeste were so caught up in their happiness that they did not read Alexander's face, but Marie and Jules, who knew him so well, exchanged glances.

"Jules . . ."

"Don't worry Marie. I'm sure it's just worry over the fact that he has to leave soon. When a man is going to go into battle he sometimes becomes introspective. I'll talk to him later."

But it was long after the party that he was able to get Alexander alone for a few minutes. Wesley had taken Celeste to the small house he had rapidly bought when he found they would be permitted to marry. Alexander had had several drinks, and that might have been a good thing at the time for combined with his anxiety and misery it loosened his tongue.

They stood together sipping their last drink for the evening.

"Alexander, you've been awfully quiet all evening. Is there something wrong, something I can help you with?"

"I doubt it, Father. I've created my own problems I'll have to find my way out myself."

"Sometimes it's good to put your problems into words. You can get a better look at them that way."

"Maybe . . . maybe I don't really want to look at them. Seeing my own stupidity can be alarming."

"I don't understand."

Alexander sipped his drink thoughtfully and for several minutes Jules thought he had no intention of speaking at all. Then Alexander walked to a chair, sat, and motioned to his father to sit across from him.

"Maybe it would be better to explain what has happened. Maybe you'll have some idea of which way I can turn, or where else I can search."

"Search . . . for whom?"

"Abby Southerland."

"Abby, why she probably is back across Southern lines and home by now. She made her escape along with her father and Paul. They must have made sure she was safely gone before they made the attempt and got caught."

"I'm afraid not, Father. Abby never left Philadelphia," he said quietly.

Jules looked blankly at Alexander for a few minutes.

"I don't understand. It was reported that the house was found empty. The three of them had fled after seeing that all their servants strategically disappeared. There was no trace of any of them until Paul and Abby's father were caught. It's just been taken for granted that she made good her escape."

"I know what was reported. I've kept close tabs on what was being said and done. I had a very special reason ... I ... I don't know if I can make you understand the reasons behind what I've done. You see, Abby never left Philadelphia ... because I've held her prisoner since the night the arrests were supposed to be made."

Jules sat back in his chair and said quietly, "Maybe you had best start at the beginning. I don't really believe what I'm hearing."

Alexander drained his glass and set it aside. Then he clasped his hands firmly before him, rested his elbows on his knees and began to talk. He told his father all that had happened from the moment he had met Abby.

Jules did not interrupt, but he very effectively read between the lines. There was no doubt in his mind that Alexander had been hurt more by what he had done than anyone else.

"What in God's name did you expect to prove by holding her prisoner?"

"All I could think of was to keep her safe, keep her from being captured. It was a nightmare I continually had that she was caught and hung. I took the first, and what I thought was the only chance I had to protect her."

"Did you believe she was going to surrender that easily? Alexander, she did not strike me as the kind of woman who would give up her loves and beliefs very easily."

Alexander gingerly rubbed a head that still had a sizeable lump on it.

"You can believe that, I'll vouch for it."

"You never told me just how she got away."

"When I found out about her father and Paul, I felt she had a right to know. I got too involved. A good whack on the head," he shrugged helplessly, "and she was gone. I've tried everything and every place. She must have had contacts somewhere. Someone had to have picked her up or she would have been somewhere in the area I found Major."

"If that is so, Alexander," his father said in a firm but sensitive voice, "it is no good to search for her. It is clear to see they had some way to get her across the lines safely. She's gone, Alexander, and the only way you will see her again is when this war is over."

"If I wait here that long, it might be too late. We know the South is losing. I need your help . . . again," Alexander laughed mirthlessly.

"What do you want, Alexander? I don't see what I can do to help you."

"I want to be with the first point of Sherman's army.

From what I understand he plans to cut straight through Georgia. If I'm at the head of that thrust I might be able to find her before it's too late."

"You might get killed doing it, too," his father said softly. "It's a very difficult thing to place your own son in such a place."

"If I told you that she is my life . . . if I told you that I need her like I need air to breathe or food to eat. Would you understand that I have to do anything I can to find her. Leading a patrol ahead of Sherman I might stand a chance of finding . . . of finding Abby there. At least then I can see she doesn't get any more hurt from this than she already has."

Jules sighed again, "I'll do what I can to have you transferred. No one would believe this. I hope you know what you're doing, Alexander."

"At this point in the game, Father, I'm not too sure. All I know is I'm going to try everything in my power to be there first."

"Well, I will talk to the powers that be in the morning. You'll be leaving soon."

He stood, and Alexander stood to face him. He laid his hand on Alexander's shoulder remembering days past.

"You will take care of yourself, son. You will not make me regret doing this by letting anything happen to you. I'm afraid I could never forgive myself and I would have a very difficult time with the guilt of knowing I could have stopped you."

"I'll do my best."

"And," Jules grinned, "maybe you'll bring us back a beautiful addition to the family."

"Again, I'll try my best," Alexander laughed. "She's

a stubborn little rebel. But this is one Yankee who does not intend to take a no or a lump on the head as a final answer.''

"Good," Jules replied. "Now you are speaking like a Dubonne. Shall we have one last drink?"

"Good idea."

Alexander poured them and handed one to his father. Silently they touched their glasses together.

"To finding Abby ... and to the end of this war," Jules said.

"Thank you, Father and ... I hope both prayers are answered."

They drank, then without another word they left the room. As they walked up the stairs, Alexander chuckled.

"What's so funny?"

"While you're shifting things about, why don't you get old Wes a few more days leave. If I'd just been married I sure would hate to leave my bride in two days."

Jules chuckled, "I'll try."

"It would be nice to see old Wes' face when he finds out."

They shared their laughter.

The buggy moved slowly through the night toward the small house Wesley had chosen for his bride. Beside him, Celeste sat quietly, her head resting on his shoulder.

"Celeste," Wes said quietly, "I'm sorry everything had to be this way."

"What are you talking about?"

"The wedding; I'm sure your parents planned something better for you. I imagine you thought of something a lot different too. If I'd just had more time."

"Wesley," Celeste laughed. "I wouldn't have wanted it to be any different. Do you really think all that fuss means anything to me? You and I, that's all that matters. That's all I've dreamed of since I was a little girl."

"You're something pretty special Celeste. I'm glad I had enough sense to finally see it."

"Well, I'll admit you were aggravatingly slow."

Wes laughed, holding the reins in one hand he put the other arm about Celeste and held her close to him.

When they reached the small house, Wes quickly stabled the horse while Celeste waited, then they walked across the small expanse of lawn to the front door.

When he unlocked the door and pushed it open, Celeste was about to enter when Wesley's hand on her arm stopped her. She looked up at him questioningly.

Without saying a word, Wesley swept her up into his arms and stepped across the threshold kicking the door closed behind him.

She looked about a dimly lit room whose light came from a low burning fire in the fireplace. Before it sat a table that held the dishes and glasses for a small supper.

Celeste smiled as she gazed into Wesley's eyes. "I should have known you would think of everything."

"I want tonight to be perfect. It's the most important night of my life," he said gently as he set her on her feet but still held her close to him. He bent his head and brushed her lips with his.

"Oh, Wes, we have so little time together, and I'm so frightened."

"Shhh, Celeste, don't be frightened. I have you now

and it's going to take more than a war to separate us. Forever is now ... and now is forever," he said softly as he enfolded her in his arms and bent to again capture her mouth with his. "This will be over soon and we will be together again."

"Will you promise me that, Wes? Promise me you'll come back to me safe."

"I will, love, I will."

She clung to him fiercely for a moment, then he held her a little away from him and in the depths of his eyes, she could see his hunger and need for her.

"Are you hungry?" he said softly.

"I'm hungry, Wes," she said gently, "but not for food ... only you."

She watched him smile in pleasure and slowly his eyes warmed as he again drew her to him.

The kiss began gently as he was aware of her uncertainty and fear. But it leaped to full desire when her lips parted beneath his and she pressed herself willingly against him.

He could hardly believe what he felt, that the slim sweet woman in his arms was filled with the same flame of desire that coursed through him.

Celeste was lost in the magic of the kiss, enclosed in the strength of his arms and willingly surrendering to the heated passion she sensed he was controlling.

With trembling fingers, Wes loosened the pins in her hair letting its glossy golden mass fall about her. He slid his fingers in it and savored the silken touch of it. Slowly he let his fingers drift to the laces that held her bound and loosened them. The gown fell unheeded at her feet.

He stared avidly at her slim golden beauty in the nearly transparent shift she wore. Touched by the firelight's glow, she was a vision that Wesley would carry with him forever.

"Celeste," he murmured, "you are so very beautiful. It's so hard to believe you belong to me. I'm afraid I'll wake up and find this is all a dream."

Her soft laugh touched him. Slim arms encircled his neck and a warm soft body was pressed against his.

"My love is real, my husband. So real I can hardly bear it. I love you, Wes."

The world faded from existence and they knew only each other and the burning mutual need they had to close away the future and live this short time they had to share.

She was dizzy with intoxicating kisses that touched her lips then randomly explored until they brought a sigh of intense pleasure. Blinded with a new and overwhelming sensation she closed her eyes and clung to him as he lifted her and carried her to the darkened room next to them.

He joined her on the bed and their bodies molded to each other breast to breast; thigh to thigh, straining to possess, to enclose each other. His hungry mouth followed his seeking hands that wanted to know all the lovely mystery of the woman who held him.

Celeste's love was a giving thing that made him nearly weep with joy. She gave in a sweet surrendering that lifted him beyond anything he had ever experienced before.

They cried out to each other in a language only the most fortunate of lovers shared. The language of pure and intense love.

She felt the shattering strength of him and held it, he felt the sweet surrender and clung to it. Their wildly beating hearts combined in the melody of their love and each breathless moment, each kiss each touch lifted them higher and higher until they were beyond all reason, all thought. Together they blended in a tempestuous completion that left them weakly clinging to each other in a careening world.

He held her sweat slicked body close to him, caressing her gently and kissing away the tears of love that touched her cheeks.

Slowly they regained their hold on reality.

Her head lay in the curve of his shoulder and her hair spilled lightly across his chest. He held her close with one arm while he absently caressed its silken strands. He could feel her warm breath on his neck as slowly it began to return to normal.

"Wes?" she whispered softly, so softly he could barely hear.

"What love?"

"I . . . I didn't disappoint you? I mean . . . I . . . I have always been afraid that when we were married I would be less than what you expected. I could not stand to lose your love."

Wesley rolled on his side pulling her beneath him. He smiled down into her eyes as he gently brushed stray hairs from her cheek.

"Celeste if you had been any more perfect, I would have died from the sheer pleasure of having you. You are all any fortunate man could want. I'm so very grateful you chose me. If I can I hope to keep your love forever like this."

She sighed contentedly and nestled against him like a warm affectionate kitten. For a while they talked of their future. They made plans for the day he would be home for good.

But conversation slowly faded from the path of renewed desire and they surrendered without hesitation or reservation. She was completely his in every way.

It was in the wee hours of the morning that her slow even breathing told him she slept. But it was a long time before sleep came to him.

They had talked of tomorrow, and of forever. But a small insistent fear touched him and he clung to her to help him fight it off ... would there be a tomorrow for them ... would there be a forever?

Twenty-five

Sherman was ready to move, and Alexander received his official orders to join Sherman's forces a few weeks before it began. A total of four armies were involved in this campaign.

The two of the Union forces were Meade's army of the Potomac and the army of the James. The latter was commanded by Major General Benjamin F. Butler, an incompetent officer, whom Grant would have very much liked to replace but whose appointment was a political necessity.

The overall plan was for Meade to advance southward toward Richmond while Butler came up the James River to attack from the southeast.

George was called back to join the forces that would attack from the southeast, but before he was called away from the area of High Oaks an event was to take place that would startle him completely and put a great deal of urgency in his return. He hoped to find Alexander as soon as possible and tell him a strange story about High Oaks and the heir to it.

It had started after Dan's late night visit to the small

gardener's cottage. He had slipped away long before dawn and without any Union soldiers ever being aware he had been there.

It was a pale gray dawn. Soft beams of early morning sun cut the air. It was a peaceful dawn, one of the very few remaining that High Oaks would see.

Catherine left the cottage; this time she locked the door behind her. She did not want to step within its walls again until Dan returned.

She walked slowly across the lawn that was still wet with dew. She was almost to the porch when she realized someone stood in the shadow of one of the huge pillars.

She stood perfectly still for a moment until he moved a little more into the light. George watched her hesitate, then walk toward him.

How beautiful she is he thought, and a pang of jealous anger held him at the man who possessed her heart. For one intense second he wished the phantom Dan Wakefield would be a casualty of the war. But as fast as the thought came, he pushed it aside. All that would be gotten from that would be a broken heart for Catherine, but he knew it would bring her no closer to him. The war had ripped apart the lives of everyone it touched. He remembered very well the arguments he had had with Alexander, and today was the first time he truly realized what Alexander had meant.

He stepped down the three steps that separated them and looked down into her wide violet eyes. He wanted to plead with her to pack what she had and come with him. He had fought too often not to know the violent disaster that was headed this way. But he knew she would smile . . . and refuse in the gentle way she had that stopped all his arguments.

High Oaks belonged to her man. Here he had left her and here he would find her when he returned.

"You're up early," she said as he stopped beside her.

"And you," he laughed as he motioned toward the small cottage. "My wayward young lady. Are you up early or coming home late."

"I'm afraid I fell asleep at the cottage and the time just fled."

"Catherine," he began.

She looked at him aware that he was going to tell her something that might make a difference in her life.

"What is it?"

"I've received orders to leave here."

"Where are you going?" she said, then she laughed, "I suppose that was very foolish of me. I'm sure you can't tell me."

"Well," he responded to her light laughter with a mild chuckle, "I can't tell you but it's because I'm not too sure myself where I'll end up. Catherine, I ... I don't suppose you or Mrs. Wakefield are going to take my advice."

"If it is to leave here, I'm sorry; Dan will be home one day. I want to be here."

"I'm afraid for the both of you. The Confederate army is moving this way. I'm sure there will be a confrontation somewhere near here. I would hate to see High Oaks be in the middle of it. But if it must be surely you can see the wisdom of your leaving."

"Wisdom," she repeated gently. "Has there really been any wisdom in all of this? No, we will stay here ... we will pray ... and we will wait."

"I envy him you know," he said softly. "I wish I had met you before you knew him. I wish I had you at home waiting for me. It would give a man incentive to lay aside his sword and stay comfortably at home."

"Thank you, George. I do hope everything goes well for you. Someday, when this is over come and visit us, I should like you to meet Dan. I think you two would get along despite your Yankee ways."

They laughed together for a moment. "I should like to meet him."

"When do you leave?"

"Tomorrow."

"When do you think . . ."

"The offensive will start . . . within two weeks, I would say."

"I will truly be sorry to see you go. I have felt you were a friend."

"I was supposed to conquer," he smiled, "but instead, I'm the conquered."

"Come," she replied, "let us share breakfast together."

He nodded, she took his arm and they walked inside.

He gave his orders after breakfast and the rest of the day he spent seeing that all preparations were cared for properly. That night, after Virginia had retired for the night, he sat with Catherine in the living room.

"Do you know Catherine, I've no idea what your Dan looks like."

"Wait," she said quickly. Then she rose and ran lightly up the steps. The only picture of Dan still at High Oaks was one in a locket that belonged to Catherine. The rest of the portraits like most of the valuable things at High Oaks had been sold long ago to pay for food and medicines.

She came back down the stairs carrying the locket.

When she reached his side, she snapped it open and handed it to him. His smile faded to stunned amazement when he looked at the picture. He had been prepared for anything but not for the officer in gray and gold whose smiling face was an exact copy of Alexander.

"My God, I don't believe this."

"What?"

"He . . . he looks so much like a friend of mine. The resemblance is astounding. If I didn't know better I would swear they were related."

On the other side of the open locket was a picture of Catherine, and George decided at that moment he would have it.

He handed the locket back to Catherine who closed it.

"My mother always used to say that everyone in the world had a double somewhere."

"Well, then, maybe I might still have the luck to run across your double some day. If I do, I will snatch her up without question."

"I shall miss your silver tongue about here. Until you came, I thought all Yankees were bloodthirsty ogres."

"Catherine, there's a lot of those on both sides. It's why I'm afraid for you."

"Don't be. We'll be all right. High Oaks is all the protection we need."

He wanted to argue with her but he knew it would be useless. He watched in silence as she wished him a good night and walked up the stairs.

The next morning he assembled his men on the front lawn of High Oaks. Both Catherine and Virginia stood on the porch to wish him goodbye.

"I've forgotten some papers," he said, and he left them on the porch and dashed up the steps. He knew he didn't have much time to do what he intended. He ran to Catherine's room. The locket lay on her dresser where she had left it the night before. There was no time to remove her picture so he grabbed up the entire locket and shoved it in his pocket, then he quickly returned to the porch.

He waved farewell to Catherine and Virginia, trying to control the worry he felt. He knew one thing for certain. When this war was over he fully intended to come back here. For two reasons; one, to make sure Catherine was all right and two, to meet the man who was the double for Alexander Dubonne for a dim suspicion had begun in the back of his mind and he wanted to look into it.

The immense house seemed lost and lonely when George had taken his men and gone. Both Virginia and Catherine watched and waited daily for any word of battles fought.

Three weeks went by. Weeks filled with an ominous quiet, then again the slow steady trickle of wounded and tired soldiers crossed High Oaks property, stopping for what help they could get and to share word of what was happening.

Again Catherine and Virginia were caught up in the tedious and overwhelming work.

Quite some distance from High Oaks a battle was taking place. A battle that would have a pronounced effect on the people of High Oaks.

Gregory Wakefield roused his men in the early morning light. They had been under enforced march most of the night, so, with very little sleep they made ready to meet the force of General Grant in a place appropriately called the Wilderness. General Grant hoped to get through the Wilderness without having to fight in that tangled mass of undergrowth. General Lee had, however, anticipated that the Union force would try this and marched to meet them.

The result was two days of furious and confused fighting under terrible conditions. It was impossible to see or to control the troop movements. The woods caught fire. Men fought blindly on unable to distinguish friend from foe, while the wounded perished in the flames.

Amid the shouts and screaming, the blistering heat and confusion Gregory did his best to keep his men under control but it was a lost cause. He would have drawn them back but could not see most of them.

A patch of white smoke cleared momentarily from a small section of sparse woods. It cleared at the exact moment that Gregory had chosen to cross it in search of three of his men he could not account for. He was less than half way across it, running low and dodging in a zigzag manner when a sharp pain in his leg caused him to fall forward to his knees. He rose again and started to run, but he was not to make the other side. A sharp excruciating pain in his chest slammed the breath from him. He staggered then fell. This time he remained still as a pool of blood seeped into the parched earth beneath him.

He was unaware, several hours later, of hands that lifted him. He was carried back behind the lines to a makeshift hospital that was more a scene from hell than the island of mercy its title proposed. There he lay over half a day before the overworked doctor had the time to see him.

He felt as if a heavy weight lay on his chest and his breathing was labored and painful.

During the hours he lay alone, he had much time to think. He demanded his mind dwell on something besides the almost unbearable pain ... and so he thought of High Oaks, of Virginia ... of the son he had stolen from another man.

Gregory was an extremely intelligent man and a very able leader. But he was a leader who knew he was defeated. He had known for a long time, but had stood as best he could and ignored the inevitable. Now he knew not only was time running out for the South, but time was running out for him as well. What filled him then was remorse for what he had done, and the deep urgent need to spend his last days at High Oaks.

He was treated by an overworked exhausted doctor who was too tired and too overwhelmed with the blood and death he was surrounded with to keep the truth from showing on his face.

For the first time in a long time Gregory Wakefield prayed. Not in fear of death, but to be allowed to find a way to the home and woman he loved. He did not want to buried here in this wilderness away from all he had known and loved.

He knew he could not even get to his feet let alone make the trip from the Wilderness to High Oaks. He needed help, and knew of no place he might turn except to the God he had not spoken to for a long time.

He spoke to the doctor about it and was rewarded by a broken unsteady laugh.

"There is nothing ah can do, Suh," he said, "if ah could find a way to send any of these boys home ah would. I'm sorry."

Despair held him, complete and utter despair. Never in his life had he felt so lost or so alone. He began to wonder, in his fevered state, if this was some brand of punishment for the sin he had committed. To take away a son from a man was a terrible thing, to lie to the boy and to someone he loved as he had to Virginia was another. He owed a debt both to Jules Dubonne and his family, and to Dan. "Dante," he said softly, "he is Dante Dubonne and he deserves the truth. He deserves the right to make his own choices. A right I never truly gave him."

His fever burned, and he clung with agonized tenacity to life and hope that somehow he would be able to find a way to be taken home.

He had no sense of time and could not tell how long he had been there. Pain and fever had darkened days to nights, and yet he clung to life, much to the surprise of the doctor who had given him up long ago and only waited for him to die to replace him in the bed by another wounded.

Gregory blinked his weary eyes open as a dark form bent over him. It was the blurred wavy pattern of a huge dark man that refused to come into focus until a gentle hand touched him and an even gentler voice spoke.

"Mistah Wakefield . . . Mistah Wakefield, suh."

The familiar voice seeped into his mind and with it came a name. He smiled and whispered gratingly with labored breath.

"Jessie!"

"Yassuh, Mistah Gregory," the voice sounded happier now. "It's me, Jessie."

"Jessie," he gasped, "what in the hell are you doing here."

"Ah's fightin' suh, same as you," came the surprising answer.

357

Gregory tried to laugh, but the pain brought an uncontrolled groan of agony.

"Fighting for what? You fighting for slavery, Jessie."

Jessie chuckled, then his voice became warm with quiet affection.

"No, suh, ah's fightin fo' what ah loves. Yo, Mrs. Virginia, and High Oaks. The only thing in this world ah'd want to protect 'sides dat boy of ours."

Tears Gregory could not control ran down his gaunt cheeks. He reached blindly and felt a surge of strength as a hard solid hand took his.

"Jessie," he ground out in an agonized sob, "I've got to go home."

"Ain't no way, suh, you cain't get yoself outah dat bed."

"Jessie, please. You've got to help me find a way. Jessie, I don't want to die here, not here among strangers. I want to be at High Oaks."

"Mistah Gregory ..."

"I've got to right a wrong, Jessie. Don't let me die with it on my soul. I'll burn in hell for it. Please Jessie ... please help me. I want to go home."

"Ah'll try suh. Yo rest easy. Ah'll try."

Jessie's dark form receded as Gregory sank into an exhausted state of half consciousness.

Jessie walked from Gregory's side determined to find a way to take him home.

It took Jessie another day to steal an officer's horse and hide it away, and yet another day to find a broken down old carriage that had been abandoned at a nearby farm.

When he made makeshift equipment to harness the horse to the carriage he brought it to the front of the hospital and informed the doctor he was there to take Gregory home.

The doctor was somewhat relieved for Gregory was dying anyhow and he had to think of the living.

It took six men to get Gregory into the carriage, not one of whom had the slightest bit of optimism that either of them would ever make it back to High Oaks.

Jessie was a man who had lived off the land and struggled against adversity all his life. He knew the way to High Oaks along back roads and through seemingly inpenetrable areas, and he used every ounce of knowhow he had.

At night he found fresh water and cleaned Gregory's wound as best he could. He scavenged for food, and slowly ... slowly they came closer and closer to High Oaks ... to home.

Gregory dwelt in a dark land of fever and pain. Often he rambled and he spoke of High Oaks. He called for Virginia and spoke to her lovingly as if she were there. He told of all that had happened and Jessie listened with a heart filled with pain at the anguish in Gregory's soul. He knew that Gregory's mind would not be at peace until he had told the truth to Virginia and Dan.

His ancestry had handed down to Jessie a deeply superstitious nature. He felt, deep in his heart, that Gregory was only able to cling to life because God wanted him to be able to leave behind the burden he had carried for so many years.

Grimly, he moved along. Determined to get Gregory home.

Often he sat on the carriage seat, moving slowly along, with tears blinding his own eyes. He remembered the beauty of High Oaks, the happiness of the family that lived there. He thought of all the beauty that was now past and would never be again.

He wondered, too, how Virginia Wakefield would accept the news that she had lost all ... High Oaks, Gregory, and the son he knew she had loved beyond ... he felt ... more than he thought was normal.

He remembered, before Dan had come, her tenuous hold on sanity after the loss of her children. If Dan were taken away from her now, after the shock of everything else, and told she was to let him go to another family, another mother, would she retain the hold she had, or would this be the last blow that would claim her mind?

The mind of a woman he respected and admired, or the soul of the man he loved. The choice was one of unbearable weight and he bore it with a feeling of deep misery.

The area about them became recognizable, and he knew he was now on High Oaks property.

No matter what he had heard he was still shocked to see the overgrown fields, the broken fences, and finally the total disaster of the shell of a house that was once the most beautiful plantation in the area. He was glad that Gregory could not see the disaster that had struck down all that had taken him a lifetime to build.

Someone must have seen him turn up the drive, for the door opened and a woman stepped out on the porch. As he drew closer he could see it was Virginia Wakefield. His heart was a leaden lump in his breast as he stopped the carriage by the porch and their eyes met.

Twenty-six

Virginia Wakefield had knelt by the small graves for over an hour, but she did not heed the time. She felt an almost unbearable tiredness, as if she no longer even wanted to breathe.

It had been nearly two months since any word of Dan had come and longer still word from Gregory.

"Where was this terrible Wilderness in which they were going to fight?" she wondered.

She gazed at the small graves and read the names on the worn stone slowly. If only Dan and Gregory were home everything would be all right. What did it matter the destruction about her? Gregory and Dan would change all that.

She smiled to herself. Catherine ... Catherine was here. When Dan came home she would marry him and they would have children. Again, she had often in the past few weeks, she heard the happy laughter of children surround her. She allowed herself, as she had often in the past few weeks, to drift into a euphoric world where the tragedy of war no longer existed and everything was alive with the bright glow of happiness.

Catherine stood on the back veranda of High Oaks and watched Virginia. She was frightened of the change in Virginia. She prayed for some word from Gregory or Dan that was the only thing that seemed to retrieve Virginia from the far away world she seemed to exist in lately.

There had been no word for weeks. Often, in the distance they could hear the muted roar of cannon and sometimes even sporadic gunfire. But no one had come near High Oaks. She was afraid to leave High Oaks and the small amount of protection it afforded, for a strange new adversary had been spawned by the war ... the scavenger. They had two small hand guns and some ammunition, and once had driven away a rather evil looking man who, she felt, would have done more than steal if given a chance.

She watched Virginia stand and slowly walk down the path toward the house. She turned and went inside her room, crossed it and walked down the long bare hall. She was halfway down the stairs when Virginia came to the bottom. "Catherine," she smiled up at her. "Are you still searching for that locket?"

Catherine remained calm and smiled, but it had been weeks since she had told Virginia about the missing locket.

She felt sure George had taken it, and had said so to Virginia. It alarmed her that Virginia refused to acknowledge the fact that any Union soldiers had been at High Oaks at all. Again the fear struck her that Virginia seemed to be losing her hold on reality more and more.

"No ... I ... I found it," she lied. "I had just foolishly misplaced it."

"That's good dear. I'm sure Dan would be upset if

you lost it. It was your engagement picture."

Again Catherine was jolted by the phantoms Virginia insisted on believing in, but she agreed with another strained smile.

Catherine was about to speak again when they heard the sound of something approaching the house. It was so strange to hear any such thing that for a moment they just stood and looked at each other. Then Virginia regained herself quickly.

"Run and get the gun Catherine," she commanded.

Catherine spun about and ran up the steps to her room. From a drawer in her dresser she withdrew the gun and ran back down the steps. She came out on the porch in time to see Jessie bring the horse to a halt.

"Jessie!" Virginia said happily. "It is good to see you. Are you well?"

"Yessum," he said and Catherine was the first to be alarmed at the solemn look on his face.

"Jessie . . . ?"

"Miz Wakefield," he said gently, "I done brought Mistah Gregory home."

Virginia's eyes moved to the carriage and her face turned pale. For a minute Jessie thought she was going to faint and he jumped quickly down. But Virginia shook off his hand and ran to the carriage.

"Gregory!" she moaned softly. Her eyes filled with tears as she reached out and touched his pale thin face. He was unconscious, had been for the last ten miles.

"Jessie, help me get him inside. We must do something."

"Miz Wakefield . . . dey ain't nuthin' yo' or me kin do," He said the words gently and was quite unprepared for Virginia's wild anger-filled face as she turned on him.

"Don't say that! Don't you ever say that! You lift him gently and bring him in the house."

Neither Catherine or Jessie said a word as Virginia turned and walked to the door.

"Hurry, or I'll have you whipped, you hear, hurry!"

Jessie's eyes met Catherine's and he saw the sadness there. Slowly he turned and climbed into the carriage. Gently he lifted Gregory in his massive arms and carried him into the house. Virginia moved ahead of him to the bedroom.

He laid Gregory on the bed and was immediately ordered by Virginia to fetch hot water and cloth for bandages. She was gently removing Gregory's filthy clothes as he left and closed the bedroom door behind him.

Catherine had stood in the hall, now they looked at each other.

"How long has she been like this?"

"It's been happening for a long time, ever since Gregory left, sometimes she has lucid days, even weeks, then she slips away again. This is the worst it's been," Catherine answered tiredly.

"He's dyin', Miss Catherine. There ain't nothin' no body kin do about it. He's only been holdin' on 'cause he wanted to die here at High Oaks, and he wanted to be with her."

"Oh, Jessie, I'm frightened. What will happen to her?"

"I doan know. They ain't nobody but God knows dat. We just stay with her. When he's gone she'll need our help."

Catherine nodded silently and they walked down the stairs to carry out Virginia's orders.

For two days more, Gregory hovered near death. It

was the third night that he opened his eyes to reality and saw Virginia seated on the edge of his bed holding his hand.

Jessie lay asleep in the far corner of the room for he had kept a vigil for nearly forty-eight hours. Catherine was asleep in the next room.

"Ginny," he rasped. She smiled with tears in her eyes.

"You haven't called me that since we were courting, Gregory. How sweet it sounds to hear you say it again."

She lifted his hand and pressed her lips to it and let her tears fall warm on his skin.

"Ginny, don't cry. I'm home?"

"Yes, my love, you're home, and I've no need for tears anymore."

"I love you, Ginny . . . more than anything in this world I love you."

"I know . . . I know," she sobbed.

Gregory realized the absence of pain, and felt it strange that everything seemed bathed in a soft golden glow. He had never seen Virginia look so beautiful in all the years they had been together. He knew she would understand what he had to say . . . and what he felt they had to do.

"Ginny, I must tell you something."

"Yes, love?"

"You must understand."

"Anything, Gregory."

"I've committed a terrible sin, and you are the only one who can help me."

"I will do anything you ask my dear."

"I lied to you."

"What?"

"I lied to you, all those years ago."

"I don't understand. What did you lie to me about?"

"About Dante."

"Dan?"

"No . . . Dante. He's Dante Dubonne."

"Oh Gregory. He has forgotten that long ago. Why do you say that now. He has no one but us. The adoption was legal. He's Dan Wakefield, and he's happy to be so."

"No . . . no . . . you see. I knew his family was alive. I traced them. They still live. He has parents, a brother and sister. He was never ours to take."

Something huge and dark shook her world to its foundations, and she felt as if she were being smothered by the thick blackness of it.

"No," she murmured softly.

"It is true. I have proof. You must get it and give it to him. Our world is destroyed. Dante must have the chance to start a new life for himself."

She could not speak, and Gregory mistook it for acquiescence.

"Ginny, you must help me. I cannot live with this guilt any longer. I cannot deny Dante what should be his. Please, Ginny . . . please."

"What do you want me to do?" she said the words in a quiet voice.

"Under the floorboards by my desk there is a tin box. In it is all the proof he will need. It has the address of his family and where he can find them. Give it to Dan when he comes home. Have him take you with him. There is no life at High Oaks anymore."

She looked at him with eyes wide with the burning terror she felt inside. Some great dark force was trying to take her son from her. She had to do something to stop it or she knew she would die.

"I . . . I will do what must be done."

"Promise me," he said weakly.

"I promise you," she replied quietly.

Relief seemed to wash all the strength from his body. He lay spent on the huge bed and Virginia sat very still. There was a screaming silence in the room, and as the stars began to disappear one by one and the gray mist of dawn began to rise, Gregory Wakefield died. He clung to Virginia's hand, his guilt washed from him, feeling he had finally righted the wrong that had been a heavy burden all the years.

Virginia cried silently, tears slipping down her cheeks to touch the cold hand she held in hers. Slowly she bent forward and closed the sightless eyes. Then she brushed a kiss against his cold lips.

She rose and quietly walked from the room without waking Jessie.

She went downstairs to Gregory's study. Where the desk had once stood she knelt on the floor and searched with her fingers for the loose floorboard. She found it and pulled it up revealing the tin box that sat in the dark recess. Slowly she lifted it and walked to the fireplace. There were still red embers in it from the evening fire Jessie had built. She sat in front of it and opened the box.

She read every word of what was written on the papers within. Then with slow deliberation she tore each one in two. Piece by piece she fed them into the fire and watched closely making sure each piece was completely burnt.

When it was finished she sat for a long time and

stared into the fire, satisfied that no one would ever know the secret she held. Dan was hers, and she would let no power on this earth take him from her.

Again she began to weep, slow bitter tears.

"I'm sorry Gregory. I love you and I'm sorry. Even if you can never forgive me, I cannot let him go. He is all I have left . . . oh, Gregory, he is all I have left."

Jessie woke with a quick start. He sat up and looked toward the bed. He knew the moment he saw the still form that Gregory had gone from them. He felt a deep burning sadness at the passing of a good man.

It was only after he rose and walked to the bed to assure himself it was true that he missed Virginia. It surprised him that she was no longer at Gregory's side. He began to worry about her mental condition. If she had been beside Gregory when he died her mind might have finally slipped beyond help.

He went to Catherine's door and knocked. When she appeared she was bleary-eyed from deep exhausted sleep.

"Jessie?"

"He's gone, Miz Catherine. I doan know zactly when. Sometime in the night. You gotta come with me."

"Virginia?"

"I'm fraid fo' her Miz Catherine. She was with him when I fell asleep."

"Where is she now?"

"I doan know."

"We'd best go find her."

They went down the stairs and looked in every room. Jessie was the one who saw the torn up floor board and the empty box that sat beside the now dead fire.

" 'Pears she was burnin' somethin'," he said, a puzzled

frown between his eyes.

"Jessie, I'm frightened for her, we must find her."

Jessie turned and looked at her. "I 'spect we both know where she is."

"The cemetery?"

He nodded. Without another word they left the room. They went out the back door and from where they stood they could see Virginia standing on the hill where she had so often stood before. They looked at each other and without speaking they started up the hill.

They came to Virginia's side. She stood, with her shawl wrapped tight about her as if it helped to contain the deep grief she felt.

"Miz Wakefield," Jessie said gently. She turned her head to look at Jessie. She smiled, and the smile made Catherine shiver as if a cold hand touched her.

"Jessie," Virginia said softly, "you must bury him here, beside our children."

"Yessum," he replied but Catherine could see he was shaken by this cool tearless response.

"Dan will come home soon. He will want to come here to see where his father lies. We must take care of everything."

"Virginia," Catherine said as she laid her hand on Virginia's arm. "Come back to the house and lie down for a few minutes. You need some rest."

Virginia smiled again, the strange ethereal smile. "No, Catherine. We must see that Gregory is dressed properly. Everything must be done right. Jessie, I want you to make the coffin immediately."

"Yessum," he replied, but his anguished gaze was locked on Catherine. He could not understand this tearless woman and he was afraid of what he could not see but could feel like a strong current.

"Go, Jessie," Catherine replied, "I'll take care of her."

Jessie nodded. He turned and walked down the hill. It took him some time to find enough material to make the coffin. It was over three hours before he had it put together. In this time Virginia and Catherine had washed Gregory and dressed him in his uniform.

Jessie came in to tell them he had the coffin ready.

"Bring it in here, Jessie," Virginia said.

"Yessum."

Jessie carried the box in and set it beside the bed. Carefully Virginia lined the box with her shawl. Together they lifted Gregory and laid him in it and Catherine and Jessie stood and watched while Virginia carefully wrapped him. Then she placed a warm blanket over him as if she were afraid he might get cold.

"I done dug the grave Miz Wakefield," Jessie said. "I'll carry him up now."

Both Jessie and Catherine felt a moment of sheer panic when Virginia replied in a calm voice.

"Maybe we had best wait for Dan to come home. A son should be here when his father is buried."

Catherine held back the gasp of shock. She gathered her wits quickly.

"Dan won't be home for some time, Virginia. We must show proper respect for Gregory. I'm sure Dan would be the first to understand. He is a good son and will be here as soon as he can. He would want you to go on and do what is right."

"Of course," Virginia said calmly, "go on, Jessie."

Jessie hefted the coffin to his shoulder as if its weight were nothing. Both Catherine and Virginia followed him slowly up the hill. With a gentleness born of love he eased the coffin into the grave he had dug.

Then he stood, unsure if he should begin to put the dirt in.

Virginia knelt and lifted a handful of dirt and slowly dropped it into the grave. It rattled sharply against the wood.

"Goodbye for now, Gregory, my love, you rest on High Oaks and Dan and I shall be here always to protect it. I love you, Gregory."

The words were said so softly that Catherine could barely hear them.

Virginia turned away from the open grave and Catherine joined her as she walked slowly down the hill.

"We'll go and wait for Dan, Catherine," she said. "He'll be home soon and High Oaks will be happy again for this time he will never . . . never go away again."

Jessie heard these words and felt a depth of sorrow he had never felt in the worst moments of his life for he knew High Oaks had lost both master and mistress this day.

Slowly he lifted the shovel and began to shovel the dirt back into the grave. Each thud seemed to echo the dark gloom that had descended on the world.

"Dat boy come home he gonna have a hard thing to face. He been strong all his life, I sho hopes he come home with enough strength left to face all this losin'. Lawd, iffen yo gwine to look down on dat boy do it now when he has all dis blackness to face."

He shoveled slowly and methodically. When he finished he stood looking at the mount of fresh earth, then brushing the blinding tears he turned and left Gregory Wakefield in peace with his beloved High Oaks.

Twenty-seven

At a place called Cold Harbor, Grant ordered a frontal assault on Lee's entrenchments. His men knew it was suicidal; and, the night before, they sat up calmly writing their names and addresses on slips of paper and pinning them to their coats so that their dead bodies might be recognized on the field.

War-weariness and depression spread over the land. The very appearance of the armies in the field reflected the fatigue. Gone were the fine uniforms, the epaulettes, the shining sabers. The picture-book war was over.

The men looked dirty and tired and toiled along in loose columns and were remarkable for a most wonderful collection of old felt hats in every stage of dilapidation. Their clothes were torn, dusty, and shabby. They fought as loyally and as doggedly as ever, but the glamour was gone. War had become a grim unending business of slaughter.

George sat with several men about a low burning fire. It was late at night and the conversation had slowed to an occasional question and a softly muttered reply.

He sat with Catherine's small gold locket in his hand and gazed at the face at which he would never tire of looking. She smiled serenely back at him. As always he allowed his mind to fabricate his own personal dream. She was his and she waited for his return. He would allow the fantasy to go only so far and then he let Dan's level gaze draw him back to reality. It did no good to allow his dreams to carry him too far.

He wondered what she was doing now. Occasionally, he wondered if Dan Wakefield sat with the Confederates less than 10 miles from them. There was even a moment he lost the battle for control and envisioned Dan as a fatality in the soon-to-come conflict.

He still could not believe the resemblance between Dan Wakefield and Alexander. It was a thing he intended to tell Alexander about as soon as he saw him again. He would show him the picture in the locket. Maybe when the war was over, they could go back to High Oaks. He had a deep suspicion that somehow Dan and Alexander were related.

He snapped the locket shut and put it in his breast pocket. He spread his blanket just out of range of the light and the fire. He lay on his back with his hands folded behind his head and watched the stars begin to appear one by one.

He allowed his mind to drift back, back to the days he had been the gallant cavalier in blue. He laughed in pity at his own foolishness and remembered how Alexander had felt about war. It had been a hard and bitter lesson for him, but he knew now his feelings about war were somewhat the same as Alexander's had been. It was another thing he promised himself to talk to Alexander about. He had had enough of the touch of war, and when it was over, he intended to leave the military. He knew it would not make his father very happy, but he knew he was sick to death of the brutality and bloodshed he had seen.

He was about to drift into sleep when he heard his name called. He sat up.

"Over here!" he called.

He couldn't make out the identity of the man who walked toward him until he crossed beside the fire.

"Wes! What the hell are you doing out here? I thought you were with Cable's outfit."

"Was till four weeks ago. Got transferred out here. Looks like they expect a lot to happen around here in a few days."

"God, I haven't seen you since . . . I don't even remember the last time."

"It's been a long time," Wes laughed. "I heard you were here so I decided to look you up. I've been searching for you all day."

"Have you seen Alexander lately?"

"He was home last time I was."

"He all right?"

"Pretty much so the last time I saw him."

"Mr. and Mrs. Dubonne, they're all right?"

"Yep."

"And," George laughed, "the beautiful Celeste, has she found another handsome civilian to squire her around while you're gone."

"She better not have," Wes laughed in response. "She's wearing my wedding ring. I'm afraid I'd have to shoot one civilian dead."

"Married! I'll be..." he reached to shake Wes' hand. "Congratulations, you lucky son of a gun. How'd you manage that? I thought her parents would never let her go."

"My absolute charm and irresistibility," Wes grinned.

George made a derisive sound.

"I was ready to get down on my knees and beg, but it was Alexander who turned the tables, of course, he threatened my life at the same time," Wes added.

"You're in a good position," George chuckled.

"No problem. Treating Celeste good is about the easiest thing I've ever had to do in my life. When this thing is over I'm going to spend the rest of my life doing everything in my power to keep her happy."

"Yeah... if this thing is ever over. I'm beginning to wonder if we've all died and this is the everlasting hell old Rev. Thomas told us we'd be livin' in if we didn't mend our ways."

"They're dug in pretty good over there."

"They are. I expect we'll attack in the morning."

They remained silent for several moments, each one visioning the next day's battle.

"George?"

"Yeah?"

"You've had a lot of military training, been in a lot of battles."

"Yes."

"You ever get scared?"

"Me!... hell yes. Sometimes I wondered if anyone next to me could hear my teeth chatter. Why, did you think you were alone?"

375

"Kinda."

"Everybody's scared Wes . . . everybody."

"Yeah, I guess so," he rose. "I'll see you in the morning, George. Good night."

"Wes . . ." George said, but Wes had already turned and was walking away.

After a few minutes, George rolled again in his blanket and slept.

It was long before dawn when the camp was stirred awake and began to prepare to attack the Confederate fortifications.

George looked for Wes for a while but couldn't find him, then after a while there was too much confusion and too much for him to do to search any longer.

He put it aside promising to find him when the battle was over. He made all his preparations and was ready to move his men at the order. He sat on his horse, and wondered why . . . this time . . . he felt no fear . . . no fear at all. The bugle sounded the charge. The charging cheer rang out loudly. The line of blue clad soldiers rushed forward and the Confederate pickets emptied their rifles, jumped from their rifle pits and ran back toward their main line which was still silent except the artillery. This was severed rapidly . . . the line of blue swept on, in good order, cheering loudly and continuously. They drew near the Confederate earthworks. Cannon cut gaps in the ranks. Then the heads of Lee's infantry rose above the entrenchments, and the Union soldiers could see the glint of sun on their polished rifle barrels. A cloud of smoke curled along the works and the blue clad warriors began to tumble in large numbers.

The field grew hazy with smoke. Rifles were tossed high in the air. Battle flags went down with a sweep to again appear and plunge into the smoke. Wounded men straggled out of the battle ... the fire grew steadily fiercer and fiercer ... the day drew to a close ... night settled down, and the fight still went on.

The Confederate fire was murderous and slowly the Union force was driven back and the assault was abandoned.

It was early dawn and the rising white mist covered the ground. It was a seething hell of groaning, moaning wounded.

Men searched for wounded friends, sometimes finding them alive and sometimes finding them dead. Either way, they were lifted gently and carried behind the lines.

Wes sat with his back braced against a tree. A dark stain on the sleeve of his left arm spoke eloquently of a wound that caused him to grit his teeth in pain. He was too weak from the loss of blood to move and he wondered with an almost detached feeling, if he would bleed to death before someone came to help.

The sun was nearly overhead when he was found. His head spun dizzily and he groaned as he was lifted and carried to where a doctor could examine him.

Once it was cleaned and bound and the bleeding was stopped, his wound became at least bearable.

"You won't be hugging any pretty girls along the way, but it'll take you home, boy," the doctor smiled at him and passed on.

It was toward early evening, and Wes sat beside a small campfire. He recognized the young soldier that was walking toward him as one of George's men. When the man spotted Wes he moved quickly in his direction. He knelt on the ground beside Wes.

"Hi, Lyman. Good to see you made it."

"Thanks, I've been sent to find you."

"Sent, by whom?"

"Lt. McClellan . . . he's been hit."

Wes' eyes searched the others and the truth was evident in them.

"Bad?"

"Yes . . . real bad. He wants to see you."

"Lyman . . . is he . . . ?"

"He's dyin' if that's what you mean." Lyman said bitterly. "One of the best officers we ever had, and one fine man." He spat. "This God damn war is goin' to last forever."

Wes got to his feet without another word and followed Lyman through the debris and bodies. After quite some time they came to a hastily pitched tent around which sat several men in absolute silence.

"He's inside," Lyman said softly. "You best go in. I don't think he has much time and there seems to be something important he wants to say to you."

Wes nodded, then he inhaled a deep breath, pushed aside the flap of the tent and stepped inside.

Several blankets padded the ground and George lay on them covered with several more. Wes could hear his heavy raspy breathing. He went to his side and knelt on the ground beside him.

"George . . . George it's me, Wes. You wanted to talk to me?"

George's eyes opened heavily, as if it took all the effort he had. Slowly they focused on Wes' face.

"Wes . . . ?"

"Yes, I'm here. Is there something you want me to do?" Tears stung his eyes and he licked dry lips.

"Letters . . . in my . . . pocket."

"All right George. Rest easy, the doctor will . . ."

No . . . no time . . . the letters . . . some for my parents . . . one for Catherine Markland. When this is over . . . you see . . . she gets it."

"I don't know her, George. Tell me where to find her. I'll take the letter to her personally."

"High Oaks . . . plantation . . . Dan Wakefield . . . Virginia."

"I'll take care of it."

"Wes . . . in my pocket," he motioned feebly to his breast pocket. Wes reached for him and took out the locket.

"Catherine . . . give the . . . locket to Alexander . . . tell him . . . go . . . High Oaks . . . something he should. . . ." The words remained unfinished and George's breath rattled to a rasping halt. Wes held his own breath in agony waiting for the next one . . . it never came.

Wes remained quiet for a moment, then he reached into George's other pocket and took out the letters. Two were addressed to his parents, one to Alexander, and one to Catherine Markland, High Oaks Plantation.

"I swear, George, I'll see they get these. I swear to God, George I'll see they get them.

Slowly he rose, put the letters in his pocket. He looked at the locket in his hand, but at this moment grief held him and he did not have the courage to open the locket and look at the face of the girl whose name had been the last one George had spoken.

He put the locket in his pocket and left the tent.

The men surrounding the tent looked at him questioningly, but he shook his head negatively. Then without another word, he walked away.

Wes was given leave to go home until his wound was healed, but there was no means of transportation in existence. Each man had to fend for himself.

It was over a week before Wes could get a ride on a supply wagon that was going his direction. It took him less then half the way where he lost three more days trying to find another ride.

In short jumps he finally made it to within twenty miles of Philadelphia. From there he had to walk. His wound, uncared for from the day after the battle had begun to give him a great deal of trouble. By the time he reached the outskirts of Philadelphia he was running a fever that made his ears buzz and caused him to stumble often as he walked.

It was Celeste that was uppermost in his mind. When he felt himself weakening he concentrated only on one thing. Celeste was near, Celeste would ease the pain and the loneliness, Celeste . . . Celeste . . . Celeste.

He staggered to the door of his own house without really knowing where he was. The world spun about him and pain sliced through his body which burned with fever.

He did not know that he had to lean against the door frame to pound feebly on the door for he could not seem to find the handle.

The world slipped away from him and he sagged to his knees as the door swung open. He looked up into

Celeste's wide shocked eyes, murmured her name softly and fell forward. It was the last thing he would remember until nearly a week later.

Celeste gave a small cry of surprise and fell on her knees beside Wes. "Wes!" she cried as she lifted his head to rest against her.

He seemed to hear her voice but he did not have control over his body. He did not know he responded to her urging and regained his feet. She got him to their bedroom where he collapsed across the bed and let total darkness overtake him.

Celeste had never seen any man in the condition Wesley was in now. She did not panic, but set about taking the filthy vermin infested clothes from him. She had difficulty with his large frame, but after a while she had the clothes in a pile she intended to burn immediately.

She heated water and bathed him, then forced a half of a glass of straight bourbon past his lips.

Once she had the wound cleaned, and had his feverish body bathed and safely between the blankets he seemed to rest easier, but it was a long time before he stopped calling her name over and over and fell into a deep heavy sleep.

She had gone through the pockets of his clothes before she had burnt them. She laid the letters aside, admired the locket for a few minutes and wondered it if were a gift for her. Then she laid it aside for the top priority now was Wes' health. She would ask him about the locket later.

She sent a message both to Wes' parents and to hers. They came immediately.

Though they helped her every way they could they could not get her to leave his side as long as the fever raged.

She would speak softly to him as he thrashed about the bed. She bathed him again and again in cool water and kept him clean and warm.

Hour after hour she kept a vigil. But on the third day she was in a state of complete exhaustion. She could not understand why, though the fever was going down, he seemed to be calling out for something and reaching for some unknown thing.

She was so tired, and her eyes felt heavy and burned like fire. She listened to Wes' incessant mumbling and heard him move on the bed.

She went to the side of the bed and lay beside him.

His good arm came about her and she was shocked with the force of it as he drew her against him. Then, suddenly, she understood, for he sighed deeply and his body became still. He held her close, and soon his breathing was calm and normal as his body and mind drifted into deep relaxing sleep. She too could not keep her eyes open any longer. When her mother came in to check on them later she found them quietly and peacefully asleep in each other's arms. Silently she tiptoed from the room and closed the door softly behind her.

It was to a bright sunlit room that Wes opened his eyes much later.

Celeste was seated on a chair beside his bed. She came to him immediately and took his hand in hers. They smiled at each other, unable to say any words that could describe how they felt.

She forced him to eat some warm soup, and when he had obediently done so and was contentedly resting again she began to question him.

He told her about the battle, his wound and George's death. Then he told her about the locket.

"I'm supposed to give it to Alexander the next time I see him. Then I'm to tell him to go to High Oaks Plantation."

"Why?"

"I don't know. It's something to do with the locket and a girl named Catherine."

"Can I open it, Wes?"

"I don't see why not. It can't do any harm to look, can it?"

She went to the dresser and picked up the locket. When she opened it her smile faded and her face turned pale.

"Celeste?"

She went to him and handed him the locket. He stared in surprise and profound disbelief at the face of Alexander . . . in a Confederate uniform.

Twenty-eight

Abby was completely amazed at the Countess' ability for survival. Not only survival but the ability to find the best wherever she went.

Assured that they would run into all kinds of difficulty crossing the lines, it was the Countess who handled everything.

She disappeared one morning, then returned late in the afternoon with official passes to go South without question. The passes were for the Countess and her retinue. Abby then became a maid in her household, a maid who could not speak English.

The search for Abby had been intense, so the Countess provided her with a gold blonde wig and the costume of a maid. She kept herself in the background each time they ran across a patrol of Union soldiers.

It amused her that they flirted shamelessly with her while they talked among themselves about the escaped spy for which they were to keep watch.

Yvonne flirted herself, mostly to gain information about where the spy was most closely watched for ... these were the routes they by-passed, choosing much safer and less travelled roads.

Abby seemed drawn by the fierce need to stand on the soil of Fernhill. She wanted to go home. Somehow she deluded herself into believing when she was home it would ease the hollow loneliness within her and fill the darkness in her heart.

Yvonne knew this wasn't so and knew also that Abby's thoughts and emotions were held not by some place but by someone.

They had finally crossed the last barrier of Union lines and were on Southern soil. Abby discarded her disguise and breathed a sigh of relief. There was continual and devastating evidence of the war all around them. Fields left to overgrow, houses deserted and some destroyed.

Each one she saw shattered Abby's reserve a little more. As familiar territory came into view a whole new fear gripped Abby. Would she find Fernhill intact? Or would it be in the same condition she had seen some of the others.

Yvonne had been watching her closely as they travelled. Constantly she had shrewdly dodged Abby's continual questions about why she should be travelling with a known rebel spy to a nearly defeated South.

As they neared Fernhill Abby again asked her, and this time she received an answer ... such as it was.

"It is a terrible thing this making of war, is it not?" the Countess said softly as her eyes scanned a particularly ravaged area. "I can remember ..." Abby began, then she let the words die unspoken.

"You can remember what, Abby?"

"This land when it was beautiful . . . so very beautiful."

"You must have had a wonderful childhood here."

"Yes, I did. Maybe that's why I believe you must cling to the land you love, the home you love. It is important to have such roots to hold you."

"More important than anything else?" the Countess asked softly.

Abby was silent for a minute, then she said, "Yes."

"Do you honestly believe that?"

"I . . . I must."

"Why must you . . . or have you already been faced with a choice?"

"I don't know what you're talking about. I came home because it is just that . . . my home. I have done much to try to protect it. Once I was no longer effective I had no other choice but to return."

"Abby . . . I will tell you something I have not told many other people. It is not a place that gives you joy and peace. It is the people who share it with you. No matter where you are if you are with people who care for you, love you, you will be happy. I have been to the very best, and I have known the very worst, and each time I remember with love it is a person, not a place."

Abby's eyes darkened with pain and she remained silent.

"If," the Countess continued, "I had a choice of where to spend the rest of my life, I would rather have a cottage with the man I love than a mansion filled with loneliness and anger."

"Are you saying I should forget the place in which I was born?"

"If it is destroyed Abby . . . will it destroy you?"

"Destroy me—how?"

"Fill you with hatred and anger. Turn your mind to vengeance."

"Should one surrender completely to the enemy?"

"Enemy?" the Countess said softly. "Are there many, or is there only one."

"I cannot turn back," Abby whispered.

"Tell me something cherie, it has puzzled me from the first moment we met."

"What?"

"Why you were where you were, and why you were not caught with your father."

Abby remained silent for some time.

"Do you not trust me with that answer? I feel we are friends who can speak plainly to each other."

"It is a part of the story that is too painful to remember."

"But you do remember, every day I see it in your eyes. I would help you, cherie. I have known a love for one man, a man I had to leave."

Abby turned to look at the Countess.

"I had to make a choice. I had given my word of honor to a cause. I could not just walk away from that. My father gave his life for it. Could I forget that? I . . . I want to go home."

"To see if it was worth it? To find if you had made the right choice? To prove to someone that you are so strong you do not need him or anyone else."

"He was a Yankee!"

"But you loved him?"

"No! No! He was the enemy. I had no right to love

him. I could not give him all of myself. I was a traitor! A traitor! I lay in a Yankee's arms while my father died for all he believed in.''

"Ah," the Countess said gently. "And so now we are a martyr for your father's life. You atone for a sin . . . even if that sin was only loving.''

"I had no right.''

"You had every right! A man is not just a Yankee or a Rebel, he is not just North or South, he is not just friend or enemy. If you love you love for no reason except it was meant to be.''

"What do you know!" Abby said angrily as tears touched her eyes.

"I shall tell you what I know, cherie," she said gently. "I was born so desperately poor that I thought money was the only safety. Like your Fernhill, money was my strength and sanctuary. I met a man and loved him desperately . . . but he was poor also. I met another who offered me all the wealth I would ever want. But after two years of marriage to him I found out what hell could be like. You see, he had bought me . . . and he never let me forget it. Then, he died and left me all his money. I thought I would find the one I loved and be happy. But you see . . . he would not be bought, and he no longer trusted me. He left me and went to someone else who had a free and honest love to give. Cherie, go to your Fernhill, then think if what you have given up is worth the sacrifice.''

Abby closed her eyes and pulled the shawl she wore tighter about her. She remained silent now and gazed quietly at the abandoned land about her. Where her thoughts roamed, Abby did not know, she only knew she had opened wide a door Abby wanted to remain closed and locked. Doors that admitted Alexander. Once he was inside them she could not force his memory to leave.

She heard his gentle voice plead with her to stay with him. She felt the strength of his arms about her and the hard yet sensitive mouth that had claimed her.

It took her several silent hours to firmly force him to a dark closet of her heart and lock the door against his memory.

The land grew more and more familiar. She began to identify childhood landmarks.

Then she waited in breathless expectation as they turned a sharp curve in the road then left it to turn up the drive to Fernhill.

Her breath was caught in her breast by a hard painful hand as she gazed at the evidence of violence and disaster about her. The dismal ruin that faced her brought tears to her eyes.

This home had been bright and shining, a vision of social elegance. What was elegant four years before was total desolation now.

It was completely deserted, the windows mostly boarded up, the ones that weren't stood open without sign of the fragile imported glass that had graced them.

Inside debris littered the floor. The huge staircase had several broken steps and the beautiful hand carved railing that had been there was entirely gone.

Abby drifted from room to room trying to tread gently, for each step seemed to echo through the house like ancient sighing ghosts. Outside she checked the outbuildings; most that were still standing were skeletal ruins. The slave quarters, once bustling with life were silent forms of crumbling brick.

The area was grown up, almost completely reverted to its natural state.

Abby sat on the front porch, stunned at the emptiness. The Countess sat beside her while her servants began to prepare a meal. They worked outside with the equipment they always carried along, for the kitchen which, as usual, was a small building detached from the main house, and completely gutted by fire.

"It is a shame. Such a waste," she said.

"Oh Yvonne, you should have known it before the war. It was so beautiful."

"Time changes everything. There is nothing you can do about it."

"I will rebuild it."

"Impossible! What will you use for money?"

"I will sell a small piece of it. Enough to hire help."

"The war is not over yet, cherie. They may come again. What will you do for protection?"

"After all we have been through do you doubt I will protect myself?"

Yvonne sighed, there was no use at the moment to try and talk sense to Abby. She was going to use Fernhill as a shield and there was nothing she could say at the moment to stop her. She wondered who the Yankee was who had driven her so. She also wondered, if he loved her enough, would he follow her here?

"This Yankee, cherie, is he someone whose name you would prefer not to tell me?"

"It doesn't matter anymore Yvonne. He is someone I will never see again. Our worlds were too far apart. He asked more than I could give . . . or I asked more than he could give."

"His name, cherie?" she reminded softly.

"Dubonne ... Alexander Dubonne."

Abby continued to talk about the repairs she meant to perform, unaware that Yvonne had become strangely quiet and gazed at her now with an unreadable look in her eyes.

"How far are we away from a town?" she asked Abby.

"Atlanta is not far."

"It would be the safest place I imagine."

"If any place is safe," Abby replied, then she turned to Yvonne. "Safest place for what?"

"For me, cherie, I am not used to such ... primitive discomforts. I will leave some of my people with you temporarily, but I shall find accommodations in Atlanta. If you were wise you would join me there."

"No ... I'm home. I'm home to stay and no one, not even the whole Yankee army will drive me from here again. I ... I thought perhaps you might stay ... just for a while."

"Cherie," Yvonne said gently. "I like you very much. I admire your courage, it is why I helped you to escape. I thought maybe you would understand when you arrived here that you need more than an empty house and a piece of land to make you happy. I will not make it easier for you to hide behind Fernhill. If I stay here you will use me as you plan on using Fernhill. I shall go to Atlanta. We can visit each other and I will be near if you feel you want to change your mind. I will not be part of your shield, or your source of camouflage so you do not have to face your thoughts and your emotions ... even if you become angry with me I cannot stay."

"I cannot be angry with you, you have saved my life and I am grateful for all you have done for me."

"We will stay for a day or two to see you are all right . . . cherie, consider what I have said. Be honest with yourself . . . and with him."

"I will think about it," Abby said firmly.

The Countess laughed.

"You are a stubborn one, are you not? Your voice tells me you will do no such thing."

Now they both laughed together. Then they were brought food and since both were hungry and they did not want to come to an argument they concentrated on eating and discussing the beauty that lay about them.

Yvonne had agreed to stay two days. She set her servants about cleaning up the downstairs rooms and at least two of the multitudes of bedrooms.

The middle of the second day found her issuing orders that would leave Abby half the provisions they had carried.

Abby had walked across the fields alone, at first to see if anything at all showed signs of growing. It was her first opportunity alone since she had arrived. She walked slowly, enjoying the quiet and peace. A thin strip of woods bordered the field through which she walked. It was another place she had often played as a child. She decided to seek the cool shade of the trees.

She reached the edge of the field and stepped into the darker shadows of the trees. There was a trace of a path and she walked along it several feet before she realized something that brought her up short. The path showed all appearances of being well used . . . recently.

She looked about her, but there was no sign of

anyone. A bubbling creek ran through the woods and she crossed it still following a path that seemed more and more traveled upon yet there was no sign of life anywhere.

The woods thickened for a while and she almost lost the path in the dimness, then she could see the rays of the sun piercing the thinning trees.

Again the woods thinned and the path became clear. She was moving uphill, and when she reached the top she found herself in a small clearing. The clearing was not what stopped her, but the small cabin that sat in the center of it did.

For several minutes, she just stood in absolute surprise staring at it. She knew one thing for sure, when she and her father had left the plantation, it had not been there.

A thin spiral of smoke came from the chimney.

She took no more than three steps into the clearing when she heard the brush snap behind her. She never got a chance to turn around before a voice stopped her.

"Ya'all stay where yo are and doan move," came a voice that sounded familiar to her. She spun about with a happy smile on her face.

"Loel!" she cried. The slim girl that stood before her was a more grown up, much prettier Loel, but Loel it was.

"Miz Abby!"

Loel ran to her side, but stopped unsure before her. It was Abby who took the last two steps and threw her arms about her. They hugged each other fiercely. "Loel, what are you doing here? Are you alone?"

"No'um, after you left we wuz sent back home.

Dem . . . dem Yankees came. After a while our men come. Dey fought here. When dey ruined da cabins we come here . . ."

"We? Who is we?"

"Ol Zak, ya'all 'member him?"

"Yes."

"My brother Noah, his woman Hannah, my daddy."

"You've been living in this cabin since then?"

"Yes 'um, we was afraid the Yankees would come back, 'sides . . . we din think it right to stay in da big house . . . not since yo'all been gone. Daddy din think it was right."

"Where is everyone else?"

"Dey's in da cabin."

"Well let's go. I've got to talk to them."

They walked to the cabin. Surprise and happiness greeted Abby. Questions were asked and answered both by Abby and the others.

"What yo'all gwine do Miz Abby now yo Daddy's dead?" Loel's father asked.

"I'm going to rebuild Fernhill and run it just like my father did."

"Wif what yo gwine to run it chile?" he asked gently.

She met his eyes and lifted her chin stubbornly. She spoke softly . . . but firmly.

"You're free, Moses, so are your children. I'm not telling you what to do any more, I'm asking. Come and help me with the plantation. And I'll give you this property your cabin is on and five acres of land. Does that sound fair?"

"Sounds mo' than fair. We'll help yo wif da plantin' and workin' on da house . . . but we lives in our own home. Ya'all see Miz Abby. It be da first real home my chillun know. Noah he one fine boy, and his woman Hannah she gonna gibe him a chile soon. Maybe dat's why we help you, 'cause we know how it feel to come home."

"Thank you, Noah . . . thank you," she held out her hand and after the first sign of shock left his eyes, he took her slim hand in his hard calloused ones.

Abby brought them all back with her and after they had looked around at the damage and decided what needed the most work the soonest they began to make a plan as to how the work was to be divided and who was to do what. Abby insisted on carrying her end of the work and only Yvonne knew she threw herself so deeply into it because of fear. Fear that she would find Fernhill a hollow victory and that her need for Alexander would destroy what barriers of peace she had erected.

The Countess left for Atlanta, promising to send Abby word soon about the war and what was happening.

Abby missed her bright bubbling company from the moment she was gone. She refused to admit she was afraid, but it lingered just below the surface of her mind.

At night the huge house was left to her alone as Moses and his family found their way back to the cabin. Abby would stand on the veranda and look out across the now overgrown lawn. She would listen to the sounds of night. It was then that Alexander touched her memory, no matter how she tried to keep him away.

If she closed her eyes she could feel his presence like a tangible thing. The feel of his hard protective arms that she craved. The touch of his lips on hers with the sensitive gentleness that had made her his.

She stood now, bathed in the pale moonlight and allowed him to invade her thoughts and emotions for what she vowed would be the last time.

She savored the memory of their shared love, relived every moment until the presence of him in her mind overwhelmed every sense.

Reluctantly she pulled herself away from thoughts of what she could no longer have. She had to face the fact that a world of different ideas and ideals separated them. She hated the war that had made them enemies, that had given them so much only to brutally snatch it away. Would he remember when the war was over or would he hate her for running away. Would he forgive her or would he simply wipe her from his life?

She ached with the need she could barely control. She went back inside her room leaving the huge windows open to the still night breeze.

She had just blown out the candle when a sound from outside made her freeze motionless. It was the slow but steady sound of a horse coming up the drive.

The Countess had left her a pistol and ammunition and she was not afraid to use it. She ran to her bureau drawer and took the gun out. She loaded it quickly then stepped outside her bedroom door into the dark hall.

Whoever was there had just walked up on the front porch. She walked slowly down the stairway.

Her eyes were used to the dark now. She stood at the bottom of the steps and listened.

Whoever it was still stood outside the door.

Moonlight began to fill the room with pale light as the huge full moon began to rise higher in the night sky.

Her nerves were taut and her hand was wet with sweat as she held the gun before her.

The knob of the door turned slowly and with a small creaking sound it swung open.

He stood in the doorway, and she didn't know at that moment whether to scream or to cry. The broad shoulders were familiar as was the glow of moonlight on his golden hair.

She knew him as only a woman would know the man she had shared the depths of love with.

She took a step forward with the gun leveled before her. He saw her then and stopped for a second, then he took three steps toward her before her voice stopped him again.

"Get out of here, Yankee . . . before I kill you."

He smiled and began to walk toward her.

"Oh, no, Abby, we do not play the enemies again. I've found you, my love, and unless you pull that trigger, I am about to force your unconditional surrender."

Twenty-nine

Sherman started his march toward Atlanta. With him rode a man who was as determined to put a finish to the war as Sherman was, only for a different reason.

Alexander knew that Abby's home was on the direct path to Atlanta, and he wanted to find her more than anything in the world.

The road to Atlanta for him would be one of blood and fear, but he knew he would face it because there was no other way.

Another thing held him in deep but silent fear. He knew of the violence that rode with Sherman. They were an army that would live off the land—in every way.

Nightmares held him when he thought of Abby alone facing the wrath of an avenging and powerful army such as Sherman's was.

He fought in each battle as they moved slowly South. After each battle Alexander would search the area about them and find the names that belonged to the homes they passed.

Word of this strange activity finally came to

Sherman's ears. It was quite late one evening, after a day of inactivity, that Alexander was summoned.

He was surprised, and couldn't think of anything that his commanding officer could want to talk to him about. In his estimation, Sherman had a difficult situation well in hand and he couldn't see him asking for advice, especially from a young lieutenant who was quite recently attached to his army.

The commander, to Alexander, was one of the most picturesque figures of the war. He was tall and lank, not very erect, with hair like thatch which he continually rubbed with his hands until it stood unruly and erect. A rusty beard trimmed close, a wrinkled face, sharp and prominent red nose, small bright eyes, coarse red hands and a black felt hat slouched over the eyes.

Alexander stood stiffly at attention before Sherman who gazed at him in silence until Alexander felt sweat prickle on his brow.

"I have heard of some strange activities of yours, sir," Sherman said at last.

"Me, sir?"

"You, sir."

"I've no idea what the major general is talking about, sir."

"You don't?" Sherman said as he walked around him and stood behind his back which made Alexander even more nervous.

"No, sir."

"Lt. Dubonne, is it not?"

"Yes, sir."

"I must tell you something you don't seem to know Lt. Dubonne."

"Yes, sir."

"I am a man who makes a point of knowing what goes on around me. I find a general is much more effective if he knows all about the area in which he intends to operate . . . and the men who will be with him."

"Yes sir," Alexander replied, a puzzled note in his voice. "But I don't understand, sir. Is the major general upset with me in some way?"

"Not upset," Sherman replied. "A little disappointed maybe."

"Disappointed?"

"That one of my officers would not remember my sources of intelligence and take it upon himself to conduct a search . . . in enemy territory, I might add, for something which," Sherman chuckled, "I could have told him the location of had he asked."

Alexander stood rigidly still. He wasn't quite sure of what Sherman knew and did not know, and he was not about to volunteer any information.

Sherman reappeared in front of him, and to Alexander's relief he saw a benevolent gleam in his eyes and a half smile on his face.

"Lt. Dubonne . . . Alexander, you are a good officer. I've watched you for some time. I had occasion to meet your father several times. I admire his military brains, have in fact used some of his advice. That is why I took it upon myself to ask a few questions."

He waited for a few minutes, then knew Alexander was going to offer nothing.

"The name of Miss Southerland's plantation is Fernhill. It's just outside of Atlanta. Atlanta . . . is our destination within the next few months."

Alexander felt a quiver of intense relief flow through him. Now he knew where she was. All he had to do was to get to her before disaster struck.

"Thank you, sir," he replied quietly.

Sherman laughed. "I only told you this because I want your undivided attention between here and Atlanta. We are facing an enemy that is clever, determined and as courageous as any enemy can be. It is a long way to Atlanta."

"You have my undivided attention, sir."

"About Miss Southerland's ... ah ... extra-curricular activities. Your father, myself, and a few other friends have seen to a pardon. Her father's life was enough of a price to pay. That, and the desolation of her homeland. No woman could be asked any more than what she has already given."

"Abby is ... rather stubborn, sir. She will probably defend her home with a gun herself. In fact she'll probably shoot me as soon as she sees me."

"Now that little problem, sir," Sherman laughed, "is all yours. All I want from you between here and Atlanta is your attention to duty. I want you to get to Atlanta safe. The outcome of your personal war is up to you and the lady in question." He winked. "Can this Yankee capture and hold a rebel force by himself?"

"I will certainly put up quite a battle sir," Alexander grinned.

"Good! You are dismissed."

Alexander saluted sharply and turned to leave.

"Alexander?"

"Yes, sir."

"Good luck. Maybe ... maybe this is the kind of thing

that will help draw our severed country back together."

"Yes, sir . . . thank you, sir."

He left his commanding officer's tent with a new sense of determination. He would find Abby, he would find her in time, and he would force her to listen and understand that their love was bigger and stronger than any force that stood against it.

Kenesaw Mountain, New Hope Church, Sherman continued his march. Relentlessly he moved on and on facing Confederates defenses that were protected by well-formed breastworks.

The Confederate army was well entrenched and had a spirit among themselves that surprised the Union forces.

But still the juggernaut of Sherman's force continued to move on. Then he faced his promised land as he came to the outskirts of Atlanta, less than eight miles from the city. The domes and spires of Atlanta glittered in the sunlight before him.

He rode at the extreme front and eagerly they pressed their skirmishers forward after the rapidly retreating Rebels. Suddenly they came upon a high bluff overlooking the Chattahoochee and looked southward across the river at the beautiful city of Atlanta. Such a cheer went up that it could be heard in the entrenchments of the doomed city itself.

Sherman stepped nervously about, his eyes sparkling and his face aglow—casting a single glance at Atlanta, another at the river, and a dozen at the surrounding valley to see where he could best cross the river.

But sight was far from conquest, and when they met the gallant defense and were hurled back, they finally settled down for a siege.

Now was Alexander's first opportunity to be free of duty for a short time and to again set out on his search for Abby. He needed the location of the plantation and the quickest and safest route. These were supplied by Sherman himself who sent Alexander a well marked map along whose edge he had written "Good luck and Godspeed."

He knew it would be best to go at night, so he waited impatiently for the sun to set.

He rode along a dark dirt road, bounded on both sides by thick stands of trees. He was as alone here as if he were the only man on earth.

He wondered if Abby felt as alone as he, and once his mind was on her he found it difficult to try to think of anything else.

When he turned up the drive that led to Fernhill he stopped his horse and sat for a moment gazing at what once must have been a most beautiful sight. A flood of deep sympathy moved through him at the sense of loss Abby must feel.

The house was dark, and he wondered if Abby were there. Was it all in vain? Had she been forced to go somewhere else for safety?

Resolutely he nudged his horse into motion and rode up the drive. The moon, large and full, sent an almost day brightness across the porch. He stood at the door for a few minutes praying silently that Abby would be there, and that he could find the way to reach her passionate rebel heart. He knew one thing for certain, he would not leave this place unless Abby came with him, he also knew he would not take no for an answer again . . . even if she had a larger weapon to use than the last time.

He reached out and turned the knob, pleased that the door was not locked, then by the light of the moon he could see the lock had been broken long ago.

He stood for a few minutes until his eyes became accustomed to the inner darkness. Then he saw her and his heart swelled with the intensity of relief and pleasure he felt.

He ignored the gun she held, for all he could see now was her slim dark beauty. All he could feel was the joy of knowing she was alive and well. He wanted to take her in his arms, to tell her how sorry he was for all that had happened. He wanted to comfort her and to love her ... so he started toward her and was brought up short by her cold voice demanding that he leave.

This time he smiled and as he started toward her again he told her firmly that she would have to shoot him to stop him.

She backed away slowly as he came toward her.

"It's no use, Abby," he said gently. "Shoot, or put the gun away. I've searched too long, I've waited too long. All the lonely nights and days, all the times we should have been together where we belong. I will not let you go again, not ever again."

He heard the low muffled sob as she continued to back away.

"The victor Alexander? Are you here to finish the destruction? Are you here to gloat?"

"You know that isn't so," he said softly as he continued to move slowly toward her. "Of all the people in world you know how I hated this. I would never have destroyed this beauty, and above all I would never have hurt you if I had had a choice."

She trembled violently and tears glazed her cheeks. To him, she had never looked lovelier, and he had never wanted her more than he did at this moment.

Abby could feel his strength envelop her as it always had. She felt a need to feel the strength of those arms hold her and lift her beyond this grief and pain. How desperately she wanted his love to ease her fears. Yet she could not, would not surrender her ideals. She could not bear the thought of surrendering Fernhill to the enemy again.

"Yankee!" she said in defensive anger.

He was close to her now. In a sudden move he jerked the gun from her hand. With his other hand he grasped her arm and pulled her into his arms.

"Yes, Rebel, Yankee. But one who loves you with all his heart."

It was useless for her to struggle as his mouth swept down to possess hers. After the kiss began there was no more struggle. The gun dropped unnoticed between their feet as her arms encircled his neck and she returned the kiss with a passion that inflamed him. He held her close and heard her muffled tears, he felt her body tremble against his and knew her grief, felt it as she did. He knew she wept not only for herself but for all the senseless loss. All the beauty and peace in her world had been destroyed. She stood in the ashes of her world, stood and faced the enemy who had destroyed it. Faced him and heard him speak of love and sorrow. It was almost more than she could bear.

She stood a little away from him. "How...how did you get here? How did you know...I don't understand."

"I'm with Sherman. He's just outside of Atlanta. It's a matter of time, Abby, until he takes Atlanta. For all intents and purposes it's a sign of the end."

"But you . . ."

"I told you once before, Abby, that I'd not let anything separate us. That includes a trifle like a war, and a mountain like your damned rebel pride. I love you, have loved you from the beginning. I told you I'd follow you wherever you went. I meant what I said. We have something wonderful and to me very precious. I won't let you or Lee's whole army stop it."

He moved closer to her, gently he reached out and brushed tears from her cheeks, then he lay his hand against her cheeks.

"I don't know what you've felt about me since we've been separated Abby, I only know what I've felt. A deep and awful loneliness and emptiness. I know without hesitation or doubt that you are the only thing that can fill that emptiness. Look at me Abby," he said tenderly. "Look at me and tell me that you don't love me, that you don't need me as much as I need you. Tell me that with truth in your voice and I'll go away. I'll leave you here to mourn in peace."

His attack breached her defenses. She could not say the words, could not lie about her loneliness. About the way she had failed to find the peace at Fernhill she had expected to help support her decision.

He came even closer and his overpowering sense of strength rocked her world. Her reserves shuddered dangerously before the onslaught of his love.

"Alexander," she whispered.

"Tell me, Abby," he demanded quietly. "You have to say the words that send me away, because unless you can say you don't want me I'm not going to leave."

"I can't," she sobbed helplessly. "I can't."

She whispered his name again as she heard his warm laugh and felt his arms reach for her.

Again their lips met, this time with a vibrant renewal of lost love. Her lips, moist and salty with her tears trembled beneath his. She clung to the hardness of him and felt the deep loving warmth with which he enclosed her.

He held her a little away from him and smiled down at her. "I thought I had lost you. You've no idea how desperate I was. I would have done anything to have found you that night. Why did you run from me, Abby? Didn't you know in your heart I would never let you go?"

"I . . . I thought I could do so much, Alexander. I thought I would find a way when I came home. I thought Fernhill would fill the emptiness leaving you made. It didn't. I know now that there is a need within me that only you can fill."

He drew her back into his arms and held her tight, brushing his lips across her hair. "I have come a long way to hear you say that, love. Maybe now you realize that there can never be enmity between us. There is no battle. Despite all that is happening around us we are where we belong, in each other's arms. I intend to see it stays that way for balance of our lifetime."

"It has been so lonely here without you. Do you have to go back soon?"

"I'll keep in contact, when something begins I'll have to go. Until then . . . rebel or no rebel," he smiled,

"This Yankee is here to stay for as long as possible. At least," he whispered, "we have tonight. Abby, listen to me," he said quietly. "When this is over I'll help you rebuild."

"You would do that for me, Alexander?"

"I would do just about anything to make you happy again, to make you forget the nightmare you have been through."

She closed her eyes and savored the sound of the steady beat of his heart. It was the only firm source of strength in her rocking uncertain world. "I love you, Yankee," she smiled. "Whatever happens in our future, for now I love you ... and I need you, Alexander ... I need you to hold me and to tell me it will be all right."

Alexander lifted her chin with his hand and kissed her gently. For a moment he left her to go and close the door he had left standing open. Then he went back to her side and took her hand in his.

"For tonight the war ... the Union ... the Confederacy ... nothing exists but us. Tomorrow we will face the world, for tonight I have you, Abby, and that's all I'll ever really need."

Silently they walked up the stairs together and closed the world away and began a night of long desired and long awaited love.

They came together with forceful hunger the first time, as if all their pain and loneliness could be washed away in the almost violent possession of each other.

Later it became a gentle blending and a joyous union that buried forever all resistance that had ever existed between them.

Much later, in the wee hours of the morning, they lay

together, content to hold one another, ignoring the fact that morning would come.

Contrary to their wishes the sun skimmed the horizon and sent its first tentative rays to disturb the lovers. They stirred to wakefulness with no desire to leave the warm sanctuary they had found.

For a while they talked in soft whispers, as if their voices would shatter the spell in which they existed. They caressed with intense pleasure, their lips gently seeking each other.

Between their gentle touches he questioned and she told the story of her escape and her journey back to her beloved plantation.

"You must meet the Countess, Alexander. She is the most mysterious most self reliant and surprising woman I've ever met."

"I must, and I must thank her for seeing to your safety, although I'd argue the point of her qualities. I might agree if I had not met you first. You are definitely the most surprising woman I've ever met!" He nuzzled her ear in playful pleasure while his hands renewed their quest for warm and inviting memories. "Abby is there anything to eat in this house?"

She laughed gaily as she hugged him. "How dare you speak of food at a time like this?"

He chuckled and squeezed her tight enough to bring a protesting gasp.

"I've used up all my strength woman. I need something to renew my energy."

"Well, if you must, you must," her blue eyes glittered in wicked pleasure. "I certainly don't want you to run short of energy. There must be something downstairs to renew you."

"How would you like breakfast in bed?" he grinned.

"What a delightful thought."

"Lie still, I'll go get something. We'll eat right here."

She watched him rise and dress and start for the door. "Don't you want me to help you?"

At the door he turned and smiled. "I want you right where you are. I thought of this scheme just to keep you there. Clever aren't I? I'll be back soon. Don't move."

She laughed as he closed the door behind him and snuggled down beneath the blanket missing his warmth already.

He whistled lightly to himself as he went down the steps. He searched through what supplies there were in the house realizing how slim they were. He gathered some food and a bottle of wine he rescued from a nearly depleted cellar. He started back up the steps with his arms laden when a hard cold voice voice froze him midway.

"Stay where yo is, Yankee. Doan move or ah blow yo head off sure."

Thirty

Alexander obediently froze. He was not sure who or how many stood behind him, but without half his clothes, and with no weapons at all he was not about to do anything to alarm them.

"What you done wif Miz Abby? Where she at? If yo hurt her, Yank you'all bettah say yo prayers quick."

"I didn't harm her. She's upstairs. Let me turn around, I'll explain who I am and why I'm here."

Alexander started to turn but the voice held him.

"Doan move Yank. I 'spect yo do and I blow a hole in you. Where Miz Abby at?"

"She's . . . she's in bed," Alexander replied knowing how damning it sounded. He had a pretty good idea what was going through the mind of the voice behind him. He heard a soft whisper behind him and a stir of movement. He was right about one thing, there was more than one. He wondered if they were scavengers, blue or gray, just how safe Abby would be if he didn't at least try to warn her. Then his mind remembered what the voice had said . . . Miss Abby . . . they knew her.

He was about to speak again when he felt someone close to him. Then a very pretty black girl was at his side.

"Yo'all stan' here. Mah pappy has a gun on your back. Ah'll go see Miz Abby is all right. Iffen she ain't pappy gwine to blow you so full of holes they gonna hafta pick up the pieces all over Gawja."

"She's all right, I'm telling you," he said angrily, "let me explain."

The girl's dark eyes watched him intently, then suddenly with a flash of slim dark legs she ran up the steps and was gone.

Alexander stood silent, aware of the eyes that bored holes in his back. To him it was an eternity before the girl reappeared with an amused Abby behind her.

"Abby, for God's sake tell them who I am."

She grinned in devilment, "Should I tell them you're nothing but a Yankee who forced himself in and did away with my virtue during the night?"

He heard the click of the gun being cocked and his shoulders twitched as if he could almost feel the ball between them.

"Abby," he said threateningly. She laughed now and the black girl's teeth flashed white in a smile.

"It's all right, Moses. This is one Yankee I can guarantee is a friend of mine."

Alexander sighed with relief and turned to look at the man who stood below him.

He smiled, "Good morning."

"Mawnin' ... Miz Abby yo' wan to tell us what this Yankee doin'."

"Put your gun away, Moses," Abby said, "and I'll tell

you everything."

Moses set the gun aside, but he kept one dark eye on Alexander.

It was some time before Alexander saw the look change from outright hostility to grudging acceptance.

As far as Alexander was concerned Sherman could have laid siege to Atlanta for months and he would have been content. He knew when Atlanta weakened and fell he would have to move on with Sherman.

He worried about Abby's safety when he had to leave for she adamantly refused to leave. It was Moses who tried to assure Alexander that he and his family would take care of her.

Two days later, Alexander returned to camp. He told Abby he would return as soon as possible.

The siege continued, as the railroad system collapsed civilians within the city went hungry. Meal sold for one hundred dollars a bushel, bacon thirteen dollars a pound and flour fifteen hundred dollars a barrel.

The Confederacy watched with the thoughts in their minds "No money in the treasury, no food to feed General Lee's army—no troops to oppose General Sherman. Is the cause really hopeless? Is it to be abandoned this way?"

But sight was far from conquest. And Sherman's army had to admire the tremendous defense the Atlanta rebs had.

Alexander returned again and again, but he and Abby both knew the time was running short.

Day after day the Confederates struck back blindly at

the federal forces only to be beaten back with bloody losses.

Sherman edged south of the city and cut its last outside connections; this left the Confederate army outside its defenses. Then the whole force of the two armies met each other. Sherman charged, not one instant did his force hesitate—it moved steadily forward to the enemy's works—over the works with a shout—over the cannon—over the rebels—hand to hand battle ... and the despairing cries of surrender soon stopped it. The firing ceased and one thousand rebels were ... prisoners of war—Atlanta surrendered and Sherman moved in.

Alexander rode with him and was appalled at the rout. Soldiers were ordered to "forage liberally on the country" and they did. The most brutal foraging of the war was to be done by Sherman's cavalry.

When he left the city, behind him lay the smoldering ruins of Atlanta, Georgia.

After they had swept through Atlanta, Sherman's plans were to capture Savannah. Alexander requested permission to go back to Fernhill just for a few days before they moved on. He didn't expect it, but Sherman granted it anyway.

Abby had heard by now of the terrible destruction of Atlanta. She was struck with a deep poignant grief. It was as if some deep part of her had been wounded. She watched daily for any sign of Alexander and when he came she threw herself into his arms. She did not cry, or even speak, but he knew what she was feeling.

"Alexander," she said quietly, "how long ... can you stay with me ... just for a day?"

"Three days," he replied quietly. "Three days, then I have to go."

"Three days," she replied as she rested her head against his chest. They stood for a moment simply holding each other. He knew that at this moment it was what she needed most.

"You rode with him?" she questioned softly then she laughed. "How stupid of me. You had no choice, of course you rode with him."

"Abby, I'm sorry. I can't ask you to understand, but this has to be ended. The Confederacy is too brave and too stubborn to surrender while they can still fight. He has to do this—it has to end! It has to."

She looked up at him, her eyes filled with tears, for a moment it surprised her that his eyes were strangely moist too.

"I'm sorry, Abby, truly sorry. I know how you must feel, how I would feel if everything I knew was destroyed."

"Alexander . . . I want to go into Atlanta."

"No, Abby, no. You don't need to see that. It won't do any good and it only makes bad memories worse."

"I have a friend in Atlanta, a woman who helped me get home when the whole Union army was looking for me. I owe her that much. At least to see . . . if she's . . . I owe her that much."

"I can't let you go into that dead city. I can't . . . I won't."

"If you don't go with me, Alexander I shall wait until you are gone and go by myself."

Their eyes held, and he knew she spoke the truth.

"All right Abby. I'll go with you." He drew her back

into his arms and held her. She heard the rumble of laughter deep within.

"What's funny?"

"I think General Lee chose the wrong defense for Atlanta. He should have called on you. You're stubborn enough to have just beat Sherman off."

She started to speak resistance, but he stilled her words by binding him close to her and kissing her into silence.

Alexander lifted her in front of him and they rode in silence to the city of Atlanta. He knew there was no way to prepare her for the grim destruction she would find.

Homes stood in ruins. What cannon ball did not destroy, fire had. Sherman had devoured the land. Everything that had been edible, every sweet potato, all cattle, hogs, sheep and poultry had been carried away, as were more than ten thousand horses and mules. The foraging done was more than twenty million dollars worth, and the remainder was simply waste and destruction.

Refugees had left the city by the hundreds, some of them even resorted to looting to find enough to exist on until they found some other source of existence.

They moved slowly through the town, he remembering the force of destruction and she remembering a beautiful city that now stood in ruins.

There were some who stayed, because they had nowhere to go, or because they refused to be pushed from their city even by the monstrous army of Sherman.

One after another they questioned them until they found word. Abby's questions were answered, Alexander's were at best ignored, and at times he could see the glitter of hatred in their eyes. He wondered if the hatred would ever go away. It left a deep hollow fear within him.

It seems the Countess had gone from Atlanta at the first word of Sherman's final drive. Where she had headed no one knew. Abby was glad she was safe, and she wondered if she would ever hear from her again.

They rode back to Fernhill. Both of them knew when he left this time it would be a long time before they would see each other. It was a silent spectre that lurked between them that they did not want to face.

That night they sat together before a low burning fire. He held her close to him and they both were caught in the fear of parting.

"Abby?"

"What?"

"I'm afraid to leave you here alone. I'm afraid of the way things will be when I'm gone."

"I'll be all right Alexander. Moses and his family will help me."

"You're not safe in this house. After something like this, there's always scavengers, from both sides. How can I go and leave you knowing things are this way. Look at the night I came. If I had been more than one you wouldn't have had a chance."

"I've already asked Moses and his family to move in here with me. They agreed to until you come back. I'll be safe, Alexander, don't worry. I'll be safe."

He moved from his chair to the floor in front of the fire. Then he reached out a hand and she smiled and put hers in it. He drew her down beside him.

She lay beside him and he gazed down into her eyes.

Gently he brushed his fingers along her cheeks, committing every plane to memory.

"Abby," he whispered as he bent forward and kissed her cheek and her slim throat. "I love you so much my dear sweet Rebel. I love you so much. You're part of every breath I take. I would give my life to see you safe."

She lifted her arms about his neck. "Don't say that Alexander. If anything happened to you the best part of me would die. I want us to pretend ... pretend this is our home, yours and mine. No war exists. There is nothing beyond that door but a new and wonderful world for us to share. Tonight will be the first night of the rest of our lives. We begin ... now."

Slowly he bent his head to lightly taste her lips with his. The kiss was feather light and the brilliant sweetness of it brought a surrendering moan of agony from her.

"Oh, Alexander, take away the shadows and the fear ... only you can ... only you."

The touch of his mouth on hers became a flame that licked into life a blaze of emotion that swept them away. His mouth possessed hers hard and seeking, finding a response as demanding as his. The smoldering fires of love burst into an explosive blinding need that consumed them both.

The aching sweet surrender blended them into one in a thunder of roaring passion. Like a joyous renewal of life, like a homecoming after bitter loss it lifted them to soar heavenward like eagles lost to the darkness of earth to fly brilliantly among the stars. His open hungry mouth on hers filled her veins with passion like a heady wine. The masculine scent of him intoxicated her and left her drunk with the need of him. She clung to him like the tendrils of a slim vine about a great oak.

They came together, fused into one like molten metal. Their bodies blended each possessing, each surrendering all.

They were weak and clinging to one another yet reluctant to part even for a moment. They lay together and watched the flames die and burning embers glow. For a time she slept, warm and secure in the curve of his arm. He held her, unable to sleep, watching her slow even breathing and framing each moment in his heart to carry with him through the long lonely nights ahead.

They carried their game of pretense through the next day, laughing and talking together. Walking the barren fields, holding hands, talking in low laughing whispers. They played together like children, filled with the joy of each other, and knowing that another day would separate them.

Moses knew of the happiness Alexander had brought to Abby. He had seen her laugh as she had a long time ago and he knew this Yankee was good for her. He and Alexander had an opportunity to talk for a moment alone. Abby was asleep and Alexander took a moment to walk in the cool night air. When he stepped out on the porch he immediately sensed someone's presence. Then he saw Moses seated in the shadows with a gun across his lap.

"Good evening, Moses."

"Evenin'."

"You on guard?" Alexander smiled. He could hear Moses' chuckle.

"I been guardin' that li'l gal a whole lot longer 'en yo' has Yank."

"Aren't you ever going to call me anything but Yank? I get the feeling you don't like me Moses."

" 'Spect I didn't at first. Now ..." he shrugged.

"Now?"

Moses rose from his chair and walked over to stand beside Alexander.

"Now I see's what yo doin'. I see's her laughin' and happy. I see's her eyes shinin' with love the way a pretty woman's eyes should. I see's yo' kin make her happy, and I see's she needs yo'. 'Spect that's a good enough reason fo' not shootin yo in de first place."

Alexander stood quiet for a moment. He leaned against a huge pillar and gazed at the brilliant stars.

"Moses."

"Yassah?"

"Take good care of her while I'm gone," he said quietly. "I don't want her hurt any more. Keep her safe until I get back and I swear I'll spend the rest of my life making her happy and helping her to forget all that's happened."

Moses looked at Alexander and their eyes held for several silent minutes then he said softly, "Yassah 'spects ah'll do dat, just like I think yo' means what yo' say. She be safe ... I take good caar of her."

"Thanks," Alexander replied. He turned to walk back into the house. "Good night, Moses."

"Good night ... Mistah Alexander, sleep well."

Alexander smiled at the use of his name, laughing at why it meant so much to have this itinerant black man speak to him by name and with respect.

He walked quietly up the steps and into the room he shared with Abby. She lay asleep on the bed. He stood beside it and looked down at her.

Pale moonlight lit the room with a white glow. Gently he took the covers and pulled them away. She lay slim and beautiful, her body washed with the moon's glow seemed to glimmer gold and white. Her dark hair spilled across his pillow and he gently reached out and touched the silken mass.

She stirred restlessly, and he slipped out of his clothes and lay down beside her, drawing her into his arms. He closed his eyes to enjoy the cool feel of her body pressed against him. He inhaled the sweet scent of her and savored the pleasure of touching her smooth skin. He caressed her and bent his head to trace warm kisses on her neck and the smooth skin of her shoulder. He smiled as he felt her grow still, then her arms crept up to draw his head down to hers. She murmured his name and her parted lips accepted his most willingly.

It was a gentle possession, and his quiet touch as he joined their bodies made her want to weep. It was not a thing of wildness and flame, but a sweet and loving blending. Slowly, he immersed himself within her, holding her close and touching her with a tender and sensitive oneness.

He wanted to pour all his longing, all his love, all his need within her to hold until he could find his way to her again, and to fill him with her sweetness.

Afterward, they slept, and the hours fled. Night faded before the rising sun.

Abby wakened first. She lay curled close to Alexander. For a long time she lay still fighting the terror she did not want him to see in her eyes.

Today he would leave her and only God knew if they would ever see each other again. Agony filled her as she envisioned him dead on some faraway battlefield. It made her cold and she involuntarily shivered.

She felt his arm tighten about her and a gentle kiss brushed against her hair.

"You knew?"

"I shall always know. I love you so much I can feel your fear. Don't be afraid, Abby. I'll be back. I will have left the most important part of my life here. A part I cannot exist without. I'll be back to claim it again."

"Alexander . . . come back to me safely."

"I will love, I will."

She clung to him and he to her for another breathless moment.

"I have to get up, Abby."

"I know."

She watched him rise and begin preparations. He shaved, washed and dressed and began to pack what things he had. He came to the side of the bed and she started to rise. He put a hand against her shoulder and pressed her back against the pillow.

"Stay here, Abby. It will be easier for us both."

He sat on the edge of the bed and took her hand in his. He kissed it, then turned it over and placed a kiss in her palm. He closed her hand and smiled down into her eyes.

"Hold this for me, love. I shall want it back as soon as I return."

She gave a choking sob and threw herself into his arms.

He rocked her gently for a moment then he kissed her tear touched lips. She closed her eyes as he laid her back against the pillows. She felt the cold emptiness of her arms as soon as he left them. Then . . . the soft click of the closing door told her he was gone.

The pain of it brought a low moan of anguish. She could not bear the pain of it. She leaped from the bed and grabbed her robe. Slipping it on, she ran to the window.

He was already mounted and riding away. She watched his tall broad form until he disappeared.

Tears blinded her eyes and she could no longer see.

"Alexander . . . I love you . . . oh, you damn Yankee don't let anything happen to you . . . come back safe . . . oh, Alexander come back safe."

She lay on the bed for a long time allowing her tears to overcome her. She wept until she was exhausted. Then with grim determination she rose, washed and dressed.

She went downstairs and out on the porch where she found Moses waiting for her.

"There are a lot of things to do around here, Moses and I think it's time we got started."

"Yassum," he replied. He smiled at her and she returned it.

"We're not defeated, Moses, and we never shall be."

"No, Ma'm yo sho won't. It gonna take mo than what 'ole Sherman kin do to break us."

"Only," she laughed shakily, "I don't know just where to begin."

"Suppose yo let Moses show yo. We gonna make this place grow again. I go and get the rest of my family. We come over here and work until Mistah Alexander get back. Then yo two kin get started buildin a family of yo own. Yassum, dis here place gonna shine again some day. We uns may be down now but we sho ain gonna stay dat way."

She nodded and watched Moses walk across the field toward his cabin.

A whole new strength began to fill her. Soon Alexander would come back and they would begin a life together. Someday they would have children and Fernhill would be filled with laughter and peace.

She looked across her land and felt a surge of courage it always brought. She had turned her back on defeat and faced the future with prayer and hope.

Thirty-one

Everywhere, except before Richmond, Southern armies were in retreat. Lee! Lee! was the cry. Yet a glance at the tattered veterans in the vermin infested trenches about Richmond should have warned that not even Lee could do the impossible.

The condition of the army was daily becoming more desperate. Starvation, literal starvation, was doing its deadly work. So depleted and poisoned was the blood of many of Lee's men from insufficient and unsound food that a slight wound, which would probably not have been reported at the beginning of the war, would often cause blood-poisoning, gangrene, and death.

It was a harrowing but not uncommon sight to see these hungry men gather the wasted corn from under the feet of half fed horses, and wash and parch it to satisfy in some small measure their craving for food. Lee himself dared not hope, he could only promise, "I shall endeavor to do my duty and fight to the last."

Lee knew if Petersburg fell, Richmond could not be defended ... and Petersburg fell. The Confederate army retreated.

By the following morning they were gone from Richmond, and army officers were burning supplies that might fall into enemy hands. The wildest confusion prevailed.

That afternoon the Federal troops took possession of Richmond. Wes Rainey rode into Richmond with the conquering Federals. When they entered they found a city of ruins. No sound of life, but the stillness of a catacomb ... a wide vista of desolation. A white smoke-wreath rose occasionally. A gleam of flame shot a grotesque picture of broken arches and ragged chimneys into his brain.

Alexander with Sherman's force was moving up from the South. In their camp also was an intense stillness as if the prelude to some shattering event.

Alexander sat just outside his tent. He had just received a packet of letters, some of them months old. His mother and father, Celeste ... and a larger thicker one from Wes. He opened it first. It contained another closed letter addressed to Alexander and a short letter from Wes.

He unfolded Wes' and read first. The words leaped from the page striking him a fierce blow and drawing a soft sound of pain. George was dead. Grief struck him and memories of beautiful days past. George had been his closest friend and companion. He read Wes' words through tear blurred eyes. Wes told him where and how George had died, and that some of his last thoughts had been of Alexander.

"... George has written to you of something very strange. In fact he spoke to me of it. He gave me a locket that contains a picture that bears an ungodly resemblance to you. He has asked me to bring it to a woman in Virginia at a place called High Oaks. He wanted you to go also. I shall carry out his wishes after the war is over. I hope both you and Celeste will go along. It is a mystery that needs solving . . .

He went on to tell Alexander of his wound and the battle and his short stay at home. He closed with a hopeful prayer that Alexander was well and would keep himself safe, and that the war would be over soon and they would all be together again.

He laid aside Wes' letter, and read his parents letter first, then Celeste's. He found it hard to open George's letter. After a while he lifted it with a trembling hand and tore it open. He took the page out and began to read.

Dear Alexander:

I am writing this letter before a battle so please excuse the atrocious writing. I have only the stub of a pencil and my lap for a desk which makes things difficult. I know I haven't written for a long time but tonight I have the need to speak to an old friend.

It seems so long ago since we had any time to talk together. A lifetime has passed, a lifetime of pain and misery . . . and learning.

Do you remember our continual personal argument about the waging of war? Oh, Alexander, I was so caught up in the pageantry and false bravado of everything. I don't think I had the slightest idea of man's inhumanity to man until now. I have fought and found it unrewarding. I have killed and been sickened unto death over what I have done. I have seen war at its grimmest and I cannot bear the ugliness of it. Worst of all, I have led men to their deaths, and later written letters to their families . . . I have suddenly found I have nothing to say to them that I can justify at all.

I am tired, and I want to go home. I want to walk in the cool air and breathe peace. I want to see my family and friends again. I want to marry and give life instead of being the producer of death.

I write these things to you for I know you are the only one who truly understands. It is a dark time for me, and yet I am no longer afraid.

We must talk, when this is over and we have again regained our sanity. When we are home again.

I have seen Wes, and I have told him of a strange occurrence. When you get back you must take a short trip to Virginia. I was there for a while and I have run across a man who is your absolute double. It would be interesting for you to meet him.

I have also met the woman of my dreams. To my despair, she is promised to this Dan Wakefield who is your copy. Her name is Catherine, and she is very beautiful. I only wish it could be; maybe, when this is over I shall go to High Oaks and compete for her hand. It would be the culmination of all my battles. But the reward could be the greatest of my life.

Well, I am exhausted and I guess I had better

get some sleep. Tomorrow promises to be quite a battle. I must give credit to these Rebels, they fight with unending courage. They have my admiration for their single-minded devotion.

God bless you and keep you safe my friend until we meet again.

George.

Alexander held the letter in his hand. He braced his arms on his knees and bowed his head to rest against them. A hard lump in his breast made it difficult to breathe. He wanted to cry but a heavy dryness possessed him and he could only remain still as the pain washed over him. He allowed his memory to go back to the carefree days when he and George were young together. The sheer waste of life paralyzed him with anguish. He thought of his torn country and the torn lives.

He thought of Abby and cursed the war that separated them. Sleep was a difficult thing for him that night. It was filled with restless nightmares.

The next morning Sherman was again on the move. The huge hand of fate closed about the ragged Confederate army. The South resisted furiously.

Sherman met another wing of Lee's retreating force. Alexander led his men into a battle that, as George had said, drew his deep admiration for the remnants of Lee's force.

The men came with a loud Rebel yell; their gray uniforms seemed black amidst the smoke; their preserved colors torn by grape and ball, waved defiantly; twice they halted, and poured in volleys, but came on again like a surge from the fog, depleted but determined. It was an awful instant; the rebels could stand no more; they reeled, swayed, and fell back broken and beaten. A few more volleys, a new and irresistible charge by the Federals, and a shrill warning command to die or surrender; and, with a sullen and tearful impulse ... muskets were flung upon the ground.

After the battle, when silence fell over the camp of the Union army, Alexander sat numb with exhaustion and wondering if the rebel army would have the strength to resist again. He knew of the carnage, was sick with the blood and fear of battle. Silently he prayed deeply that this would be the end.

Many miles away a carriage rode up the long drive to High Oaks. Catherine watched it come. Very few people in the South had a carriage and she had no idea who could be coming to visit her.

She stood on the porch and shaded her eyes with her hand. She heard the door of the house open and close and she turned to see Virginia walking toward her.

The change in Virginia in the past few months could still shake her. Virginia smiled, but it was a habitual empty smile. She was pale and extremely thin. Often she sat in absolute silence, her eyes seeing inward to something Catherine could not share. Daily she went to the cemetery where she would place fresh flowers on Gregory's grave, then sit and talk to him as if he were present. This alarmed both Jessie and Catherine but there was no way they could stop her. The conversations were always about Dan ... sometimes as if Dan were already home ... and sometimes as if he were lost to them completely . . . but always they were of Dan. It stretched Catherine's already frayed nerves near the breaking point.

They knew of the continual retreat and defeat of Lee's army and silently carried visions in their heads and hearts of where Dan could be at the moment . . . and what condition he was in.

"Who is it, Catherine? We certainly are not prepared for guests, why I haven't had the guest rooms cleaned in weeks."

Catherine sighed, patiently saying nothing about the fact that almost all the rooms in the house were empty and there was nothing, not even food, to prepare for guests.

"It's all right, Virginia, I'm sure it's just someone passing through. Maybe they have come to give us news."

"Of Dan!" Virginia cried excitedly. "Oh, I do hope it's word of Dan. My son," she said in an aggrieved voice, "has not written to me. I shall have to speak firmly to him about that as soon as he comes home. I taught him better than that. Gregory will be upset."

Catherine choked back an answer, and her eyes burned with helpless tears. She too prayed for word of Dan, for if Dan came back maybe Virginia would regain her equilibrium and happiness of a sort could touch High Oaks again.

The carriage rolled to a halt and the driver jumped down and ran to open the door. Catherine watched a beautiful blonde woman step down. She was a complete stranger to Catherine.

Richly dressed and completely poised and beautiful

431

she walked up the steps.

"This is High Oaks, is it not?" she spoke with a French accent.

"Yes, it is," Catherine replied. "I am Catherine Markland and this is Virginia Wakefield."

"I am quite pleased to meet you. I have been told much about you by a good friend of both of us ... Abby Southerland."

"Abby!" Catherine smiled and her eyes lit with pleasure. "Abby is my cousin. Do come in ..."

"I am Countess LeClerc. I traveled home with Abby. We became separated during the siege of Atlanta."

"I'm sure you can tell us a great deal about what is happening," Virginia said brightly. "Please come in, let us have tea and chat."

Catherine could see surprise, then instant sympathy touch the Countess' eyes, and she was grateful that she masked both emotions quickly and smiled at Virginia.

"Thank you," she said softly, "you are very gracious."

Virginia led the way and Catherine and the Countess followed. Catherine was grateful for Virginia's sake that they did have a small amount of tea. Virginia served it in cracked cups which she totally ignored. She chattered on about Yvonne staying as their guest for a few days.

"Thank you for your hospitality. I should be grateful for a few days respite from traveling ..." she looked at Catherine ... "and for some time to talk."

It was much later, toward early evening that they found the chance to talk alone. Virginia had been coaxed by Catherine to go to her room and rest, for Catherine could see the vague troubled look and she knew it heralded another visit to the cemetery.

Catherine and the Countess walked beneath the shade of the high oaks that lined the drive.

"She is . . . unwell?" the Countess ventured.

"She has been through a great deal, enough to crush the mind of stronger people."

"But, she is not your responsibility, no?"

"She is Dan's mother."

"Ah."

"That is not the only reason. She was . . . is a beautiful kind and gentle person. She has been good to me always. I cannot leave her like this. When Dan comes home things will be different . . . she will be different."

"Tell me what has happened, cherie. Abby speaks of Dan Wakefield, his parents and you, her favorite cousin, with a great deal of love and respect."

Catherine told her everything that had happened at High Oaks from the day war was declared until that moment. Her voice choked and quieted when she spoke of Gregory's death and the long frightening time since Dan had been heard from.

"Sometimes no news is the better news."

"I hope you are right. Please, tell me what happened at Atlanta, and about Abby."

She spoke of Abby with a great deal of affection. She told Catherine all she knew about what Abby had done, and of the Yankee she was in love with.

"A Yankee," Catherine whispered.

"A man," the Countess countered. "When this war is over, if God pleases, maybe they can start a new life together. Should you not bury the hatred then . . . or will he always be . . . a Yankee."

"I don't know ... I don't know. The world now is such a tragic mixed up place."

"Do you think your Dan would accept him not as an enemy ... a Yankee ... but as a man?"

"I don't know that either. Dan has suffered a terrible loss. How will he feel when he comes home and finds his father dead and his mother ..."

"Everyone has suffered losses, but can we exist if we keep hatred alive? Maybe your Dan and Abby's Yankee can be the first to accept each other."

"Well," Catherine smiled, "since they will be related to each other I certainly hope you are right."

They walked along in silence for a while, each caught up in private thoughts. Each unaware of the violent shock the future was to hold.

Catherine was surprised to find the Countess intent on doing her share of what work was needed to keep them alive. She had expected her to be someone they would have to cater to during her stay. She was also surprised to see that not only did she want to help she was quite capable of doing anything she set her mind to.

Jessie too was surprised that the beautiful visitor from ... somewhere ... knew how to milk a cow, and laughingly proved it on the one and only cow High Oaks had left.

Catherine never went into town. She was afraid that someone would question her about Virginia and she did not want to have to answer their prying questions.

Jessie was the one who went to sell what they had to sell and to buy what necessities they did not grow.

There were no luxuries bought. No clothes or shoes, nothing they could do without. What few dresses

Catherine had left were worn and repaired so often that they were in danger of complete disintegration.

The Countess unpacked the trunks that had been laced to the back of her carriage and revealed several beautiful dresses.

She insisted that both Catherine and Virginia were to select one for themselves.

"I have many at home, and it will give me great pleasure to give you one. As a guest you must do what you can to make me happy, no?"

Since the Countess herself had the same golden coloring as Catherine her clothes complimented Catherine. She chose a pale blue gown, but folded it gently to put away.

"Cherie?"

"I'll save it . . . for when Dan comes home," she said softly.

"Of course, cherie . . . I understand."

Life became slow, quiet and tedious. Virginia seemed to slip deeper and deeper into her private world. More and more often they would find her seated by Gregory's grave speaking softly of how things would be better when Dan . . . her son . . . came home.

Often they had trouble coaxing her away. And they were afraid her physical health was slowly following her mental one.

Jessie was already hitching up the horse to the wagon. He smiled at her when she approached. She knew Jessie had always been a free man, and that he could have left them and done better on his own. She also knew he stayed mostly for Dan's benefit. He had loved Dan since he was a boy and he would help protect what was his while he was away fighting.

"Mawnin', Miz Catherine."

"Good morning, Jessie."

"You're almost ready to leave?"

"Yessum."

"Don't forget the flour, Jessie, we're out of bread."

"Yessum."

"And could you see if they have a little molasses. If you find some I'll make you some of that gingerbread you like so well."

Occasionally bits and pieces of news came through . . . defeat at Petersburg . . . defeat at City Point . . . defeat at Five Forks . . . defeat . . . defeat.

No one knew what was true and what was not, yet the same idea began to drift through again and again. The North had taken Richmond. Lee's army was on its last final march.

Catherine could only pray, and sometimes she was too emotionally drained to even do that.

She had wakened early in the morning which was a habit for her. She liked the early morning and often sat on the back veranda which faced east to watch the sun rise.

She rose now from her seat on the veranda and walked down the steps and across the back lawn. Jessie was going to town today and she was going to remind him of a few things they needed.

"Well," he grinned. "I 'spect ah'll jes have to find some. My mouth sho got a taste for sum o' that."

"Jessie . . . see if there's any news."

"Yo'all know I does that all de time."

"I know," she sighed, "I just hope . . .

"Miz Catherine, yo' rest yo' mind. Dat boy gwine ta come back to yo. Yo'all been gettin' thin and pale. He gonna think ol' Jessie doan know how to care for his lady while he's gone. Yo' best eat some more befo' yo disappear."

She laughed. "I'll try Jessie, I'll try."

She watched him ride away and turned to walk back to the house. Her eyes caught a movement and she knew Virginia was again talking to Gregory. She was too tense to go and try to coax her away. Let her talk to him she thought. Maybe she's happy and that's more than most of us can say. She walked back into the house and started her chores and preparations for meals. She moved tiredly about. She was not hungry and realized she had begun not to care if she ate or slept.

Virginia came back into the house just as the Countess appeared from upstairs. They sat around the table to share morning tea and the small amount of bread left.

Virginia was rambling on about Dan and Gregory until Catherine wanted to scream at her to stop.

Then they heard Jessie shout from outside and exchanged surprised glances. Then they ran to the porch. Jessie was just leaping down. He stood at the bottom of the steps and looked up at the three women who waited breathlessly.

"It's over! Da war's over. Lee done surrendered. The fightin's all done."

"Jessie!" Catherine cried.

"It's true. Lee surrendered."

Catherine buried her face in her hands and cried in agonized relief.

"Dan!" Virginia cried, "my son is coming home."

Then they fell into each others arms crying both with the pain of defeat and with the joy of knowing the dying was done ... and Dan would be coming home.

Thirty-two

Dan had marched until he was so exhausted he did not know how much distance he had covered. One plodding step after another. They were retreating ... again. They had been on continual retreat since Richmond had fallen. They were hounded now by the Union army. There was no peace, no time to stop, to rest.

Through the weeks that would come to be known as "the weeks of the flying fights" the Union army hounded the Confederates. At Jetersville, at Saylers Creek, at Farmville. Lee found the enemy continually pursuing, still preventing him from turning south to join Johnston.

His army was disappearing. Dan's own veteran division had numbered sixty-nine hundred on January thirtieth, after Five Forks and Fort Gregg and in flight it now had twenty-six hundred officers and men.

Lee's only hope was to follow the railroad, but on April eighth Federal cavalry reached Appomattox Station ahead of him.

There could be no escape, the last battle was fought. The battle did nothing but cost a few more Confederate lives. Dan could remember ... and the pain of it crushed him. As all others, when the line broke he had run ... he had run with tears in his eyes, blindly. It was over ... Lee had to surrender. In the house at Appomattox Lee and Grant met.

The entire army of northern Virginia was surrendered, to be released on parole. Before leaving Lee requested rations for his hungry men.

April 12 was the day appointed for the surrender of Confederate arms. There was much ceremony by the Union army. But for the Confederates not a sound of trumpet nor roll of drum nor a cheer ... but an awed stillness, rather breath-holding as if it were the passing dead.

They fixed bayonets, struck arms, then hesitantly removed cartridge boxes and laid them down. Lastly ... they tenderly folded their flags, battle worn and torn, blood-stained heart-holding colors, and laid them down. Some with burning tears in their eyes. They pressed them to their lips. And only the Union flag greeted the sky.

Suddenly, after all the battles, the marching, the hunger and cold, it was over. Dan was free to go home and he was momentarily stunned with the immensity of the situation.

He had nothing but the tattered and worn clothes on his back. His boots had been nearly worn through. All the food he had were the rations from Grant's army, and he was faced now with the long walk home.

He left Appomattox the next morning and began the

journey. He trudged dusty roads, occasionally received a ride short distances on wagons. Most of the time was spent on foot. To make matters worse it began to rain and he spent a night in a deserted barn.

Sleeping on the ground, stretching his food, he continued on. There were times when he fell in with others who were headed home. They spoke of many things, of battles fought, of home, of loved ones . . . but never of surrender. The word meant nothing to them yet.

Slowly he neared High Oaks. The vision of High Oaks and Catherine had become blurred in his mind. He saw the destruction about him, but could not put High Oaks, his safety, his rock of security, in the same condition as everything else about him.

He stepped on High Oaks land and felt the first real sense of peace he had known in a long time.

He had run out of food three days before and had nothing in his stomach but water he had drunk from a stream several hours before. His ears buzzed with the dizziness of hunger, but he continued to walk because he felt safety, peace, food and love were waiting at High Oaks.

He walked the wasted fields toward the house that stood in the distance. As he neared the house sights of destruction began to seep into his brain. The house stood tall and quiet. It was as if it were a ghost-like mirage. Pain twisted his heart and he stood frozen for a moment in the grief of all that was lost.

It was that moment the front door opened and Catherine came out on the porch. She must have seen him coming from a distance. To her he must have looked like another rag-tag soldier walking across High Oaks property on his way home.

She shielded her eyes with her hand, then suddenly she stiffened as Dan began to move rapidly toward her, his hand raised.

"Catherine!" he called. He heard her cry out, then, she was off the porch and running toward him.

She lifted her skirts and flew across the ground. Suddenly she was in his arms, crying his name over and over. He crushed her to him and filled his senses with the sweetness of her.

His eyes were hot and blurred with tears as hers were. They could not even see each other, but it was not necessary. There was no necessity to see ... only to feel.

He never wanted to let her go; feverishly he kissed her, her cheeks, her soft surrendering lips. He kissed her again and again hungrily. "Catherine," he whispered between kisses, "Catherine my sweet, my love Catherine."

"Oh Dan," she sobbed, "you're home, thank God you're home safe."

He held her a little away from him and his eyes devoured her, absorbing her slim golden beauty as if he wanted to print it within his heart.

"It's over Catherine, it's over. I'm home to stay. There will be no more separations for us."

"You're home, you're home, you're here. Nothing else matters in the world now. You're home, Dan my love and you'll never have to go away again." He drew her into his arms again, savoring the feel of her slim body pressed against his. Then he bent his head and covered her mouth with his in a long lingering kiss that brought him home completely.

They stood for several minutes just holding each other, drawing strength from each other. Then he slid his arm about her waist and they started to walk toward the house.

"It's ... It's all so changed," he said, then he laughed harshly, "that was a stupid thing to say, we've all changed. Our whole world, everything we know is changed." He paused for a moment then drew her tighter against him. "All except you Catherine. You're still beautiful, and still my rational common sense hold on everything."

"I've been so frightened Dan. I'm afraid all my stability and common sense have been teetering on the edge. I need your strength to help keep me going. Now you are here I can begin to live again."

"Live again," he said softly, "we've lost so much Catherine. Will we ever be able to live again? Maybe ... Now that I can see, feel and taste High Oaks ... Maybe I'll be able to help my father and mother rebuild High Oaks ... It will never be the same again, but at least we can find some happiness in each other."

She stopped walking and looked up into his eyes. She, in her joy of having him home, had forgotten the tragedy of High Oaks. Dan read her face well, much too well. He stood frozen in fear of what her words would be.

"Catherine?" he said, afraid of what was coming "... tell me," he added gently. "My mother?"

Catherine shook her head negatively.

"My father," he said in an agonized voice.

She wanted to say something to ease the pain she saw

in his eyes, but there were no words that could soothe the depth of loss he felt.

"Tell me what has happened Catherine," he said gently, aware of how hard it must be for her.

She began to speak quietly, and he made no sound, did not try to interrupt her until she told him of how Jessie had brought Gregory home.

He wept silent, bitter tears, but still he did not speak. Then she told of how Virginia had been so wounded by Gregory's death that she had lost control of her emotions.

"Dan . . . She's been hurt. With everything that has happened to her life. To High Oaks, and Gregory's death. It has been almost too much for her. It's you Dan, you're the only hold she has on sanity. Once she knows you're home, once she knows you're safe . . . maybe she too can begin to live again."

Again he drew her tighter against him and bent to kiss her gently but lingeringly. "Let's go find her Catherine. It's about time we got started in putting our lives back together."

They walked up the front steps and opened the door. Inside they were met by silence. Then a sound came from the kitchen. Dan walked over and pushed the door open.

Jessie had just finished putting down an armload of wood by the kitchen fireplace. He turned as the door opened, then gazed in open mouthed amazement for a second, then gave a shout of happiness.

Dan crossed the room and threw both arms about Jessie in a bear hug. Jessie too clung to the boy he had helped to raise and whom he loved.

"Jessie, it's good to see you."

"Sho boy, it does this ole heart good to see yo's well and home. Dis here place ain't the same without your wild ways 'round here. Yo well boy? Yo'all right? Yo sho looks powerful skinny and hungry. Come to think of it yo looks like yo'all needs a bath too."

"Well you're right on just about all counts. I need a bath, I need clean clothes, I need some food. But the most important thing I need I've got. Catherine ... you, Jessie, Catherine told me. You brought my father home. I'm grateful Jessie."

"He belong buried here. He wanna come home to die. I couldn't let him die out there. He was a good man, ain't no way I could leave him there."

"Well I'm grateful," Dan repeated. "You've always been my best friend Jessie, I guess now you're more important in my life."

"Jessie," Catherine said. "Where's Virginia?"

"Ah 'spects Miss Catherine, she's up there with him. She always is first thing in the morning. She ain't come down yet."

He spoke to Catherine, but his eyes held Dan's.

"I'll go with you Dan," Catherine said.

"No," he whispered softly, "No, let me talk to her alone first. Where is she?"

"Up on the hill where your father's buried."

Dan touched Catherine's cheek lightly, then without speaking again he left the room. Jessie and Catherine stood looking at each other in mute agony as they heard the outer door close.

Dan stood on the back porch and gazed up the hill to where he could see Virginia standing in the small cemetery. She stood with her back to him. Her shoulders slumped and she looked so lost and dejected that it made him wince. Then he began to walk slowly across the lawn and up the hill.

Virginia vaguely heard him coming, but she thought it was either Catherine or Jessie. She stiffened in resistance for she knew they would try to draw her away from Gregory. She needed to be near Gregory, for he was the only one who knew her guilty secret.

Dan stood behind her, reluctant to shock her. Then he spoke softly, "Mother?"

His voice entered her mind like a bolt of lightning, and she felt as if a huge hand had closed about her heart and was stopping her breathing. She spun about, her eyes wide with pleasure.

"Dan!" she cried, "my son! Dan, oh, Dan."

He took her gently in his arms and held her close to him, feeling her thin arms grip him and her body tremble against him like a leaf in a hurricane.

She cried, thick heavy sobbing tears, her body quivered with the intensity of them. It hurt him to feel the pain that was within her.

"Mother, don't cry anymore, please. I know how hurt you are, but Father wouldn't have wanted you like this. We'll start over, the three of us, and we'll make High Oaks a place to be proud of. Don't cry."

Virginia tried to regain control of herself, she lifted her head and looked into his eyes. The emerald eyes sparkled back at her with sympathy and understanding and love. She lifted her hand and pressed it against his cheek.

"I knew you would come back. I knew God couldn't

be so cruel as to take my husband and my son. Dan ...
You won't ever leave us? I have told your father over
and over ... When Dan comes home ... He'll make
everything all right."

That she was grasping at shadows was clear to him,
for no one could make everything all right again. But
her speaking of Gregory as if she could contact him
made him shiver in alarm. Catherine had told him of her
condition, yet he was still unprepared for what he saw
now. She had slipped beyond reality, and built a shaky
world on him alone. It frightened him in a way that the
war never had. If he failed her somehow would she slip
beyond help? He knew he would do everything in his
power to prevent that. Yet a strange premonition held
him.

"Come mother, let's go back to the house."

"Of course," she replied. "You must be tired and
hungry. I'll have a meal prepared for you."

Again her regression to the way things had been
struck him, but he remained silent.

She took his arm and began to walk back down the
hill with him. "You must meet our guest Dan. She's a
countess. I've been waiting for you to come back. We
should really have a party. Invite all our friends. The
Masons, the Waverleys ... oh, and the Everly boys ..."

"Mother," he said gently," the Everleys ... they
both died at Gettysburg."

She looked at him vacantly, as if his words ruffled a
memory she had safely put away. Then she smiled and
continued talking as if he had never spoken.

"The Countess is a lovely lady. She has been visiting
with the Southerlands ... You remember the Souther-

lands don't you? Why, I believe you'all had a crush on her at one time."

"Abby," he said softly. He remembered Abby. She was so beautiful, he had fancied himself in love with her. He smiled, thinking of Catherine, and the rare beautiful thing they shared. No, he had never loved Abby, but the time had been one of gay carefree pleasure, and he had been so young and carefree then. Four years ago, it felt like an eternity. In four years he had lost his youth.

They went in the house and crossed the wide hall to the sitting room. Dan observed how she totally ignored all the debris and destruction about her.

The Countess had come downstairs to find Jessie and Catherine seated at the kitchen table sipping coffee.

"Good morning," she smiled. "Has Virginia not come down yet?"

"Yes, she's at the cemetery." Catherine replied. A note of sadness appeared in Yvonne's eyes.

"'Tis a shame."

"It might be different now. Dan is with her. He came home his morning."

"How wonderful."

"More than wonderful," Catherine replied. "Very near a miracle."

At that moment Dan and Virginia walked into the room. When Jessie and Catherine's eyes rose to meet them the Countess turned. Her eyes grew wide and she made a startled cry of absolute shock. Her gaze welded on Dan in absolute disbelief.

"Countess, what's wrong?" Virginia said.

Dan laughed embarrassedly, "I know I don't look too good, but surely not enough to frighten you."

As rapidly as she had lost control she regained her composure. Her face grew impassive and her eyes revealed nothing of the rapid thoughts that filled her mind at the sight of Dan Wakefield.

"But of course not," she smiled, "even under the disreputable exterior one can see the oh so handsome young man."

Her French accent revived some old memories for Dan who immediately called on his French.

"Madam, vous etes de bonne, grace j'espere reparer de bonne heure le degats. Dites-moi pourquoi je faisais peur a vous."

"Oh sir," she laughed, "it would not be kind to speak French in front of the others. We will speak the English. No?"

"Yes, of course," Dan said, but he watched her for a quiet moment.

Dan was urged upstairs where a tub of hot water was provided. He found some remains of his clothes and after his bath and shave he dressed. Downstairs a meal, the best they could provide, was set before him. He ate so much that everyone laughingly declared he would burst should he swallow one more mouthful.

He was fussed over, pampered and gently cared for the balance of the day. At the end of it he finally urged his mother, Jessie and the Countess to bed.

"I'll be here in the morning, and for all the mornings the rest of our lives." he said.

They reluctantly agreed, and only because they could clearly see he wanted to be alone with Catherine.

When they left Dan and Catherine stood across the room and gazed at each other.

"Catherine . . . come and walk with me."

"Walk . . . where?"

"I . . . I never got to say goodbye to my father."

"Of course. I understand," she said softly.

He reached out his hand and she walked across the room and took it. They walked up the hill to stand beside Gregory's grave. They were silent for a long time.

"He loved High Oaks so much," Dan said quietly, "and he trusted me, loved me so much he gave it to me."

"It was not misplaced love or trust Dan. He chose well."

He put his arms about her and held her close to him.

"I need you Catherine. I've been afraid a lot of times in my life, but nothing like this. Father gone, mother . . . like she is. I don't want to lose High Oaks."

"You won't Dan. You're not alone. Jessie and I are here. We love you, we have faith in you, and we'll help you any way we can."

He smiled as his arms tightened about her.

"If you tried for a million years you could never imagine how much I love you. I used to sit around the fire at night and remember how soft your skin is . . . how blue your eyes are, and how remarkably soft your hair is. I could actually feel it if I thought hard enough."

She remained quiet, her arms about his waist and her head lay against his chest.

"I love you Catherine," he said softly.

"I know Dan . . . I know."

"Tomorrow we'll go into town and find the reverend. If you agree we'll be married right away. Let's begin everything together. Let's rebuild High Oaks together."

"Yes Dan ... Yes."

He tipped up her chin with gentle fingers, and kissed her.

"I want you Catherine, for all the lost and lonely nights I spent without you."

"And I have waited so long ... so very long," she replied. "Remember the gardener's cottage on my father's plantation?"

"Could I forget the night I first found you."

"And the small cottage here at High Oaks?"

He chuckled. "I had a devil of a time trying to get away that night. I thought they would find me and shoot me."

"I locked the door that night, and I've never been back since."

"Shall we go and see if everything is still the same?" He whispered.

"Yes," came the soft reply.

"They walked down the hill with their arms about each other. Catherine went into the house and found the key. Then they walked across the lawn to the cottage.

From a window on the second floor the Countess stood and watched the lovers disappear inside the cottage. There was a frown between her eyes as she watched. After a few minutes she dropped the curtain she had held aside and walked to her bed.

She sat down, her face showing signs of sincere puzzlement.

"Alexander Dubonne," she said softly, "I wonder ... Alexander ..."

Thirty-three

The end of the war was greeted by Alexander with a surge of joy that was beyond control. It was over! He could go to Abby, try to convince her to come home with him. He didn't know if he would have any success in getting her away from Fernhill, but he intended to try.

The first thing he did was to sit down and write his parents a letter to explain why he intended to take a detour on the way home.

My Dear Family:

You will have to excuse the quick letter. We celebrated the end of this disastrous war just a little too much last night and my hands are a little shaky today, not to mention that my eyes are a little blurry.

The war is over. I can hardly believe it. I'm afraid I'll wake up tomorrow and find this is a dream and we're still involved in this nightmare. Anyway, on top of all the great news that the war is over, I have something else I have to tell you.

Under normal circumstances I could be home in less than four weeks, but I'm afraid I won't be.

Father, since you might understand this better than the others you might take the time to explain in more detail what I'm going to tell you. I'm on my way to Georgia. I'm on my way to Fernhill plantation where I expect to find the woman I intend to make my wife.

Once I persuade Abby to become my wife I'll bring her home with me. Since that might take some time all I can say is I'll be there as soon as circumstances permit.

You all know I love you very much, and it would take something remarkable to keep me from coming straight home . . . but then Abby is remarkable and I can't see the balance of my life without her.

I'll see you as soon as I possibly can.

All my love,
Alexander

He posted the letter, gathered his few belongings necessary for travel and made arrangements for the balance of his things to be shipped home.

He had nothing but military apparel, and didn't bother to buy civilian clothes. Still in uniform, as soon as his work was finished and he was granted permission to leave, he mounted his horse and headed for Fernhill, for Abby, and for a happy future.

At Fernhill Abby stirred restlessly in bed, but sleep

seemed to be evasive. Finally she rose and walked to the window and looked out over the land.

It was well past dawn and she could hear stirrings downstairs. Someone briskly chopped wood somewhere out of her sight, and she could hear Loel singing in the kitchen.

How wonderful this all would be if only Alexander were here to share it with her.

She turned from the window and dressed, then she went downstairs. No matter how often she walked through the house she could not get used to its deserted, uncared for look. Memories of its past rare beauty always lingered in her mind.

She knew she would never be able to restore its old beauty, but with Alexander to help her they could turn it into something much better than what it was.

She walked to the kitchen, and Loel turned to smile at her from the stove where she was preparing breakfast.

"They ain't much this mawnin' Miss Abby, but we got some eggs and I done made some fresh bread yesterday."

"Just some coffee Loel, is there any?"

"Yessum, they is, but coffee ain't enough for all the workin' yo' do. You'all got to eat sompthin'."

"I'm not hungry."

"You'all ain't ate worth a shoot since dat Yankee done gone. He gonna come back and find yo' so puny and sickly he gonna skedaddle for home without thinkin' about marryin' you."

"Don't worry about that Yankee Loel," Abby laughed.

"Yessum. Noah done gone to town today. He gonna

swap dat ole gun of pa's fo' some seed if he can. Pa says better to plant some seed than to aim dat gun at someone.''

"Your father is right. I wish I had known he was going. There might be some things in the house he could have bargained with. Well maybe next time." Abby sat down at the table, and Loel placed a cup of coffee in front of her.

"Any sugar?"

"No'um dey ain't any. Ain't been any fo' a week."

"Ummm. Maybe Noah will think to try and get a little," she sighed. "What I would give for a cup of that foamy chocolate Josie used to make ... or one of those sweet sticky little buns."

"Yes'um, sometimes in da kitchen Josie used to slip me one ... dey sho was good."

"Everything was good ... it seems like ..."

She shook away the memories and rose.

"It does no good to dwell in the past. Those days are gone forever, and we have to make the best of what we have. Alexander will come back one day, and we'll work together to make it all it was. Someday things will be good again."

"Miss Abby?"

"What?"

"Dat man ... Mr. Alexander ... no matter what yo' thinks ... He still a Yankee. What makes yo' think he gonna stay here and work like a field hand? He gonna wanna go nawth ... Home ... Where he kin do what he wants, where he'll be with his own kind."

Abby looked at her angrily. "Alexander knows how much Fernhill means to me ... he'll stay ... he'll help me."

"What about what's important to him? Or don't that count?"

"It'll be important to him," Abby said, but sudden doubt weakened her voice. "It will," she added softly.

Pity sparkled momentarily in Loel's eyes for a moment before she turned back to the stove.

"Yes'um."

Abby stood up and walked out of the kitchen. She stepped out on the back porch and closed the kitchen door behind her. Loel's words had opened startling new thoughts she didn't like. She knew she could never leave Fernhill, not in its darkest hour.

Moses stood in the shade of a large tree slowly and solidly chopping wood for the stove. She walked down the steps and crossed the lawn to stand near him.

"Good morning Moses."

"Mawnin' Miss Abby."

"Loel said you sent Noah to find some seeds."

"Yes'um, it's near time fo' plantin' iffen we wants to eat. The few scrawny chickens and that ole cow we got ain't enough to keep us goin'."

"How are we going to plow?"

" 'Spect me and Noah kin do it. Only we gonna plow one field here and one by our cabin. When yo' man comes home we'll be leavin'."

"You . . . you prefer that cabin to here?"

"Miss Abby," he said gently, "we'uns doan belong in dat big house. 'Sides dat it got too many memories hauntin' it. Miss Abby, yo' be mad iffen I say my piece?"

"No Moses, go on, say what you want."

"Sell dis place Miss Abby. Go wif dat boy and start a new life. I kin see from when he was here. Dat boy, he loves yo' a powerful heap."

"If he loves me won't he be willing to stay here and help me?"

He looked at her and smiled. "Does yo' measure love like dat? Yo put a price on it? Are yo' goin' to ask what he wants or jus' tell him what yo wants?"

"Don't be silly Moses, of course I'll ask him. But . . . But I need him here," she added.

Moses was about to answer her when a loud shout rang out. Both Abby and Moses spun about and watched Noah running in their direction. He was breathless, but grinning broadly as he came to their side.

"Pa . . . Miss Abby . . . de wah . . . it's ober! It's ober!"

"Noah!" Abby cried.

"Yessum, Lee done surrendered at Appomattox. It's ober."

"Surrender," Abby whispered. She turned and walked off across the field toward the woods.

She walked without seeing for her eyes were blurred with hot tears. All for nothing, she thought, all the death, the destruction, the waste. Her father . . . his life gone for a cause that lay defeated.

She stood in the shade of a tree and leaned against it. A soft moaning sob escaped her lips, then was followed by another and another until she sagged to her knees crying abandonedly.

It was over two hours later that she lay exhausted against the thick roots of the tree. She opened her eyes to see the sun high overhead, sending its rays down through the trees.

"Alexander," she whispered as she slowly rose to her

feet. "Alexander."

She started for home, sure that Alexander was her answer to every problem. The touch of his hand, his strength were all she would ever need. "Soon," she murmured. "He'll come soon."

The days began to move along . . . slowly, agonizingly slow. Every day Abby watched the road . . . and every night she went to bed with a prayer on her lips that the next day would be the one.

Days blended into weeks and still there was no sign of Alexander. Many men crossed her land on their journey home. She watched the bitterness of defeat unfold before her and she held herself together with only one thought . . . Alexander.

She had been in the fields planting with Noah, Loel and Moses. She stood and pressed her hands to her aching back, then stretched to relieve the taunt tired muscles unused to such work. She gazed toward the house in time to see a carriage turn up the drive. She was shocked for a moment, then the only reasonable thought came to her mind.

"Alexander!" she whispered, then she ran. She stumbled on the newly turned earth, but kept her feet. Again she was flying across the field.

She came to a stop a few feet from the carriage half crying, half laughing. A look of surprise crossed her face as the carriage door opened and Yvonne stepped out.

"Yvonne," Abby said.

"Bon jour cherie," she called. "You are pleased to see me, no?"

"Yes, yes, I am." Abby laughed as they threw their arms about each other.

"I didn't know where you had gone. I came to Atlanta to find you," Abby said.

"I left just before the final attack."

"Where did you go?"

"Well my dear, that is a long and very interesting story. If I may come in and talk I will tell you."

They went inside and once comfortably seated Abby began to ask questions. "Where did you go?"

"I took the chance of visiting your cousin Catherine Markland at High Oaks."

"High Oaks," Abby replied. "Catherine is staying at High Oaks?"

"She is. I stopped by her parents' home, but it was completely destroyed and they were living with her uncle. That is why I went on to High Oaks. I met your young friend Dan Wakefield."

"Is everyone . . . everything all right at High Oaks?"

Yvonne shook her head negatively and told her about Virginia's condition and Gregory's death and the terrible condition High Oaks itself was in.

"The only good thing was when Dan returned home. He and Catherine were married a day later. They are extremely happy with each other. I left the day after the wedding to come here."

"I don't understand, why should you want to come back here?"

"Because I know the man you love will come here someday; I have something to tell him that shall be, at the least a shock, and at the most one of the happiest things in his life."

"Alexander?"

"Yes, Alexander Dubonne."

459

"Why do you think he will come here?"

"You told me more than you knew you did. I think he loved as deeply as you. Knowing that I think he will come."

"I hope you're right, but it's been weeks and there is no sign of him."

"Time cherie ... give him time. Come, tell me what you have been about since we parted. You look like a skinny little farm girl."

"I guess that's what I am," Abby laughed, "but we have to survive don't we?"

Yvonne smiled and sat back in her chair and listened to Abby talk. She thought of the surprise she had in store for Alexander.

"Cherie, this Alexander, he can offer you so much more than this. Don't be a fool like some die-hard rebels, live your life in the future, not in the past. Let him give you the good life you deserve."

"You sound like Moses and Loel," Abby laughed.

"Maybe they love you too," Yvonne replied softly.

"I'm going to ask Alexander to stay ... if he comes ... we'll ... we'll work it out."

"My dear," Yvonne said gently, "don't be a fool. Find happiness and hold on to it. Life is too short to mourn the past too long."

"I'll decide later ... when Alexander comes ... If," she whispered, "if he comes."

Alexander traveled as quickly as his war weary horse could carry him. He camped out under the stars at night, and tried to stay out of the path of soldiers returning home. A lone Yankee traveling in rebel territory would not have fared well at the moment.

It was difficult to travel so, and it slowed his progress a great deal. He chafed under the wasted time, but continued to use prudence.

He was elated and somewhat proud of himself when he crossed onto what he knew was Fernhill property. It would only be a matter of an hour or so until he would be near enough to see the house.

He crested the last hill, a smile on his face, and his heart singing Abby's name over and over.

Then the smile faded, and the song was stilled as he stared with disbelieving eyes at the scene that lay before him.

What had once been a magnificent house, and had been brutalized but left intact, lay before him a mass of blackened ruins. It had been burnt so that all that was left standing was a chimney and a few blackened ruins.

He nudged Major into a ground consuming run and stopped by what would have been the front porch. The only thought in his mind was Abby . . . Where was Abby?

He dismounted and walked among the ruins. Then suddenly another thought came to him. There was still a remnant of warmth he could feel as he walked through the ruins. It was still warm . . . then the burning had to have been done in the past day or at the most two.

He knew there were bands of scavengers about, deserters from both sides, who took the South's desperate helplessness as an opportunity to loot, to burn, even kill.

Terror filled his heart as it pounded relentlessly Abby . . . Abby . . . Abby.

He didn't know from which direction they had come or gone. He had no idea where to begin a search, yet he mounted his horse and prepared to begin.

He rode past the house, across the fields and toward the woods. Then a man stepped from the edge of the woods, and in an instant he recognized him ... Moses. Moses waved to Alexander who was beside him in minutes.

"Mister Alexander, Ah's been watchin fo' yo' for days. Ah's sho glad to see yo'all done come."

"Abby! Moses where Abby? Is she all right?"

"Well suh, she is an she ain't."

"She's been hurt!"

"No suh, she all right. She jus had all de fight and de spirit whupped outta her."

"What happened Moses?"

"Bunch of scavengers. Good thing I seed 'em comin'. I got everybody out the back way. But Miss Abby, she seed 'em loot and burn the house. She done cried like she was dyin'. Since den she been grievin'. I sho am glad yo's here. Maybe yo kin help her. I sho prayed to de Lawd you'd come and do dat."

"Where is she Moses?"

"She done took to walkin' down by de stream. Yo'all kin find her her down there."

Alexander handed the horse's reins to Moses and walked toward the stream. When he found it he walked along its edge until he saw her.

She was seated at the water's edge. She was gazing down into the water and he felt he had never seen anyone look so crushed and defenseless as Abby did then. He knew she had received the final hurt that had broken her.

He walked toward her but she was so deep in her thoughts she didn't hear him. He could see the tears on her cheeks and the way her hands lay listlessly in her lap.

She is the South, he thought. Lost, forlorn and broken. Was he the conqueror? His mind and heart revolted against such an idea. They were one, as their torn country should be, and he had to find the words to mend the wounds.

He walked slowly to her side, but still her reverie was so deep she did not hear. He knelt in front of her.

She looked up at him with pain deadened eyes. There was a weariness about her as if she had fought a terrible fight with all her strength and lost.

"Alexander," she whispered in a hoarse tear ridden voice.

He held out his hand. "Take my hand Abby," he said in a firm commanding voice. She reacted automatically, without thought, and reached out her hand to him.

"Hold it! Hold it tight," he commanded, and he felt her hand grip a little more firmly.

"You're not alone, Abby. This is not the end, it's the beginning. Together we can face it. Look at me Abby."

Her wide blue eyes met his firm gaze. "I love you. I won't lose you, and I won't let you defeat yourself. We can put the past behind us Abby ... I won't let you go," he added gently. "Do you hear me, my love? I won't let you go."

He stood, drawing her with him. They stood facing each other, then with a low moaning sob she was in his arms, whispering his name again in painful hope as his mouth met hers.

He held her against him and caressed her hair gently as she cried. He said nothing, only let her wash away the pain that had burst its confines and enveloped her. When she could cry no more, when her body lay weakly against his, when he could feel her trembling cease, only then did he cup her face in his hands and hold her eyes with his.

"All the pain and misery are over Abby. Stay with me, start a new life with me . . . Please love, I need you, maybe more than you do me. I love you Abby."

He kissed her gently. "For now we'll start with today. We'll leave the past and the future to themselves. There's just today, just you and me."

"I've been so lost, so frightened," she sighed.

"I know love, I know."

"I thought . . ."

"What?"

"That you might never come back."

"Little fool. I can't exist anywhere else than with you. I'll always be here Abby, you can hold onto that . . . Hold on to me, love, as I do you. We don't need anything else but each other."

"Yes. . . Yes Alexander, hold me . . . Hold me and I'll believe."

He held her close and for a while they remained silent. Then she spoke quietly.

"What will we do Alexander?"

"For now, we'll go home . . . We'll get married, and one day we'll rebuild. Your heart is here, and I don't want you to lose Fernhill. After that," he laughed, "we'll just let the future happen." He took her hand,

"Suppose we go back and tell Moses you're all right. He's been worried to death about you."

"Dear Moses, what a rock of strength he has been. Without him and his family I don't know what would have become of me."

"Don't worry, I intend to thank him properly. I'll see he gets all he needs to get his farm running."

"You will have to thank the countess too."

"Countess?"

"Countess LeClerc," Abby replied. "She's been a good friend. In fact the only reason she was here was to talk to you. It seems she knows some deep dark secret she says you should know."

"Sounds interesting," he replied.

"Yes, it makes me wonder what I don't know about your past. Tell me Alexander, what secret does a Countess know that she has to travel from High Oaks to tell you."

"My love," he chuckled, "I've never met a Countess in my life, and I can't imagine a secret that links me to High Oaks, a place I've never seen before."

He put his arm about her waist and they walked through the woods to Moses' cabin.

Alexander could not quite make out the features of the woman in the doorway, for she stood on the shadowed porch. They grew close and the woman stepped out into the sunshine.

Alexander stopped and his face registered shock. Yvonne laughed and walked up to him. No French accent was apparent as she laughed and said:

"Hello . . . Alexander Dubonne. I've come to repay a very old debt."

Alexander gasped in surprise. "Belle!"

465

Thirty-four

"Belle?" Abby repeated in shock, but already Alexander was laughing. If that took her by surprise, Yvonne and Alexander embracing each other did more.

"Belle, what in God's name are you doing here? . . . and a Countess?"

"The title is legitimate Alexander. Can you imagine Belle Thompson a member of royalty?"

They stood laughing together, and Abby felt a twinge of jealousy. At that moment Alexander turned to her, put his arm about her waist again, and drew her closer to him.

"My darling," he said, "Belle is a very old friend of mine from home. I imagine she has quite a story to tell us."

Belle laughed, "I am a friend to both of you, and I shall prove it shortly."

"This promises to be quite interesting. Abby says you have something important to tell me. Some deep dark secret."

"Let's go inside and sit down." Belle said, "I'll tell

you how I got to be where I am, and then, I want you to be sitting down when I tell you my other piece of news. If you aren't it might knock you off your feet."

"Good heavens, that does sound intriguing," he replied. "What . . . ?"

"Never mind Alexander, one story at a time," Belle replied as she took hold of his other arm and they walked into the cabin together.

Inside, Abby asked Loel to make some coffee. They sat about the rough hewn table.

"Now suppose you start at the beginning," Alexander said.

"First," Belle said as she reached across the table to touch Abby's hand. "You must understand that Alexander was kind to me at a time when I desperately needed kindness. I am grateful for the opportunity to repay him in some way for all he has given me."

Abby smiled, but Alexander knew he was going to be in for some discomfort later. He knew quite well the sweet smile on Abby's face was not exactly compatible with what was going on inside. He held her hand beneath the table; and gave it a reassuring squeeze, and the eyes she turned to him were clear, and open . . . and told him nothing at all.

Belle went on with her astounding story.

"When I left Philadelphia I had a great deal of money, for I had sold everything that . . ." she cast a quick look at Alexander, "that I had. I knew it would not last long if I just stayed in New York and spent it. I decided to build it into a chance at something better . . . And I did. I sailed to France . . . not as Belle Thompson, but as Lady Claire, recent widow of a younger son of a wealthy family. Thanks to Alexander's teaching and his books I did well. I set up a small salon and in no time I met Count LeClerc. He was handsome and wealthy . . . and we fell in love. I was afraid his family would never accept me if they knew who I really was. I kept the secret . . . or thought I did . . . until after we married. On our wedding night he informed me that he knew who I was but he loved Belle Thompson as much as he did Lady Claire and he would keep my secret too." Her eyes darkened with memories. "We were happy . . . for over two years we were happy, then . . . he was riding, he always loved his horses . . . somewhat like you Alexander. . . . The horse threw him, and he died instantly."

"Oh Belle, I'm so sorry," Abby said softly.

"I was lost . . . and to my distress I found that his family had finally discovered my true identity. They were enraged, and I thought I would have to return to America as poor as when I had been born. But to his family's distress I found that he had set up a source of money for me they could not touch. I left France, wealthy, independent . . . and with nowhere to go. It was then I met Col. Matthew Brady."

Alexander gave a startled look at the mention of the name. "Lincoln's right arm in the espionage department?" he questioned.

Abby's eyes widened and Belle's eyes were filled with genuine distress. "I'm sorry Abby, but I hope you will understand. What you did for the South I did for the North. It had been planned that I should meet you, and we thought those plans had gone awry when your father was captured. It was only fate that led me to you that night."

"You used me," Abby said quietly.

"Abby I have a very genuine affection and admiration for you. I could have turned you in and been lauded as a heroine. Instead I helped you come home. As you, I wanted only these hostilities to end. If I sent messages North it was for the purposes of ending all this. Please, Abby, try to understand."

"I do," Abby whispered in a painful voice.

"Go on Belle," Alexander said, as he again gave Abby's hand a comforting squeeze.

"When I knew Alexander was the man you loved I thought it best that I did not return from Atlanta. I was curious about your friends so I traveled there. I was to receive the shock of my life when I arrived at High Oaks. The war ended and Dan Wakefield came home. I think the rest of this story will give you the biggest and I hope the happiest surprise of your life, Alexander. You have one of the strangest attachments to High Oaks that anyone could ever dream of."

"High Oaks. Dan Wakefield. Those two names have cropped up in my life quite often."

"How?" Belle asked.

"Abby seemed startled at my resemblance to him when I first met her. Then a friend of mine wrote me a letter and mentioned again resemblance. I guess we must look pretty much alike."

"The resemblance doesn't end there."

"What do you mean?" Abby questioned.

"Alexander, do you remember a long time ago you showed me the medal you wore around your neck?" Belle said.

Alexander felt Abby's hand slip from his and groaned

inwardly at the explaining he was going to have to do later.

"Yes."

"Well . . . after Dan and Catherine were married, the day after, in fact, we had a little scare. During the night there was a small fire. It was not enough to do any harm, but it brought Dan running. He had his shirt off. I saw something then that put all the pieces together for me. A day or so later I had a chance to question Dan Wakefield alone. It seems Dan was an orphan the Wakefields adopted . . . It also seems they found him . . . literally found him half dead. They could find none of his family and so after a long time they legally adopted him and his name became Dan Wakefield."

"I don't know what this has to do with me, Belle. I never met this Dan Wakefield in my life."

"Oh yes Alexander, you have," Belle answered softly, "you have."

"If I did I don't remember."

"It's a memory you put away a long time ago. You see, what I saw around his neck was a medal exactly like yours, and what I found out when I questioned him was that his name before he became Dan Wakefield was . . . Dante Dubonne."

Alexander stared at her in profound shock, his face grew pale and his voice trembled as he replied.

"Belle! Dear God, is this some kind of joke? It's impossible. Dante . . . alive? But . . . I saw him go over-board in a storm so fierce no one could have survived it."

"You saw him go overboard . . . you and your family thought he died. He didn't. He was washed ashore very near dead."

"But ... why didn't he tell them who he was ... where we were? We would have come for him.

"Alexander, I'm not sure of the answer to that but I have my suspicions. There is much more I have to tell you, then you can make your own decisions."

Alexander's face was still ashen and he repeated in an awed voice. "Dante ... My brother ... alive ... I just don't believe this. I must go there right away. I must see for myself. All these years I thought ... My God I must go to him."

"Wait Alexander," Belle said. "There is so much more you should know."

She went on to tell him about what Dante's life had been, how he had been raised and how he loved High Oaks and his adopted parents.

"But it is not fair to Mother and Father ... To Celeste and to me. It is not fair to Dante either. What kind of people could keep us a secret, keep us apart, and how did they do it? Dante was nine, but he was bright. He would have found us."

"I believe he might have been led to either by one or both of the Wakefields. I think they told him you were gone, maybe drowned in a shipwreck. It is the only logical way."

"But that's outrageous!" Alexander said angrily. "They had no right ..."

"I know Alexander," Belle said gently, "but listen to the rest of the story."

She went on to explain as much of Dante's past as she had gotten from him without telling him the reason why. He had told her of his choices, of his growing love for

High Oaks and for Gregory Wakefield. In the end she told Alexander of Gregory's death and Virginia's condition.

"If you go there, seeking a brother, and Dante is he ... then you might just be pushing Virginia Wakefield into complete insanity. Dan loves her. He would not be able to forgive you easily for that. He is a man of honor. Could he turn his back on High Oaks, and on a woman he knew as mother for so many years when she is ill and needs him?"

Alexander rose abruptly and walked to the window. Abby and Belle exchanged glances both of fear and expectancy. Alexander folded his arms and rested them on the window sill, then, for a moment he rested his head against them as he spoke softly and agonizingly.

"Dante ... My God ... brother. All these years ... All these wasted years. I thought you were dead."

He turned to face Abby who had risen and come to stand behind him.

"Do you realize," he said in a bitter voice, "for four years my brother and I have been fighting each other. Good Lord we could have killed each other and never known."

Abby came to him and put her arms about his waist. He held her close and rubbed his chin absently against her hair. "My own brother ... I could have killed him."

Belle saw the terror-stricken misery of his eyes and she too rose. "What are you going to do Alexander?"

He seemed to be deep in thought for several minutes, then he said in a quiet firm voice.

"I've got to see him. I have to let him know we're alive."

"And Virginia Wakefield?"

"Dammit! She has no right! She has stolen from us what no human has the right to steal. Why should I care what happens to her? She deserves what she gets."

Abby looked up in surprise, then she reached up and lay her hand against Alexander's cheek. Her eyes held his and she could see the glitter of uncertain pain in them.

"You don't mean that Alexander," she said. "You are too compassionate a man to feel that way."

"Abby, what do you expect from me?" he said in a choked voice. "He's my brother. We were close, as close a brothers can be. She has taken years away from us."

"Maybe," Abby said gently. "God has taken people who had plenty to give to people who had nothing. You heard Belle tell you of the Wakefield children who died. Can you not feel what they must have felt when Dante seemed to be given to them. All they had to do was to tell one lie and a son could be theirs. I know you, Alexander my love, and I know you will find a way that will hurt no one."

Their eyes locked and held. She read his pain and anger accurately, but she had already read his heart a long time ago and she knew he would not let a fragile sick woman pay a price such as Virginia would, should she know the truth.

He inhaled a ragged breath and held Abby tighter as if he wanted to draw strength from her. Loel and Belle exchanged glances of relief.

"I will have to think," Alexander said. "I don't know what to do. All I can think of now is the grief and pain we all felt when we lost him. Give me some time."

"Of course you need time. This has been a tremendous shock. One does not have a brother return from the dead every day. Is there anything I can do to help?" Belle said.

"No," Alexander said. "No . . . I . . . I'm going for a ride. I have to be alone for a while. I have to think."

"Alexander . . ." Abby began.

"Abby," he said gently, "just give me some time. I'm trying to understand all of this. Just give me a little time."

She nodded with tears in her eyes. He brushed her lips with a gentle kiss, then left the cabin. Abby stood for a minute watching the closed door.

Belle came and stood beside her. "He is right Abby. Give him some time. He must find his own way."

"I know . . . I wish I could help him."

"He knows he has your strength too. He'll be back soon."

Abby nodded and they returned to their seats at the table. A deep silence fell over the room. A silence Abby found difficult to bear.

"Belle?"

"Yes?"

"Will you . . . will you tell me how you and Alexander met?" she smiled.

"I do believe Alexander has enough difficulties now. I don't want to make them any worse."

"You were lovers?"

"We were children. Abby he did not love me, not as he loves you. We gave to each other at a time when there was a need. He forgot me, he could never forget you. Did he not follow you, did he not fight for your

474

love? I can see his eyes when he looks at you. He loves you deeply."

"I would just like to know," Abby repeated.

"All right, I shall tell you, if you promise not to remind him of me . . . at least not too often."

"Only when necessary," Abby smiled again, then they both laughed and Belle told her the entire story.

Alexander rode for a while. There was a violent tumult within him. He had to forcefully restrain himself from going back to the cabin, getting Abby and going to High Oaks no matter what the cost to anyone.

He thought of Dante as he had been when they were children. They had been so very close. He relived their childhood, their escape from France, and then the dreadful storm that had separated them. Could he sacrifice another life to this tragedy? He knew he couldn't, yet he didn't know what to do.

He had to find a way, for now that he knew Dante was alive he knew he could never go home and face his family without him.

He dismounted by the stream, tied his horse and walked the dark quietness of the woods for a while in deep thought.

The sun grew dark as it began to descend below the hills. Long shadows fell across the clearing and still there was no sign of Alexander's return.

Abby insisted the others go to bed. She lit one candle, then stepped out on the porch. She sat on the top step watching the woods.

The pale full moon rose, lighting the area with a white

misty glow. Abby became worried. She walked slowly down the steps and across the clearing. She had not quite reached the edge of the woods when a rustling sound came to her. In another moment Alexander appeared. She breathed a sigh of relief as he rose toward her.

He rode to her side, then he reached down and effortlessly lifted her to the saddle in front of him. Major, well trained to his master's commands stood perfectly still. Without saying a word Alexander wrapped his arms about her. He bent his head and touched her mouth with his in a gentle kiss.

"Ummmmm," he murmured, "I had forgotten just how sweet you are my love."

"Alexander, I have been worried half to death about you and all you can think of now is kissing me."

"Best thought I've had in weeks," he chuckled. "If I had someplace to take you I should like to turn a kiss into some of the even sweeter memories I have."

"Alexander," she sighed as she rested her head against his chest. "You wonderfully impossible man. Will you tell me what you have decided to do?"

"Yes," he whispered, "as soon as you kiss me again."

Impatient to hear what his plans were Abby drew his head down to hers and kissed him.

"There! Now tell me."

"Abby," he laughed, "by no possible stretch of anyone's imagination could that be called a kiss. If you want information, madam, you shall have to do better than that. I remember kisses past that carried me through an entire war. I'll take one of those please."

Exasperated, but knowing he would not budge from his desires she put both arms about his neck, melted against him and lifted her mouth to touch his. Her lips parted beneath his questing ones in a searing hot kiss that sent every sense he had soaring. Tongues met, touched and sought to inflame. She heard the soft sound of passion as he crushed her to him and his lips played upon hers until she too was lost in the blazing need she felt.

He released her lips reluctantly, and she caught her breath as she dizzily returned to reality.

"Now."

"Now," he said huskily as he nuzzled her ear and let his hands caress her gently. "Let us get on to more important things."

"Alexander," she said with a threatening laugh, "you deceiving Yankee, tell me what you plan on doing or I swear I shall shoot you yet."

"Woman, you are still a stubborn rebel."

"And you are a Yankee with a one track mind," she laughed. Then her voice became gentler as she said, "Alexander please, I'm worried about you."

"Don't be, love. It was a terrible shock, especially the fact that we have fought each other for so long. But I will not destroy another life."

"What will you do?"

"I have to see him Abby, I have to. I have to let him know we are here and have never forgotten him. Especially now, that so much of his world has been destroyed. I want to know him, I want to help rebuild his life. I want to tell my . . . our parents so that one day we can find a way to be together as a family should be. I can understand how the Wakefields felt, but before God, Abby, they had no right to take Dante from us. I won't hurt her, but maybe fate will find a way to reunite us. Until then, without her knowing, I've got to see him."

"Have you thought of a way to do this?"

"Yes. Belle can act as liaison. She can go with me and arrange a meeting between Dante and me without anyone knowing."

"You and Belle?"

"Yes."

"Oh Yankee," she whispered softly, "if you think I plan on letting you and Belle travel to High Oaks together you are sadly mistaken. You belong to me Yankee, and I don't intend to let you forget it."

"Jealous, love?" he chuckled.

"Because I know she still loves you? Because I know she would grab you up in a minute if I let you go? I'm not jealous Yankee, nor am I stupid. If you go, I go with you. Dan knows me well. I can act as liaison between you."

"Uh huh, and it's a long way to Richmond from here."

"It is."

"We may have a chance to renew the relationship between North and South."

"We may," she replied softly as slowly he bent his head to again touch her lips with his.

"God," he groaned, "I wish there was some place besides that crowded cabin to go."

"Why Yankee," she chuckled, "you are on Southern soil. It's summer and the ground is warm."

"I've a blanket in my bedroll," he suggested hopefully.

"Sounds inviting," she murmured. "I know of a great huge tree where you can find soft ground and shelter among its roots."

"Abby," he whispered, "I have never been much interested in the trees that grew around here until now. Suppose you show me just where this tree is?"

With Abby giving directions he guided his horse back through the trees. After several minutes they found the huge tree of which she spoke. He dismounted, and lifted her down beside him taking every opportunity to hold her and kiss her warmly as he did. She spread the blanket while he unsaddled and hobbled Major so he would not stray. She stood by the blanket and watched him walk toward her. The pale moonlight came down through the trees in random beams that lit the area with a pale white glow.

Then suddenly he was beside her and with a soft whisper of her name he drew her gently against him. She could feel the warmth of him and the deep masculine scent of him filled her being with a heady heart-stirring need.

She closed her eyes as his fingers gently pulled the pins loose from her hair. It tumbled about her, and he slid his hands into its luxuriant depths and lifted her face so that their lips could blend again in a shattering kiss that left her breathless and clinging to him. He had to control himself with fierce effort, for it had been so long since he had possessed her that it set the blood flowing hotly in his veins and stirred his body to a flaming need of her.

Gently he began to remove the restricting clothes that were between them, savoring each touch of her smooth skin as he did. It took him only moments to discard his. He drew her cool soft body against him and could have cried out in the sheer joy of it.

"Abby . . . I've needed you for so long, loved you for so long that I can hardly believe you are here and this is not a dream."

"It's a dream I have shared for a long time my Yankee . . . too long. I love you Alexander . . . I love you."

He drew her down on the blanket with him and pulled her into the curve of his arm, nestled warmly against him. His hands, warm and strong, gently caressed her.

His kisses grew hungry, seeking, and fierce. She could have cried out with the exquisite pain of his possessive need, yet her hunger leaped to meet his in a fiery passion. They were heedless of anything but each other and the violent consuming flame that devoured all sense of time and place.

They came together in an almost violent surge of passion, possessing each other in a mutual sense of love and need.

Rocketed to the heavens, to plummet helplessly into a cauldron of ecstasy they clung to one another in a consuming climax that left them weak and clinging helplessly to one another as slowly their senses and breathing spiraled downward to normal. Yet it was a long time before either was capable of speech.

He held her close against him, reluctant for the world to intrude on their happiness.

He pulled the blanket over them and held her warm and safe against him.

"Alexander?"

"Yes."

"When do we go?"

"I guess as soon as possible," he sighed. "We have one thing to do first."

"What?"

"We are getting married tomorrow. I want to capture you permanently before anything else can happen."

"Then?"

"Then we go to High Oaks ... and home."

She sighed and snuggled closer to him for warmth, and for a time she slept. He held her and watched the moon rise high in the night sky.

As he watched he wondered what Dante was doing, and thinking of what he would say to a brother who, just weeks before, had been the enemy. Could they find a way together to help rebuild the lives that had been torn apart first by fate and then by war ... he hoped so ... he prayed so.

Thirty-five

It was in the wee hours of the morning that they both felt the chill of the cooling earth. Alexander wakened, and for a few moments he lay still and quiet, enjoying Abby as she lay curled against him and remembered many lonely nights and mornings that he had felt empty and alone.

Reluctantly, he gently shook Abby awake. He watched with pleasure as her sleepy blue eyes opened and lit with love when she saw him.

"Much as I hate to leave here," he said gently as he held her close to him, "I'm afraid we must go."

She shivered with the sudden cold and moved closer to him.

"That is a sure way to keep us here another hour or so," he whispered.

"Alexander, how good it is to wake up secure and safe knowing you're here, that you'll never leave again."

"I know. I guess I realized I was lonely for you but, not as much as I am now. I'm so grateful it is all over and we are still together. There were times when I was afraid it would never be."

He kissed her. "Cold or no, woman, we have to get

up. It's only an hour or two 'til dawn and I'm sure Moses and his family are early risers."

Abby dressed quickly as did Alexander for they were thoroughly chilled. He saddled Major, mounted, and drew Abby up before him.

He let Major pick his way slowly back to the cabin. He enjoyed the quiet solitude and Abby's slim body nestled close to him.

She too felt the strength and security of the hard muscular arm that held her close to him.

They arrived at the cabin before dawn. When he lifted her from the saddle, Alexander took the last opportunity to kiss her one last time before they went inside.

Inside, Abby set about making some breakfast. Alexander had groaned about his hunger. By the time the scent of fresh coffee and food being prepared filled the air, the others came stumbling sleepily one by one from their rooms.

Once breakfast was over, Alexander questioned Moses as to how soon they could find a reverend to marry him and Abby.

"We want to be married before we go."

"Won't take Noah no time atall to go and fetch him."

"Thanks, Moses."

When Moses sent Noah, Abby and Belle went for a short walk to talk for a while. It was then that Alexander took Moses aside and had a long talk with him. What he said brought a wide smile and a look of deep respect to Moses' face.

"Now, this is to be a secret between us, Moses. I don't want Abby to know yet."

"Yassah, ma mouth is shut. I'll do what you want."

"Good. I knew I could count on you."

"What yo decided to do, boy, 'bout your brother?"

"I'm going to High Oaks with Abby as soon as the wedding is over. Abby will arrange a meeting between . . . Dante and me without Mrs. Wakefield knowing. Once Dante and I are together again, we'll figure out what is best to do. I . . . I don't know how he'll feel, but I've got to let my parents and sister know he's alive. It's not fair to them to go on believing he's dead. Somewhere, somehow, there has to be a way for us all to be together again without hurting anyone. I don't know how, but, I'll find a way."

"Sho, boy, I 'spects Gawd wants yo'all to be together or he wouldn't have let you find out."

"It's a strange thing, Moses," Alexander said thoughtfully.

"What?"

"I've always hated war, hated the idea of killing anyone. When I fought I forced myself to think of them as enemies. I made myself shoot at what I would allow myself to think of as only gray uniforms. Now, I find my brother wore such a uniform. The idea of brother killing brother is beyond all reason. It makes me feel I was right in the first place. They are not enemy, or gray uniforms, they are brothers. I hope I never have to be part of such a thing again. My brother will always be an example to me of what I was doing when I raised a gun toward another."

"Yo' is right, boy. Killin' is bad no matter what reason a man puts to it. War is a bad thing, but, a war where a man fights agin his own is real bad. Ain't too many gets a lesson like yo and yo brother did. It's sho a hard way to learn."

"It sure is," Alexander replied.

Abby and Belle returned. Over an hour later Noah reappeared with the reverend in tow.

The ceremony was quick and simple and because of her silence, Alexander was sure Abby was hurt and disappointed. When the reverend had signed the papers and handed them to Alexander, he paid him an exorbitant fee which shocked the preacher who left with profuse thanks.

Alexander drew Abby aside. He put his arm about her and pulled her close to him.

"Abby, I'm sorry."

"For what?" she asked in surprise.

"For all the rush, for the reverend, for not taking you home and having a proper wedding. I'm sure this is not what you had planned on."

"Oh, Alexander," she laughed as she hugged him fiercely. "Can I tell you the truth?"

"What truth?"

"I always swore I'd never get married. It was the farthest thing from my mind. I had never thought of fancy weddings or pretty gowns. I was going to be the first woman in politics and I didn't have time for all that nonsense."

"Good God, I hope there's been more changes than wedding plans."

She cocked an eyebrow at him. "I shall let you worry about that for a while."

"I'm not too sure," Alexander groaned as he tightened his hold about her. "That the war is really over."

They laughed together and then Loel called them to eat the small amount of food she had been able to prepare.

"I think," Alexander said, "that we had best get started. It's a long way from here to Richmond. There's

485

no need to pack much, Abby. We'll buy another horse so we can travel quickly and whatever you might need, we'll buy along the way.''

"You might need a couple of extra blankets," Belle said with a chuckle.

"Why?" Alexander slipped neatly into her trap. "We'll be staying in boarding houses mostly along the way."

"Oh," Belle said innocently. "I thought you might be camping out on the way. It does get chilly at night . . . doesn't it?"

Alexander wanted to laugh, but since Abby was already blushing and her eyes held his, he choked the laughter back.

"No need for the blanket, Belle," he said in a voice so filled with humor that Abby eyed him suspiciously.

Belle offered him one of her horses in exchange for enough money to purchase another when she decided what her destination would be. They would purchase another saddle in Atlanta.

Abby and Alexander said goodbye to Moses and his family. Belle walked with them to their horses.

"Where will you go now, Belle?" Alexander asked. "What will you do?"

"I always land on my feet, Alexander, like a cat. Someone told me once no one could defeat me but myself. I am far from defeated. Maybe I shall visit you one day."

"You will always be welcome in our home, Belle," Abby said.

"And where will home be?" Belle questioned gently.

Abby smiled. "Any place that Alexander chooses for it to be."

Belle smiled again, more at the gaze of absolute love Alexander gave Abby than what she had said. She walked to Alexander's side. Putting her arms about his neck, she kissed him a very long and deep kiss goodbye.

"Goodbye, you two. May God bless you."

"Thank you, Belle," Abby replied.

They rode away, stopping once at the end of the drive to wave.

When they arrived in Atlanta, Abby was tired . . . or so she claimed. Alexander found a room and while Abby was having a bath, he set out to purchase a saddle. It took him over an hour to do so for despite the fact he had removed his uniform jacket, his military bearing and Northern accent labeled him Yankee. And, a Yankee found things a little difficult in Georgia at that time.

When he returned to their room, he found another tub of hot water prepared for him and a tray of warm food Abby had had prepared and brought up.

"I thought we might have supper here, alone together," she said. "After all, it is our honeymoon."

"It is, Mrs. Dubonne," he replied as he took her warm body in his arms. "We could stay here for a few days but the atmosphere outside this room is rather chilly. Abby, once this is over, we'll have a proper honeymoon. For now, if you'll bear with me, I want to get to Dante as soon as we can."

"Of course you do. I understand, Alexander. You get in the tub and wash the day's travel away, then we'll eat. I'm famished."

He discarded his clothes and sank gratefully into the hot water. He watched Abby. By the glow of the candlelight her skin shone like pale cream. She had brushed her clothes and hung them so they would be wearable the next day. All she wore was a filmy chemise that left very little to Alexander's imagination. She was busy arranging the dishes on the table and missed completely the devilish gleam in Alexander's eyes.

"Abby," he said nonchalantly. "Be a good wife and scrub my back will you? I can't seem to reach where it's the most uncomfortable."

She came and knelt beside the tub, took the rag and soap in her hand and lathered it briskly. His wondering gaze roamed warmly over half revealed curves and his heated blood urged him to much closer contact. He lifted his hand from the water and ran his wet fingers across her shoulder and down across the rise of her breast to the small valley between.

"Alexander, do sit still. You'll get me wet."

But now he had reached out to grip both wrists and the soap fell into the water. All pretense was lost as he drew her close and claimed her mouth with his.

"Alexander!" she yelped in surprise. But she was already too late, for strong arms gripped her and lifted her over the edge of the tub to plant her firmly in his lap. She fought momentarily but soon realized all fighting was useless. After a few minutes, her slim arms encircled his neck and she relaxed against him.

"Since I am already soaked, it seems of no use to fight."

"I always knew you were a clever girl," he chuckled as his lips nuzzled gently along her slender throat. With a quickness that made her gasp, he slipped the wet chemise over her head and cast it aside.

Now he drew her more firmly against him. Closing his eyes, he savored the feel of the slim, slippery curves beneath his roaming hands and the soft breasts that pressed firmly against his chest.

Slowly, as if all time in the world were theirs, he caught her warm, moist mouth with his. Nibbling gently and running his tongue lightly over her half parted lips, a gentle touch of a kiss, again and again and again, each a little firmer, each a little more seeking, each a little hungrier.

Now he felt her body quiver to warm stirring life as she moved more urgently against him and her mouth sought more of the exquisite pleasure his kisses gave.

"Miss Dubonne," he whispered. "Do you realize we have been married over eight hours and this is the first real opportunity I've had to kiss you?"

"My darling," she murmured. "Eight hours, the beginning of a lifetime."

"A beautiful beginning," he replied as he kissed her again. "Shall we continue in the beautiful manner in which we started?"

"Yes," she whispered, her lips against his. "Yes."

His kisses became deeper, warmer and his hands sought to draw the depths of pleasure from her.

Considerable splashing occurred and half the water in the tub found its way to the floor before it occurred to both of them that they were in the most ridiculous place in the world to make love.

No matter how they moved, they found it to be impossible. Abby pressed her face against Alexander's shoulder to stifle her nearly uncontrollable laughter. Alexander cursed heartily once then gave in to the laughter that overwhelmed him. They clung to each other for a minute weak with laughter at their remarkable situation.

Their laughter died as their eyes met. Slowly he rose

from the tub and drew her up to stand beside him. He placed both hands on her hips and bent forward to taste again the sweetness of most willing lips.

"Abby, my sweet, you could never imagine how very much I love you and how grateful I am that you have given up everything to come with me."

"I've given up nothing but memories, my husband, and you are more real, more wonderful than any."

His eyes held hers, telling her the truth of his love more deeply than words could ever do. She smiled as she read them and knew that all her choices had been right. That Alexander and his love for her were the road to freedom.

Slowly he bent and lifted her in his arms. While their eyes held and he rocked her gently against him, he took the few steps to the bed. There he lay her gently down following her until their bodies touched and her arms rose to draw him even closer.

Leisurely they sought to discover the pleasure their touch brought to each other. He wanted to know her, to plumb the depths of her need, to fill her with the deep sense of belonging and love that she gave him.

The joy of her filled him until he could not seem to bear the intense pleasure, yet he sought more. The sweet, slim body beneath him sought his with an urgency that set him trembling in passion. He heard her sighs of pleasure, felt her tremble and cling to him as he blended their bodies together in a rising song of ecstasy.

A sonata of love washed through them as they moved together in a crescendo of pleasure. They clung blindly as the flight of passion drew them higher and higher, then left them to drop breathlessly to reality.

They lay very still, holding each other, aware of the

rare and intensely beautiful emotion they shared so completely.

Alexander drew the blankets over them and they lay entwined, reluctant to even let sleep cheat them of one precious moment of their love for each other.

"Alexander?"

"Ummm?"

"It's a long way to Richmond."

"Yes, it is," he smiled as he drew her tight. "A lot of miles. A nice long honeymoon."

Her arms tightened about him and she laughed softly. He found he liked the sound of her laughter.

"Alexander?"

"What now, curious one?"

"What are you really going to do at High Oaks? I mean, you never really told me what your plans are."

"I thought I would find a nice out of the way place near Richmond and rent it. You could then go on to High Oaks. I'll leave the hour to you for you'll know the right moment. When it comes, you make the arrangements for us to meet. I think it would be best if you brought him to me. But, if you think another way will work let me know and we'll make what arrangements are necessary."

"What do you think will happen?"

"I . . . I don't know, Abby. I know what I want to happen. I want Dante to come home with me. To see the parents he should have been with all his life."

"I guess I feel a little sympathy for the position Dante is in but I want to know how and why this terrible thing came about. How two people took such a terrible step by separating a boy from his family and never telling him the truth."

"Maybe he doesn't have the answers himself. Then what will we do?"

"I guess I'll have to cross that bridge when I get to it. Abby, I don't know what else to do. God, he's my brother and I want him to be part of our family again. Maybe . . . Maybe I'll write to my parents and have them come here . . . I don't really know what I'll do."

"Tell me about him, Alexander. I don't really know that much about you even. What were you like as children? What was your home like . . . Tell me about this brother you love and maybe I'll know you better too."

"Dante," Alexander said reminiscently. "He was always trailing after me all the time. I guess it made me feel good that he wanted to copy me. I guess it kind of made me more responsible too. I was always afraid I'd make a mistake and he'd be the one to suffer for it. He was a determined boy all the time, never wanting anything to beat him." He went on to tell her many incidents of their youth including the time Dante had jumped Alexander's pony without lessons or parental permission. "He rode well, right from the first it was obvious he'd be a good rider . . . He was a kind, decent kid, Abby, and . . . we loved each other. Even then, even when we were so young, we loved each other. After he was washed overboard I almost found it impossible to go on. It was as if I had lost a part of me. I'm sure if Celeste and I felt that way, for my parents it must have been worse. Then to find that he's been alive all this time, that someone had just . . . just taken him away from us. The immensity of it boggles my mind. I'll never understand anyone who could do that . . . never."

Abby remained silent for she knew he was fighting a battle within himself, for despite what he said, she knew he was loving enough and compassionate enough to understand. That's what was hurting him, the fear that he would understand and as a result lose his brother again.

She listened as he told her how it had been when Dante had been lost. He told her of the journey from France, of the gift of the three identical medals. In a painful, quiet voice he told her of the storm and the agonizing moment when Dante was washed away and lost to them . . . until now.

When he finished they both remained silent, for she knew there was no way to ease his pain until he faced his brother again.

After a long while, she could tell by his slow even breathing that he slept.

Alexander knew that it would take them more than a month to travel the distance to High Oaks. He made arrangements to go part of the way by train, shipping their horses with them in a cattle car. It would cut a great deal of time from their travel and now, as far as Alexander was concerned, time was of the essence.

They took the trip in short jumps, Alexander watching sharply for any sign of exhaustion from Abby. Occasionally, he would stop for a day or two to allow themselves to rest and to purchase Abby clothes and discard the ones she was wearing. Alexander kept his uniform in half decent condition for he found the conqueror could usually have his way among the conquered no matter where they traveled.

Alexander did not want to be seen in the territory immediately surrounding High Oaks for anyone who knew Dan Wakefield could only look at Alexander and realize the connection. He did not want word of him to travel ahead and alarm either Virginia or Dante.

They arrived in the outskirts of Richmond in the early afternoon. It took Alexander a very short time to find and rent a small house well away from the densely traveled roads.

He questioned Abby on the location of High Oaks and found it was only a little less than a day's ride away.

They sat in the small house and ate a light supper Abby had prepared. Neither ate much for neither could keep their minds off the meeting that would take place in the near future.

"Do you know the way from here to High Oaks?" he questioned Abby.

"Yes, I do."

"I'll ride with you most of the way, then I'll return here. Do you think you can get him to come without . . . Virginia Wakefield knowing?"

"I'll do my best. How much do you want me to explain to him . . . and Catherine, his wife, do you want me to tell her too?"

Alexander paced the floor for a few minutes in deep thought. Then he went to Abby and took her shoulders in his hands.

"Abby . . . I know he must love this place and he must care a great deal for the people who have cared for him for so long and have given him so much. Would you understand if I told you I didn't want him to be faced with decisions until we meet and talk. I don't want this to be any harder on him than it has to. Do you think you can bring him here without giving reasons at all?"

"I will try to think of something," she replied. "But, I doubt very much if I can bring Dan . . . Dante . . . without Catherine. She has a right to make this decision with him ... She is his wife, Alexander."

"Of course, you are right."

"When do you want me to go?"

"It's best to start in the morning. For now, you had best get some rest. It will be a long, hard trip for you."

"Yes ... long ... and very hard."

"Abby?"

"What?"

"I want you to know how much I appreciate all you are doing. It is beyond duty even for a loving wife such as you."

"I do love you, Alexander, and I want you to be happy. You never will be now that you know your brother is alive unless you see him. If it makes you happy, it will make me happy too."

"When this is over, Abby," he whispered as his arms came about her to hold her close, "I promise I'll do everything in my power to keep you happy."

"I know, Alexander ... I know." She walked with him to their bedroom and for a few more hours they shut the harsh world away.

Morning came too soon for either of them. They rose and prepared for travel in silence. By dawn they were on their way.

When they were only a few miles from High Oaks, Abby pulled her horse to a stop.

"Alexander, you had best leave me here. Any closer and someone will recognize your face and begin asking questions."

He nodded, and he leaned toward her and kissed her.

"Good luck. Abby, hurry home."

"I will," she replied. Without another word she urged her horse ahead. He watched her until she was out of sight. He returned to the small house that seemed suddenly cold and empty.

The day passed and he spent most of it pacing the floor. When night fell, he knew it would be impossible to sleep. He lit a fire in the small fireplace and sat contemplating it. He knew it would be the following night, maybe longer, before Abby would return.

He must have fallen asleep in the chair for the next thing he knew sunlight touched him. The fire was cold, dead ashes. He was faced with a long, empty day with nothing to do but to think.

He prepared food to occupy his time and his hands but found he had no appetite for it when he was done.

He paced, he sat, he thought until his nerves screamed with the tension.

To him the sun seemed to hang in the sky. Would night never come? He wondered if Abby had gotten there safely. He wondered what excuse she would use. He worried over the results of this meeting. His nerves were frayed and he would have given his soul for a drink.

Finally, the sun began to set but there was no sign of Abby. Hours ticked slowly by. The night stretched on and on until he could have wept with frustration.

Again, without the benefit of a fire, he fell asleep in the chair. Again he was awakened by the early morning sun.

Now a new and unreasonable fear set in. What had happened at High Oaks to keep Abby there?

The morning passed and the afternoon and slowly drifted into early evening.

The sun was red on the horizon when he heard the sound of an approaching horse and buggy.

His heart leaped to his throat as he stood and faced the door. Slowly the door swung open.

Thirty-six

Dan sat heavily down on a fallen log and sighed as his tired body relaxed. He watched Jessie across the field from him moving with relaxed ease as he continued to work. It always amazed him how much more work Jessie could accomplish in a day than he. Jessie would laugh at this question.

"Doan worry, boy, yo gets the hang of it quick enough. It jus takes a little mo time. Yo ain had enough 'sperience yet. But, doan worry," he'd chuckle. "Yo sho gonna get it."

He spread his hands out before him, palms up, and looked at the bleeding blisters. Jessie had assured him these would harden with time but he wondered just how long it would take. To him it felt as though he had been working for years instead of weeks.

Every time he looked at the overgrown fields and the destruction that needed repairs he felt a sense of futility. He was not enough for High Oaks. It needed many hands. Besides he had no money to afford the cheapest labor. They, he and Jessie, had plowed two small fields and had traded or sold as much as they could to the Yankees who occupied Richmond. He found this difficult to do and if he had not desperately needed the seed, he would never been able to swallow his pride and do it.

Jessie had smiled at his first proud resistance then he had opened Dan's eyes to the fact that pride would not put food on the table. It had been a very hard thing to swallow but he had.

The fields they had planted began to spring to new life. They divided their work between caring for them and trying to do as much repair on the house that he could.

When he thought of the house, he thought of Catherine for to him they were united. He had never seen anyone work as hard as Catherine did to make the large, half empty house a home. But when he thought of them he thought also of his mother. It irritated him that he could become so angry with her. Virginia did not seem to realize any longer that there had been such tragic changes at High Oaks. She treated everyone about her like slaves, including Catherine, who took it with a smile, but it annoyed Dan.

He worried that his mother's condition seemed to be deteriorating and he didn't know what to do about it. He had no idea it was guilt that was steadily eating away at her soul. She knew Gregory had wanted Dan to know the truth and the secret, held within her, was slowly tearing her apart.

Dan looked up to see Jessie approaching with a wide smile on his face. He smiled back and rose slowly and stiffly.

"Yo'all restin' again, boy? We ain't gonna get nuthin' done you keep settin' down all de time."

"Damnit, Jessie," Dan laughed. "Don't you ever get tired? I swear you work like an ox and you expect a poor inexperienced man like me to keep up."

"Yo' poor boy," Jessie chided ruthlessly. "Yo' needs beauty rest I 'spects. Well, it's nigh on to eatin' time. We'll go back to de house and see what dey got."

"No sympathy," Dan groaned. "You've got no sympathy. You're a hard driver."

"Doan need no sympathy," Jessie chuckled. "Yo gots enough fo yourself, you doan need none o mine."

Dan had to laugh with him as they started back across the fields toward the house.

"Jessie, I sure would like to go fishing like we used to on a beautiful day like this."

"Yassah, mebbe we get this field cleared before sundown we could go. A good fish would taste mighty fine. But we gets the work done first."

Dan turned an exaggerated frown on him.

"This work isn't ever going to get done if we don't get some help. Two of us just isn't enough."

"Dan, boy, I was here with yo daddy when he built this place. He started with less'en yo' got. He had nuthin' but a piece of land. He worked like a hoss and he built one fine place. Yo kin do it too, yo just doan know you kin."

"My father was a special kind of man," Dan said softly.

"So is yo', boy, so is yo."

Dan laughed. "You and Catherine, you'll never let me slip will you?"

Jessie laughed in return. "Now yo' talkin' about one fine person. Yo' sho is lucky to get that gal. She gwine to keep yo' goin' no matter what. She one fine lady. She strong, where a woman should be strong, in her heart and in her lovin' yo'."

"Now, on that point I agree with you. She is one fine lady. I just wish I could give her more than just a lot of work and puttin' up with . . . " he stopped, aware he was about to say something against his mother and he loved her too much to do that. Yet he knew Jessie knew what he was going to say.

They remained silent as they returned to the house. They washed their hands and faces clean at the pump in the back yard before they entered the house.

When they walked into the kitchen, Catherine was preparing food. The table was set for the three of them.

Dan looked at Catherine closely and saw the sweaty brow that made her hair curl wetly on it, at the slim tanned arms and efficient hands. To him she looked so fragile that it frightened him. She had always been slim but now she was thinner than usual. He went to her and put an arm about her waist and drew her close to kiss her gently.

"You look tired," he said.

"I'm fine, Dan," she smiled. "I'm really very much stronger than you think."

"Where's Mother?"

He did not miss the quick look between Jessie and Catherine.

"She . . . She isn't really feeling well, Dan, this heat . . . She had a tray in her room."

"Which you made and carried up to her. You sweat and work and wait on her hand and foot."

"Dan, she isn't well."

"Mentally no, but, physically she's as strong as you are. Maybe a little work would repair some of the damage!"

"Dan!"

"I'm sorry, Catherine. It's just that . . . I hate to see you like this. It's not what you deserve."

She put both arms about him and smiled up into his eyes.

"Dan, look at us. We have much more than most people around here. We've been able to survive and keep High Oaks. We have each other. I'm happy. I know so many who have lost the ones they love. You're safe, we're together. It's enough, Dan. Be happy like I am."

He held her close and smiled. "You always make me feel like king of the mountain. You're always right too. I guess we do have more than most. I just don't like to see you have to work so hard."

"You were spoiled before," she laughed. "A little work never hurt anyone."

"What do you know?" he chuckled. "You've never worked with Jessie on your back."

Jessie watched with a pleased smile. This woman was good for Dan. She made him smile, even laugh. It gave him a great deal of pleasure to watch them together. Then he thought of Virginia Wakefield and a frown creased his brow. He tried to remember some of Gregory's ramblings as he brought him home. There was something strange and mystifying here. Sometimes he felt an unseen force that seemed to linger in the room when Virginia was present.

Jessie's ancestors had handed down a firm belief in good and evil spirits. He had a strong feeling that something reached from Gregory's grave to Virginia. He was afraid, only because it seemed to tangle about Dan and Catherine. He would fight whatever it might be for these two were closer to him than any children of his own could have been.

"I'm going upstairs to talk to Mother. I'll be right down."

Both Catherine and Jessie were silent for a long time after Dan had left the room.

"Oh, Jessie," she said softly.

"I know, Missy. I know. Dat boy hurtin' but he gots to find his own way. Yo' helps him, but she don't. She just think about herself and what she might lose. I 'spects she don't rightly 'preciate yo either cause you takes him away from her. She sick wif somethin' and she wan' to hold dat boy too close. It ain't natural."

"Maybe . . . Maybe it will all pass. Maybe as time goes on she'll get better."

" 'Spects yo' doan believe dat anymore than I do. Somethin' eatin at dat woman. I wisht I knew what it was. Da truth would make it easier on everyone."

Catherine made no reply for it was the echo of suspicions that were also in her mind. She went about silently putting the food on the table.

Dan went up the stairs realizing, as he had for some time, that he was reluctant to go into his mother's room. The way she seemed to exist in another unrealistic world disturbed him. It gave him a twinge of guilt. He rapped lightly on the door and when she answered he opened it and walked in.

"Dan." She smiled and stretched out a hand to him. He walked to the edge of the bed and took it then sat down beside her.

"My goodness, Dan, have you been to the stables again? You are filthy. I must ask you not to hang around the stables too often."

"Mother . . ." he began, wanting to tell her the stables were long gone. He couldn't. "You're looking well this morning," he lied. "Couldn't you have come down and had dinner with us? It's hard for Catherine to carry your meals up all the time."

Virginia was pale and her hair was wild and uncared

for. She had grown very thin despite the food she ate.

"Dan . . . I must speak to you of something else."

"Yes, Mother?"

"That . . . slave . . . That Jessie. I don't think it's proper for you to hang around with him. People will talk."

He flushed with anger he tried to control.

"Mother, in the first place Jessie is not a slave, he's the best friend I have. In the second place, he's the only one Catherine and I have to help us here. Without Jessie's help, I would lose High Oaks. I need him, Mother, much more than he needs me. There are no people to talk and I don't give a damn if anyone does. I don't see anyone else offering a hand besides Jessie. The rest can go to . . ." He stopped.

"Dan! I won't have you shouting like that! Good heavens, Dan, it's only for your own good that I tell you this. A plantation owner hobnobbing with the blacks . . . it just isn't done. What would your father think if he knew?"

"Father would understand, Mother. Maybe that was one of his failings, he loved so much that he would do anything not to hurt anyone. I know he was that way with you and God only knows all the things he did for my good. He would understand exactly what I'm trying to do. To rebuild High Oaks, start a new family and make a whole new life."

She gazed at him, to his shock, with a look of intense fear in her eyes. He was immediately sorry for the harsh words he had said that disturbed her so.

"I'm sorry, Mother. I didn't mean to shout at you. I'm just a little tired, that's all. Please forgive me."

"Of course, Dan, of course." But her voice was vague

and she again had the faraway look in her eyes. He stood up and looked down on her, his eyes filled with pity.

"Won't you try to come down this afternoon for a while? I'm sure Catherine would be happy to help you dress and brush your hair."

"Yes . . . Yes, Dan, I will. You go on and have your dinner."

He bent and kissed her, sensitively aware of some kind of pain yet unable to reach her. He walked to the door and left. He did not see the look of near panic in her eyes as she watched him go.

"A new family . . . a new life . . . No, Dan, no. You belong to me. You belong to me," she whispered.

Dan reappeared in the kitchen and the three of them sat and ate in silence. After the meal he and Jessie returned to work.

Despite what she said, Virginia did not come down the balance of the day. Instead, she rose from her bed and agitatedly paced the floor wringing her hands and mumbling softly to herself.

Below, Catherine could hear her footsteps pacing, pacing. She had heard this before but had not told Dan. She did not want him anymore upset and worried than he was.

Late that night, when Dan and Catherine had gone to bed, Virginia slipped from her room. She crept silently down the steps and left the house.

Jessie, who was not abed yet, he enjoyed a late night smoke before sleeping, stood in the shadows of the house. He was surprised to see Virginia walk ghost-like across the lawn and up the hill to the cemetery. He was deathly afraid for this woman's safety in her state and the effect it would have on Dan should something happen to her. So, quietly, he followed her intending on remaining out of sight until she safely returned home.

She walked up the hill to the cemetery. It had been bordered by an iron fence and along the fence several trees had been planted to bring cool shade to those who lay beneath them. It was behind one of these that Jessie hid himself and watched. It was a very quiet night with little or no breeze and her voice carried quite clearly to him. It gave him a severe sense of shock when he realized she was having a conversation with Gregory Wakefield as if he were alive and stood beside her.

"I cannot let him go, Gregory. I cannot. He belongs to me ... No, no, I will not tell him the truth, you cannot make me ... You are angry, Gregory, I know ... But, I burnt all the papers ... He will never know his family still lives ... He does not need them ... Those terrible parents who pushed him into the sea ... His brother and sister? ... No, he does not need them ... He has High Oaks ... and me ... only ... only that woman ... that Catherine. I know she is telling him things about me ... But it's all right, Gregory ... I'll get rid of her ... Then Dan will have everything he needs ... High Oaks ... and me ... No. No! No! Gregory, I cannot ... I cannot! All the proof is gone! It's gone! All he has is the medal and no one will ever tell him of the others."

Jessie stood frozen, perspiration prickled on his skin. He was frightened of what he knew was a complete loss of sanity. Some evil existed here. He trembled when he heard her refer to Catherine and the fact that she had calmly decided to "get rid of her". . . How? What did she plan to do to sweet, gentle Catherine? What papers had she burnt? Why had she kept such a dark secret for so long? Dan's family ... they lived ... and Virginia never intended for him to know. Jessie knew he had to do something but, he didn't know what. He only knew someone had to protect Catherine and Dan from disaster.

He slipped back down the hill before Virginia, leaving her on the hill in communion with the ghost that haunted her.

He knew in his heart that Gregory Wakefield had intended Dan to know. He remembered that Virginia had been alone with him the night he died. He must have told her the truth, given her evidence. That must have been what she burnt, never intending Dan to know.

Jessie lay sleepless for a long time, but by dawn he had made his decisions. Even if Dan hated him for what he must do to Virginia, still he had to tell them the truth. Not for Dan to leave High Oaks and find his true parents, but to protect him and Catherine from disaster for he knew now Virginia Wakefield had slipped beyond anyone's help. He also knew the unbalanced mind was capable of harming Catherine.

He rose long before the dawn. He walked the fields of High Oaks and thought of the happy days it had known.

Gregory and Virginia had made it beautiful, had given it an heir to keep it strong. But, they had stolen a life . . . and he realized High Oaks was not worth the loss Dan had been forced to suffer.

He had grown to love both High Oaks and the people who had rescued him. But, he had not been given a choice.

He knew now that he was going to tell Dan and Catherine what he knew. From there he would let Dan make his own choices. At least Dan would be more aware of his mother's condition . . . and able to protect Catherine from harm.

He saw a light in the kitchen and walked toward the house. From outside he was surprised to see that it was Virginia who was in the kitchen.

He did not want to face her at the moment. He argued with himself that it was because he wanted to talk to Dan and Catherine first, but, inside was a deep twisting fear of insanity and the aura of evil that lingered about it.

He watched from outside as she puttered about the kitchen, then the light was extinguished. He could hear her walk across the room and up the stairs.

He found the palms of his hands were sweaty and he shivered a little in the cool morning air.

Soon Catherine and Dan would come down to start breakfast and prepare for the day's work. He would wait and he would tell them then.

He heard footsteps on the stairs and knew it was Catherine. They were light and, as usual, Catherine was up first to make sure Dan ate well before he started to work.

To Jessie it seemed an unbearably long time before he heard a heavier footfall and knew Dan was up.

He was about to come around the house and enter through the front door when he looked down the long drive of High Oaks and saw a rider approaching.

From the distance he could tell it was a woman. He stood and watched until he could recognize her. By the time she reached the porch, he was there waiting with a broad smile on his face.

"Good mawnin', Miss Abby. It sho is fine to see you 'round here again. It been a long time."

"Jessie," Abby smiled, her blue eyes lighted with pleasure at seeing an old remembered face. "It's good to see you. How is . . . everything," she finished quietly and he knew she must have some knowledge of what had been happening here.

"Not too bad, Miss Abby. Does yo know about Mistah Gregory?"

"Yes, I heard from a friend. I'm sorry, Jessie. I know you cared for him a great deal. It's a tragic loss."

"Yessum, it is dat."

"Virginia?"

"She . . . she been poorly lately. When Mistah Gregory go some part of her died. She been here in body, but her soul, it done gone wif him."

"How terrible . . . Dan? . . . Catherine?"

Dey's well. Dose two younguns been married goin' on two months now. Dat boy, he workin' his fool head off trying to get dis place back to producin' again."

"Well, I have to talk to Dan. Are they up yet?"

"Yessum, Miss Catherine she been in the kitchen for a while makin' breakfast. I heard Dan come down a little bit ago. Shall I go tell em yo'all's here?"

"No, let me go in and surprise them." She dismounted and came to stand beside him on the porch.

"Dat gonna be one fine surprise. Dey needs a little pleasure 'bout now," he smiled.

She walked ahead of him into the house, trying not to see the emptiness, the destruction and the feeble attempts at resurrection.

When she pushed the kitchen door open it was without sound. Dan and Catherine were standing with their arms about each other and he was kissing her in a most thorough fashion.

"That's no way to get breakfast cooked," Abby laughed.

They leaped apart like children who had been caught in mischief. Simultaneously they cried out.

"Abby!" They both rushed to her side and she was enclosed in warm embraces and kisses.

"You two look wonderful. I'm so glad to see you."

"You're the one who looks wonderful," Catherine said.

"Let's quit with the compliments," Dan laughed. "The bunch of us look like something left over from a war." They all laughed together.

"Have you eaten, Abby? Are you hungry?" Catherine asked.

"I could use a little breakfast."

Soon they sat about the table and were eating and talking at the same time. Jessie decided to wait until later to talk to Dan. Abby's astute gaze did not miss Catherine and Dan's continual reference to Jessie and his help. She realized immediately she had an ally in Jessie. She took the first opportunity she could to whisper urgently to Jessie.

"Jessie, I have to talk to you alone."

He showed no outward sign but, answered in a quiet whisper, "Under de tree out by de ole barn."

She nodded and moved away from him. It wasn't until Catherine decided to take a tray to Virginia and Dan accompanied her that she slipped out. She found Jessie waiting.

Slowly and deliberately she explained exactly why she was here and the story she had to tell Dan.

"It might be a chance for him to get a whole new start, both for High Oaks and for him and Catherine. I'm sure his real parents would understand the love he has for this place. They would not want to take him away from it. They would only want to fill his life with all the love they could not give over the years."

"Miss Abby, dey might feel dat way and Dan, he might

too. But, his mammy gwine to be bad. She ain gwine to give him up. Anybody tries . . ."

"But, Jessie, she doesn't have to give him up. Doesn't she understand?"

"No, M'am," he said quietly. "She doan understand."

It sobered Abby and she stood silently as he went on to explain all he had overheard in the cemetery. Abby's face turned pale as she began to fully realize what Virginia had done to Dan.

"We have to tell him. We have to take him to meet Alexander. If we do not, Alexander will come here."

"Yessum, but you got to do it without her knowin'. I doan know what she do if she find out but, it might be sumpthin' bad."

"Yes, Jessie. Can you help me get Dan alone?"

"Yessum, I'll try."

They walked back to the house together unaware of the eyes that watched them intently from the second floor window.

For the balance of the day, to Dan's surprise, Virginia came downstairs and after she greeted Abby warmly, she refused to leave Dan's side.

She insisted on helping a surprised Catherine and Abby with dinner and chatted at the meal as if nothing in their world had ever changed.

Jessie was suspicious that Virginia knew, somehow, that what Abby was here for concerned her son.

When he could whisper to Abby he suggested that to ease Virginia's fears, Abby should spend the night. The next day he would find a way to get Dan from Virginia's watchful eye.

Abby agreed, assured in her mind that Alexander would understand if she were gone overnight.

She was given a room, and Virginia stayed awake and up until Abby walked up the stairs. Jessie, Dan and Catherine went to bed. The house became still and quiet.

Abby stood at her window thinking of Alexander and Dan. The only thing that kept them apart was the instability of Virginia's mind. She also knew that Alexander would come here if she weren't back in a few days. She was really frightened of what might happen then.

She was about to turn and go to bed when she saw Virginia walk across the lawn and up the hill to the cemetery. A genuine feeling of fear touched her. It was too late to protect Virginia Wakefield. Now, she had to do what she could to protect Dan and Catherine and still give them the future they deserved.

She slept restlessly with wild, dark dreams she could not remember when she awoke in the morning. Determinedly, she went downstairs to face what had to be faced and put an end to it.

She found no one in the kitchen so she walked across the room and out the back door onto the porch. Still she saw no one. She turned to walk back into the house and came face to face with Virginia, a cold maniacal gleam in her eyes and a pistol in her hand that pointed at Abby's heart.

Thirty-seven

Abby stared in disbelief. This was not the beautiful and kind Virginia Wakefield. This woman who looked at her with wild eyes and a half smile on her lips. Abby opened her mouth to speak.

"Shhhh, don't say a word," Virginia whispered. "You would not like to waken everyone would you? I have been waiting to talk to you alone."

"With a pistol, Virginia?" Abby questioned.

Virginia ignored Abby's question. "What are you doing here, Abby?"

"I have just come to visit my cousin and to see you and Dan again. I heard of Gregory's death . . . I'm sorry."

"No . . . No, Abby," Virginia replied quietly. "I saw you talking to that slave yesterday. You all—him, Catherine and you, you'll tell him lies . . . lies. You'll make me give him up. He's mine, he's my son! And no one else can have him."

Abby saw an imperceptible movement behind Virginia. She knew someone was there, but she didn't know who. She had to keep Virginia talking.

"No one wants to take him from you Virginia."

"Yes, yes they do."

"Why do you think that? I have visited you so many times before?"

"Before . . . It was different before. Gregory was here then . . . so long ago. He knew how to keep Dan here . . . he kept the secret."

"Secret? What secret?"

Abby had seen a glimpse of gray, she knew it was Dan who stood in the shadows of the dark kitchen and listened.

"I'll not tell you . . . Gregory tried. But I'll not tell anyone."

"You cannot keep your secret any longer Virginia. Too many people besides me know. We have told others. Virginia, let us help you. Dan doesn't have to go away, but he has to know the truth."

Dan had come down the stairs without putting on his boots. He did not want to waken Catherine so he slipped quietly from the room. He opened the kitchen door and the sight that greeted his eyes froze him in his tracks. His mother, pointing a pistol at Abby. He could not believe his eyes. He knew his mother was strangely ill, but he did not know it was this bad. He was about to speak when their words held him immobile. He stood in profound shock . . . and listened.

"He only needs to know that I am his mother, and High Oaks is his. He has to stay here."

"He will stay here. He will care for you, but he must know that his real family is still alive."

"No!"

"I am Alexander Dubonne's wife. I have seen the medal he wears about his neck. I know that Dan wears the same medal. I know they are brothers. Alexander has come to see him. Virginia, please. There is love to be shared. We all can help you. We all can fill this house with happiness, but that happiness cannot be built on a lie. Dan has parents who thought him dead, a sister and brother who loved him too. He has a right to that. They have a right

513

too. You have a right for all you have given him. Share him Virginia . . . please . . . before you lose him."

Dan could not believe all he was hearing. His parents, still alive! Alexander, Celeste, still alive! And all these years he had been lied to, deceived.

"I will just say you had to leave quickly." Virginia continued, as she raised the barrel of the gun and held it steady. "No one will ever know."

"It will be no use to kill me Virginia, Alexander will come for me. There is no way that Dante will not learn the truth, from me, from him . . . or from Jessie. Do you intend to kill us all?"

"If I have to."

"No, Mother," Dan's voice came from behind her. She whirled about and faced Dan with tears in her eyes.

"Give me the pistol, Mother," he said gently. Abby could hear the love in his voice. "There is no one or nothing that could make me love you or High Oaks less. I will always be your son."

"Dan," she moaned softly, as he reached out and took the pistol from her. She trembled violently and he came to her and held her in his arms. She clung to him in desperation and cried in a heart-breaking way, that stirred pain in both Dan and Abby.

"Mother, if you tell me the truth you will feel so much better. I know now it has been this secret that has hurt you so badly. Talk to me . . . I will understand."

"You won't leave me here alone?"

"No Mother. This is my home. Catherine's and mine. But I must know the truth. Will you tell me?"

She nodded and he led her to a chair. When she sat down he knelt in front of her, and held her hands in his and listened while she washed away the guilt and fear that had been her companion for so long.

He did not interrupt, nor did he question her, for he knew all she was saying was truth.

The last whispered words fell from her lips. She seemed utterly spent. He rose and very gently lifted her up into his arms and carried her to her room. There he laid her on her bed and sat down beside her, holding her hand.

"Mother you must rest now, sleep, and I shall stay here beside you."

"You won't go?" she pleaded in a pathetic child's voice.

"No, I won't go."

Slowly her eyes closed and she slept. He sat beside her ... for hour after hour he sat. Abby and Catherine and Jessie looked in occasionally, but he waved them away. He needed the time with her to prove to her he would not leave and maybe help her regain her hold on sanity. He also used the time to think of how he could do what he knew he had to do.

It was late afternoon when she wakened. She saw him seated beside her. The smile she gave him was a well-remembered smile of love.

"Dan ... Can you ever forgive us? We never meant to hurt anyone. We needed you so."

"There is no question of forgiveness any longer Mother. We must do our best to repair the damage as much as we can. I cannot blame either of you for loving, or for needing. I could not love you less, and I love High Oaks."

"What will you do Dan ... Dante?"

"Just Dan Mother," he smiled. "Will you understand?"

"Maybe now I can try."

"I have to see them Mother. But remember, High Oaks will always be my home. I will come back. Can you trust me now? I will go ... but I will return."

"As a boy, it always seemed important to you, the truth. I suppose you cannot lie now. Will you go alone?"

"Catherine and Jessie will stay here with you. My . . . Alexander is in Richmond. I will go with Abby to meet him, then I will ask him to come here. We will make our plans together when I get back."

"All right Dan . . . I shall wait for you."

He kissed her, then he rose from the bed and left the room. Virginia closed her eyes in the first peaceful sleep she had known since Gregory had died leaving her the secret that had nearly cost her life.

Dan explained to the three impatient people who waited for him what had happened, and what he intended to do.

"When shall we leave, Dan?" Abby said.

"Early in the morning if that's all right with you."

She nodded, then she and Jessie went to bed, leaving Catherine and Dan alone. He held out his arms to her and wordlessly she went to them.

The next morning Abby and Dan left High Oaks early. They rode alone in silence. Dan deep in lost childhood memories of the brother he was about to meet again after all the years.

When they arrived at the house where Alexander waited he felt tense and a little frightened. He walked across the porch alone for Abby had decided to wait and give the brothers time alone.

Dan reached for the knob with a hand that trembled. He opened the door, and stepped inside.

They stood facing each other for a heart stopping moment. Tears blinded both their eyes.

"Alexi," Dan whispered. Hearing the name only Celeste and Dante ever used stirred Alexander with a blinding surge of forgotten love.

Suddenly they reached for each other, for words could not be found to say what they felt. They embraced fiercely, crying unashamedly as they clung to each other. For a long moment they held each other tight, then Alexander looked at his long lost brother. The tears streamed down their cheeks and they laughed and cried all in the same moment.

"Dante ... Dante. We thought ... It's a miracle! A miracle."

Now they began to talk, tumbling words spoken simultaneously. Laughing questions answered before they were finished. Dante asked of their parents, of Celeste. Alexander asked of his past years.

Finally they regained control of their emotions. Abby entered and the three of them sat about and talked for several hours. It seemed Alexander and Dante could not get enough questions and answers.

"Dante, you must come home with me now. Mother and Father will be wild with joy, and Celeste, she's married now, she'll be so happy."

"Alexi," Dante began hesitantly ... Then he explained all that had happened before he had come to meet them.

"I owe them my life Alexi, and I love High Oaks. It is the only home I know. We must go there first, you and I, then I shall go with you. But in the end I will return to High Oaks. It was given to me in trust. I cannot break that trust. I want to rebuild it with my own hands. I want to make it what it was before the war. Do you understand?"

"Yes, yes Dante, I do. We'll go there. I want to see this High Oaks of yours, and I want to meet your Catherine. We have a whole lifetime to catch up on. Let's begin as soon as possible."

The three of them returned to High Oaks, where they found a renewed happiness that had not been there for a long time.

Catherine, Abby and Virginia made a supper of all the good things they could provide. During the meal

Alexander and Dante chattered constantly, while the others listened delighted in the outpouring of love and memories shared.

It was in the early hours of the morning that they all found their way to beds.

Alexander agreed to stay two weeks so that Dante could show him all of High Oaks and tell him his plans for it.

They spent hours riding together, walking together and working together.

Always talking, laughing as if they could not get enough of each other.

But not once did they mention the war or the opposite sides on which they had fought.

It was night before they were to leave for Philadelphia that they found the courage to talk about it.

They were walking together and this time both were silently at peace with all about them.

"High Oaks was so very beautiful and so productive before . . ." Dante began.

"Before this stupid tragedy of a war," Alexander added.

"Tragedy . . . yes that's what it was. Such an ungodly terrible waste."

"Dante . . . when I found out who you were . . . Well I really realized the terrible futility of war. We are brothers, yet we might have faced each other in battle. We might even have killed one another. It is a thing I have sworn I shall never be part of again."

"I'm going to spend the rest of my life trying to blot it from my mind."

Dante said, "It has taken a great deal from me . . . You should have known my foster father, Alexi . . . you would have liked him. He was a peaceful and gentle man, like you. He taught me to build not to destroy. I stand with you brother. I shall never raise a gun to another man again."

"Well," Alexander laughed, "the Dubonnes stand in agreement. It's a good beginning of a whole new life."

"Tell me about Celeste's husband."

"Wes? He's a wonderful husband, Celeste is happy. She'll be so much happier when she sees you. I find I can hardly wait."

"I'm a Rebel about to be outnumbered by Yankees." Dante laughed.

"If Abby and you are examples, you have nothing to worry about. You can handle anything we Yankees have to give. Abby is one Rebel that never gives up on anything."

"We've been so damn lucky Alexi."

"Yes, we have."

"Let's spread the good luck around and keep the Rebels and the Yankees united from now on."

"Amen brother . . . Amen."

They had agreed to start early the next morning, so daylight found them seated about the breakfast table in laughing conversation.

They looked at each other in surprise when the sound of an approaching buggy could be heard.

They all went to the front porch to see, for visitors were an uncommon event yet. They were more surprised to find two buggies coming up the drive. Alexander was the first one to recognize them.

"It's Mother and Father in the first and I'll bet it's Wes and Celeste in the other."

Dante went to stand beside Alexander, with Catherine's and Virginia's hands in his.

When the carriages came to a stop Alexander was there first to assist his mother down. She held Alexander's hand tight, but her eyes were on Dante. So many emotions washed through her that at first she did not hear Alexander speak.

"Mother, Father, what are you doing here?"

Marie was breathless as she watched Dante walk slowly down the steps to stand beside Alexander.

Her eyes filled with disbelieving tears and a soft sound came from her.

"We had a visitor Alexander," Jules said in a taut whisper. "A woman by the name of LeClerc. She had a very strange story to tell us. That, and a locket Wes brought home has brought us here."

Marie had reached a hesitant hand toward Dante as Wes and Celeste came to stand by her side. Eyes wide with amazement they all seemed paralyzed into disbelieving immobility until Dante smiled, walked to Marie, took her hand and spoke softly.

"Mother."

"Dante!" Marie cried and she was in Dante's arms, laughing and crying at the same time, and whispering his name over and over.

It seemed to release them from their disbelief for they crowded about him now and he tried to embrace them all at the same time.

For a moment pandemonium reigned as they all tried to ask questions at the same time. Then Dante drew Virginia and Catherine beside him.

"It is a very strange thing," he laughed, "but I should like to introduce my mother . . . to my mother."

Marie and Virginia stood looking at one another, then Marie went to her and they embraced. Both wept with emotion they could not control.

"We must talk, you and I," Marie said. "I should like to hear about our son's childhood."

"Yes," Virginia replied. "I have a great deal I must explain to you, and a great debt to repay. We have not much to offer, but you are welcome to stay with us at High Oaks."

"Thank you," Marie replied gently. "I should love to."

Now Marie turned to Catherine. "And you are Dante's wife. How lovely you are."

"The Dubonnes have excellent taste in women, Mother," Alexander laughed. "That can be judged by Father's choice of you, Dante's choice of Catherine, and my good fortune in Abby . . . my wife."

They all laughed, then Celeste spoke happily. "The men have no better taste than the women," she said brightly. "The example, Mother's choice of Father and mine in Wes."

It was a joyous gathering and they spent the balance of the day exchanging stories of all that had passed. They could not seem to get enough of each other and well past midnight were still reluctant to separate and go to bed. The house did not settle to quiet slumber until the early hours of the morning.

Strangely it was two, Wes and Catherine who still could not find restful sleep. Catherine decided to get some air and maybe she would be able to sleep better. She left Dante sound asleep, donned her robe, and walked down to the garden. There she sat on a bench and contemplated all the strange events that had happened that had drawn all the people asleep in High Oaks together.

She was startled by a sound and turned to see Wes walking toward her.

When he reached her side he spoke quietly.

"I'm sorry, I didn't mean to startle you, or frighten you. I could not sleep, and I was on the veranda when I saw you walk down here. It was my first opportunity to see you alone. I have something to tell you, and to give you that I thought you might want to be kept private."

"I don't understand. You have something to give me?"

"Let me explain first," he said. "Do you mind?" he questioned as he motioned to the seat beside her.

"No, of course not. Please, sit down."

He sat down beside her and quietly began to explain his friendship with George, his being there when George died, and the things George had given him to return to her. Then he took the letter and the locket and handed them to her. She accepted them with silent tears in her eyes.

"Catherine . . . His last words were of you. He loved you I think. I think he also knew how hopeless it was. I'm sorry to bring you such sadness after all this happiness, but I promised him you would get both the locket and the letter."

She held the locket and the letter in her hands with painful tears that fell unreserved down her cheeks.

She remembered George, the Yankee who had occupied High Oaks for a short time. She remembered him as a kind gentle man. The lie to the terror the Yankees had brought to the South.

"Thank you," she said softly. She sat looking at the letter and the locket for some time, then she realized Wes had quietly gone.

She lay the locket in her lap and opened the letter. By the light of a full moon she read . . . She wept as she read and her hands trembled with the knowledge of grief and love enclosed in the pages.

My very dear Catherine:

I will say that on these pages, for I know when you read them I shall be only a memory. I will also say I love you. I think I fell in love with you the very first day I set foot on High Oaks. I admire your loyalty, and I envy your man who holds your love. I would trade places with him gladly, be on the losing side of the war, if I had you to come home to. That is a very difficult thing for a man with the military background I have had to say.

I have been trained to war, and I have thought it a

route to completeness and strength. I find it a very hollow victory. In the past few months I have realized the truth of life. It is not to conquer or to outmaneuver. It is to love and to be loved. To build, not to destroy. To create life not to end it.

What I would give, my Catherine, to be able to relive my life . . . to be able to undo the hurt that has been done you. To know you before your heart belonged to your Dan.

I have gazed at your picture in the locket I stole from you. The more I look at him beside you the more I know you were meant to be. I have a suspicion my dear that there is a secret in this that should be surprising. When I get home I intend to see it is looked into. I believe there is much more to your Dan's mysterious origins than anyone knows. In fact I think I hold the secret.

It's a thing I should like to see be true, for maybe I can help in some small way to rebuild what I so very carelessly and foolishly helped to destroy.

I fight with a new reality now. The reality that I do not face any other enemy than myself. I no longer have the heart for battle. I want only to go home . . . maybe find a woman like you to share the balance of my life.

Think of me with a kind heart my Catherine, and know that I would change it all if I could. I came to you a victor . . . I left defeated. I left my heart at High Oaks . . . with you.

You and Dan, despite what you have been through, will never be defeated. I know that now.

A friend, a long time ago, tried to tell me that war was an evil destructive thing. I know now he was right.

Please forgive me for all past hurt, and let me wish

you the kind of future you deserve. Have hope Catherine, and be happy.

All my love
George McClellan

She let the letter drop to her lap, and buried her face in her hands and wept anew for all the destruction the war had caused . . . even for the victors. She washed herself clean of any bitterness that might have lingered. She was about to return to her room when she saw Dante walking toward her. She rose and watched him come.

When he reached her side he smiled and reached out to draw her into his arms.

"I woke and found you gone. It made me realize again how lonely that bed and my arms are without you," he whispered as he kissed her gently. "I saw you talking to Wes and when he left you were crying . . . Why Catherine? Can you tell me? I don't want you unhappy, even for a moment."

"Oh, Dan . . . Dante . . ."

"Dan it's always been, Dan it will be to you. A name doesn't matter."

"I'm not unhappy. I have you . . . We have a whole new future to build."

"A whole new future," he mused. "Sometimes I can't believe it. I have so much Catherine, you, High Oaks, two mothers," he laughed, "father, and a brother and sister I thought I had lost a long time ago. It seems like a dream."

"You're not angry with Gregory now that you know the truth?"

"No . . . I might have been once, but there's too much happiness now to dwell on the pain. I shall only remember him for the love he gave me and the future of High Oaks. I shall forget everything else. We'll begin again."

She slid her arms about his waist and smiled up at him.

"I love you Dan . . . more at this moment, I think, than I have ever loved you before. You are strong with the kind of strength I need. I want to be part of you and High Oaks forever. Part of the future we can all build together."

He kissed her again, and, with their arms about each other they walked back across the garden to the home that held their hearts.

Catherine put the locket and the letter in a chest. Someday she would look at it again, maybe read the letter again . . . But not now. For her there was only one thought that held her . . . Dan, their love, and tomorrow.

Epilog

Alexander picked up a newly arrived letter from the table addressed to him. When he read it his smile broadened and he gave a low laugh of complete pleasure.

He took the stairs two at a time and moved rapidly down the hall to the door of the room he and Abby shared. It stood open a little, so he pushed it wider. Abby sat at her dressing table absently brushing her hair. Her face had a far away dreamy look, and he knew of what she thought ... Fernhill and a lost home she missed so deeply, although she tried her best to keep it from him. It had been over a year and a half since they had come to his home, and still he knew her heart missed Fernhill deeply.

He walked silently across the room to stand behind her. She raised her blue eyes to him in the mirror and smiled as he rested one hand on her shoulder and gently caressed her hair with the other.

"Good morning," he said quietly. "Have I told you in the past few hours how very beautiful you are and how much I love you?"

She placed her hand over his and smiled.

"Even if you have it is a thing I never grow tired of hearing."

He drew her up and held her close, kissing her deeply. Then he held her a little away from him.

"I want you to pack some clothes!" he said. "We are going away for a few weeks.

"Away, where?"

"That my sweet," he laughed as he drew her back into his arms, "is a surprise. I have been planning it for a long time. Now it's all ready."

"What?" she laughed. "Tell me."

"Nope, I will show you. We're leaving tomorrow so you'd best hurry."

"Alexander!"

"Sorry love, I've no intentions of telling you, and we are leaving tomorrow even," he said as his eyes roamed warmly over her half dressed state, "if I have to take you as you are."

He remained firm no matter how she tried to coax answers from him. She gave up, packed a few clothes, and they left the following day. They traveled south, and soon she realized they were headed toward Fernhill.

She grew silent, not wanting to tell him of the pain returning to the ruins of her beloved home was causing. He felt her silence, but remained quiet himself. They had traveled to Atlanta by train. Once there he had hired a carriage and now they drove slowly down the road to Fernhill.

When they crested the hill that led to Fernhill she closed her eyes. She could not bear it, and a small protesting sound came from her. She clasped her hands tightly in her lap.

Then she felt the buggy come to a halt. Alexander sat in silence, and reluctantly she opened her eyes to face what she knew she must.

She gasped, and felt a hard constriction in her breast that nearly stopped her breathing.

It sat before her, complete and gloriously beautiful. Fernhill, tall and magnificent, with its white pillars and wide green lawns ... its shade trees and gardens, the long winding drive ... everything the same as it had been before the war, before its destruction.

Tears she could not retain fell heedlessly down her cheeks as she turned brilliant love filled eyes toward a smiling Alexander.

"Alexander," she cried.

"I had Moses make everything as close as he and Loel could remember. I wanted to give you some small happiness for all the joy you've given me."

"Oh Alexander," the words caught in her tears and she could barely speak. Oh my dear Yankee. You . . . You're . . . You're so wonderful! I love you."

Her arms came about his neck and he laughed happily as his arms closed about her. He could feel the joy that coursed through her, and he exulted in the pleasure he had given her.

Their lips blended in a deep and promising kiss.

Reluctantly he let her go for the moment until he drove the buggy to the door. It was flung open by a grinning Moses, with a delightful Loel behind him. Abby left the buggy quickly and embraced them both as she laughed and cried.

Alexander came to stand behind her.

"Moses, you've done a remarkable job. It looks magnificent."

"Thank yo suh. I tried to do mah best. Loel done help me wif de inside. It sho took a lot of men and a lot of money, but yo done it suh! yo done it."

"Show us the rest Moses." Alexander replied.

Moses and Loel went in and Abby was about to follow when Alexander's restraining hand stopped her. She looked up at him questioningly.

With a laugh he swung her up into his arms.

"This our home, love," he said as his lips brushed hers. "I want it right. I want the happiness we have now to live here forever."

"My dear beloved Yankee," she whispered as she clung to him, "It will . . . It will."

He carried her inside, and they shut the world of lost wars and unhappiness out. Together they would make a new beginning for Fernhill, for the South, and for their love.

HIV Manual

FOR HEALTH CARE
PROFESSIONALS

Richard D. Muma, MPH, PA-C
Assistant Director and Assistant Professor
Department of Physician Assistant
College of Health Professions
Wichita State University
Wichita, Kansas

Barbara Ann Lyons, MA, PA-C
Associate Professor
Department of Physician Assistant Studies
School of Allied Health Sciences
The University of Texas Medical Branch
Galveston, Texas

Michael J. Borucki, MD
Assistant Professor
AIDS Care and Clinical Research Program
Division of Infectious Diseases
Department of Internal Medicine
The University of Texas Medical Branch
Galveston, Texas

Richard B. Pollard, MD
Professor
Microbiology and Internal Medicine
Chief, AIDS Care and Clinical Research Program
Division of Infectious Diseases
Department of Internal Medicine
The University of Texas Medical Branch
Galveston, Texas

Appleton & Lange
Stamford, Connecticut

Notice: The authors and the publisher of this volume have taken care to make certain that the doses of drugs and schedules of treatment are correct and compatible with the standards generally accepted at the time of publication. Nevertheless, as new information becomes available, changes in treatment and in the use of drugs become necessary. The reader is advised to carefully consult the instruction and information material included in the package insert of each drug or therapeutic agent before administration. This advice is especially important when using new or infrequently used drugs. The authors and publisher disclaim all responsibility for any liability, loss, injury, or damage incurred as a consequence, directly or indirectly, for the use and application of any of the contents of the volume.

Prentice Hall International (UK) Limited, *London*
Prentice Hall of Australia Pty. Limited, *Sydney*
Prentice Hall Canada, Inc., *Toronto*
Prentice Hall Hispanoamericana, S.A., *Mexico*
Prentice Hall of India Private Limited, *New Delhi*
Prentice Hall of Japan, Inc., *Tokyo*
Simon & Schuster Asia Pte. Ltd., *Singapore*
Editora Prentice Hall do Brasil Ltda., *Rio de Janeiro*
Prentice Hall, *Upper Saddle River, New Jersey*

Library of Congress Cataloging-in-Publication Data

HIV manual for health care professionals / Richard D. Muma . . .
  [et al.]. — 2nd ed.
     p.   cm.
  Includes bibliographical references and index.
  ISBN 0-8385-3773-1 (alk. paper)
  1. HIV-positive persons—Care—Handbooks, manuals, etc.
I. Muma, Richard D.
  [DNLM: 1. HIV Infections—nursing.   WC 503 H6764 1997]
RC607.A26H576   1997
616.97′92—dc20
DNLM/DLC
for Library of Congress   96-41640

Acquisitions Editor: Cheryl L. Mehalik
Production Editor: Jeanmarie M. Roche
Designer: Janice Barsevich Bielawa

PRINTED IN THE UNITED STATES OF AMERICA

CONTENTS

CONTRIBUTORS

Mary L. Adair, PA-C
Physician Assistant
AIDS Healthcare Foundation
National Coordinator
Physician Assistant AIDS Network
Los Angeles, California

Eric N. Avery, MD
Assistant Professor
Department of Psychiatry and Behavioral Sciences
Associate Member
Institute for the Medical Humanities
The University of Texas Medical Branch
Galveston, Texas

Salah Ayachi, PhD, PA-C
Associate Professor
Physician Assistant Studies
School of Allied Health Sciences
Physician Assistant
AIDS Care and Clinical Research Program
Division of Infectious Diseases
Department of Internal Medicine
The University of Texas Medical Branch
Galveston, Texas

Michael J. Borucki, MD
Assistant Professor
AIDS Care and Clinical Research Program
Division of Infectious Diseases
Department of Internal Medicine
The University of Texas Medical Branch
Galveston, Texas

John G. Bruhn, PhD
Provost and Dean
Pennsylvania State University, Harrisburg
Middletown, Pennsylvania

Pamela Burian, PA-C
Physician Assistant and Coordinator
Women's Services
AIDS Healthcare Foundation
Volunteer Faculty
Family Medicine
University of Southern California
Los Angeles, California

Bernadette Montgomerie Canales, RN
Research Nurse
AIDS Care and Clinical Research Program
Division of Infectious Diseases
Department of Internal Medicine
The University of Texas Medical Branch
Galveston, Texas

Roberto Canales, PA-C
Lecturer
Department of Physician Assistant Studies
School of Allied Health Sciences
Physician Assistant
AIDS Care and Clinical Research Program
The University of Texas Medical Branch
Galveston, Texas

Janice G. Curry, BS, PA-C
Physician Assistant and Clinical Study
       Coordinator
AIDS Care and Clinical Research Program
Division of Infectious Diseases
Department of Internal Medicine
The University of Texas Medical Branch
Galveston, Texas

John E. Fuchs, Jr., PharmD
Clinical Research Specialist
Department of Internal Medicine
Assistant Professor
Department of Pharmacology and Toxicology
The University of Texas Medical Branch
Galveston, Texas

Mary Lou Galantino, MS, PT
Associate Professor
Program in Physical Therapy
Richard Stockton College of New Jersey
Pomona, New Jersey
Clinical Specialist
Garden State Infectious Disease Clinic
Kennedy Health Care Systems
University of Medicine and Dentistry of New Jersey
Vorhees, New Jersey

Kathryn B. Grayce-Barnes, BS, PA-C
General Practitioner
Knouse, Hidalgo, and Associates
Levittown, Pennsylvania

Stephen G. Hausrath, MD
Assistant Professor
AIDS Care and Clinical Research Program
Division of Infectious Diseases
Department of Internal Medicine
The University of Texas Medical Branch
Galveston, Texas

Salme E. Lavigne, RDH, MS
Associate Professor and Chairperson
Department of Dental Hygiene
College of Health Professions
Wichita State University
Wichita, Kansas

Barbara Ann Lyons, MA, PA-C
Associate Professor
Department of Physician Assistant Studies
School of Allied Health Sciences
The University of Texas Medical Branch
Galveston, Texas

Richard D. Muma, MPH, PA-C
Assistant Director and Assistant Professor
Department of Physician Assistant
College of Health Professions
Wichita State University
Wichita, Kansas

Miguel A. Ortega, ACSW, LMSW-ACP
Supervisor
Department of Social Work
The University of Texas Medical Branch
Galveston, Texas

David P. Paar, MD
Assistant Professor of Medicine
AIDS Care and Clinical Research Program
Division of Infectious Diseases
Department of Internal Medicine
The University of Texas Medical Branch
Galveston, Texas

Cody Patton
Director
HIV Care Coordination Team
Interfaith Ministries
Wichita, Kansas

Richard B. Pollard, MD
Professor
Microbiology and Internal Medicine
Chief, AIDS Care and Clinical Research Program
Division of Infectious Diseases
Department of Internal Medicine
The University of Texas Medical Branch
Galveston, Texas

Timothy F. Quigley, PA-C
Clinical Educator
Department of Physician Assistant
College of Health Professions
Wichita State University
Wichita, Kansas

Karen S. Stephenson, MS, PA-C
Associate Professor
Department of Physician Assistant Studies
School of Allied Health Sciences
Physician Assistant
Department of Pediatrics
The University of Texas Medical Branch
Galveston, Texas

Peggy Valentine, EdD, PA-C
Associate Professor
Physician Assistant Department
Director
National AIDS Minority Information and
    Education Program
Howard University
Washington, D.C.

PREFACE

The care of chronically ill patients with many complex problems can be difficult for a single clinician to manage. Often, many types of health care providers are needed to help manage the numerous medical and psychosocial concerns of the patient. Such is the care of HIV-positive patients; it is multifaceted and multidisciplinary.

HIV Manual for Health Care Professionals is intended for a variety of health care disciplines. When the first edition of the book was published, we found it to be useful in training health care professionals from many arenas because the book is a multidisciplinary approach to the primary care of HIV-positive patients.

This edition provides useful and practical information to the clinician on how to manage the HIV-positive and/or AIDS patient. A common comment from students and clinicians is that it is readable and provides current and concise information on all aspects of care.

All parts of the book provide a step-by-step approach to care, whether it be managing *Pneumocystis carinii* pneumonia, deciding on treatment for HIV, prevention counseling, or crisis intervention, as with suicide. In response to readers of the first edition and the dramatic changes made in HIV research over the last 3 years, we have added content that covers protease inhibitors, viral loads, prevention of opportunistic infections, psychiatric care and management, rehabilitation, nutrition, and an extensive resource list.

HIV Manual has also been reorganized into a user-friendly format. In doing so, the book has been arranged to coincide with the way clinicians care for patients (that is, evaluate, diagnose, treat, and counsel). Part I, **Overview**, begins with a chapter on the multidisciplinary approach to HIV patient care, and it is here where one can see how important a team approach is in managing HIV-positive patients. After the introductory material, the reader can review the current epidemiology, immunology, etiology, and pathogenesis of HIV, if necessary. Part II, **Evaluation,** includes chapters covering the systematic approach to the care of adults, children, and women. Each chapter has specific protocols aimed at streamlining the care of these patient groups. Part III, **Diagnosis and Treatment,** covers in great detail the common diseases directly or indirectly associated with HIV. It is here where the reader will find information needed to manage these diseases. The remaining chapters in this section offer information on special issues frequently encountered in the care of HIV-positive patients, such as recognition and management of adverse drug reactions and interpreting laboratory data. This is followed by material on treatment of the primary infection, and information is given on current treatments such as protease inhibitors.

Part IV, **Counseling and Prevention,** contains extensive chapters on pre- and post-test counseling; social worker assessment and intervention; psychiatric care; social and psychological aspects of care; and prevention. Part V, **Supportive Care,** covers specific procedures and their protocols performed by nurses; nutritional needs of HIV-infected patients; rehabilitation issues; and an extensive resource list for provider and patients.

Each chapter is referenced with current reviews and studies on the corresponding topic for the individual who wishes to pursue any topic in greater detail.

The overall goal of this book is to provide the health

care student or clinician with concise, up-to-date information on the HIV infection, so that the care of HIV-infected patients can be optimized.

Richard D. Muma
Barbara Ann Lyons

ACKNOWLEDGMENTS

This book is dedicated to HIV-positive patients and their health care providers.

We have been inspired by patients, their families and significant others, and their health care providers. We wish to thank the many individuals who have shared their experience and knowledge with us, including the input of our students who have helped shape the contents of this book.

We also acknowledge the cooperation of our contributing authors and the continuing support of our faculty colleagues. We would like to thank our editor, Cheryl Mehalik of Appleton & Lange, for her interest in the book and her helpfulness throughout the production of the manuscript.

Preparation of this book was supported in part by the United States Department of Health and Human Services, Health Resources and Services Administration, Bureau of Health Professions, grant numbers 5D21 PE16001-11; 5D21 PE16001-12; and 1U76 PE00238-01.

part I

OVERVIEW

one CHAPTER

Overview of HIV/AIDS

Richard D. Muma • Richard B. Pollard

■ Trends

On June 5, 1981, the *Morbidity and Mortality Weekly Report* (*MMWR*) carried an article reporting five cases of *Pneumocystis carinii* pneumonia (PCP) in homosexual men.[1] Within a short time, similar cases had been reported in New York City and San Francisco, while other reports included cases of perianal herpes and uncontrollable diarrhea, all unresponsive to treatment and occurring in homosexual men.

Additionally, other rare opportunistic infections such as *Mycobacterium avium-intracellulare* were reported increasingly in adults, and several patients were infected with *Cryptosporidium*, a disease so rare that only a few cases were known to have occurred in prior years. Reports of non-Hodgkin's lymphoma and Kaposi's sarcoma (KS) in homosexual men further complicated the puzzling medical picture. These occurrences marked the emergence of what appeared to be a new disease, known as acquired immunodeficiency syndrome (AIDS).

Since the recognition of AIDS and its causative agent, human immunodeficiency virus (HIV), more than 500,000 cases have been diagnosed in the United States.[2,3] Many more are expected to be diagnosed well into the next century.

With any disease, trends in its occurrence tend to change over time. AIDS is no different. In 1981, 189 cases of AIDS were reported to the Centers for Disease Control from 15 states and the District of Columbia; 76 percent of cases were reported from New York and California.[4] Ninety-seven percent of cases reported were among men, 79 percent of whom reported being homosexual or bisexual; no cases were reported among children.[4] In 1990, more than 43,000 cases were reported from all states, the District of Columbia, and U.S. territories; more than 11 percent of adolescent and adult cases were in women; and nearly 800 cases were in children.[4] Currently, children account for more than 7000 cases.

In order to further understand the impact of HIV infection, one can examine mortality and loss of productivity. In 1993, AIDS became the leading cause of death in persons between ages 25 and 44 years.[5] As of 1994, it was the leading cause of death in all men in this age group and the third leading cause of death in women.[5] In black women, ages 25–44, it is the leading cause of death.[5] Also, as of 1994, AIDS was the fourth leading cause of years of potential life lost before age 65, which reflects, in part, lost productivity.[5] This statistic does not, however, reflect the additional loss of productivity which occurs due to illness before death.

Although most cases are still concentrated in high population centers, more are being diagnosed in rural United States.[6] This new development will likely place an extra burden upon specialists and primary care providers already practicing in underserved areas. The worldwide nature should be mentioned as well. This infection has rapidly spread through areas of the world with large medically underserved and economically disadvantaged populations. This pattern of rapid expansion, especially in Africa, South America, and Southeast Asia, is expected to continue.

It should be mentioned that some of the patients currently seeking HIV care were infected before the discovery of the virus and before significant public health measures were developed. Hence, predicting the future course of the infection is hampered by the lack of data concerning new HIV infections occurring today that will only present for medical attention some years from now. Therefore, these individuals will not be represented in the demographic statistics until they seek medical care. This lag period makes the development of public health strategies for this particular situation much more complicated than for other infectious agents.

The other major influence of the changing epidemiology has been a shift in the burden of HIV care, which has occurred since the epidemic began. Although many of the early patients, who were injecting drug users and indigent, required the use of public hospital facilities, a large number of the initially infected male homosexuals were employed and had health care insurance. The patients acquiring HIV infection today, because of socioeconomic status and racial and other demographic factors, are expected to primarily use public health facilities. This will further increase the influence of the epidemic on large public hospitals, university referral centers, and in an overall sense, involve a patient group that has limited access to adequate health care.

Another major shift in HIV care has been the rapid development of therapies for the primary infection as well as for many opportunistic infections. The development of therapies in this particular arena has been both dramatic and rapid. Although no single therapeutic advance has altered the course of the epidemic, new single-agent and combination-agent therapy directed at HIV, as well as the development of preventative therapy for many of the opportunistic infections, have dramatically affected the outcomes of many patients with HIV infection.

Of major concern, however, is the ability to provide access to the advances being made both at the research and clinical level. The newer combinations of therapy frequently are very expensive. The dramatic discovery, which showed the administration of zidovudine (Retrovir) to an infected mother can prevent infection in the newborn, has re-emphasized this issue. Both identification of therapy for infected mothers, as well as providing expensive antiviral therapy, has caused controversy in this country and in countries where even single agent therapy is not available. Differences in access to health care and medications despite rapid and dramatic advances will require aggressive efforts to provide medications through alternative programs.

■ Health Care Providers

Almost every group of health care providers has been involved in the care of HIV-infected patients to date. The physician groups most affected, and involved early, included adult and pediatric infectious disease specialists and oncologists. These two groups continue to be very active in AIDS care and research. In addition, a large group of primary care physicians, including general internists and family practitioners, has increasingly provided health care for this ever-increasing patient population.

Physician extenders have also been affected by the

HIV epidemic. Nurse practitioners and physician assistants have been heavily involved in the care of patients with HIV infection. Such individuals have been particularly useful and skillful in providing primarily outpatient care. Both groups have been involved in clinical research projects and have proven to be an excellent resource.

The impact on the nursing profession has also been significant. Many institutions have developed specialized nursing units, inpatient and outpatient, and nurses have been required to develop significant knowledge concerning the care of HIV-infected individuals. In addition, nurses have also served as a major resource for clinical research and have contributed greatly to the development of new knowledge.

Social workers make up another affected group. They have participated heavily in the development of resources for HIV-infected patients. Social workers have played a major role in the identification of public assistance programs and the enabling of patients to become users of Medicare, Medicaid, housing, free medication programs, and the like. Many institutions have developed specialized social workers who deal primarily with HIV-infected patients.

Additional groups of health care providers, such as occupational therapists and physical therapists, have also participated in the care of HIV-infected individuals, particularly those patients who have prolonged hospital stays that require rehabilitation in order to maximize their ability to function. Dietitians provide consultation and prescribe dietary regimens for those individuals who need to gain weight or require parenteral nutrition. Hospital-based clergy, ethicists, and other individuals in the medical humanities have also participated in the development of policies for the provision of care for large numbers of HIV-infected individuals. This latter group has provided comfort to individual patients as well as assistance in developing appropriate policies for health care providers.

■ Predicting the Future

Although it is difficult to predict the future in any medical area, it would seem obvious that this epidemic will be marked considerably by therapeutic advances. These will no doubt occur in a progressive fashion, with the development of a universally effective solution to HIV infection probably not forthcoming in the near future. More likely, there will be the continued development of combinations of therapeutic agents directed at the primary infection, along with the development of multiple therapies for opportunistic infections and continued emphasis on the development of prophylactic agents for opportunistic infections.

Patients identified earlier in their HIV infection will continue to have an increasingly improved prognosis and a prolonged life span. Their quality of life will also begin to be affected significantly, with fewer hospitalizations and a much greater emphasis on outpatient therapy. The necessity for detection of HIV-infected individuals as these therapies become widespread will require aggressive attempts to identify infected patients much earlier than at present. As the patient numbers increase, a significant amount of attention to the development of medication resources will be required. Newer therapies, which will be expensive and yet prolong life, will require consideration for their adequate provision. In general, there should be optimism that this infection will be affected by therapeutic advances and increases in knowledge about HIV itself and the immunologic perturbations associated with infection. This may translate into a chronic manageable disease with a significantly prolonged life span for each HIV-infected individual. One can be cautiously optimistic that dramatic but gradually progressive changes will occur until this epidemic is controlled by changes in medical therapy over the foreseeable future.

The following text, which will attempt to bring together fundamental information regarding HIV and AIDS, is intended as a guide to assist the clinician in understanding the epidemiology, etiology, clinical manifestations, treatment, and management of HIV and AIDS. Because the data regarding HIV and AIDS are changing almost daily as new information is uncovered, future research could reveal information that is contrary to that presented in this text or that alters the significance of particular facts or theories. To the best of our knowledge, the information that follows is accurate at the time of this printing.

References

1. Centers for Disease Control. *Pneumocystis* pneumonia—Los Angeles. *MMWR*. 1981;30:250–252.
2. Centers for Disease Control and Prevention. First 500,000 AIDS cases—United States, 1995. *MMWR*. 1995;44:849–853.
3. AIDS: 15 years into the epidemic. *Patient Care*. 1996; 30:8–9.
4. Centers for Disease Control. Update: Acquired immunodeficiency syndrome—United States, 1982–1990. *MMWR*. 1991;40:358–369.
5. Centers for Disease Control and Prevention. Update: mortality attributable to HIV infection among persons aged 25–44 years—United States, 1994. *MMWR*. 1996;45:121–125.
6. Centers for Disease Control and Prevention. AIDS map. *MMWR*. 1996;45:316.

two

CHAPTER

Epidemiology of HIV/AIDS

Richard D. Muma

■ Statistics

As mentioned in the previous chapter, the number of AIDS cases has increased rapidly. Between June 5, 1981 and June 30, 1996, 548,102 AIDS cases (ages 0 to 12, 7,296 cases; ages 13 and older, 540,806 cases) were reported in the United States.[1] More than one million (Fig. 2–1) have been reported worldwide; however, the World Health Organization (WHO) estimates this number to be closer to 4.5 million.[2] The number is expected to grow considerably over the next several years, as WHO estimates that at least 18.5 million adults and 1.5 million children are infected with HIV worldwide.[2] Some researchers estimate that by the year 2000, 40 million persons may be infected with HIV.

Among men aged 25 to 44 years, HIV infection was the leading cause of death for all men (23 percent of deaths) and for white and black men (20 percent and 32 percent of deaths, respectively; Fig. 2–2).[3] HIV infection was the third leading cause of death for all women in this age group (11 percent of deaths), the fifth leading cause

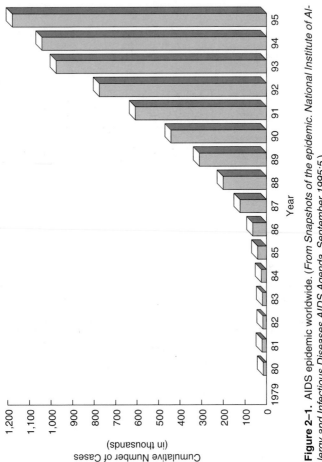

Figure 2-1. AIDS epidemic worldwide. (*From Snapshots of the epidemic. National Institute of Allergy and Infectious Diseases AIDS Agenda. September 1995:5.*)

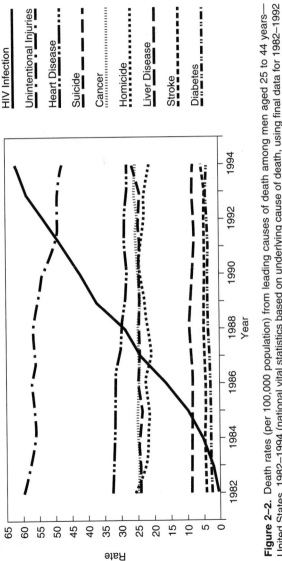

Figure 2–2. Death rates (per 100,000 population) from leading causes of death among men aged 25 to 44 years—United States, 1982–1994 (national vital statistics based on underlying cause of death, using final data for 1982–1992 and provisional data for 1993–1994). (*From Centers for Disease Control and Prevention. Update: Mortality attributable to HIV infection among persons aged 25–44 years—United States, 1994. MMWR. 1996;45:121–125.*)

for white women (6 percent of deaths), and the leading cause for black women (22 percent of deaths; Fig. 2–3).[3]

In 1994, the death rate from HIV infection per 100,000 population among persons aged 25 to 44 years was almost four times as high for black (177.9) as for white men (47.2), and nine times as high for black (51.2) as for white women (5.7; Fig. 2–4).[3]

■ Origin, Transmission, and Transmission Groups

Manifestations of AIDS were noted as early as 1979 after various reports from Africa, Haiti, and the United States documented rare opportunistic infections and neoplasms in supposedly healthy individuals. Epidemiologic evidence suggests that the virus may have first appeared in Africa.[4] However, many different theories have been hypothesized to explain the origin of the disease. Viruses that strongly resemble HIV endemically infect African green monkeys without causing disease in them. It is postulated that a mutation in one of these viruses resulted in HIV and was transmitted to humans, most likely by trauma.

AIDS cases have occurred in six major transmission groups.[1] These groups are arranged in a hierarchy so that patients with multiple risks are placed in only one group. The distribution of AIDS patients by groups in the United States is outlined in Table 2–1. The majority of U.S. AIDS cases occur in men who have sex with men and injecting-drug users. This is beginning to change as more cases are reported in heterosexual males and females.[1] Because the interval from infection until symptoms is estimated to be 11+ years, these changes in HIV transmission patterns will not be reflected in the AIDS statistics for another decade.

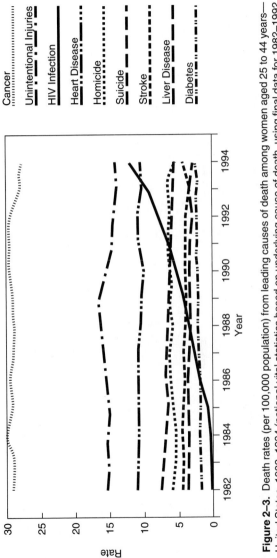

Figure 2–3. Death rates (per 100,000 population) from leading causes of death among women aged 25 to 44 years—United States, 1982–1994 (national vital statistics based on underlying cause of death, using final data for 1982–1992 and provisional data for 1993–1994). (*From Centers for Disease Control and Prevention. Update: Mortality attributable to HIV infection among persons aged 25–44 years—United States, 1994.* MMWR. *1996;45:121–125.*)

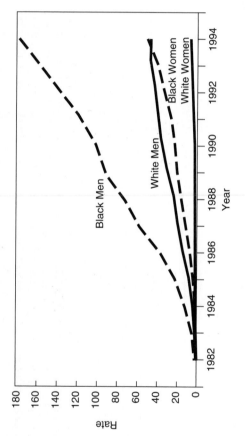

Figure 2–4. Death rates (per 100,000 population) from HIV infection among persons aged 25 to 44 years, by sex, race (data unavailable for races other than white and black), and year—United States, 1982–1994 (national vital statistics based on underlying cause of death, using final data for 1982–1992 and provisional data for 1993–1994). (*From Centers for Disease Control and Prevention. Update: Mortality attributable to HIV infection among persons aged 25–44 years—United States, 1994.* MMWR. *1996;45:121–125.*)

TABLE 2–1. AIDS CASES BY GROUPS. UNITED STATES (MALE AND FEMALE) THROUGH JUNE 1996

AIDS Cases	No.	%
HIV Exposure Category		
Men who have sex with men	274,192	50.0
Injecting drug use	137,753	25.1
Men who have sex with men and inject drugs	35,218	6.4
Hemophilia	4,280	1.0
Heterosexual contact	44,980	8.2
Transfusion recipients/Blood components	7,684	1.4
Pediatric cases	7,181	1.3
Undetermined (reflects both adult and pediatric cases)	36,814	6.7
Total	548,102	100
Vital Status		
Living	205,112	37.4
Deceased	342,990	62.6
Total	548,102	100.0

From reference 1.

■ Modes of Transmission

HIV is transmitted in limited ways: through sexual contact, through infected blood components and clotting factor concentrates, and perinatally. HIV has been isolated from a number of body fluids, including blood, saliva, semen, urine, cerebrospinal fluid, and sweat. The virus preferentially infects CD4+ lymphocytes and conceivably could be recovered from any site where such cells are found. However, such findings are not necessarily significant in the context of public health.

Actions and/or behaviors that are considered high

risk and are frequently associated with HIV infection include vaginal and/or receptive anal intercourse and other potentially traumatic sexual activities with HIV-infected individuals. Examples include the following.

- *Anilingus:* Encircling the anal area with the tongue.
- *Cunnilingus:* Tonguing the vagina/clitoris (more risky during menstrual period).
- *Fellatio:* Tonguing and sucking the male genital area (more risky if partner ejaculates in the mouth).
- *Fisting:* Putting hand, fist, or forearm into the rectum or vagina.
- *Urolagnia:* Urinating on the skin or in body cavity (more risky if there are open cuts in the skin, mouth, vagina, or rectum).
- *Rectal and/or vaginal placement of objects:* Placing objects (sex toys) may cause tears in the mucosa, which could serve as a portal of entry for the virus.
- *Needle sharing and frequent injection of IV drugs.*
- *Blood transfusions prior to mid-1985:* Blood components that presumably have transmitted HIV include whole blood, red cells, platelets, and plasma.
- *Maternal–fetal transmission:* HIV-infected women transmit HIV to the fetus or infant either in utero or at delivery in 15 to 30 percent of cases.[5]

Actions and/or behaviors that are considered low risk and usually not associated with HIV infection include the following.

- *Occupational transmission:* The collective evidence strongly suggests that the risk to health care workers of occupational transmission (needle sticks) of HIV is low (0.3 percent)[6] and can be most effectively reduced by following recommended guidelines for the care of HIV-infected persons and the handling of their specimens (see Chapter 16).

- *Casual contact:* There is no evidence that AIDS or HIV can be transmitted through air, food, water, fomites, arthropods (mosquitos), or casual contact (hugging or kissing).

◼ Demographic Characteristics of AIDS in the United States

Age

Approximately eighty-eight percent of all AIDS patients reported to the Centers for Disease Control (CDC) are between the ages of 20 and 49.[1]

Gender

Approximately 82 percent of AIDS patients are male.[1] Of these men with AIDS, 51 percent have sex with men. Men in other transmission groups account for 7 percent of the total cases. Females account for 18 percent of the total, or 82,198 cumulative cases.[1]

Race

For all AIDS cases, 47 percent occur in whites, 34 percent in African-Americans, 18 percent in Hispanics, and 1.0 percent in Asians/Pacific islanders and American Indians/Alaskan natives.[1]

◼ Geographic Distribution in the United States

Although the AIDS epidemic in the United States was recognized initially in the Northeast and West, and rates remain highest in the Northeast, the findings from AIDS surveillance document that the greatest proportionate increases in the HIV epidemic have occurred in the South and Midwest—areas that account for the largest proportion of the U.S. population.[1] As of October 1995, 31.2 percent were reported in the Northeast, 9.8 percent in the Midwest, 33 percent in the South, 22.7 percent in the West, and 3.2 percent in U.S. territories (Fig. 2–5).

■ Diseases Associated With AIDS

Until 1992, the three most commonly reported diseases on death certificates among patients dying with HIV were pneumocystosis, Kaposi's sarcoma, and pneumonia of unspecified origin.[7,8] Pneumocystosis, initially the most common, accounted for one third of HIV-related deaths.[8] However, by 1992 pneumocystosis accounted for less than half this proportion.[8] The percentages of cryptococcosis and candidiasis decreased to a lesser extent.[8] A complete picture of the trends in the prevalence of infectious diseases and cancers occurring in HIV-infected individuals is shown in Figure 2–6. It is postulated that the decreasing frequency of death associated with pneumocystosis is because individuals are now receiving chemoprophylaxis and are being diagnosed and treated earlier.[8] This may also explain the decrease in prevalence of cryptococcosis and candidiasis.[8]

■ CDC AIDS Definition for Adults

In the mid-1980s the CDC developed a surveillance case definition for AIDS in adults and adolescents (aged 13 and over), and children (less than 13 years of age), in order to track the disease. The definition for children is discussed in Chapter 6. The adult and adolescent definition was based on the early observation that patients with

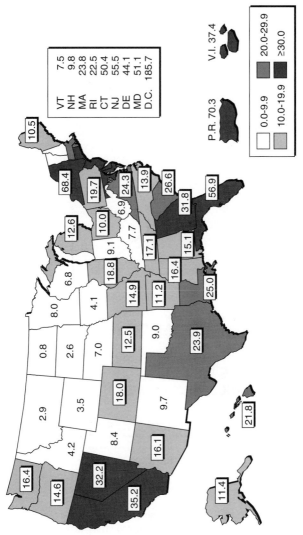

Figure 2–5. AIDS cases per 100,000 population—United States, January to December 1995. *(From Centers for Disease Control and Prevention. AIDS map. MMWR. 1996;45;316.)*

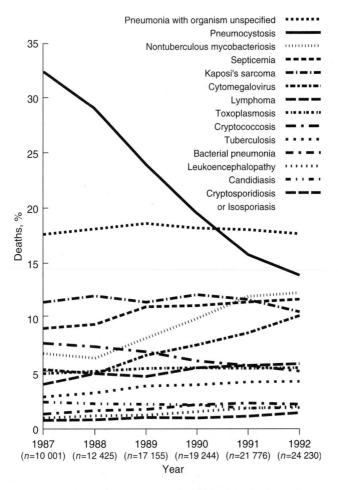

Figure 2–6. Infectious diseases and cancers reported among people dying of HIV infection in the United States, 1987 to 1992. (*Reproduced with permission from Selik RM, Chu SY, Ward JW. Trends in infectious diseases and cancers among persons dying of HIV infection in the United States from 1987–1992. Ann Intern Med. 1995;123:933–936.*)

AIDS developed certain opportunistic illnesses secondary to a specific defect in a cell-mediated component of the immune system. If no other cause for the cellular immune dysfunction was present, the diagnosis of one of 12 opportunistic illnesses was considered indicative of AIDS. In 1987 the CDC revised this definition (Box 2–1) to include HIV dementia, HIV wasting syndrome, and other illnesses.[9] More recently the CDC has expanded the AIDS surveillance definition to include all HIV-infected persons who have fewer than 200 CD4 cells/mm^3, or a CD4 cell percentage of total lymphocytes of less than 14.[10] This expansion also includes three conditions—pulmonary tuberculosis, recurrent pneumonia, and invasive cervical cancer—and retains the 23 conditions in the case definition published in 1987.[9,10]

The expansion of the surveillance case definition for AIDS has resulted in moderate increases in reported AIDS cases after first being changed in 1987, and dramatic increases after the change in 1993 (Fig. 2–7). The 1993 change has primarily reflected reports of HIV-infected persons in whom severe immunosuppression had been diagnosed.[11] Refer to Chapter 5 for the new CDC classification system and how it reflects the new AIDS case definition.

■ **Box 2–1**
List of Conditions in the 1987 AIDS Adult and Adolescent Surveillance Case Definition

- Candidiasis of bronchi, trachea, or lungs
- Candidiasis, esophageal
- Coccidioidomycosis, disseminated or extrapulmonary

■ *Box 2–1 continued*

- Cryptococcoses, extrapulmonary
- Cryptosporidiosis, chronic intestinal (>1 month duration)
- Cytomegalovirus disease (other than liver, spleen, or nodes)
- Cytomegalovirus retinitis (with loss of vision)
- HIV encephalopathy
- Herpes simplex: chronic ulcer(s) (>1 month duration); or bronchitis, pneumonitis, or esophagitis
- Histoplasmosis, disseminated or extrapulmonary
- Isosporiasis, chronic intestinal (>1 month duration)
- Kaposi's sarcoma
- Lymphoma, Burkitt's (or equivalent term)
- Lymphoma, immunoblastic (or equivalent term)
- Lymphoma, primary in brain
- *Mycobacterium avium* complex or *M. kansasii*, disseminated or extrapulmonary
- *Mycobacterium tuberculosis*, disseminated or extrapulmonary
- *Mycobacterium*, other species or unidentified species, disseminated or extrapulmonary
- Pneumocystis carinii pneumonia
- Progressive multifocal leukoencephalopathy
- *Salmonella* septicemia, recurrent
- Toxoplasmosis of brain
- Wasting syndrome caused by HIV

From reference 9.

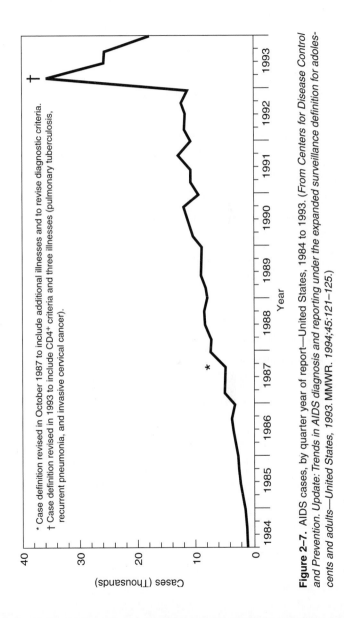

Figure 2-7. AIDS cases, by quarter year of report—United States, 1984 to 1993. (*From Centers for Disease Control and Prevention. Update: Trends in AIDS diagnosis and reporting under the expanded surveillance definition for adolescents and adults—United States, 1993. MMWR. 1994;45:121-125.*)

References

1. Centers for Disease Control and Prevention. *HIV/AIDS Surveillance Report*. 1996;8:1–33.
2. World Health Organization global AIDS statistics. *AIDS Care*. 1995;7:547.
3. Centers for Disease Control and Prevention. Update: Mortality attributable to HIV infection among persons aged 25–44 years—United States, 1994. *MMWR*. 1996;45:121–124.
4. Anderson RM, May RM. Understanding the AIDS pandemic. *Sci Am*. 1992;5:58–66.
5. Davis SF, Byers RH, Lindegren ML, et al. Prevalence and incidence of vertically acquired HIV infection in the United States. *JAMA*. 1995;274:952–955.
6. Centers for Disease Control and Prevention. Case-control study of HIV seroconversion in health-care workers after percutaneous exposure to HIV-infected blood—France, United Kingdom, and United States, January 1988–August 1994. *MMWR*. 1995;44:929–933.
7. Centers for Disease Control and Prevention. HIV/AIDS Surveillance Report. February 1993:1–33.
8. Selik RM, Chu SY, Ward JW. Trends in infectious diseases and cancers among persons dying of HIV infection in the United States from 1987–1992. *Ann Intern Med*. 1995;123:933–936.
9. Centers for Disease Control. Revision of the CDC surveillance case definition for acquired immunodeficiency syndrome. *MMWR*. 1987;36:1s–15s.
10. Centers for Disease Control and Prevention. 1993 revised classification system for HIV infection and expanded surveillance case definition for AIDS among adolescents and adults. *MMWR*. 1992;41(RR-17):1–19.
11. Centers for Disease Control and Prevention. Update: Trends in AIDS diagnosis and reporting under the expanded surveillance definition for adolescents and adults—United States, 1993. *MMWR*. 1994; 43:826–831.

three

CHAPTER

Immunology

Michael J. Borucki

Immunity is a normal adaptive response, intended to protect the body from invasion by microbes and transformed (tumor) cells. A variety of rare, inherited, disorders cause well-characterized immunodeficiency syndromes whose symptoms begin in childhood; agammaglobulinemia and severe combined immunodeficiency are examples. Acquired immune defects are those that arise later in life, without evidence of immunodeficiency during the childhood years. The acquired immunodeficiency syndrome, caused by the lentivirus HIV, is characterized by the development of clinically diverse infections and neoplasms that occur opportunistically, that is, only in the setting of profound immunodeficiency.

Acquired immune defects have been associated with a variety of conditions: old age, diabetes, renal failure, lymphoreticular malignancies, malnutrition, autoimmune diseases, splenectomy, burn injuries, immunosuppressive therapies (corticosteroids, lympholytic agents, cytotoxic agents, total nodal irradiation), and AIDS. Thymic involution and depressed delayed-type hypersensitivity responses are well recognized sequelae of immune senescence. Patients with advanced age and HIV infection progress more rapidly than do young adults with HIV infection. Prior to the AIDS epidemic, malnutrition was the most common cause of an acquired immune defect. Malnutrition has been associated with a variety of immunologic defects, including decreased secretory IgA, decreased interferon elaboration, hypocomplementemia, and diminished phagocytosis. Malnutrition complicates many HIV-related processes, such as wasting, esophageal diseases, and diarrhea diseases.

Immunity can be broadly divided into two types, natural and specific. Natural immunity refers to those immune responses, such as natural killer cells and complement activation, that are nonspecific and occur without the immune system being "primed." Nonspecific indicates that the same immune responses occur irrespective of the nature of the foreign antigen. Complement activation, for example, follows the same cascade whether elicited by transplant rejection, tumor growth, or gonococcemia. Natural immunity is not histocompatibility complex-restricted.

Specific immunity is a response to exposure by a specific antigen (priming) and develops in two parallel arms, one humoral ("humor" meaning soluble, referring to antibodies) and the other cellular. "Humoral" and "cellular" refer to the effector arm of the immune response; humoral immunity is effected through antibody production, and cell-mediated immunity (CMI) is effected through immune cells, largely through cytotoxic T cells. Both arms of specific immunity are dependent upon cells for the development of the immune response. The initiation of specific immunity follows the recognition, processing, and presentation of foreign antigens by antigen-presenting cells (APCs). The prototypic APC is the monocyte/macrophage; however, other cell types may participate in antigen processing and presentation, including Langerhans' cells, dendritic cells, and microglial cells. The APCs phagocytose the foreign antigen (whether bacteria, virus, fungus, parasite, tumor cell, transplanted tissue, or foreign body), process the antigen, and then display (present) the antigens on their surface. Major histocompatibility complex proteins (MHCs) are intimately involved in antigen presentation. MHCs are divided into two major classes. MHC class I proteins are expressed on the surface of all nucleated cells and are important in self-recognition and MHC restriction. MHC class II protein expression is largely limited to the surface of immune cells. Antigen presentation allows for other cells of the immune system (especially B and T lymphocytes) to recognize these antigens and react to them. As they mature, the B and T cells become committed to a specific antigen, and once mature are primed to specifically recognize and target this one antigen. They may respond to very closely related antigens but will not respond to antigens that are very much different than the principal target antigen. The ability of the immune response to recognize the vast diversity of antigens in our environment depends on the above scenario being repeated again and again for each new antigen encountered. It is believed that the human immune system is capable of recognizing perhaps 100 million different antigens. Specific immunity to a new antigen, the "neoantigenic" response, takes a discrete period of time to develop, typically 7 to 10 days.

Once stimulated by the interaction with the APC, B and T cells that recognize the antigen continue the immune cascade, which includes clonal expansion. One cell divides into many progeny cells, the "clone," all capable of interacting with the exact same antigen. In the case of B cells, they mature to plasma cells, each bearing and capable of secreting antibodies targeting the specific antigen. In the case of T cells, the end product is a cytotoxic T cell targeting cells for destruction that display the specific antigen (tumor cells or infected cells, for example). Effective cytotoxic T-cell responses depend on other components of the cell-mediated immune cascade, including helper cells and cytokines, to develop fully.

The cellular arm is a bit more complex and involves many distinct populations of cells with different functions; three of which are helper, suppressor, and cytotoxic functions. The helper and suppressor functions serve to regulate the intensity of the cellular immune response. The helper cells help or increase the intensity of the CMI response. The suppressor cells suppress or decrease the intensity of the immune response. Additional regulation of the cellular immune response occurs through a variety of cytokines, principally the interferons and interleukins. Multiple layers of regulation are imposed because immunity resembles a "double-edged sword." Although immunity clearly benefits the host, the potential for deleterious effects, as manifested by the autoimmune diseases (i.e. rheumatoid arthritis, systemic lupus erythematosus), also exists.

T cells are often characterized by the markers they bear on their surfaces. For example, all mature T cells bear an MHC class II protein on their surface called CD2 (previously known as T3 or OKT3). Subpopulations of T cells may display other MHC class II markers such as CD8 (T8 or OKT8) or CD4 (T4 or OKT4). These surface markers may suggest differing functions of these subpopulations of T cells; for example, most T cells with helper activity are CD4+ cells. Other markers suggest cellular activation (HLA-DR), memory cells (CD45RO, CD29), and other functions. CD4+ cells represent one critical component of the immune response, as they are central to the coordination of the cell-mediated immune response (Fig. 3–1).

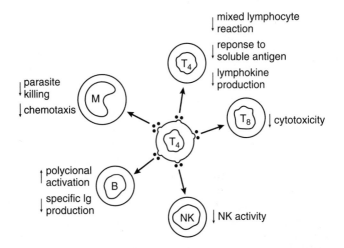

Figure 3–1. HIV infects both monocytes/macrophages (M) and CD4+ T cells (T4), comprising immune responsiveness in general and neoantigenic responses in particular. The CD4+ T-cell plays a central role in the orchestration of the immune response. Quantitative and qualitative defects in CD4+ T cells produce a variety of immune defects, including decreased mixed lymphocyte reaction, decreased responsiveness to soluble antigens, disordered lymphokine production, decreased specific cytotoxicity, decreased natural immunity, polyclonal B-cell activation, impaired specific immunoglobulin synthesis, decreased killing of intracellular pathogens, and decreased chemotaxis.

The laboratory determination of a CD4 count represents the determination of the number of cells that express both CD2 (T cells) and CD4 (helper T cells) in a given volume of blood (usually per cubic millimeter). Similarly, the T4% represents the percentage of CD4+ cells among the CD2+ cells.

HIV infects both macrophages and CD4+ T cells. As such, HIV infection perturbs both antigen processing and the first critical cell-to-cell interaction in the cellular immune cascade. The defects in monocytes are largely qualitative, resulting in the functional defects of impaired killing of intracellular parasites and defective chemotaxis. The defects in CD4+ T cells are both qualitative and quantitative, impairing both the function of CD4+ T cells and a decrease in the number of CD4+ cells over time.

Natural immunity, mediated by natural killer (NK) and lymphokine-activated killer (LAK) cells, may be important to host defense from viral infections. Natural killer cells are a functionally defined subset of non-T, non-B lymphocytes of bone marrow origin, which lyse selected target cells, including transformed and virus-infected cells. Patients congenitally lacking NK cells are susceptible to infection by herpesviruses. Natural killer cells can be distinguished from other lymphocyte subsets by their granular morphology and by the expression of the surface-marker antigens CD3−, CD16+, CD56+ and possibly CD57. Natural immunity is suppressed in HIV infected individuals primarily because of a qualitative defect of both NK and LAK cells. The functional defect includes a hyporesponsiveness to interferon-alpha, which is thought to be related to the loss of CD4+ cells. Although NK cells are not normally considered susceptible to HIV infection, infection of NK cells by human herpesvirus 6 induces expression of CD4, an antigen not constitutively expressed by NK cells, thereby predisposing NK cells to infection by HIV.[1]

Cytokines are soluble factors employed in the signalling between immune cells in the development of an immune response. In parallel with the intracellular messengers that facilitate cellular activation, the cytokines may be thought of as extracellular messengers that facilitate the activation of functionally related cell groups. The susceptibility of peripheral lymphocytes to programmed cell death appears to be regulated by diverse cytokines. T-cell help for cell-mediated and humoral immunity develops in a balanced fashion, modulated by the type 1 and type 2 cytokines. Macrophage activation is favored by the type 1 cytokines: interferon-gamma, interleukin-2, and tumor necrosis factor-alpha. Macrophage function is suppressed by the type 2 cytokines: interleukin-4, interleukin-10, and interleukin-13. Decreased production of type 1 cytokines impairs the development of cell-mediated immune responses. In addition to regulating immune responses, cytokines contribute to the regulation of HIV expression. HIV replication is regulated by many factors, including external stimuli (such as cytokines), host cellular factors, and viral gene products.

Cytokines may directly affect HIV expression. Interferon-gamma induces HIV expression from chronically infected monocytes. Granulocyte monocyte colony-stimulating factor (GM-CSF) and interleukin-6 (IL-6) increase virus expression in monocytes predominantly by post-transcriptional mechanisms. Tumor necrosis factor alpha (TNF-alpha) upregulates HIV expression in chronically infected T-cell and monocyte cell lines by induction of transcription activating factors, which bind to the NF-kappaB binding site in the HIV long terminal repeat. Tumor necrosis factor-alpha synergistically increases HIV expression when combined with either IL-6 or GM-CSF. Tumor necrosis factor-alpha may be produced to excess in HIV-infected individuals. Tumor necrosis factor-alpha induction is not limited to stimulation by HIV. Heterogeneous microbial infections upregulate HIV through the production of cytokines, thereby accelerating lymphocyte depletion and immunodeficiency. This has caused some authorities to speculate that AIDS is a disorder of the immune network caused by HIV, whose pathogenesis is best considered a "cytokine disease."

Other cytokines inhibit HIV expression. Interferons alpha and beta decrease HIV expression in acutely and chronically infected cells by inhibiting viral assembly, budding, and release. Transforming growth factor-beta (TGF-beta) downregulates constitutive and inductive expression of HIV by transcriptional and post-transcriptional mechanisms. Under certain circumstances, TGF-beta may enhance HIV replication.

CD4+ T-cell depletion in the peripheral blood is the hallmark of progressive HIV infection. Current estimates suggest that, in HIV-infected individuals, on the order of one billion CD4+ T cells are destroyed every day.[2] The idiotypic network model suggests that both HIV genetic variation and the immune response to HIV are under constant co-selective pressure, which ultimately exhausts all possible immune responses against HIV and allows immunologic escape.[3] HIV can cause CD4+ T-cell depletion both by direct and indirect mechanisms.

Direct CD4+ T-cell destruction may follow disruption of the cell membrane as a consequence of viral budding. The integrity of the cell membrane may also be affected by insertion of viral envelope proteins into the cell membrane. Compromise of the cell membrane can allow ion flux, loss of critical ion gradients, and cell death. Cytoplasmic accumulation of unintegrated viral DNA may lead to cytotoxicity. Similarly, intracellular binding of HIV envelope components with CD4 may cause cytotoxicity. The CD4 envelope complexes may disrupt nuclear cytoplasmic transport by occupying the nuclear pores.

HIV may cause CD4+ T-cell depletion by indirect mechanisms as well. Destruction of uninfected CD4+ T cells may occur as a consequence of autoimmune phenomena or syncytia formation. Uninfected CD4+ T cells may bind free gp120 and become targets for lysis by antibody-dependent cellular cytotoxicity.

In lymph nodes, the frequency of HIV-1 infected CD4+ T cells is substantially higher (from 1/2 to 1 log) than in the peripheral blood. High levels of HIV-specific mRNA, which suggests active viral replication, may be routinely detected by in-situ hybridization and RNA PCR in lymphoid tissue even when peripheral blood lymphocytes appear to have a modest viral burden. In patients with early-stage disease, a heavy viral load resides in the lymphoid organs, suggesting that these tissues act as major reservoirs for HIV.[4,5]

Follicular dendritic cells, within the lymph nodes, are large cells with both CD4 and receptors for the constant fragment of immunoglobulins (Fc) expressed on the surface. Homing receptors on lymphocytes are one reason why lymphocytes are intensely concentrated in lymph nodes. The physical proximity also increases the efficiency of cell-to-cell interactions and of the cytokine interactions of the immune response. The follicular dendritic cells have many invaginations on the surface, which aid in trapping infectious agents for phagocytosis by macrophages. For most infectious agents this arrangement assists in the development of the immune response. The surface expression of both CD4 and Fc receptors causes the follicular dendritic cells (FDC) to accumulate high concentrations of HIV. In addition to trapping HIV, the FDC are also infected by HIV.[6] The FDC also increase in number within the lymph nodes and probably contribute to the generalized adenopathy characteristic of earlier stages of HIV infection. As HIV infection progresses, the lymph nodes involute as the cellular constituents are progressively destroyed. Because lymphocytes regularly pass through the lymph nodes, CD4+ T cells that come in contact with the FDC are likely to become infected.

Qualitative abnormalities also occur in CD4+ T cells. T-cell hyporesponsiveness to soluble antigens occurs early in the course of HIV infection. Defective T-cell cloning also supports functional impairment of CD4+ T cells. In vitro exposure of cells to specific HIV proteins, in the absence of actual HIV infection, inhibits antigen-specific responses. HIV envelope protein may interfere with the interaction between CD4 and MHC molecules required for efficient antigen presentation. CD4 receptor density may be decreased on HIV-infected CD4+ T cells. Binding of gp120 to CD4 may disrupt postreceptor signal transduction.

Cytotoxic T-cell responses are important in controlling HIV infection by suppressing viral replication and by destroying HIV-infected cells. Lentiviral infections, in general, are associated with exuberant cytotoxic T-cell responses. Cytotoxic T-cell (CTL) activity is associated with the early, asymptomatic stage of disease. Following primary infection with HIV, the development of CTL activity is associated with a rapid decrease in HIV replication. Cytotoxic T cells recognize a variety of HIV proteins, including envelope protein, polymerase, group-associated antigen, and regulatory components. CTL responses may accelerate the process of immunodeficiency by targeting CD4+ cells for destruction. One study found that immunologically normal HIV-infected individuals were typically devoid of CTL responses to HIV.[7] Furthermore, although CD8+[8] T cells are critical to suppressing HIV replication, this may be independent of anti-HIV CTL activity. Adequate understanding of protective cellular immune responses is needed to foster successful vaccine development [9] and immunotherapeutics.[10]

Autoimmune phenomena are well recognized in the setting of HIV infection. Anti-cardiolipin antibodies (ACA) have been described in the patients with HIV infection. In one small series, over half of HIV infected individuals were IgG-ACA positive.[11] Antibodies directed at HIV envelope glycoprotein gp120 may cross-react with major histocompatibility class II beta chains.[12] Immunoglobulins have been demonstrated on CD4+ T cells of HIV-infected patients. The presence of surface immunoglobulins on CD4+ T cells has been correlated with decreased CD4+ T-cell numbers.[13] Autoimmunity may also contribute to apoptosis.[14] One model of HIV-induced autoimmunity suggests that HIV variants, which undergo constant evolution (or selection), continuously stimulate, infect, and deplete susceptible CD4+ T cells. Indeed, HIV viral variation has been correlated with more rapid CD4+ T-cell loss.[15] Suppressor T cells undergo a parallel, but mirror-image, evolution until immunity against HIV cross-reacts with selected suppressor T-cell clones.

Apoptosis, or programmed cell death, is a prominent cause of CD4+ T-cell depletion in HIV infection.[16] Morphologically, apoptosis is characterized by cell crenation, nuclear condensation, and membrane bleb formation. Programmed cell death naturally occurs in immature thymocytes. It is the process of clonal depletion, or negative selection, of autoreactive T cells, leading to the establishment of self-tolerance. Apoptosis also occurs in mature CD4+ T cells following CD3 receptor cross-linking. In HIV-infected individuals, cross-linking of CD4 may occur as a result of binding of gp120 to CD4, priming the cell for apoptosis following antigenic stimulation of the T-cell receptor. Apoptosis occurs following acute HIV infection of lymphocytes in vitro. In vitro data suggest that minute concentrations of gp120 are sufficient to prime T cells for apoptotic death. Apoptosis may also be induced, in vitro, by HIV-1 TAT protein.[17] Apoptotic death may be effected through intracellular oxidative stress and free radical formation. Anti-oxidants, such as N-acetylcysteine, may be protective against apoptosis in some in vitro models.[18] Spontaneous apoptosis of cultured CD4+ and CD8+ T cells from HIV-infected individuals has also been observed. The loss of CD4+ Th1 responses in HIV-infected individuals is thought to result from activation-induced apoptosis of CD4+ Th1 cells. Expression of the marker CD95, or Fas, is increased in T cells primed for apoptotic death. Interleukin-12 appears to protect against this effect in CD4+ T cells.[19]

Superantigens may be involved in the immuno-pathogenesis of HIV infection. In mice, a retrovirus-encoded superantigen promotes a typical superantigen effect; the expansion of cells expressing specific T-cell receptor beta-chain variable (V_{beta}) regions. In humans infected with HIV, V_{beta} selection may occur, and may be an HIV retroviral superantigen effect; however, this remains controversial.[20,21] It is thought that superantigens function as activators of specific V_{beta} T-cell subsets, which may lead to T-cell anergy. Additionally, HIV replication may be increased up to 100-fold in human T-cell lines expressing specific V_{beta} regions.

T helper (Th) clones develop along one of two generalized pathways, the type 1 response (Th1) or the type 2 response (Th2). Differing patterns of cytokine secretion first suggested the difference. In general, the Th1 response promotes IgG2a production and the development of cellular immunity. By contrast, the Th2-type response promotes IgE, eosinophil, and mast cell production. The Th1 response is favored by cytokines which promote macrophage activation; the Th2 response is favored by cytokines which suppress macrophage activation. Interleukin-12, a cytokine elaborated by macrophages, promotes the development of the Th1 response. Interferons alpha and beta also promote the development of the Th1 response. Th1 and Th2 responses are antagonistic: Th1 responses suppress the development of Th2 responses, and vice versa. The progressive defect in cell-mediated immunity that occurs in the setting of HIV infection is thought to favor the development of Th2 responses and the further suppression of Th1 responses. That HIV promotes a Th1/Th2 switch is subject to debate.[22]

An improved understanding of the immunopathogenesis of HIV infection has spawned new areas of research to decipher the role of immunity in HIV infection by exploring cytokine therapies, cytokine inhibitors, ex-vivo cell expansion, antioxidants, selective immunosuppressives, and vaccines as therapeutics.

References

1. Lusso P, Malnati MS, Garzino-Demo A, et al. Infection of natural killer cells by human herpesvirus 6. *Nature.* 1993; 362:458–462.

2. Ho DD, Neumann AU, Perelson AS, et al. Rapid turnover of plasma virions and CD4 lymphocytes in HIV-1 infection. *Nature.* 1995;373:123–126.

3. Hoffmann GW. The T cell receptor and AIDS pathogenesis. *Scand J Immunol.* 1995;41:331–337.

4. Pantaleo G, Graziosi C, Demarest JF, et al. HIV infection is active and progressive in lymphoid tissue during the clinically latent stage of disease. *Nature.* 1993;363:355–358.

5. Embretson J, Zupancic M, Ribas JL, et al. Massive covert infection of helper T lymphocytes and macrophages by HIV during the incubation period of AIDS. *Nature.* 1993;363:359–362.

6. Patterson S, Gross J, English N, et al. CD4 expression on dendritic cells and their infection by human immunodeficiency virus. *J Gen Virol.* 1995;76:1155–1163.

7. Ferbas J, Kaplan AH, Hausner MA, et al. Virus burden in long-term survivors of human immunodeficiency virus (HIV) infection is a determinant of anti-HIV CD8+ lymphocyte activity. *J Infect Dis.* 1995;172:329–339.

8. Toso JF, Chen CH, Mohr JR, et al. Oligoclonal CD8 lymphocytes from persons with asymptomatic human immunodeficiency virus (HIV) type 1 infection inhibit HIV-1 replication. *J Infect Dis.* 1995;172:964–973.

9. Schnittman SM, Fauci AS. Human immunodeficiency virus and acquired immunodeficiency syndrome: An update. *Adv Intern Med.* 1994;39:305–355.

10. Valentine FT, Kundu S, Haslett PAJ, et al. A randomized,

placebo-controlled study of the immunogenicity of human immunodeficiency virus (HIV) rgp160 vaccine in HIV-infected subjects with $\geqq 400/mm^3$ CD4 T lymphocytes (AIDS Clinical Trials Group protocol 137). *J Infect Dis.* 1996;173:1336–1346.

11. Coll-Daroca J, Gutierrez-Cebollada J, Yazbeck H, et al. Anti-cardiolipin antibodies and acquired immunodeficiency syndrome: Prognostic marker or association with HIV infection? *Infection.* 1992;20:140–142.

12. Pugliese O, Viora M, Camponeschi B, et al. A gp120 HIV peptide with high similarity to HLA class II beta chains enhances PPD-specific and autoreactive T cell activation. *Clin Exp Immunol.* 1992;90:170–174.

13. Muller C, Kukel S, Bauer R. Relationship of antibodies against CD4+ T cells in HIV-infected patients to markers of activation and progression: Autoantibodies are closely associated with CD4 cell depletion. *Immunology.* 1993;79:248–254.

14. Zagury JF, Cantalloube H, Achour A, et al. Striking similarities between HIV-1 Env protein and the apoptosis mediating cell surface antigen Fas. Role in the pathogenesis of AIDS. *Biomed Pharmacother.* 1993;47:331–335.

15. Wolinsky SM, Korber BTM, Neumann AU, et al. Adaptive evolution of human immunodeficiency virus-type 1 during the natural course of infection. *Science.* 1996;272:537–542.

16. Ameisen JC. From cell activation to cell depletion. The programmed cell death hypothesis of AIDS pathogenesis. *Adv Exp Med Biol.* 1995;374:139–163.

17. Li CJ, Friedman DJ, Wang C, et al. Induction of apoptosis in uninfected lympocytes by HIV-1 TAT protein. *Science.* 1995;268:429–431.

18. Malorni W, Rivabene R, Santini MT, Donelli G. N-acetycysteine inhibits apoptosis and decreases viral particles in HIV-chronically infected U937 cells. *FEBS Lett.* 1993;327:75–78.

19. Estaquier J, Idziorek T, Zou W, et al. T helper type 1/T helper type 2 cytokines and T cell death: Preventive effect of interleukin 12 on activation-induced and CD95 (Fas/APO-1)-mediated apoptosis of CD4+ T cells from human immunodeficiency virus-infected persons. *J Exp Med.* 1995;182:1759–1767.

20. Boldt-Houle DM, Rinaldo CR Jr, Ehrlich GD. Random deple-

tion of T cells that bear specific T cell receptor V_{beta} sequences in AIDS patients. *J Leukoc Biol*. 1993;54:486–491.

21. Akolkar PN, Chirmule N, Gulwani-Akolkar B, et al. V_{beta}-specific activation of T cells by the HIV glycoprotein gp160. *Scand J Immunol*. 1995;41:487–498.

22. Romagnani S, Maggi E, Del Prete G. An alternative view of the Th1/Th2 switch hypothesis in HIV infection. *AIDS Res Hum Retrovirus*. 1994;10:3–9.

four

C H A P T E R

Etiology and Pathogenesis

Michael J. Borucki

The human immunodeficiency virus (HIV) is a member of the lentivirus genus of the retrovirus family. HIV has no known animal reservoirs, though similarities between human and simian lentiviruses suggest they arose from a common ancestor. HIV is directly transmitted from person to person most commonly by intimate sexual contact, maternal–fetal transmission, or injection drug use (by sharing hypodermic syringes contaminated with blood). In the United States, blood products have been tested for HIV since the enzyme-linked immunosorbent assay (ELISA) became available in 1985. Although the HIV screening ELISA is not a perfect test, the sensitivity and specificity of the currently available tests exceed 99.7 percent. As a consequence, transfusion-associated cases of HIV transmission are now rarely seen in clinical practice.

Following initial infection with HIV, an acute viral syndrome may be noted, with headaches, muscle aches, sore throat, lymphadenopathy, and a nonpruritic macular rash involving the trunk. Most commonly the acute illness is modest and nondescript enough so as to go unnoticed among the many colds and flu-like illnesses that the average adult will experience. The acute illness is accompanied by rapid viral replication, and HIV may be detected in the blood by culture, p25 antigen assay, or polymerase chain reaction (PCR) amplification of viral RNA or proviral DNA. Seroconversion, with the HIV ELISA becoming reactive, typically follows in 1 to 4 weeks.

A variable period of clinical latency, characterized by the absence of signs or symptoms attributable to HIV, follows the acute infection and typically lasts a decade or longer.[1-4] It was previously believed that the period of clinical latency was accompanied by a significant degree by viral latency. Although a prolonged period of clinical latency occurs, viral latency, the absence of actively replicating HIV virus, does not. HIV certainly exists in a latent, proviral form, but the contribution of viral latency to HIV disease progression is now speculative. Recent studies of HIV viral kinetics suggest that the period of clinical latency is characterized by the ongoing destruction of CD4+ cells by the continuous, rapid replication of HIV.[5,6] This represents a significant change in our understanding of HIV disease pathogenesis. Previously, some investigators speculated that HIV was necessary, but not sufficient, to lead to the destruction of the immune system. Earlier theories of AIDS pathogenesis centered on co-pathogenesis, antigenic overload, and other factors in addition to HIV that might be necessary to develop AIDS. With our current knowledge of the aggressive and unrelenting replication of HIV, it is quite clear that HIV is necessary and sufficient to cause AIDS. Indeed, more interest may now be focused on how the immune system, in the face of continuous destruction of CD4+ cells, manages to maintain immunity for so long. Peripheral blood lymphocytes constitute only about 1 to 3 percent of the total body lymphocyte population. Lymphocytes within lymph nodes may harbor 10 times as high a viral burden as the peripheral blood lymphocytes.

Following the phase of clinical latency, prodromal signs, then overt signs, and eventually late-stage signs of AIDS occur. Prodromal signs may include one or more of the following: progressive generalized adenopathy, oral candidiasis, thrombocytopenia, cervical dysplasia, recurrent vulvovaginal candidiasis, pelvic inflammatory disease, zoster, nocardiosis, listeriosis, bacillary angiomatosis, or oral hairy leukoplakia. In general, these signs should prompt the clinician to consider underlying HIV infection, particularly when noted in young adults with unknown HIV status. The overt signs of AIDS include all of the AIDS-defining illnesses, of which *P. carinii* pneumonia is the classic indicator illness (see Chapter 2 for tabulation of other AIDS-defining illnesses). The late-stage signs include those AIDS-defining illnesses that occur in AIDS patients with the most profound immunodeficiency: AIDS dementia, progressive multifocal leukoencephalopathy, *M. avium* disease, and cytomegalovirus disease. Typically, patients with HIV infection become at risk for AIDS-defining illnesses when the absolute CD4+ cell count remains below 200. Late-stage manifestations are typically noted when the absolute CD4+ count remains below 50.

In addition to the CD4+ count, a number of other surrogate markers have been demonstrated to have prognostic value, including beta-2-microglobulin and neopterin. Increased levels of HIV p25 antigen, syncytia-inducing phenotype, and HIV quantitative microcultures have also been correlated with more rapid progression to AIDS. Many investigators have recently evaluated the utility of HIV-RNA PCR as a marker for disease progression. Despite varying methods, populations, and assays the results are remarkably uniform; HIV viral burden as measured by RNA PCR is the best predictor of disease progression. The measurement of a single HIV viral burden has greater predictive value than any other marker, and may predict outcomes as much as a decade away.[7] When combined with the absolute CD4+ cell count, a very complete model of the risk of disease progression can be developed.

HIV, like all viruses, is an obligate intracellular parasite whose replication is dependent on the host cell. The life cycle of HIV occurs in eight major steps; binding, uncoating, reverse transcription, integration, transcription, protein synthesis, assembly, and budding (Fig. 4–1). Viral glycoprotein gp120 binds to the host cellular receptor, the

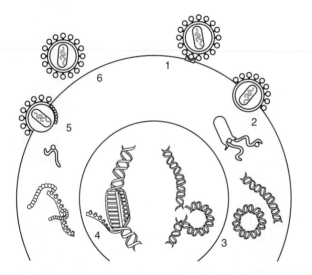

Figure 4–1. Life cycle of retroviruses. 1. Binding of viruses to target cell. 2. Uncoating of virus and transcription of viral RNA to DNA by reverse transcriptase. 3. Transportation of viral DNA to the nucleus and integration into host genome. 4. Transcription and protein synthesis. 5. Assembly of viral proteins and RNA at cell surface. 6. Budding of mature viral particle from host.

CD4 protein. Following binding, the viral lipid bilayer fuses with the host cell lipid bilayer uncoating the core of the HIV virion. Within the cytoplasm of the host cell, preformed reverse transcriptase enzyme uses the viral RNA as a template to reverse transcribe viral RNA to proviral DNA. The proviral DNA is then transported to the nucleus of the host cell. Another viral enzyme, HIV integrase, now produces a nick in the host cell DNA and inserts the proviral DNA into the gap. As the host cell grows and divides, it passes along copies of the integrated proviral DNA to progeny cells. The proviral DNA may remain latent for a variable period of time until an unknown signal promotes the emergence from latency. Once proviral DNA is transcribed to mRNA, the process of translation of the genetic code to viral proteins can begin. The precursor protein translates are subsequently cleaved by HIV viral proteinase into the various enzymatic, structural, and coat proteins. The structural proteins then coordinate the assembly of the HIV virus at the host cell surface. As the assembly completes, the forming virus buds from the surface of the infected cell and is released in the extracellular space. The newly formed virus is then ready to start another cycle of virus growth.

HIV, in common with other retroviruses, is organized into three major gene sequences: the group-associated antigens (GAG), polymerase (POL) region, and envelope (ENV) region (Fig. 4–2). The group-associated antigens comprise the major structural proteins of HIV; the capsid (CA, p25), the matrix (MA, p17), and nucleocapsid (NC, p6 and p9). The two viral RNA strands are closely associated with the nucleocapsid proteins. These structural proteins define the shape of the HIV virion and enclose the enzymatic and genetic materials of the virus. The matrix protein is responsible for incorporation of the coat (envelope) proteins during viral assembly. The GAG gene products are highly conserved. The HIV-RNA PCR ampli-

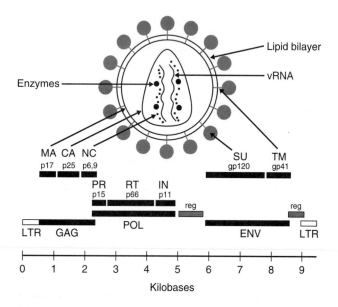

Figure 4–2. A schematic of the HIV virion is presented at the top of the figure. The middle of the figure illustrates the major gene products: the matrix (MA), capsid (CA), nucleocapsid (NC), proteinase (PR), reverse transcriptase (RT), integrase (IN), surface (SU), and transmembrane proteins and glycoproteins. The relative size (in kD) of the products is indicated below the gene product abbreviations (such as p17 under MA). Pointers indicate the structural features of the virion. The bottom of the figure is a linear map of the generalized HIV genome; GAG, POL, and ENV open reading frames are indicated as solid bars. The frame shift is indicated by the discontinuity of the GAG:POL bars. The open bars at either end of the linear map represent the long terminal repeat (LTR) segments. The regulatory genetic elements, which are small sequences and may be spliced (including segments in the central area and the LTR), are indicated by the dotted bars and are labeled "reg."

fies a sequence within the GAG gene. In translation, a frame shift occurs downstream of the major GAG antigens. The frame shift occurs somewhat inefficiently, resulting in an excess production of GAG proteins relative to POL and ENV proteins. GAG products are synthesized at a ratio of 20:1 compared to the GAG:POL transcripts. The mature virion also contains more capsid than polymerase and more polymerase than envelope proteins at a ratio of roughly 100:10:1. The increased production of some viral proteins makes some HIV antigens easier to detect than others. The laboratory determination of an "HIV antigen" assays for the GAG capsid protein, HIV p25 (older literature and clinical practice may refer to p25 as p24).

The polymerase gene codes for three major HIV proteins: reverse transcriptase (RT, p66), integrase (IN, p11), and proteinase (PR, p15). These are the active, enzymatic components of the virus. All of the currently licensed antiretrovirals are directed at polymerase targets, either at reverse transcriptase (nucleoside therapies and non-nucleoside reverse transcriptase inhibitors, or NNRTIs) or proteinase (proteinase inhibitors). The POL gene products have the least antigenic or genetic diversity (best conserved) of any HIV component. Many copies of these proteins are packaged into the capsid of the virus. After HIV is internalized, and following the dissolution of the capsid, the enzymatic components are immediately available. As a consequence, reverse transcription of viral genetic RNA to proviral DNA and subsequent proviral DNA integration into host chromosomal DNA can occur in the absence of protein synthetic steps. The HIV gene products are translated as a group, and the GAG components are translated as a single 55-kD protein. The 55-kD GAG precursor is subsequently cleaved into the individual GAG proteins by the proteinase. The same is true of the 160-kD

ENV precursor, which is subsequently cleaved into its 120- and 41-kD component glycoproteins. Reverse transcriptase is an RNA-dependent DNA-polymerase with RNase H activity. It has no exonuclease, or error-correcting, activity. The HIV reverse transcriptase is a sloppy enzyme; it has a base misincorporation (error) rate of about 1 per thousand to ten thousand bases. Because the HIV genome is approximately 9.8 kilobases in length, errors in genetic transcription are the norm. Estimates range from 2 to 10 errors per genome reverse transcript. Given the rapid rate of viral replication and the high error rate, it has been estimated that all possible genomic errors might occur in 2 to 3 days.[8,9] Indeed, rapid evolution of viral variants has been demonstrated to occur during the course of primary infection, and more importantly within 2 to 4 weeks following the start of some antiretroviral therapies.[5] Viral load markers may guide response following the introduction of antiretroviral therapy.[10] Two to three point mutations in the reverse transcriptase or proteinase gene products may be sufficient to produce high-level resistance to currently available therapeutics. Furthermore, base changes that alter the antigenic profile of the virus may allow it to escape from effective immunity. The high error rate of reverse transcription, then, provides a significant survival advantage to the HIV virus.

The envelope gene codes for just two glycosylated proteins, the surface (SU, gp120) and transmembrane (TM, gp41) glycoproteins. These glycoproteins are displayed on the exterior of the virus, external to the lipid bilayer. They are involved in binding to the CD4 protein receptor on CD4+ T cells and cells of monocyte macrophage lineage. The transmembrane glycoprotein is thought to be involved in syncytia formation. The envelope gene products have significant genetic and antigenic diversity; different isolates of HIV may have 50 percent diversity of the ENV gene components. Neutralizing antibodies are typically directed to the hypervariable antigenic domains of these proteins. Vaccine therapies and vaccines, per se, have primarily targeted immunity to these proteins.

The HIV genome also contains a number of regulatory elements, both positive (promoting) and negative (repressing) for viral replication. A number have been well characterized: TAT (transactivator), TAR (TAT response region), REV (regulator of expression of virus), RRE (REV response element), VIF (virus infectivity factor), and NEF (negative factor). The name NEF is a bit of a misnomer because NEF-deleted mutants exhibit high rates of viral replication. Other regulatory sequences have been identified—among them VPR, VPU, VPX, and TEV—whose effects are less well characterized. Interested readers are referred to one of the many excellent reviews of the microbiology of HIV.[11]

References

1. Bucquet D, Deveau C, Belanger F, et al. Multicenter French cohort of adults with HIV infection. Description and course after 4 years of follow-up. *Presse Med.* 1994;23:1247–1251.

2. Sabin C, Phillips A, Elford J, et al. The progression of HIV disease in a haemophilic cohort followed for 12 years. *Br J Haematol.* 1993;83:330–333.

3. Lee CA, Phillips AN, Elford J, et al. Progression of HIV disease in a haemophilic cohort followed for 11 years and the effect of treatment. *Br Med J.* 1991;303:1093–1096.

4. Rutherford GW, Lifson AR, Hessol NA, et al. Course of HIV-I infection in a cohort of homosexual and bisexual men: An 11-year follow-up study. *Br Med J.* 1990;301:1183–1188.

5. Wei X, Ghosh SK, Taylor ME, et al. Viral dynamics in human immunodeficiency virus type 1 infection. *Nature.* 1995;373:117–122.

6. Ho DD, Neumann AU, Perelson AS, et al. Rapid turnover of plasma virions and CD4 lymphocytes in HIV-1 infection. *Nature.* 1995;373:123–126.

7. O'Brien TR, Blattner WA, Waters D, et al. Serum HIV 1 RNA

levels and time to development of AIDS in the Multicenter Hemophilia Cohort Study. *JAMA*.1996;276:105–110.

8. Coffin JM. HIV population dynamics in vivo: implications for genetic variation, pathogenesis, and therapy. *Science.* 1995;267:483–489.

9. Perelson AS, Neumann AU, Markowitz M, et al. HIV-1 dynamics in vivo: Virion clearance rate, infected cell life-span, and viral generation time. *Science.* 1996;271:1582–1586.

10. Saag MS, Holodniy M, Kuritzkes DR, et al. HIV viral load markers in clinical practice. *Nat Med.* 1996;2:625–629.

11. Levy JA. Pathogenesis of human immunodeficiency virus infection. *Microbiol Rev.* 1993;57:183–289.

part II

EVALUATION

five
CHAPTER

Evaluation of Adults

Richard D. Muma

In areas of high endemicity, the resources of available specialists have already been overwhelmed by the rapidly growing pool of patients. Consequently, primary care providers, rather than specialists, are increasingly involved in the care of HIV-infected individuals. As the epidemic continues, primary care health care workers will need an increased understanding of the evaluation and management of patients with HIV.

Once an individual has been diagnosed with HIV, the initial evaluation should be undertaken as rapidly as possible. The initial and subsequent evaluations require the following approach.

- Evaluation of the immune system and classification by CDC grouping (Table 5–1).

Parts of this chapter are reprinted with permission from *Physician Assistant* 1991;15(1):23–32 and 1991;15(2):15,19–22.

TABLE 5–1. 1993 REVISED CLASSIFICATION SYSTEM FOR HIV INFECTION AND EXPANDED AIDS SURVEILLANCE DEFINITION FOR ADOLESCENTS AND ADULTS[a]

	Clinical Categories		
CD4 T-cell Categories	**(A) Asymptomatic, Acute (Primary) HIV or PGL[b]**	**(B) Symptomatic, Not (A) or (C) Conditions[c]**	**(C) AIDS-Indicator Conditions[d]**
(1) Greater than or equal to 500/mm^3	A1	B1	C1
(2) 200–499/mm^3	A2	B2	C2
(3) Less than 200/mm^3; AIDS indicator T-cell count	A3	B3	C3

For classification purposes, category B conditions take precedence over those in category A, and category C conditions take precedence over category B. For example, someone treated for persistent vaginal candidiasis but who has now developed PCP will remain in category C.

[a] C1–C3, A3, and B3 illustrate the expanded AIDS surveillance case definition. Persons with AIDS-indicator conditions (categories C1-C3) as well as those with CD4 T-lymphocyte counts less than 200/mm^3 (categories A3 and B3) are now reportable as AIDS cases in the United States and territories, effective January 1, 1993.

[b] PGL, persistent generalized lymphadenopathy. Clinical category A includes acute (primary) HIV infection.

[c] Examples include bacillary angiomatosis, oral candidiasis, vulvovaginal candidiasis, cervical dysplasia, cervical carcinoma in situ, constitutional symptoms or diarrhea lasting longer than 1 month, oral hairy leukoplakia, herpes zoster involving at least two distinct episodes or more than one dermatome, idiopathic thrombocytopenia, listeriosis, pelvic inflammatory disease, and peripheral neuropathy.

[d] A list of these conditions can be found in Chapter 2.

Adapted from the Centers for Disease Control and Prevention. 1993 revised classification system for HIV infection and expanded surveillance case definition for AIDS among adolescents and adults. MMWR. 1992;41(RR-17):1–19.

- Identification and treatment of infectious and neoplastic complications.
- Initiation of approved anti-HIV therapy.
- Consideration of experimental measures.

This particular methodology will allow the clinician to rapidly evaluate the immune system and identify treatable HIV-related disease processes so that either conventional chemotherapy or experimental chemotherapy can be instituted as soon as possible. Evidence suggests that early evaluation of individuals infected with HIV is of increased benefit[1,2] through earlier identification and treatment with anti-HIV drugs. These results are encouraging and should prompt individuals at risk (Box 5–1) to obtain early HIV testing, evaluation, and intervention.

When a patient is suspected to be HIV positive or has been diagnosed with the HIV infection, a baseline evaluation should be performed to determine the extent of the primary disease and diagnose secondary complications. The initial visit should consist of a thorough history and physical exam, baseline laboratory evaluation, patient education, and a psychosocial evaluation.

■ History

The history is the most important aspect of the evaluation, as it will suggest specific diagnostic and therapeutic interventions beyond the baseline evaluation. Although the history may be lengthy, it is important to identify and record those aspects of the medical history that may be individual baseline parameters to help differentiate them from those related to HIV.[2,3] The most important aspects of the history include HIV risk factors, past medical history (especially sexually transmit-

■ **Box 5–1**

HIV RISK GROUPS

- Sexually active individuals who practice unprotected sex
- Injecting drug users who share needles
- Hemophiliacs and blood transfusion recipients who received blood products prior to April 1985
- Sexual partners and children of the above

ted and injecting drug use diseases), and a thorough review of systems.

Risk Factors

Information obtained from the patient should first include risk factors for acquiring HIV such as homosexual activity, injecting drug use (IDU), and parenteral inoculation of body fluids. Obtaining the risk factor from the patient is not only for epidemiologic purposes but also helps to identify special complications inherent to a particular risk group. For instance, homosexual patients often find themselves isolated from their family, friends, and significant others when the diagnosis becomes known. If this information is obtained early in the history, these stresses may be more readily recognized, and appropriate psychological referral can be made as needed. Patients at risk because of IDU may continue to abuse drugs and need referral to a drug treatment program. This information may help explain and potentially alleviate problems such as patient noncompliance with follow-up frequently seen with IDU patients.

Medical History

A history of sexually transmitted diseases (STDs) including chancroid, condyloma, herpes, gonorrhea, and syphilis should also be obtained. Information regarding the treatment of syphilis is particularly important in this population, given the high occurrence of latent and neurosyphilis, and should include the agent, route, and duration of treatment.

A history of other disease processes such as tuberculosis, salmonellosis, zoster, and hepatitis B should be obtained from the patient, because these diseases may also impart significant morbidity.

Other disease processes may appear in association with immunosuppression. In particular, inquiries should be made regarding a history of any recurrent or unusual infections such as the following.[3]

- Tuberculosis, zoster, and genitorectal herpes
- Acute and chronic skin disorders such as molluscum contagiosum, folliculitis, venereal warts, seborrheic dermatitis, and fungal infections
- Oral, vaginal, or rectal candidiasis
- Diarrhea caused by *Giardia lamblia*, *Entamoeba histolytica*, *Salmonella*, *Shigella*, or *Campylobacter*
- Bacterial pneumonia, aseptic meningitis, and sinusitis

A history of any of these infections may suggest a subtle impairment in immunity, and if such problems have occurred remotely, this may suggest long-standing immune impairment potentially attributable to HIV infection.

Women should be asked questions regarding menstrual history, last menstrual period, method of birth control, the number and dates of pregnancy and abortions, and living children and their ages. Recurrent or severe vaginitis may affect women with HIV, and a history of vaginal discharge and pruritus should be sought (refer to Chapter 7).

Review of Systems

Next, the history should focus on a review of body systems to screen for previously undiagnosed or intercurrent illnesses. Before particular systems are assessed, a general review of systems should be done. Inquiry should be made regarding weight loss, weakness, fatigue, fever, chills, and night sweats. These general symptoms may not be specific for a particular disease, but more often than not, one or all of them will be present if an infectious process or neoplasm is developing. The body systems targeted should routinely include those systems that are most often involved by the infectious or neoplastic complications that occur in HIV-infected individuals. These include the central nervous, respiratory, cardiovascular, genitourinary, and gastrointestinal systems, and the skin.

Direct inquiry should be made of 17 "cardinal" symptoms at the initial and at each follow-up visit. This list, although not intended to be exhaustive, may rather serve as an example of an abbreviated review of systems that allows for rapid screening for the major complications of HIV infection in symptomatic individuals. These symptoms are the very minimum that should be asked about at every visit. The 17 symptoms and some of their associated differential considerations are presented in Box 5–2.

Because of the diverse pathology referable to the central nervous system (CNS), gastrointestinal system (GI), and pulmonary system, these three organ systems warrant special attention.

Central nervous system symptoms are frequently problematic in that baseline symptoms such as chronic headaches and symptoms specifically referable to HIV are

■ **Box 5-2**

Review of Systems

1. *Weight loss:* Opportunistic infection, tuberculosis, neoplasms, worsened malabsorptive diarrhea, depression, or as a CDC category C manifestation.

2. *Anorexia:* Hepatitis, carcinoma, disseminated opportunistic infection, AIDS dementia complex (ADC), metabolic disturbances such as diabetes, uremia, electrolyte abnormalities, depression, overuse of psychoactive pharmaceuticals, or illicit stimulant use.

3. *Increasing debility:* Neuromuscular complications of AIDS, AZT myopathy, steroid myopathy, ADC, Addison's disease, undiagnosed or spreading carcinoma, progressive multifocal leukoencephalopathy, cardiomyopathy, or overmedication.

4. *Adverse drug experiences:* Experimental therapeutics, "black market" remedies, over-the-counter drugs, or illicit drug use/abuse.

5. *Fevers:* Opportunistic infection (particularly *P. carinii*, disseminated fungi, mycobacterioses), infections with more "conventional" pathogens, non-Hodgkin's lymphoma, drug fever, or as a CDC category B manifestation of disease.

6. *Rigors:* Bacterial infections, catheter infections, phlebitis, endocarditis, mycobacteriosis, disseminated fungal opportunists, or malaria (if traveled or resided in an endemic area).

7. *Night sweats:* Tuberculosis, disseminated fungal infections, pyogenic infections, or lymphoma.

■ *Box 5–2 continued*

8. *Headache:* Meningitis (tuberculous, fungal, or aseptic), mass lesions (toxoplasmosis, nocardiosis, or lymphoma), or more "conventional" causes (tension, vascular, or cluster headaches).

9. *Change in vision:* Retinitis caused by cytomegalovirus or toxoplasmosis, ethambutol-induced optic neuritis, zoster ophthalmicus, or syphilitic, herpetic, fungal, or tuberculous involvement of the uveal tract.

10. *Diplopia:* Intracranial mass lesions from toxoplasmosis, nocardiosis, or lymphoma or extracranial involvement of the extraocular muscles.

11. *Dysphagia:* Esophageal involvement by *Candida*, herpes simplex virus, lymphoma, Kaposi's sarcoma, or AZT-induced erosions.

12. *Dyspnea:* Pulmonary involvement by *P. carinii*, cytomegalovirus, typical tuberculosis, atypical mycobacterioses, histoplasmosis, cryptococcoses, coccidioidomycosis, lymphoma, Kaposi's sarcoma, nonspecific interstitial pneumonitis, or edema from left ventricle failure.

13. *Diarrhea:* Salmonellosis, shigellosis, traveler's diarrhea, typical and atypical mycobacterioses, strongyloidiasis, giardiasis, amoebiasis, cryptosporidiosis, isosporiasis, cytomegalovirus, pseudomembranous colitis (following antimicrobial therapy), Addison's disease, malabsorption, excesses of caloric supplementation, hypervitaminosis D, or as a CDC category B manifestation.

■ *Box 5–2 continued*

14. *Changing lymphadenopathy:* CDC category A manifestation of disease if persistent and involving multiple noninguinal sites, lymphoma, "reactive" (in association with severe dermatitis), pseudolymphoma (associated with phenytoin), cytomegalovirus or Epstein-Barr mononucleosis, toxoplasmosis, syphilis, or disseminated tuberculous or fungal disease.

15. *Oral lesions:* Thrush, oral hairy leukoplakia, histoplasmosis, herpes simplex, aphthous lesions, Kaposi's sarcoma.

16. *Rashes:* Seborrheic dermatitis, papular eruption of HIV, tinea, scabies, secondary syphilis, zoster, disseminated herpes simplex, folliculitis, disseminated fungal infections, Kaposi's sarcoma, thrombocytopenia purpura, drug reaction (especially to sulfa antimicrobial, ampicillin, amoxicillin, and phenytoin).

17. *Change in mental status:* AIDS dementia complex, intracranial mass lesions, progressive multifocal leukoencephalopathy, neurosyphilis, *Toxoplasma* encephalitis, herpes encephalitis, meningitis, Addison's disease, metabolic aberrations (electrolyte, glucose, uremia, hypoxia, acidosis), Wernicke's encephalopathy, sepsis, psychoactive drug excess.

often difficult to separate. Chronic headaches could be little more than chronic tension headaches, but could be one manifestation of an intracranial neoplasm or abscess. A careful review of systems may offer focal or localizing symptomatology to support a mass lesion—for example, diplopia, blurred vision, seizures, unilateral weakness, dysarthria, or a change in personality. CNS symptoms may be broadly divided into those that typically present with meningeal findings, those with focal findings, and those that are infrequently associated with focality of symptoms or exam. Intracranial focal processes include toxoplasmosis, non-Hodgkin's lymphoma, herpes encephalitis, and progressive multifocal leukoencephalopathy. Meningeal symptoms predominate with cryptococcal, tuberculous, or aseptic meningitis. The nonfocal dementing illnesses include primary HIV disease, syphilis, drug effects, electrolyte disturbances, hypoglycemia, and hypoxia.

Gastrointestinal symptoms may be broadly divided into an acute dysenteric pattern, with prominent fevers, abdominal pain, and a mucous to bloody diarrhea; and a chronic pattern, with diarrhea present in excess of 2 weeks without associated fevers and without an abrupt change in volume or frequency. Dysenteric illness suggests the classical diarrheal pathogens of the immunocompetent host: salmonellosis, shigellosis, amoebiasis, traveler's diarrhea, and pseudomembranous colitis. Chronic diarrhea is more commonly a primary manifestation of HIV infection or caused by cryptosporidiosis, isosporiasis, atypical mycobacterioses, or malabsorption.

Pulmonary symptoms such as cough and dyspnea suggest a wide range of processes that may be broadly divided into those that are frequently associated with fevers and those that are not. All of the opportunistic infections—whether fungal, viral, parasitic, or mycobacterial in origin—are typically associated with fevers. By contrast, intrapulmonary disease from Kaposi's sarcoma or non-Hodgkin's lymphoma, or compromised left ventricular function from cardiomyopathy, are uncommonly associated with fevers.

■ Physical Examination

The physical exam should be thorough and directed toward the body systems discussed previously. Thus, the major foci of the physical examination of the HIV-positive patient should include the mouth, eyes, skin, lungs, heart, lymph nodes, abdomen, central and peripheral nervous system, rectum, and genitalia.

Mouth

When inspecting the mouth, particular attention should be given to white plaques on the buccal mucosa, soft and hard palates, and the tongue. White, plaque-like lesions are most commonly oral *Candida* but may represent oral hairy leukoplakia. Oral hairy leukoplakia usually develops on the lateral aspects of the tongue and, unlike oral *Candida,* is not easily removed by scraping. Other common oral findings in the mouth include ulcerative lesions, which may indicate herpes simplex, aphthous ulcers, or histoplasmosis. Purple or brown raised lesions in the oral cavity should be considered Kaposi's sarcoma until proven otherwise.

Eyes

Clinical abnormalities that can occur can be caused by microvascular abnormalities such as cotton wool spots. Cytomegalovirus and Kaposi's sarcoma are also common. Less common causes include toxoplasmosis, herpes simplex, zoster, *Cryptococcus, Candida, Mycobacterium avium-intracellulare,* and tuberculosis.

Of these possibilities, cytomegalovirus retinitis remains the most common cause of vision loss in AIDS patients. Funduscopic findings usually consist of extensive perivascular exudates and hemorrhages. Cotton wool spots may also be associated with active retinitis. An important feature of cytomegalovirus retinitis, which distinguishes it from toxoplasmosis, candidiasis, and other causes, is the frequent absence of vitreous inflammatory response. In cytomegalovirus retinitis, the retina is easily visualized.

Extraretinal ocular disease is most commonly caused by Kaposi's sarcoma. Kaposi's sarcoma most commonly involves the skin, but mucosal disease may involve the gastrointestinal tract, oropharynx, or conjunctival structures.[4] Although Kaposi's sarcoma, in this particular presentation, does not usually cause significant discomfort or pain, it does commonly cause unacceptable cosmeses.

Skin

Examination of the skin is challenging because common skin disorders may present in an exaggerated manner, making them difficult to diagnose. Common skin lesions include herpes simplex, herpes zoster, condyloma, abscess formation (particularly perirectal abscesses), folliculitis, secondary syphilis, scabies, paronychia/onycholysis, tinea versicolor, Kaposi's sarcoma, seborrheic dermatitis, and xerosis.[5] These present more often in individuals with a compromised immune system (CD4 cell count less than 200/mm^3). In addition, patients with a CD4 count less than 200/mm^3 may have lesions that present atypically, such as severe ulcerative lesions caused by herpes simplex.

Lungs

As a group, pulmonary diseases cause the majority of morbidity and mortality in patients with AIDS. Index diagnosis and recurrences of *P. carinii,* in particular, are common. Other opportunistic organisms that cause pulmonary infections include cytomegalovirus, *Mycobacterium tuberculosis*, nontuberculous mycobacteriosis, histoplasmosis, cryptococcosis, and coccidioidomycosis.[6] Neoplasms and lymphoproliferative disorders such as lymphoma, Kaposi's sarcoma, and lymphoid interstitial pneumonitis can also cause pulmonary disease. Careful examination of the lungs, including auscultation for wheezing and crackles, should be routinely performed, especially when there is a history from the patient of nonproductive cough, fever, dyspnea, or tachypnea.

Heart

Cardiovascular complications of HIV are uncommon. Tuberculosis and other fungal organisms may, however, cause pericardial effusions; thus, a complex cardiac exam should be done. It is important to note that the survival of AIDS patients with pericardial effusion is significantly shorter than the survival of those without effusion.[7] A more worrisome problem, particularly in intravenous drug users, is the possibility of bacterial endocarditis and its complications. A cardiomyopathy has been associated with HIV, and although uncommon, it connotes a very poor prognosis.

Lymph Nodes

Inspection of lymph nodes should be considered routine because many of the AIDS-defining illnesses can cause enlarged lymph nodes. Changes in lymph nodes can be associated with viruses, specifically cytomegalovirus,

Epstein-Barr virus, and HIV. As a general rule, soft, mobile, and tender nodes have viral etiologies, whereas firm, tender, or fixed nodes may indicate problematic secondary processes such as bacterial, fungal, or mycobacterial infections or neoplasm. Hard, fixed, and nontender nodes usually indicate neoplastic involvement. One should be concerned especially if the nodes begin to change (increase in size or become asymmetrical). All major nodal groups should be surveyed.

Abdomen

The abdomen should be inspected for masses, organomegaly, ascites, and tenderness. Hepatosplenomegaly may be associated with viral hepatitis and disseminated fungal or mycobacterial infections. Masses or extensive organomegaly usually indicate neoplastic or fungal involvement. Most commonly, in patients with diarrhea, a nondescript pain is elicited on the exam, usually in the lower quadrants, and may indicate a colitis caused by parasites, bacteria, or viruses. Malabsorption may also cause diarrhea without associated physical findings. Ascites may complicate prominent hepatic involvement by fungi, tuberculous and nontuberculous mycobacteriosis, Kaposi's sarcoma, or lymphoma.

Central and Peripheral Nervous System

Neurologic manifestations, both central and peripheral, occur commonly; therefore, close attention should be focused toward the neurologic exam. A complete neurologic exam should be done, including evaluation of the cranial nerves, motor and sensory systems, reflexes, gait, station, cerebral function, and special maneuvers such as testing for meningeal signs (Brudzinski's and Kernig's signs). When indicated, referral for a neuropsychological exam should be considered, especially when a cognitive/

motor/behavioral disorder is suspected, as in AIDS dementia complex (ADC). Distinct as well as subtle changes may be seen on these exams.

The most common neurologic manifestation in AIDS patients is ADC.[8-11] The changes seen are mild at the beginning, and progress throughout the course of the disease to a more severe state. These changes may be difficult to distinguish from other causes of neurologic dysfunction. Early in the course of the disease, there may be impairment in both verbal and motor response seen on the exam. At this point, slurred speech and difficulty coordinating hand movements may be observed. The impairment is more obvious when the disease has progressed over several months. With progression, motor exam abnormalities may show slowing of finger opposition, wrist rotation, and foot tapping. Much later in the course of the disease, ataxia and clumsiness may progress to paraparesis and urinary/fecal incontinence.

Secondary neurologic manifestations may be easier to diagnose because they more commonly cause symptomatology. Diseases such as central nervous system toxoplasmosis, primary brain lymphoma, herpes encephalitis, and progressive multifocal leukoencephalopathy typically present with focal deficits.[8] Cryptococcal meningitis, aseptic meningitis, and neurosyphilis may have focal findings as well, but will often have a subacute presentation with more mild findings such as meningeal signs and altered mental status.

Vacuolar myelopathy may also occur and should be differentiated from other causes of CNS dysfunction. This degenerative condition, in which an open space forms in the spinal cord tissue, is characterized by a progressive spastic paraparesis and upper motor neuron deficits. Ataxia and hyperreflexia have also been described.

Peripheral manifestations caused by HIV include sensory neuropathies and inflammatory demyelinating polyneuropathies. Patients often describe paresthesias, painful dysesthesias, and muscle weakness in the extremities. However, in the latter case, the weakness may be generalized. Neurologic exam findings may show mild to marked motor deficits and absent or decreased reflexes.

Genitalia and Rectum

Both the genitalia and rectum should be inspected and palpated for lesions consistent with herpes, scabies, syphilis, tinea, chancroid, condyloma, and Kaposi's sarcoma. All but the latter are frequently seen in these areas. Kaposi's sarcoma may be seen in the later stages of the disease. A rectal exam should be performed in all patients. In men, prostatitis and proctitis should be looked for; in both sexes, a stool test for occult blood to rule out gastrointestinal bleeding should be performed.

■ Laboratory and Diagnostic Evaluation

In concert with the goals of performing a complete history and physical examination, the laboratory studies stress the rapid evaluation and the early identification of concurrent illnesses. It is believed that early intervention and treatment may improve the long-term survival of patients infected with HIV. Thus, patients may be evaluated as one of two major groups as defined by history and physical exam (Box 5–3). The two major groups are (1) patients who are asymptomatic and at risk for HIV, and (2) patients who are symptomatic and HIV positive and/or suspected to have an AIDS-related condition. The first group will most likely include an abbreviated laboratory evaluation, whereas symptomatic individuals or those with known AIDS will require a more extensive

■ Box 5–3

Laboratory and Diagnostic Evaluation

ASYMPTOMATIC PATIENTS AT RISK FOR HIV

- CBC with differential
- Liver transaminases (AST/ALT)
- Syphilis screen (RPR or VDRL), confirmation by FTA-ABS
- Serology for CMV and toxoplasmosis
- HIV ELISA and Western blot confirmation
- Prior exposure hepatitis panel
- Tuberculin skin test (TST)

SYMPTOMATIC AND HIV POSITIVE AND/OR SUSPECTED TO HAVE AN AIDS-RELATED CONDITION

- CBC with differential
- Liver transaminases (AST/ALT)
- Syphilis screen (RPR or VDRL), confirmation by FTA-ABS
- Serology for CMV, EBV, HSV, toxoplasmosis, cryptococcus
- Prior exposure hepatitis panel
- Tuberculin skin test (TST)
- CD4/CD8 subsets
- Plasma HIV RNA (viral load)
- Fungal immunodiffusion titer
- Chest x-ray
- Electroencephalogram

workup. Figure 5–1 may serve as a guide for follow-up visits.

Asymptomatic and High-risk Patients

If patients are at risk for HIV infection but their antibody status is unknown, they should be screened for HIV using the enzyme immunoassay (EIA) to detect HIV antibodies.[12,13] Confirmation of HIV antibodies can be followed up with a Western blot. (Note: Seronegative patients must be counseled that testing does not substitute for prevention of AIDS; continued high-risk behavior poses a hazard regardless of the frequency of testing.) At risk patients as well as known seropositive patients should be screened for sexually transmitted diseases, hepatitis, and tuberculosis. A complete blood count (CBC) with differential should be routinely performed because of the increased incidence of anemia, thrombocytopenia, and neutropenia that occurs in the latter stages of HIV infection.[14] Serum for liver transaminases (AST and ALT) and hepatitis (A, B, and C) is needed to assess ongoing liver function and prior/present infection with hepatitis, particularly hepatitis B.[15,16]

Evaluation for sexually transmitted diseases should begin with screening for syphilis with nontreponemal tests such as the RPR (rapid plasma reagin) or VDRL (Venereal Disease Research Laboratory) with a confirmatory FTA-ABS (fluorescent treponemal antibody absorption) test as indicated. This is extremely important, because HIV-infected patients with early syphilis are at increased risk for neurologic complications and have higher rates of treatment failure.[17] Any suspicious lesion or discharge should be further evaluated for syphilis with darkfield microscopy and for *N. gonorrhea, Chlamydia,* and herpes simplex by appropriate culture. All patients should undergo PPD skin testing for tuberculosis, as *M.*

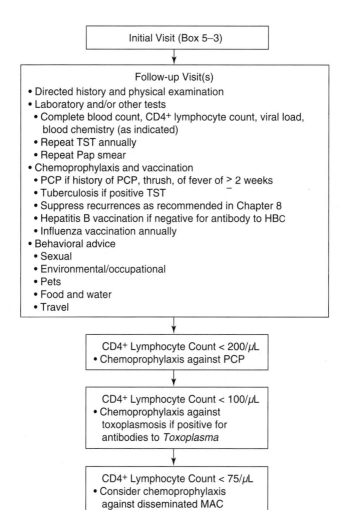

Figure 5–1. Follow-up visits. (*With permission from USPHS/IDSA guidelines for the prevention of opportunistic infections in persons infected with human immunodeficiency virus: An overview.* Clinical Infectious Diseases. *1995;21(suppl):S15.*)

tuberculosis causes frequent morbidity in this patient population.[18,19]

Patients With Symptomatic HIV Infection or AIDS

Any patients who have a social history and symptoms compatible with a disease associated with HIV should be evaluated using a separate protocol (Box 5–3) to screen for HIV-related illnesses and diagnose already existing conditions. Like the asymptomatic and high-risk individual, this group of patients should also have blood drawn for complete hemogram, liver transaminases, and hepatitis and syphilis serology. In addition, this group of patients may benefit from having blood drawn for cytomegalovirus (CMV) and herpes simplex virus (HSV) antibodies. Infections with HSV and CMV are common in patients at risk for AIDS.[20] Disease occurs following reactivation and may cause significant morbidity and mortality,[21] may adversely affect cell-mediated immunity,[22,23] and may augment infection with HIV.[24]

Determination of the absolute CD4 cell number is the principal means of determining if sufficient immune dysfunction has occurred to warrant therapy, because most antiretroviral therapies like zidovudine (ZDV) are not initiated until some evidence for immunosuppression has occurred.[1,2] However, CD4 cell numbers are less useful in determining an individual's risk for progressing to AIDS. New data suggest that monitoring for the presence of HIV RNA in plasma may be more useful in determining progression.[25–27]

The CD4 cell plays a central role in the cell-mediated immune system. Defects in cell-mediated immunity allow for the development of diseases in patients with AIDS (*P. carinii, Toxoplasma gondii,* cytomegalovirus, and others). The CD4/CD8 ratio may be helpful as well, and is usually inverted with advanced disease. The normal range for the absolute CD4 count ranges between 500 and 1000/mm^3 but may vary somewhat from lab to lab. Most individuals do not develop opportunistic infections until the absolute CD4 count drops consistently below 200/mm^3.

Fungal studies are usually reserved for individuals who present with symptoms suggestive of a disseminated mycosis, such as fever of unknown etiology, but can be obtained at baseline for future comparison. A fungal immunodiffusion is an inexpensive means of determining prior infection with common fungal organisms, such as histoplasmosis, cryptococcosis, coccidioidomycosis, and blastomycosis. If a patient complains of a headache and fevers, a serum cryptococcal antigen may be a useful screening test.[28] The antigen appears to be a rapid, sensitive, and specific test for active disseminated cryptococcal disease. If a patient appears to have a fungal or acid-fast systemic fungal infection, bone marrow biopsies may be helpful by identifying organisms on stains or as isolates. Additional blood and urine cultures should be ordered for fungal isolates and acid-fast organisms.

Another baseline study should include a toxoplasmosis titer, because disease caused by toxoplasmosis also occurs principally through reactivation of an old infection. This organism most commonly causes abscess formation or encephalitis[29] in the compromised host but can also cause retinitis[30] and pneumonitis.

Unfortunately, an elevated toxoplasmosis titer by itself is not diagnostic for an active infection, but is in a clinically compatible setting. For *toxoplasma* encephalitis, computerized tomography (CT) of the head to demonstrate ring-enhancing lesions or a biopsy demonstrating infected brain tissue is needed. The latter is usually not indicated if the lesions decrease in size after appropriate treatment.

As mentioned earlier, symptoms suggestive of pulmonary disease should receive special consideration.[31] Most of the diseases that patients encounter are pulmonary in nature. Whether the patient has pulmonary symptoms or not, a baseline chest x-ray should be ordered for comparison in the future, and may be particularly useful if changes of old histoplasmosis or tuberculosis are present. This becomes important when minimal changes are seen on chest films even in the presence of an active pulmonary infection. Special attention should be taken when a diffuse interstitial pattern is seen on a chest x-ray (see Chapter 8, Figures 8–1 and 8–2). Organisms such as *P. carinii,* CMV, and histoplasmosis should be included in the differential. Other findings that should increase suspicion of an active pulmonary process include the presence of granulomata, cavities, and hilar enlargement. Any of these findings may suggest a mycobacterial infection or fungal infections such as histoplasmosis, although pneumatocele associated with pneumocystis carinii pneumonia (PCP) may mimic cavitary disease. The definitive diagnosis of any uncertain chest x-ray abnormality should be made by bronchoscopy with a bronchoalveolar lavage (BAL).[32,33]

Occasionally, transbronchial biopsy is necessary to define more focal disease. Sputum analysis may be helpful if pulmonary tuberculosis is suspected, but is less useful when diseases such as PCP, CMV, and fungal infections such as histoplasmosis are present. An arterial blood gas may be helpful to assess the possibility of hypoxia and may prompt empiric treatment while awaiting definitive diagnosis. If there is not a significant amount of hypoxia and the patient is clinically stable, a bronchoscopy should be obtained first for the diagnosis.

Like pulmonary infections, diarrhea also causes significant morbidity in patients with HIV and deserves equal attention.[34,35] If a patient presents with a history of diarrhea that does not resolve spontaneously, evaluation of the cause is indicated. Pathogens causing diarrhea in HIV patients are broad and may include parasites, bacteria, or viruses. To define the etiology, samples should be obtained for ova and parasites, AFB smear, cryptosporidiosis, and culture for enteric pathogens such as *Salmonella, Shigella, Campylobacter,* mycobacteriosis, and *E. coli.* If the diarrhea persists and no pathogen is identified, then a barium enema can be obtained to look for mucosal abnormalities followed by endoscopy for biopsy of involved areas. Fortunately, most cases of diarrhea have confirmed etiologies by microbiologic evaluation of stool samples.

Another adjunct when initially evaluating the HIV-positive patient is the electroencephalogram (EEG). Because dementia associated with HIV is common, particularly in patients with full-blown AIDS, the EEG may be able to pick up early changes consistent with AIDS dementia complex. If dementia is present, the EEG may reveal mild to severe slowing of brain wave activity. Although not wholly diagnostic for ADC, an EEG may be more helpful in following the progression of the dementia. A more helpful diagnostic tool in diagnosis of ADC is a computed tomogram (CT) of the head: cerebral atrophy can be demonstrated in most cases of advanced ADC.

■ Psychosocial Evaluation and Patient Education

Patients who have been diagnosed in any group or stage of the HIV infection may eventually begin to develop physical as well as psychosocial problems. Both of these issues are usually related, and tend to rise and fall in level of importance in relation to the fear of the unknown. Some of the specific issues that patients will have to deal with include deteriorating health, treatment options, death and dying, loss of job and financial security, loss of emotional or family support, relationship problems, and changes in lifestyle (see Chapters 13 to 15).[36] It is important that the health care professional working with this population be extremely sensitive to these issues and be able to understand and identify the resources available to the client (refer to Chapter 20). Also at this point, there should be a discussion with the patient on HIV prevention. This can be accomplished by spending a brief amount of time at the end of each patient encounter. Minimum information to the patient should include discussion on modes of transmission (Box 5–4), protective measures, and safe sex (see Chapter 16).

■ Summary

Rapid evaluation is the key when caring for those who are infected with HIV. Additionally, an awareness of new developments and often subtle signs of early complications of HIV infection will provide an important advantage for patients.[1] Being able to provide adequate care for those

---

■ Box 5–4
Modes of HIV Transmission

- Vaginal and/or receptive anal intercourse
- Infection/percutaneous exposure with HIV-infected blood or blood products
- Maternal–fetal transmission.

who may present for care is probably the most important, as a recent study suggests that access to medical care may explain improved survival among patients.[37,38]

References

1. Gold JW. HIV-1 infection: Diagnosis and management. *Med Clin North Am*. 1992;76:1–18.

2. Pottage JC, Samet JH, Soloway BH. The asymptomatic patient. *Patient Care*. 1996;30:27–51.

3. Clement M, Franke E, Wisniewski TL. Managing the HIV-positive patient. *Patient Care*. 1989;23:51–87.

4. Odajynk C, Muggia FM. Treatment of Kaposi's sarcoma: Overview and analysis by clinical setting. *J Clin Oncol*. 1985;3:1277–1285.

5. Jewell ME, Sweet DE. Oral and dermatologic manifestations of HIV infection. *Postgrad Med*. 1994;96:105.

6. Marchevsky A, Rosen MJ, Chrystal G, et al. Pulmonary complications of the acquired immunodeficiency syndrome: A clinicopathologic study of 70 cases. *Hum Pathol*. 1985;16:659–670.

7. Heidenreich PA, Eisenberg MJ, Kee LL, et al. Pericardial effusion in AIDS: Incidence and survival. *Circulation*. 1995;92:3229–3234.

8. McArthur JH, Palenicek JG, Bowersox LL. Human immunodeficiency virus and the nervous system. *Nurs Clin North Am*. 1988;23:823–841.

9. Berger JR. Neurologic complications of human immunodeficiency virus infection. *Postgrad Med*. 1987; 81:72–79.

10. Price RW, Sidtis J, Rosenblum M. The AIDS dementia complex: Some current questions. *Ann Neurol*. 1988; 23(suppl): 27–33.

11. Navia BA, Jordan BD, Price RW. The AIDS dementia complex, 1. Clinical features. *Ann Neurol*. 1986;19:517–524.

12. Centers for Disease Control. Public Health Service guidelines for counseling and antibody testing to prevent HIV infection and AIDS. *MMWR*. 1987;36:509–515.

13. Centers for Disease Control. Interpretation and use of the Western blot assay for serodiagnosis of human immunodeficiency virus type-1 infections. *MMWR*. 1989;38:1–7.

14. Murphy MF, Metcalfe P, Waters AH, et al. Incidence and mechanism of neutropenia and thrombocytopenia in patients with human immunodeficiency virus infection. *Br J Haematol.* 1987;66:337–340.

15. Rustgi VK, Hoofnagle JH, Gerin JL, et al. Hepatitis B virus infection in the acquired immunodeficiency syndrome. *Ann Intern Med.* 1984;101:795–797.

16. Alter MJ, Hadler SC, Margolis HS, et al. The changing epidemiology of hepatitis B in the United States. *JAMA.* 1990;263:1218–1222.

17. Centers for Disease Control. 1993 Sexually transmitted diseases treatment guidelines. *MMWR.* 1993;42:37–39.

18. Burwen DR, Bloch AB, Griffin LD, et al. National trends in the concurrence of tuberculosis and acquired immunodeficiency syndrome. *Arch Intern Med.* 1995;155:1281–1286.

19. Centers for Disease Control and Prevention. Surveillance of tuberculosis and AIDS co-morbidity—Florida, 1981–1993. *MMWR.* 1996;45:38–41.

20. Holmberg SD, Stewart JA, Gerber AR, et al. Prior herpes simplex virus type 2 infection as a risk factor for HIV infection. *JAMA.* 1988;259:1048–1050.

21. Suttman U, Willers H, Gerdelmann R, et al. Cyomegalovirus infection in HIV-1 infected individuals. *Infection.* 1988;16: 111–114.

22. Schrier R, Rice G, Oldstone M. Suppression of natural killer cell activity and T cell proliferation by fresh isolates of human cytomegalovirus. *J Infect Dis.* 1986; 153:1084–1091.

23. Carney W, Rubin R, Hoffman R, et al. Analysis of T lymphocyte subsets in cytomegalovirus mononucleosis. *J Immunol.* 1981;126:2114–2116.

24. Mosca JD, Bednarik DP, Raj NBK, et al. Herpes simplex virus type-1 can reactivate transcription of latent human immunodeficiency virus. *Nature.* 1987;325:67–70.

25. Saksela K, Stevens CE, Rubinstein P, et al. HIV-1 messenger RNA in peripheral mononuclear cells as an early marker of risk for progression to AIDS. *Ann Intern Med.* 1995;123:641–648.

26. Greene WC. Predicting progression to AIDS. *Ann Intern Med.* 1995;123:726–727.

27. Schooley RT. Correlation between viral load measurements and outcome in clinical trials of antiviral drugs. *AIDS.* 1995;9(suppl 2):S15-S19.

28. Kovacs JA, Kovacs A, Polis M, et al. Cryptococcosis in the acquired immunodeficiency syndrome. *Ann Intern Med.* 1985;103:533–538.

29. Levy RM, Rosenbloom S, Perrett LV. Neuroradiologic findings in AIDS: A review of 200 cases. *Am J Roentgenol.* 1986; 147:977–983.

30. Friedman AH. The retinal lesions of the acquired immunodeficiency syndrome. *Trans Am Ophthal Soc.* 1984;82:447–492.

31. Murray JF, Garay SM, Hopewell PC, et al. Pulmonary complications of the acquired immunodeficiency syndrome: An update. Report of the second National Heart, Lung, and Blood Institute workshop. *Am Rev Respir Dis.* 1987;135:504–509.

32. Barrio JL, Harcup C, Baier HJ, et al. Value of repeat fiberoptic bronchoscopies and significance of nondiagnostic bronchoscopic results in patients with the acquired immunodeficiency syndrome. *Am Rev Respir Dis.* 1987;135:422–425.

33. Golden JA, Hollander H, Stulbarg MS, et al. Bronchoalveolar lavage as the exclusive diagnostic modality for *Pneumocystis carinii* pneumonia: A prospective study among patients with the acquired immunodeficiency syndrome. *Chest.* 1986;90:18–22.

34. Borich A, Kotler DP. Combating chronic diarrhea in AIDS patients. *Phys Assist.* 1990;14:101–114.

35. Soave R, Johnson WD. Cryptosporidium and *Isospora* infections. *J Infect Dis.* 1988;157:225–229.

36. Baker J, Muma RD. Counseling patients with HIV infection. *Phys Assist.* 1991;15:40.

37. Chaisson RE, Keruly JC, Moore RD. Race, sex, drug use, and progression of human immunodeficiency virus disease. *N Engl J Med.* 1995;333:751–756.

38. Wu C. AIDS progression depends on quality of care. *Science News.* 1995;148:198.

SIX CHAPTER

Evaluation of Children

Karen S. Stephenson

■ The Epidemiology of Pediatric AIDS

The first pediatric AIDS case was identified in 1982. Through June 1996, 7,296 cases were reported, with a steadily growing number of new cases per year.[1] Of this group, 57 percent were black, 23 percent were Hispanic, and eighteen percent were white. Asians/Pacific islanders made up 0.56 percent of the total, and American Indians/Alaska natives made up 0.3 percent of the total. Fifteen children (0.2 percent of the total) did not have race or ethnicity indicated.

The most common exposure category for these cases was intravenous drug use by the mother, and the second most common was the mother having sex with an intravenous drug user.[1] The only race/ethnicity group for which IV drug use was not the most common was Asians/Pacific islanders. In this group, the mother was at risk for HIV, but the risk was not specified.

Children (those below 13 years of age) usually acquire the disease by perinatal routes, transfusion, and treatment of hemophilia. As of December 1995, percentages for these means were 90, 5, and 3 percent, respectively.[1] Another 1 percent of the infections have no determined cause.[1] Three means of transmission between mother and child include placenta, contact with mother's blood at delivery, and breast feeding. Cesarean sections will not prevent infection at delivery.[2] Children may also acquire infection from sexual exposure, including assault.[3]

■ Diagnosis

The mean age for diagnosis of perinatally infected children is 17 months. There are quite a variety of symptoms noted depending upon the age of the child at presentation. Infants may demonstrate mucocutaneous candidiasis, failure to thrive, hepatosplenomegaly, or respiratory distress secondary to *Pneumocystis carinii* pneumonia (PCP). Toddlers may have parotitis, generalized lymphadenopathy, recurrent bacterial infection, neurologic disease, or development abnormalities. For older children, symptoms may include failure to thrive, hepatosplenomegaly, chronic interstitial pneumonia, or a combination of these.[3]

■ Laboratory Evaluation

CD4+ (helper) lymphopenia with decreased absolute numbers of CD4+ lymphocytes and an inverted CD4+ to CD8+ ratio are hallmarks of HIV infection. However, children with HIV infection may have a normal CD4+ cell count. B cells may also undergo change; commonly there is hypergammaglobulinemia, but the opposite may occur as well.[3] Table 6–1 contains age-specific normal CD4+ counts.

TABLE 6–1. IMMUNOLOGIC CATEGORIES BASED ON AGE-SPECIFIC CD4+ T-LYMPHOCYTE COUNTS AND PERCENT OF TOTAL LYMPHOCYTES

Immunologic Category	Age of the Child					
	< 12 months		1–5 years		6–12 years	
	µL	%	µL	%	µL	%
No evidence of suppression	> 1500	≥ 25	> 100	≥ 25	> 500	≥ 25
Evidence of moderate suppression	750–1499	15–24	500–999	15–24	200–499	15–24
Severe suppression	< 750	< 15	< 500	< 15	< 200	< 15

With permission from reference 4.

■ HIV Testing in Children

Detection of HIV infection in infants is difficult because the child passively acquires antibodies from the mother. These maternal antibodies may last for as long as 18 months,[5] but uninfected children usually serorevert to a negative status at around 9 to 10 months.[3] Antibodies present after 18 months is part of the definition of an HIV infection in children as recently recommended by the CDC.

Recent studies[6] have demonstrated wide variability in seroreversion rates among different populations and the method of testing (ELISA versus Western blot). A study by Chantry and others[6] recommended that ELISA rather than Western blot (WB) be used to follow antibody status in infants. In that study, 6.2 percent of infants reverted to negative status by ELISA testing, but remained WB-positive at 18 months of age. The mean age for seroreversion by ELISA was 11.6 months for the Chantry study and 10.3 months in the European Collaborative Study.

The only characteristic thought to be related to the rate of seroreversion supported in this study was the initial cord blood HIV titer as measured by ELISA. None of the following characteristics measured in this study were significantly related to this seroreversion: maternal gamma-globulin levels, maternal CD4+ counts, maternal alcohol use, gestational age of infant, diarrhea, or failure to thrive.

Because the maternal antibodies are of the IgG class, efforts at testing have been directed toward measuring the infant's evidence of infection. This is particularly important to the infant because decisions about treatment must be made as soon as possible, and there are risks with administration of antiretroviral medications, such as zidovudine (AZT, ZDV, Retrovir). The potential benefits for early treatment to the infant have been identified by the American Academy of Pediatrics. These include reduced morbidity and dissemination of information regarding the risk of HIV transmission. The parents can be educated about the risk of transmission from breast milk, during subsequent pregnancies, and from sexual activity by the mother and the father.[7]

The decision about early treatment is complicated by the fact that only one third of infants exposed to the virus perinatally become infected. The estimates range from 12.9 to 39 percent,[5] and the remaining infants gradually clear the mother's IgG antibodies from their bloodstreams.[3]

Several methods of testing are used to evaluate an infant for signs of an infection. These include detecting HIV-specific antigen (HIV p25 antigen ELISA), detecting HIV-specific DNA using the polymerase chain reaction (PCR), detecting anti-HIV IgA antibodies, demonstrating the virus itself by culture, and Elispot/IVAP (in vitro antibody production).[4]

Of these, viral culture and PCR measurements are the most sensitive and specific means of detecting an HIV infection.[4] The p25 antigen ELISA is not as sensitive as the other commonly employed methods because of the presence of immune-complexed p25. The p25 antigen is a protein from the virion, but two problems exist with the test: p25 may not be present in asymptomatic patients,[3] and it may not be detectable in the presence of high levels of HIV-specific antibodies.[8] The test has been modified to dissociate these complexes with an improvement in the test's sensitivity.[4]

The HIV-DNA polymerase chain reactions (PCR) measures DNA that is incorporated into the human DNA by HIV. Because it is a relatively small amount of DNA, it must be amplified for measurement. Because DNA, rather than antibodies, is measured, this test provides a more specific test for the infection, but it is not very sensitive during the neonatal period. The results can be obtained in one day and only require a small amount of blood. Because of the small amounts of DNA measured, though, it is possible to have contamination from other studies (that is, to measure DNA that actually belongs to another person) unless great care is taken in performing the test.[8]

Viral cultures are also available. They take 7 to 28 days to complete and represent a significant risk to those monitoring the culture. They are also expensive and detect an infection in a newborn about 50 percent of the time.[8]

Blood thought to contain the HIV virus can be cultured to detect the presence of lymphocytes producing antibodies, but not the antibodies themselves. This is known as an in vitro production assay (IVPA), and a product known as Elispot is available for IVPA testing. Maternal antibodies may interfere with this test, or there may be a false-negative result during asymptomatic periods when no antibodies are produced by activated lymphocytes.[8]

The antibody assay used for adults detects IgG class antibodies, but that measurement is not appropriate for infants. Attention has now been directed toward antibodies produced by the infant, including IgM and IgA antibodies.[8] Evaluation of these two antibodies indicates that IgA measurements will be a more reliable test. IgG from the mother can block binding of IgA and IgM, but IgA persists in the baby's blood longer than IgM. This testing for IgA is presently not reliable for infants less than 3 months of age because evaluations have revealed that IgA antibodies are frequently not present before 3 months of age.[9]

In summary, all of these methods are improving abilities to identify an HIV infection in children but are the least sensitive for newborns (those infants to 2 months of age). The PCR and viral cultures detect 50 percent of infections during this period, whereas HIV-specific IgA and p25 assays are positive for fewer than 10 percent of newborns. In vitro antibody production is also not reliable during this period. On the other hand, most assays (PCR < IVAP < IgA, and culture) have 75 to 100 percent sensitivities by 6 months of age.[8]

Even in circumstances where testing specific for children less than 18 months of age is not available as described, patterns of change for the maternal HIV antibodies can help predict those who will seroretrovert or not. In a group of infants born to HIV-positive mothers in South Africa,[10] babies later found to be uninfected and infected lost maternal antibodies at the same rate for the first 3 months. By 6 months, the uninfected infants lost antibodies at a greater rate, but the most significant change between the two groups occurred between 6 and 9 months. The authors noted that the antibody trend in their study reflected trends noticed in HIV-positive children in the United States and Europe. Infants who are 6 to 9 months of age may have already sustained PCP pneumonia, and the trends noted in the maternal antibodies that might imply an HIV infection may occur too late in the child's life to begin PCP prophylaxis.

■ Classification for HIV Infection in Children

In 1987, the CDC developed a classification system for HIV in children. More recently, the classification was modified to evaluate the child by the following criteria: infection status, immunologic status, and clinical status.[4] Infection status is determined by the presence of HIV and/or HIV antibodies by the testing described. The child may be perinatally exposed, a serorevertor, or HIV infected. This decision cannot be based on one measurement but must be made over time based on the pattern of seroreversion over the first 18 months of the child's life. A child who is HIV-infected must have two separate measurements that are positive by HIV culture, HIV PCR, or HIV p25 antigen, or meet the 1987 surveillance case definition for HIV. The child who is over 18 months of age can be HIV infected by two measurements of HIV (ELISA then confirmed by WB). See Box 6–1 for a summary of the classification of infection status for children exposed to HIV.

Children who are HIV positive must also be monitored for their immunologic status as measured by CD4+ lymphocytes. As is the case with adults, the HIV gradually infects the T lymphocytes and reduces their numbers. Children, though, have different normal levels based on their age. Normal levels, both absolute and percentage counts, have been established for children and allow for categories of no evidence of suppression, moderate suppression, and severe suppression.[4] The levels were established from both North American and European clinical

■ **Box 6–1**

Diagnosis of HIV Infection in Children

DIAGNOSIS: HIV INFECTED

A. A child < 18 months of age who is known to be HIV seropositive or born to an HIV-infected mother

AND

has positive results on two separate determinations (excluding cord blood) from one or more of the following HIV detection tests: HIV culture, HIV polymerase chain reaction, and HIV antigen (p25)

OR

meets criteria for acquired immunodeficiency syndrome (AIDS) diagnosis based on the 1987 AIDS surveillance case definition

B. A child ≥ 18 months of age born to an HIV-infected mother or any child infected by blood, blood products, or other known modes of transmission (e.g., sexual; contact) who:

is HIV-antibody positive by repeatedly reactive enzyme immunoassay (ElA) and confirmatory test (e.g., Western blot or immunofluorescence assay [IFA])

OR

meets any of the criteria in A above.

■ *Box 6–1 continued*

DIAGNOSIS: PERINATALLY EXPOSED (PREFIX E)

A child who does not meet the criteria above who:

is HIV seropositive by EIA and confirmatory test (e.g., Western blot or IFA) and is < 18 months of age at the time of test

OR

has unknown antibody status, but was born to a mother known to be infected with HIV.

DIAGNOSIS: SEROREVERTER (SR)

A child who is born to an HIV-infected mother and who:

has been documented as HIV-antibody negative (two or more negative EIA tests performed at 6 to 18 months of age or one negative EIA test after 18 months of age);

AND

has had no other laboratory evidence of infection (has not had two positive viral detection tests, if performed)

AND

has not had an AIDS-defining condition.

With permission from reference 4.

studies. If the absolute and percentage counts of CD4+ lymphocytes place the child in different categories, the child should be placed in the more severe category.[4]

The third means of classification is based on the clinical categories. The four categories (N, A, B, and C) range from children who have no signs of HIV infection (N) to children who are severely symptomatic (C). See Boxes 6–2 and 6–3 for the specifics of these categories. The immunologic and clinical categories are then used to classify children with HIV (Table 6–2).[4]

■ Infectious Complications of HIV Infection in Children

Pulmonary complications include *Pneumocystis carinii* pneumonia (PCP), lymphoid interstitial pneumonia, tuberculosis (TB), and respiratory syncytial virus.[3] As in adults, PCP is the leading AIDS-indicator disease, and lymphoid interstitial pneumonia is the second most common in children. This second disease is not part of the syndrome associated with AIDS in adolescents and adults (Table 6–3).[1]

Pneumocystis Carinii Pneumonia

As is the case with adults, PCP is the most common serious opportunistic infection in children, and usually occurs in the first year of life for children who are HIV infected.[11] In addition, many children die within 2 months of a PCP infection. Prophylaxis for PCP can postpone this infection, and the initiation of treatment is based on the CD4+ count of the child.

PCP presents with fever, a nonproductive cough, and tachypnea. Interstitial changes and air bronchograms can be seen on chest x-ray. The diagnosis is made by

■ Box 6–2

Clinical Categories for Children With HIV
Infection

CATEGORY N: NOT SYMPTOMATIC

Children who have no signs or symptoms considered to be the result of HIV infection or who have only one of the conditions listed in category A, below.

CATEGORY A: MILDLY SYMPTOMATIC

Children with two or more of the conditions listed below but none of the conditions listed in categories B and C.

- Lymphadenopathy (≥ 0.5 cm at more than two sites; bilateral = one site)
- Hepatomegaly
- Splenomegaly
- Dermatitis
- Parotitis
- Recurrent or persistent upper respiratory infection, sinusitis, or otitis media

CATEGORY B: MODERATELY SYMPTOMATIC

Children who have symptomatic conditions other than those listed for categories A or C that are attributed to HIV infection. Examples include but are not limited to:

- Anemia (< 8 g/dL), neutropenia ($< 1,000/\text{mm}^3$), or thrombocytopenia ($< 100,000/\text{mm}^3$) persisting ≥ 30 days
- Bacterial meningitis, pneumonia, or sepsis (single episode)

■ *Box 6–2 continued*

- Candidiasis, oropharyngeal (thrush), persisting (> 2 months) in children > 6 months of age
- Cardiomyopathy
- Cytomegalovirus infection, with onset before 1 month of age
- Diarrhea, recurrent or chronic
- Hepatitis
- Herpes simplex virus (HSV) stomatitis, recurrent (more than two episodes within 1 year)
- HSV bronchitis, pneumonitis, or esophagitis with onset before 1 month of age
- Herpes zoster (shingles) involving at least two distinct episodes or more than one dermatome
- Leiomyosarcoma
- Lymphoid interstitial pneumonia (LIP) or pulmonary lymphoid hyperplasia complex
- Nephropathy
- Nocardiosis
- Persistent fever (lasting > 1 month)
- Toxoplasmosis, onset before 1 month of age
- Varicella, disseminated (complicated chickenpox)

CATEGORY C: SEVERELY SYMPTOMATIC

Children who have any condition listed in the 1987 surveillance case definition for acquired immunodeficiency syndrome with the exception of LIP (Box 6–3).

With permission from reference 4.

■ **Box 6-3**

Conditions Included in Clinical Category C for Children Infected With HIV

CATEGORY C: SEVERELY SYMPTOMATIC[a]

Serious bacterial infections, multiple or recurrent (any combination of at least two culture-confirmed infections within a 2-year period), of the following types: septicemia, pneumonia, meningitis, bone or joint infection, or abscess of an internal organ or body cavity (excluding otitis media, superficial skin or mucosal abscesses, and indwelling catheter-related infections).

Candidiasis, esophageal or pulmonary (bronchi, trachea, lungs).

Coccidioidomycosis, disseminated (at site other than or in addition to lungs or cervical or hilar lymph nodes).

Cryptococcosis, extrapulmonary.

Cryptosporidiosis or isosporiasis with diarrhea persisting > 1 month.

Cytomegalovirus disease with onset of symptoms at age > 1 month (at a site other than liver, spleen, or lymph nodes).

Encephalopathy (at least one of the following progressive findings present for at least 2 months in the absence of a concurrent illness other than HIV infection that could explain the findings): (1) failure to attain or loss of developmental milestones or loss of intellectual ability, verified by standard developmental scale or neuropsychological tests; (2) impaired brain growth or acquired microcephaly

■ *Box 6–3 continued*

demonstrated by head circumference measurements or brain atrophy demonstrated by computerized tomography or magnetic resonance imaging (serial imaging is required for children < 2 years of age); or (3) acquired symmetric motor deficit manifested by two or more of the following: paresis, pathologic reflexes, ataxia, or gait disturbance.

Herpes simplex virus infection causing a mucocutaneous ulcer that persists for > 1 month; or bronchitis, pneumonitis, or esophagitis for any duration affecting a child > 1 month of age.

Histoplasmosis, disseminated (at a site other than or in addition to lungs or cervical or hilar lymph nodes).

Kaposi's sarcoma.

Lymphoma, primary, in brain.

Lymphoma, small, noncleaved cell (Burkitt's), or immunoblastic or large cell lymphoma of B-cell or unknown immunologic phenotype.

Mycobacterium tuberculosis, disseminated or extrapulmonary.

Mycobacterium, other species or unidentified species, disseminated (at a site other than or in addition to lungs, skin, or cervical or hilar lymph nodes.)

Mycobacterium avium complex or *Mycobacterium kansasii*, disseminated (at site other than or in addition to lungs, skin, or cervical or hilar lymph nodes).

Pneumocystis carinii pneumonia.

Progressive multifocal leukoencephalopathy.

■ *Box 6–3 continued*

Salmonella (nontyphoid) septicemia, recurrent.

Toxoplasmosis of the brain with onset at > 1 month of age

Wasting syndrome in the absence of a concurrent illness other than HIV infection that could explain the following findings: (1) persistent weight loss > 10 percent of baseline OR (2) downward crossing of at least two of the following percentile lines on the weight-for-age chart (e.g., 95th, 75th, 50th, 25th, 5th) in a child > 1 year of age OR (3) < 5th percentile on weight-for-height chart on two consecutive measurements, ≥ 30 days apart PLUS (a) chronic diarrhea (at least two loose stools per day for > 30 days) OR (b) documented fever (for ≥ 30 days, intermittent or constant).

[a] See the 1987 AIDS surveillance case definition for diagnosis criteria.
With permission from reference 4.

identifying characteristic cysts in respiratory secretions. Some children, though, will require bronchoscopy or lung biopsy to establish the diagnosis. Trimethoprim-sulfamethoxazole is the treatment of choice in children. Children have fewer side effects with this regimen than do adults; pentamidine carries significant risks including hypoglycemia, pancreatitis, and renal failure.[3]

Treatment for children with PCP is TMP (20 mg/kg per day) and SMZ (100 mg/kg per day) in four divided daily doses intravenously for 21 days. If TMP-SMZ is not appropriate for a patient, intravenous pentamidine (4 mg/kg per day) in one daily dose for 12 to 14 days can be used. However, pentamidine has a high rate (50 to 60 per-

TABLE 6–2. PEDIATRIC HIV CLASSIFICATION

| Immunologic Category | Clinical Categories | | | |
	N: No Signs/ Symptons	A: Mild Signs/ Symptoms	B: Moderate Signs/ Symptoms[a]	C: Severe Signs/ Symptoms[a]
No evidence of suppression	N1	A1	B1	C1
Evidence of moderate suppression	N2	A2	B2	C2
Severe suppression	N3	A3	B3	C3

Children whose HIV infection status is not confirmed are classified by using the above grid with a letter E (for perinatally exposed) placed before the appropriate classification code (e.g., EN2).

[a] Both category C and lymphoid interstitial pneumonitis in category B are reportable to state and local health departments as AIDS.

With permission from reference 4.

cent) of adverse side effects. Pentamidine can be given intramuscularly, but painful sterile abscesses may develop.[12]

It is also important to provide adequate nutrition and pulmonary support for children with PCP. Children should be given 150 to 200 kcal/kg per day if they weigh less than 10 kg, and 100 to 150 kcal/kg per day if they weigh more than 10 kg. Children receive pulmonary support with intubation and mechanical ventilation based on their oxygen levels and the pH of the arterial blood.[12]

Lymphoid Interstitial Pneumonia

Lymphoid interstitial pneumonia (LIP) is a slowly progressive disorder with cough and mild hypoxemia. There is frequently a generalized adenopathy and salivary

**TABLE 6–3. LEADING AIDS-INDICATOR DISEASES
REPORTED IN CHILDREN FOR 1995**

HIV wasting syndrome	18%
Pneumocystis carinii pneumonia	18%
HIV encephalopathy (dementia)	17%
Bacterial infections, multiple or recurrent[a]	15%
Lymphoid interstitial pneumonia and/or pulmonary lymphoid hyperplasia[a] (presumptive)	13%
Candidiasis of esophagus (presumptive)	9%

These data are based on the 800 pediatric cases reported to the CDC for 1995.
[a] Not indicators for AIDs in adolescents or adults.
With permission from reference 1.

gland enlargement; digital clubbing is present in the late stages of the disease. A chest x-ray will show small nodules and fine reticular densities.[3] Sputum examination reveals lymphocytes, plasma cells, and macrophages.

Because there is no specific etiologic agent for LIP, treatment of the complications is by administering the appropriate antimicrobial agent (bacterial or viral), oxygen, and bronchodilators as indicated. LIP has also improved after treatment with zidovudine.[13]

Tuberculosis

In the pediatric patient, tuberculosis is not yet frequently associated with the HIV infection as it is in adults, but TB is expected to become more common. This is in part because of the difficulties in confirming the diagnosis of tuberculosis in children. During the years 1985 to 1988, 90 percent of adults with TB were confirmed bacteriologically, whereas only 28 percent of children less then 15 years of age were.[14] In addition, several factors may cause the skin test to be falsely negative; these include a period of nonreactivity 10 weeks after HIV-infected persons contract TB, persons with recent live virus immunizations (MMR),[15] and being in the newborn age group.

Tuberculosis infections and HIV infections in children follow a pattern opposite that noted in adults. In adults, the tuberculin bacillus is usually acquired when the person is immunocompetent and represents an activation of a latent disease, whereas the child is usually infected with HIV *in utero,* perinatally, or from family members. Because the child's immune system is not competent when TB is contracted, there may not be a positive skin test, pleural effusion, or lymphadenopathy.[14]

Children usually acquire their infection from members of their household, and the parent or parents at risk to transmit the HIV infection are also at risk for tuberculosis. Children with HIV and/or tuberculosis could be identified by careful follow-up of the contacts of an adult with tuberculosis. This surveillance is important because children may have nonspecific symptoms. Constitutional symptoms such as low-grade fever, cough, weight loss, night sweats, and failure to thrive may occur; other pulmonary symptoms are usually absent. Those pulmonary symptoms that have been observed with TB include wheezing, decreased breath sounds, tachypnea, and respiratory distress. These symptoms result from bronchial obstruction.[16]

The chest x-ray may or may not reveal substantial pathology. The initial infection may cause no visible changes, though hilar adenopathy may develop. In most children, the hilar adenopathy resolves, but in others, the adenopathy may lead to bronchial obstruction, perforation of the bronchus, and caseation. With proper treatment (isoniazid, rifampin, and pyrazinamide), these changes usually resolve.[16]

Recent recommendations about the use of skin testing and interpreting the results have been made to guide health care professionals in establishing the diagnosis of TB.[17] The Mantoux (PPD) provides a quantitative response to the TB antigen; the multipuncture tests (Monovac or Tine) are no longer recommended because they do not provide a quantitative response. All children should be evaluated for their risk for TB, and testing should be based on the circumstances for each child. Children with family members with TB, children with x-ray evidence of TB, and children who are from or travel to endemic countries should be tested immediately. Children who should be tested annually are those who are HIV positive and/or are incarcerated adolescents. Children exposed to adults at high risk should be tested every 2 to 3 years. Children with relatively low risk should be tested sometime between ages 4 and 6 years and again sometime between 11 and 16 years. Limiting the testing of children with low risk is meant to conserve resources for those people at high risk. It must also be acknowledged that those at high risk for HIV and TB may not use health care frequently. Health care professionals should use every opportunity to evaluate high-risk children for TB. The use of mailed-in cards by parents to report to the result of the TB skin test is no longer recommended.

The induration that defines a positive TB skin test is based on factors that define high risk for TB as well as the immunocompetence of the person being tested.[17] Children who have TB, have family members with TB, and who are immunocompromised for any reason may only muster a 5-mm response, and therefore that measurement is considered positive. Children who are 4 years of age or less, with chronic medical problems (diabetes, renal failure, and malnutrition), and children exposed to adults at high risk are considered to have a positive test at 10 mm of induration. Those children who are over 4 years of age and have no risk factors are considered positive at 15 mm of induration.

Children who may have received one or more BCG vaccinations should also receive PPD testing.[18] The BCG vaccines may vary in their effectiveness from 0 to 80 percent, and approximately one third of the world's population has a TB infection. The number of immunizations or scars is thought to affect the amount of induration that indicates infection even after vaccination. In Turkey, children may have no vaccination or may have as many as three. In a group of 3548 children, no scar produced a mean induration of 3.2 mm +/− 3.9; one scar, 6.3 +/− 7.8; two scars, 10.7 +/− 6.2; and three scars, 14.8 +/− 4.3. This subsequent increase in induration based on the number of scars is called the booster effect. This booster effect may also be caused by infection with nontuberculous mycobacteria. Starke and others[18] consider 12 mm of induration independent of the time period between immunization and testing as indicating TB infection, though these recommendations are based on one BCG vaccine.

Tuberculosis in children was concentrated in seven states in 1993: California, Texas, New York, Illinois, Florida, Georgia, and Pennsylvania. These states contain 45 percent of the U.S. population, but have 66 percent of the cases of TB in children.[19] In a study of pediatric TB cases in New York City, many of the children and their adult caregivers were not tested for HIV because of concerns for confidentiality, nor was the adult source identified. It is also important that cultures be done to identify the drug sensitivities of the TB mycobacterium causing the infection. This is even more important when the caregivers who expose the child are at risk for concurrent HIV because of IV drug use or have other risk factors, such as incomplete treatment for TB. Many children with TB are brought for evaluation of illness and TB is discovered as part of the evaluation. As mentioned earlier, the symptoms of TB may be only constitutional symptoms (such as fever or weight loss) rather than the pulmonary symptoms noticed in immunocompetent adults.

In a recent study of 12 children who have both AIDS and TB, most of the classical findings in tuberculosis were not present, in part because the children were all anergic from AIDS.[20] Most of the children presented with fever and tachypnea, had chronic lung disease that masked any x-ray evidence of TB, and had negative TB and anergy skin tests. Most of the x-rays showed diffuse lung infiltrates like those found in LIP and PCP. All of the children were immunosuppressed based on their CD4+ counts and three children presented with extrapulmonary TB. Four of the children had strains resistant to at least one antitubercular drug.

Respiratory Syncytial Virus

Respiratory syncytial virus (RSV) is a common respiratory infection in infants and young children, and most infections occur during fall and early spring. The usual clinical course includes 1 to 2 days of rhinitis, dry cough, and mild to moderate fever; the symptoms usually resolve in 3 to 7 days. Thirty to 40 percent of children go on to develop pneumonia and bronchiolitis; this then leads to signs of respiratory distress including cyanosis, tachypnea, inspiratory rales and expiratory wheezing, retractions, and cough.[21]

Radiographic findings include hyperinflation, increased bronchial markings, or pneumonia. The diagnosis can be confirmed by rapid antigen testing. Arterial blood gases are needed to assess the severity of respiratory distress, and hospitalization may be necessary. These children may need antiviral therapy with ribavirin by infant oxygen hood.[21] A small-particle aerosol generator

(Viratek SPAG-2) should be used to provide the medication for 12 to 18 hours a day at a rate of 190 Tg/L of air for at least 3 days and no longer than 7 days. The vial (6 g/vial) of ribavirin (Virazole) is diluted into sterile water and given with the aerosol generator that accompanies the medicine. Side effects from this drug include hypotension, cardiac arrest, digitalis toxicity, anemia, reticulocytosis, rash, conjunctivitis, and worsening of respiratory status. This drug is reserved for patients with severe lower-tract RSV infections.

Children who are HIV positive or who have AIDS also experience the spectrum of response to an RSV infection. Most children tolerate the infection without complications, but children with concurrent pneumonia or PCP infection are more likely to develop respiratory distress or failure and may require antiviral therapy.[3]

Congenital Syphilis and AIDS

In addition to acquiring an HIV infection from their mothers, infants may also be exposed to other sexually transmitted diseases. These include syphilis, gonorrhea, and hepatitis B infections.[3] In addition, the numbers of congenital syphilis cases reported to the CDC have been rising rapidly since 1986.[22] Two thirds or more of infants exposed to untreated syphilis become infected, and 38 to 64 percent of these infants are asymptomatic.[23] As in HIV, this condition occurs most commonly among African Americans, then Hispanics, and thirdly, Caucasians.[24] The child is at greatest risk of infection during the mother's primary syphilis episode (the appearance of a chancre).

There are a wide variety of findings associated with congenital syphilis. These variations are secondary to the maternal stage of syphilis, stage of pregnancy at the time of infection, rapidity of maternal diagnosis and treatment, adequacy of the maternal treatment for the fetus, maternal reinfection, immunologic reaction of the fetus,[25] and use of erythromycin to treat maternal syphilis.[24] Erythromycin is no longer recommended for treatment of syphilis because infants developed syphilis despite their mothers' treatment.[24]

The most common signs of congenital syphilis are condylomata lata, periostitis or osteochondritis, persistent rhinorrhea, and other manifestations listed in Table 6–4. Some of these signs are shared with infection with HIV. The classical signs of congenital syphilis do not appear until age 2 years or later.[25]

As for HIV infections in newborns, establishing the diagnosis is complicated by the maternal IgG antibodies to syphilis that cross the placenta. Despite this, prenatal screening remains the most important tool for treating the infection as quickly as possible, though pregnant women at greatest risk for syphilis may not seek prenatal care. Serum from the infant (rather than cord blood) should be analyzed for both VDRL and FTA-ABS tests. Because of the maternal antibodies, the infant's VDRL should be at least fourfold that of the mother's titer. In addition, CSF analysis should be done with a nonquantitative VDRL test rather than rapid plasma reagin or FTA-ABS.

There is now an IgM antibody test that is particularly valuable for establishing the diagnosis when the mother's VDRL titer remains elevated or stable despite adequate treatment or when there is a discrepancy between the infant's and mother's titers. Confirmation of congenital syphilis can be done by darkfield testing of exudate or serum for *Treponema pallidum*.[25] Presumptive diagnosis can be established by criteria from the CDC (Table 6–4).[25] PCR testing for *T. pallidum* DNA is also being used to identify whether the infant is infected or just has mother's antibodies, as in HIV. During primary syphilis, though,

TABLE 6–4. CLINICAL FINDINGS OF CONGENITAL SYPHILIS

Signs of Early Congenital Syphilis	Signs of Late Congenital Syphilis (after 2 years)
Stillbirth	Frontal bossing
Funisitis	Short maxillae
Placentitis	Saddle nose
Enlarged placenta	Protruding mandible
Focal proliferative villitis	High-arched palate
Endovascular proliferation	Hutchinson teeth[a] (peg-shaped upper incisors)
Relative immaturity of villi	
Nonimmune hydrops fetalis	Mulberry molars
Intrauterine growth retardation	Perioral fissures (rhagades)
Hepatosplenomegaly with or without jaundice	Clutton joints (bilateral knee effusions)
Generalized lymphadenopathy	Higoumenakis sign (sternoclavicular thickening)
Bone abnormalities	Saber shins
Diaphyseal periostitis	Flaring scapulas
Osteochondritis	Interstitial keratitis[a]
Wimberger sign	Neurologic abnormalities
Mucocutaneous lesions	Mental retardation
Mucous patches	Eighth cranial nerve deafness
Pigmented macules (condylomata lata)	Hydrocephalus
Vesiculobullous rash	
Any unexplained rash involving palms and soles	
Intractable diaper rash	
Persistent rhinitis (snuffles)	
Nephrotic syndrome	
Pneumonitis ("pneumonia alba")	
Neurologic abnormalities	
Pseudoparalysis (postneonatal Erb palsy)	
Leptomeningitis	
Ophthalmologic abnormalities	
Failure to thrive	

[a]Components of the Hutchinson triad.
With permission from reference 25.

the risk of transmission is much higher than HIV, and is estimated to be between 75 and 100 percent.[24]

For children with exposure to syphilis *in utero,* the maternal sera is more likely to be positive than is cord sera or neonatal sera. In a group of infants at a Bronx Hospital, several reasons were identified for producing a false-negative neonatal RPR.[26] These include prematurity (less than 28 weeks) in which there are low levels of antibodies crossing the placenta, mother's infection acquired just prior to delivery so there is not enough time for development of antibodies, immunodeficiency from HIV, a prozone phenomenon, or maternal treatment. It is also possible that maternal treatment may result in negative sera but there may be long bone evidence of congenital syphilis in the infant. Because of the risk of missing an infant with congenital syphilis secondary to false-negative sera, the CDC and the American Academy of Pediatrics recommend that all of the following situations warrant evaluation of the infant: mother RPR positive and untreated, mother whose syphilis was treated with erythromycin, treatment of mother within one month of delivery, pregnant mother treated appropriately but no documentation of falling titers, or syphilis treatment prior to pregnancy but no evidence of falling titers. Finally, any infant with a negative evaluation from a group at high risk for syphilis should be evaluated for IgM antibodies. These seronegative infants should be followed closely during the first year of life.

Evaluation of congenital syphilis includes a thorough physical examination for any of the physical findings associated with this condition, long bone radiographs, simultaneous VDRL titers for mother and infant, confirmatory FTA-ABS and IgM studies of FTA-ABS, CSF analysis for cell count, protein level, and VDRL (Table 6–5). Other testing may be clinically indicated, and all infants should receive an antibody titer for HIV. Infants

TABLE 6–5. EVALUATION FOR EARLY CONGENITAL SYPHILIS

1. Maternal history, including results of serologic testing and treatment
2. Thorough physical examination
3. Long-bone radiographs
   Diaphyseal periostitis
   Osteochondritis
   Wimberger sign
4. Nontreponemal antibody titer: VDRL test (simultaneous quantitative serum titer for mother and neonate)
5. Treponemal antibody titer
   FTA-ABS test
   FTA-ABS on 19S-IgM fraction of serum (CDC)
6. CSF analysis
   Cell count
   Protein level determination
   VDRL test
7. Other tests as clinically indicated
   Chest radiography
   Complete blood cell count: Leukemoid reaction with or without monocytosis or lymphocytosis, Coombs-negative hemolytic anemia
   Platelet count (thrombocytopenia)
   Liver function tests
   Urinalysis
8. HIV antibody test

With permission from reference 25.

may also require extensive testing to confirm the HIV infection for the same reasons necessary for syphilis (maternal antibodies).[25]

The newborn must be treated for probable neurosyphilis infection, and there may be difficulties in establishing this condition. See Figure 6–1 for an algorithm for treatment. Each child should have a CSF evaluation done; the characteristic findings include a positive VDRL titer of

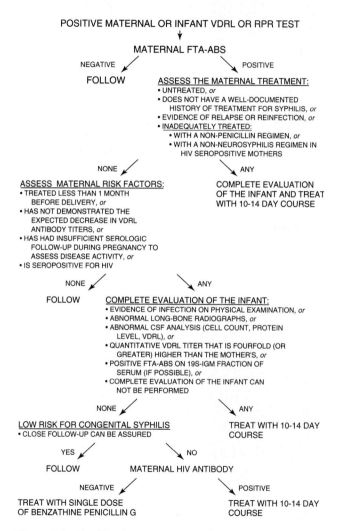

Figure 6–1. Algorithm for management of newborn infant born to mother with positive nontreponemal (VDRL or rapid plasma reagin) test result. (*With permission from reference 25.*)

the fluid, a mononuclear pleocytosis (5 to 100 cells/mm^3), a moderately elevated protein level (30 to 75 mg/mL), and a normal glucose concentration. The CDC has recognized the difficulties in diagnosing neurosyphilis in infants with congenital syphilis and now recommends treatment with aqueous crystalline penicillin G or procaine penicillin G for a minimum of 10 days so as to also treat a CNS infection.[25]

This recommendation especially applies to infants who have no physical or laboratory evidence of congenital syphilis but who do have a positive HIV antibody test with antibodies from mother and/or infant. Each infant with HIV antibodies should have CSF analysis for neurosyphilis. These two sexually transmitted diseases share many of the same epidemiologic characteristics, but the concurrent HIV infection is thought to alter the manifestations of syphilis by impairing cell-mediated immunity to the syphilitic spirochete. The open chancre is thought to also enhance the introduction of HIV. The B-cell abnormalities associated with the HIV infection (hypergammaglobulinemia) may lead to unusually high VDRL titers.[25]

Treatment for the newborn with congenital syphilis must recognize the ambiguity in properly identifying infants who have neurosyphilis (Fig. 6–1). Some treatment failures have been reported with benzathine penicillin G, and this antibiotic does not establish levels in the CSF adequate to eradicate the spirochete. The CDC now recommends 100,000 to 150,000 units/kg per day IV of aqueous crystalline penicillin G, or 50,000 units/kg per day IM of procaine penicillin G for 10 to 14 days.[25] A recent study reported by Stoll has demonstrated that aqueous crystalline penicillin G is more effective in eradicating syphilis in the CSF than benzathine penicillin G.[24]

Difficulties in treating the infant's mother who has both an HIV infection and a syphilis infection may compromise treatment of the infant. Research has demonstrated that HIV-positive patients have a greater number of treatment failures in early syphilis for those given benzathine penicillin G, and this treatment will then not adequately eradicate the illness in the child.[25]

These difficulties with treatment make it imperative that all infants born to women with a positive reaction to syphilis be monitored closely (Fig. 6–2). Whether or not the infant had evidence of congenital syphilis, each child should be seen at 1, 2, 3 (or 4), 6, and 12 months of age, and a VDRL titer should be done at each visit. For those infants born to a mother whose serum was VDRL positive

FOLLOW-UP FOR UNTREATED INFANTS: VDRL AND FTA-ABS TITER AT 1, 2, 4, 6, AND 12 MONTHS	FOLLOW-UP FOR TREATED INFANTS: VDRL TITER AT 1, 2, 4, 6, AND 12 MONTHS, and CSF ANALYSIS EVERY 6 MONTHS
• VDRL TITER IS DECREASING BY 3–4 MONTHS OF AGE, and • VDRL IS NEGATIVE BY 6 MONTHS OF AGE, and • FTA ABS IS NEGATIVE BY 12 MONTHS OF AGE	• VDRL TITER IS DECREASING BY 3–4 MONTHS OF AGE, and • VDRL IS NEGATIVE BY 6 MONTHS OF AGE, and • CSF VDRL IS NEGATIVE BY 6 MONTHS OF AGE, and • CSF CELL COUNT IS DECREASING, and • CSF CELL COUNT IS NORMAL BY 2 YEARS OF AGE
Yes / No	No / Yes
UNINFECTED REEVALUATE AND RETREAT WITH A REGIMEN RECOMMENDED FOR SYPHILIS OF MORE THAN 1 YEAR'S DURATION	ADEQUATELY TREATED

Figure 6–2. Follow-up management for an infant examined or treated for congenital syphilis. (*With permission from reference 25.*)

but FTA-ABS negative, the VDRL should be falling by 3 to 4 months of age and gone by 6 to 12 months of age.[24] If not, the infant should be fully reexamined and treated. If the infant continues to have maternal FTA-ABS antibodies beyond 1 year of age, that should be considered a treatment failure. Finally, if a mother develops secondary or tertiary syphilis after treatment for primary syphilis, her infant must be reevaluated.[25]

Those who have evidence of congenital syphilis should also be followed with VDRL titers. The titers should be nonreactive by 6 months. Infants with CSF abnormalities should be followed every 6 months until the fluid is normal. If the CSF VDRL is positive at 6 months, the infant should be treated again. In addition, the CSF abnormalities should be returning to normal at each examination. If not, or if the CSF cell count is abnormal at 2 years of age, the infant should be treated again. The child should also be followed for evidence of neurologic or ophthalmologic abnormalities associated with syphilis.[25]

■ Prophylaxis for *Pneumocystis Carinii* Pneumonia

As in adults, PCP is the most common AIDS-associated condition in children, but they are less able to cope with infection. In cases reported to the CDC, 35 percent of children with PCP died within 2 months of their diagnosis. Trimethoprim-sulfamethoxazole (TMP-SMZ) at a dose of 150 mg/m^2 TMP and 750 mg/m^2 SMZ in divided doses either daily or three consecutive days per week is effective in preventing PCP. See Table 6–6 for therapy alternatives.

Absolute and percentage counts of CD4+ lymphocytes are used as one measure of immunosuppression and are used as guidelines for starting PCP prophylaxis (Table 6–7).[27] Since the initial guidelines were released for CD4+

TABLE 6–6. DRUG REGIMENS FOR PCP PROPHYLAXIS

Recommended Regimen (children ≥ 1 month of age)

Trimethoprim/sulfamethoxazole (TMP-SMZ) 150 mg TMP/m^2 per day with 750 mg SMZ/m^2 per day given orally in divided doses twice a day (BID) 3 times per week on consecutive days (e.g., Monday, Tuesday, Wednesday).

Acceptable alternative TMP-SMZ dosage schedules:
150 mg TMP/m^2 per day with 750 mg SMZ/m^2 per day given orally as a single daily dose 3 times per week on consecutive days.

150 mg TMP/m^2 per day with 750 SMZ/m^2 per day orally divided BID and given 7 days/week.

150 mg TMP/m^2 per day with 750 mg SMZ/m^2 per day given orally divided BID and given 3 times per week on alternate days (e.g., M-W-F).

Alternative Regimens, if TMP-SMZ Not Tolerated

Aerosolized pentamidine (≥ 5 years of age) 300 mg given via Respirgard II inhaler monthly.

Dapsone (≥ 1 month of age) 2 mg/kg (not to exceed 100 mg) given orally once daily.[a]

If neither aerosolized pentamidine nor dapsone is tolerated, some clinicians use intravenous pentamidine (4 mg/kg) given every 2 or 4 weeks.

[a] Please note the increase of dapsone to 2 mg in the latest recommendations.
With permission from references 11 and 27.

levels that warrant PCP prophylaxis, some children have developed PCP with CD4+ levels above those recommended for prophylaxis.[11] Apparently, the CD4+ count for these children drops just before the PCP develops, but some infants less than 12 months of age and diagnosed with PCP have CD4+ counts greater than 1500 cells/μL. In addition, some of these children with PCP were not known to be HIV exposed in enough time to provide prophylaxis. The rate of PCP rises sharply at age 2 months and most commonly occurs in children 3 to 6 months of age.[27]

TABLE 6–7. USING CD4+ COUNTS TO GUIDE PROPHYLAXIS FOR PCP

Age	PCP Prophylaxis	CD4+ Monitoring
Birth to 4–6 weeks	No prophylaxis	At 1 month of age
4–6 weeks to 4 months	Begin prophylaxis	At 3 months of age
4–12 months		
HIV +	Prophylaxis	At 6, 9, and 12 months of age
No signs of HIV infection[a]	No prophylaxis	None
1–5 years	Prophylaxis if CD4+ count < 500 or < 15 percent	Every 3–4 months
6–12 years	Prophylaxis if CD4+ count < 200 or < 15 percent	Every 3–4 months

[a] Please see Box 6–1 for ruling out HIV infection in infants.

■ Antiretroviral Therapy for Children

Two types of treatment are available to reduce the numbers of circulating HIV in someone infected with the virus. The older group of medications act by inhibiting reverse transcriptase and are known as nucleoside analogues; zidovudine and didanosine are two medications in this class. Newer drugs, called proteinase inhibitors, also prevent replication of the virus. Saquinavir is an example of this type of drug. These medications encourage weight gain, reduce hepatosplenomegaly, reduce the effects of encephalopathy, reduce the amount of p25 antigen in the blood and cerebrospinal fluid, reduce the numbers of virus detected in the blood, and improve CD4+ counts.[28]

Until recently, two medications were approved by the Food and Drug Administration for use in children. These drugs were zidovudine (ZDV or AZT) and didanosine (ddI); both inhibit reverse transcriptase. ZDV can be used beginning at 3 months of age, but ddI is not recommended until 6 months of age for those children who do not tolerate ZDV. The first type, reverse transcriptase inhibitors, has not been studied as extensively in children as in adults, though clinical trials do demonstrate an improvement in the child's condition while receiving the medication. In a review of clinical trials of zidovudine,[29] improvements were noted in neurodevelopmental abnormalities, cognitive abilities, appetite and weight gain, as well as decreased lymph node and liver size, decreased immunoglobulin values, and increased CD4+ cell counts. Oral zidovudine also brought about reductions in p25 antigen levels in CSF as well as reversal of the CSF cultures for HIV for most of the children (6 of 7) who were enrolled in a recent clinical trial. This results in improvement in neuropsychological activity, even when the most common AIDS-indicator disease in this clinical trial was encephalopathy. These studies evaluated children from infancy to preteens, and different dosages, both oral and intravenous, were used. As in adults, higher levels resulted in anemia and neutropenia for a significant number of children. The usual oral dosage for these clinical trials was 180 mg/m^2 every 6 hours or four times a day. The best dosage for infected children must still be determined.[30] Other side effects from ZDV include nausea, myalgia, insomnia, and severe headaches.[31] Eventually, HIV will become resistant to these medications by mutating.

Stavudine (d4T) was recently studied in children by

Kline and others.[28] This is another nucleoside analogue like ZVD and ddI, but was better tolerated than the older medications. Thirty-seven children, ages 7 months to 15 years, were given one of four dosing schedules based on experience with adults until most children tolerated 1 mg/kg per day. They then received escalating doses of 2 to 4 mg/kg per day until clinical or immunologic problems developed. The median number of weeks on therapy was 37, and most of the side effects noticed were thought to be secondary to HIV rather than the medication. There were no dose-related side effects noted in the study, and this implies that this may be a safer reverse transcriptase type medication for children.

The newer group of medications, protease inhibitors, are just being approved for use in adults. Several have just been approved for adults: saquinavir, ritonavir, and indinavir. The combination of the first two drugs appears to be better than each separately because ritonavir protects saquinavir from liver degradation.[32]

Several studies have also demonstrated that double or triple therapy with reverse transcriptase inhibitors has a synergistic effect, that is, a substantial reduction in viral load and for a longer period of time. In a recent report, deliviridine was used in combination with ZVD or ddI and there was a 68 percent reduction in viral load that lasted for a year.[32]

■ Immunizations for HIV-positive Children

Children with the HIV infection are at high risk for fulminant cases of childhood illnesses, including a fatal outcome from measles and chickenpox.[3] Hence, immunizations become more important and should be carefully considered when treating patients (Table 6–8).[33]

TABLE 6–8. RECOMMENDED IMMUNIZATION SCHEDULE FOR HIV-EXPOSED/INFECTED INFANTS

Age (months)	Immunization (dose)	Age (months)	Immunization (dose)
Newborn	Hep B (1)[a]		
1	Hep B (2)	7	Influenza (1)[b]
2	DTP (1), Hib (1)[c]	8	Influenza (2)[b]
3	EIPV (1)[c]	12	Hib (3 or 4),[c] MMR[e]
4	DTP (2), Hib (2)[c]	15	EIPV (3), DTAP (4)[f]
5	EIPV (2)[c]	18	DTAP (4)[f]
6	DTP(3), Hib (3), Hep B(3) [c,d,g]	24	Pneumococcal, 23-valent[h]

DTAP, diphtheria and tetanus toxoids with acellular Pertussis; DTP, diphtheria-tetanus-pertussis; EIPV, enhanced inactivated polio vaccine: Hep B, hepatitis B; Hib, hemophilus influenzas type b; MMR, measles-mumps-rubella. This schedule differs from that recommended for immunization of immunocompetent children in the following ways: (1) EIPV replaces oral polio vaccine, and the first two doses of EIPV may be given at 3 and 5 months instead of 2 and 4 months; (2) the second dose of Hep 5 vaccine is given at 1 month; and (3) pneumococcal vaccine is recommended. This schedule is designed to deliver vaccine to HIV-infected children as early as possible and to limit the number of injections to two per visit.

[a] Infants born to mothers positive for hepatitis B surface antigen should receive hepatitis B immune globulin within 12 hours of birth in addition to Hep B vaccine.

[b] Primary immunization against influenza for children < 9 years of age requires two doses of vaccine, the first of which can be given as early as 6 months of age. Subsequent vaccination should be undertaken annually, before the influenza season.

[c] DTP and Hib vaccines are available together or separately. With the combined DTP-Hib vaccine, a single injection on each occasion is sufficient and can be given at 2, 4, and 6 months. Administration of EIPV as a second injection at 2 and 4 months can replace separate immunizations at 3 and 5 months.

[d] The need for a third dose of Hib vaccine depends on which formulation was used previously. Regardless of whether the primary series requires two or three doses, a booster dose is required at 12 to 15 months.

[e] HIV-infected children should receive prophylactic immunoglobulin after exposure to measles, whether or not they have been vaccinated against measles.

[f] DaTap can be administered at either 15 or 18 months. Alternatively, a fourth dose of DTP can be given as early as 12 months.

[g] If DTP and Hib are given as separate injections at 6 months, the third dose of Hep B vaccine may be postponed until the next visit.

[h] Some authorities recommend revaccination for HIV-infected children vaccinated > 6 years previously.

From reference 33.

TABLE 6–9. RECOMMENDED FOLLOW-UP SCHEDULE FOR ASYMPTOMATIC INFANTS BORN TO HIV-SEROPOSITIVE MOTHERS (CONSENSUS OF PEDIATRIC INFECTIOUS DISEASES TRAINING PROGRAM DIRECTORS)

Evaluations	No. of Times Performed during the First Year of Life	Ages (months) Recommended for Evaluations	No. of Times Performed during the Second Year of Life	Age (months) Recommended for Evaluation
History and physical examination	3–12	0, 3, 6, 9, 12	2–5	15, 18, 21, 24
Neurodevelopmental testing	0–12	6, 12	1–4	24
Complete blood count and platelet count	1–6	0, 3, 6, 9, 12	0–4	15, 18, 21, 24
Renal function tests	0–5	0, 6, 12	0–4	18, 24
Liver function tests	0–5	0, 6, 12	0–4	18, 24
Serum immunoglobulins	0–6	6, 12	0–4	24
Lymphocyte subsets	0–6	0, 3, 6, 9, 12	0–4	15, 18, 21, 24
Lymphocyte proliferation assays	0–4	NR	0–3	NR
HIV antibody (ELISA)	0–6	0, 3, 6, 9, 12	1–4	15, 18, 21, 24
HIV antibody (Western blot)	0–6	If + ELISA	0–4	15, 18, 21, 24

HIV p25 antigen assay	0–6	0, 3, 6, 9, 12	0–4	15, 18, 21, 24
HIV peripheral blood culture	0–5	0, 3, 6, 9, 12	0–4	15, 18, 21, 24
HIV PCR assay	0–5	0, 3, 6, 9, 12	0–4	15, 18, 21, 24
Lumbar puncture	0–1	12	0–1	24
Electroencephalograph	0–2	12	0–2	24
Chest radiograph	0–2	12	0–2	24
Head computed axial tomographic scan and/or MRI	0–1	12	0–1	24
Electrocardiography/ECHO	0–2	12	0–2	24

NR, not recommended.
With permission from reference 30.

■ Periodic Evaluation of Infants Born to HIV-positive Mothers

Table 6–9 summarizes the evaluation of an infant born to an HIV-positive mother.[30]

■ Psychosocial Aspects of HIV in Children and Adolescents

Children with HIV/AIDS frequently have developmental delays and progressive loss of cognitive function. Delays are most common in fine and gross motor skills as well as speech. These may be directly related to CNS infection with HIV. Manifestations of infection include microcephaly and radiographic evidence of cerebral atrophy. School-age children also perform poorly when undergoing testing for intelligence.[34]

Children are also at risk for depression because they have a chronic disease that at present is universally fatal. Common symptoms include apathy, withdrawal, and anorexia. Children and adolescents may also develop dementia and psychosis. Little has been done to study these conditions directly in children and adolescents, but they have been observed to have similar symptoms to adults with AIDS who suffer from AIDS dementia or encephalopathy. Treatment includes rehabilitation, psychopharmacology, and psychotherapy.[34]

■ Prophylaxis for Opportunistic Infections in Children

Recently, the CDC released recommendations for treatment of opportunistic infections in HIV-positive persons.[33] Several of the conditions are covered by TMP-SMZ given to protect against PCP. Some conditions contain recommendations for adults but the regimens have not been studied in children. Others can be covered by immunizations and/or immunoglobulins. For a complete description of the recommendations, please refer to the CDC guidelines.[33]

Those conditions that may also be covered by TMP-SMZ for PCP include toxoplasmic encephalitis, bacterial respiratory infections (except resistant *Streptococcus pneumoniae*), and some bacterial enteritis.

Those conditions that can be postponed with immunoglobulins include varicella-zoster virus. For conditions that can be prevented or postponed with immunizations, refer to Table 6–8.

Treatments for the following have been recommended in adults but not fully studied in children: *Mycobacterium avium* complex with rifabutin, cryptococcus with fluconazole after an episode, coccidioidomycosis with fluconazole after an episode, and cytomegalovirus disease with ganciclovir after an episode.

Cryptosporidiosis, microsporidiosis, and bartonellosis do not have an effective treatment currently.

Some other conditions with specific treatments though not recommended for prophylaxis include tuberculosis with single or multiple drugs based on drug sensitivities, herpes simplex virus with acyclovir, and candidiasis with an antifungal (nystatin, topical clotrimazole, ketaconazole, fluconazole, or itraconazole). For treatment regimens, please see Table 6–10 for prophylaxis prior to occurrence of these infections and Table 6–11 for prophylaxis for recurrences.[33]

TABLE 6–10. PROPHYLAXIS FOR FIRST EPISODE OF OPPORTUNISTIC DISEASE IN HIV-INFECTED INFANTS AND CHILDREN

Pathogen	Indication	Preventive Regimens	
		First Choice	Alternatives
Strongly Recommended as Standard of Care			
Pneumocystis carinii	All infants 1–4 months old born to HIV-infected women; HIV-infected or HIV-indeterminate infants < 12 months old; HIV-infected children 1–5 years old with CD4+ count of < 500 µL or CD4+ percentage of < 15 percent; HIV-infected children 6–12 years old with CD4+ count of < 200/4µL or CD4+ percentage of < 15	TMP-SMZ, 150/750 mg/m²/day in 2 divided doses PO TIW on consecutive days (AII); acceptable alternative schedules for same dosage (AII); single dose PO TIW on consecutive days, 2 divided doses PO qd, or 2 divided doses PO TIW on alternate days	Aerosolized pentamidine (children ≥ 5 years old), 300 mg qm via Respirgard II nebulizer (CIII); dapsone (children ≥ 1 month old), 2 mg/kg (not to exceed 100 mg) PO qd (CIII); IV pentamidine, 4 mg/kg every 2–4 weeks (CIII)
Mycobacterium tuberculosis			
Isoniazid sensitive	TST reaction of ≥ 5 mm or prior positive TST result without treatment or contact with	Isoniazid, 10–15 mg/kg (maximum, 300 mg) PO or IM qd × 12 months or	Rifampin, 10–12 mg/kg (maximum, 600 mg) PO or IV qd × 12 months (BIII)

	case of active tuberculosis	20–30 mg/kg (maximum, 900 mg) PO BIW × 12 months (BIII)	Uncertain
Isoniazid resistant	Same as above; high probability of exposure to isoniazid-resistant tuberculosis	Rifampin, 10–12 mg/kg (maximum, 600 mg) PO or IV qd × 12 months (BII)	None
Multidrug resistant (isoniazid and rifampin)	Same as above; high probability of exposure to multidrug-resistant tuberculosis	Choice of drugs requires consultation with public health authorities	None
Varicella-zoster virus	Significant exposure to varicella with no history of varicella	VZIG, 1 vial (1.25 mL)/10 kg (maximum, 5 vials) IM, give ≤ 96 hours after exposure, ideally within 48 hours (AI) (Children routinely receiving IVIG should receive VZIG if the last dose of IVIG was given > 14 days before exposure)	None
Various pathogens	HIV exposure/infection	Immunizations	None
Recommended for Consideration in All Patients			
Toxoplasma gondii	IgG antibody to *Toxoplasma* with severe immunosuppression (CD4+ count of < 100/µL)	TMP-SMZ, 150/750 mg/m²/day in 2 divided dose: PO TIW on consecutive days (CIII); accept-	Dapsone (children ≥ 1 month old), 2 mg/kg or 15 mg/m² (maximum, 25 mg) PO qd

TABLE 6–10. *(continued)*

Pathogen	Indication	Preventive Regimens	
		First Choice	**Alternatives**
	(Prophylaxis may be considered at higher CD4+ counts in the youngest infants, but no relevant data are available)	able alternative schedules for same dosage (CIII): single dose PO TIW on consecutive days, 2 divided doses PO qd or 2 divided doses PO TIW on alternate days	*plus* pyrimethamine, 1 mg/kg PO qd, *plus* leucovorin, 5 mg PO every 3 days (CIII)
Mycobacterium avium complex	CD4+, count of < 75/μL	Children 6–12 years old: rifabutin, 300 mg PO qd (BI); children < 6 years old: 5 mg/kg PO qd when suspension is available (BI)	All ages: azithromycin, 7.5 mg/kg in 2 divided doses PO qd (CIII); Clarithromycin, 5–12 mg/kg PO qd (CIII)

Not Recommended for Most Patients, Indicated for Consideration Only in Selected Patients

Pathogen	Indication	First Choice	Alternatives
Invasive bacterial infections	Hypogammaglobulinemia	IVIG, 400 mg/kg qm (AI)	None
Candida species	Severe immunosuppression	Nystatin (100,000 U/mL), 4–6 mL PO q6h; or topical clotrimazole, 10 mg PO 5×/day	Ketoconazole, 5–10 mg/kg PO q 12–24 hours (CI); fluconazole 2–8 mg/kg PO qd (CI)

Organism	Indication		
Cryptococcus neoformans	Severe immunosuppression	Fluconazole, 2–8 mg/kg PO qd (BI)	Itraconazole, 2–5 mg/kg PO q 12–24 hours (CIII)
Histoplasma capsulatum	Severe immunosuppression, endemic geographic area	Itraconazole, 2–5 mg/kg PO q 12–24 hours (CIII)	Fluconazole, 2–8 mg/kg PO qd (CIII)
Coccidioides immitis	Severe immunosuppression, endemic geographic area	Fluconazole, 2–8 mg/kg PO qd (CIII)	Itraconazole, 2–5 mg/kg PO q12–24h (CIII)
CMV*	CD4+ count of < 50 mL and CMV antibody positivity	Children 6–12 years old: oral ganciclovir under investigation	None
Influenza A virus	High risk of exposure (e.g., institutional outbreak)	Rimantadine or amantadine 5 mg/kg qd (maximum, 150 mg) in 2 divided doses PO for children < 10 y old; for children ≥ 10 y old, 5 mg/kg up to 40 kg, then 200 mg in 2 divided doses PO qd	None

Not all of the recommended regimens reflect current Food and Drug Administration-approved labeling. BIW, twice weekly; CMV, cytomegalovirus; IVIG, intravenous immune globulin; qm, monthly; TIW, three times weekly; TMP-SMZ, trimethoprim-sulfamethoxazole; VZIG, Varicella-zoster immune globulin. The Respirgard II nebulizer is manufactured by Marquest, Englewood, CO. Letters and Roman numerals in parentheses after regimens indicate the strength of the recommendation and the quality of the evidence supporting it (see text). The efficacy of parenteral pentamidine (e.g., 4 mg/kg qm) is controversial. TMP-SMZ and dapsone/pyrimethamine (and possibly dapsone alone) appear to be protective against toxoplasmosis, although relevant data have not been prospectively collected. Daily treatment with TMP-SMZ reduces the frequency of some bacterial infections. Patients receiving sulfadiazine/pyrimethamine for toxoplasmosis are protected against PCP and do not need TMP-SMZ. Protection against *T. gondii* is provided by the preferred antipneumocystis regimens. Dapsone alone cannot be recommended on the basis of currently available data. Pyrimethamine alone probably provides little, if any, protection. Ketoconazole and fluconazole are preferred for prophylaxis of esophagitis and severe mucocutaneous infection. * Data on oral ganciclovir are still being evaluated; the durability of its effect is unclear. Acyclovir is not protective against CMV. *With permission from reference 33.*

TABLE 6–11. PROPHYLAXIS FOR RECURRENCE OF OPPORTUNISTIC DISEASE (AFTER CHEMOTHERAPY FOR ACUTE DISEASE) IN HIV-INFECTED INFANTS AND CHILDREN

| | | Preventive regimens | |
Pathogen	Indication	First Choice	Alternatives
Recommended for Life as Standard of Care			
Pneumocystis carinii	Prior PCP pneumonia	TMP-SMZ, 150/750 mg/m²/day in 2 divided doses PO TIW on consecutive days (AI); acceptable alternative schedules for same dosage (AI); single dose PO TIW on consecutive days, 2 divided doses PO qd, or 2 divided doses PO TIW on alternate days	Aerosolized pentamidine (children ≥ 5 years old), 300 mg qm via Respirgard II nebulizer (AI); dapsone (children ≥ 1 month old), 2 mg/kg (not to exceed 100 mg) PO qd (CIII) IV; pentemidine, 4 mg/kg every 2–4 weeks (CIII)
Toxoplasma gondii	Prior toxoplasmic encephalitis	Sulfadiazine, 85–120 mg/kg in 2–4 divided doses PO qd *plus* pyrimethamine. 1 mg/kg or 15 mg/m² (maximum, 25 mg) PO qd plus leucovorin, 5 mg PO every 3 days (AII)	Clindamycin 20–30 mg/kg in 4 divided doses PO qd, *plus* pyrimethamine, 1 mg/kg PO qd, plus leucovorin, 5 mg PO every 3 days (AII)

Pathogen	Indication	Preventive measure (first choice)	Alternative
Mycobacterium avium complex	Prior disease	Clarithromycin, 30 mg/kg in 2 divided doses PO qd *plus* at least one of the following: ethambutol, 15–25 mg/kg in PO qd; clofazimine, 50–100 mg PO qd; rifabutin, 300 mg PO qd; ciprofloxacin, 20–30 mg/kg in 2 divided doses PO qd (CIII)	None
Cryptococcus neoformans	Documented disease	Fluconazole, 2–8 mg/kg PO qd (CIII)	Itraconazole, 2–5 mg/kg PO ql2-24h (CIII): amphotericin B 0.5–1.5 mg/kg IV q.w.-TIW (AI)
Histoplasma capsulatum	Documented disease	Itraconazole, 2–5 mg/kg PO ql2-24h (CIII)	Fluconazole. 2–8 mg/kg PO qd (CIII); amphotericin B, 1.0 mg/kg IV q.w. (AI)
Coccidioides immitis	Documented disease	Fluconazole, 2–8 mg/kg PO qd (CIII)	Amphotericin B, 1.0 mg/kg IV qw (AI)
Cytomegalovirus[1]	Prior end-organ disease	Ganciclovir, 10 mg/kg in 2 divided doses: IV qd for 1 week, then 5 mg/kg IV qd; *or* Foscarnet 60–120 mg/kg IV qd (AI)	None

TABLE 6–11. (continued)

Pathogen	Indication	Preventive regimens	
		First choice	Alternatives
Salmonella species (non-typhi)	Bacteremia	TMP/SMZ, 150/750 mg/m² in 2 divided doses PO qd for several months (CIII)	Ampicillin, 50–100 mg in 4 divided doses PO qd (CIII); chloramphenicol. 50–75 mg/kg in 4 divided doses PO qd (CIII) (For children > 6 years old, consider ciprofloxacin, 30 mg in 2 divided doses PO qd (CII)

Recommended Only if Subsequent Episodes Are Frequent or Severe

Pathogen	Indication	First choice	Alternatives
Invasive bacterial infections	More than 2 infections in 1 year period	IVIG, 400 mg/kg qm (AI)	TMP-SMZ 150/750 mg/m² PO qd (AI)
Herpes simplex virus	Frequent, severe recurrences	Acyclovir, 600–1,000 mg in 3–5 divided doses PO qd (CIII)	
Candida species	Frequent, severe recurrences	Ketoconazole, 5–10 mg/kg PO q 12–24 hours, or fluconazole, 2–8 mg/kg PO qd (BI)	

Not all of the recommended regimens reflect current Food and Drug Administration-approved labeling. IVIG, intravenous immune globulin; qm, monthly; qw, weekly; TIW, three times weekly; TMP-SMZ = trimethoprim-sulfamethoxazole. The Respirgard II nebulizer is manufactured by Marquest, Englewood, CO. Letters and Roman numerals in parentheses after regimens indicate the strength of the recommendation and the quality of the evidence supporting it (see text). Only pyrimethamine/sulfadiazine confers protection against PCP. Although the clindamycin/pyrimethamine regimen is an alternative for adults, it has not been tested in children. However, these drugs are safe and are used for other infections. Ciprofloxacin should not be given to children < 6 years of age. Rifabutin (5 mg/kg PO) qd may be given to children < 6 years of age when a suspension becomes available. [1]Oral ganciclovir has not been studied in children. Choice of drug should be determined by susceptibilities of the organism isolated.

With permission from reference 33.

References

1. Centers for Disease Control and Prevention. *HIV/AIDS Surveillance Report.* 1996;8:1–33.
2. Caldwell MB, Rogers MF. Epidemiology of the pediatric AIDS infection. In: Edelson PJ, ed. Childhood AIDS. *Pediatr Clin North Am.* 1991;38:1–16.
3. Burroughs MB, Edelson PJ. Medical care of the HIV-infected child. In: Edelson PJ, ed. Childhood AIDS. *Pediatr Clin North Am.* 1991;38:45–68.
4. Centers for Disease Control and Prevention. 1994 Revised classification system for human immunodeficiency virus infection in children less than 13 years of age. *MMWR.* 1994;43:1–10.
5. European Collaborative study. Children born to women with HIV-1 infection: Natural history and risk of infection. *Lancet.* 1991;337:253–260.
6. Chantry CJ, Cooper ER, Pelton SI, et al. Seroreversion in human immunodeficiency virus-exposed but uninfected infants. *Pediatr Infect Dis J.* 1995;14:382–387.
7. American Academy of Pediatrics, Task Force on Pediatric AIDS. Perinatal human immunodeficiency virus (HIV) testing. *AAP News.* 1992;8:20–25.
8. Rogers MF, Chin-Yin O, Kilborne B, Schochetman G. Advances and problems in the diagnosis of human immunodeficiency virus infection in infants. *Pediatr Infect Dis J.* 1991:10:523–531.
9. Weiblen BJ, Lee FK, Cooper ER, et al. Early diagnosis of HIV infections in infants by detection of IgA antibodies. *Lancet.* 1990;335:988–990.
10. Moodley D, Bobat RA, Coutsoudis A, Coovadia HM. Predicting perinatal human immunodeficiency virus infection by antibody pattern. *Pediatr Infect Dis J.* 1995;14:850–852.
11. Grubman S, Simonds RJ. Preventing Pneumocystis carinii pneumonia in human immunodeficiency virus infected children: New guidelines for prophylaxis. *Pediatr Infec Dis J.* 1996;15:165–168.
12. Sanders-Laufer D, DeBruin W, Edelson PJ. *Pneumocystis carinii* infections in HIV-infected children. In: Edelson PJ, ed. Childhood AIDS. *Pediatr Clin North Am.* 1991;38:69–88.

13. Pitt J. Lymphocytic interstitial pneumonia. In: Edelson PJ, ed. Childhood AIDS. *Pediatr Clin North Am.* 1991;38:89–95.

14. Braun MM, Cauthen G. Relationship of the human immunodeficiency virus epidemic to pediatric tuberculosis and *Bacillus Calmette-Guerin* immunization. *Pediatr Infect Dis J.* 1992;11:220–227.

15. American Thoracic Society and the Centers for Disease Control. Diagnostic standards and classification of tuberculosis. *Am Rev Respir Dis.* 1990;142:725–735.

16. Starke JR. Modern approach to the diagnosis and management of tuberculosis in children. *Pediatr Clin North Am.* 1988;35:441–464.

17. Committee of Infectious Diseases, American Academy of Pediatrics. Update on tuberculosis skin testing of children. *Pediatrics.* 1996; 97:282–284.

18. Ildririm I, Hacimustafaoglu M, Ediz B. Correlation of tuberculosis induration with the number of *Bacillus Calmette-Guerin* vaccines. *Pediatr Infect Dis J.* 1995;14:1060–1063.

19. Driver CR, Luallen JJ, Good WG, et al. Tuberculosis in children younger than five years old: New York City. *Pediatr Infect Dis J.* 1995;14:112–117.

20. Chan SP, Birnbaum J, Rao M, Steiner P. Clinical manifestation and outcome of tuberculosis in children with acquired immunodeficiency syndrome. *Pediatr Infect Dis J.* 1996;15:443–447.

21. Kuzal RJ, Clutter DJ. Current perspectives on respiratory syncytial virus infections. *Postgrad Med.* 1993;93:129–141.

22. Centers for Disease Control. Congenital syphilis, New York City, 1986–1988. *MMWR.* 1989;38:825–829.

23. Zenker PN, Rolfs RT. Treatment of syphilis, 1989. *Rev Infect Dis.* 1990;12(suppl 6):S590-S609.

24. Stoll B. Congenital syphilis: Evaluation and management of neonates born to mothers with reactive serologic tests for syphilis. *Pediatrics.* 1994;13:845–852.

25. Ikeda MK, Jenson HB. Evaluation and treatment of congenital syphilis. *J Pediatr.* 1990;117:843–852.

26. Chhabra RS, Brion LP, Castro M, et al. Comparison of maternal sera, cord blood, and neonatal sera for detecting presumptive congenital syphilis: Relationship with maternal treatment. *Pediatrics,* 1993;91:88–91.

27. Centers for Disease Control and Prevention. 1995 revised guidelines for prophylaxis against Pneumocystis carinii pneumonia for children infected with or perinatally exposed to human immunodeficiency virus. *MMWR.* 44:1–11.

28. Kline MW, Dunkle, LM, Church JA, et al. A phase I/II evaluation of stavudine in children with human immunodeficiency virus infection. *Pediatrics.* 1995;96:247–252.

29. McKinney RE Jr., Maha MA, Conner EM, et al. A multicenter trial of oral zidovudine in children with advanced human immunodeficiency virus disease. *N Engl J Med.* 1991;324: 1018–1025.

30. Prober CG, Gershon AA. Medical management of newborns and infants born to human immunodeficiency virus-seropositive mothers. *Pediatr Infect Dis J.* 1991;10:684–695.

31. Richmond DD, Fischl MA, Grieco MH, et al. The toxicity of azidothymidine (AZT) in the treatment of patients with AIDS and AIDS-related complex: A double-blind, placebo controlled trial. *N Engl J Med.* 1987;317:192–197.

32. Sharp V, Ferri RS. AIDS Update. *Clinician Rev.* 1996;6:115–119.

33. Centers for Disease Control and Prevention. USPHS/IDSA guidelines for the prevention of opportunistic infections in persons infected with human immunodeficiency virus: A summary. *MMWR.* 1995;44:1–34.

34. Speigal L, Mayars A. Psychological aspects of AIDS in children and adolescents. In: Edelson PJ, ed. Childhood AIDS. *Pediatr Clin North Am.* 1988;35:441–464.

SEVEN

CHAPTER

Evaluation of Women

Mary L. Adair • *Pamela Burian*

■ The Epidemiology of AIDS in Women

Women are currently the fastest growing group being infected with human immunodeficiency virus (HIV). Although women made up only 7 percent of the total cases of AIDS in the United States through 1985, women represented 18 percent of all cases by 1994. The estimate of HIV-infected women who had children in 1994 was 7000. AIDS went from being the tenth to the third leading cause of death among women 25 to 44 years old in 1994, and continues to increase. In some areas, such as New York City and New Jersey, AIDS is now the leading cause of death among women in this age group.[1]

According to the CDC, white, non-Hispanic women make up 22 percent of cases of AIDS in women, Hispanic women 20 percent of cases, and black, non-Hispanic women 57 percent of cases. Although women of color represent 21 percent of all U.S. women, they represent 77 percent of cases of AIDS. Risk factors for acquiring HIV infection were reported as 38 percent heterosexual contact, 41 percent injection drug use, 2 percent contaminated blood or blood products, and 19 percent no exposure identified. It is assumed that the majority of those cases with no known exposure were sexually acquired.

To date there has been one documented case of female-to-female transmission of HIV.[2] Although it is assumed that transmission between women is low, it should be considered a possible means of HIV transmission. Recognition and further investigation of female-to-female transmission will better allow us to address risk behaviors and interventions.[3]

■ Identification of HIV-positive Women

Historically, women have not been diagnosed until they were further along in the course of AIDS. Factors contributing to late diagnosis may include poor access to health care, poor use of health care, and the low degree of suspicion of HIV-related disease by health care providers of women. Also, women at high risk, as well as many health care professionals, may be unaware of the early manifestations of HIV.

Gynecologic symptoms are often the first sign of HIV infection in women. These may include recurrent vulvovaginal candidiasis and pelvic inflammatory disease, especially those cases with tubo-ovarian abscess and genital herpes simplex, and especially those unresponsive to standard therapies. All women with a known sexually transmitted disease should also be counseled for HIV testing.

The CDC recommends that all women of childbearing age with high-risk behaviors should be counseled and tested for HIV. We would recommend, however, that all women who are or have been sexually active be counseled and tested for HIV.

Although the issue of mandatory HIV testing of newborns and pregnant women is controversial, the United States Public Health Service recommends that (1) all pregnant women should be routinely counseled and encouraged to be tested for HIV; (2) testing of pregnant women and their infants should be voluntary; and (3) counseling and testing should be offered as early as possible in pregnancy and ideally before a woman becomes pregnant.[4]

■ Medical Care of HIV-infected Women

In addition to routine care for HIV disease, medical care for HIV-infected women should also include attention to their reproductive and endocrine systems. Baseline clinical evaluation of nonpregnant women is the same as men, with the addition of Pap smear and rubella antibody status.

In one study,[5] HIV-infected women had a poorer survival rate than men, even though rates of disease progression did not differ. The most common first events for women other than death were pneumocystis carinii pneumonia (PCP), invasive candidiasis (esophageal or disseminated), and wasting. Bacterial pneumonia and other mycobacterial infections were more frequent in women.

■ Gynecologic Care of HIV-infected Women

Table 7–1 gives an overview of the gynecologic care of HIV-infected women.

TABLE 7–1. GYNECOLOGIC MANAGEMENT OF HIV-INFECTED WOMEN

Examination/Counseling	Frequency
Pelvic examination (including Pap smear, syphilis serology, gonorrhea and *Chlamydia* cultures)	Every 6 months
Colposcopy	Annually and with abnormal Pap smears
Breast examination with pelvic examination. Mammogram as indicated by American Cancer Society guidelines	Every 6 months
Counseling regarding STDs, cervical dysplasia, cancer, family planning, safer sex practices	Routinely

Breasts

There is no evidence that breast cancer is increased in HIV-positive women. Recommendations for breast cancer screening are the same as for women who are HIV negative, and include medical provider examinations, breast self-examination, and mammograms based on American Cancer Society recommendations.

Menstruation

Menstrual irregularities and abnormalities are common among HIV-infected women, especially amenorrhea in late-stage HIV disease, presumably due to cachexia and/or chronic disease. Stress, wasting, and other systemic illnesses can cause dysfunction in the hypothalamic axis and lead to amenorrhea. Some medications can interfere with women's menstrual cycles, such as megestrol and opiates. Platelet disorders such as idiopathic thrombocytopenia purpura (ITP) may cause heavier menstrual cycles.[6]

Vulvovaginal Candidiasis

Vaginal candidiasis is the most common gynecologic disorder and one of the most common medical problems experienced by HIV-infected women. It often precedes oral thrush as a sign of HIV disease, and recurrent or persistent candidiasis is the most frequent early sign of HIV disease among women seeking HIV testing.

Treatment for the initial episode of vaginal candidiasis in the HIV-infected woman should be the standard topical antifungal medication such as clotrimazole (Gyne-Lotrimin). In the absence of correctable causes (oral contraceptives or antibiotics), recurrent or resistant vaginal candidiasis can be treated orally with ketoconazole (Nizoral), 400 mg/day for 14 days, or fluconazole (Diflucan), 200 mg every 4 days for three doses). Liver functions should be monitored carefully with treatment. Fluconazole as a 150-mg single dose has been approved for the treatment of uncomplicated vulvovaginal candidiasis. Ketoconazole and fluconazole are not recommended for pregnant women.[7,8]

HIV Genital Ulcers

Evaluation of ulcerative lesions in HIV-infected women should also include a darkfield exam or a direct immunofluorescence test for *Treponema* and *Hemophilus ducreyi*, viral culture, and biopsy to exclude squamous cell carcinoma.

A new entity, HIV genital ulcer, has recently been described in a few women with HIV. In this group, cultures are all negative and ulcers are unresponsive to standard treatments for chancroid, syphilis, or herpes. When given a trial of zidovudine (Retrovir), the ulcers rapidly healed. Primary HIV ulcer should be in the differential of HIV-infected women with genital ulcers. These ulcers may also appear on other parts of the body where there are mucous membranes.

Pelvic Inflammatory Disease

Pelvic inflammatory disease (PID) is a spectrum of inflammatory disorders in the genital tract of women including endometritis, salpingitis, and tubo-ovarian abscess. Chlamydia and gonorrhea are the most common causes of PID. Other causes include enteric organisms such as *Escherichia coli*, anaerobic cocci, *Mycoplasma hominis*, and *Ureaplasma urealyticum*. Of note, there have been rare case reports of PID caused by *Mycobacterium tuberculosis* in HIV-infected women. Review of a number of small reports suggest that PID may have a different initial presentation and response to treatment in some HIV-positive women and a higher incidence of surgical intervention. These data suggested that the clinical course of PID may be altered by symptomatic HIV infection, and that such patients have blunted local immune defenses resulting in a slower or inadequate response to standard medical therapy. This finding may also explain the lower incidence of gonococci and chlamydia reported by some investigators, implying that PID in HIV-infected women is frequently due to ascent of endogenous lower genital tract pathogens.

The CDC recommends hospitalization and intravenous antibiotics in the treatment of PID in HIV-infected women. Any of the currently approved treatment regimens can be used.[9]

Sexually Transmitted Diseases

Limited data is available on the course of gonococcal and chlamydia infections in HIV-infected women. Therefore, these infections should be treated with standard regimens.

Herpes simplex virus (HSV) infections are frequently seen in HIV-infected persons. HSV ulcers persisting longer than 1 month are associated with severe immunosuppression and are an AIDS-defining event. Case reports suggest that the clinical course of HSV infection may be particularly fulminant in HIV-immunosuppressed women. Women with frequent HSV recurrences are likely to benefit from prophylactic oral acyclovir therapy or other anti-herpetic medicine.

Several case reports indicate that initial treatment with a single dose of benzathine penicillin G may occasionaly fail to cure early syphilis in HIV-infected persons. This may result in relapse and progression to syphilitic meningitis or neurosyphilis. Although syphilis and neurosyphilis are generally treated with standard therapy, higher doses or longer treatment may be needed.[10]

Cervical Disease and Human Papillomavirus

Human papillomavirus (HPV) has been known since the 1970s as a sexually transmitted agent leading to cervical disease.[11] Studies have proven that HPV in the immunocompromised host has a ninefold increase in anogenital infection and a 16-fold increased incidence of cervical intraepithelial neoplasia (CIN) compared with the normal population. HPV types 16 and 18 have been found most commonly in cervical cancers, whereas types 6 and 11 are most frequently associated with benign condyloma or low-grade squamous intraepithelial lesion (SIL). Multiple studies have demonstrated that severe immunosuppression is associated with increased frequency and severity of cervical dysplasia.[12] Studies have demonstrated that HIV-positive women have a much higher incidence of multiple-type HPV infection, which may be related to increased risk of cervical cancer and resistance to standard treatments.[13]

Several studies have demonstrated a high false-negative rate of cytologic screening in predicting CIN in women who are HIV-positive when compared to colposcopy and biopsy. Therefore, a baseline colposcope examination should be considered in HIV-positive women, and for all women with abnormal Pap smears, regardless of previous cytology.

The CDC recommendations as of 1993 for screening women with HIV includes an initial Pap smear, repeated in 6 months if normal, and then annually. If inflammation/reactive atypia is present, they recommend repeat smear in 3 months and colposcopy for SIL or atypical squamous cells. However, these guidelines may overlook other important considerations, including lesions of the vulva or vaginal or perianal area that would not usually be detected with Pap smears only. The advantages of increased routine colposcopy screening include detection of other than cervical lesions, as well as earlier diagnosis and treatment of cervical lesions.[7]

A recent study found that anal human papillomavirus infection and anal cytologic abnormalities occurred more frequently than cervical abnormalities in a small group of women with HIV infection. It remains to be established whether HIV-infected women are at increased risk for anal cancer.[14]

■ Treatment

External Warts

Although there is no form of treatment that has been shown to completely eradicate warts, treatment is recommended to decrease the likelihood of progression to dysplasia, cancer, and exposure to infants during delivery. There are several treatment options, including the following.

1. Podophyllin 10 to 25 percent liquid (should not be used during pregnancy). Apply petroleum jelly on surrounding normal skin, apply podophyllin to lesions, and allow to air dry before dressing. Rinse off after 4 hours. Apply weekly for 4 to 6 weeks.
2. Liquid nitrogen or cryoprobe. Freeze for 60 seconds, thaw, and then refreeze for 60 seconds. Repeat weekly for up to six treatments.
3. Trichloroacetic acid (TCA) 80 to 90 percent liquid (safety during pregnancy not established). Apply to lesions, no rinsing required. Repeat weekly up to six times.
4. Combined cyrotherapy and topical medication. Single 60-second freeze with liquid nitrogen, followed by application of topical liquid.
5. Fluorouracil (Efudex). Apply 2 percent or 5 percent solution or 5 percent cream BID for 3 to 6 weeks.
6. Surgery, laser, or electrocautery.[15]

Internal Vaginal Lesions

Internal vaginal lesions can also be treated also with cryotherapy or, for more extensive lesions, loop extrasurgical excision procedure (LEEP), laser vaporization, or surgery.[15]

Cervical Dysplasias

Treatment is based on colposcopic examination and biopsies. Many experts now agree that cervical dysplasia or CIN and carcinoma in situ (CIS) are points on a spectrum of disease that begins as very mild dysplasia and concludes with invasive cancer of the cervix. The spectrum includes CIN I (mild dysplasia) or human papillomavirus (HPV) effect; CIN II (moderate dysplasia); CIN III (severe dysplasia) or carcinoma in situ, and invasive carcinoma. The goal of all treatment of CIN is to prevent invasive cancer. This is accomplished by either ablation (destruction) or excision (removal) of the entire transformation zone of the cervix.

Dysplasia can be treated very effectively with local destruction of the abonrmal tissue; however, invasive cancer cannot. Therefore, in choosing therapy for CIN the practitioner must always decide whether invasive cancer has been thoroughly and convincingly ruled out. For CIN I and II, cryotherapy is generally preferred. Excisional therapies such as LEEP or cone biopsy are preferred for most CIN III lesions. It is important for women to be closely followed up because of possible persistence of dysplasia or failure of the treatment. It is recommended by some that Pap smear, colposcopy, and endocervical curettage be repeated at 3 months after initial treatment, especially if the lesion was large and more than mild in severity. If the 3 to 6 month post-treatment Pap smears are negative, continue Pap smears every 6 months. Consideration should be given for annual colposcopy.[15]

Cervical Carcinoma

Invasive cervical carcinoma appears to present at a more advanced stage, with higher rates of recurrence and a higher death rate in the HIV-positive woman as compared to HIV-negative women. Treatment is essentially the same regardless of HIV-status, although the greater the immune suppression, the higher the risk of complications.

■ Pregnancy

Many women learn of their HIV status from prenatal screening. At this point, it is ideal to counsel the patient on either pregnancy termination or continuation.

HIV can be transmitted from mother to baby during pregnancy or during the birth process. HIV also can also be transmitted through breast milk. A variety of studies in the United States place the risk of vertical transmission from mother to fetus at 15 to 30 percent. Current data do not suggest that pregnancy accelerates the progression of HIV infection, although most data are from women with CD4 counts above 200. For women in more advanced stages of HIV disease, many experts are concerned that the added stress of pregnancy may lead to worse short- and long-term outcomes for the women and possibly for their babies. In February 1994, the results of a major national study from the National Institute of Allergy and Infectious Diseases AIDS Clinical Trial Group (study 076)[16] demonstrated that zidovudine (Retrovir) may reduce the transmission rate to around 8 percent. The study included relatively healthy women, with CD4 counts above 200, who had never taken zidovudine before. In the study zidovudine was given orally after 14 weeks gestation and intravenously during labor. Oral zidovudine was then initiated in the newborn for 6 weeks (refer to Table 7–2 for specific dosages).

The only significant side effect in newborns was a mild anemia that resolved when zidovudine was discontinued. There was no increase in the number of birth defects. However, it is possible that there could be long-term side effects or problems for women and babies that are not evident yet. Unanswered questions include the value of this regimen in women with lower CD4 counts or in women with previous zidovudine exposure who may have resistance, and whether there is an optimal period of antiviral activity (that is, whether zidovudine should be taken during pregnancy, during labor, and after delivery). It is unknown whether zidovudine prophylaxis during pregnancy will lead to resistance in the mother or the baby, limiting later antiviral applications.

TABLE 7–2. SUMMARY OF REDUCTION OF MATERNAL-INFANT TRANSMISSION OF HUMAN IMMUNODEFICIENCY VIRUS TYPE 1 WITH ZIDOVUDINE TREATMENT STUDY

Study Population[a]

Pregnant women at 14 to 34 weeks of gestation with CD4 counts $\geq 200/mm^3$

Study Regimen

During pregnancy:	100 mg AZT orally 5 times daily
During labor:	Loading dose of 2 mg/kg AZT, followed by continuous infusion 1 mg/kg until cord clamped
For newborns:	2 mg/kg AZT oral syrup every 6 hours starting 8 to 12 hours after birth and continuing until the infant is 6 weeks old

Study Results

Placebo group:	Estimated transmission rate: 25.5 percent (confidence interval, 18.4 percent to 32.5 percent)
AZT-treated group:	Estimated transmission rate 8.3 percent (confidence interval, 3.9 percent to 12.8 percent)
AZT side effects:	No significant difference between treated and untreated mothers. Mild, transient anemia greater in treated infants

[a] 477 women enrolled, 363 infants born at time of analysis.
Adapted from Connor EM, Sperling RS, Gelber R, et al. Reduction of Maternal-Infant Transmission of Human Immunodeficiency Virus Type 1 with Zidovudine Treatment. *N Engl J Med.* 1994;331:1173–1180

PCP prophylaxis should not be withheld from a pregnant woman with a CD4 count of less than 200. Trimethoprim-sulfamethoxazole, dapsone, or aerosolized pentamidine can all be considered safe in pregnancy, although some experts would avoid dapsone in the first trimester, and some do not like to use trimethoprim-sulfamethoxazole close to term because of the theoretical risk of kernicterus in the newborn. Treatment of opportunistic infections in the pregnant woman should not be different from the nonpregnant woman.

Studies continue at this time to investigate more about factors that may contribute to higher rates of vertical transmission including low CD4 counts, viral load and type, mother's stage of infection, and events during labor and delivery (especially premature rupture of membranes). Other studies are focusing on reducing viral load with use of other antiretrovirals (See Chapter 11).

■ Family Planning

Little information is available about optimal contraceptive use in women with HIV. Important considerations are effective protection against pregnancy, sexually transmitted diseases, transmission of HIV, and the impact of the contraceptive on the course of HIV.

Most discussions on this subject in HIV-infected women have focused on preventing the dissemination of virus rather than preventing unwanted pregnancies. Although condoms should ideally be routinely used by all HIV-infected sexually active women to prevent transmission of HIV and STD exposure, a backup method should be offered.

Many HIV-infected women do not want to become pregnant. These women need to be counseled on the different types of contraception, along with their advantages and disadvantages.

Tubal ligation is the most reliable and possibly safest method of contraception for women who do not desire future pregnancy. It is important that this option be based on a woman's own personal choosing, and not encouraged or denied based on serostatus.

The effects of hormonal therapies such as oral contraceptives, Norplant, and Depo-Provera in HIV-infected women are unknown. It is not known whether hormones, particularly oral contraceptives, have adverse interactions with commonly used HIV/AIDS drugs. Contraindications and follow-up at this time are the same as in HIV-negative women.[17]

Intrauterine devices (IUDs) are contraindicated in HIV-infected women due to the increased risk of ascending infection and PID. Spermicidal sponges are also not recommended because of studies that have found vaginal and cervical irritation resulting from the sponges that may enhance HIV transmission.

■ Psychosocial Aspects of HIV in Women

The psychosocial impact of HIV disease among women is formidable considering that women were until recently thought to be a low-risk population. Given statistics showing that HIV disease is most prevalent in people of color and poor communities, it is no wonder that access to care is the leading reason why women are first seen at a late stage of disease or presenting in the emergency room with an opportunistic infection.

Except in major urban areas, practitioners have a low suspicion of HIV-related symptoms in women, who may therefore go undiagnosed until late in their disease. Even if the woman knows her HIV status, she is more likely to be the caregiver of her partner and/or children with HIV, before seeking treatment for herself. The lack of supportive services—child care, transportation, education, and outreach programs—can lead to a feeling of isolation and shame.[18]

The issue of pregnancy in HIV-infected women is one that may bring out many of our own biases and may harm our professional relationship with these women. In many cases, women's reproductive choices have been met with insensitivity and judgments relating to cultural differences and language barriers. Pregnant women must be given information about the options available to them and the risks, benefits, and possible consequences of these options. Prenatal care, social support services, drug treatment programs, and adoption options should also be discussed where appropriate.

A very important nonmedical issue to discuss with HIV-positive patients making decisions about becoming pregnant or continuing a pregnancy, is the woman's feelings and beliefs about bearing a child who may be HIV infected. Possibilities to consider are that the woman may not survive long enough to raise the child to adulthood, and that the woman may lack the support of a partner, family member, or friends who can help with child care.[19] It has been estimated that unless the course of this epidemic changes dramatically, by the year 2000, the overall number of motherless children and adolescents will exceed 80,000. The vast majority of these children will come from poor communities of color.[20]

Access to clinical drug trials have traditionally excluded women of childbearing age for fear of tetragenic affect on a potential fetus. Therefore, much of our information regarding efficacy of medications and dosages has come from trials that did not include women.

Expansion of drug treatment programs and access to them is urgently needed. In 1989, the National Institute of Drug Abuse estimated there were 6.5 million people using drugs, which significantly impaired their health and ability to function, with only 250,000 people in treatment. Efforts to reduce injection drug use in order to decrease transmission of HIV among women are essential. The physical and psychological dependence on drugs can for many women outweigh their fear of acquiring HIV or seeking medical care. Also, women with children may be less likely to access programs for fear that their children will be taken away. Available drug treatment programs have been shown to decrease high-risk behaviors with methadone maintenance, residential therapeutic communities, outpatient programs, support groups, and acupuncture.

Women-controlled barrier methods to prevent STDs, HIV, and unwanted pregnancies are needed, especially for women with little control over their partner's resistance to condom use and also in the case of domestic violence.

■ Summary

There are still many unanswered questions regarding the natural history of HIV infection in women. There are currently two large-scale epidemiology studies underway in the United States: the HIV Epidemiology Research Study (HERS) funded by the Centers for Disease Control and Prevention, and the Women's Interagency HIV Study (WIHS) funded by the National Institutes of Health. Data from these studies are pending.

It is important for practitioners to recognize the gender-specific issues when dealing with HIV infection. The psychosocial, gynecologic, and reproductive issues make HIV infection in women unique, and a multispeciality team approach would ensure quality of care and better compliance. When working with women living with HIV disease, often one has to work within a family network.

Until increased efforts are seen directed at prevention

and education, and until health care providers show a greater willingness to consider all sexually active people at risk and in need of counseling for HIV, we will continue to see increasing infections in women.

References

1. Update: AIDS among women—United States, 1994. *JAMA.* 1995;273:267.
2. Chu SY, Conti L, Schable B, et al. Female-to-female sexual contact and HIV transmission. *JAMA.* 1994; 6:433.
3. Rich JD, Buck A, Tuomala RE, Kazanjian PH. Female homosexual transmission. *Clin Infect Dis.* 1993;17:1003–1005.
4. Focus on women's issues. *J Int Assoc Physicians AIDS Care.* 1995;1:6–10.
5. Melnick SL, Sherer R, Louis TA, et al. Survival and disease progression according to gender of patients with HIV infection. *JAMA.* 1994;272:1915.
6. Wilson S, Lein B. HIV Disease in women. Treatment issues. *Gay Men's Health Crisis Newsletter.* Summer/ Fall 1992;6.
7. Korn AP, Landers DV, et al. Gynecologic disease in women with HIV-1. *J AIDS Retrovirol.* 1995;9:361–370.
8. Minkoff H, DeHovitz J. Care of women infected with the human immunodeficiency virus. *JAMA.* 1991; 266:2253–2258.
9. McCormack, William M. Pelvic inflammatory disease. *N Engl J Med.* 1994;330:115–119.
10. Drugs for sexually transmitted disease. *Med Lett Drugs Ther.* 1994;36:1–6.
11. Johnson CJ, Burnett AF, Willet GD, et al. High frequency of latent and clinical human papillomavirus cervical infections in immunocompromised human immunodeficiency virus-infected women. *Obstet Gynecol.* 1992;79:321–327.
12. Matorras R, Ariceta JM, Rementeria A, et al. Human immunodeficiency virus-induced immunosuppression: A risk factor for human papillomavirus infection. *Am J Obstet Gynecol.* 1991;164:42–44.
13. Koutsky LA, Holmes KK, et al. A cohort study of the risk of cervical intraepithelial neoplasia grade 2 or 3 in relation to papillomavirus infection. *N Engl J Med.* 1992;327:1272-1278.

14. Williams AB, Darragh TM, Vranzan K, et al. Anal and cervical human papillomavirus infection and risk of anal and cervical epithelial abnormalities in human immunodeficiency virus infected women. *Obstet Gynecol.* 1994;83:205–211.

15. Wright VC, Lickrish MB, eds. Basic and Advanced Colpoposcopy. Houston, TX: Biomedical Communication Inc.; 1989:161–222.

16. AZT reduces rate of maternal transmission of HIV. *NIAID News,* February 21, 1994.

17. Denenberg R. Female sex hormones and HIV. *AIDS Clin Care.* 1993;5:69–71.

18. Schable B, Diaz T, Chu SY, et al. Who are the primary caretakers of children born to HIV-infected mothers? Results from a multistate surveillance project. *Pediatrics.* 1995;95: 511–515.

19. Arras JD. AIDS and reproductive decisions: Having children in fear and trembling. *Milbank Q.* 1990; 68:353–381.

20. Michaels D, Levine C. Estimates of the number of motherless youth orphaned by AIDS in the United States. *JAMA.* 1992;263:3456–3461.

part III

DIAGNOSIS AND TREATMENT

eight

CHAPTER

Diagnosis and Treatment of HIV-Related Conditions

Richard D. Muma • Michael J. Borucki • Salah Ayachi • Roberto Canales • Stephen G. Hausrath • Salme E. Lavigne • David P. Paar

In the presence of HIV and immunosuppression, many opportunistic and neoplastic conditions have an increased ability to manifest themselves. Pneumocystosis and Kaposi's sarcoma are still two common conditions, but with the advent of chemoprophylaxis and anti-HIV therapy both have declined somewhat in prevalence.[1] Other frequently reported HIV-related conditions include bacterial pneumonia, nontuberculous mycobacteriosis, septicemia, cytomegalovirus, lymphoma, toxoplasmosis, cryptococcosis, *Mycobacterium tuberculosis*, progressive multifocal leukoencephalopathy, candidiasis, and cryptosporidiosis.[1]

Even though all of these conditions, and others discussed in the chapter, have distinct pathologic findings, they often share signs and symptoms, making their diagnosis difficult to establish. Even more problematic is that some of the signs and symptoms of these conditions are not dissimilar to those of other viral infections including HIV itself.

This chapter will attempt to bring together essential information regarding the most common HIV-related conditions. It is hoped that after reviewing this material the reader will have a better understanding of some of the more common HIV-related conditions.

■ HIV and Persistent Generalized Lymphadenopathy

As early as 1979 and 1980, with the discovery of HIV, clinicians began observing persistent generalized lymphadenopathy (PGL) in otherwise healthy homosexual men.[2] Today, PGL is defined as palpable lymphadenopathy of 1 cm or greater in size involving two or more extrainguinal sites and persisting for more than 3 months in the absence of a concurrent illness or condition other than HIV infection to explain the findings.[3] In 1993, PGL was been placed in group "A" of the CDC classification system for HIV infections.[4]

Clinical Manifestations

Lymphadenopathy may either be discovered by the patient or noted during a routine physical exam in an asymptomatic individual.[2] Symptoms such as fatigue, malaise, low-grade fever, and occasional night sweats may accompany the lymphadenopathy in some patients, as well as a sore throat, fever, and myalgias at the onset of PGL or within few months of onset.[2] Lymph nodes are characteristically firm, nontender, and freely mobile, ranging from 1 to 5 cm in size and involving multiple sites such as the cervical, supraclavicular, posterior auricular, submandibular, axillary, occipital, and epitrochlear locations.[2]

Diagnosis

Before the diagnosis of PGL can be made, a patient must have palpable lymph nodes of 1 cm or greater involving two or more extrainguinal sites and persisting for more than 3 months in the absence of a concurrent illness or condition other than HIV infection.[2]

Treatment

There is no treatment protocol for patients with PGL. The primary consideration is of alternate causes of adenopathy, such as syphilis, toxoplasmosis, hepatitis B, Epstein-Barr virus, cytomegalovirus, drug reactions, histoplasmosis, tuberculosis, and *Cryptococcus*. Routine follow-up every 3 months, accompanied by an evaluation of the immune system (CD4/CD8 ratio, absolute CD4, viral load, white blood cell count, hemoglobin/hematocrit, and platelets), is suggested for asymptomatic patients (see Chapter 5). For patients who are symptomatic and showing signs of progression of their HIV infection (decrease in CD4) and PGL, further evaluation, depending on the patient's symptoms, may be necessary.

■ *Pneumocystis Carinii* Pneumonia

Pneumocystis is generally accepted as being a protozoan, although other authors may classify it as a fungus. Evidence exists to support either substantiation.[5] The incidence of *Pneumocystis* infection is uncertain. In non-HIV infected population, serologic studies show that up to 75 percent of children develop detectable antibody by 2 to 4 years of age. This suggests that although disease caused by *Pneumocystis* is rare, infection may be common. In humans, the disease occurs worldwide in all age groups, either as epidemics in crowded nurseries or as sporadic cases among older children and adults. Epidemics in nurseries, as well as clustering of cases in cancer wards, suggest the possibility of airborne or respiratory spread. Historically, *Pneumocystis carinii* was a significant pathogen primarily in malnourished and impoverished children living in orphanages.[5]

Pneumocystis carinii pneumonia (PCP) remains the most serious opportunistic infection affecting HIV-infected adults and children despite recommendations for chemoprophylaxis for both groups.[6–9] In both age groups, at least half of all cases of PCP occur in persons with previously undiagnosed HIV infection.[6] This is mostly attributed to late identification of HIV-infected individuals and lack of appropriate medical care once identified.[10] Mortality rates, however, have improved with the advent of chemoprophylaxis, with PCP causing only 14 percent of AIDS-related deaths, down from the previous 32 percent.[1,10] The prognosis is better with an initial episodes, than with the second and third episodes, but this may relate more to advancing immunosuppression than anything else. Thus, it is appropriate to devote considerable attention to the manifestations, diagnosis, and therapy of this process in an effort to decrease the morbidity and mortality that *Pneumocystis* causes in this population.[11]

Despite intense interest in attempting to unravel the biology and pathophysiology of PCP, the clinician remains confronted with several puzzling features of the illness:

- The organism cannot be reliably cultured.
- Serologic testing is imprecise and insensitive, and for diagnostic purposes is not routinely available.

- In AIDS patients, the signs and symptoms of the illness are frequently subtle and indistinct.
- Recurrent episodes of pneumonia are uniquely common in AIDS patients, and simultaneous occurrence with other pulmonary processes, such as pulmonary Kaposi's sarcoma or cytomegalovirus pneumonitis, complicates management of the illness.[11–18]

Clinical Manifestations

The classic signs and symptoms of PCP are an abnormal lung exam with fever, shortness of breath, nonproductive cough, and dry rales. Alternatively, there may be a subtle, prolonged preclinical course; mild hypoxia, normal chest x-ray film, fever, and cough may be minimal. Investigation of new minor symptoms often leads to early diagnosis.

Typically, the chest x-ray film shows a diffuse interstitial infiltrate, although discrete areas of pneumonia may be seen (Figs. 8–1 and 8–2). The presence of an effusion or of a nodule is sufficiently rare as to suggest an alternate diagnosis. The results of gallium scanning are abnormal in a significant number of cases, even those in which the chest x-ray is normal. However, false positives are common with the gallium scan, occurring in approximately half of the cases.

Diagnosis

The definitive diagnosis of PCP is established by demonstrating the presence of organisms. Fiberoptic bronchoscopy is the procedure of choice.[11] Bronchoalveolar lavage via bronchoscopy has nearly 90 percent sensitivity[11] and significantly less morbidity, making it the diagnostic procedure of choice. Open-lung biopsy is rarely necessary.

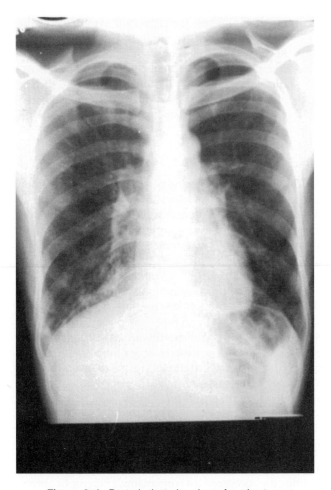

Figure 8–1. Posterior/anterior view of a chest x-ray from a patient with PCP showing diffuse interstitial infiltrates. (*With permission from* Phys Assist. *1991;15:15.*)

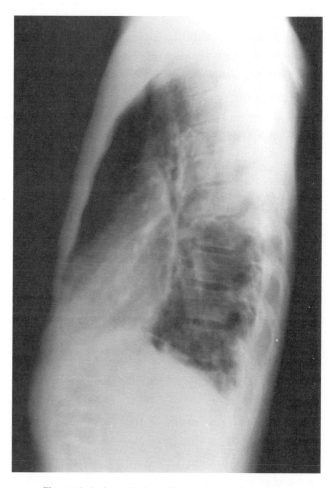

Figure 8–2. Lateral view of a chest x-ray from a patient with PCP showing diffuse interstitial infiltrates. (*With permission from* Phys Assist. *1991;15:15.*)

Treatment

First line therapy can be initiated with intravenous pentamidine isethionate (Pentam) (3–4 mg/kg per day) or intravenous trimethoprim and sulfamethoxazole (Bactrim or Septra) (TMP-SMZ; 15 to 20 mg of trimethoprim per kg per day, and 75 to 100 mg of sulfamethoxazole per kg per day).[19] The efficacy of these two regimens is similar; there is an 85 percent or greater rate of response during the first episode and somewhat poorer results for subsequent episodes. The addition of corticosteroid is beneficial in cases where the PO_2 is less than 70 mm Hg or the A-a gradient exceeds 35 mm Hg. Second line therapies for mild to moderate PCP in those who are intolerant to first line therapy include: clindamycin (Cleocin) with primaguine, dapsone with trimethoprim, or atuvaquone (Mepron). For moderate to severe disease trimetrexate (Neutrexin) is an alternative therapy.

A slow response to therapy is common, and radiographic evidence of improvement may be delayed. The optimal duration of therapy is unclear, but a minimum of 2 weeks for mild disease, and 3 weeks for more severe disease, is recommended. Repeat chest x-ray should be obtained at the beginning of therapy to measure response. Fevers and dyspnea commonly take 5 to 7 days to resolve.

Prevention

For primary prophylaxis (CD4 cell count < $200/mm^3$; or unexplained fever for 2 weeks or oropharyngeal candidiasis) and secondary prophylaxis (prior history of PCP), it is recommended to use oral TMP-SMZ DS, one daily (Tables 8–1 and 8–2).[20] For those allergic to TMP-SMZ, aerosolized pentamidine (Nebupent), dapsone, or atovaquone may be used.

TMP-SMZ Toxicities

- Rash
- Fever
- Leukopenia
- Hyponatremia
- Abnormal liver-function tests

Pentamidine Toxicities

- Leukopenia
- Azotemia/kidney failure
- Elevated levels of transaminases
- Dysglycemia
- Hypotension

Atovaquone Toxicities

- Rash
- Nausea
- Diarrhea
- Headache
- Vomiting
- Fever

■ Histoplasmosis

Infection with *Histoplasma capsulatum* has been encountered in many areas of the world but is much more frequent in certain areas such as the United States.[21] Within the United States, infection is more common in the Ohio and Mississippi river valleys and the broad area surrounding them. *Histoplasma* prefers a moist environment to grow, particularly when enriched by droppings from birds or bats. The fungus has been isolated from many sites; one common example is dirt from chicken coops and caves. *Histoplasma* is introduced into the body through inhalation; infection begins in the lungs and can become systemic.

TABLE 8–1. PROPHYLAXIS FOR FIRST EPISODE OF OPPORTUNISTIC DISEASE IN HIV-INFECTED ADULTS AND ADOLESCENTS

		Preventive Regimens	
Pathogen	Indication	First Choice	Alternatives
Strongly Recommended as Standard of Care			
Pneumocystis carinii[a]	CD4+ count of < 200/μL or unexplained fever for ≥ 2 w or otopharyngeal candidiasis	TMP-SMZ, 1 DS PO qd (AI)	TMP-SMZ, 1 SS PO qd (AI) or 1 DS PO tiw (AII); dapsone, 50 mg PO bid or 100 mg PO qd, (AI); dapsone, 50 mg PO qd, plus pyrimethamine, 50 mg PO qw plus leucovorin, 25 mg PO qw (AI); dapsone, 200 mg PO qw, plus pyrimethamine, 75 mg PO qw, plus leucovorin, 25 mg PO qw (AI); aerosolized pentamidine, 300 mg qm via Respirgard II nebulizer (AI)
Mycobacterium tuberculosis[b] Isoniazid-sensitive	TST reaction of ≥ 5 mm or prior positive TST result	Isoniazid, 300 mg PO, plus pyridoxine, 50 mg PO qd × 12	Rifampin, 600 mg PO qd × 12 months (BII)

Pathogen	Indication	First Choice	Alternatives
	without treatment or contact with case of active tuberculosis	months (AI); *or* isoniazid, 900 mg PO, *plus* pyridoxine, 50 mg PO biw × 12 months (BIII)	
Isoniazid-resistant	Same as above; high probability of exposure to isoniazid-resistant tuberculosis	Rifampin, 600 mg PO qd × 12 months (BII)	Rifabutin, 300 mg PO qd × 12 months (CIII)
Multidrug-resistant (isoniazid and rifampin)	Same as above; high probability of exposure to multidrug-resistant tuberculosis	Choice of drugs requires consultation with public health authorities	None
Toxoplasma gondii[c]	IgG antibody to Toxoplasma and CD4+ count of < 100/µL	TMP-SMZ, 1 DS PO qd (AII)	TMP-SMZ, 1 SS PO qd *or* 1 DS PO tiw (AII); dapsone, 50 mg PO qd *plus* pyrimethamine, 50 mg PO qw *plus* leucovorin, 25 mg PO qw (AI)

Recommended for Consideration in All Patients

Pathogen	Indication	First Choice	Alternatives
Streptococcus pneumonias[d]	All patients	Pneumococcal vaccine, 0.5 mL im x 1 (BIII)	None
Mycobacterium avium complex	CD4+ count of < 75/µL	Azithromycin, 1200 mg PO qw	Clarithromycin, 500 mg PO bid (CIII); Rifabutin, 300 mg PO qd (BII)

TABLE 8-1. *(continued)*

Not Recommended for Most Patients, Indicated for Consideration Only in Selected Populations or Patients

Pathogen	Indication	Preventive Regimens	
		First Choice	**Alternatives**
Bacteria	Neutropenia	Granulocyte colony-stimulating factor 5–10 μg/kg sc qd x 2–4 w; *or* granulocyte macrophage colony-stimulating factor, 250 μg/m² iv over 2 h qd x 2–4 w (CIII)	None
Candida species	CD4+ count of < 50/μL	Fluconazole, 100–200 mg PO qd (CI)	Ketoconazole, 200 mg PO qd (CIII)
Cryptococcus neoformans[e]	CD4+ count of < 50/μL	Fluconazole, 100–200 mg PO qd (BI)	Itraconazole, 200 mg PO qd (CIII)
Histoplasma capsulatum[e]	CD4+ count of < 50/μL endemic geographic area	Itraconazole, 200 mg PO qd (CIII)	Fluconazole, 200 mg PO qd (CIII)
Coccidioides immitis[e]	CD4+ count of < 50/μL endemic geographic area	Fluconazole, 200 mg PO qd (CIII)	Itraconazole, 200 mg PO qd (CIII)
CMV[f]	CD4+ count of < 50 μL and CMV antibody positivity	Oral ganciclovir, 1 g PO tid (CIII)	None

Pathogen	Indication	First choice	Alternatives
Unknown (herpes viruses?)[g]	CD4+ count of < 200/μL	Acyclovir, 800 mg PO qid (CIII)	Acyclovir, 200 mg PO tid/qid (CIII)

Recommended for Consideration[h]

Pathogen	Indication	First choice	Alternatives
Hepatitis B virus[d]	All susceptible (anti-HBc-negative) patients	Energix-B, 20 μg im × 3 (BIII); or Recombivax HB, 10 μg im × 3 (BIII)	None
Influenza virus[d]	All patients (annually, before influenza season)	Whole or split virus, 0.5 mL im/y (BIII)	Rimantadine, 100 mg PO bid (CIII); or amantadine 100 mg PO bid (CIII)[i]

Not all of the recommended regimens reflect current Food and Drug Administration-approved labeling. Anti-HBc, antibody to hepatitis B core antigen; biw, twice weekly; CMV, cytomegalovirus; DS, double-strength tablet; qm, monthly; qw, weekly; ss, single-strength tablet; tiw, three times weekly; TMP-SMZ, trimethoprim-sulfamethoxazole; TST, tuberculin skin test. The Respigard II nebulizer is manufactured by Marquest, Englewood, CO; Energix-B by SmithKline Beecham, Rixensart, Belgium; and Recombivax HB by Merck & Co., West Point, PA. Letters and Roman numerals in parentheses after regimens indicate the strength of the recommendation and the quality of the evidence supporting it. A = Supported by evidence that is both statistically and clinically persuasive, are strongly recommended, should always be offered, and are considered standard of care; B = recommended for consideration; C= considered optional; D = should generally not be offered; E = contraindicated. Roman numeral rating I–III refer to the quality of evidence that forms the basis for recommendations regarding the use of a product or measure for preventing opportunistic infections in HIV-infected persons.

[a] Patients receiving dapsone should be tested for glucose-6-phosphate dehydrogenase deficiency. A dosage of 50 mg qd is probably less effective than a dosage of 100 mg qd The efficacy of parenteral pentamidine (e.g., 4 mg/kg/qm) is uncertain. Inadequate data are available on the efficacy and safety of atovaquone or clindamycin/primaquine. Sulfadoxine/pyrimethamine (Fansidar, Roche Laboratories, Nutley, NJ) is rarely used because it can elicit severe hypersensitivity reactions. TMP-SMZ and dapsone/pyrimethamine (and possibly dapsone alone) appear to be protective against toxoplasmosis. TMP-SMZ may reduce the frequency of some bacterial infections. Patients receiving therapy for toxoplasmosis with sulfadiazine/pyrimethamine are protected against *P. Carinii* pneumonia and do not need TMP-SMZ.

TABLE 8–1. *(continued)*

[b] Directly observed therapy is required for 900 mg of Isonizid biw; isoniazid regimens should include pyridoxine to prevent peripheral neuropathy. Exposure to multidrug-resistant tuberculosis may require prophylaxis with two drugs; consult public health authorities. Possible regimens include pyrazinamide plus either ethambutol or a fluoroquinolone.

[c] Protection against *T. gondii* is provided by the preferred antipneumocystis regimens. Pyrimethamine alone probably provides little, if any, protection. Dapsone alone cannot be recommended on the basis of currently available data.

[d] Data are inadequate concerning clinical benefit of vaccines against *S. pneumoniae*, influenza virus, and hepatitis B virus in HIV-infected persons, although it is logical to assume that those patients who develop antibody responses will derive some protection. Some authorities are concerned that immunization may stimulate the replication of HIV. Prophylaxis with TMP-SMZ may provide some clinical benefit by reducing the frequency of bacterial infections, but the prevalence of *S. pneumoniae* resistant to TMP-SMX is increasing. Hepatitis B vaccine has been recommended for all children and adolescents and for all adults with risk factors for hepatitis B infection.

[e] There may be a few unusual occupational or other circumstances under which prophylaxis should be considered; consult a specialist.

[f] Data on oral ganciclovir are still being evaluated; the durability of its effect is unclear. Acyclovir is not protective against CMV.

[g] Data regarding the efficacy of acyclovir for prolonging survival are controversial; if acyclovir is beneficial, the biologic basis for the effect and the optimal dose and timing of therapy are uncertain.

[h] These immunizations or chemoprophylactic regimens are not targeted against pathogens traditionally classified as opportunistic but should be considered for use in HIV-infected patients. While the use of those products is logical, their clinical efficacy has not been validated in this population.

[i] During outbreaks of influenza A.

From CDC. *USPHS/IDSA guidelines for the prevention of opportunistic infections in persons infected with HIV: A summary. MMWR. 1995;44:24–25.*

TABLE 8–2. PROPHYLAXIS FOR RECURRENCE OF OPPORTUNISTIC DISEASE (AFTER CHEMOTHERAPY FOR ACUTE DISEASE) IN HIV-INFECTED ADULTS AND ADOLESCENTS

Pathogen	Indication	Preventive Regimens	
		First Choice	Alternatives
Recommended for Life as Standard of Care			
Pneumocystis carinii	Prior *P. carinii* pneumonia	TMP-SMZ, 1 DS PO qd (AI)	TMP-SMZ, 1 SS PO qd (AI) *or* 1 DS PO tiw (AII); dapsone 50 mg PO bid *or* 100 mg PO qd (AI); dapsone, 50 mg PO qd, *plus* pyrimethamine, 50 mg PO qw, *plus* leucovorin, 25 mg PO qw (AI); dapsone, 200 mg PO qw, *plus* pyrimethamine, 75 mg PO qw, *plus* leucovorin, 25 mg PO qw (AI); aerosolized pentamidine, 300 mg qm via Respirgard II nebulizer (AI)
Toxoplasma gondii[a]	Prior toxoplasmic encephalitis	Sulfadiazine, 1.0–1.5 g PO q6h, *plus* pyrimethamine, 25–75 mg PO qd, *plus* leucovorin, 10–25 mg PO qd-qid (AII)	Clindamycin, 300–450 mg PO q6-8h, *plus* pyrimethamine, 25–75 PO qd, *plus* leucovorin, 10–25 mg PO qd-qid (AII)

TABLE 8-2. *(continued)*

| Pathogen | Indication | Preventive Regimens | |
		First Choice	*Alternatives*
Mycobacterium avium complex[b]	Documented disseminated disease	Clarithromycin, 500 mg PO bid, *plus* one or more of the following: ethambutol, 15 mg/kg PO qd; rifabutin, 300 mg PO qd; ciprofloxacin, 500–750 mg PO bid (BIII)	Azithromycin, 500 mg PO qd, *plus* one or more of the following: ethambutol, 15 mg/kg PO qd; rifabutin, 300 mg PO qd; ciprofloxacin, 500–750 mg PO bid (BIII)
Cytomegalovirus[c]	Prior end-organ disease	Ganciclovir, 5–6 mg/kg iv 5–7 d/w or 1,000 mg PO tid (AI); *or* foscarnet, 90–120 mg/kg iv qd (AI)	Sustained-release implants
Cryptococcus neoformans	Documented disease	Fluconazole, 200 mg PO qd (AI)	Itraconazole, 200 mg PO qd (BIII); amphotericin B, 0.6–1.0 mg/kg iv qw-tiw (AI)
Histoplasma capsulatum	Documented disease	Itraconazole, 200 mg PO bid (AII)	Amphotericin B, 1.0 mg/kg iv qw (AI); fluconazole, 200–400 mg PO qd (BII)
Coccidioides immitis	Documented disease	Fluconazole, 200 mg PO qd (AII)	Amphotericin B, 1.0 mg/kg iv qw (AI); itraconazole, 200 mg PO bid (AII); ketoconazole, 400–800 mg PO qd (BII)

Salmonella species (non-typhi)[d]	Bacteremia	Ciprofloxacin 500 mg PO bid for several months (BII)	None

Recommended Only if Subsequent Episodes are Frequent or Severe

Herpes simplex virus	Frequent/severe recurrences	Acyclovir, 200 mg PO tid or 400 mg PO bid (AI)	None
Candida species (oral, vaginal, or esophageal)	Frequent/severe recurrences	Fluconazole, 100–200 mg PO qd (AI)	Ketoconazole, 200 mg PO qd (BIII); itraconazole, 100 mg PO qd (BIII); clotrimazole troche, 10 mg PO 5×/d (BII); nystatin 5×10⁵U PO 5×/d (CIII)

Not all of the recommended regimens reflect current Food and Drug Administration-approved labeling. DS, double-strength tablet; qm, monthly; qw, weekly; SS, single-strength tablet; tiw, three times weekly; TMP-SMZ, trimethoprim-sulfamethoxazole. The Respirgard II nebulizer is manufactured by Marquest, Englewood, CO. Letters and Roman numerals in parentheses after regimens indicate the strength of the recommendation and the quality of the evidence supporting it. (Refer to table 8–1 for explanation)

[a] Only pyrimethamine/sulfadiazine confers protection against *P. carinii* pneumonia.

[b] The long-term efficacy of any regimen is not well established. Many multiple-drug regimens are poorly tolerated. Drug interactions (e.g., those seen with clarithromycin/rifabutin) can be problematic. Rifabutin has been associated with uveitis, especially when given at daily doses of > 300 mg or along with fluconazole or clarithromycin.

[c] Ganciclovir and foscarnet delay relapses by only modest intervals (often only 4–8 weeks). Ocular implants with sustained-release ganciclovir appear promising.

[d] Efficacious eradication of *Salmonella* has been demonstrated only for ciprofloxacin.

From CDC. USPHS/IDSA guidelines for the prevention of opportunistic infections in persons infected with HIV: A summary. MMWR. 1995; 44:26.

Clinical Manifestations

The vast majority of infections present with a fever of uncertain origin with localizing findings as the infection progresses, or with cough, fever, and malaise. Chest x-ray findings include hilar adenopathy with or without one or more areas of pneumonitis. Acute disseminated histoplasmosis may be mistaken for miliary tuberculosis with severe disease. Common findings include fever, emaciation, hepatosplenomegaly, lymphadenopathy, jaundice, anemia, leukopenia, and thrombocytopenia.

Diagnosis

Serologic tests and clinical manifestations may leave one to suspect histoplasmosis, but definitive diagnosis requires demonstration by culture or histology.[22] In disseminated histoplasmosis, cultures of bone marrow, blood, urine sediment, and biopsy specimens are usually positive.

Treatment

All patients with disseminated or chronic pulmonary histoplasmosis should receive intravenous amphotericin B (Fungizone).[19] The therapy usually takes 10 to 12 weeks and requires doses of 0.4 to 0.6 mg/kg per day (total dose of 1.0 to 1.5 g). Maintenance therapy is required, and amphotericin B (50 to 100 mg intravenously) can be given weekly or biweekly. Itraconazole (Sporanox, 200 to 400 mg in divided doses orally with food daily) for 3 months, or until the infection has resolved, is the preferred maintenance agent for *Histoplasma* because of efficacy and the convenience of oral dosing. This drug appears to be effective for maintenance too, and 200 mg twice a day has been proven effective.[23]

Prevention

Although HIV-infected persons living in or visiting histoplasmosis-endemic areas cannot completely avoid exposure to *H. capsulatum*, they should avoid activities known to be associated with increased risk (such as cleaning chicken coops, disturbing soil beneath bird-roosting sites, and exploring caves).[20] According to the CDC, no recommendation can be made regarding chemoprophylaxis for HIV-infected persons in histoplasmosis-endemic areas or for histoplasmin-positive persons in nonendemic areas.[20] However, there may be a few unusual occupational or other circumstances under which prophylaxis should be considered.[20] If this is the case, a specialist should be consulted (Tables 8–1 and 8–2).

Amphotericin B Toxicities

- Decreased renal function
- Hypokalemia
- Thrombocytopenia
- Flushing
- Generalized pain
- Convulsions
- Chills
- Fever
- Phlebitis
- Headache
- Anemia
- Anorexia
- Itraconazole toxicities
- Nausea
- Rash
- Vomiting

Itraconazole Toxicities

- GI upset
- Rash

- Edema
- Malaise
- Fever
- Headache
- Dizziness
- Psychiatric effects
- Hypertension
- Hypokalemia
- Hepatic dysfunction
- Impotence
- Hepatitis

■ *Mycobacterium tuberculosis*

After decades of steady decline, *Mycobacterium tuberculosis* has been on the rise in the United States since 1985.[24–26] This increase reflects the interaction of the concurrent HIV epidemic, a rise in homelessness, and the discontinuation of many statewide TB control programs in the 1970s.[27] 1993 was the first year since 1985 that saw a decline in new cases from the previous year, although the incidence was still 14 percent greater than that reported for 1985.[28] Reports of multidrug-resistant strains of tuberculosis have complicated this disease, which poses an urgent public health problem.[29] In response to some of these issues, the World Health Organization has declared tuberculosis a global emergency.[30] Tuberculosis now effects more than one third of the world population.[31]

Persons with HIV infection are at increased risk for TB resulting from both newly acquired disease and from reactivation of latent infections.[24]

Clinical Manifestations

Disseminated disease or limited extrapulmonary tuberculosis (especially in the lymph nodes) occurs in 70 to 80 percent of HIV-infected patients with tuberculosis. Even when the initial presentation involves the lung, an atypical picture is common. Classical upper-lobe apical disease and cavitation are infrequent; the chest x-ray films may reveal only adenopathy or middle-lobe or lower-lobe infiltrates indistinguishable from those produced by other opportunistic infections. Symptoms usually include fever, night sweats, cough, and weight loss, again making the diagnosis of tuberculosis difficult to separate from that of other opportunistic diseases.

Diagnosis

The diagnosis of tuberculosis should be made by bronchoscopy or through biopsy of involved organs. Sputum smear and culture should be obtained but are less helpful, because of the often disseminated nature of the disease in HIV-infected individuals. Tuberculin skin test (TST) is also less helpful in the HIV-infected individual, because of the decreased ability to react to antigen skin testing in general. However, patients who are HIV positive and TST positive should receive appropriate therapy. Blood cultures are occasionally positive, and new tests (RNA-DNA probes) may allow rapid diagnosis of mycobacterial infection and identification of the species of mycobacteria from a variety of body fluids. Cultures and acid-fast bacillus smears of all suspicious areas should be obtained.

Treatment

Although tuberculosis is increasingly common among AIDS patients, the number of available antituberculosis antibiotics has increased very little since the 1970s.[19] The available treatment is as follows:

- Isoniazid (INH)—5 to 10 mg/kg per day; usually 300 mg orally daily for 6 months to 12 months, and

- Pyridoxine (vitamin B$_6$)—50 mg orally daily for 6 months or as long as on INH treatment, and
- Rifampin (Rifadin)—9 mg/kg per day; usually 600 mg orally daily for 6 months to 12 months, and
- Ethambutol (Myambutol)—15 mg/kg per day, usually 800 to 1200 mg orally daily for 2 months and/or
- Pyrazinamide (PZA)—25 mg/kg per day orally daily for 2 months (in areas of INH resistance exceeding 4% a four drug regimen should be instituted).
- For multidrug resistant tuberculosis, five to six drugs are recommended, which include isoniazid, rifampin, pyrazinamide, ethambutol, an aminoglycoside (amikacin, streptomycin, kanamycin, capreomycin), and a quinolone (ciprofloxacin, ofloxacin, levofloxacin). The exact drug combination is under investigation and awaits the results of current clinical trials. If a patient presents with resistant strains of TB, an expert in this area should be consulted.

Prevention

If an individual has a TST of 5 mm or more, or has a prior positive TST result without treatment or contact with a case of active tuberculosis, the regimen prescribed should be INH 300 mg orally daily for 12 months plus pyridoxine 50 mg orally daily while on INH (Tables 8–1 and 8–2).[20] In individuals who cannot tolerate INH, prophylactic treatment may be completed with rifampin (600 mg PO qd).

Isoniazid Toxicity
- Peripheral neuropathy
- Skin rash
- Hepatotoxicity
- Pyridoxine deficiency

Rifampin Toxicity

- Hepatotoxicity
- Gastrointestinal upset
- Fever

Ethambutol Toxicity

- Reduced visual acuity
- Optic neuritis
- Gastrointestinal upset
- Peripheral neuritis
- Gout

Pyrazinamide Toxicity

- Hepatotoxicity
- Fever
- Rash

■ Central Nervous System Toxoplasmosis

The most common cause of focal encephalitis in patients with AIDS is reactivation of a latent infection with *Toxoplasma gondii*.[32] Human infection usually occurs following ingestion of tissue cysts in undercooked or raw meat, organ transplantation, fecally contaminated food, goat's milk, or transmission of trophozoite from mother to fetus in utero.[33,34] The cat is the definitive host for *Toxoplasma*.[35] Infection usually occurs at a young age and remains dormant in individuals with healthy immune systems. However, in patients infected with HIV and a depressed immune system, this protozoan infection becomes reactivated.[35]

Clinical Manifestations

Symptoms range from mild headache and fever to focal neurologic deficits, seizures, and in some cases, coma. Ex-

TABLE 8–3. MAJOR NEUROLOGIC MANIFESTATIONS OF HIV INFECTION

Diagnosis	CD4+ Count (cells/mm³)	Presenting Symptoms	Neurologic Signs	Diagnostic Studies	Therapy
HIV dementia	< 200	Memory loss, gait disorder, behavioral change	Dementia, spasticity, psychosis	CT/MRI: brain atrophy, white matter abnormalities; CSF; increased β_2-microglobulin	High-dose zidovudine clinical trial
Toxoplasma encephalitis	< 200	Headache, fever, confusion, lethargy, seizures	Dementia, ataxia, hemiparesis	Serum *Toxoplasma* antibodies; CT/MRI; multiple enhancing lesions, edema	Pyrimethamine, sulfadiazine: clindamycin
CNS lymphoma	< 100	Headache, confusion, lethargy, memory loss, seizures	Dementia, hemiparesis, aphasia	CT/MRI: enhancing lesions (especially if single); stereotactic biopsy	Radiotherapy
Progressive multifocal leukoencephalopathy	< 100	Lethargy, confusion, weakness	Hemiparesis, ataxia, visual disturbance	CT/MRI: multiple hypodense, nonenhancing white matter lesions; stereotactic biopsy	High-dose zidovudine, Ara-C (IV, IT): clinical trial
CMV encephalitis	< 50	Rapidly progressive confusion, apathy, weakness	Dementia, cranial neuropathies, spasticity	CT, MRI: periventricular and meningeal abnormalities; CSF: CMV culture, PCR; electrolyte abnormalities	Ganciclovir, foscarnet

	CD4 count	Clinical features	Diagnosis	Treatment
Vacuolar myelopathy	< 200	Gait dysfunction, lower extremity weakness and stiffness, urinary dysfunction	MRI/CSF: normal or nonspecific abnormalities	Baclofen, physical therapy
Cryptococcus neoformans meningitis	< 200	Lethargy, confusion, meningeal signs, cranial nerve palsies	CSF India ink, serum and CSF *Cryptococcus neoformans* antigen and culture	Amphotericin B (plus or minus flucytosine), fluconazole
Neurosyphilis	Any	Headache, memory loss, visual disturbances	Dementia, stroke, meningeal or myelopathic signs, cranial nerve palsies	CSF: increased leukocyte count, increased protein; serum and CSF VDRL	IV penicillin (plus probenecid)
Distal symmetrical polyneuropathy	< 200	Distal numbness, paresthesias, pain	Stocking-glove sensory loss, decreased ankle reflexes	EMG: distal axonopathy	Neurotoxin withdrawal, analgesics, tricyclic antidepressants, anticonvulsants, capsaicin
Inflammatory demyelinating polyneuropathy	> 500, < 50	Progressive weakness, paresthesias	Weakness, areflexia, mild sensory loss	CSF: increased leukocyte count, elevated protein; EMG: demyelination	Early (increased CD4 count): plasmapheresis, IVIg steroids; late (decreased CD4 count) ganciclovir

TABLE 8-3. *(continued)*

Diagnosis	CD4+ Count (cells/mm³)	Presenting Symptoms	Neurologic Signs	Diagnostic Studies	Therapy
Mononeuropathy multiplex	> 500, < 50	Facial weakness, foot drop, wrist drop	Multifocal cranial and peripheral neuropathies	EMG: multifocal axonal neuropathy; nerve biopsy: inflammation, vasculitis, CMV inclusions	Early: none; late: ganciclovir
Progressive polyradiculopathy	< 50	Lower extremity weakness, paresthesias, urinary dysfunction	Flaccid paraparesis, saddle anesthesia, decreased reflexes, urinary retention	CSF: increased leukocytes (PMNs), CMV culture; PCR; EMG: polyradiculopathy	Ganciclovir, foscarnet
Myopathy	Any	Muscle weakness, myalgia, weight loss	Proximal muscle weakness	Increased creatine kinase; EMG: irritative myopathy; muscle biopsy: myofiber degeneration, inflammation, inclusions	Zidovudine reduction or withdrawal, corticosteroids

CMV, cytomegalovirus; CNS, central nervous system; CSF, cerebrospinal fluid; CT, computed tomography; EMG, electromyography; IT, intrathecal; IV, intravenous; IVIg, intravenous immunoglobulin; MRI, magnetic resonance imaging; PCR, polymerase chain reaction; PMN, polymorphonuclear leukocytes.
With permission from Simpson DM, Tagliati M. Neurologic manifestations of HIV infection. Ann Intern Med. 1994;121:770.

tracerebral involvement and coexistent chorioretinitis are occasionally reported. (Table 8–3).[35]

Diagnosis

The most useful diagnostic test for toxoplasmosis has been the CT scan or MRI (Fig. 8–3). Lesions are usually multiple, ring enhancing with contrast, associated with cerebral edema, and located in cortical or subcortical regions of the brain, such as the basal ganglia.[35,36] Serologic tests are of value in the diagnosis of toxoplasmosis in AIDS. However, antibody to toxoplasma is prevalent in the general population, and its presence, therefore, has a low predictive value for active infection. Alternatively, very few patients with AIDS and toxoplasmosis are seronegative for toxoplasmosis, so a negative toxo-IgG strongly suggests an alternate etiology. The clinical and radiologic picture of toxoplasmosis of the central nervous system can be mimicked by several other conditions, including lymphoma, histoplasmosis, nocardiosis, CNS cryptococcus, progressive multifocal leukoencephalopathy, tuberculosis, cytomegalovirus, Kaposi's sarcoma, and hemorrhage.[32,35] Because noninvasive tests lack specificity, definitive diagnosis requires biopsy of the brain, either by open excision or by stereotactically guided needle. However, because of the potential morbidity resulting from brain biopsy and the possibility of false-negative results, some centers favor empirical therapy in patients with positive serologic findings, mass lesions of the CNS, and a clinical picture compatible with toxoplasmosis.[36]

Treatment

Treatment with oral pyrimethamine (Daraprim, 200 mg loading dose, then 25 mg/day) and sulfadiazine (100 mg/kg per day up to a maximum of 8 g/day) is usually

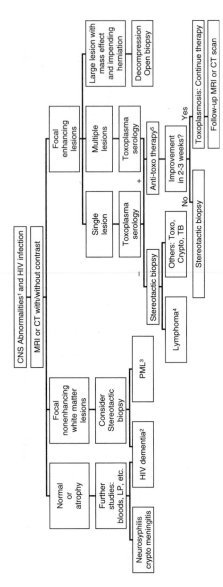

Figure 8-3. Algorithm for the management of brain lesions in patients with HIV infection. [a](Headache, mental status alteration, focal neurologic signs. [b]High-dose zidovudine, clinical trial. [c]Antiretroviral, Ara-C (intravenous, intrathecal) clinical trial. [d]Pyrimethamine + sulfadizine or pyrimethamine + clindamycin. [e]Radiation therapy. CNS, central nervous system; Crypto, *Cryptococcus neoformans*; CT, computed tomography; IT, intrathecal; IV, intravenous; LP, lumbar puncture; MRI, magnetic resonance imaging; PML, progressive multifocal leukoencephalopathy; TB, tuberculosis; Toxo, toxoplasmosis. (*With permission from Simpson DM, Tagliati M. Neurologic manifestations of HIV infection. Ann Intern Med. 1994;121:775.*)

effective.[19,32] Folinic acid (Leucovoran, 5 to 10 mg orally per day) is commonly given in anticipation of megaloblastic anemia[32,36] caused by pyrimethamine. Clindamycin (450 mg orally every 8 hours) appears to be an effective alternative to sulfadiazine in the sulfa-allergic patient.[19,32,36] The optimal duration of therapy is unknown and should be guided by radiographic and clinical evidence of resolution. In most cases, striking clinical and radiographic improvement is apparent within 2 weeks. Pyrimethamine, sulfadiazine, and folinic acid should probably be continued for life. Relapses are frequent, and maintenance therapy, if tolerated, is required. The long half-life of pyrimethamine may make intermittent therapy feasible. One approach is to give 25 mg of pyrimethamine and 2 g of sulfadiazine three to seven times a week.

Prevention

Any individual with the serologic presence of IgG antibody to *Toxoplasma* and a CD4 count of less than $100/mm^3$ should be placed on TMP-SMZ orally daily (Tables 8–1 and 8–2).[20] In TMP-SMZ intolerant individuals, serious consideration should be given to TMP-SMZ desensitization for its benefits in multiple opportunistic pathogen prophylaxis (Refer to Chapters 10 and 17 for further discussion). Atovaquone would be a preferred anti-PCP prophylactic in a toxoplasma seropositive individual in preference to either dapsone or aerosolized pentamidine. Patients who own cats should exercise reasonable caution while emptying or otherwise working with litter boxes, as close contact with cat feces is an established means of transmission in certain settings.[37] Daily emptying of litter boxes combined with prompt handwashing can serve to further diminish the risk of toxoplasmosis in those who do empty litter boxes.[20,37]

Pyrimethamine Toxicities

- Skin rash
- Myelosuppression
- Megaloblastic anemia

Sulfadiazine Toxicities

- Renal insufficiency
- Hemolytic anemia
- Agranulocytosis
- Aplastic anemia
- Thrombocytopenia
- Eosinophilia
- Skin rashes
- Liver toxicity

■ Cryptococcal Meningitis

The incidence of cryptococcal infection was rising prior to the beginning of the AIDS epidemic in 1981, presumably because of the increasing use of immunosuppressive therapy in cancer and organ transplantation patients.[38] AIDS, however, has resulted in an alarming acceleration of this trend.[38] *Cryptococcus neoformans* is the causative agent in cryptococcosis, a fungal infection that can become systemic but has a marked predilection for the brain and the meninges.

Clinical Manifestations

The presentation of cryptococcal meningitis in patients with HIV infection ranges from fulminant disease with extensive extraneural involvement to an extremely subtle disease process characterized by mild clinical depression, absence of meningeal signs, and little or no headache and fever (Table 8–3).[32,38] A high index of suspicion and a low threshold for the performance of a lumbar puncture are required for early diagnosis. The less common, fulminant presentation is characterized by multiple sites of involvement (the central nervous system, blood, skin, lung, liver, spleen, and bone) and a rapidly deteriorating clinical course.

Cryptococcal meningitis should be considered in patients who present with one or more of the following: headache, meningismus, photophobia, mental status changes, seizures, or focal neurologic deficits. The diagnosis should also be considered in patients with unexplained fever in the absence of neurologic signs and symptoms, and computed tomographic findings of hydrocephalus or mass lesions should prompt careful evaluation for cryptococcal infection.

Diagnosis

Cerebrospinal fluid (CSF) examination must be performed to exclude the diagnosis (Fig. 8–3).[23] The diagnosis may be made after revealing a positive CSF India ink stain, or a CSF cryptococcal antigen titer of more than 1:8, or a positive CSF culture.[32]

Treatment

One treatment regimen for cryptococcal infections is amphotericin B. Most patients receive a total of 1.0 to 1.5 g of amphotericin B intravenously over at least 6 weeks (0.4 to 0.7 mg/kg per day for 2 to 3 weeks, and then 0.3 to 0.4 mg/kg per day), but various factors, such as the speed of clinical response and drug toxicity, may influence decisions about therapy.[19,32]

Therapy with amphotericin B is not curative, and relapse occurs in more than half the patients. Some authorities recommend concomitant therapy with 5-flucytosine (100 to 150 mg/kg per day for 2 to 3 weeks).[19,32] A newer oral antifungal agent, fluconazole[19,32] (400 mg/day orally), has been approved for both the acute and chronic infection. The overall response rate is essentially equal to that with amphotericin B. Fluconazole can be given 400 mg IV once a day for the acute infection as well. Between 200 and 400 mg of fluconazole will need to be continued to prevent relapse (usually for life).[19,32]

Prevention

Individuals with a CD4 count of less than $50/mm^3$ should be considered for prophylaxis. First choice for prophylaxis is fluconazole 100 to 200 mg orally daily (Tables 8–1 and 8–2).[20] Itraconazole, 200 mg orally daily, may be given as an alternative.[20] Although HIV-infected persons cannot avoid exposure to *C. neoformans* completely, avoiding sites that are likely to be heavily contaminated, such as areas contaminated with pigeon droppings, may reduce the risk of infection.[20]

Amphotericin B Toxicities
- Decreased renal function
- Hypokalemia
- Thrombocytopenia
- Flushing
- Generalized pain
- Convulsions
- Chills
- Fever
- Phlebitis
- Headache
- Anemia
- Anorexia

Fluconazole Toxicities

- Nausea
- Headache
- Skin rash
- Vomiting
- Abdominal pain
- Diarrhea
- Elevated transaminases

■ Primary Brain Lymphoma

Primary brain lymphoma (PBL) was one of the first malignancies to be associated with AIDS.[39] Lymphoma generally develops late in HIV disease in association with CD4 cell counts of less than 100/mm³. Scientists have detected the presence of Epstein-Barr virus (EBV) in CNS lymphoma tissue, and some report that EBV in the CSF has diagnostic value.[32] Primary brain lymphomas have a younger age distribution, there is a very high frequency of extranodal involvement, and the prognosis is extremely poor.

Clinical Manifestations

Like other intracranial mass lesions, primary CNS lymphomas commonly produce focal neurologic signs and symptoms (Table 8–3). Hemiparesis, aphasia, and convulsions are usually attributable to supratentorial lesions. Although uncommon initially, seizures occur in patients at some point in illness. Clinical signs of meningeal involvement are uncommon; their presence should alert the clinician to other causes, such as meningitis from opportunistic pathogens or meningeal metastasis from systemic lymphoma. Confusion, lethargy, and memory loss suggest dysfunction of both cerebral hemispheres, and are frequently caused by brain edema, bilateral tumor infiltration, or a coexisting disease.

Primary CNS lymphomas in AIDS patients generally follow a more fulminant course than is seen in immunocompetent patients. In a few reported cases, the clinical progression was extraordinarily rapid, and severe neurologic deficits developed over several days. Commonly, neurologic symptoms precede the diagnosis of AIDS. One should be highly suspicious of CNS lymphoma when evaluating neurologic symptoms in patients with risk factors for AIDS who do not have other manifestations of the syndrome.

Diagnosis

In order to make a definitive diagnosis, tissue must be obtained. Biopsy of a suspected primary brain lymphoma is at times difficult and often leads to inconclusive results. CT scans can also be useful in determining the diagnosis (Fig. 8–3). Although the radiographic findings are variable, intraparenchymal lesions almost always intensify after intravenous administration of contrast material. The enhancement is usually nodular or patchy, although ring and periventricular enhancement patterns have been seen in a number of cases. When lumbar puncture can be safely performed, cytologic examination of CSF is a relatively noninvasive method for establishing the diagnosis; however, it lacks sensitivity, as malignant cells are not frequently present in the CSF.

Treatment

Left untreated, the disease is rapidly fatal, and long-term survival is rare. Radiation therapy has been used in a number of patients with some success; however, relapses are very common. Chemotherapy has been attempted in the treatment of AIDS-related lymphoma, however, because of poor response, heightened toxicities, and concern over worsening immunosuppression, it is not frequently recommended.

■ AIDS Dementia Complex

As we have seen, AIDS patients are susceptible to a variety of opportunistic infections and neoplasms of the central nervous system. These patients may also develop a subacute or, more commonly, a chronic progressive CNS disorder characterized by cognitive, motor, and behavioral dysfunction.[40–42] Indeed, this disorder, which the medical community has named AIDS dementia complex (ADC), is by far the most common CNS complication in persons with AIDS. ADC is a unique clinical syndrome with a distinct spectrum of underlying neuropathology. Evidence suggests that rather than being a sequela of immunosuppression, ADC may be caused by infection of the brain with HIV.[41,43]

ADC is a clinical term that is largely synonymous with, or incorporates, other designations, such as subacute encephalitis or encephalopathy, AIDS dementia, AIDS encephalopathy, and HIV-associated cognitive/motor complex. Although ADC may develop before any of the systemic complications initially used by the CDC to define AIDS, it occurs principally in patients already diagnosed with AIDS and is accompanied by morbidity comparable to that of other AIDS-related illnesses. The current CDC definition recognizes ADC as a criterion for AIDS. Dementia is included in the term because cognitive impairment is the most notable and most disabling aspect of the disorder.[42] The word *complex* is included because other neurologic manifestations, such as organic psychosis or progressive paraparesis related to myelopathy, are also prominent features that may dominate the clinical presentation and course.[42]

TABLE 8–4. AIDS DEMENTIA COMPLEX: CLINICAL ASPECTS

Symptoms

Cognitive—poor concentration, forgetfulness, slowness

Motor—loss of balance, clumsiness, leg weakness

Behavioral—apathy, reduced spontaneity, social withdrawal

Signs

Mental status—inattention, psychomotor slowing, impairment of processing; global dementia, mutism, organic psychosis

Motor findings—impaired rapid movements, ataxia, tremor, hypertonia, paraparesis, incontinence, myoclonus

Neuropsychological test profile—impaired sequential, alternation problem solving and complex sequencing; slow verbal fluency and fine motor control

Overall character—subcortical dementia with diffuse cognitive deficit, psychomotor slowing, motor impairment, behavioral apathy

Neuroradiological findings

CT and MRI of the head—cerebral atrophy (Fig. 8–4)

EEG—slowing of brain wave activity

Clinical Manifestations

The clinical features of ADC are sufficiently uniform to allow the definition of a distinct clinical syndrome (Table 8–3 and 8–4).[32] Signs and symptoms include memory loss, gait disorders, behavioral changes, spasticity, and psychosis. These manifestations, although not all inclusive, begin subtly and progress to severe cognitive and motor retardation.

Diagnosis

Neurodiagnostic studies (CT and MRI) are useful for ruling out neurologic complications and for supporting the diagnosis of ADC (Figs. 8–3 and 8–4). They also may provide insight into some aspects of the pathobiology of the disease.

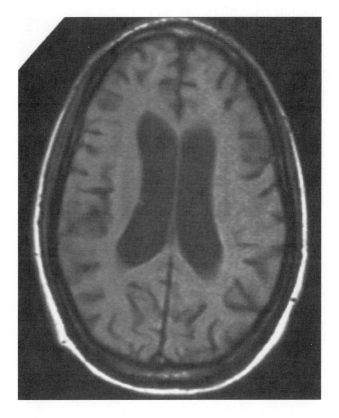

Figure 8–4. MRI demonstrating cerebral atrophy. (*With permission from* Patient Education: A Practical Approach. 1996; p 148.)

Treatment

At present, the treatment of ADC is limited to the management of symptoms. Antiretroviral therapy has been introduced for AIDS, and there is some evidence that such treatment helps ameliorate ADC. Zidovudine (200 mg every 4 hours while awake) benefits some patients with ADC. This drug penetrates relatively well into the brain and holds promise of retarding CNS infection. In persons with progressive HIV dementia despite these high doses of zidovudine, or in those who cannot tolerate zidovudine, therapy with an alternative antiretroviral agent, such as didanosine (Videx), zalcitabine (Hivid), or preferably stavudine (Zerit) may be initiated.[32]

■ Other Neurologic Manifestations

There are many other neurologic manifestations of HIV infection not discussed in detail, but summarized in table format. These include progressive multifocal leukoencephalopathy, CMV encephalitis, vacuolar myelopathy, distal symmetrical polyneuropathy, inflammatory demyelinating polyneuropathy, manoneuropathy multiplex, progressive polyradiculopathy, and myopathy. Please refer to Table 8–3 for details on each disorder.

■ Cytomegalovirus

Cytomegalovirus (CMV) is infectious for humans of all ages beginning with the gestation period. First called salivary gland virus after it was found to cause subclinical salivary gland infection as well as a fatal, disseminated cytomegalic inclusion disease in newborn infants, CMV has subsequently been shown to cause a wide spectrum of diseases including congenital malformations, a mononucleosis syndrome in adolescents and young adults, and fatal disseminated infection in immunocompromised patients. The name refers to the characteristic enlargement of infected cells. Infection usually occurs after close and prolonged contact, and evidence suggests that CMV may be sexually transmitted. The virus has been isolated in saliva, semen, urine, cervical secretions, and feces. Primary infection may also occur after exposure to fresh blood or blood products. Cytomegalovirus infection in AIDS patients can occur as a new infection or more commonly through reactivation of latent virus obtained earlier in life. Approximately 50 to 70 percent of U.S. adults are CMV seropositive.

Cytomegalovirus belongs to the herpes virus group of double-stranded DNA viruses. It produces large intranuclear and smaller cytoplasmic inclusions in infected cells. The intranuclear inclusions are typically central and surrounded by a clear halo, producing the characteristic "owl's eye" appearance. Cytomegalovirus is a major cause of dysfunction in a wide variety of organs in patients with AIDS. Because CMV is so common as a latent virus in the general population, and because cell-mediated immunity is the important element in host defense for controlling its proliferation, it is not surprising that it is a major pathogen. The most common areas affected by cytomegalovirus include the retina, lung, gastrointestinal tract, and less frequently, the liver. Up to 20 percent of patients with AIDS may develop CMV disease, and CMV is the most common cause of blindness in AIDS.

Clinical Manifestations

Patients may have fever, weight loss, and severe malaise with primary infection but may complain of shortness of breath (CMV pneumonia), diarrhea (CMV colitis), vision changes (CMV retinitis), or even dysphagia (CMV esophagitis), depending on the location of the infection.

Diagnosis

The definitive diagnosis should be made through histopathologic evidence (showing the presence of CMV inclusion bodies in tissue) and culture. Infection can also be diagnosed by demonstrating a fourfold rise in antibody titer, but serologic studies may be less reliable in patients with AIDS. In the retina, the classic "crumbled cheese and ketchup" appearance of exudate with heme is diagnostic to a trained observer.

Treatment

Ganciclovir (Cytovene), an acyclovir derivative, has been approved for individuals infected with CMV.[19] The initial dosage is 10 mg/kg per day IV divided into two doses for 14 days. Maintenance therapy is required to prevent relapse, and recommended doses are 5 mg/kg per day. Foscarnet, 90 mg/kg IV every 12 hours for 2 to 3 weeks for induction, and 120 mg/kg per day IV for maintenance, has also been approved for CMV infections, usually in those who have failed ganciclovir.[44] Oral ganciclovir (1 g three times daily or 500 mg six times daily while awake) may be used as an alternate to IV therapy for maintenance treatment of CMV retinitis in whom retinitis is stable following appropriate induction therapy and for whom the risk of more rapid disease progression is balanced by the benefit of avoiding daily IV infusions.[45,46]

The United States Food and Drug Administration (FDA) recently approved Vitrasert, a therapeutic eye implant that delivers ganciclovir (Cytovene) directly to the eye in those with active retinitis.[46] The implant offers another alternative to current IV ganciclovir treatments that must be administered three or more times weekly. The implant is inserted in the posterior segment of the eye, and it lasts for 5 to 8 months. AIDS patients newly diagnosed with CMV retinitis who received Vitrasert in clinical trials were able to significantly delay disease progression, compared with patients on IV ganciclovir.

Cidofovir (Vistide) has also been recently approved by the FDA for treatment of CMV retinitis.[46] Cidofovir was shown in three studies to delay the progression of CMV retinitis significantly in newly diagnosed as well as relapsing patients whose disease has progressed despite treatment with ganciclovir or foscarnet. Cidofovir has a much longer half-life, requiring less frequent dosing (once a week), compared to ganciclovir and foscarnet requiring surgical implantation of a chest catheter for frequent drug delivery.[46]

Prevention

Oral ganciclovir (1 g three times daily) is indicated for the prevention of CMV disease in patients with advanced HIV infection who are at risk for developing CMV disease.[45]

Ganciclovir Toxicities

- Myelosuppression
- Rash
- Nausea/vomiting
- Renal insufficiency
- Suppression of spermatogenesis

Foscarnet Toxicities

- Renal dysfunction
- Renal failure
- Seizures
- Tetany

- Hypocalcemia
- Hyperphosphatemia

Cidofovir Toxicities

- Renal failure

■ Cryptosporidium

Cryptosporidium is a coccidian protozoan belonging to the class sporozoa.[47] This organism is an intracellular parasite usually infecting cells of the intestine and associated glands. *Cryptosporidium* causes acute, self-limiting diarrhea in nonimmunocompromised individuals. In HIV-infected persons, *Cryptosporidium* can cause severe, protracted, and debilitating diarrhea. Less commonly, a more indolent chronic form of diarrhea can been seen. Although symptomatic disease is largely limited to diarrhea, widespread extraintestinal infection with this organism may occur.

Transmission of *Cryptosporidium* from animals to humans is well documented, and animal handlers are known to be at high risk for acquiring the infection.[48] Although this was initially thought to be the primary mode of transmission, it now appears that many humans do not acquire the pathogen from infected animals.[49] Day-care center outbreaks, nosocomial acquisition, and clustering of cases among close contacts appear to be important modes of transmission.

Clinical Manifestations

Cryptosporidial infection in humans is characterized by watery diarrhea, cramping abdominal pain, weight loss, and flatulence.[50] Most patients report exacerbation of diarrhea and abdominal cramps with food ingestion.

Nausea, vomiting, myalgia, and malaise may also be present.[50]

Diagnosis

The diagnosis is made by the examination of the stool with the use of acid-fast staining. Multiple stool examinations are needed, because the organisms may be shed intermittently; even intestinal biopsy may occasionally miss the organisms.

Treatment

Effective therapy for diarrhea induced by *Cryptosporidium* is not yet available, although more than 20 agents have been used. Some used include spiramycin, azithromycin, paramomycin, bovine immunoglobulin, diclazuril, and letrazuril.[19] For now, symptomatic relief with diphenoxylate and atropine sulfate (Lomotil), loperamide (Imodium), or octreotide (Sandostatin, 50 to 100 µg subcutaneously three times daily) is used.

■ *Mycobacterium avium* Complex

The *Mycobacterium avium* complex (MAC) includes both the organisms *M. avium* and *M. intracellulare,* and sometimes includes *M. scrofulaceum,* which are classified as acid-fast, slowly growing bacilli.[51] Until the onset of the AIDS epidemic, infections with MAC were primarily limited to the lungs in patients with underlying pulmonary disease. Other less frequent manifestations of infection with MAC in persons without AIDS included lymphadenitis, bone and joint infections, and genitourinary tract disease. Disseminated MAC infections rarely were reported prior to 1981. However, with the increasing incidence of AIDS, disseminated MAC infection has become common.[52,53] It is, therefore, important for clinicians caring for patients with AIDS to be familiar with this important disease process associated with AIDS.

MAC includes the most noted nontuberculosis mycobacteria in the environment and has been isolated from a variety of sources including soil, dust, sediments, water, and aerosols.[54,55] For humans, the most likely source of exposure to MAC appears to be contaminated water.[56] In patients with AIDS, MAC involvement of the bowel is often extensive, suggesting that the gastrointestinal tract may be the site of initial infection, with dissemination to other organs occurring thereafter.[57]

Clinical Manifestations

Because patients with AIDS frequently have multiple simultaneous opportunistic infections, it is difficult to determine precisely which symptoms can be attributed to infection with MAC; persistent fever, weakness, malaise, anorexia, weight loss,[58] and diarrhea[51] appear to be the most common. Fever is almost universally present and may be the only symptom. Often the patient will present with fever of unknown origin. Night sweats are also commonly seen. Diarrhea can vary in volume, consistency, and frequency. Although the most frequent presentation is watery, nonbloody diarrhea, MAC can cause colitis as well as malabsorption syndrome. Weight loss can be dramatic, with loss of more than 15 percent of body weight over several weeks. Patients presenting with a wasting syndrome should be evaluated for the presence of disseminated mycobacterial infection. Other, less frequent manifestations include lymphadenopathy, hepatomegaly, splenomegaly,[51] and cutaneous and oral lesions. Although found in the lung, *M. avium-intracellulare* rarely causes serious pulmonary disease in HIV-infected patients.[51]

Diagnosis

The identification of clinically significant mycobacteria can be achieved within a few hours, once sufficient growth is available, using nonradioactively labeled DNA probes.[59] A definitive laboratory diagnosis of disseminated MAC should take no longer than 4 weeks.[51] Biopsy of the liver, lymph nodes, or bone marrow and culture of the blood can establish the diagnosis. The presence of large numbers of mycobacteria, often with little or no granuloma formation, is striking in cases of infection with these agents. Large foamy macrophage teeming with acid-fast bacilli are often seen. This is to be contrasted with the paucibacillary histologic presentation of *M. tuberculosis.* Large numbers of AFB on stains of the bone marrow suggest MAC rather than *M. tuberculosis.*

Treatment

Clarithromycin (Biaxin) has been shown to be a promising agent for the treatment of MAC[19]; 500 mg should be given orally twice a day with one of the following:

- Ethambutol (Myambutol)—15 to 20 mg/kg orally daily
- Rifabutin (Mycobutin)—150 mg orally twice a day
- Ciprofloxacin (Cipro)—750 mg orally twice a day

Prevention

New evidence suggests that azithromycin (Zithromax) 1200 mg every week is most beneficial for prevention of MAC in patients with a CD4 cell count less than $75/mm^3$. However, oral rifabutin (Myobutin, 300 mg every day) may also be considered for the prevention of disseminated disease (Tables 8–1 and 8–2).[20] Clarithromycin 500 mg orally twice a day may also be given for prophylaxis as well.

■ Oral Manifestations

It is well documented in the literature that the oral cavity may show some of the first signs of HIV infection.[60–63] All health care providers must be aware of these signs, which in some cases may be AIDS defining. Palliative treatment for these oral manifestations must be pursued early in patient care in order to improve the quality of life for the patient. With increasing immunosuppression, the gingival and periodontal status will deteriorate, leading to eventual destructive bone loss and deep pain in the jaws. Invasion by *Candida albicans* usually occurs early in the history of the disease.[63–65] Although oral candidiasis is not an AIDS-defining condition, it has been reported to be the earliest oral manifestation.[63] Oral hairy leukoplakia is the next most common oral lesion to appear and has been associated with the Epstein-Barr virus.[66,67] Oral herpes simplex viral lesions often appear in patients who have had previous exposure to the herpes simplex virus (HSV). Usually these lesions are larger and persist longer than in patients who are not immunosuppressed. Fifteen to twenty-five percent of the AIDS population will develop Kaposi's sarcoma,[66,68] which in the majority of cases will occur in the head and neck region.[69] Table 8–5 is a modification of a well-documented and relatively succinct classification of the oral manifestations of HIV developed by the European Economic Community (EEC) and the World Health Organization (WHO).[70] It summarizes numerous oral manifestations that have been documented in HIV/AIDS patients in varying degrees of frequency. Further discussion and treatment considerations will be provided for the more commonly occurring conditions.

TABLE 8–5. ORAL MANIFESTATIONS OF AIDS

	Fungal Infections	Viral Infections	Bacterial Infections	Neoplasms	Other Conditions
Commonly Associated With HIV	Candidiasis pseudomembranous erythematous hyperplastic angular cheilitis	Herpes simplex virus (HSV) Cytomegalovirus (CMV) Epstein-Barr virus (hairy leukoplakia)	HIV necrotizing gingivitis HIV-necrotizing periodontitis LGE (linear gingival erythema) HIV periodontitis	Kaposi's sarcoma	
Less Commonly Associated With HIV	Histoplasmosis Cryptococcosis Geotrichosis	Varicella zoster virus Human papillomavirus Verruca vulgaris Condyloma acuminata Focal epithelial hyperplasia	Actimomycosis Cat-scratch disease Sinusitis Submandibular cellulitis Infections caused by *Enterobacterium cloacae* *Escherichia coli* *Klebsiella pneumonia* *Mycobacterium avium intracellulare*	Non-Hodgkin's lymphoma Squamous cell carcinoma	Facial palsy Trigeminal neuropathy Recurrent aphthae ulcers (major apthae) Delayed healing Xerostomia Salivary gland enlargement Necrotic ulcerations

Oral Candidiasis

As one of the earliest signs of HIV, oral candidiasis prevalence ranges of 43 to 93 percent in seropositive individuals have been reported[6] and have been associated with progressive loss of immunity. There are four forms of candidiasis currently recognized: erythematous candidiasis, pseudomembranous candidiasis, hyperplastic candidiasis, and angular cheilitis. The most common form is pseudomembranous candidiasis, which is a yellow-white, loosely adherent plaque that wipes off easily and may be located anywhere in the mouth.[71] The erythematous form is seen clinically as red lesions most commonly occurring in the palate and the dorsum of the tongue. It was previously referred to as "atrophic candidiasis."[65] One explanation of the high occurrence of candidiasis suggested by researchers is that zidovudine therapy, which a number of HIV-positive individuals participate in, produces iatrogenic anemia, which has been significantly associated with HIV-related oral candidiasis.[72,73]

The presence of oral candidiasis has been shown to increase the risk for HIV-associated periodontal diseases; thus, control of this fungal infection is imperative for maintenance of oral health.[73,74] Recommended antifungal treatment consists of either topical applications of drugs such as mycostatin (Nystatin, one or two pastilles orally 4 or 5 times daily) or systemic administration of either ketoconazole (Nizoral, 200 to 400 mg orally daily for 14 days) or fluconazole (Diflucan, 200 mg orally on day 1, then 100 mg orally daily for 14 days).

Oral Hairy Leukoplakia

Oral hairy leukoplakia, seen worldwide in AIDS populations, has been considered predictive for the presence of HIV or AIDS infection.[75] Oral hairy leukoplakia (HL) is a white lesion of the tongue that does not rub off. It is occasionally seen in other parts of the mouth such as the buccal or labial mucosa or the pharynx.[67] The surface may be smooth, corrugated, or markedly folded and hairy. The folds tend to run vertically along the lateral surfaces of the tongue, and the surface is often very thick with hairlike projections.[76] Studies have revealed the presence of the Epstein-Barr virus in the majority of HL lesions; however, the significance of this finding has not yet been established.[66,67]

Treatment is not usually required because of its asymptomatic nature. In severe cases, however, oral acyclovir has been recommended, and more recently a 25 percent solution of topical podophyllin resin has been shown to be effective in resolving HL.[77]

Oral Herpes Simplex Virus

Individuals previously infected with the herpes simplex virus (HSV) who become HIV infected are susceptible to a dramatically altered course of this recurrent disease.[78] Lesions may be very widespread and are seldom confined to just the palatal gingiva. Clustered vesicles and erosions may involve the entire hard palate, lower labial mucosa, or the buccal mucosa unilaterally. HSV lesions may also occur as a coinfection with cytomegalovirus with a high rate of recurrence.[79,80] Recommended treatment for HSV is oral acyclovir (Zovirax, 200 mg orally five times a day) .

The CDC case definition for AIDS includes patients who are HIV positive and have had oral or esophageal herpetic lesions that have persisted for longer than 1 month.[81]

Kaposi's Sarcoma

Kaposi's sarcoma, a rare but frequently occurring neoplasm in the AIDS population, occurs most commonly in the head and neck region.[69] A recent study has shown a possible association between Kaposi's sarcoma (KS) and a herpesvirus-like DNA sequence.[82]

Clinically, KS occurs most commonly on keratinized tissues such as the hard palate or the gingiva and appears as a multicentric vascular-like neoplasm that may be red, blue, black, or purple and may be flat or raised.[66,69,76] Progressive lesions may become ulcerated and painful and may bleed.

Treatment for KS may include surgical excision, radiation therapy, intralesional injections, and systemic chemotherapy.[69] Therapy is usually palliative, as complete remission of the disease is rare. If radiation therapy is the treatment of choice, all caregivers must be aware of the side effects and possible complications. Severe mucositis and xerostomia tend to occur in all irradiated patients and may become so severe that treatment must be discontinued.[69,83] The patient with severe mucositis who has been previously prescribed a chlorhexidine (CHO) oral rinse should discontinue its use, as the alcohol content in CHO further aggravates the lesions. Salivary substitutes that contain methylcellulose or povidone iodine rinse may be palliative substitutes for the CHO.

The danger of osteoradionecrosis is a major consideration for the irradiated patient. Consultation with a dental specialist prior to radiation therapy is a must, in order to determine the periodontal status of the tissues and allow for extraction of teeth with a poor prognosis. This type of intervention will reduce the risk for osteoradionecrosis.

HIV Gingivitis or Linear Gingival Erythema

An unusual form of gingivitis, HIV gingivitis, was first described by Winkler and Murray as a distinct erythematous band at the marginal gingiva associated with petechiae.[72] This definition has more recently been expanded to include the presence of linear gingival erythema (LGE) and one of the following:

1. Punctate erythema of the attached gingiva
2. Diffuse erythema of the attached gingiva
3. A well-defined red band along the free gingival margin that does not bleed on probing in 50 percent or more sites[84]

Recommended treatment of LGE includes meticulous home care and indefinite twice-daily rinsing with chlorhexidine digluconate (CHO).

HIV-associated Periodontitis

Individuals with HIV infection exhibit a more distinct form of periodontitis than those not infected. Characteristics include the presence of HIV-associated gingivitis or LGE and attachment loss where the recession is at least twice the probing depth on one of two forms: reverse architecture, such as depression in place of the interdental papilla; or cratering in the area of the interdental col.[84] Severe clefting often accompanies the recession, indicating major bone loss. Treatment of this form of periodontal disease includes nonsurgical periodontal therapy, usually performed by a dental hygienist or periodontist, and meticulous home care strategies.

Necrotizing Ulcerative Periodontitis

The criteria for necrotizing ulcerative periodontitis, a new classification of periodontal disease, includes the criteria for HIV-associated periodontitis plus one of the following:

- Exposed bone
- Ulceration/necrosis of the attached gingiva
- Complaints of severe deep-bone pain[84]

Systemic metronidazole therapy for 4 to 5 days, along with povidone iodine irrigations, has been shown to provide relief for symptoms of this condition.

Recommended Oral Care of the HIV/AIDS Patient

When first diagnosed as HIV positive, all patients should be referred to a dental professional for close observation and therapy. Maintenance of immaculate oral hygiene will preserve the dentition and delay oral manifestations considerably. All patients must be placed on a routine regimen of twice daily rinses with chlorhexidine digluconate to control oral bacterial growth, regular brushing with a soft-bristled toothbrush, and daily flossing.

It is imperative that the oral care of the HIV/AIDS patient be a multidiscipline effort between the medical and dental teams. Consultation regarding the patient's CD4+ count, medications prescribed by either team, and new lesions signaling further immunocompetence should be discussed across disciplines. Once the CD4 count drops below 200, prophylactic antibiotic coverage prior to any invasive dental procedures such as scaling and root planing (nonsurgical periodontal therapy) must be provided with a broad-spectrum antibiotic such as cephalexin (Keflex) to protect against further infection. It is also noteworthy to mention that one of the oral manifestations of zidovudine, which HIV-infected patients take, is oral ulcerations. These may become very painful for the patient and prevent proper nutrition. Chlorhexidine rinses should be discontinued with the appearance of any oral ulcerations, as the alcohol content will further irritate the lesions. Combination therapy with systemic metronidazole and povidone iodine rinses have been shown to be effective in reducing the pain and duration of these lesions.[83,85] Topical corticosteroids such as fluocinonide (Lidex) may also provide relief.[60]

Close observation of the oral cavity in the HIV-infected individual is highly recommended for both dental and medical teams. After initial periodontal therapy, which is usually provided by a dental hygienist, the suggested return for supportive or maintenance therapy is at 1-month intervals.[86] This will provide optimal care for the patient and maintain close surveillance for any oral manifestations requiring further intervention.

■ Dermatologic Manifestations

The skin is a commonly affected organ in patients who are HIV positive. Some dermatologic diseases, such as shingles, can serve as markers of underlying HIV infection; others, such as an epidemic form of Kaposi's sarcoma, are diagnostic of AIDS.

Most skin disorders found in immunosuppressed patients can also be seen in immunocompetent hosts. In the HIV-infected immunosuppressed individual, these diseases are more extensive and refractory to treatment. Skin lesions that are most common in HIV patients can be divided into three broad categories: infectious, noninfectious, and neoplastic lesions.

Viral Infections

Varicella (Herpes) Zoster Virus. Clinical zoster occurs as a reactivation of varicella zoster virus (VZV, HZV, shingles), and is seen with increased frequency in immunosuppressed patients. In HIV-negative patients, zoster occurs commonly in the elderly but very infrequently in those under 35 years of age. Clinicians should be alerted to looking for underlying HIV disease in any young patient who presents with zoster.

Zoster occurs only in patients who have previously

been infected with VZV ("chickenpox"). Upon resolution of the chickenpox, the virus travels from the cutaneous lesions to sensory neurons and into the dorsal root ganglia, where it remains dormant. In the normal host it takes years for the virus to reactivate, at which time the patient develops shingles. As with most diseases, the clinical course may vary. However, most patients experience a prodrome of sensory disturbances in the distribution of the involved dermatome(s) prior to the appearance of lesions. The patient may report burning, tingling, or pain and tenderness to palpation in the affected area, followed by appearance of the lesions 3 to 5 days later.

The lesions most often begin as papules and evolve into vesicles with an erythematous base. The vesicles may evolve into multiple small pustules that later begin to crust and then resolve. New lesions may appear for another 5 to 7 days. Oral acyclovir (Zovirax) at 800 mg five times daily for 10 days is the therapy of choice. In some cases, patients may require a longer course of treatment.

Varicella zoster may involve a single dermatome or multiple dermatomes and can be recurrent or disseminated. Unidermatomal zoster is the most common and is easy to define. The lesions involve one dermatome and do not cross the midline. Multidermatomal zoster involves two or more dermatomes. Recurrent zoster is diagnosed in patients with multiple bouts of shingles. In disseminated zoster, 20 or more lesions are found in widely scattered areas from the primary dermatomes.

Occasionally patients will develop disseminated disease involving visceral organs, especially the lungs and CNS. Visceral involvement without cutaneous dissemination occurs very rarely.

Both postherpetic neuralgia and scarring from VZV are more common in HIV-positive than in immunocompetent patients.[87] Some experts feel postherpetic neuralgia may last for weeks to months and can effectively be treated with the tricyclic antidepressants (amitriptyline or imipramine) or antiepileptics (phenytoin or tegretol).

Herpes Simplex Virus. With increasing immunosuppression, herpes simplex virus (HSV) recurrences can be progressive and persistent. Active lesions in the HIV-positive population are typically reactivation of latent infection. Acyclovir-resistant strains complicate the picture by confusing the diagnosis and occasionally presenting with atypical features.

The acute vesicular eruption rapidly evolves into chronic, nonhealing ulcerations. The most common sites of infection, in order of frequency, are the perianal, genital, and orofacial areas. Erosions at these sites can enlarge and deepen and, if left untreated, can coalesce into lesions up to 20 cm in diameter.[88] Lesions may also extend from the oropharynx to the esophagus, causing herpetic esophagitis accompanied by severe odynophagia. Secondary bacterial infections, particularly of perianal ulcers, occur commonly and may mask the underlying process.

Acyclovir, available in three formulations in the United States, as topical (ointment), intravenous, and oral forms, is used to control mucocutaneous herpetic lesions. Oral acyclovir, 200 mg five times a day for 10 days, is recommended for most cases of HSV.[89] In individuals with frequent and severe recurrences, prophylactic oral acyclovir may be indicated with 200 to 400 mg two to five times a day. Severe disease may require IV acyclovir at 5 to 10 mg/kg every 8 hours for 14 days, followed by the oral regimen. Failure to respond requires immediate evaluation for acyclovir-resistant strains. Oral antibiotics should be added to this regimen if secondary infection is suspected. The goal of therapy in acute episodes is to reduce virus shedding, local symptoms (pain), and time to healing.[89]

Molluscum Contagiosum. Molluscum contagiosum is a cutaneous poxvirus infection that, in healthy patients, is usually sexually transmitted and self-limiting. However, in the HIV-infected patient the clinical course differs significantly. Whether the lesions represent *de novo* infection or reactivated latent infections remains to be determined. However, its predilection for trunk and face, along with its occurrence in advanced symptomatic HIV disease, favors the latter. The incidence of molluscum increases as CD4 cell numbers decrease to levels below 250.[87]

Molluscum presents as flesh-colored, umbilicated papules, 1 to 3 mm in diameter, distributed usually to the face, neck, scalp, and trunk. Atypical lesions of up to 10 mm commonly occur in the HIV-positive population. Diagnosis is usually made clinically, but early biopsy is recommended for atypical lesions, which may be confused with cutaneous cryptococcosis, histoplasmosis, coccidioidomycosis, verruca, or squamous cell carcinoma.

Treatment modalities include liquid nitrogen, electrocoagulation, and curettage. Retin-A in a 0.01 percent cream applied once daily may suppress new lesions. In most instances, however, a cure is not accomplished.

Human Papillomavirus. Human papillomavirus (HPV) manifestations, such as verrucae vulgare (common warts) and condylomata (anogenital warts), are common in HIV-infected patients. They occur in the same physical distribution as in HIV-negative patients but are more numerous and refractory to treatment.[87]

Verrucae vulgare lesions of the hands are extremely common and typically coalesce into large plaque-like areas. Flat warts of the beard and plantar surfaces are also frequently seen. Treatment is often unsuccessful, and recurrence is the norm. Management options for these lesions include cryotherapy, electrodesiccation, laser therapy, and the application of keratolytics.

Condylomata acuminata or anogenital warts are sexually transmitted and can be found on the skin, oropharynx, genitalia, and/or anal area. These flesh-colored lesions may not become apparent for weeks to years after the patient has been infected with HPV. They normally first appear as flesh-colored, pink, or red papules and may develop into the common "cauliflower-like" mass. Condyloma treatment options include cryotherapy, electrocautery, laser surgery, and topical podophyllin. Intralesional interferon is also being used in clinical trials. Even after appropriate treatment, condylomata recur in a large number of patients. Patients are usually referred to a dermatologist.

HPV infection of the cervix is considered to be the most common cause of squamous cell abnormalities on Papanicolaou smears.[90] As a result, women with HIV infection should obtain regular Pap smears every 6 to 12 months. It is important to keep in mind that squamous cell carcinomas may also present as rapidly growing genital vegetative lesions near the vulva and/or anus.[90,91]

Secondary Syphilis. Condylomata lata are associated with secondary syphilis. Warty lesions in moist areas may become relatively elongated, making it difficult to distinguish condylomata lata from condylomata acuminata.[92] However, secondary syphilis lesions tend to be flatter and more grayish on exam and can be positively identified by abrading and examining the lesions under darkfield to identify the spirochetes.[92] The diagnosis should also be confirmed by standard serum testing for syphilis.

Scabies. Scabies is caused by a mite (arthropod) and spread by skin-to-skin contact as a result of overcrowding, sharing of bed linens, and/or sexual activity. The presence of the mite, its eggs, and its waste products causes an allergic response characterized by severe intractable pruritus. Characteristic lesions are "burrows," brownish erythematous papules, and vesicles. Sites of predilection are the hands, interdigital webs, and flexor surfaces of the wrists, nipples, axilla, buttocks, penis, and feet. Diagnosis is established by scraping of burrows or papules and microscopic examination to reveal the eggs or parts of the mite body.[93]

Treatment is with a scabicide such as 1 percent lindane (Kwell) lotion or 5 percent permethrin (Elimite) cream. Lindane is contraindicated in pregnant women and very young children because it is absorbed through the skin and can cause severe adverse effects ranging from irritability to seizures and even death.[93] Permethrin is less absorbed through the skin resulting in fewer side effects, but it should be used with caution in infants and pregnant women. Treatment success depends on patient compliance with the directions for proper application, treatment of individuals who share the same bed, and disinfection of clothing and bedding materials. Patients treated with either scabicide should be informed that the pruritus may last for several days to 2 weeks after adequate treatment. Therefore, adjunct treatment with antihistaminics and a topical antipruritic lotion containing pramoxine or menthol should be used to relieve the symptoms. Secondary bacterial infections should be treated when they occur.

Norwegian scabies, also known as "crusted" scabies, is a severe variant of scabies. Norwegian scabies produces lesions consisting of widespread hyperkeratotic crusted nodules and plaques that frequently involve the nails. Whereas in the immunocompetent patient the lesions contain 5 to 10 organisms, in the HIV-positive individual the lesions are heavily infested with mites and contain tens of thousands of these organisms.[93] As a result, patients are highly contagious, requiring isolation measures and prophylactic treatment of exposed contacts.

Treatment of crusted scabies is more difficult because of the large numbers of mites. However, it appears that soaking the skin in lukewarm water for 10 minutes prior to application of the scabicide improves the clinical response; the agent is applied again in 12 hours and left on for another 12 hours. One week following therapy, skin scrapings should be performed and the patient retreated if mites are still present.[93]

Fungal Infections

Candida. Candidiasis can present as a mucocutaneous, perianal, or vaginal infection. The lesions usually appear as erythematous, tender patches in the groin, axillary, or inframammary areas with satellite papules in the periphery. In the male, *Candida* can produce balanitis and distal urethritis. In females, vaginal candidiasis is common and can be recurrent and extremely bothersome. *Candida* can also produce acute or chronic paronychia. Treatment of *Candida* infections includes drying of wet areas and application of antifungal powders (nystatin) and creams (clotrimazole). If topical agents fail to clear the infection, oral fluconazole, 100 to 200mg every day for at least 14 days, may be used. Oral agents such as griseofulvin, 500 mg every day for at least 6 months, are usually needed to treat onychomycosis and paronychial infections.

Tinea. Dermatophyte tinea infections are quite common in the HIV-infected host and present in the same manner as their HIV-negative counterpart. Tinea pedis ("athlete's foot") is seen most often, and presents with the usual skin cracking evolving into maceration of the interdigital areas. When the infection involves the sole of the foot, dry scaling develops, especially in the lateral aspects of the sole, giving it a "moccasin" appearance. Complications of tinea pedis infection include fungal invasion of the toenails (onychomycosis).[94]

Tinea cruris ("jock itch") is also common in HIV-infected hosts. Typically, it presents as erythematous, scaly, pruriginous plaques with sharply demarcated borders. It appears in the genitocrural folds and may extend to the inner thighs and scrotum. In the severely immunosuppressed patient, the erythema may not be present, and the lesions may not show the area of central clearing that is typical of tinea cruris.[91]

Tinea corporis ("ringworm") usually first appears as scaly, annular, plaque-like lesions with central clearing. Like tinea cruris, tinea corporis may look atypical if the patient is severely immunosuppressed. In this instance, lesion borders may not be elevated, and the central clearing may not be present.[91]

Normal treatment modalities can be used in attempts to eradicate these fungal infections. Topical antifungal creams (naftifine 1 percent twice daily) can be used to treat tinea pedis and tinea cruris; however, for tinea corporis, a systemic antifungal such as fluconazole, 50 mg orally every day for 1 month, may need to be added.[91]

Systemic Fungal Infections. Several systemic fungal infections can manifest as cutaneous lesions. Cryptococcosis occurs in approximately 10 percent of all patients with AIDS. Most of the cases involve the CNS, but the skin may also be involved with lesions much like those of molluscum contagiosum.[87] They appear as umbilicated white papules or occasionally as papules with a central area of crusting. These lesions are found most often on the face and usually occur in groups. Cutaneous cryptococcosis is always associated with systemic infection. Patients with cryptococcosis are hospitalized and treated with amphotericin B followed by oral fluconazole for maintenance therapy.[91]

Histoplasmosis is another common fungal infection that presents with cutaneous lesions in about 10 percent

...on of these factors. Treatment modalities in-
...uent application of emollients, proper nutrition,
...ance of drying soaps.

...nges. Multiple nonspecific hair changes have
...observed in HIV-infected patients. These may
...lopecia, loss of luster, and straightening of previ-
...ly hair. These are felt to be secondary to a com-
...of HIV infection of the follicular epithelium and
...al abnormalities. Many patients also experience
...n of eyelashes because of prolonged anagen
...growth,[87] a phenomenon called trichomegaly.

...uptions

...lated eruptions are quite common in HIV-infected
... The rash usually consists of pruritic pink to red
...s or papules and may last for several weeks to
...after discontinuation of the offending drug. The
...ommon agent implicated in drug eruption is
...oprim-sulfamethoxazole (Bactrim, Septra) used
...? treatment and prophylaxis. Others include clin-
...n, cephalexin, and rifabutin. Treatment for drug
...n normally consists of discontinuation of the of-
...g drug and medication with antihistamines as
...1.

...s–Johnson Syndrome. Stevens–Johnson syn-
... may be described as an allergic, idiopathic, or
...exposure reaction involving rash, usually erythema
...orme, with involvement of two or more mucous
...branes, and accompanied by fever.[98] Erythema mul-
...ne lesions usually begin as round to oval macules
...apules, varying in size from less than 1 cm up to 1 to
...in diameter, and may develop into blisters (bullous
...ema multiforme) affecting the knees, elbows, palms,

of patients with disseminated histoplasmosis. Lesions can present as papules, papulonecrotic lesions, cup-shaped papules, vegetative plaques, or diffuse purpura-like lesions.[91] Histoplasmosis is also treated with amphotericin B, followed by itraconazole (Sporanox) for maintenance.

Noninfectious Manifestations

Seborrheic Dermatitis. An "exaggerated dandruff" condition, seborrheic dermatitis (SD) affects those areas of greatest sebaceous activity (nasolabial folds, eyebrows, and mustache). In patients with AIDS, the incidence of SD has been estimated at 40 to 80 percent, whereas in HIV-seropositive patients the incidence is 20 to 40 percent, as compared to only 3 to 5 percent in those who are immunocompetent.[95] SD manifests with greasy scales. The etiology is thought to be multifactorial and partly related to overgrowth of several different cutaneous fungi.

Generally, treatment consists of 1 percent hydrocortisone cream applied to the affected areas two or three times each day. Because SD is thought to have a fungal component, many clinicians are beginning to use a combination of hydrocortisone and antifungal cream. It must be stressed that treatment for SD is only palliative, not curative. Once treatment is stopped, the lesions will recur.

Psoriasis. Psoriasis is a papulosquamous dermatosis that is also associated with HIV infection. As with most other dermatoses, psoriasis presents with increased severity and frequency with diminished CD4 cell numbers.[87] As a result, a new onset of explosive psoriasis, or a sudden exacerbation in an individual with previous chronic stable psoriasis, should alert the clinician to undiagnosed HIV infection. In immunocompetent patients, psoriasis is usually mild and limited to the elbows, knees, and lumbosacral areas and affects 1 to 2 percent of the general population.[96]

Psoriatic lesions in HIV-positive patients are identical to those seen in the general public, although the clinical disease differs in that several subsets of lesions may be found in the same patient. Patients may have papules (guttate), pustules, plaques, extensive exfoliative erythroderma, or some combination of these. Typical nail changes are seen, ranging from pitting to severe destruction.

Treatment is complicated in that most regimens, including ultraviolet B (UVB), involve some degree of immunosuppression. Care must be taken to use the lowest effective dosages. Therapeutic modalities include emollients, salicylic acid ointment, topical corticosteroids, crude coal tar, ultraviolet light, and etretinate.

Zidovudine at high doses (200 mg four times a day) has been used for prompt symptomatic relief of pruritus and clearing of lesions in 6 to 8 weeks. Methotrexate is contraindicated, as it has been associated with rapid immunosuppression and death.[95]

Eosinophilic Pustular Folliculitis. Eosinophilic pustular folliculitis (EPF), also commonly referred to as HIV-associated eosinophilic folliculitis, is a chronic and extremely pruritic eruption that is clinically similar to bacterial folliculitis. Lesions begin as small papules or pustules that typically involve the face, neck, trunk, or extremities. It is not unusual for patients with EPF to present with lichenified or even ulcerated areas secondary to intense scratching of the lesions. The exact etiology of EPF is unknown, but histopathologic findings include innumerable eosinophils within the fundibula of hair follicles.[87] Occasionally the follicles may rupture, resulting in perifolliculitis.

Treatment of EPF is difficult. Oral antihistamines can be used to alleviate some of the pruritus. Phototherapy

with UVB is the treatment of ch
taken with caution because of t
tion of latent HIV infection and
population. In many instances, c
continued, the symptoms reappe

Pruritic Papular Eruption of HIV.
tion (PPE) is a poorly defined ch
matitis seen frequently (up to
HIV-infected patients. The etiolog
the accompanying pruritus is unkr

The eruption consists of sym
to erythematous papules involving
extremities to varying degrees. I
changes including multiple excoria
tory hyperpigmentation, and prur
typically seen. The eruption may ne
coalesce to form plaques. The cours
wanes over periods of 1 to 24 months

Typical histologic features incl
middermal perivascular and perifol
infiltrates with variable numbers of
common conditions that can be mistal
eosinophilic folliculitis and drug erupt

Treatment includes phototherapy
times a week, topical corticosteroids, en
histamines. Results are variable; the pru
fractory to most standard oral and top
Spontaneous resolution may occur at an
clinical course.

Xerosis. Severe xerosis is extremely cc
infected hosts. Several different reasons fc
the skin have been postulated, including r
tion of sebum and sweat, epidermal cell
mality, poor nutrition or poor absorption o

combinat
clude fred
and avoi

Hair Cha
also beer
include a
ously cu
bination
nutrition
elongati
phase o

Drug E
Drug-re
patients
macule
months
most c
trimeth
for PC
damyc
eruptic
fendin
neede

Steve
drom
drug
multi
mem
tiforr
and
2 cm
eryth

and soles. Mucosal involvement varies from oral blisters and erosions to hemorrhagic conjunctivitis and stomatitis. Although most cases in immunocompetent children and adults are due to infections, in most adults the syndrome is either idiopathic or drug-related. In those cases due to infections, numerous viruses, fungi, and bacteria have been implicated.[98]

Neoplastic Manifestations

Kaposi's Sarcoma. Kaposi's sarcoma (KS) is a multifocal neoplasm that can affect any organ in the body but most commonly involves the skin.[99] It can present in a variety of forms, colors, shapes, and distribution patterns. KS is the only opportunistic disease than can occur in the setting of normal CD4 counts. Histologically, KS lesions consist of small vascular spaces, multiple abnormal lymphocytes, spindle-like cells, blood vessels, and extravasated red cells.[87] Many researchers have sought an infectious agent in the pathogenesis of KS; HPV is currently thought to be the likely culprit. Some feel that herpes viruses may indirectly affect the development of KS through activation of leukocytes and induction of soluble factors.[87]

KS skin lesions normally begin as tiny macular violaceous areas that may enlarge and possibly become elevated to form plaque-like lesions, which sometimes evolve further into nodules. KS lesions are typically nonpruritic, painless, and may have some surrounding edema, which is felt to be secondary to lymphatic obstruction. Although painless, KS lesions may become ulcerated and thereby cause local pain. Suspicious lesions should always be biopsied. Mucous membrane, gastrointestinal, and pulmonary involvement, ranging from involvement of the oral cavity, stomach, colon, small intestine, large bowel, to the lungs, may be found in advanced cases.

Treatment options include observation, excision, radiation, and chemotherapy. Excision is reasonable only for small lesions that the patient wishes to have removed for cosmetic purposes. Radiation is also used primarily for smaller lesions, because complete resolution of larger lesions with radiation is rare. Chemotherapy is normally reserved for patients with rapidly progressing lesions or patients with visceral involvement. Alpha interferon is effective in controlling KS in patients with high CD4 counts. Multiple agents have been studied, including bleomycin, vincristine, vinblastine, and adriamycin, among others, all with varying degrees of success. Even with a good response to chemotherapy, KS will usually relapse quickly after the therapy has been discontinued.

■ Hepatitis

Hepatitis A virus (HAV), hepatitis B virus (HBV), hepatitis C virus (HCV), hepatitis delta virus (HDV), and hepatitis E virus (HEV) are five serologically distinct hepatotropic viruses that cause acute viral hepatitis. HBV, HCV, and HDV are also associated with chronic infection that can lead to cirrhosis, hepatic failure, and hepatocellular carcinoma. Hepatitis that is not due to one of these five viruses is called non-A–E hepatitis. Recently, a group of RNA viruses has been described that appear to be responsible for at least a portion of these cases of non-A-E hepatitis. These viruses are called hepatitis GB virus A (HGBV A), HGBV B, HGBV C, and hepatitis G virus (HGV). Because the mode of transmission of some of these viruses is similar to that of the human immunodeficiency virus type 1 (HIV), some individuals may be co-infected with HIV and one or more of these hepatitis viruses.

This section will provide an overview of the clinical course, diagnosis, and therapy of infection with the hepatotropic viruses and will review what is currently known about co-infection with HIV and the hepatitis viruses.

Epidemiology

Hepatitis A virus is spread predominantly by the fecal–oral route. Contaminated water supplies and food-stuffs and common source epidemics have been described. Specific risk factors that have been associated with HAV include contact with another person with hepatitis, male homosexuality, foreign travel, contact with children attending a day-care center, and illicit drug use.[100]

HBV is spread predominantly by the parenteral route. Risk factors include exposure to blood or blood products (transfusions, hemophiliacs, renal dialysis, and oncology ward patients), exposure to contaminated needles and syringes (injecting drug users, health care workers), and multiple sexual contacts. Thus, hemophiliacs, injecting drug users, and gay men are at risk for both HIV and HBV infection.[101]

The risk factors for acquiring HCV infection are the same as for HBV infection; however, sexual transmission occurs less efficiently and less commonly than HBV.[102] In one retrospective serologic survey of injecting drug users and gay men, 73 and 16 percent, respectively, were positive for HCV antibody.[103]

The acquisition of HDV is closely linked to that of HBV infection. HDV is endemic in certain areas, especially the Mediterranean area, the Middle East, and less so in southern Italy and northern Africa. Delta hepatitis is rare in the United States but does occur in injecting drug users and their sexual partners, hemophiliacs, and multiple transfusion recipients. It is uncommon in gay men.[104]

Hepatitis E virus is an enterically transmitted virus

that is spread through fecal contamination of drinking water. It has been responsible for large epidemics of acute viral hepatitis in third world countries.[105] One seroepidemiologic survey demonstrated that over 20 percent of 162 gay men being tested for HIV infection in Italy had evidence of past infection with hepatitis E virus, and that coinfection with HIV and HEV was common in gay men, but much less common in men who had acquired their HIV through intravenous drug use.[106] This suggests that HEV may be transmitted by sexual practices that result in fecal–oral contact; this mode of transmission has been described for other enterically transmitted pathogens among gay men.

Clinical Manifestations

Acute Hepatitis. The clinical course of acute viral hepatitis caused by any of the above viruses can be divided into four phases: incubation period, the preicteric phase, the icteric phase, and convalescence. After an incubation period that varies depending on the type of hepatitis, symptoms of the preicteric phase include malaise, weakness, anorexia, nausea, vomiting, and pain in the right upper quadrant. The icteric phase begins with jaundice and lasts up to 3 weeks. Symptoms begin to abate soon after jaundice appears. During the convalescent phase, symptoms disappear. Only 20 to 50 percent of cases of viral hepatitis are icteric. The remaining infections are asymptomatic or are associated with inconsequential symptoms.[101]

The major laboratory abnormalities associated with acute viral hepatitis include elevations in the hepatic transaminases and bilirubin. The hepatic transaminases begin to rise during the late incubation period and peak in the early icteric phase. These may increase to greater than 100 times normal. Alkaline phosphatase may increase, but only one to three times normal. Bilirubin may rise to 20 times normal in the icteric phase.[101]

Chronic Hepatitis. Following exposure to HBV, there is a well-defined immunologic response that results in resolution of illness and protective immunity. The first serologic marker of HBV infection is hepatitis B surface antigen (HBsAg), which is a protein found on the surface of the virus particle. This often persists in serum throughout the period of clinical illness. During convalescence, the disappearance of HBsAg and the appearance of antibody directed against HBsAg, anti-HBsAg antibody (HBsAb), mark resolution of the infection. From 5 to 10 percent of patients with acute HBV infection do not clear HBsAg and become chronically infected.[101]

Chronic HBV infection leads to either chronic persistent hepatitis (CPH) or chronic active hepatitis (CAH). Both are characterized by asymptomatic periods and periods of disease exacerbation during which fatigue, low-grade fever, right upper quadrant pain, and abnormalities in hepatic transaminases and bilirubin occur.[106]

Chronic persistent and chronic active hepatitis can be distinguished histopathologically. Chronic persistent hepatitis is characterized by mild inflammation in portal triads and hepatic lobules, but there is little or no hepatocyte necrosis. Chronic active hepatitis, on the other hand, is associated with more extensive inflammatory infiltration of portal triads and hepatic lobules. In addition, there is necrosis of hepatocytes at the junction of portal triads and hepatic lobules and extension of necrosis throughout the lobules. The final result of hepatocyte necrosis is cirrhosis, the replacement of necrotic hepatocytes with fibrous material. It is estimated that cirrhosis occurs in 2.5% of patients with chronic HBV infection.[107]

How co-infection with HIV affects the course of acute and chronic HBV infection is currently a matter of active investigation. In one serologic survey of patients with HIV infection, the prevalence of HBsAg was more than twice as great in the group with AIDS as compared to the group with HIV infection but no AIDS. This suggests that advanced immunosuppression may make it less likely for patients to clear HBV infection or more likely to reactivate latent infection.[108]

In another study, the histologic and immunohisto-chemical characteristics of HBV infection were compared in a group of 20 men with HIV infection and a group of 30 men without HIV infection. Although the liver biopsies of the men with HIV infection had less inflammation and necrosis, there was greater tissue expression of HBeAg and HBV DNA polymerase, indicating that HBV replication was greater in patients co-infected with HIV. It was postulated that the lower level of inflammation and necrosis reflected impaired cytotoxic T-lymphocyte activity, a function that is impaired in those with HIV infection and that appears responsible for hepatocyte destruction in patients with chronic HBV infection.[109] Whether the greater degree of viral replication ultimately leads to accelerated hepatic dysfunction remains to be seen.

HCV has a great propensity to cause chronic infection. Fifty percent or more of those affected will develop chronic infection, and up to 25 percent of these will develop cirrhosis. Chronic HCV infection is one of the most common causes of cirrhosis in the United States. The histopathologic appearance is similar to that of chronic HBV infection.[102] The effect of co-infection with HIV on the course of chronic HCV infection has not been well described.

Hepatitis delta virus (HDV) can only infect people who are HBsAg positive, because the presence of HBV is required in order for HDV to replicate. Acute delta hepatitis occurs in two forms, co-infection and superinfection. In co-infection, there is simultaneous occurrence of acute HBV and acute HDV infection. Acute co-infection is usually self-limited and rarely leads to chronic hepatitis. Superinfection occurs when acute HDV infection occurs in a chronic HBV carrier. Superinfection results in chronic HDV infection in over 80 percent of cases. Chronic HDV hepatitis is often severe and leads to cirrhosis and other complications.[104] There is some evidence to suggest that co-infection with HIV adversely affects the outcome of HDV infection.[110]

HBGV C appears to cause chronic infection, because viral RNA can be demonstrated in the serum of infected individuals for years, but most infected individuals appear not to have clinically detectable liver disease. These viruses appear to be transmitted parenterally.[111] There is no published information on the course of individuals infected with both HIV and HBGV C.

Diagnosis

Acute and chronic viral hepatitis due to hepatitis viruses A to E can be diagnosed serologically. Table 8–6 lists the serologic tests that are commonly used for diagnosis of acute infection with one of the hepatotropic viruses. In general, when someone presents with acute hepatitis, serologic studies for HAV, HBV, and HCV should be obtained. If there is evidence for acute infection with one of these viruses, then the diagnosis is established. If all of these are negative, then studies for HEV should be considered. Currently, diagnostic studies for HEV infection include a total immunoglobulin assay and electron microscopy of stool to detect virions. These are available through the CDC in Atlanta. The CDC requests that state health departments be contacted in order to access these tests. In most cases, diagnosis of HDV infection is done when a patient is already known to have chronic HBV infection. HDV serology may be obtained when there is unexplained worsening of chronic HBV infection.

Some antibody detection tests detect total im-

TABLE 8–6. SEROLOGIC TESTS USED TO DIAGNOSE ACUTE VIRAL HEPATITIS

Virus	Acute Infection	Past Infection	Comment
HAV	Anti-HAV IgM	Anti-HAV IgG	—
HBV	HbsAg Anti-HBc IgM	HbsAb Anti-HBc IgG	A few patients with acute HBV infection may be HBsAg negative, but the presence of anti HBc IgM confirms the diagnosis of acute HBV infection.
HCV	Anti-HCV Ig	Anti-HCV Ig	The current antibody test does not distinguish between IgM and IgG antibodies.
HDV	Anti-HDV Ig	Anti-HDV Ig	HDV infection is relevant only when HBV infection is also present.
HEV	Anti-HEV Ig	Anti-HEV Ig	HEV in the stool by electronmicroscopy can confirm acute infection. State health departments should be contacted when diagnostic tests for HEV infection are needed.

HBsAg, hepatitis B virus surface antigen; HBsAb, hepatitis B virus surface antibody; HBc, hepatitis B core antigen; Ig, immunoglobulin (IgM is not distinguished from IgG).

munoglobulins (Ig), but cannot differentiate between IgM and IgG antibodies. Thus, interpretation of the test will depend on the clinical circumstances. For instance, if a person presents with a syndrome that is consistent with acute hepatitis, and HAV and HBV serology is negative, then a positive HCV Ig suggests that HCV is responsible for the acute hepatitis.

Currently, there are no commercial tests for the diagnosis of non-A–E hepatitis; detection of viral RNA by the polymerase chain reaction is a research tool for the investigation of this infection.

Chronic viral hepatitis may be diagnosed following an epidose of acute hepatitis or may be discovered in the evaluation of a patient with unexplained hepatic transaminase elevations. Table 8–7 reviews the diagnosis of chronic viral hepatitis.

Management

Acute Hepatitis. There is no specific therapy for acute viral hepatitis. Supportive therapy, including intravenous fluids, antiemetics, mild analgesia, and antipyretics, may be necessary in some cases. It may be prudent to stop potentially hepatotoxic medications until transaminase levels approach normal values.

Chronic Hepatitis. Interferon alfa is approved by the United States Food and Drug Administration for the treatment of chronic HBV and HCV infections; it is used as an investigational agent for chronic delta hepatitis. Interferon is administered subcutaneously. Side effects include fever, myalgia, fatigue, hair loss, and bone marrow suppression. Only a fraction of patients treated with interferon have a sustained virologic cure. The currently recommended regimens of interferon for chronic HBV and HCV infections are listed in Table 8–8.

TABLE 8–7. SEROLOGIC TESTS USED TO DIAGNOSE CHRONIC VIRAL HEPATITIS

Virus	Tests	Comment
HBV	HBsAg	Persistence of HBsAg for greater than 6 months establishes the diagnosis of chronic HBV infection.
HCV	Anti-HCV Ig	Persistently or intermittently elevated hepatic transaminases in conjunction with a positive HCV Ig suggests the diagnosis of chronic HCV infection. This can be confirmed by detecting viral RNA in the serum.
HDV	Anti-HDV IgG	The diagnosis of chronic HDV is made in the setting of known chronic HBV infection.

In the trials that were used to support the approval of interferon for HBV and HCV infections, the response to therapy was measured by comparing pre- and post-treatment transaminases and liver histopathology obtained at biopsy. Conversion from hepatitis B e antigen (HBeAg) positive to HBeAg negative was also a criterion for response in the HBV trials. Until recently, it has been unclear whether therapy that was deemed successful by these criteria actually provided benefits to patients in terms of decreasing the long-term complications of chronic HBV and HCV infections. Recently a long-term study of patients who had been successfully treated with interferon for chronic HBV infection demonstrated that therapy was beneficial because patients who converted to HBeAg negative lived longer with fewer complications from their HBV infections.[112] The same sort of long-term follow-up report for HCV patients treated with interferon is needed to determine what the real utility of interferon for chronic HCV therapy is.

TABLE 8–8. DOSES OF INTERFERON CURRENTLY RECOMMENDED FOR THE THERAPY OF CHRONIC HBV AND HCV INFECTIONS

Infection	Dose of Interferon	Comment
Chronic HBV	3 million units subcutaneously daily for 6 months.	Approximately one third of patients respond to therapy with a loss of HBeAg; co-infection with HIV is a predictor of poor response to therapy.
Chronic HCV	3 million units subcutaneously 3 times per week for 6 months.	Fifty percent of those treated show an initial response, but relapse is frequent after therapy is stopped; longer duration of therapy may be associated with a sustained response. Co-infection with HIV probably makes a sustained response to therapy less likely.

Summary

Hepatitis viruses A to E are hepatotropic viruses that cause acute viral hepatitis. Of these, HBV, HCV, and HDV may lead to chronic viral hepatitis. These three viruses occur in patients who are co-infected with HIV. The available evidence suggests that co-infection with HIV may have an adverse effect on the course of chronic viral hepatitis, although more data are clearly needed to substantiate this statement. Presently, interferon is the main therapy for chronic viral hepatitis. Some reports suggest that HIV infection is a predictor of poor response to interferon in patients with chronic HBV infection. More research is needed to define the effect that HIV infection has on the natural history and therapy of chronic viral hepatitis.

■ Syphilis

It is no surprise that HIV infection and syphilis are part-nered. They are both commonly transmitted in the same way, and, actually, syphilis is the easier of the two to transmit or receive. There are epidemiologic data linking them closely, showing that HIV's transmissibility is en-hanced when the chancre of syphilis is present. This sec-tion is an attempt to describe the diagnosis and treatment of syphilis in a patient with HIV infection.[113–132]

Syphilis, the many and varied presentations, is caused by the spirochete *Treponema pallidum.* It is re-stricted to humans and has been described since the days of Columbus. It has long been termed "the great mim-icker," meaning that the clinical manifestations are many and, unfortunately, almost never specific. The diagnosis is almost always presumed rather than proved, simply be-cause the organism cannot be cultivated in vitro.

Clinical Manifestations

Primary Syphilis. Usually obtained through sexual con-tact, the organism invades the bloodstream through mu-cous membranes or abraded skin. Typically, the site of entry will develop a small raised papule (never a vesicle) that quickly erodes to develop into an ulcer. It usually has thickened borders and appears quite clean. It is described as painless, but this is not universal. Many reports of mul-tiple lesions occurring in patients with HIV infection are available now. This initial infection occurs over a period of days. The actual incubation period is not known in pa-tients infected with HIV but is believed to be as short as 3 days or as long as 90 days. The duration of these lesions is also not really known in HIV-infected patients, but it can be prolonged. These lesions are highly infectious, and a diagnosis can be made directly with a darkfield microscopic evaluation of a scraping. The characteristic, small, helical organisms should be easily seen.

This phase of the disease is called primary syphilis. It is important to understand that although the clinical disease at this point is localized, the organism is by this time widespread, carried through the bloodstream to virtually all parts of the body. Treated or untreated, these lesions of primary syphilis heal. There may be regional lymphadenopathy, but it is not usually tender. It does not suppurate, as the lymphadenopathy associated with the painful ulcer of chancroid will. Clinically, the patient will have no signs or symptoms of any syphilitic disease. The host defenses will develop a humoral antibody response. Although case reports of HIV-infected patients without serologic evidence of syphilis but showing various signs of disease have been published, it appears this is a very rare occurrence. This clinically silent time is referred to as latent syphilis. In the pre-AIDS era, patients who were either inadequately treated or whose immune defenses failed to contain the disease progressed then to secondary syphilis.

Secondary Syphilis. Secondary syphilis is a clinically apparent phase involving the skin. The rash usually develops first on the trunk and then becomes diffuse. An important aspect is that it very often involves the palms and soles. The most characteristic rash is a pigmented macular eruption, although it may be papular or even sometimes pustular. Importantly, it is never vesicular. The organism is present in these lesions, and they are infectious. More often than not, the patient will have additional features of the infection such as fever, weight loss, and malaise. By the time of the development of the rash, the patient will have serologic evidence of infection. Again, rare cases without such evidence are described but are not the rule. The diagnosis then is not usually difficult to make, given the characteristic appearance and distribution of the rash and serologic evidence of syphilis. In questioning the patient, however, a history of primary syphilis, or chancre, will not always be obtained. In some patients the initial infection may have been so trivial as to have come and gone unnoticed. It is not clear whether HIV-infected patients if untreated will pass through this phase, as every time it is brought to medical attention they are treated. If untreated, it can progress to a fulminant and fatal infection. What does seem clear is that not all patients develop secondary syphilis.

Latent Syphilis. The literature and the textbooks separate two phases of latent syphilis: early latent and late latent. Early latent syphilis describes the silent period during which recurrences of the skin and mucous membrane lesions are likely to recur. In the pre-AIDS era, this was thought of as 1 to 4 years from the time the rash of secondary syphilis developed. Late latent syphilis was then described as the longer period that follows, when recurrences of the dermatologic features were not likely. These terms may not apply to HIV-infected patients. It has been clearly shown now that the progression of the stages of syphilis is altered when HIV is present. The symptomatic periods can be prolonged and the silent periods abbreviated. Put simply, HIV-infected patients can progress rapidly through these stages, and secondary syphilis may never be manifested. There may even be recurrences of what appear to be primary syphilis. It is probably best to describe the clinically silent but serologically evident state as simply latent syphilis.

Tertiary Syphilis. Tertiary syphilis designates clinically apparent disease. Most often this is a neurologic manifestation, but not always. There are case reports of syphilitic arthritis, hepatitis, splenic abscesses, and in the pre-AIDS era, tertiary syphilis included the cardiovascular manifestations of aortitis and luetic aneurysm. This term, tertiary syphilis, is not specific or very descriptive. It is meant to define a patient with a long exposure to the organism, and the development of advanced disease. It is much more useful now to specifically describe the clinical manifestations in an HIV-infected patient, which more often than not will be neurologic. This simplification must be guarded, however, with the understanding that the less common and sometimes unusual presentations will be found sometimes. It still may be called "the great mimicker."

Neurosyphilis. Neurosyphilis, a specific form of tertiary syphilis, indicates disease of the central nervous system caused by the treponeme. Traditionally there were features of neurosyphilis that were thought of as occurring earlier and features that occurred later. Again, these temporal descriptions have broken down in the HIV epidemic, and any of the neurologic manifestations are best simply described as neurosyphilis. There may be features of meningitis, encephalitis, or of parenchymal lesions of the spinal cord. The organism produces a vasculitis, and the result may be inflammation, hemorrhage, or infarction. In addition, primary neuronal destruction also occurs. In reviewing a series of surveys, the common symptoms often were mental status changes, seizures, visual disturbances, cranial nerve palsies (including decreased hearing), and motor abnormalities, specifically hemiparesis. In older reports (pre-AIDS), features of ataxias, gait disturbances, and bladder and bowel incontinence are discussed. Tabes dorsalis specifically refers to the loss of neurons in the dorsal columns, and is characterized by "lightning-like" shooting pains and the loss of sensation and proprioception, usually in the lower limbs. Physical findings of neurosyphilis include abnormal fundi, sometimes with papilledema or findings of optic neuritis, abnormal pupillary reflexes, specifically irregular small pupils (the Argyll-Robertson pupils) that react poorly to light but will constrict in accommodation, and the various motor, sensory, or cognitive findings mentioned above.

Diagnosis

Above all, a high index of suspicion is needed to bring together the presenting symptoms, physical evidence, and serologic findings necessary to accurately diagnose syphilis.

Primary syphilis is usually evident if complained of and can best be diagnosed with confidence through the use of the dark-field microscopic evaluation of a scraping of the lesion. Generally, most patients will have serologic evidence of disease, but in HIV-infected patients this is not always going to be the case.

Secondary syphilis in its classic form as described earlier should also be easily diagnosed. A full-thickness skin biopsy will show characteristic histologic features, and special stains very often can demonstrate the presence of the organisms. Serologic assays are invariably positive in secondary syphilis. Some difficulty in diagnosis may occur when the presentation is less than classic. The lesions may be atypical: raised plaques rather than macules, pustular lesions, involvement of the oropharynx as the prominent site, and the usual involvement of the palms and soles absent. Still, the serology and the use of the biopsy should provide sufficient proof of the diagnosis.

Latent syphilis will only be discovered when screening serologic tests return positive. It is imperative to understand that treatment for this phase is always indicated. Although the patient appears asymptomatic, the organisms are present, and the goal of treatment is eradication of this occult infection and the prevention of progression to the manifestations of tertiary syphilis, which in the HIV-infected patient means neurosyphilis.

Neurosyphilis can be diagnosed when a patient presents with positive serology, any of the neurologic findings mentioned above, and abnormal findings of cerebrospinal fluid examination. The presenting complaint may be sudden or indolent, and fever may or may not be present. Surveys have not yet answered whether there is a correlation between neurosyphilis and the CD4 cell count. Currently the diagnosis should be considered regardless of the stage of HIV infection. Certainly patients have been described with neurosyphilis and no previous history of opportunistic infections. There will be some difficulty diagnosing neurosyphilis with confidence. It is considered always to be present if the CSF Venereal Disease Research Laboratory (VDRL) test is positive, regardless of the dilution present. The difficulty arises when HIV-infected patients present with serologies that are positive for syphilis and neurologic findings but the CSF VDRL test is negative.

The central nervous system is believed to be involved in at least half of the HIV-infected population. The various pathologic processes possible are too numerous to list, but the important point is that abnormalities in the cerebrospinal fluid in an HIV-infected patient may be the rule rather than the exception. Therefore, in entertaining a diagnosis of neurosyphilis in an HIV-infected patient with neurologic findings, it is imperative at least to exclude as many of the more common CSF infections as possible. An MRI of the head will be the most useful imaging study, as it is sensitive to the findings of toxoplasmosis, lymphoma, and most importantly, progressive multifocal leukoencephalopathy. Assaying the CSF for the presence of cryptococcal antigen will effectively rule out cryptococcosis. Bacterial and especially mycobacterial cultures of the CSF will help at least lower the likelihood of these infections, but a skin test for TB and a careful history of previously treated TB are also important. In the end it may be impossible to rule out mycobacteriosis, and the patient may deserve treatment for this as well as neurosyphilis. Last, a diligent search for evidence of cytomegalovirus (CMV) infection should be made. This would include a dilated retinal exam, blood buffy coat, and urine cultures for cytomegalovirus. Recent surveys have clearly shown that CMV can and does sometimes cause a parenchymal vasculitis with findings essentially indistinguishable from those of neurosyphilis.

Asymptomatic neurosyphilis deserves some special comment here. Because the progression of syphilis is hastened in the HIV-infected patient, the CDC has recommended that all patients with latent syphilis undergo lumbar puncture. When the CSF VDRL test is found to be positive, a diagnosis of asymptomatic neurosyphilis is made. That patient should be treated as having neurosyphilis. It is difficult to decide how to manage an asymptomatic patient with latent syphilis given a negative CSF VDRL test and CSF pleocytosis and/or an elevated CSF protein. At this time no data can be found that give an adequate solution to this problem. The posture of our experience is this: given an HIV-infected patient with serologic evidence of latent syphilis and a normal neurologic exam, if a lumbar puncture is performed, and the CSF VDRL test is negative, but other abnormalities are present, a search is begun for the other causes of the abnormalities listed earlier. If no other pathology is found, the patient is treated as described for latent syphilis and followed closely, with a repeat lumbar puncture planned in about 6 months. If the serum titers have responded to therapy, and the CSF VDRL test remains negative, the patient is only watched. If there has been no response serologically to the treatment, and CSF abnormalities persist, treatment for neurosyphilis would be recommended.

Serologic tests (Table 8–9) used in the diagnosis of syphilis are available in two kinds: tests that detect antibodies directed against the treponeme itself, and tests that detect antibodies directed against a cardiolipin-lecithin antigen. It is simply a fortune of nature that there is a cross-reactivity between the body's immune response to the treponeme and the cardiolipin-lecithin antigen, which is cheaper and much more available than the assays using the treponemal antigens. Both kinds of assays have their special utilities.

Treatment

The principle of therapy (Table 8–10) is to deliver enough of the right drug to the right place for long enough to eradicate any infection. However, antibiotic therapy is not the only factor in clearing the infection. Host responses clearly are involved, and in the course of HIV infection are always changing. So at this time, no controlled trials

TABLE 8–9. SEROLOGIC TESTS FOR SYPHILIS

Assay	Significance
Treponemal assays[a] MHA-Tp FTA-ABS	Highly sensitive and specific for syphilis. Indicative of prior infection with syphilis. Not useful in monitoring response of therapy. Once reactive, these tests remain reactive for life. Most useful to confirm reactive or weakly reactive non-treponemal assays.
Nontreponemal assays VDRL and RPR	Both generally signify the presence of infection and are titered out. These titers then change with therapy, providing evidence of effectiveness.

[a] The treponemal tests are inherently more sensitive. Following treatment, the nontreponemal assays will often become nonreactive, whereas the treponemal assays may persist for life. It is for this reason that the nontreponemal assays can be used to monitor the effectiveness of therapy.

TABLE 8–10. TREATMENT OF SYPHILIS[a]

Primary syphilis Secondary syphilis Latent syphilis	2.4 million units of benzathine penicillin IM once a week for 3 consecutive weeks
Asymptomatic neurosyphilis	Ceftriaxone 1g IM or IV each weekday for a total of 14 doses
Symptomatic neurosyphilis	Aqueous penicillin 4 million units IV every 4 hours for 10 days

[a] There is no alternative to penicillin/ceftriaxone for use in HIV-infected patients at this time that can be recommended on the basis of any published experience. In the case of penicillin-allergic patients, skin testing should be done and consideration given to desensitization. In desperate cases, chloramphenicol might be considered. Tetracyclines and macrolides are not bactericidal and should not be considered. For treatment of pregnant women and children, refer to Chapters 6 and 7 for recommendations.

of any regimen for any stage of syphilis are available to guide therapy. Retrospective data, anecdotal reports, and expert consensus is combined to offer some guidance. As new information becomes available, these guidelines may change.

References

1. Selik RM, Chu SY, Ward JW. Trends in infectious diseases and cancers among persons dying of HIV infection in the United States from 1987–1992. *Ann Intern Med*. 1995;123:933–936.

2. Mathur-Wagh U, Mildvan D. HIV infection and persistent generalized lympadenopathy. In: Wormser GP, Stahl RE, Bottone EJ, eds. AIDS and Other Manifestations of HIV Infection. Park Ridge, NJ: Noyes Publications; 1987:398–407.

3. Centers for Disease Control. Classification system for human T-lymphotropic virus III/lymphadenopathy-associated virus infections. *MMWR*. 1986;35:334–339.

4. Centers for Disease Control and Prevention. 1993 revised classification system for HIV infection and expanded sur-

veillance case definition for AIDS among adolescents and adults. *MMWR.* 1992;41(RR-17):1–19.

5. Armengol CE. A historical review of *Pneumocystis carinii*. *JAMA.* 1995;273:747.

6. Kaplan JE, Masur H, Holmes KK, et al. USPHS/IDSA guidelines for the prevention of opportunistic infections in persons infected with human immunodeficiency virus: An overview. *Clinical Infectious Diseases.* 1995;21(suppl 1):S12–S31.

7. Centers for Disease Control. Guidelines for prophylaxis against *Pneumocystis carinii* pneumonia for persons infected with human immunodeficiency virus. *MMWR.* 1989;38(suppl):1–9.

8. Centers for Disease Control. Recommendations for prophylaxis against *Pneumocystis carinii* pneumonia for adults and adolescents infected with human immunodeficiency virus. *MMWR.* 1992;41(RR-4):1–11.

9. Centers for Disease Control. Guidelines for prophylaxis against *Pneumocystis carinii* pneumonia for children infected with human immunodeficiency virus. *MMWR.* 1991;40 (RR-2):1–13.

10. Gallant JE, Masur H, Powderly WG. Prophylaxis: Who, what, when, and why? *Patient Care.* 1996;30: 77–97.

11. Suffredini AF, Masur H. *Pneumocystis carinii* infection in AIDS. In: Wormser GP, Stahl RE, Bottone EJ, eds. AIDS and Other Manifestations of HIV Infection. Park Ridge, NJ: Noyes Publications; 1987:445–477.

12. Cushion MT, Walzer PD. Cultivation of *Pneumocystis carinii* in lung derived cell lines. *J Infect Dis.* 1984;149:644.

13. Latorre CR, Sulzer AJ, Norman LG. Serial propagation of *Pneumocystis carinii* in cell line culture. *Appl Environ Microbiol.* 1977;33:1204–1206.

14. Pifer LL, Woods D, Hughes WT. Propagation of *Pneumocystis carinii* in Vero cell culture. *Infect Immun.* 1978; 20:66–68.

15. Hughes WT. Serodiagnosis of *Pneumocystis carinii*. *Chest.* 1985;87:700.

16. Kovacs JA, Hiemenz JW, Machner AM, et al. *Pneumocystis carinii* pneumonia: A comparison between patients with the acquired immunodeficiency syndrome and patients with other immunodeficiencies. *Ann Intern Med.* 1984;100:663–671.

17. Wharton JM, Coleman DI, Wofsey CB, et al. Trimethoprim-sulfamethoxazole or pentamidine for *Pneumocystis carinii* pneumonia in the acquired immunodeficiency syndrome: A prospective randomized trial. *Ann Intern Med*. 1986;105:37–44.

18. Stover DE, White DA, Romano PA, et al. Spectrum of pulmonary diseases associated with the acquired immune deficiency syndrome. *Am J Med*. 1985;78:429–437.

19. Sepkowitz KA, Armstrong D. Treatment of opportunistic infections in AIDS. *Lancet*. 1995;346:588–589.

20. Centers for Disease Control and Prevention. USPHS/ IDSA guidelines for the prevention of opportunistic infections in persons infected with human immunodeficiency virus: A summary. *MMWR*. 1995;44(RR-8):24–26.

21. Chinn H, Chernoff DN, Migliorati CA, et al. Oral histoplasmosis in HIV-infected patients. *Oral Surg Oral Med Oral Pathol Oral Radiol Endod*. 1995;79:710–714.

22. Salzman SH, Smith RL, Aranda CP. Histoplasmosis in patients at risk for the acquired immunodeficiency syndrome in a nonendemic setting. *Chest*. 1988;93:916–921.

23. Wheat J, Hafner R, Wulfsohn M, et al. Prevention of relapse of histoplasmosis with itraconazole in patients with the acquired immunodeficiency syndrome. *Ann Intern Med*. 1993;118:610–616.

24. Hoffman ND, Kelly C, Futterman D. Tuberculosis infection in human immunodeficiency virus-positive adolescents and young adults: A New York City cohort. *Pediatrics*. 1996;97:198–203.

25. Centers for Disease Control and Prevention. Essential components of a tuberculosis prevention and control program. *MMWR*. 1995;44(RR-11):1–16.

26. Centers for Disease Control and Prevention. Screening for tuberculosis and tuberculosis infection in high-risk populations. *MMWR*. 1995;44(RR-11):19–32.

27. Brudney K, Dobkin J. Resurgent tuberculosis in New York City. *Am Rev Respir Dis*. 1991;144:745–749.

28. Centers for Disease Control. Expanded tuberculosis surveillance and tuberculosis morbidity—United States, 1993. *MMWR*. 1994;43:361–366.

29. Centers for Disease Control. National action plan to combat multidrug-resistant tuberculosis. *MMWR.* 1992;41:(RR-11) 1–71.

30. Williams RG, Douglas-Jones T. Mycobacterium marches back. *J Laryngol Otol.* 1995;109:5–13.

31. Sudre P, Dam G, Kochi A. Tuberculosis: A global overview of the situation today. *Bull World Health Organ.* 1992;70:149–159.

32. Simpson DM, Tagliati M. Neurologic manifestations of HIV infection. *Ann Intern Med.* 1994;121:769–785.

33. Lenox TH, Haverkos HW. Toxoplasmosis in AIDS. In: Wormser GP, Stahl RE, Bottone EJ, eds. AIDS and Other Manifestations of HIV Infection. Park Ridge, NJ: Noyes Publications; 1987:642–654.

34. Sacks JJ, Roberto RR, Brooks WF. Toxoplasmosis infection associated with goat's milk. *JAMA.* 1982;248:1728.

35. Mariuz PR, Luft BJ. Toxoplasmosis encephalitis. In: Volberding P, Jacobson MA, eds. AIDS Clinical Review 1992. New York: Marcel Dekker; 1992:105–130.

36. Cohn JA, McMeeking A, Cohen W, et al. Evaluation of the policy of empiric treatment of suspected toxoplasmosis encephalitis in patients with acquired immunodeficiency syndrome. *Am J Med.* 1989;86:521–527.

37. Wallace MR, Rossetti RJ, Olson PE. Cats and toxoplasmosis risk in HIV-infected adults. *JAMA.* 1993;269:76–77.

38. Masci JR. Clinical aspects of cryptococcosis in AIDS. In: Wormser GP, Stahl RE, Bottone EJ, eds. AIDS and Other Manifestations of HIV Infection. Park Ridge, NJ: Noyes Publications; 1987:680–697.

39. Snider WD, Simpson DM, Aronyk KE, et al. Primary lymphoma of the nervous system associated with the acquired immunodeficiency syndrome. *N Engl J Med.* 1983;308:45. Letter.

40. McAllister RH, Harrison JG, Johnson M. HIV and the nervous system. *Br J Hosp Med.* 1988;40:21–26.

41. Rosenblum BC, Levy RM, Bredesen DE, eds. AIDS and the Nervous System. New York: Raven Press; 1988:203–219.

42. Muma RD, Lyons BA, Borucki MJ, Pollard RB. AIDS dementia complex: A diagnostic and therapeutic challenge. *J Am Acad Phys Assist.* 1991;4:102–108.

43. Price RW, Sidtis J, Rosenblum M. The AIDS dementia complex: Some current questions. *Ann Neurol.* 1988; 23:527–533.

44. Jacobson MA. Foscarnet therapy for AIDS-related opportunistic herpesvirus infections. In: Volberding P, Jacobson MA, eds. AIDS Clinical Review 1992. New York: Marcel Dekker; 1992:173–189.

45. Newsline. Physician Assistants' Prescribing Reference. New York: Prescribing Reference; 1996:A-25,151.

46. Sharp V, Ferri RS. Cytomegalovirus. *Clinician Rev.* 1996;6:116.

47. Leger L. Caryospora simplex, coccidie monosporee et la classification des coccidies. *Arch Protistenkd.* 1911;22:71–78.

48. Current WL, Reese NC, Ernst JV, et al. Human cryptosporidiosis in immunocompetent and immunodeficient persons: Studies of an outbreak and experimental transmission. *N Engl J Med.* 1983;103:256–259.

49. Hunt DA, Shannon R, Palmer SR, et al. Cryptosporidiosis in an urban community. *Br Med J Clin Res.* 1984;289:814–816.

50. Soave R. Cryptosporidiosis in AIDS. In: Wormser GP, Stahl RE, Bottone EJ eds. AIDS and Other Manifestations of HIV Infection. Park Ridge, NJ: Noyes Publications; 1987:713–735.

51. Inderlied CB, Kemper CA. Disseminated *Mycobacterium avium* complex infection. In: Volberding P, Jacobson MA, eds. AIDS Clinical Review 1992. New York: Marcel Dekker; 1992:131–172.

52. Blaser MJ, Cohn DL. Opportunistic infections in patients with AIDS: Clues to the epidemiology of AIDS and the relative virulence of pathogens. *Rev Infect Dis.* 1986;8:21–30.

53. Wallace JM, Hannah JB. *Mycobacterium avium* complex infection in patients with the acquired immunodeficiency syndrome: A clinicopathologic study. *Chest.* 1988;93:926–932.

54. Fry KL, Meissner PS, Falkinham JO. Epidemiology of infection by non-tuberculous mycobacteria. VI. Identification and use of epidemiologic markers for studies of *Mycobacterium avium, M. intracellulare,* and *M. scrofulaceum. Am Rev Respir Dis.* 1986;134:39–43.

55. Ichiyama S, Shimokata K, Tsukamara M. The isolation of *Mycobacterium avium* complex from soil, water, and dusts. *Microbiol Immunol.* 1988;32:733–739.

56. DuMoulin GC, Stottmeier KD. Waterborne mycobacteria: An increasing threat to health. *ASM News.* 1986;52:525–529.

57. Damsker B, Bottone EJ. *Mycobacterium avium-Mycobacterium intracellulare* from the intestinal tracts of patients with acquired immunodeficiency syndrome: Concepts regarding acquisition and pathogenesis. *J Infect Dis.* 1985;151:179–181.

58. Modilevsky T, Sattler FR, Barnes PF. Mycobacterial disease in patients with human immunodeficiency virus infection. *Arch Intern Med.* 1989;149:2201–2205.

59. Gonzales R, Hanna BA. Evaluation of Gen-Probe DNA hybridization systems for the identification of *Mycobacterium tuberculosis* and *Mycobacterium avium-intracellulare. Diagn Microbiol Infect Dis.* 1987;8:69–77.

60. Greenspan JS, Barr CHE, Sciubba JJ, Winkler JR. Oral manifestations of HIV infection: Definitions, diagnostic criteria and principles of therapy. *Oral Surg Oral Med Oral Pathol.* 1992;73:142–144.

61. Friedman RB, Gunsolley J, Gentry A, et al. Periodontal status of HIV-seropositive and AIDS patients. *J Periodontol.* 1991; 62:623–627.

62. Martinez-Canut P, Guarinos J, Bagan JV. Periodontal disease in HIV-seropositive patients and its relation to lymphocyte subsets. *J Periodontol.* 1996;57:33–36.

63. Riederer A, Groin G, Bogner J, et al. Incidence rate of HIV-positive-associated diseases in the head and neck region: A prospective study on 229 patients. Nineteenth AIDS conference, Berlin, June 1993. Abstract PO-B09-1404, p. 369.

64. Mitchell-Lewis D, Phelan J, Begg M, et al. The prevalence of oral candidiasis in intravenous drug users compared to homosexual men. Nineteenth AIDS Conference, Berlin, June 1993. Abstract PO-B09-1404, p. 369.

65. Samaranayake L. Oral mycoses in HIV infection. *Oral Surg Oral Med Oral Pathol.* 1992;73:171–180.

66. Greenspan D, Schiodt M, Greenspan JJ, Pindborg JS. AIDS and the Mouth. Munksgaard: Copenhagen; 1990:46–60.

6 7. Greenspan D, Greenspan JS. Significance of oral hairy leukoplakia. *Oral Surg Roal Med Oral Pathol.* 1992;73:151–154.

68. Beral V, Peterman TA, Berkelman RL, Jaffe HW. Kaposi's sarcoma among persons with AIDS: A sexually transmitted condition? *Lancet.* 1990;335:123–128.

69. Epstein JB, Silverman S. Jr. Head and neck malignancies as-

sociated with HIV infection. *Oral Surg Oral Med Oral Pathol.* 1992;73:193–200.

70. EEC-clearinghouse on oral problems related to HIV-infection and WHO collaborating center on oral manifestations of the immunodeficiency virus. Classification and diagnostic criteria for oral lesions in HIV-infection. *J Oral Pathol Med.* 1993;22:289–291.

71. Greenspan JS, Barr CHE, Sciubba JJ, Winkler JR. Oral manifestations of HIV infection: Definitions, diagnostic criteria and principles of therapy. *Oral Surg Oral Med Oral Pathol.* 1992;73:142–144.

72. McCarthy GM. Host factors associated with HIV-related oral candidiasis. *Oral Surg Oral Med Oral Pathol.* 1992;73:181–186

73. Tomar SL, Swango PA, Kleinman DV, Burt BA. Loss of periodontal attachment in HIV-seropositive military personnel. *J Periodontol.* 1995;66:421–428.

74. Grbic JT, Mitchell-Lewis DA, Fine JB, et al. The relationship of candidiasis to linear gingival erythema in HIV-infected homosexual men and parenteral drug users. *J Periodontol.* 1995;66:30–37.

75. Schiodt M, Bakilana PB, Hiza JF, et al. Oral candidiasis and hairy leukoplakia correlate with HIV infection in Tanzania. *Oral Surg Oral Med Oral Pathol.* 1990;69:591–596.

76. Greenspan J, Greenspan D, Winkler J, Murray P. Acquired immunodeficiency syndrome—oral and periodontal changes. In: Genco R, Goldman H, Cohen D, eds. Contemporary Periodontics. St. Louis: Mosby; 1990:298–322.

77. Gowdey G, Lee RK, Carpenter WM. Treatment of HIV-related hairy leukoplakia with podophyllum resin 25% solution. *Oral Surg Oral Med Oral Pathol Oral Radiol Endod.* 1995;79:64–67.

78. Eversole LR. Viral infections of the head and neck among HIV-seropositive patients. *Oral Surg Oral Med Oral Pathol.* 1992;73(2):155–163.

79. Flaitz CM, Nichols CM, Hickls MJ. Herpesviridae-associated persistent mucocutaneous ulcers in acquired immunodeficiency syndrome. *Oral Surg Oral Med Oral Pathol Oral Radiol Endod.* 1996;81:433–441.

80. Regezi JA, Eversole LR, Barker BF, et al: Herpes simplex and

cytomegalovirus coinfected oral ulcers in HIV-positive patients. *Oral Surg Oral Med Oral Pathol Oral Radiol Endod.*
1996;81:55–62.

81. 1993 revised classification system for HIV infection and expanded surveillance case definition for AIDS among adole-
cents and adults. *MMWR.* 1992;41(RR-17):15.

82. Tin YT, Tsai ST, Yan JJ, et al. Presence of human herpesvirus-
like DNA sequence in oral Kaposi's sarcoma. *Oral Surg Oral
Med Oral Pathol Oral Radiol Endod.* 1996;81:442–444.

83. Scully C, McCarthy G. Management of oral health in persons
with HIV infection. *Oral Surg Oral Med Oral Pathol.* 1992;73:
215–225.

84. Robinson PG, Winkler JR, Palmer G, et al. The diagnosis of
periodontal conditions associated with HIV infection. *J Periodontal.* 1994;56:236–243.

85. Greenspan D, Greenspan JS. Management of the oral lesions
of HIV infection. *J Am Dent Assoc.* 1991;122:26–29.

86. Crawford JM. Human immunodeficiency virus-associated
periodontal diseases: A review. *J Dent Hyg.* 1993;67:198–207.

87. Cockerell CJ, Friedman-Kien AE. Cutaneous signs of HIV infection. In: Broder S, Merigan TC Jr, Bolognesi D, eds. *Textbook of AIDS Medicine.* Baltimore: Williams & Wilkins;
1994:507–524.

88. Dover JS, Johnson RA. Cutaneous manifestations of human
immunodeficiency virus infection. 1. *Arch Dermatol.* 1991;127:
1383–1391.

89. Hirsch MS. Herpes simplex virus. In: Mandell GL, Bennett
JE, Dolin R, eds. Principles and Practice of Infectious Diseases. New York: Churchill Livingstone; 1995:1342.

90. Bonnez W, Reichman RC. Papillomaviruses. Mandell GL,
Bennett JE, Dolin R, eds. Principles and Practice of Infectious
Diseases. New York: Churchill Livingstone; 1995:1389.

91. Berger TG, Greene I. Bacterial, viral, fugal, and parasitic infections in HIV disease and AIDS. In: James W, ed. AIDS: A
Ten-Year Perspective. Philadelphia: Saunders; 1991:478–485.

92. Rein MF. Genital skin and mucous membrane lesions. In:
Mandell GL, Bennett JE, Dolin R, eds. Principles and Practice
of Infectious Diseases. New York: Churchill Livingstone;
1995:1059.

93. Wilson BB. Scabies. In: Mandell GL, Bennett JE, Dolin, R, eds. Principles and Practice of Infectious Diseases. New York: Churchill Livingstone; 1995:2561–2562.

94. Hay, RJ. Tinea pedis. In: Mandell GL, Bennett JE, Dolin, R, eds. Principles and Practice of Infectious Diseases. New York: Churchill Livingstone; 1995:2377.

95. Mathes BM, Douglas MC. Seborrheic dermatitis in patients with AIDS. *J Am Acad Dermatol.* 1985;13:947–951.

96. Sadick N, McNutt NS, Kaplan M. Papulosquamous dermatoses of AIDS. *J Am Acad Dermatol.* 1990;22:1270–1277.

97. Pardo RJ, Bogaert MA, Penneys NS, et al. UVB phototherapy of the pruritic papular eruption of the acquired immunodeficiency syndrome. *J Am Acad Dermatol.* 1992;26: 423–428.

98. Weber DJ, Cohen MS. The acutely ill patient with fever and rash. In: Mandell GL, Bennett JE, Dolin R, eds. Principles and Practice of Infectious Diseases. New York: Churchill Livingstone; 1995:551–552.

99. Levine AM, Gill PS, Salahuddin SZ. Neoplastic complications of HIV infection. In: Wormser GP, ed. AIDS and Other Manifestations of HIV Infection. New York: Raven Press; 1992:444.

100. Lemon SM. Type A viral hepatitis: New developments in an old disease. *N Engl J Med.* 1985;313:1059–1067.

101. Hoofnagle JH. Acute viral hepatitis. In: Mandell GL, Douglas RG, Bennett JE, eds. Principles and Practice of Infectious Diseases. New York: Churchill Livingstone; 1990:1001–1017.

102. Dienstag JL, Alter HJ. Non-A, non-B hepatitis: Evolving epidemiologic and clincial perspective. *Semin Liver Dis.* 1986;6:67–81.

103. Tor J, Llibre JM, Carbonell M, et al. Sexual transmission of hepatitis C virus and its relation with hepatitis B virus and HIV. *Br. Med J.* 1990;301:1130–1133.

104. Hoofnagle JH. Type D (delta) hepatitis. *JAMA.* 1989; 261:1321–1325.

105. Favorov MO, Fields HA, Purdy MA, et al. Serologic identification of hepatitiis E virus infections in epidemic and endemic settings. *J Med Virol.* 1992;36:246–250.

106. Montella F, Rezza G, DiSora F, et al. Association between

hepatitis E virus and HIV infection in homosexual men. *Lancet.* 1994;344:1433.

107. Hirschman SZ. Chronic hepatitis. In: Mandell GL, Douglas GR, Bennett JE, eds. *Principles and Practice of Infectious Diseases.* New York: Churchill Livingstone; 1990:1017–1024.

108. Scharschmidt BF, Held MJ, Hollander HH, et al. Hepatitis B in patients with HIV infection: Relationship to AIDS and patient survival. *Ann Intern Med.* 1992; 117:837–838.

109. Goldin RD, Fish DE, Hay A, et al. Histological and immunohistochemical study of hepatitis B virus in human immunodeficiency virus infection. *J Clin Pathol.* 1990;43:203–205.

110. Novick DM, Farci P. Croxson TS, et al. Hepatitis D virus and human immunodeficiency virus antibodies in parenteral drug abusers who are hepatitis B surface antigen positive. *J Infect Dis.* 1988;158:795–803.

111. Masuko K, Mitsui T, Iwano K, et al. Infection with hepatitis GB virus C in patients on maintenance hemodialysis. *N Engl J Med.* 1996:334:1485–1490.

112. Niederau C, Heintges T, Lange S, et al. Long-term follow-up of HBeAg-positive patients treated with interferon alfa for chronic hepatitis B. *N Engl J Med.* 1966:334:1422–1427.

113. Burgoyne M, Agudelo C, Pisko E. Chronic syphilitic polyarthritis mimicking systemic lupus erythematosus/rheumatoid arthritis as the initial presentation of human immunodeficiency virus infection. *J Rheumatol.* 1992;19:313–315.

114. Glover RA, Piaquadio DJ, Kern S, Cockerell CJ. An unusual presentation of secondary syphilis in a patient with human immunodeficiency virus infection. *Arch Dermatol.* 1992;128:530–534.

115. Rufli T. Syphilis and HIV infection. *Dermatologica.* 1989;179:117–133.

116. Lukehart SA, Hook III EW, Baker-Zander SA, et al. Invasion of the central nervous system by *Treponema pallidum:* Implication of diagnosis and treatment. *Ann Intern Med.* 1988;109:855–862.

117. Kanda T, Shinohara H, Suzuki T, Murata K. Depressed CD4/CD8 ratio in TPHA-negative patients with syphilis. *Microbiol Immunol.* 1992;36:317–320.

118. Imperator PJ. Syphilis, AIDS and crack cocaine. *J Commun Health.* 1992;17:69–71.

119. Fabian RH. Neurologic diseases associated with trophic skin lesions. In: Demis DJ, ed. Clinical Dermatology. 19th ed. Philadelphia: Lippincott; 1992;4:1–6.

120. Rompalo AM, Cannon RO, Quinn TC, Hook EW III. Association of biologic false-positive reactions for syphilis with human immunodeficiency virus infection. *J Infect Dis.* 1992; 165:1124–1126.

121. Marra CM, Handsfield HH, Kuller L, et al. Alterations in the course of experimental syphilis associated with concurrent simian immunodeficiency virus infection. *J Infect Dis.* 1992;165:1020–1025.

122. Hook EW III. Management of syphilis in human immunodeficiency virus-infected patients. *Am J Med.* 1992;93: 477–479.

123. Pereira LH, Embil JA, Haase DA, Manley KM. Prevalence of human immunodeficiency virus in the patient population of a sexually transmitted disease clinic. *Sex Transm Dis.* 1992;19:115–120.

124. DiNubile MJ, Baxter JD, Mirsen TR. Acute syphilitic meningitis in a man with seropositivity for human immunodeficiency virus infection and normal numbers of CD4 T lymphocytes. *Arch Intern Med.* 1992;152:1324–1326.

125. Holtom PA, Larsen RA, Leal ME, Leedom JM. Prevalence of neurosyphilis in human immunodeficiency virus-infected patients with latent syphilis. *Am J Med.* 1992;93:9–12.

126. Dowell ME, Ross PG, Musher DM, et al. Response of latent syphilis or neurosyphilis to ceftriaxone therapy in persons infected with human immunodeficiency virus. *Am J Med.* 1992;93:481–488.

127. Johns DR, Tierney M, Felsenstein D. Alteration in the natural history of neurosyphilis by concurrent infection with the human immunodeficiency virus. *N Engl J Med.* 1987; 316:1569–1572.

128. Katz DA, Berger JR. Neurosyphilis in acquired immunodeficiency syndrome. *Arch Neurol.* 1989; 46:895–898.

129. Musher DM, Hamill RJ, Baughn RE. Effect of human immunodeficiency virus (HIV) infection on the course of

syphilis and on the response to treatment. *Ann Intern Med.* 1990;113:872–881.

130. Manganoni AM, Graifemberghi S, Facchetti F, et al. Effectiveness of penicillin G benzathine therapy for primary and secondary syphilis in HIV infection. *J Am Acad Dermatol.* 1990;23:1185.

131. Mandell GL, Douglas RG, Bennett JE, eds. Principles and Practice of Infectious Diseases. 3rd ed. New York: Churchill Livingstone; 1990.

132. Braude AI, Davis CE, Fierer J, eds. Infectious Diseases and Medical Microbiology. 2nd ed. Philadelphia: Saunders; 1986.

nine

CHAPTER

Interpreting Laboratory Data

Janice G. Curry

Interpreting laboratory data of HIV-infected patients is often a challenging, and sometimes frustrating, endeavor. The normal value ranges are generally more variable and may need to be based on the patient's overall disease progression. What may appear to be a panic lab value may be well within a patient's norm. Conversely, a "normal" value may represent a significant change from the patient's norm. Two examples are a white blood cell count of 7.8 in a patient with advanced AIDS who normally has a total white blood cell count of 1.2, and hypocalcemia in a profoundly nutritionally depleted patient with a decreased albumin level.

Questions that should always be foremost in the clinician's mind when interpreting laboratory data are the following.

1. Is this a change for this patient or an unexpected abnormality?
2. Is the patient symptomatic? (For example, is the patient with a low hemoglobin/hematocrit having any clinical signs and/or symptoms of anemia?)

3. Could this be a drug-induced abnormality?
4. Does this lab abnormality actually represent an improvement for this patient?
5. How competent is the patient's immune system?
6. Are the lab abnormalities heralding a new opportunistic infection, or are they a manifestation of HIV itself?

If all of these factors are evaluated when interpreting data, then therapeutic treatments or additional diagnostic studies will be more appropriately instituted and occasionally avoided. HIV-related processes affect every organ system in the body; however, it does not follow that every disease or health problem is an HIV-related event. The following is a brief look at some laboratory and diagnostic abnormalities and their possible causes.

■ Establishing the Diagnosis of HIV

A variety of tests are used to establish the diagnosis of HIV. Human immunodeficiency virus can be isolated (or cultured) from concentrated peripheral blood lymphocytes and less frequently from body fluids.[1] However, culture is difficult, expensive, takes several days, is not frequently available in most laboratories, and is positive more often in the early stages of infection than in later stages.[1]

HIV viral antigen may become detectable as soon as 2 weeks after infection and usually lasts roughly 3 to 5 months. DNA probe kits are commercially available but are not used as a standard test.

The ELISA (enzyme-linked immunosorbent assay) is used most commonly to detect the presence of antibody to HIV, types 1 and 2. A reactive ELISA is used to diagnose HIV infection indirectly. A positive or reactive ELISA is repeated using the same blood sample. If repeatedly reactive, the Western blot or indirect flourescent antibody (IFA) test is performed. A positive Western blot or IFA is considered confirmatory for HIV.[2]

Three other tests are used to detect HIV antibodies. The first approved by the US Food and Drug Administration (FDA), Confide HIV Testing Service, offers an over-the-counter home blood collection kit in which the patient takes a finger-stick blood sample using an enclosed lancet and places the blood sample on a test card and mails to a participating laboratory. A test result center provides confidential test results, counseling and referral. The Orasure HIV-1 Western Blot Kit is unique in that it tests oral mucosal transudate (the patient places a pad between the lower cheek and gum for two minutes), which contains high concentrations of antibodies and is free of most of the contaminants found in saliva. The FDA has also approved the first HIV test to use urine samples to detect the presence of antibodies to HIV-1. According to the FDA all these tests have similar sensitivity and specificity to the standard office blood test.

Nonreactive HIV test results can occur during the acute stage of infection when the virus is present but an antibody response has not yet developed. This period of time before antibody is detected may be as long as 6 months. During this period, a test for HIV antigen (P25) may suggest HIV infection.[2,3] In perinatally acquired disease, where neonates have maternal HIV antibodies, many authorities rely on HIV-RNA-PCR (viral load) to detect HIV infection (refer to viral load section for further information regarding HIV-RNA).

There is also controversy whether reactivity against only a single antibody of a certain type (the core proteins GAG p15/p17 or the envelope glycoproteins gp 120/160) is sufficient to consider the test truly reactive and thus indicative of HIV infection in the absence of reactivity against antibodies to more than the single protein. When this happens, it is often considered a false positive or an "indeterminant" reaction.[1] Commercially available immunofluorescent assays have helped eliminate many indeterminant test results. This assay requires fewer steps by laboratory technicians, therefore eliminating some areas of inaccuracy.

When interpreting tests for HIV, one must remember that a positive test indicating HIV infection does not mean AIDS. AIDS is a clinical diagnosis. HIV infection is the continuum of clinical conditions ranging from the mononucleosis-like syndrome associated with seroconversion through asymptomatic HIV infection to symptomatic HIV infection, and finally to AIDS.[4]

■ Absolute CD4 Count

A method for following the progression of HIV infection is measurement of the CD4+ lymphocytes. Specific laboratory tests include the absolute CD4 counts (Table 9–1) and the CD4/CD8 ratio.[2,5] Although these values do not indicate the patient's current health, they do provide a guide to whether the patient is at a negligible, modest, or marked risk for AIDS-related opportunistic infections. Monitoring CD4 counts assists the clinician in predicting an individual's risk for the development of opportunistic infections, which is directly related to immunodeficiency.[6] The results are also a guide by which antiretroviral therapy and prophylactic treatment decisions can be made.

The CD4 count should be drawn at the time of initial evaluation and at a second visit 2 to 6 weeks later to establish a baseline (Table 9–2). Depending on clinical symptoms, CD4 counts should be drawn every 2 to 6 months after the baseline value has been established.[3,5] Once CD4 counts fall below 50, their value in relation to disease progression is somewhat reduced, and procuring

TABLE 9–1. THERAPY DECISIONS BASED UPON CD4 COUNT AND CLINICAL FEATURES

T4 Values (normal range 500–1000)	Stage and Clinical Features	Therapy Decisions
1000–500	Acute retroviral syndrome/asymptomatic. Intermittent symptoms, oral candidiasis, oral ulcers, lymphadeno-pathy, xerosis, rashes (seborrheic dermatitis, folliculitis).	Treat symptomatically.
Below 500	Asymptomatic/symptomatic. Chronic or intermittent symptoms. Lymphadenopathy, oral candidiasis, oral lesions, nausea, vomiting, diarrhea, fevers, night sweats, tuberculosis, zoster, *Nocardia*, Kaposi's sarcoma may be seen.	Begin antiretroviral therapy.
Below 200	Increasingly severe and persistent symptoms. Memory or cognitive deficits. Life-threatening infections. Increased incidence of cancers and pulmonary and CNS pathology. Increased risk of disseminated disease processes. AIDS-defining infections such as *Pneumocystis carinii* pneumonia (PCP), *Toxoplasma*, histoplasmosis, cryptococcosis.	Antiretroviral therapy and prophylaxis (as available) is crucial. Consider change in anti-retroviral if immunoclinically failing.
Below 50	Increased/high probabilities of opportunistic infections and mortality, PML, AIDS dementia, CMV, MAC, and other late-stage processes.	According to patient and disease process. Patient should maintain antiretroviral therapy and prophylactic treatments. Consider change in antiretroviral therapy or combination therapy.

TABLE 9–2. T4 VALUES VERSUS INTERVAL FOR FOLLOW-UP

T4 Value	Interval	Reason for Monitoring
> 500 Repeatedly	Every 6 months	Deciding when to institute antiretroviral therapy.
500–200	Every 3 to 6 months	Monitoring response to anti-retroviral therapy and to decide when to initiate prophy-laxis for *Pneumocystis* pneu-monia and other infections.
200–50	Every 2 to 3 months	Evaluating the need to change antiretroviral therapy, consider-ing other prophylaxis (as avail-able), and assessing the risk for opportunistic infections.
< 50 Repeatedly	?	Monitoring may only increase patient anxiety. Consider using viral load to evaluate progress.

additional levels rarely varies treatment. It should also be noted that variations of up to 15 percent for an individual may be normal. Due to this variation and the possibility of lab error, clinicians should review CD4 trends over time rather than making treatment decisions based on a single value. A possible exception to this is initiating PCP prophylaxis when the CD4 count reaches $200/mm^3$ or less.

Other laboratory tests that may help in determining how active the virus may be in an individual are the beta-2 microglobulin (B2M) and the p25 antigen.[2,6] These val-ues may be abnormal during active progression of the patient's HIV disease. Serum concentrations of B2M greater than 3 mg/L have been shown to be a predictor of the development of AIDS.[7] Detection of p25 antigen, one of the core proteins, in the serum of an HIV-positive per-son appears to reflect active HIV replication.[7]

■ Viral Load

Recently introduced and commercially available tests to quantitatively measure plasma HIV RNA levels have revolutionized HIV treatment and care.[8] Numerous studies have determined that viral load changes precede changes in CD4 counts and are more accurate in determining the relative risk for disease progression as well as the effectiveness of primary therapy.

Current consensus is that levels less than 5,000 to 10,000/copies mL correlate to minimal risk for disease progression, while levels of greater than 30,000 to 100,000 copies/mL usually indicate a high risk for disease progression. Higher viral load values over time indicate that primary therapy interventions should be changed or reevaluated and that the risk for opportunistic infections is higher.

HIV viral loads are not meant to replace CD4 counts, which are still important in guiding prophylactic treatment decisions. Their primary value is in guiding and evaluating primary HIV therapy and disease progression.

■ Abnormalities in Hematologic Studies

Clinically significant hematologic abnormalities are common in HIV infection. These abnormalities can be caused by a single or, more likely, a number of factors in conjunction such as the direct effect of HIV infection, ineffective hematopoiesis, infiltrative disease, nutritional deficiencies, peripheral destruction secondary to splenomegaly or immune dysfunction or, perhaps most importantly, drug-induced hematologic abnormalities.[6,9,10] Abnormalities are found in all stages of HIV infection and involve the bone marrow, cellular elements of the peripheral blood, and coagulation pathways.

The typical anemia, which is the direct effect of HIV infection, is normocytic and normochromic (Table 9–3). Microcytic anemia is fairly uncommon and should alert the clinician to the possibility of blood loss from Kaposi's sarcoma of the GI tract, lymphoma, or perhaps cytomegalovirus (CMV) colitis with resultant iron deficiency.[3] Because nutritional deficiency has been documented in HIV-infected individuals, folate, vitamin B_{12}, and iron studies may help in diagnosing the cause and treatment of the anemia.

Bone marrow abnormalities are common in HIV. In addition to the virus itself causing myelosuppression, in-

TABLE 9–3. ANEMIA AND HIV

Causes of Normocytic Anemia

HIV

Bone marrow infections

    Mycobacterium avium[a]

    Mycobacterium tuberculosis

    Histoplasma capsulatum[a]

    Coccidioides immitis

    Cryptococcus neoformans

    Pneumocystis carinii

    Leishmania donovani

Causes of Microcytic Anemia

Kaposi's sarcoma of the GI tract

CMV colitis

Lymphoma

Iron deficient anemia of other causes

Causes of Macrocytic Anemia

Zidovudine (AZT or Retrovir)

Vitamin B_{12} or folate deficiency secondary to malabsorption

Hemolytic anemia

Drugs: Dapsone or sulfa drugs

[a] Especially in the presence of nucleated red blood cells.

fectious processes such as the atypical mycobacteria (*M. avium* and *M. kansasii*), histoplasmosis, cryptococcosis, and B19 parvovirus are known to aggravate or cause anemia.[9] Infectious causes of anemia should always be considered when the patient has unexplained constitutional symptoms, involvement of all blood cell lines, or a consistent decrease in hemoglobin without an alternative etiology.

Granulocytopenia is another commonly encountered cytopenia in HIV infection (Table 9–4). Like other cytopenias, it may stem from HIV infection alone, be caused by a myelopathic process in the bone marrow, or more commonly be caused by drug therapy.[3,6] Only when the absolute granulocyte count falls below 750 does the risk of infection and sepsis become great.

Thrombocytopenia is the most frequent platelet abnormality associated with HIV infection. The etiology may be HIV related or may be a side effect of drug ther-

TABLE 9–4. CAUSES OF GRANULOCYTOPENIA

HIV

Malignancy

Drug-induced

  Frequent

    Chemotherapy for Kaposi's sarcoma or lymphoma

    Ganciclovir

    AZT (Retrovir) (may be more frequent/severe when used in combination with lamivudine [3TC])

  Occasional

    Pyrimethamine (especially if not given in conjunction with folinic acid)

    Interferon

    Amphotericin B

  Infrequent

    Acyclovir

    Famciclovir

    Trimethoprim/sulfamethoxazole (TMP-SMZ)

apy. HIV-related immune thrombocytopenic purpura (ITP) is a diagnosis of exclusion and is properly diagnosed only when the patient has no other condition causing the thrombocytopenia.[11] HIV-related ITP may be associated with splenomegaly and is often found in conjunction with generalized lymphadenopathy. Thrombocytopenia which is HIV related may become less frequent with the widespread use of combination antiretroviral therapy. One commonly known yet unusual phenomenon of zidovudine is that at a higher dose than normal, it may increase the platelet count. Treatment in symptomatic cases of HIV-related ITP is systemic corticosteroids. It is important to evaluate whether the patient is symptomatic. Some patients may remain asymptomatic even with platelet counts of less than 20,000. Common causes of drug-induced thrombocytopenia are TMP-SMZ, amphotericin B, pyrimethamine, and ketoconazole.

Prolonged activated partial thromboplastin times (PTT) are occasionally detected in patients with HIV infection. This is thought to be a result of "lupus-like" anticoagulants and is probably an acquired immunoglobulin that interferes with phospholipid-dependent coagulation, thus prolonging the PTT. Hemorrhagic tendencies have not been noted in these patients and invasive procedures have been performed without bleeding.[4,6]

■ Abnormalities in Renal Function

Throughout the course of their illness, AIDS patients are at a high risk for renal complications. Systemic infection, sepsis, dehydration, hypoxia, and nephrotoxic drugs combine to decrease renal function and may permanently damage the kidneys.

Hyponatremia is one of the most common metabolic problems in patients with HIV infection. Gastrointestinal salt losses from diarrhea and free water repletion are the most common causes of hyponatremia. Volume repletion with normal saline generally corrects this condition.[3] Another cause of hyponatremia is the syndrome of inappropriate antidiuretic hormone secretion (SIADH). Syndrome of inappropriate antidiuretic hormone secretion is most often caused by infection or mass lesions in the brain or lung of AIDS patients. Additionally, SIADH is associated with euvolemic hyponatremia and is primarily managed by fluid restriction.

There are numerous etiologies for lesions in the kidneys of AIDS patients that cause clinical evidence of renal disease. One of these lesions is focal segmental glomerulosclerosis.[3,4,6] Focal segmental glomerulosclerosis primarily occurs among IV drug users and in black males. It still remains controversial whether this is related to HIV or IV drug use. However, the most significant factor contributing to kidney failure is nephrotoxic drugs used in therapy for opportunistic infections (Table 9–5).

TABLE 9–5. NEPHROTOXIC DRUGS

Frequent
    Amphotericin B[a]
    Foscarnet[a]
    Pentamidine
    Aminoglycosides[a]
Occasional
    Nonsteroidal antiinflammatory drugs
    High-dose acyclovir
    Valacyclovir (Valtrex)
Infrequent
    Rifampin
    Sulfa drugs
    Flucytosine

[a] May also be associated with magnesium-wasting nephropathy.

■ Abnormalities in Liver Function

Abnormalities in liver function commonly occur in HIV and AIDS patients. Liver dysfunction may be related to preexisting hepatic disease, ethanol usage, infections, neoplasms, or drug toxicity. Three distinct clinical syndromes have been recognized: (1) diffuse hepatocellular injury, (2) granulomatous hepatitis, and (3) sclerosing cholangitis.[3,4,6] Abnormal liver function tests are frequently a result of fatty infiltration of the liver or other nonspecific changes.

Diffuse hepatocellular injury is the most common abnormality in liver function. It may be caused by drug toxicity or preexisting hepatic disease due to chronic active hepatitis B, C, or D. Frequently co-infection can be demonstrated. The clinical picture of diffuse hepatocellular disease shows low-grade fever, hepatomegaly, jaundice, and in severe cases, ascites. Rapidly rising AST (aspartate transaminase) ALT (alanine transaminase) and elevated bilirubin levels are common.[2,3,6]

Granulomatous hepatitis is associated with mycobacterial or fungal disease as well as drug toxicity. This produces an obstructive or cholestatic enzyme pattern. Peliosis hepatitis is frequently found in bacillary angiomatosis. Other infective processes that have been noted to affect the liver are CMV, MAC, and cryptosporidiosis. Fever and constitutional symptoms are prominent in infectious processes.[4,6] Liver function tests demonstrate progressively rising levels of alkaline phosphatase, and less dramatic elevations of AST and ALT. Bilirubin concentrations are less often affected.[2,4,6]

Sclerosing cholangitis has been recognized in AIDS patients. The etiologies and pathophysiology are not known. Patients present with nonspecific abdominal complaints and progressive cholestasis. Retrograde endoscopy has demonstrated single and multiple areas of narrowing or dilation of intrahepatic and extrahepatic ducts.[3] In long-term cases, progressive jaundice and liver failure develop.

Hepatotoxic medications should be withheld when the patient has clinical symptoms of hepatitis. Often the liver enzymes may be elevated as much as fourfold without any clinical signs of hepatitis. Some of the more common hepatotoxic medications are the antituberculars (rifampin, pyrazinamide, and isoniazid) and the antifungals (fluconazole, ketoconazole, and itraconazole); an infrequently toxic drug is TMP-SMZ.

■ Abnormalities in Pancreatic Function

Pancreatic disease in AIDS patients has received little attention until fairly recently.[3] Studies have estimated a 7 percent lifetime incidence rate of pancreatitis. The most common causes of elevated lipase levels, but not necessarily pancreatic disease, are the antiretrovirals didanosine (ddI, Videx), zalcitabine (ddC, Hivid), and stavudine (d4T, Zerit). Intravenous pentamidine therapy for *Pneumocystis* pneumonia has been associated with hypoglycemia because of selective damage to beta cells in the islets of Langerhans.[3,4,6] If this injury is sufficiently severe or prolonged, hyperglycemia and insulin-dependent diabetes can result. Pentamidine may also cause overt pancreatitis. The combination of zalcitabine and pentamidine should be avoided. Patients with a significant history of alcohol use should be given didanosine or combination therapy with didanosine with careful monitoring.

Lipase is a more specific marker of pancreatic function; however, in acute pancreatitis, the amylase level may rise more rapidly initially but typically returns to normal range more quickly than lipase.[2,3] An elevation in lipase and/or amylase, without clinical or symptoms signs of pancreatitis, does not necessitate discontinuation of didanosine or zalcitabine.

Systemic complications of Kaposi's sarcoma are known to affect the pancreas. Systemic CMV, MAC, and fungal infections may also injure the pancreas, although pancreatic involvement is rarely noticed until autopsy.[3,4,6]

References

1. Ravel R. Clinical Laboratory Medicine. Chicago: Year Book; 1989.
2. Fischbach F. A Manual of Laboratory and Diagnostic Tests. Philadelphia: Lippincott; 1996:512.
3. Masci J. Primary and Ambulatory Care of the HIV-infected Adult. St. Louis: Mosby; 1992.
4. Joshi V, ed. Pathology of AIDS and Other Manifestations of HIV Infection. New York: Igaku-Shoin; 1990.
5. Jewell M, Swee D. Asymptomatic HIV infection: a primary care disease. *Postgrad Med.* 1992; 92:155–166.
6. Sande M, Volberding P. The Medical Management of AIDS. Philadelphia: Saunders; 1990.
7. Polis MA, Masur H. Predicting the progression to AIDS. *Am J Med.* 1990;89:701–704.
8. Schooley RT. Correlation between viral load measurements and outcome in clinical trials of antiviral drugs. *AIDS.* 1995;9(suppl 2):S15–S19.
9. Mir N, Costello C, Luckit J, et al. HIV disease and bone marrow changes: A study of sixty cases. *Eur J Haematol.* 1989;42: 339–343.
10. Mitsuyasu R, Lambertus M, Goetz MB. Transfusion dependent anemia in a patient with AIDS. *Clin Infect Dis.* 1992;15: 533–539.
11. Ratner L. HIV associated autoimmune thrombocytopenia purpura: A review, *Am J Med.* 1989;86: 194–198.

ten

C H A P T E R

Recognition and Management of Adverse Drug Reactions and Drug Interactions

John E. Fuchs, Jr.

The goal of recommending a drug to a person is to treat a condition without creating a problem. Unfortunately, problems are inevitable occurrences in all populations that receive medications. With certain drugs, however, patients with HIV infection have a greater tendency to develop adverse reactions compared to the non-HIV patient.[1] Additionally, HIV patients may receive numerous medications to treat multiple medical problems. It is known that the greater the number of medications a patient takes, the more likely is the risk of adverse drug reactions. Because it is sometimes difficult to differentiate disease from drug-induced abnormalities, recognizing and managing an adverse reaction in a patient with multiple diseases and medications is a challenge. It is important not to forget that medications can be a problem instead of a solution.

Definition

An adverse drug reaction (ADR) is an unintended nuisance or a potentially life-threatening effect of a drug.[2] Adverse drug reactions can be classified as either related or not related to the dose (or serum level) of a drug. A characteristic of serum-level-related ADRs is improvement upon drug dosage reduction, and they may be predictable. Non-serum-level-related ADRs, such as allergic or hypersensitivity reactions, respond only to drug discontinuation, and are considered unpredictable. Sometimes, risk factors can be identified that increase the likelihood of an ADR.

■ Getting Started—Reviewing the Medication Regimen

Many ADRs are predictable from the dose, serum level, or number of medications a patient receives. In some cases, ADRs must be accepted, and one hopes that they will be mild. However, minimizing the risk or the severity of predictable adverse reactions at each patient visit can be accomplished by reviewing the medication regimen and preventing overmedication. This involves four steps:

1. Discontinuing unnecessary medications (every drug must have an active diagnosis)
2. Determining that each dose is correct for body weight, and hepatic and renal function
3. Recognizing a sign or symptom as a potential adverse drug reaction
4. Recognizing potentially significant drug interactions

■ Recognition

Recognition of an ADR begins with an index of suspicion that a particular sign or symptom is causally related to the use of a drug. Literature-documented ADRs can be helpful in diagnosing the ADR, but are not necessarily a requirement. Identifying risk factors is helpful, but is not absolute. Differentiation between ADRs and disease symptomatology is sometimes difficult but can be accomplished by:

1. Determining the onset of the complaint relative to drug use
2. Identification of risk factors that increase the likelihood of an ADR (which can be a concurrent illness)
3. Response to subsequent dose reductions and/or drug discontinuation (and perhaps reintroduction of suspected drug)
4. Ruling out concurrent disease entities with appropriate diagnostic evaluation

It is not always possible to determine the causal relationship with a drug and the ADR. A list of previously reported and common adverse drug reactions is found in Table 10–1.

■ Management

Once the ADR is recognized and is determined to be a nuisance or potentially life threatening, management usually consists of dosage reduction or drug discontinuation. Depending on available alternatives and the severity of the ADR, reintroduction of the drug at a later time could be an option, especially if the ADR is dose related. Reintroduction of a drug following a hypersensitive reac-

TABLE 10–1. PREVIOUSLY REPORTED AND COMMON ADVERSE DRUG REACTIONS

Drug	Adverse Effects
Acyclovir (Zovirax)	*Intravenous:* Thrombophlebitis, confusion, hallucinations, renal impairment, (must be diluted in 100 ml of normal saline and infused over 1 hour) *Oral:* Long term (1 to 2 years) rarely causes headache, dizziness, arthralgia
Amphotericin B (Fungizone)	Normochromic normocytic anemia, hypokalemia, hypomagnesemia, renal impairment, infusion-related fever and chills
Atovaquone (Mepron)	Nausea, abdominal pain, rash, hepatitis
Azithromycin (Zithromax)	Abdominal pain, diarrhea
Ciprofloxacin (Cipro)	(Avoid in patients < 18 years old) nausea, headache, dizziness, arthropathy
Clarithromycin (Biaxin)	Nausea, abdominal pain (increase with doses > 1 g/day), taste perversion
Clofazimine (Lamprene)	Nausea, abdominal pain, skin discoloration (pink-brown)
Cotrimoxazole (Bactrim)	*Intravenous:* Bone marrow suppression, tremor, nausea *Oral:* Rash, fever, nausea
Dapsone (Avlosulfon)	Rash, peripheral neuropathy, hemolytic anemia in patients with G6PD deficiency, methemaglobinemia
Didanosine (Videx)	Nausea, vomitting, abnormal liver function tests, pancreatitis, peripheral neuropathy
Ethambutol (Myambutol)	Peripheral neuropathy, hyperuricemia, metallic taste, optic neuritis (rare and dose related)
Filgrastim (Neupogen®)	Bone pain, hyperuricemia, altered taste perception
Fluconazole (Diflucan)	Nausea, abdominal pain
Flucytosine (Ancobon)	Nausea, neutropenia, thrombocytopenia

Foscarnet (Foscavir)	Anemia, renal dysfunction, hyper- and hypophosphatemia, hypocalcemia
Ganciclovir (Cytovene)	*Intravenous:* Neutropenia, thrombocytopenia, disorientation with high dose (15 mg/kg per day or greater) for prolonged periods (> 14 days) *Oral:* Nausea, vomiting, neutropenia, thrombocytopenia
Indinavir (Crixivan)	Nausea, abdominal pain, headache, nephrolithiasis, abnormal liver function tests
Isoniazid	Hepatitis, peripheral neuropathy, drug-induced SLE (rare)
Itraconazole (Sporanox)	Nausea, hypertriglyceridemia, hypokalemia (doses > 400 mg/day), adrenal insufficiency (doses > 600 mg/day), hepatitis (rare)
Ketoconazole (Nizoral)	Nausea, abdominal pain, hepatitis, hypertriglyceridemia, adrenal suppression (doses > 600 mg/day)
Lamivudine (Epivir)	Nausea, vomiting, headache, dizziness, neutropenia, peripheral neuropathy
Metronidazole (Flagyl)	Peripheral neuropathy (doses > 1500 mg/day)
Ofloxacin (Floxin)	(Avoid in patients < 18 years old) nausea, headache, dizziness, arthropathy
Pentamidine (Pentam)	*Intravenous:* Pancreatitis, neutropenia, hypoglycemia, hypotension, renal insufficiency *Inhalation:* Metallic taste, anorexia, bronchospasm, pancreatitis
Primaquine	Nausea, hemolytic anemia in patients with G6PD deficiency, methemaglobinemia
Pyrazinamide	Hyperuricemia, hepatitis (doses > 30 mg/kg per day), arthralgia
Pyrimethamine (Daraprim)	Megaloblastic anemia, neutropenia
Rifabutin (Mycobutin)	Nausea, rash, neutropenia, uveitis (rare), reddish-orange discoloration of urine, stool, saliva, and sweat
Rifampin (Rifadin)	Fever, rash, reddish-orange discoloration of urine, stool, saliva, and sweat; thrombocytopenia and interstitial nephritis (rare)

TABLE 10–1. (continued)

Ritonavir (Norvir)	Nausea, vomitting, anorexia, perioral paresthesias, peripheral neuropathy, dizziness, taste perversion
Saquinavir (Invirase)	Nausea, vomiting, abdominal pain, diarrhea
Sulfadiazine	Nausea, rash, neutropenia, crystalluria, renal failure
Trimetrexate (Neutrexin)	Neutropenia, thrombocytopenia, anemia
Zalcitabine (Hivid)	Peripheral neuropathy, pancreatitis, arthralgia, esophageal and mouth ulcers
Zidovudine (Retrovir)	Neutropenia, megaloblastic anemia (bone marrow recovery 14 days), headache, blue nail pigmentation, proximal myopathy of legs associated with increased CPK

tion may require a desensitization plan. Management of ADRs depends on:

1. Recognition and differentiation from disease
2. Assessing severity
3. Dosage reduction and/or drug discontinuation
4. Available alternative therapy
5. Reintroduction of drug after resolution of ADR: lower dose or desensitization

Peripheral neuropathy, pancreatitis, renal dysfunction, neutropenia, sulfonamide hypersensitivity, and drug interactions deserve further attention, as they are commonly encountered in an HIV clinical setting.

■ Peripheral Neuropathy

HIV, CMV, and vitamin B_{12} deficiencies have been associated with peripheral neuropathies in AIDS patients.[3,4] Although the etiology of peripheral neuropathy of some drugs is known, such as isoniazid, it is unclear whether other drugs associated with peripheral neuropathy induce or exacerbate existing disease. When a patient develops activity-limiting peripheral neuropathy, it is appropriate to lower dosages or withdraw the suspected neurotoxins to establish a causal relationship.

Drugs

1. Zalcitabine (Hivid)
2. Isoniazid[5]
3. Dapsone (Avlosulfon)
4. Metronidazole (Flagyl)
5. Didanosine[6] (Videx)
6. Ethionamide (Trecator)
7. Stavudine (Zerit)

8. Lamivudine (Epivir)
9. Ritonavir (transient) (Norvir)

Risk Factors for Drug-induced Peripheral Neuropathy

1. Advancing HIV disease (absolute CD4 count < 50)
2. Vitamin B_{12} deficiency
3. Previous peripheral neuropathy or concurrent neurotoxin

Recognition

1. Sensory neuropathy is the rule (tingling, numbness, burning, or pain in the feet or hands); motor involvement is rare
2. Reduced or absent achilles reflex

Management

Non-activity-limiting Neuropathy

1. Discontinue unnecessary neurotoxin.
2. Use correct dosage for body weight and renal function (Table 10–2).
3. Therapeutic trial: ibuprofen 400 to 600 mg, 3 doses/day; amitriptyline/desipramine 25 to 50

TABLE 10–2. ANTIRETROVIRAL DOSAGE REDUCTION[a]

For body weight less than 132 pounds (60 kg)	
Didanosine	125 mg twice daily
Stavudine	30 mg twice daily
For creatinine clearance 30 to 50 mL/min	
Lamivudine	150 mg once daily
Stavudine	20 mg twice daily
Zalcitabine	0.75 mg twice daily

[a]Zidovudine, indinavir, ritonavir, and saquinavir dosages are not reduced based on body weight or renal function.

mg once daily at bedtime (desipramine has less anticholinergic activity, which makes it more favorable in patients with oral candidiasis).

Activity-limiting Neuropathy (persistence > 3 days)

1. Reduce dosage or discontinue suspected drug.
2. Recovery may take over 2 weeks to several months.
3. When symptoms decrease or resolve, reintroduce drug at lower dosage.

■ Pancreatitis

Advancing HIV disease and CMV have been associated with pancreatitis in the absence of drug therapy.[7] When a patient develops clinical pancreatitis, it is appropriate to provide a drug-free period of suspected pancreatoxins to establish the causal relationship.

Drugs

1. Didanosine[8,9] (Videx)
2. Zalcitabine (Hivid)
3. Ganciclovir (Cytovene)
4. Pentamidine (intravenous)[10] (Pentam)
5. Pentamidine (inhalation)[11] (Nebupent)
6. Stavudine (Zerit)
7. Lamivudine (Epivir)

Risk Factors for Drug-induced Pancreatitis

1. Concurrent alcohol consumption
2. Hypertriglyceridemia
3. Previous pancreatitis
4. Absolute CD4 lymphocyte count less than 50

Recognition

1. Abdominal pain, nausea, and vomiting; associated with elevations in amylase, lipase, or both
2. Hypocalcemia
3. Hypertriglyceridemia

Management

1. Use correct dosage for body weight and renal function (Table 10–2).
2. Encourage patient to discontinue alcohol ingestion.
3. Asymptomatic elevations in pancreatic enzymes are more common than symptomatic pancreatitis. However, if salivary fraction of amylase has been ruled out, suspected pancreatoxins should be discontinued if enzyme(s) exceed four times the upper limit of normal to determine causal relationship.
4. Discontinue suspected pancreatoxin if patient is symptomatic and pancreatic enzymes are two times upper limit of normal to determine causal relationship.
5. When pancreatic enzymes have normalized, rechallenge with reduced dosage and repeat enzymes in 5 to 7 days if alternative therapy is unavailable.

■ Renal Dysfunction

An HIV nephropathy that usually leads to renal failure has been described, but drugs are the most common cause of renal dysfunction. Recovery from drug-induced lost renal function is the rule when the nephrotoxin is discontinued.

Drugs

1. Amphotericin B[12] (Fugizone)
2. Foscarnet (Foscavir)
3. Pentamidine (intravenous) (Pentam)
4. Acyclovir (intravenous) (Zovirax)
5. Sulfadiazine[13]
6. Cidofovir[14] (Vistide)

Risk Factors for Drug-induced Renal Dysfunction

1. Dehydration (Increase dietary sodium intake and/or infuse 500 to 2000 mL normal saline)
2. Hyponatremia
3. Concurrent nephrotoxins (aminoglycosides, vancomycin)

Recognition

1. Rise in serum creatinine greater than 0.4 mg/dL from baseline
2. Impaired urinary concentrating ability
3. Proteinuria
4. Urinary casts

Management

1. Use correct dosage for body weight and renal function (Table 10–2).
2. Correct dehydration/hyponatremia; infuse 500 to 1000 mL normal saline, then 2 to 3 L/day.

3. If rehydration is insufficient, reduce dosage appropriately or discontinue until serum creatinine has normalized.
4. Probenecid should be administered before and after cidofovir to minimize renal dysfunction. The dose is 2 g by mouth 3 hours before the infusion and 1 g at 2 and 8 hours after the end of the infusion.

■ Neutropenia

Neutropenia predisposes a patient to infection.[15,16] It is estimated that 20 to 25 percent of patients with HIV infections have low circulating neutrophils, but neutrophil function may also be impaired (chemotaxis, phagocytosis, and killing power). When a patient develops neutropenia, it is appropriate to lower the dosage, or withdraw the suspected bone marrow suppressant, or administer a neutrophilic hematopoietic factor to prevent a life-threatening infection. Hematopoietic factors may allow continuation of bone marrow suppressant.

Drugs

1. Zidovudine (Retrovir)
2. Ganciclovir (Cytovene)
3. Flucytosine (Ancobon)
4. Pyrimethamine (Daraprim)
5. Pentamidine (Pentam)
6. Sulfonamides
7. Lamivudine (Epivir)
8. Trimetrexate (Neutrexin)

Risk Factors

1. Concurrent bone marrow-suppressing agents.

Recognition

Absolute granulocyte count (ANC) less than 750 cells/mm^3 (total WBC $\times$ [% segs + % bands]).

Management

1. Use correct dosage for body weight and renal function (Table 10–2).
2. Withdraw suspected agent and administer a therapeutic alternative if available.
3. If bone marrow suppressant cannot be discontinued, administer filgrastim (gCSF) also known as Neupogen® 5 μg/kg (round off to nearest 50 μg; vial contains 300 μg/mL) subcutaneously or intravenously once daily for 3 to 4 consecutive days. Maintenance dose of gCSF are sometimes necessary and are dosed at 5 μg/kg, one to three times weekly. Monitor CBC weekly.

Note: Target ANC is 1500 cells/mm^3. Discontinue filgrastim if ANC is above 15,000 cells/mm^3. Sargramostim (gmCSF) is an alternative.

■ Sulfonamide Hypersensitivity

Sulfonamide antibiotics are used commonly in the management of HIV-related infections.[17–19] However, hypersensitivity to these drugs is common and often leads to drug discontinuation. Because sulfonamide antibiotics are inexpensive and remain the drug of choice for infections that include *Pneumocystis carinii* pneumonia and cerebral toxoplasmosis, several methods to improve tolerance have been utilized. Desensitization, which involves administering progressively larger doses at 30 to 60-minute intervals, is considered a safe and effective approach in most patients who have not had a life-threatening reaction. Published experience, as well as ours, indicates that desensitization is successful in 60 to 80 percent of patients. Up to 30 percent of patients successfully desensitized and are maintained on prophylactic therapy will have a rash and/or fever that reoccurrs within several months and may require redesensitization.

Drugs

1. Trimethoprim-sulfamethoxazole (SXT, co-trimoxazole)
2. Sulfadiazine
3. Dapsone (clinical cross reactivity with co-trimoxazole or sulfadiazine is rare)

Risk Factors

1. Progressive immunodeficiency
2. Large doses of sulfonamide
3. Coexisting CMV or Epstein-Barr virus infections
4. Glutathione deficiency
5. Slow acetylator phenotype

Recognition

Maculopapular rash and/or fever that resolves within 5 days of sulfonamide discontinuation.

Management

1. Desensitization can be performed at home, in an outpatient clinic, or in a hospital. Patients with a previous history of a life-threatening reaction should be desensitized *only* if absolutely necessary and *only* in a location that contains monitoring and resuscitative equipment.
2. The patient should consent to the procedure.
3. Desensitization protocol (see Chapter 17).

4. After successful desensitization, patients should receive *daily* doses of the sulfonamide antibiotic as interruption in the regimen for 48 hours increases the likelihood of hypersensitivity reoccurrence.

■ Viral Protease Inhibitors

Protease inhibitors (PI) possess inhibiting properties not only of HIV protease, but also of the drug-metabolizing enzyme systems of the liver.[20–23] Hepatic enzymes, also known as P450 cytochrome (CYP), are responsible for metabolizing drugs to inactive molecules.[24] PIs have their highest affinity for the CYP3A4 enzyme system, a moderate affinity for CYP2C9 and CYP2D6, and the least affinity for CYP1A2. The higher affinity a PI has for a particular enzyme, the less enzyme will be available to metabolize co-administered drugs. Hence, drugs that utilize the P450 enzyme systems can be expected to accumulate to potentially harmful levels.

Drugs

1. Indiavir (Crixivan)
2. Ritonavir (Norvir)
3. Saquinavir (Invirase)

Risk Factors for Drug Interactions With Protease Inhibitors

Co-administered drugs that require the cytochrome P450 enzyme system for metabolism.

Recognition and Management

(See Table 10–3.)

TABLE 10-3. DRUG INTERACTIONS WITH PROTEASE INHIBITORS

Protease Inhibitor (A)	Co-Administered drug (B)	Effect	Action
Indinavir, ritonavir, saquinavir	Terfinadine, astemizole, cisapride	Increased blood levels of (B)	AVOID
Indinavir, ritonavir, saquinavir	Rifampin	Decreased serum levels of (A)	AVOID
Ritonavir, saquinavir	Tricyclic antidepressant drugs	Increased blood levels of (B)	Reduce (B) dose by 50 percent
Ritonavir, saquinavir	Rifabutin	Increased blood levels of (B)	AVOID
Indinavir	Rifabutin	Increased blood levels of (B)	Reduce Rifabutin dose by 50 percent
Indinavir	Ketaconazole	Increased blood levels of (A)	Reduce Indinavir dose to 600 mg every 8 hours

References

1. Kovacs JA, Hiemenz JW, Macher AM, et al. Pneumocystis carinii pneumonia: A comparison between patients with the acquired immunodeficiency syndrome and patients with other immunodeficiencies. *Ann Intern Med.* 1984;100: 663–671.

2. McQueen EF. Pharmacological basis of adverse drug reactions. In: Speight TM, ed. Avery's Drug Treatment: Principles and Practice of Clinical Pharmacology and Therapeutics. 3rd ed. Baltimore: Williams & Wilkins; 1987:229.

3. Cornblath DR, McArthur JC. Predominant sensory neuropathy in patients with acquired immunodeficiency syndrome and AIDS related complex. *Neurology.* 1988;38:794–796.

4. Simpson DM, Olney RK. Peripheral neuropathy with human immunodeficiency virus infection. *Neurology Clin.* 1992;10: 685–711.

5. Gibson FD, Phillips S. Peripheral neuritis after long term isoniazid. *Geriatrics.* 1966;21:178–181.

6. Kiebartz KD, Siedlin M, Lambert JS, et al. Extended follow up of peripheral neuropathy in patients with AIDS and ARC treated with didanosine. *J Acquir Immune Defic Syndr.* 1992;5: 60–64.

7. Schwartz MS, Brandt LJ. The spectrum of pancreatitis disorder in patients with AIDS. *Am J Gastroenterol.* 1989;84:459–462.

8. Rathburn CR, Martin ES. Didanosine therapy in patients intolerant of or failing zidovudine therapy. *Drug Intell Clin Pharm.* 1992;62:1347–1351.

9. Maxson CJ, Greenfield SM, Turner JL. Acute pancreatitis as a common complication of didanosine in AIDS. *Am J Gastroenterol.* 1992;87:708–713.

10. O'Neil M, Selub SE, Hak LF. Pancreatitis during pentamidine therapy in patients with AIDS. *Clin Pharmacol.* 1991;10: 56–59.

11. Murphy RL, Noskin GA, Ehrenpreis ED. Acute pancreatitis associated with inhaled pentamidine. *Am J Med.* 1990;5N: 553–556.

12. Heidemann HT, Gerkens JF, Spickard WA, et al. Amphotericin B nephrotoxicity in humans decreased by salt repletion. *Am J Med.* 1983;75:476–481.

13. Simon DI, Brosios FC, Rothstein DM. Sulfadiazine crystalluria revisited. *Arch Intern Med.* 1990;150:2379–2384.

14. Flaherty JF. Current and experimental therapeutic options for cytomegalovirus disease. *Am J Health Syst Pharm.* 1996;53(suppl 2):S4–S11.

15. Murphy MF, Metcalfe P, Waters AH, et al. Incidence and mechanism of neutropenia and thrombocytopenia in patient with human immunodeficiency virus infection. *Br J Haematol.* 1987;66:337–340.

16. Israel DS, Plaisance KI. Neutropenia in patients infected with human immunodeficiency virus. *Clin Pharmacol.* 1991;10:268–279.

17. Gluckstein D, Ruskin J. Rapid oral desensitization to trimethoprim-sulfamethoxazole: Use in prophylaxis for pneumocystis carinii pneumonia in patient with AIDS who was previously intolerant to TMP-SMZ. *Clin Infect Dis.* 1995;20:849–853.

18. Nguyen MT, Weiss PJ, Wallace MR. Two-day oral desensitization to trimethoprim-sulfamethoxazole in HIV-infected patients. *AIDS.* 1995;9:573–575.

19. Bachmeyer D, Salmon C, Barre C, et al. Trimethoprim-sulfamethoxazole desensitization in HIV-infected patient: An open study. *AIDS.* 1995;9:299–312.

20. Danner SV, Carr A, Leonard JM, et al. A short-term study of the safety, pharmacokinetics, and efficacy or ritonavir, an inhibitor of HIV-1 protease. *N Engl J Med.* 1995;333:1528–1533.

21. Kumar GN, Rodrigues AD, Buko AM Denissen JF. Cytochrome P450-mediated metabolism of the HIV-1 protease inhibitor ritonavir in human liver microsomes. *J Pharm Exp Ther.* 1996;277:423–431.

22. Product information. Merck & Co., March 1996.

23. Product information. Roche Laboratories, November 1995.

24. DeVane CL. Pharmacogenetics and drug metabolism of newer antidepressant agents. *J Clin Psych* 1994;55(suppl):38–45.

eleven

CHAPTER

Treatment of the Primary Infection and Vaccines

Richard B. Pollard

■ HIV Treatment

Efforts to control HIV infection through the development of antiretroviral medications as well as consideration of the use of immunomodulators have been intensive in the arena of HIV infection. The developments of therapies in this area have been both gratifying and frustrating. HIV has the ability to produce mutant resistant viruses that do not respond to antiviral chemotherapeutic agents. This has resulted in mixed results, with new agents inducing enthusiasm and then frequently turning out less promising after being developed. However, the overall development of such interventions must be considered remarkable, with significant numbers of new agents recently approved and on the horizon for the foreseeable future. This is much different than in the early years, in which only one agent, zidovudine (Retrovir, AZT), licensed in 1987, was recognized to be active, one to which resistance occurs relatively rapidly and which should not be used as single-agent therapy.

Probably the other most important development over the last decade has been the understanding of the disease process gathered through large-scale clinical trials. This has developed into a sophisticated process, where information about the utility of new agents can now be produced rapidly. In addition, active agents are approved for usage in accelerated fashion by regulatory authorities. Many thousands of patients have participated in such clinical trials, and their willingness to do so has certainly enhanced the progress of drug development.

Clinical Markers and Response to Therapy

In addition to development of new agents, the clinical trials process has also identified the comparative reliability of markers that one might use to decide relative activity and efficacy of various agents. It has become clear that although the ultimate standard for a new agent is its ability to effect clinical disease and influence mortality, the development of more rapidly changing measurements that appear to correlate with clinical events has hastened the development of new therapeutic interventions. The initial studies ranged from those with zidovudine, which showed an effect on mortality, to measurements of clinical progression (mainly the development of certain opportunistic infections and other softer signs of progressive HIV infection).[1-4] Recently, it has become obvious that waiting for clinical progression to decide whether one is responding to a particular agent is no longer acceptable, and that other measurements should be used in addition to measurements of clinical disease. However, the influence on clinical disease is still an important measurement of drug activity.

The most commonly used endpoint, termed by some a surrogate marker, has been CD4 cell counts. The CD4 counts progressively decline in the course of HIV infection, and their level predicts the risk for development of certain opportunistic infections as well as clinical decline.[5] Changes in CD4 count, either naturally induced by continued HIV replication or enhanced with the use of effective antiretroviral therapy, became a standard for measuring response to new agents. This measurement is a more sensitive marker of the activity of antiviral agents as compared to disease progression. In addition, there appear to be some limits on the ability of antiviral agents to influence CD4 counts. For example, even with development of newer triple combinations therapies, patients may have increases in CD4 count but they may not return to normal levels.[6] The meaning of such partial responses is poorly understood. The measurement of CD4 counts, however, does remain an important part of evaluating the relative stage of HIV infection in an infected individual and response to active antiretroviral therapy.

The last several years has produced a new understanding of HIV infection, with data suggesting that there is a constant rapid turnover of high numbers of virus particles and CD4 cells.[7,8] It is through these data that we now have a different understanding of the pathogenesis of HIV infection. It is an ongoing, long-term interaction, with multiple virus particles infecting susceptible cells and those cells being destroyed, with virus produced and affecting additional cells. This interaction takes place continuously for a prolonged period, until the immune system is unable to continue the constant requirement to produce such cells or the viral infection overwhelms the immune system's ability to control the infection.

The measurement of virus load, which has become relatively common, is the tool that many investigators, clinicians, and patients have been searching for. Data from multiple sources, including clinical trials and pathogenesis studies, suggest that measurement of the virus load in the blood, particularly the plasma levels of virus, is reflective of the amount of virus in the body, and that it can be rapidly influenced by active therapeutic interventions. It should also be mentioned that with this new understanding of pathogenesis of HIV, it is currently accepted that there is much more virus present in the lymphoid tissue, which is a source of continued virus replication and immunologic damage. However, the levels in the peripheral blood are felt to accurately reflect the levels in the total body. With the development of reliable techniques to quantitate virus load, this measurement has been validated as the most sensitive marker to use during intervention with antivirals and for prognostic staging of a particular patient. This technique is necessary to select patients who should be begun on therapy and for determining the influence of therapy, including when to alter individual therapeutic regimens. Data from prospective cohort follow-ups have demonstrated that patients with higher virus load are much more likely to progress, and that this measurement is much more predictive than the relative level of CD4 cells.[9] This is illustrated by the fact that patients with very high virus load, even those who have greater than 500/mm^3 CD4 cells, are at much higher risk of progression than those with lower levels of virus. In addition, virus load is relatively stable, if certain considerations for the use of the test are routinely used. For instance, the test should be performed on an individual patient using the same assay methodology, and preferably the same laboratory to avoid variability. A recent working group has recommended that patients who are being considered for therapy have this test twice at baseline, 3 to 4 weeks after beginning therapy to assess the efficacy of the therapy, and every 3 to 4 months thereafter.[10] This is similar to the frequency at which CD4 cells are measured. Changes of virus load of greater than a half-log are indicative of response to therapy, or suggestive of higher risk of clinical progression if it is increasing. With some newer therapies, very substantial decreases in virus load can be obtained. It is also apparent from multiple clinical trials that changes in virus load occur much more rapidly than changes in CD4 count or clinical disease. It is felt by many that routine monitoring of virus load will allow for an enhancement of the impact of therapeutic interventions and translate into prolonged beneficial effects with the numerous agents that are now available.

Antiviral Agents

As a reflection of the rapid progress in the development of antiviral agents, a list of agents that are either currently approved or should be approved in the near future is presented in Table 11–1. This list has expanded over the past year, with multiple new agents being approved. It should also be recognized that there are additional agents in each of the three classes listed in the table that are under active development. Some have interesting properties that will permit their licensure and use in the clinical arena. Two major targets in HIV replication have been used to develop therapies. The process of reverse transcription, where viral RNA is transformed into a complimentary DNA through the use of a virus-encoded enzyme, reverse transcriptase, has been the target of most drug development. Two classes of agents, nucleoside analogs and nonnucleoside reverse transcriptase inhibitors, act at this particular enzyme site and inhibit HIV replication. Each of the compounds listed in Table 11–1 has particular characteristics, patterns of activity, pharmacokinetics, and

TABLE 11–1. ANTIRETROVIRAL AGENTS

Medication	Usual Dosage	Adverse Affects
Nucleoside Analogs		
Zidovudine (Retrovir)	200 mg tid	Anemia, headaches, nausea, myositis
Didanosine (Videx)	200 mg bid	Pancreatitis, diarrhea, peripheral neuropathy
Zalcitabine (Hivid)	0.75 mg tid	Peripheral neuropathy, pancreatitis, oral ulcers
Stavudine (Zerit)	40 mg bid	Peripheral neuropathy
Lamivudine (Epivir)	150 mg bid	Nausea, headache
Protease Inhibitors		
Saquinavir (Invirase)	600 mg tid	GI disturbances
Indinavir (Crixivan)	800 mg q 8 hr	Hyperbilirubinemia, nephrolithiasis
Ritonavir (Norvir)	600 mg bid	GI disturbances, perioral paresthesias
Nonnucleoside Analogs		
Nevirapine (Viramune)	200 mg bid	Rash, diarrhea, drug fever
Delavirdine (Rescriptor)	400 mg tid	Rash, elevated liver enzymes

patterns of resistance that distinguishes it from the others. Therefore, as these agents are more widely used in clinical practice, their individual characteristics can be utilized to suggest combinations of agents, and combinations that might not be optimal.

Studies using the most recently developed class, HIV protease inhibitors, have resulted in licensure of three drugs in recent months. A particular advantage of protease inhibitors, not only because they are very active in suppressing HIV replication, is that when combined with reverse transcriptase inhibitors, in certain situations at least an additive to synergistic inhibition of HIV replication is produced. Therefore, the use of reverse transcriptase inhibitors plus protease inhibitors has been shown to produce dramatic results.[6,11] In addition, other targets for development of antiviral drugs, including compounds that inhibit early attachment and other targeted enzyme systems, such as integrase enzyme, another virally coated enzyme, are being explored to develop even more new therapeutic options. As many of the agents described have recently entered into clinical usage, much additional experience with regard to their individual characteristics, and in particular their use in combinations, will be acquired. Perhaps the most exciting development is the observation that with the use of certain combinations, particularly reverse transcriptase inhibitors and protease inhibitors, a significant number of patients have their virus load decreased to undetectable levels for some prolonged period of time.[6] Of continued concern, however, is the development of resistance to individual agents. This will be more fully explored as they are increasingly used in clinical practice.

Recommendations

There are various recommendations with regard to the use of antiretroviral therapies that are becoming clarified as data accumulate. When to start therapy has not been completely answered.[12,13] In particular, early studies with single nucleoside analog therapies such as zidovudine suggested that treating patients with greater than 500/mm^3 CD4 cells, while producing some immunologic effects, did not influence clinical progression. Only with a CD4 count less than 500/mm^3 did clinical benefit occur. However, certain patients who have greater than 500/mm^3 CD4 cells and very high virus load should be considered as candidates for early intervention with antiretroviral therapy. The precise viral load, which should trigger such intervention in individuals of greater than 500/mm^3 CD4 cells, has not been identified, but certainly patients with greater than 30,000 HIV RNA copies/mL represent a subpopulation at much higher risk of progression. Perhaps even a lower threshold of virus load will ultimately become utilized. Patients who also have less than 500/mm^3 CD4 cells are felt to be candidates for therapy.

The particular type of therapy to begin is unknown; however, there is much enthusiasm for combination therapy with two nucleoside analogs for this group of patients. Findings from two large studies, the AIDS Clinical Trial Group (ACTG) 175 and the Delta study, confirmed that patients starting or remaining on zidovudine alone did worse than patients on combination nucleoside regimens, some of which included zidovudine.[14,15] It is recommended that patients not receive zidovudine monotherapy for longer than 12 weeks. Whether or not other single-agent therapy in patients beginning antiretroviral therapy should be used is still under investigation. In particular, measurements of viral load should be carefully monitored in any patient beginning therapy, and if there is not a significant decrease in viral load (more than 0.5 log or greater), alternative therapy should be considered. In addition, patients who have rapidly decreasing CD4 cell counts should be considered for combination therapy.

For patients already on antiretroviral therapy, virus load monitoring once again becomes very important. With data rapidly accumulating, it is clear that waiting for changes in CD4 count or especially changes in clinical condition are not acceptable. As virus load monitoring becomes more widely available, virus load measurements will be used to decide if patients have received optimal benefit from specific regimens, in particular to decide when patients are failing and should have additional intervention. Because of the expense of the regimens containing multiple antiretroviral agents, the most aggressive regimens—which might include two reverse transcriptase inhibitors plus a protease inhibitor—are being reserved for patients who are somewhat more advanced and who have not achieved adequate responses with other therapies.

There are several other important considerations for certain groups of patients that are worthwhile mentioning. In particular, the group of patients with late-stage HIV infection with less than $100/mm^3$ CD4 cells has been a population that was relatively unresponsive to antiretroviral agents. Such patients frequently were receiving single-nucleoside therapies that produced little change in CD4 cell count or in clinical outcome. Many such patients—if treated with triple combination regimens, best termed highly active antiretroviral therapy, which include two nucleoside analogs plus a protease inhibitor—will have major changes in virus load, CD4 cell count, and potentially clinical outcome. It is not uncommon to observe in such patients two to three log drops in virus load, CD4 cell count increases by $100/mm^3$ to $200/mm^3$, and resulting improvement in clinical state.[6] The precise clinical benefit of such changes is not known, but there is increasing optimism that this group of patients will benefit significantly from these therapies. Also, patients who have dramatic alterations in their antiretroviral regimens seem to have greater benefit than those who simply switch to one new drug or add one drug to a previous regimen. Patients who have had changes in two to three compounds seem to have greater benefit.

The recent observation that a certain percentage of patients will become negative with currently available virus load measurements, and that they stay negative for some prolonged period of time, is particularly encouraging. How this will influence the emergence of resistance, and whether patients can actually stop therapy at some interval to see how quickly the virus rebounds, are subjects of current clinical investigation. The fact that experts are actually raising such questions is a reflection of having antiviral regimens that, in combination, can produce such dramatic effects.

Other Treatment

There are several other instances where therapeutic intervention is under exploration and where suggestions are that aggressive therapy may produce benefit. The first of these is in patients with a primary HIV infection where they appear with documented seroconversion from seronegative to seropositive. It is felt that this group of patients, if aggressively treated, may have very substantial clinical benefits. Active investigation on whether to start such patients on triple drug regimens very early, almost at the time they are recognized, is the appropriate intervention. The chance of dramatically changing the patient's viral load, which could produce profound alterations in clinical progression, could prove to be very beneficial. A second area of major clinical advancement has been the identification that vertical transmission from infected mother to infant can be significantly altered with the use of antiretrovirals. The only placebo-controlled trial to date is one that used zidovudine in mothers and their infants in a situation in which the mothers had intermediate HIV infection.[16] A two-thirds reduction in transmission to susceptible infants was reported. Further aggressive studies of the use of other antiretrovirals during pregnancy are underway, and continued development of improved therapy in this situation should occur. In mothers who have received zidovudine, consideration of the use of other compounds might produce a greater decrease in the chance of transmission. A third situation where more aggressive therapy has been suggested is in the area of post-exposure prophylaxis. A small observational study has suggested that zidovudine has activity in preventing transmission to health care workers who have needle stick injuries. It has recently been recommended that such health care workers with significant exposure to HIV infection be treated with at least dual combination therapy, with consideration for using a third agent.[17] It is not clear outside the needle stick injuries whether such therapy is warranted for other types of exposure (blood exposure to intact skin, for example).

The spectrum of the available drugs, and the possibility of therapeutic interventions in treating HIV infection, is rapidly changing. As mentioned, it is expected that additional compounds will soon be available for use. This will require that practitioners become familiar with each one of the available drugs and learn to use as single agents and in combination with others. Each compound, as in other areas, has particular pharmacokinetic properties and toxicities that will require in-depth understanding, particularly as these agents are used together. Also, when they are used with other compounds to treat or prophylax opportunistic infections, expertise will be required. Therefore, it will be important for practitioners to continually attempt to keep current with therapeutic agents and their implications if they are to provide optimal care for their patients.

■ Vaccines and Immunotherapy

The area of therapeutic vaccines has remained under intense investigation. However, no recommendation has been made to offer HIV-infected individuals a vaccination.[18] The use of HIV-containing therapeutic vaccines is an attempt to enhance the host's own immune response so that this response can control HIV replication. To date, no therapeutic vaccine has been shown to decrease virus load or result in enhanced overall immune responses (CD4 cells or clinical outcome). There is information that suggests that HIV-infected individuals can produce immunologic responses to vaccines that they receive; however, this has not translated into the development of improvement in their own HIV infection. Therapeutic vaccines remain a subject of continued research interest and several large-scale trails are underway. The major application for HIV vaccines is in prevention of primary infection in susceptible exposed individuals. Large-scale studies to determine the appropriate vaccine to use in preventative endeavors are also underway.

Another major area of investigation is with immunotherapy with various agents that might enhance host responses to HIV infection or improve immunologic function. Studies that will use human monoclonal antibodies directed against HIV infection to enhance the ability of the patients to neutralize their own HIV will begin shortly. In addition, techniques such as expansion of CD4 or CD8 cell populations that are targeted against HIV are under investigation. Such cell populations are expanded outside the patient's body, and then reinfused in an attempt to enhance specific responses to HIV and to help the host control the infection. Other interventions, such as administration of Interleukin 2, which has been shown to increase CD4 cells, are also being studied.[19] However, the development of very active antiretroviral therapy has changed many of the current plans to use such immunologic intervention. Such interventions are now being designed to see what they add to the antiviral and immunologic response induced by antiretroviral therapy instead of determining what they might do alone.

One of the most active areas of exploration in the laboratory is to try to understand the immune competence of the cell populations that are being enhanced following the administration of highly active antiretroviral therapy. Investigations are underway to understand the functionality of the cells produced, and to understand the nature of the particular cell populations that reemerge after virus replication has been effectively inhibited. Such data will enhance our understanding of the pathogenesis of HIV infection.

References

1. Fischl MA, Richman DD, Grieco MH, et al. The efficacy of azidothymidine (AZT) in the treatment of patients with AIDS and AIDS-related complex: A double-blind placebo-controlled trial. *N Engl J Med*. 1987;317:185–191.

2. Fischl MA, Richman DD, Hansen H, et al. The safety and efficacy of zidovudine (AZT) in the treatment of subjects with mildly symptomatic human immunodeficiency virus type 1 (HIV) infection: A double-blind, placebo-controlled trial. *Ann Intern Med*. 1990;122:727–737.

3. Volberding PA, Lagakos SW, Koch MA, et al. Zidovudine in asymptomatic human immunodeficiency virus infection: A controlled trial in persons with fewer than 500 CD4-positive cells per cubic millimeter. *N Engl J Med*. 1990;322:941–949.

4. Volberding PA, Grimes JM, Lagakos SW, et al. A comparison of immediate with deferred zidovudine therapy for asymptomatic HIV-infected adults with CD4 cell counts of 500 or more per cubic millimeter. *N Engl J Med.* 1995;333:401–407.

5. Hughes MD, Stein DS, Gundacker HM, et al. Within-subject variation in CD4 lymphocyte count in asymptomatic human immunodeficiency virus infection implications for patient monitoring. *J Infect Dis.* 1994;169:28–36.

6. Guliek R. Mellors J. Havlir D, et al. Potent and sustained antiretroviral activity of indinavir (IDV) in combination with zidovudine (ZDV) and lamivudine (3TC). Third Conference on Retroviruses and Opportunistic Infections, January 28 to February 1, 1996, Washington, DC. Abstract LB7.

7. Ho DD, Neumann AU, Perelson AS, et al. Rapid turnover of plasma virions and CD4 lymphocytes in HIV-1 infection. *Nature.* 1995;373:123–126.

8. Wei X, Ghosh SK, Taylor ME, et al. Viral dynamics in human immunodeficiency virus type 1 infection. *Nature.* 1995;373:117–122.

9. Mellors JW, Rinaldo CR Jr., Gupita P, et al. Prognosis in HIV-1 infection predicted by the quantity of virus in plasma. *Science.* 1996;272:1167–1170.

10. Saag MS, Holodniy M, Kuritzkes DR, et al. HIV viral load markers in clinical practice: Recommendations of an international AIDS society–USA expert panel. *Nat Med.* 1996;2:625–629.

11. Collier AC, Coombs R, Schoenfeld DA, et al. Treatment for human immunodeficiency virus infection with saquinavir, zidovudine, and zalcitabine. *N Engl J Med.* 1996;334:1011–1017.

12. Sande MA, Carpenter CCJ, Cobbs CJ, et al. Antiretroviral therapy in adult HIV-infected patients: Recommendations from a state-of-the-art conference. *JAMA.* 1993;270:2583–2589.

13. Carpenter CCJ, Fischl MA, Hammer SM, et al. Antiretroviral Therapy for HIV Infection in 1996. *JAMA.* 1996;276:146–154.

14. Hammer S, Katzenstein D, Hughes M, et al. Nucleoside monotherapy (MT) vs. combination therapy (CT) in HIV infected adults: A randomized, double-blind, placebo-controlled trial in persons with CD4 cell counts 200–500/mm^3. 35th Interscience Conference on Antimicrobial Agents and Chemotherapy, September 17 to 20, 1995, San Francisco. Abstract LB1.

15. Gazzard B, on behalf of the International Coordinating Committee, Chelsea and Westminster Hospital, London. Further results from European/Australian Delta Trial. Third Conference on Retroviruses and Opportunistic Infections, January 28 to February 1, 1996, Washington, DC. Abstract LB5a.

16. Connor EM, Sperling RS, Gelber R, et al. Reduction of maternal–infant transmission of human immunodeficiency virus type 1 with zidovudine treatment. *N Engl J Med.* 1994;331:1173–1180.

17. Centers for Disease Control and Prevention. Update: Provisional recommendations for chemoprophylaxis after occupational exposure to human immunodeficiency virus. *MMWR.* 1996;45:468–472.

18. Pollard RB, Forrest BD. Immunologic therapy for HIV-infected individuals, 1993–1994. *AIDS.* 1994;8:S295.

19. Kovacs JA, et al. Increases in CD4 T lymphocytes with intermittent courses of interleukin-2 in patients with human immunodeficiency virus infection: A preliminary study. *N Engl J Med.* 1995;332:567.

part IV

COUNSELING AND PREVENTION

twelve
CHAPTER

HIV Counseling and Testing

Timothy F. Quigley

The goals of HIV counseling and testing are twofold: to help uninfected individuals initiate and sustain behavioral changes that reduce their risk of becoming infected, and to assist HIV-infected individuals to avoid transmitting the virus to others.[1] Counseling and testing can also help infected individuals to access medical care prior to progression to AIDS.

Primary care providers have a unique responsibility of initiating HIV counseling and testing routinely with their patients.[2] Each clinical encounter should be viewed as a potential opportunity to offer prevention information and to assess risk for HIV infection.[3] Because the primary care provider occupies a position of trust for the patient, an opportunity exists for intimate communication and personalized education.[4]

Prior to HIV counseling, the clinician should take a thorough drug and sexual history.[4] This assessment allows the clinician to ascertain what risks the individual may have for HIV. These questions may be difficult for the clinician to ask as well as for the individual to answer.

It is best to start with open-ended questions and continue with specific, nonjudgmental questions. For instance, instead of asking individuals if they are "gay" or homosexual, ask if they have sex with men, women, or both.[4,5] The clinician should ask about the number of sexual partners and whether each partner injects drugs, is promiscuous, is at risk for HIV, or is bisexual.[5] When individuals may be unsure concerning these behaviors in their partners, testing should probably proceed, as not all people would willingly disclose this information to their sexual partners.

When asking about drug use, it may be easier to start with questions about prescription drugs and work toward asking about IV and illicit drug use. Concurrently with drug/sexual partner questioning, the clinician can include education about how drugs and alcohol interfere with judgment and may promote unsafe sexual practices.

Assessing a patient's complete drug and sexual history, and providing appropriate counseling, requires some subtlety of approach because the risk factors for HIV often involve socially unacceptable behavior.[5] Clinicians need to be aware of their own values and attitudes about sexuality, drug use, and other lifestyle issues that may bias the provider's counseling.[2] A nonjudgmental attitude in an atmosphere of respect and compassion will allow the provider to deliver the best counseling and testing services for patients at risk for HIV infection.

In addition to the development of a trusting relationship, the clinician needs to be sensitive to cultural issues, social taboos, gender roles, and the potential for discrimination in housing, employment, and health care. A flexible, individualized approach combined with listening—not lecturing—to the patient will produce the best results (Box 12–1). Avoid using technical jargon. Speak in a direct manner to the patients, using language they can understand.[4]

■ **Box 12–1**

Effective HIV Counseling

- Identify biases, overcome inhibitions
- Be nonjudgmental, compassionate
- Give personalized, individualized message
- Be culturally and linguistically appropriate
- Develop skills in sexual and drug history taking
- Use open-ended questions
- Develop cooperative strategy
- Foster trusting, respectful atmosphere
- Identify referral sources
- Inform of anonymous testing sites
- Reinforce message with handouts
- Emphasize confidentiality

If the medical, drug, and sexual history reveals a risk for HIV infection (Table 12–1), the patient should be offered testing or referral to an anonymous HIV testing site.[6] Issues of confidentiality should be explained to the patient, including the possibility that positive results may be legally given to insurers, other health care providers, state agencies, and public health authorities as required or permitted by law.

The Centers for Disease Control and Prevention (CDC) recommend that all pregnant women receive voluntary HIV testing in light of research demonstrating the efficacy of antiretroviral therapy in prevention of HIV transmission in utero (see Chapter 7).[7] In addition, pa-

TABLE 12–1. INDICATIONS FOR HIV TESTING

Engaged in sex in last 14 years, unless mutually monogamous with uninfected partner
Vaginal or anal intercourse without condom
Use of drugs or alcohol at time of sexual activity
Use of intravenous drugs in last 14 years
Blood transfusion between 1978 and 1985
Homosexual/bisexual
Pregnant women
Women planning pregnancy
Women of childbearing age with HIV risk factors
Persons planning marriage
Patients with STDs
Large number of sexual partners
Sexual partners have HIV risk factors
Adolescents and young adults
Diagnosed with tuberculosis
Hospital patients, age 15 to 54
Unstable psychiatric patients
Prostitutes or those who trade sex for drugs
Persons in correctional institutions
Children of HIV-positive mothers
Hemophiliacs
Persons from countries with high HIV rate
Persons who consider themselves at risk

From reference 6.

tients of hospitals with a high HIV or AIDS rate may be encouraged by hospital policy to receive HIV counseling and testing.[8,9] Adolescents, prisoners, homeless individuals, prostitutes, and blood plasma donors pose special counseling and testing challenges (Table 12–2).

Pretest Counseling

Risk assessment and prevention education are essential elements of the pretest counseling visit. Clear, concise,

TABLE 12–2. SPECIAL POPULATIONS: COUNSELING AND TESTING ISSUES

Homosexual/bisexual	Reticence to discuss sexuality Prior exposure to homophobic health professionals Fear of discrimination[10]
Women	Often tested later in infectious process[10] May need to promote female-dependent prevention methods Lesbian/bisexual women may have past or current risk factors
Pregnant women	Need to prevent HIV and STD during pregnancy Zidovudine therapy effective during pregnancy if HIV positive[7]
Adolescents/young adults	Risky behavior is common Need repeated discussions about risk factors Want provider to initiate discussion about HIV and STDs[12]
Hospital patients	If high HIV or AIDS seroprevalence rate, CDC encourages policies to offer HIV counseling and testing to all patients[8,9]
Prisoners	Problems with confidentiality, discrimination, retribution
Homeless/street persons/prostitutes	Often noncompliant May need repeated counseling, testing, and referral[10]
Blood/plasma donors	If p24 antigen test is positive, donors often have high titers and may be at high risk for transmitting HIV infection[13]

understandable definitions of HIV and AIDS are important at this encounter. The clinician needs to help the patient identify risk behaviors and jointly formulate a written Risk Reduction Plan to minimize further opportunities for infection.[1,3] Because some patients will fail to return for the test results, it is important to give comprehensive, individualized prevention messages[4] (Box 12–2). Discussion of safe sexual practices, discontinuing intravenous drug use, and the effects of drugs and alcohol on judgment of safe sex should be done at this time (Table 12–3).

When discussing HIV testing, the clinician should counsel the individual on the advantages and disadvantages of being tested as well as the limits of the test (see Chapter 9). Advantages of being tested include resolving uncertainty and preventing further HIV transmission.

■ **Box 12–2**

Essentials of HIV Prevention

- Abstain from sex
- Maintain mutually monogamous relationship
- Limit number of sexual partners
- Use condoms regularly and correctly
- Avoid anal sex
- Abstain from drug use
- Don't use intravenous drugs
- Don't share needles
- Bleach clean needles
- Get treatment for drug problem

TABLE 12–3. PRETEST COUNSELING

Introduce prevention message
Define HIV and AIDS
Identify risk activities
Define transmission
Explain what a negative test means
Define window period for seroconversion
Explain what a positive test means
Explain how a test can help
Conduct risk assessment
Develop risk reduction plan
Identify anonymous testing sites
Discuss confidentiality
Discuss advantages and disadvantages of testing
Discuss patient's likely reaction to negative test
Discuss patient's likely reaction to positive test
Give written materials to patient
Obtain and document written consent for test
Arrange return appointment
Advise against blood/plasma/organ donation

The patient may benefit from receiving medical care early if the test result is positive, before AIDS develops.[5] Testing may also assist women with risk factors if they are planning a pregnancy. Disadvantages of testing include the psychological trauma and the potential for social ostracism, familial estrangement, and insurance and employment discrimination.

While assessing risk factors and the timing of risk behaviors, the clinician and patient will need to discuss the "window period" for seroconversion, and then plan the most appropriate time for testing. If the individual has had a recent exposure to HIV (within the past 6 weeks) the test result may be negative. The individual should be counseled to be retested in 3 to 6 months.

In addition to patient education about the meaning of negative results and the "window period," patients should be counseled about the meaning of positive HIV testing; that is, they may be infected with the virus, they can transmit the virus if infected, they will need medical care and planning for reproductive health issues, and they could still live for many more years depending on the progress of the infection. This information will help the patient prepare psychologically for a positive test. This pretest counseling session is also the time to assess the patient's coping skills and possible reactions to a negative or positive test, and to facilitate the development of a personalized plan to deal with the results.[3] Patients may be encouraged to bring a support person to the post-test counseling session.[1]

Before testing the patient should be asked to give written, informed consent for the procedure. This is the time to again discuss confidentiality and the possibility of authorized, legal disclosures of a patient's serostatus to other health care providers, insurers, and public health authorities. Patients should be informed of the opportunity for free and/or anonymous testing sites. The consent form for HIV testing should include the purpose of the test and what the results—positive, negative, and indeterminate—mean.[5] The form should note that the individual has been counseled prior to testing and will be counseled on the results of the test.

At the conclusion of the pretest counseling session, the patient should receive a return appointment, a copy of the informed consent form, a copy of the individualized Risk Reduction Plan, and written materials to reinforce the prevention message of the counseling session. In addition, the patient should be advised against blood, plasma, or organ donation while awaiting the test results.

Post-Test Counseling

The purposes of post-test counseling are to help uninfected persons begin behavior changes to reduce their risk of becoming infected, to arrange medical care for HIV-positive individuals, to prevent transmission of HIV from those infected, and to ensure referral of as many sex- and needle-sharing partners as possible.[1]

Both the CDC and the Canadian Medical Association highly recommend that clinicians give a patient the HIV test results in the context of an in-person, face-to-face interview. This setting insures confidentiality, permits a better appreciation of the patient's reaction, enables adequate counseling, allows for better interpretation of the test results (Fig. 12–1), allows the clinician to address the patient's immediate emotional concerns, and facilitates reinforcement of the HIV prevention messages given in the pretest counseling session.[1,10] The FDA's approval of over-the-counter home HIV testing kits, however, will undoubtedly increase the number of HIV-positive individuals who will learn their test results without benefit of personal pre- or post-test counseling.

Negative Test Result

The patient who has engaged in risky behaviors and is awaiting HIV test results will likely be anxious, eager, and apprehensive. The clinician should give the test results at the beginning of the visit in a direct and clear manner.[10]

After informing individuals that the result is negative, assess their feelings and continued risk factors (Table 12–4). If they are concerned about a false negative, schedule a follow-up test in 3 to 6 months.[4] Remind all seronegative individuals that if the HIV exposure has occurred recently (within the past 6 months) they may not have seroconverted. A follow-up HIV test should be scheduled in

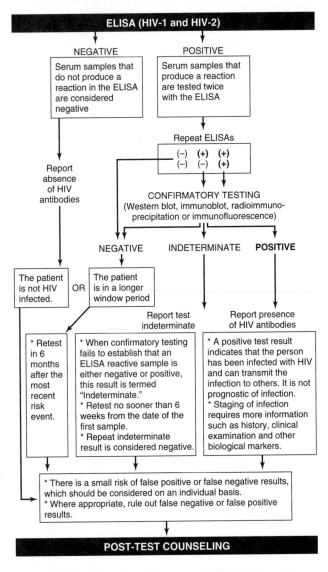

Figure 12–1. Interpretation of ELISA (HIV-1 and HIV-2). (*With permission from reference 10.*)

TABLE 12–4. COUNSELING IF HIV NEGATIVE

Reinforce prevention messages
Review risk reduction plan
Assess window period and risk behaviors
Schedule repeat test if necessary
Recommend STD screening
Refer for drug treatment if necessary

3 to 6 months. Use this time to reiterate the ways that they can protect themselves from HIV infection, and review and modify their risk reduction plan as necessary. Some patients may perceive their negative test results as an opportunity to make dramatic lifestyle changes such as entering drug treatment or avoiding high risk sexual activities. Be prepared to facilitate these behavior changes by making appropriate referrals for off-site prevention or treatment facilities.

Positive Test Result

Bad news, such as HIV-positive test results, should be delivered to the patient directly in a face-to-face visit. Listen, respond to questions, and allow time for the patient's emotional response (Table 12–5).[10]

The clinician should be prepared for a variety of reactions and emotions after informing individuals that they are seropositive for HIV.[5] Individuals could have feelings of anger, fear, guilt, denial, or combinations of emotions. They could even become suicidal. Therefore, it is important to let individuals have time to discuss their feelings. Some persons, however, will not say anything, and the clinician may have to help elicit their feelings. Some individuals may feel that they are being punished. It is important to let them know that infection with HIV is a consequence of a behavior, not a punishment.

As the newly diagnosed HIV-positive patient may be

TABLE 12–5. COUNSELING IF HIV POSITIVE

Give results in person
Be direct with test results
Be prepared for emotional crisis
Listen to patient, explore feelings
Assess psychological response
Evaluate suicide potential
Emphasize availability of crisis support
Provide hope, reassurance
Review meaning of positive test
Discuss infection control
Explain reduction of risk behavior
Give reproductive counseling
Advise healthy lifestyle changes
Discuss partner notification plans
Advise medical evaluation
Give written referral list
Schedule repeat counseling as needed
Ensure follow-up
Consider blood draw for CD4 count

overwhelmed with emotions, the first post-test counseling visit may be mostly supportive in nature.[10] The clinicians should only give as much information as the patient can handle in that visit, emphasizing hope and "taking it one day at a time" as the patient adjusts to the diagnosis. Encourage productive living with HIV, and inform the patient that he or she may remain healthy and active for many years. Stress that being infected with HIV is a chronic disease, not a death sentence.[2]

Review what a positive test means: that the patient is infected and infectious, that the virus can be transmitted in pregnancy, and that blood, plasma, and organ donation should be avoided. Preventive measures must be reemphasized regarding safer sex and safer drug practices. Patients should be advised on lifestyle measures such as nutrition, stress reduction, immunizations, and avoidance of drugs and alcohol, to avoid further compromising the immune system. In addition, patients should be given information about thorough cooking of meat and eggs, safe disposal of cat and bird litter, and not sharing razors and toothbrushes.

Referral for a comprehensive medical evaluation is essential for all newly diagnosed HIV-positive individuals. Diagnostic testing to evaluate T-cell subsets and concomitant infections (such as TB, hepatitis, STDs, toxoplasmosis) is necessary to determine the need for antiretroviral or prophylactic therapy.[11]

Seropositive individuals must be reminded to tell their partners that they need to be tested.[4,5] This includes those with whom they shared needles and their sexual partners. It may be helpful for individuals to role-play how they will tell their partner(s), or they may want the clinician to help disclose this information. If individuals will not tell their partner(s), try to persuade them to do so. If this does not work, inform seropositive individuals that it may be necessary for the clinician to inform the partner(s). This should be only as a last resort, and in most cases this is not done because of confidentiality issues. However, this could be done with appropriate consent.

Individuals should be asked about their support systems[4] and be given written information about support groups as well as telephone numbers for the AIDS hotline or a crisis clinic (see Chapter 20).

It is often necessary to arrange more than one posttest counseling visit.[5] Individuals may not be able to absorb all the information at one time. It is helpful to review the information and have them repeat it to ensure that the information they have is correct. One method for ensuring follow-up is to draw blood for a CD4 count before the patient leaves the office, scheduling another visit to discuss results and reiterate the prevention and treatment messages.[4]

If a patient doubts the positive HIV test results, the clinician will need to explore the patient's reasoning in order to assess the need for repeat testing. Individuals should be advised about the process of multiple tests to confirm positive results and the very small likelihood of a false-positive test. For the patient with no identifiable risk factors, or if there is a possibility of lab error or mislabeled samples, repeat testing should be considered.[1]

Exhaustive efforts should be made to contact all patients who don't return to receive the results of their HIV testing. Follow-up attempts should be documented in the medical record.[1] Testing sites should evaluate carefully for institutional barriers such as long waits, inconvenient hours, or inaccessible locations that discourage return visits.[3]

In the rare event of an inconclusive HIV test, the clinician will need to explain to the patient that the test may represent a false-positive test or a test where the antibodies have not yet fully developed. The patient should be counseled to continue risk reduction behaviors, and to return for repeat testing in 6 weeks. Psychiatric referral or interim counseling may be necessary to assist the patient in dealing with the diagnostic uncertainty. Be sure to give the patient a list of hotline and crisis intervention numbers.[1]

References

1. Centers for Disease Control and Prevention. HIV Counseling, Testing, and Referral Standards and Guidelines. Atlanta: U.S. Department of Health & Human Services, Public Health Service, CDC, 1994:1–2, 7–11.
2. Andrews LJ, Novick LB. HIV Care, A Comprehensive Handbook for Providers. Thousand Oaks, CA: Sage; 1995:1–11.

3. Centers for Disease Control and Prevention. Technical guidance on HIV counseling, 1993. *MMWR.* 1993;42:11–17.

4. Kassler WJ, Wu AW. Addressing HIV infection in office practice. *Primary Care.* 1992;19:19–33.

5. Fang CT, Gostin LO, Sandler SG, Schlotterer WL. HIV testing and patient counseling. *Patient Care.* 1989;23:19–44.

6. Centers for Disease Control. Public health service guidelines for counseling and antibody testing to prevent HIV infection and AIDS. *MMWR.* 1987;36:509–515.

7. Centers for Disease Control and Prevention. U.S. Public Health Service recommendations for human immunodeficiency virus counseling and voluntary testing for pregnant women. *MMWR.* 1995;44:1–12.

8. Centers for Disease Control and Prevention. Recommendations for HIV testing services for inpatients and outpatients in acute-care hospital settings; and technical guidance on HIV counseling. *MMWR.* 1993;42:1–17.

9. Janssen RS, St Louis ME, Satten GA, et al. HIV infection among patients in U.S. acute-care hospitals: Strategies for the counseling and testing of hospital patients. *N Engl J Med.* 1992;327:445–452.

10. Canadian Medical Association Expert Working Group on HIV Testing. Counseling Guidelines for HIV Testing, May 15, 1995.

11. Pottage JC, Samet JH, Soloway BH. The asymptomatic patient. *Patient Care.* 1996;30:27–51.

12. Rawitscher LA, Saitz R, Friedman LS. Adolescents' preferences regarding human immunodeficiency virus (HIV)-related physician counseling and HIV testing. *Pediatrics.* 1995;96:52–58.

13. Centers for Disease Control and Prevention. USPHS guidelines for testing and counseling blood and plasma donors for human immunodeficiency virus type 1 antigen. *MMWR.* 1996;45:1-9.

thirteen
CHAPTER

Social Worker Assessment and Intervention

Miguel A. Ortega

The role of the social worker in the treatment of those affected by HIV is multifaceted. Social work practice consists of professional interventions that enhance the development, problem-solving, and coping capacities of people. The profession promotes the effective and humane operation of medical, social, and educational systems that link people to resources and services; educates people about how to better use them; and contributes to the development and improvement of social policies and programs.[1] In the medical setting, social workers are involved in evaluation of patients' coping abilities, support network, resource systems, and their basic needs including financial, emotional, employment, and adjustment needs.

The initial evaluation done by a social worker is a complete psychosocial history that may include a personal history, family history, dynamics of relationships, educational and employment history, understanding of medical situation, past and present coping strategies and mechanisms employed, and resources presently being used to meet needs. With this information the professional social worker should assess the following.

1. Level of understanding the HIV-positive individual has of his or her medical condition
2. Makeup and dynamics of personal support system and networks
3. Past coping mechanisms, with focus on what is needed to handle present situation
4. Level of financial security and resource needs
5. Advocacy and educational needs within medical resource systems

This evaluation, combined with the social worker's knowledge about the roles and duties of the other professionals involved (physicians, nurse practitioners, physician assistants, and rehabilitation specialists), allows the social worker to provide direct interventions such as counseling, medical regimen education, advocacy, and referral. The social worker also provides consultative services to the other members of the team regarding the special needs or social circumstances of the individual patient, family, or significant others. This service includes being information brokers of current programs and the eligibility criteria for each program. In order to expand on the chapters regarding psychiatric care and psychosocial issues (Chapters 14 and 15), this chapter focuses on how to evaluate the impact of those issues on the HIV-positive patient, as well as specific interventions and resource tips.

■ Evaluation of the Person Who Is HIV-positive or Has AIDS

Identifying the diagnosis (HIV/AIDS) and whether it is a new diagnosis for the patient will help establish the potential need for crisis intervention. Although we all cope differently, the social worker needs to be prepared for dealing with an emotionally devastated individual. Determining the extent of the patient's knowledge and understanding of the diagnosis allows for the identification of the following.

1. Continued educational needs regarding health status and assistance with reframing of perspectives
2. Communication and assertiveness skills needed to enhance the patient's abilities to become a partner in his or her own care
3. The need for "safer sex" counseling and education

Determining the patient's current emotional state requires the social worker to investigate the presence of denial, anger, guilt, hopelessness, or other signs of clinical depression, including suicide risk factors. This allows for identifying and supporting the emotional well-being of the patient. Because of its severity, special attention is given to suicide risk. Individuals are considered to be at risk for suicide if they have perceived social isolation and lack available social supports.[2] The evaluation should focus on the following factors.

1. A noted past history of suicidal ideations or attempts, impulse control problems, known clinical depression, substance abuse, and/or a psychiatric diagnosis

2. An increase in personal losses in the past 6 months with significant impact, including deaths, loss of financial support, and/or loss of physical and mental capacities

3. Changes in sleep, eating, social, or recreational habits that are found to be inhibiting the ability to function

4. Coping patterns that are inappropriate, such as substance abuse or violence

5. Direct statements made regarding a desire to die or give up

If the patient is thought to be at risk, special attention needs to be given to evaluating the patient's support network, coping skills, changes in behavior, hygiene, and emotional status. If the patient states that suicide is the intent, then the worker needs to assess the following.

1. The difference between ideation, threats, and gestures

2. Lethality and availability of the means chosen

3. Detail of plan

4. Preparation (developing wills, giving away belongings)

5. Desire and ability

6. Intent to live or die

The evaluation of the social support system and basic needs (Box 13–1) of the patient includes identification of pertinent persons making up the system, their roles, how they see themselves in this system, and the strengths and weaknesses of the system itself. This may include strong family ties or friendships that may affect physical and emotional health. Obtaining a good understanding of the openness of communication related to the disease identifies individuals who may be experiencing denial, rejec-

■ **Box 13–1**
Evaluation of Basic Needs

- Living arrangements
- Financial situation
- Medical situation
- Transportation
- Activities of daily living

Note: A patient's own perceptions of his or her physical functioning, compared to the social worker's observations, gives insight into self-image and denial. This should also be based on the findings of the occupational and physical therapists as well as work evaluations for the purpose of career counseling or adaptation to working with disabilities. Consider a referral to the state vocational and rehabilitation agency, and counseling regarding awareness of rights guaranteed under the Americans with Disabilities Act.

tion, isolation, a need for counseling regarding partner notification, or a mechanism to vent fears. The ability of the support system to meet the patient's needs will identify the need for referrals to agencies and programs to help meet those needs. If community agencies are already involved, this knowledge indicates the individual's ability to use available resources appropriately.[3]

Behaviors that affect the patient's health and/or medical treatment need to be identified and assessed.

These include, but are not limited to, use of injected drugs, other substance use, unprotected high-risk sexual practices, and noncompliance with medical regimens. This information is useful to the medical team, and identifies possible obstacles and challenges in assisting the individual to address these and other issues.

The final part of the assessment should include a discussion of the direction the patient wants to take from this point on regarding treatment and other life issues. The social worker should allow the patient to prioritize the identified needs. It is important to note that because of time constraints involved in doing a thorough assessment, the patient's identified needs and concerns may be all that are dealt with in the initial interview. The larger assessment may need to be done in a second, scheduled interview.

■ Interventions

Patient education about the HIV/AIDS disease process, with an information packet specific to the patient's situation (stage of illness, social situation, and language and cultural context) is necessary. This provides written reinforcement to verbal education. It allows individuals to educate themselves at a pace with which they can cope, and provides them with materials to begin to educate family and loved ones.

Interventions for patients in denial about their diagnosis or risk groups may also help with the acceptance of the diagnosis and enhance transmission precautions. The first step is education, followed by continual reinforcement of the realities of early intervention and treatment. Open discussions about their diagnosis and the possibility of rejection and death can lead to acknowledgment. In order to establish trust, an open atmosphere, with nonjudgmental materials and staff, is essential.

Patient empowerment and self-advocacy gives individuals control over their own lives. This empowerment makes coping easier when feelings of hopelessness exist or if the terminal nature of the disease is the issue. Basic topics to cover with patients include taking personal responsibility for their own medical treatment, nutrition, exercise, and stress reduction. Interventions could include educational pamphlets, seminars, assertiveness skill training, meditation, religion, and spiritual healing.

Discussion of issues relating to large, bureaucratic clinics or hospital systems can maximize the appropriate use of the available health care services. It can also increase the ability to cope with large and continuously changing teaching and health care institutions and understanding how health care systems function.

Grief counseling for losses such as the death of loved ones from AIDS, finances, professional identity, physical functioning, appearance, independence, control of life, social support, and family support is an important skill in the social worker's repertoire. Interventions may include crisis intervention techniques to allow for controlled venting of emotions, referral to various agencies and programs to address financial and career losses, and referrals to support groups for ongoing assistance to deal with the loss or losses.

Some individuals faced with HIV/AIDS may have feelings of guilt that can be related to the possibility of spreading the disease, unresolved identity issues, survivor's guilt, or lack of independence.

The resolution of guilt can be facilitated by allowing individuals to express their feelings in a supportive environment. Patients should consider specialized therapy or support group involvement, as well as plan for the possibility of dependence and discuss what things can be done to prolong activity and control, and to remain independent mentally with physical limitations.

If the patient is a substance abuser and acknowledges that use or abuse is a problem that needs addressing, a referral to an appropriate substance abuse program is indicated. If the patient is in denial concerning substance usage, the intervention should be to reinforce the clinician's concerns about the effects of substance use on the disease and the treatment. Although change is not possible unless the patient is willing to verbalize a problem, attempts to educate the patient should continue.

Counseling patients on the disclosure of the diagnosis to family, friends, and employers involves decision counseling. To start, help the individual ascertain why disclosure is necessary at this time. Is it work related? A need for support? Out of fear or uncertainty? Pamphlets or other written materials on this topic may be helpful to the patient. This will give the patient basic information and steps in identifying to whom, when, where, and how to disclose this information. The decision should be planned and not a single-session decision.

It is imperative that all health care professionals be able to manage the suicidal patient. Suicide ideations, gestures, or threats that occur during telephone follow-up calls should be treated as real. A crisis intervention technique should be used (Boxes 13–2 and 13–3).

■ Box 13-2

Steps in the Management of the Suicidal Patient

1. Make someone aware that you are handling a suicide and have a trace placed on the call if notified by telephone.
2. Notify the mental health authorities.
3. Ask the patient to delay the suicide plan.
4. Check for detail of plan, availability and lethality of plan, and desire to die.
5. Assess whether substances have already been used, such as alcohol or cannabis, that may further impair the patient's ability to reason.
6. If a telephone contact, check to see if the patient is alone or if others are at the patient's location.
7. Help the patient identify the level and sources of stress.
8. Actively help the patient review options to solve current problem.
9. Use the patient's personal resources and your professional resources to try and resolve the most pressing issues.
10. Contract with the patient not to proceed with the suicide plan for a set period of time and to follow through with the resource plan. Be certain that the patient is able to be realistic.
11. If a phone trace is possible, keep client on the telephone line until the mental health authorities arrive.
12. Refer for appropriate psychiatric evaluation.

■ **Box 13–3**

Long-Term Management Issues
in Suicide

1. If the patient is suicidal, inform the patient's clinician of the suicide risk and refer to an appropriate psychiatric service, such as a crisis clinic, or consult psychiatry.
2. If the patient is clinically depressed, inform the patient's clinician and request psychiatric consultation. Follow the patient to reinforce the psychiatric plan and offer case management services.
3. If the patient is undergoing multiple stressors, help the patient identify issues and begin a plan to deal with each one. Refer the patient to a support group for HIV-positive persons and follow up weekly by phone and in clinic with regard to follow-through with referrals, plans made in counseling sessions, and emotional status.

References

1. National Association of Social Workers. A definition of social work practice. NASW Standards for the Classification of Social Work Practice—Policy Statement IV. Washington, DC: NASW;1981:6.
2. Dilley JW, Pies C, Hellquist M. Face to face: A guide to AIDS counseling. *HIV Dis Suicide.* 1989;5:154–155.
3. Green G. Editorial review: Social support and HIV. *AIDS Care.* 1993;5:87–104.

fourteen

Psychiatric Care

Eric N. Avery

For front-line practitioners, knowledge about and comfort with common psychiatric problems is critical to the successful care of the HIV-infected patient. Childhood histories of abuse (sexual, verbal, emotional, and physical), personality disorders, mood and anxiety disorders, and substance abuse, produce behaviors that put individuals at risk for HIV. Increasing numbers of new HIV-infected patients, as high as 54 percent in one study,[1] present with psychiatric disorders.[2] Some were present before exposure to HIV.[3,4] Other disorders emerge during the course of HIV disease. All psychiatric disorders can decrease quality of life, complicate treatment adherence, and pose difficulties in the management of patients.[5]

For those without preexisting psychiatric problems, the considerable psychological stress of infection with HIV exhausts coping mechanisms, provokes anxiety, insomnia, and grief. Adjustment disorders are common. Rates of depression are higher in patients infected with HIV than in patients with other medical conditions. For those individuals infected for a long time, survivor guilt, death, and dying issues become important stressors.

With the emergence of cognitive decline and dementia, a result of direct HIV infection of the brain, behavior may change, and depression, mania, and psychosis may develop. Delirium can be produced by systemic and intracranial infections, cancers, drug withdrawal states, endocrine disorders, disorders of fluid and electrolytes, metabolic encephalopathies, and as the side-effect of medications.

HIV-infected patients with psychiatric disorders are often difficult to manage in high-stress, crowded clinics. Patient with behavior disorders and addictions are often less responsive to educational efforts designed to change the sex and drug use behaviors. Because these patients continue to expose others to HIV infection, ethical and legal problems emerge for the health care professional.

The most common psychiatric disorders and standard treatments for them are presented in the following sections. A high index of suspicion for these disorders, a standard set of diagnostic criteria, and experience with a limited group of psychotropic medications will allow one to treat these disorders, improve the quality of life, and improve functioning of patients. When attempts at psychiatric primary care fail, referral to a mental health professional with expertise in HIV psychiatry is indicated.

■ Mood Disorders

Major Depression

The most frequent request for psychiatric help with HIV-infected patients is to evaluate and treat depression. Primary care practitioners can diagnosis and treat this disorder. But in order to do so, a high index of suspicion must be present. Health care providers should not fall prey to the notion that "depression is understandable" for those coping with HIV. There are many causes for a depressed mood in HIV-infected patients (Box 14–1), and each has its own treatment strategy. Major depression, a course of significant co-morbidity, is present in 8 percent to 33 percent of patients with HIV and AIDS.[6] With HIV progression, the chance of developing a major depression increases; however, studies have not shown that depression contributes to immunosuppression.[7] Because major

---

■ Box 14–1
Differential Diagnosis of Depressed Moods in HIV Patients

- Despondency/demoralization
- Dysthymia (chronic low mood)
- Adjustment disorder/minor depression
- Major depression, recurrent major depression
- General anxiety disorder
- Bipolar disorder—depressed phase
- Organic mood disorder "secondary depression" (infections, medication side effects, and mass lesions of CNS)
- Malnourishment/weight loss associated with HIV
- Sleep disorder
- Psychoactive substance abuse
- Bereavement

depression responds well to antidepressant therapy, it is important to diagnosis and treat it.

Clinical Manifestations. By the *Diagnostic and Statistical Manual* fourth edition (DSM-IV) criteria,[8] at least five or more symptoms (Table 14–1) should be present most of the day, during the same 2-week period, and should represent a change from previous functioning. At least one of the symptoms is either depressed mood or loss of pleasure. A useful mnemonic for depression is SIGECAPSS (Table 14–1).

   None of these symptoms is pathognomonic for major depression. In medically ill people with AIDS, the symptoms of fatigue, anorexia, and poor sleep are common and not necessarily associated with depression. In this group of ill patients, decreased mood or loss of pleasure, low self-esteem, irritability, and increased thoughts about death are most helpful in evaluating for the presence of a major depression. A previous history of depression and/or a family history of depression must be present. Because thoughts of death are more common in those infected with HIV,[9] and suicide rates are higher in this patient popula-

TABLE 14–1. SYMPTOMS OF DEPRESSION

Mnemonic	Symptom
Sleep	Insomnia or hypersomnia
Interest	Diminished interest in daily activities
Guilt	Guilt feelings, low self-esteem, worthlessness
Energy	Fatigue or loss of energy
Concentration	Diminished concentration, indecisiveness
Appetite	Weight loss/gain or change in appetite
Psychomotor	Motor agitation or retardation
Suicide	Recurrent thoughts of death
Sex drive	Decreased libido

tion than other depressed individuals, remember to carefully evaluate for the presence of suicidal thoughts or plans.

Treatment. Treatment for major depression is usually pharmacologic with adjunctive psychotherapy. Tables 14–2 and 14–3 list antidepressants that are most commonly used. Any antidepressant can be used, but the choice of an agent is based upon the advantageous use of their different side-effect profiles. In medically ill AIDS patients, lower doses are usually required. The art of using these medications is to get the patients through the side effects of these drugs, which can emerge early in the course of treatment. Frequently, the side effect will go away as the patient adjusts to the medication.[10] Figure 14–1 gives a helpful algorithm for any treatment selection.

The tricyclic antidepressants often have more distressing side effects than the newer selective serotonin reuptake inhibitors (SSRIs). For example, doxepin (Sinequan) is very sedating, and causes constipation and weight gain. Because of the sedating side effect, low doses of doxepin (25 to 50 mg) can be used to help improve sleep. To treat a major depression, higher dosing is required, producing often uncomfortable side effects. To use doxepin's side effects to your advantage, choose it for an agitated, depressed patient who is losing weight and has a problem with diarrhea. Doxepin can help decrease agitation, improve sleep, produce weight gain, and because of its constipating side effects, can slow persistent diarrhea. Low doses of desipramine (Norpramin, 25 to 50 mg) can help with pain of peripheral neuropathy. A common side effect, dry mouth, can make thrush worse in AIDS patients, a reason for not using this class of drugs.

Warning: All the tricyclic antidepressants can be lethal in an overdose, so avoid their use in patients with suicidal thoughts.

TABLE 14–2. SELECTED TRICYCLIC ANTIDEPRESSANTS

Name	Starting Dose	Therapeutic Dose	Advantages	Side Effects
Amitriptyline (Elavil)	10–25 mg qhs	100–300 mg (depression) 25–150 mg (insomnia)	Most sedating, promotes sleep, therapeutic blood level (200–250 ng/mL)	Sedation, dry mouth, orthostasis, constipation
Doxepin (Sinequan)	10–25 mg qhs	150–300 mg (depression) 25–150 mg (insomnia)	Promotes sleep, weight gain, therapeutic blood level (200–250 ng/mL)	Dry mouth, constipation, orthostasis, sedation
Imipramine (Tofranil)	10–25 mg qAM or qhs	150–300 mg qAM or qhs	Promotes sleep, therapeutic blood level (200–250 ng/mL)	Dry mouth, orthostasis, sedation
Nortriptyline (Pamelor)	10–25 mg qAM or qhs	75–150 mg qAM or qhs	Promotes sleep, therapeutic blood level (50–150 ng/mL)	Dry mouth, orthostasis, sedation.
Desipramine (Norpramin)	10–25 mg qAM	150–300 mg qAM (depression) 25–50 mg qAM (neuropathy)	May promote sleep, therapeutic blood level (125–200 ng/mL)	Dry mouth, orthostasis, sedation

TABLE 14-3. NEWER ANTIDEPRESSANTS

Name	Starting Dose	Usual Therapeutic Dose	Advantages	Most Common Side Effects
Fluoxetine (Prozac)	10 mg qAM	20 mg qAM	Little sedation, long half-life	Insomnia, agitation, nausea, anorexia, sexual dysfunction
Sertraline (Zoloft)	25 mg qAM	50–150 mg qAM	Little sedation, few side effects	Insomnia, agitation, nausea, anorexia
Venlafaxine (Effexor)	37.5 mg bid	75 mg bid or tid	Little sedation, few side effects	Insomnia, nausea, agitation
Paroxetine (Paxil)	10 mg qd	20–40 mg/day	Little sedation, few side effects	Insomnia, nausea, agitation
Trazodone (Desyrel)	50 mg qhs (for sleep)	50–200 mg qhs (for sleep)	Helps with insomnia	Sedation, SSRI-induced rare priapism
Nefozadone (Serzone)	50–100 mg qhs	200–400 mg qhs (divided dose)	Fewer sexual side effects	Sedation

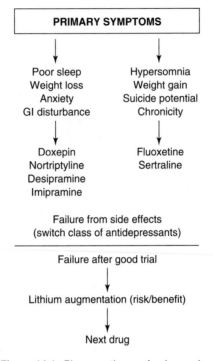

Figure 14-1. Pharmacotherapy for depression.

SSRIs are safer to use in potentially suicidal patients. Because of their energizing side effects, they should be taken early in the morning. They are helpful in depressed, fatigued patients. Because of the long half-life of fluoxetine (Prozac), use it in patients who occasionally skip doses. Occasionally, a patient will experience sedation on sertraline (Zoloft). If this happens, switch the dosing time to night. Sexual dysfunction (anorgasmia, decreased libido, and erectile failure) side effects can be a problem in the male patients. A new antidepressant, nefazodone (Serzone), has fewer of these side effects.

Always begin treatment with low doses and slowly increase over 6 to 10 days to therapeutic levels. This reduces the chance of disturbing side effects interfering with treatment compliance. To effectively treat a depression, therapeutic blood levels of the antidepressants must be reached. Blood level testing is available and very useful for the tricyclic antidepressants. Obtain the blood level 12 hours after the last dose taken. Medically ill patients may develop therapeutic blood levels at lower doses because of altered metabolism or excretion.

Impatience for results leads to increasing doses too fast, resulting in unpleasant side effects and patients discontinuing treatment. The rule of treating depression in HIV-infected patients is to "go low, go slow." Supportive psychotherapy can help get patients through the first month of treatment while you wait for blood levels to rise and an improvement in symptoms. Focus on the target symptoms of the depression (such as decreased interest, low self-esteem) in follow-up visits as a measure of improvement. If unacceptable side effects occur and if the patient can not tolerate treatment, or if the drug is failing after an adequate trial, discontinue the drug slowly, and allow for a short washout period before switching to another antidepressant. There are a variety of approaches to failed treatment (ie, lithium [Lithobid] augmentation), but primary care providers are advised to seek psychiatric consultation until they have experience with this drug.

Warning: Drug interactions with new protease inhibitors are common. For example, co-administration of tricyclic antidepressants with a protease inhibitor (Ritonavir) produces high antidepressant blood levels. Decrease the tricyclic dose by half and monitor blood level.

Psychostimulants (Table 14–4) deserve special attention in the care of HIV-AIDS patients. They can be effec-

TABLE 14–4. STIMULANTS

Name	Dose	Side Effects
Methylphenidate (Ritalin)	5–20 mg 8:00 AM and 1:00 PM (10–40 mg dose range— 4-hour effect)	Insomnia, irritability, drug–drug interaction tachycardia, addiction
Dextroamphetamine	2.5–5 mg/day (5–40 mg/day) (12-hour half-life)	Agitation, dizziness, anorexia, weight loss, headache, addiction

tive, rapid-acting antidepressants for the HIV-infected patient. They also can be a very helpful "pep pill" for the fatigued AIDS patient who is not depressed. Methylphenidate (Ritalin) is the medication of first choice for people with AIDS suffering from severe depression and fatigue. Stimulants are also useful for patients with mild neurocognitive deficits (mental slowing).[11,12] Ritalin can be used on an as needed basis for a 4-hour effect (increased mood, mental stimulation, and increase in energy). The afternoon dose should be taken early or insomnia will result. Loss of appetite is an unwanted side effect of dextroamphetamine. Be cautious if prescribing stimulants to patients with substance abuse histories and in patients with seizure disorders. In late-stage patients with confusion, stimulants can worsen the confusion. Some patients experience sedation. Many states restrict their use and a triplicate prescription may be required.

Depressed Mood Associated With Hypogonadism

The most common endocrine abnormality found in men with HIV is a low testosterone level.[13] It is more prevalent in men with AIDS,[14] and is clinically significant because not only is low testosterone linked to sexual dysfunction (diminished sexual interest, erectile and orgasmic dysfunction) but also to decreased energy, depressed mood, and muscle weakness. The causes of hypotestosternemia are multiple in patients with HIV. Depression, ingestion of megestrol (Megace, an appetite stimulant), and advanced HIV illness can result in low testosterone levels.[15] In depressed patients with decreased libido, treatment with antidepressants can revive libido in 9 to 10 days. In nondepressed patients who complain of decreased libido from hypotestosternemia, testosterone cypionate can be used for replacement (200 to 400 mg IM every 2 weeks). Blood levels between dosing should be between 1000 and 1900 ng/dL. Side effects include soreness at the injection site, irritability, being easy to anger, feeling hyperactive, and acting uncharacteristically bossy.[16] A testosterone transdermal system (Testoderm) is available and is designed to deliver 4 to 6 mg/day through daily application of a patch to a shaved scrotum. Patients using the patch commonly report scrotal itching, discomfort, or irritation. However, most men on replacement therapy note the positive effects on libido, energy, mood, and muscle mass, which outweigh the discomfort and inconvenience of use.

Bipolar (Manic-Depressive) Disorder

Clinical Manifestations. Mania is characterized by an elevated mood, increased energy, increased sense of well-being, poor judgment, and rapid thoughts and speech. There is a decreased need for sleep; delusions and hallucinations may be present. Manic states with or without psychosis may be the initial presentation of HIV infection.[17] In bipolar depression, the opposite downward mood swing may follow or precede the mania phase. This depression is similar to the major depression described in the preceding section. Mixed or rapidly cycling moods from mild highs to lows is called cyclothymia.

Treatment. Lithium is the mainstay of the treatment of bipolar disorders. Several anticonvulsants (carbamazepine, valproic acid, and divalproex sodium) can be used (Table 14–5). All should be monitored closely.

Before initiating lithium treatment, obtain tests (CBC, BUN, UA, serum creatinine, T3, T4, serum Na, and EKG) to monitor for concurrent conditions. Results of these tests will serve as a guide to lithium administration.

Rates of mania may be increased in late-stage AIDS patients with dementia.[18] In these late-stage patients, lithium levels can fluctuate, so monitor the blood levels and clinical response, and reduce doses if needed. Low doses of antipsychotics may be used in these patients with mania and dementia, but monitor for central nervous system side effects including neuroleptic malignant syndrome (Table 14–6).[19]

■ Anxiety Disorders

Clinical Manifestations

Anxiety is an unpleasant and unjustified sense of apprehension, often accompanied by physiologic symptoms. There are a number of distant psychiatric syndromes with anxiety as the predominant symptom (Box 14–2). The rates of various anxiety disorders in patients with HIV range from 2 to 28 percent.[20,21]

The very real threat of living with a chronic, life-threatening illness, the multiple psychosocial stressors associated with this disease, and the deaths of friends often produce an anticipatory anxiety, fear, and worry. Chronic, mild anxiety characterized by tension, irritability, and apprehension is common among patients living and coping

TABLE 14–5. DRUGS USED TO TREAT BIPOLAR DISORDER

Name	Starting Dose	Dose Range	Blood Level	Side Effects	HIV Precautions
Lithium carbonate (Eskalith, Lithobid)	300 mg bid	600–1200 mg qd (divided doses)	0.5–1.5 mEq/L	Lethargy, nausea, tremor, urine frequency	Toxicity, diarrhea, dehydration
Carbamazepine (Tegretol)	100 mg bid	200–1000 mg qd (divided doses)	6–12 µg/mL	Nausea, dizziness, vomiting, sedation	Bone marrow suppression
Divalproex sodium (Depakote), valproic acid (Depakene)	250 mg qd	1000 mg (divided doses)	50–100 µg/mL	Nausea, vomiting, sedation	Monitor blood levels

TABLE 14–6. DRUGS USED TO TREAT "LATE STATE MANIA"

Name	Starting Dose	Dose Range	Side Effects
Haloperidol (Haldol)	0.5 mg qhs	1–2 mg qd	Extrapyramidal syndrome (EPS), akathesia, and neuroleptic malignant syndrome
Flupherazine (Prolixin)	0.5 mg qhs	1–2 mg qd	EPS, akathesia
Thioridozine (Mellaril)	10 mg qhs	10–100 mg qd (divided doses)	Orthostatis, hypotension, sedation

with HIV. Severe anxiety with its associated motor and autonomic symptoms can be both physically painful and terrifying.

Treatment: General Principles

Treatment is based upon evaluation of the patient's complaints and making an accurate diagnosis. If you just treat the common shared symptom of anxiety using a benzodiazepine, this will not treat the often co-morbid causative syndrome. Depression and panic disorders can present with anxiety as the chief complaint. Use an antidepressant, not a benzodiazepine, for these patients. Somatic disorders, pulmonary and cardiovascular compromise, thyroid disease, endocrine disorders, and CNS lesions can also present with anxiety symptoms. These patients need treatment of the underlying disorder, not a masking of the anxiety symptoms with a tranquilizer. Demoralization, grief, obsessional and borderline personality traits, and drug intoxication can also present with anxiety symptoms. Benzodiazepines can worsen anxiety in these patients.

■ **Box 14–2**
   Anxiety Disorders

- Acute stress disorder
- Adjustment disorder, anxious
- Anxiety and depression
- Generalized anxiety disorder
- Panic disorder
- Obsessive-compulsive disorder
- Posttraumatic stress disorder
- Phobic disorder
    Simple phobia
    Social phobia
    Agoraphobia
- Anxiety disorder due to medical condition
- Substance-induced anxiety disorder

To treat anxiety, try to begin with a nonpharmacologic approach, such as relaxation training and supportive individual or group psychotherapy.[22] If these approaches fail, an antianxiety agent or an antidepressant can be added. A few commonly used drugs for treating anxiety in HIV/AIDS patients are listed in Table 14–7. It is wise to know how to use a few benzodiazepines well. All benzodiazepines relieve anxiety symptoms but have varying half-lives (Table 14–8). In HIV/AIDS patients who often are on multiple medications, it is preferable to use benzodiazepines with shorter half-lives to avoid drug buildup.

TABLE 14–7. STANDARD DRUGS FOR ANXIETY DISORDERS

Agent	Usual Initial Dose	Dosage Range	Chief Limitations
Tricyclic antidepressant: imipramine (Tofranil)	10–25 mg qd	150–300 mg	Jitteriness; TCA (tricyclic anti-depressants) side effects
Benzodiazepine: clonazepam (Klonopin) lorazepam (Ativan)	0.25 mg qAM 0.5 mg qd	1–3 mg/day 0.5–3.0 mg/day	Abuse, tolerance, dependence Psychomotor and memory impairment
Nonbenzodiazepine: buspirone (Buspar)	5 mg tid	15–60 mg/day	Dysphoria; cannot miss doses; slow to relieve anxiety symptoms

TABLE 14–8. CHARACTERISTICS OF COMMONLY USED BENZODIAZEPINES

Drug	Half-life (hr)	Dose Equivalent (mg)	Onset	Typical Route of Administration
Triazolam (Halcion)	2–4	0.25	Fast	PO
Oxazepam (Serax)	5–15	15	Slow	PO
Lorazepam (Ativan)	10–20	1.0	Intermediate	IV, IM, PO
Alprazolam (Xanax)	12–15	0.5	Fast	PO
Clonazepam (Klonopin)	15–50	0.25	Intermediate	PO
Diazepam (Valium)	20–100	5.0	Fast	PO, IV

The common practice of using benzodiazepines in patients infected with HIV often creates tolerance, dependence, and addiction to the drug. Several benzodiazepines commonly used to treat anxiety—such as alprazolam (Xanax), diazepam (Valium), and triazolam (Halcion)—can induce depression and can be particularly psychologically addicting. Triazolam can induce memory impairment and daytime anxiety. In patients with HIV-associated cognitive loss and dementia, the use of benzodiazepines should be avoided because they depress cortical function, produce disinhibition, and impair memory. Patients taking benzodiazepines, should be followed closely and patients should be told at the onset that the use of these agents is for the short term. Providers should discuss the possibility of tolerance and psychologic addiction and establish a timetable to taper and discontinue their use. Anxious HIV patients with histories of or current drug and alcohol abuse and dependence pose special problems. The use of benzodiazepines potentiates alcohol. Referral to a drug abuse specialist should be considered. In these patients, low doses of trazodone (Desyrel), 25 to 50 mg bid or tid, can help decrease anxiety and are not addicting.

Warning: Many of the benzodiazepines use liver enzymes (cytochrome P-450 3A), which are inhibited by protease inhibitors ritonavir and indinavir. Co-administration is contraindicated (Table 14–9). Because lorazepam, temazepam, and oxazepam are metabolized either solely or primarily by liver conjugation, pharmacokinetic interaction is not to be expected; therefore, these benzodiazepines can be used with protease inhibitors.[23]

Specific anxiety disorders will now be discussed.[24]

Adjustment Disorder With Anxious Mood

Clinical Presentation. A diagnosis of adjustment disorder with anxious mood should be considered in patients

TABLE 14–9. CONTRAINDICATED DRUG–DRUG INTERACTIONS

Indinavir	Ritonavir
Midazolam (Versed)	Alprazolam (Xanax)
Triazolam (Halcion)	Chlorazepate (Tranxene)
	Diazepam (Valium)
	Estazolam (Prosom)
	Flurazepam (Halcion)
	Midazolam (Versed)
	Triazolam (Halcion)
	Zolpidem (Ambien)

who have symptoms of anxiety, who are experiencing a major psychosocial stressor (HIV), and do not meet the criteria for an anxiety disorder. For a patient to qualify for the diagnosis of adjustment disorder, the anxiety must begin within 3 months of the onset of the stressor and cause occupational and/or social impairment.

Treatment

Nonpharmacologic Approaches

- Counseling
- Relaxation training
- Coping strategies

Pharmacologic Approaches

- A brief course of a benzodiazepine
- A tricyclic antidepressant in patients with more chronic anxiety symptoms or contraindications to benzodiazepine

Generalized Anxiety Disorder

Clinical Presentation. Generalized anxiety disorder (GAD) is characterized by excessive cognitive anxiety associated with physical symptoms of anxiety. GAD is continuous rather than episodic. Panic attacks are absent. The dominant feature of GAD is a persistent worried mood that is unrelated to another mental disorder. The worried mood persists for at least 6 months.

Patients with GAD exhibit six or more symptoms and have no other disease causing these symptoms. Symptoms include irritability; difficulty falling asleep; diminished ability to concentrate; shortness of breath, palpitations, or dizziness; excessive sweating, flushing, or dry mouth; frequent urination, nausea, or diarrhea; muscle aches or tension; restlessness or tension; and fatigue or difficulty relaxing.

Treatment

Nonpharmacologic Approaches

- Supportive counseling or psychotherapy
- Self-regulatory therapies (progressive relaxation, biofeedback, or meditation)
- Behavior therapy
- Exercise

Pharmacologic Approaches

- Benzodiazepine
- Tricyclic antidepressant
- Nonbenoxdiazepine anxiolytic

Panic Disorder With or Without Agoraphobia

Clinical Presentation. Panic disorder is characterized by unexpected, unprovoked attacks of cognitive and physical symptoms of anxiety. The attacks reach a symptomatic peak within 10 minutes of onset and taper off within 60 minutes. They occur, on average, two to four times per week. In a true panic attack, at least four of the characteristic symptoms mentioned earlier are present.

Treatment

Nonpharmacologic Approaches
- Patient education
- Behavior therapy to treat phobic avoidance
- Psychotherapy

Pharmacologic Approaches
- Benzodiazepines
- Tricyclic antidepressants

Phobia Disorders: Simple Phobia, Social Phobia, and Agoraphobia

Clinical Presentation. A phobia is a persistent, excessive, and unreasonable fear of a circumscribed stimulus that leads an individual to avoid the stimulus. Common simple phobias include fears of animals or insects, heights, and air travel.

Social phobia is a common disorder, characterized by episodes of intense anxiety related to the actual or anticipated social situations, involving possible scrutiny by others. Presentations of social phobia seen frequently in primary care practice are performance anxiety, such as excessive fear of speaking in front of a group, and avoidance of routine activities, such as eating or writing while observed, because of concerns about behaving in a way that might be humiliating or embarrassing. Although social phobia is a distinct diagnosis, some of its symptoms occur in other disorders. Symptoms of exposure to the phobic stimulus include blushing, tachycardia and palpitations, tremulousness, perspiration, and dyspnea.

Treatment

Nonpharmacologic Approaches

- Behavior therapy techniques such as exposure, social skills training, systematic desensitization, "flooding," anxiety management training, and relaxation training
- Cognitive restructuring

Medications from the following drug classes have also been studied in the treatment of panic disorder.

Pharmacologic Approaches

- Beta blockers
- Monoamine oxidase (MAO) inhibitors
- Benzodiazepines

Posttraumatic Stress Disorder

Clinical Presentation. Posttraumatic stress disorder (PTSD) can occur following a traumatic event that is outside the range of normal human experience (such as an accident, natural disaster, assault, rape, or incest). Diagnosis of HIV can be the traumatic event causing this disorder. The patient may have either been the direct victim of the trauma or witnessed it. Patients exhibit at least one symptom indicating persistent reexperiencing of the trauma, and display at least three symptoms of persistent avoidance of stimuli associated with the trauma or a numbing of general responsiveness. In addition, two persistent symptoms of increased arousal since the time of the trauma are present for at least 1 month.

Symptoms include the following.

- Sleep disturbance
- Social withdrawal or distancing
- Behavioral change, including outbursts, irritability, or physical abusiveness

- Alcohol or drug abuse
- Antisocial behavior or violation of the law
- Depression or suicidal idea or attempts
- High levels of anxious arousal or psychological instability
- Nonspecific somatic complaints (such as headache)

Treatment

Nonpharmacologic Approaches

- Psychotherapy
- Support groups
- Relaxation techniques or biofeedback
- Frequent visits with the primary care provider

Pharmacologic Approaches

- Tricyclic antidepressants, monoamine oxidase (MAO) inhibitors, and benzodiazepines have been used in both acute and chronic PTSD

Obsessive-Compulsive Disorders

Clinical Presentation. The essential feature of obsessive-compulsive disorder (OCD) is the presence of recurrent obsessions or compulsions that are sufficiently severe to cause marked distress, consume more than an hour a day, or interfere significantly with the patient's normal routine, functioning, or relationships.

Obsessions are recurrent, intrusive, and unwanted ideas, thoughts, images, or impulses. Compulsions are behaviors that may seem purposeful, but are performed in ritualistic manner. The rituals are observable or mental behaviors that are repeated in a stereotypic or rule-guided manner to reduce or neutralize anxiety associated with obsessions.

Treatment

Nonpharmacologic Approaches

- Behavior therapy (exposure and response prevention)
- Psychotherapy

Pharmacologic Approaches

- Tricyclic and SSRI antidepressants are occasionally helpful, particularly when depression is prominent
- Neuroleptic agents are rarely effective and should be avoided
- Benzodiazepines may be helpful only briefly during periods of intense anxiety

■ Substance Abuse and Other Behavioral Disorders

The rates of substance abuse and dependence are high in people infected with HIV. Nationally, almost one-half of all new diagnoses of infection with HIV are related to substance abuse.

Clinical Presentation. Substance abuse is defined as the inability to regulate the use of a substance in the face of problems (health, legal, work, social life, and relationships) that are the result of, or occur with, the use of the substance. Control of the use of the substance is lost, tolerance develops, and craving and/or withdrawal symptoms develop when the substance is not used. There is also preoccupation with the substance.

Treatment. In order to interrupt the pattern of abuse, attention must be directed to the behaviors that sustain it. Frequently, co-morbid diseases (depressions, anxiety disorders, personality disorders) are also present and need to be treated.

Attention should first be paid to the behavior—the loss of control—that sustains the abuse. Then the co-morbid disorders can be treated. The goal of the first treatment sessions is to show patients that they have lost control of their behavior. Serious consequences will follow if the abuse is not stopped. The patient should be persuaded to relinquish control to the treatment team and plan, and to follow their recommendations for the period of time. Treatment involves three phases: (1) detoxification (inpatient/outpatient), (2) monitoring maintenance and preparing for release, and (3) eliminating contributory co-morbidity.

After the abuse behavior is stopped, and withdrawal symptoms treated if needed, the treatment team, including all members of the clinic, should provide encouragement and support for the abstinence. Urine toxicology screens are often useful to maintain treatment compliance.

It is helpful to rely heavily on the use of community resources (Alcoholic Anonymous, Narcotics Anonymous, and other support services available to the HIV-infected patient), to aid patients. Frequent, brief visits to monitor abstinence are important. Health care providers need to be wary of prescribing medication that can be abused or that might potentiate a relapse. Minor tranquilizers, stimulants, and pain medication use, should be avoided or closely monitored.

The third phase of the treatment plan is to treat co-morbid conditions, such as mood or anxiety disorders. Sometimes changes in social networks (work, job, living situation) are needed.[25,26] When relapse occurs, persist in working again through the phases of treatment. For many HIV patients, their goal of living and dying "clean and sober" can be achieved.

■ Psychosis

Psychosis describes a degree of severity of dysfunction and is not a specific disorder. In patients infected with HIV, a number of disorders can cause psychosis (Table 14–10). A full-blown psychosis may appear in HIV-infected individuals in the absence of delirium, iatrogenic source, or substance use disorder. The prevalence of psychosis in late-stage AIDS is 0.1 to 5 percent.[27,28]

TABLE 14–10. CAUSES OF PSYCHOSIS IN THE HIV-INFECTED PATIENT

Primary psychiatric disorder (schizophrenia, bipolar disorder)

Secondary to substance abuse

Psychoneurotoxicity secondary to antiviral agents, chemotherapeutic agents, steroids

Secondary to CNS disorders

AIDS dementia complex

Dementia associated with opportunistic infection and cancers

Infections
    Fungal: *Cryptococcus, Candida albicans*
    Protozoal: toxoplasmosis
    Bacterial: *Mycobacterium avium-intracellulare*
    Viral: herpes, cytomegalovirus, papovavirus (progressive multifocal leukoencephalopathy)

Cancers
    Primary cerebral lymphoma
    Disseminated Kaposi's sarcoma

Delirium
    Alcohol or drug withdrawal
    Fluid, electrolyte, and acid–base disorders
    Endocrine disorders
    Metabolic encephalopathies: hypoxia; hepatitis; renal, pulmonary, or pancreatic insufficiency

Clinical Manifestations. The psychotic patient has difficulty functioning because of emotional and thinking difficulties. The patient has an impaired sense of reality. Hallucinations, delusions, and bizarre talk and behavior may be present. The patient may be confused and disoriented.[29]

Psychosis can be part of a group of major mental disorders that may be preexisting in HIV patients, such as schizophrenia or delusional (paranoid) disorders. However, psychosis also may be due to a general medical condition[30] or be caused by the patient's use of substances (cocaine or alcohol). Medications often used to treat HIV and accompanying opportunistic infections can cause psychotic side effects (Table 14–11).

In treating HIV patients' psychosis, it is important to recognize the difference between delirium and dementia. Delirium is usually reversible if the underlying cause is identified and treated. Delirious patients may have bizarre behavior and be difficult to control, or they may be somnolent and even appear normal during the day, but decompensate dramatically during the night (sundowning). The characteristics of delirious patients are the following.

1. Clouding of consciousness
2. Attention deficit
3. Psychotic symptoms
4. Perceptual disturbances/visual hallucinations
5. Sleep-wake alterations
6. Disorientation
7. Memory impairment (recent)
8. Fluctuations of symptoms

Dementia presents a different clinical picture. There is a broad loss of intellectual functions due to a diffuse organic disease of the cerebral hemispheres. Dementia de-

TABLE 14–11. HIV-RELATED DRUGS CAUSING PSYCHOTIC SIDE EFFECTS

Drug	Neuropsychiatric Effects
Acyclovir	Visual hallucinations, depersonalization, tearfulness, confusion, hyperesthesia, hyperacusia, thought insertion, insomnia, agitation
Alpha-interferon	Depression, weakness
Amphotericin B	Delirium, peripheral neuropathy, diplopia, weight loss, loss of appetite
Corticosteroids	Depression, euphoria, psychosis
Ganciclovir	Manic psychosis, agitation, delirium, irritability
Isoniazid	Depression, agitation, hallucinations, paranoia, impaired memory
Pentamidine	Hypoglycemia, hypotension (leading to CNS dysfunction)
Protease inhibitors	Fatigue, headache, insomnia
Trimethoprim-sulfamethoxazole	Depression, loss of appetite, insomnia, apathy, headache
Zidovudine	Headache, restlessness, severe agitation, insomnia, mania, depression, irritability

velops slowly. The characteristics of these patients are as follows.

1. Memory loss (recent)
2. Changes in mood and personality
3. Loss of orientation
4. Intellectual impairment
5. Compromised judgment
6. Psychotic symptoms

HIV dementia is a chronic, debilitating encephalitis with a distinct clinical and neuropathologic syndrome characterized by a trend of cognitive, behavioral, and motor symptoms (see Chapter 8). Psychosis may be a part of the clinical presentation.[31,32]

Treatment. Because psychotic symptoms may arise in multiple ways during the course of HIV disease, treatment begins by working through a differential in order to make an etiologic diagnosis. It is a mistake to move too quickly to a diagnosis of HIV dementia. This devastating disorder is a diagnosis of exclusion and should be arrived at only after you have considered other causes of behavioral problems and mental status changes.

In assessing "psychotic" symptoms in the HIV-infected patient, a careful history should assess for any previous history of psychotic illness, drug or alcohol abuse, and early signs of HIV-associated dementia. Family members or significant others are very helpful to elicit information from. Psychiatric consultation should be obtained if psychiatric hospitalization is indicated or if early attempts to control symptoms with antipsychotics fail.

Antipsychotics, also called major tranquilizers, are indicated for the treatment of psychosis, mania, delirium, and agitation. While the organic causative workup is in progress, antipsychotics are useful for decreasing psychotic symptoms.[33] If neurologic symptoms are absent, patients can tolerate doses equivalent to those in the general population. However, be observant for side effects (Table 14–12). Until one familiarizes oneself with using antipsychotic medications, psychiatric consultation is helpful.

If neurologic symptoms are present, as in patients with HIV-associated dementia, dosing should be done cautiously, using low doses.[34] Side effects (anticholinergic and extrapyramidal) are more common in these patients. Always be aware of neuroleptic malignant syndrome when using antipsychotic medications in patients with AIDS.[35] Key elements of this syndrome are as follows.

TABLE 14–12. TYPES OF EXTRAPYRAMIDAL SYMPTOMS/SIDE EFFECTS OF MAJOR TRANQUILIZERS

Type	Onset	Clinical Course
Dystonia	1–5 days	Acute, spasmodic, painful
Parkinsonism	5–30 days	Occurs throughout treatment
Akathesia	5–60 days	Persists during treatment
Neuroleptic malignant syndrome	Weeks	Mortality rate is 20–30 percent, symptoms last 5–10 days

1. Rapidly developing (hours to 1 to 2 days) after starting antipsychotic medications
2. Muscular rigidity and cogwheeling
3. Fever, confusion, sweating, and tachycardia
4. Rhabdomyolysis with myoglobinemia and very elevated CPK

This condition is fatal if not treated immediately, which includes the administration of bromocriptine or dontrolene (7.5 to 45 mg tid), stopping antipsychotics, and providing appropriate medical support.

Another use of low doses of antipsychotics is to control agitation, severe anxiety, and brief psychotic episodes in HIV patients with borderline personality disorders.

The choice of major tranquilizers, as with all other psychiatric drugs, is based on the side effect profile. Midrange potency agents such as molindone (Moban) and thiothixene (Navane) have been effective and well tolerated (Table 14–13). Haloperidol (Haldol), a more potent antipsychotic, is helpful for the more agitated psychotic patient (Table 14–14). Haloperidol has been associated with a higher incidence of extrapyramidal reactions and with neuroleptic malignant syndrome.[36] Benzotropin (Cogentin), 0.5 mg to 1.0 mg bid, can be added as

TABLE 14–13. MIDRANGE POTENCY ANTIPSYCHOTIC AGENTS

Name	Starting Dose	Dose Range
Thiothixene (Navane)	2–5 mg qd	2–15 mg qd
Molindone (Moban)	25–50 mg qd	24–100 mg qd
Haloperidol (Haldol)	0.5–2 mg qd	2–20 mg qd

prophylaxis against the development of extrapyramidal reactions.

■ Insomnia

Most patients complain of sleep problems at some point during the course of HIV disease.[37] Anxiety, depression, medications, and the HIV infection are common causes.

Clinical Manifestations. The sleep disorder in the HIV-infected patient can take several forms. Initial sleep disturbances (cannot get to sleep) are often anxiety related. Middle insomnia is restless, interrupted sleep. Late insomnia, waking early in the morning and not being able to go back to sleep, is often associated with a major depression. Hypersomnia, or wanting to sleep all of the time, is often caused by fatigue associated with late-stage AIDS. Sleep deprivation can cause significant psychiatric morbidity and requires evaluation.

When evaluating a person with a sleep disorder, ask about the use of substances that interfere with good sleep. Common substances are alcohol and stimulants (caffeine and nicotine). If a patient uses any of these, especially before sleep, a withdrawal state occurs during the night

TABLE 14–14. GUIDELINES FOR HALOPERIDOL USAGE

Level of Agitation	Starting Dose
Mild	0.5–2 mg
Moderate	2–5 mg
Severe	5–10 mg

1. In the medically ill, use low-range starting dose.
2. Allow 30 minutes between doses.
3. For continued agitation, double previous dose.
4. After three doses, give 0.5 to 1 mg of lorazepam IV concurrently, or alternate lorazepam with haloperidol every 30 minutes.
5. Once the patient is calm, add up the total milligrams of haloperidol given, and administer the same number of milligrams over the next 24 hours.
6. Assuming the patient remains calm, reduce the dose by 50 percent every 24 hours.
7. The oral dose given is twice the intravenous dose.
8. If haloperidol is used intravenously, clear the IV line with normal saline prior to bolus infusion.

when the level of the substances in the body decreases. This causes the person to wake up. Prescribed medications like zidovudine (Retrovir), didanosine (Videx), dapsone, fluconazole (Diflucan), acyclovir (Zovirax), and isoniazid can also interfere with sleep.

Treatment. As for the other psychiatric disorders, the first principle of treatment is to evaluate the underlying cause of the sleep disorder, and to correct it if possible. If you cannot, and decide to treat the insomnia, there are two approaches: sleep hygiene (Box 14–3) and pharmacologic (Table 14–15). When using medications to treat insomnia,

■ Box 14–3

Sleep Hygiene Rules for HIV/AIDS Patients

1. Do not take naps during the day, even if tired.
2. Do not sleep late in the morning, even if you get to sleep late. This can result in a complete sleep-wake reversal.
3. Never try to make yourself sleep. The more you try, the less it works. Trying to make yourself sleep increases arousal and is counterproductive.
4. Eliminate the bedroom clock. Do not pressure yourself to sleep.
5. Exercise. Sleep is related to your core body temperature. When you exercise, your body core temperature increases. A cooling of your body temperature, which follows exercise, will occur about 6 hours later, and should help improve your sleep. Therefore, exercise at least 4 to 6 hours before you sleep for optimum results.
6. A hot bath for 20 minutes, 2 to 4 hours before bedtime, will also lead to a drop in your body temperature that will aid in sleep. Do not take a hot bath just before sleep.
7. Avoid coffee, alcohol, soda, tea, nicotine, and chocolate before bed. Alcohol, while initially sedating, actually disrupts sleep.
8. Regularize bedtime. Wake up at a set time, and bedtime will gradually regulate itself.
9. Eat a light bedtime snack. Hunger disrupts sleep. Drinking a glass of warm milk after a high-carbohydrate snack with 50 mg of pyroxidine (vitamin B_6) may induce sleep. Vitamin B_6 may be decreased in HIV patients, thus contributing to sleep disturbance.

■ *Box 14–3 continued*

10. Schedule your "thinking" time during the day or early evening. Do not wait until bedtime to think about worries or to plan tomorrow's activities.

11. Try relaxation training and tapes. In order for these to work, you must become proficient. One-time use does not usually work. Deep relaxation can be practiced during the day and used at nighttime to help with sleep.

12. Keep a sleep log for 1 week. Take it to your health care provider.

13. Treatment is necessary if sleep efficiency is less than 85 percent.

Sleep efficiency = $\dfrac{\text{time in bed} - \text{time awake}}{\text{time in bed}} \times 100$

their side effect profiles, half-lives, and abuse potential determine choice (Table 14–15).

Antihistamines such as Benadryl and Atarax can be sedating. Both have anticholinergic side effects (sedation, blurred vision, dry mouth) and should be avoided in the medically ill or organically impaired. If used, Atarax has fewer anticholinergic properties and is preferable. These medications are available over the counter and are non-addicting.

Trazodone, although not effective as an antidepressant, is an excellent, nonabusable agent to help HIV patients sleep. Tolerance does not develop. Withdrawal side effects do not occur if stopped. It is nonlethal in an overdose. However, priapism is a rare side effect in men, so warn patients in advance to discontinue its use immedi-

TABLE 14-15. SEDATING HYPNOTICS

Name	Dosage	Side Effects
Antihistamine:		
hydroxyzine (Atarax)	25–100 mg qhs	Nonaddicting, dry mouth, blurred vision, confusion
diphenhydramine (Benadryl)	50–100 mg qhs	Nonaddicting, dry mouth, blurred vision, confusion
Benzodiazepine:		
triazolam (Halcion)	0.125–0.5 mg qhs	Rapid effect, short half-life, memory impairment
temazepam (Restoril)	15–30 mg qhs	Rapid effect, long half-life
lorazepam (Ativan)	0.25–2 mg qhs	Slow onset, long half-life, daytime sedation, tolerance, dependence
Antidepressant:		
trazodone (Desyrel)	25–150 mg qhs	Very sedating, nonabusable, priapism
amitriptyline (Elavil)	10–50 mg qhs	Lethal in overdose, morning sedation
doxepin (Sinequan)	10–50 mg qhs	Lethal in overdose, morning sedation, dry mouth

ately and to seek medical care if changes in erections occur.

The sedating tricyclic antidepressants can be useful with sleep, but again they should be used selectively to maximize their side effects. For example, if neuropathy, diarrhea, and pruritus occur with insomnia, doxepin is a good choice. However, tricyclic antidepressants can be lethal in overdosage, and because of their anticholinergic side effects they should be avoided.

Hypnotic benzodiazepines (short acting, sleep inducing) are commonly prescribed for insomnia. Precautions already mentioned about their use and abuse potential apply. Because of the rapid development of tolerance to these medications and the patient's tendency to increase the dosage to help with sleep, warn patients in advance about this problem. When prescribing benzodiazepines, it can be helpful for the patient to take a "drug holiday" during the week. Sleep quality will be poor on the nonuse nights; however, on the nights when used, the lower dose will remain effective.

Triazolam in medically ill patients with AIDS is likely to cause memory impairment, withdrawal problems, delirium, confusion, and hallucinations, and therefore should be avoided. Triazolam and temazepam are contraindicated in patients on protease inhibitors. Lorazepam and oxazepam can be used instead.

References

1. Lyketsos CG, Hanson A, Fishman M, et al. Screening for HIV infection: The need for a psychiatric presence. *Int J Psychiatry Med.* 1994;24:103–112.

2. Chuang HT, Jason GW, Pajurkova EM, Gill MJ. Psychiatric morbidity in patients with HIV infection. *Can J Psychiatry.* 1992;37:109–115.

3. Perry S, Jacobsberg JB, Fishman B, et al. Psychiatric diagno-

sis before serological testing for human immunodeficiency virus. *Am J Psychiatry*. 1990;147:89–93.

4. Kalichman SC, Kelly JA, Johnson J, et al. Factors associated with risk for human immunodeficiency virus (HIV) infection among chronically mentally ill adults. *Am J Psychiatry*. 1993;151:121–127.

5. Lyons JS, McGovern MP. Use of mental health services by dually diagnosed patients. *Hosp Community Psychiatry*. 1989;40: 1067–1069.

6. Markowitz JD, Rabkin JG, Perry SW. Treating depression in HIV-positive patients. *AIDS*. 1994;8:403–412.

7. Perry S, Fishman B. Depression and HIV, how does one affect the other? *JAMA*. 1993;270:2609–2610.

8. American Psychiatric Association. Diagnostic and Statistical Manual of Mental Disorders. 4th ed. (DSM-IV). Washington, DC: American Psychiatric Press; 1994.

9. O'Dowd MD, Biderman DJ, McKegney FP. Incidence of suicidability in AIDS and HIV-positive patients attending a psychiatry outpatient program. *Psychosomatics*. 1993;34:33–40.

10. Treisman GJ, Fishman M, Lyketsos K. Mental health care of HIV patients. *AIDS Clin Care*. 1994;6:63–66.

11. Fernandez F, Adams F, Levy JK, et al. Cognitive impairment in AIDS-related complex and its response to psychostimulants. *Psychosomatics*. 1988;29:38–46.

12. Holmes VF, Fernandez F, Levy JK. Psychostimulant response in AIDS-related complex patients. *J Clin Psychiatry*. 1989;50:5–8.

13. Hellerstein M. Endocrinology abnormalities. In: Cohen PT, Snade M, Volberding P, eds. The AIDS Knowledge Base. Boston: Massachusetts Medical Society; 1990:1–5.

14. Dobs AS, Dempsey MA, Ladenson PW, Polk BF. Endocrine disorders in men infected with human immunodeficiency virus. *Am J Med*. 1988;84:611–616.

15. Wagner G, Rabkin JG, Rabkin R. Illness state, concurrent medications, and other correlates of low testosterone in men with HIV illness. *J Acquir Immune Defic Syndr*. 1995;8:204–207.

16. Rabkin JG, Rabkin R, Wagner G. Testosterone replacement therapy in HIV illness. *Gen Hosp Psychiatry*. 1995;17:37–42.

17. Gabel RH, Barnard N, Norko M, O'Connell R. AIDS presenting as mania. *Compr Psychiatry*. 1986;27:251–254.

18. Kieburtz K, Zettelmaier AE, Ketonen L, et al. Manic syndromes in AIDS. *Am J Psychiatry*. 1991; 148:1068–1070.

19. Halman MH, Worth JL. Manic syndromes in patients with HIV-1 infection. Scientific Program and Abstracts of the 39th Annual Meeting of Psychosomatic Medicine. San Diego, 1992.

20. Williams JBW, Rabkin JG, Remien RH, et al. Multidisciplinary baseline assessment of homosexual men with and without human immunodeficiency virus infection. *Arch Gen Psychiatry*. 1991;48:124–130.

21. Atkinson JH, Grant L, Kennedy CJ, et al. Prevalence of psychiatric disorders among men infected with human immunodeficiency virus. *Arch Gen Psychiatry*. 1988;45:859–864.

22. Perry S, Fishman B, Jacobsberg L, Frances A. Effectiveness of psychoeducational interventions in reducing emotional distress after human immunodeficiency virus antibody testing. *Arch Gen Psychiatry*. 1991; 48;143–147.

23. Gerber J. Drug interactions with HIV protease inhibitors. In: Improving Management of HIV Disease. International AIDS Society; 1996;4.

24. McGlynn TJ, Metcalf H, eds. Diagnosis and Treatment of Anxiety Disorders: A Physicians' Handbook. Washington, DC: American Psychiatric Press; 1989.

25. Treisman GJ, Lyketsos CG, Fishman M, et al. Psychiatric care for patients with HIV infection. *Psychosomatics*. 1993;34:432–439.

26. Cabaj RP. Management of anxiety and depression in HIV-infected persons. *J Int Assoc Physicians AIDS Care*. 1996;2:11–16.

27. Sewell DD, Jeste DV, Atkinson JH, et al. HIV-associated psychosis: A longitudinal study of 20 cases. *Am J Psychiatry*. 1994;151:237–242.

28. Zegans LS, Coates TJ. Psychiatric manifestations of HIV disease. *Psychiatr Clin North Am*. 1994;17:17–33.

29. Tomb D. Psychiatry. 5th ed. Baltimore: Williams & Wilkins; 1995;20–28.

30. Harris MJ, Jeste DV, Gleghorn A, Sewell DD. New-onset psychosis in HIV-infected patients. *J Clin Psychiatry*. 1991;52: 369–376.

31. Navia BA, Jordon BD, Price RW. The AIDS dementia complex, 1. Clinical features. *Ann Neurol*. 1986;19:517–524.

32. Grant L, Atkinson JH. Psychobiology of HIV infection. In: Kaplan HI, Sadock BJ, eds. Comprehensive Textbook of Psychiatry. 6th ed. Baltimore: Williams & Wilkins; 1994.

33. Sewell DD, Jeste DV, McAdams LA. Neuroleptic treatment of HIV-associated psychosis. *Neuropsychopharmacol*. 1991; 10:223–229.

34. Fernandez F, Levy J, Mansell PWH. Management of delirium in terminally HIV/AIDS patients. *Int J Psychiatr Med*. 1988;19: 165–172.

35. Breitbart W. AIDS and neuroleptic malignant syndrome. *Lancet*. 1988;24:1488–1489.

36. Hriso E, Kuhn T, Masden JC, et al. Extrapyramidal symptoms due to dopamine-blocking agents in patients with AIDS encephalopathy. *Am J Psychiatry*. 1991;148:1558–1561.

37. Norman SE, Chediak AD, Kiel M, Cohen MA. Sleep disturbances in HIV-infected homosexual men. *AIDS*. 1990;4:775–781.

fifteen
CHAPTER

Social and Psychological Aspects of Care

John G. Bruhn

AIDS has had profound medical, psychological, and social ramifications. AIDS has become a political issue in both the public and private sectors, and serious social problems have resulted, both from the fears of contagion and from the initial appearance of the syndrome among stigmatized minorities.[1] Significant psychological concerns have arisen among health care workers as a result of prejudice and fears of contagion. These issues have added to the psychological and social burdens of patients with AIDS, who face a debilitating disease with a poor prognosis.

■ Psychological Adaptation

The psychological adaptation to any severe life-threatening disease depends upon factors derived from three major areas. These factors are medical (symptoms, clinical course, and complications, particularly of the central nervous system); psychological (personality and coping; interpersonal support); and sociocultural (social stigma attached to the disease and affected groups). The frequent complications of the central nervous system may impair the patient's behavior. As evidence of the link between the central nervous and immune systems continues to grow, the implications for hypothesizing a relationship between stress and the clinical course of AIDS become more promising—as do the indications for using stress-reduction strategies. There is some evidence that risk reduction measures may positively affect the clinical course.

The medical or disease-related factors are the primary determinants of adaptation because they constitute the altered physical state and medical circumstances to which the patients must adapt. These key factors are the impact of diagnosis; common symptoms and events in the clinical course; nature of the frequent psychological distress and psychiatric disorders; central nervous system complications; and the responses of caregivers.

The diagnosis of AIDS is a catastrophic event because it is known to have a rapid downhill course, no definitive treatment, and an extremely poor prognosis. The diagnosis is usually made over the course of weeks to months, and the clinical course can range from being asymptomatic; to experiencing frequent infections, swollen nodes, and general malaise; to complete debility. After a diagnosis of AIDS is made, each new symptom, infection, loss of weight, or fatigue is regarded as a sign of progression of disease. The characteristic skin lesions of Kaposi's sarcoma, when present, provide visible evidence of the diagnosis. Transmission of AIDS through sexual contact or body fluids often leads to self-imposed or clinician-recommended limitation of social and intimate contacts. Guidelines for "safe sex" may require marked alteration of sexual behavior, the need to reveal one's medical status to partners, and accepting a monogamous relationship or celibacy.

The sociocultural burden of the diagnosis of AIDS results from several sources. The social stigma associated with the contagious aspect causes altered behavior in others, including avoidance of physical and social contact. Although this is painful enough for adults, even children with AIDS have become isolated from schools and from other children by frightened parents.

The diagnosis may force the patient's identification as a likely member of a stigmatized minority (homosexual, drug user, or recent immigrant). Families may abruptly learn of a lifestyle they find difficult to accept. In the largest risk group, homosexual and bisexual men, the diagnosis may create a crisis in which an otherwise private sexual preference is revealed. Drug users are already the objects of negative societal attitudes and have little advocacy in society. Haitians, even long-term residents, have been the focus of prejudicial treatment. Hemophiliacs and recipients of blood transfusions receive the most sympathetic response because of the perceived random nature of the exposure. Although some persons have acquired AIDS through blood transfusions, the main tendency of the public is "to blame the victim" for having AIDS. Sexual transmission of AIDS by prostitutes may cause an association of the disease with this socially ostracized group.

Patients with AIDS are vulnerable to rejection and feelings of guilt, arising from concerns that their behavior, particularly sexual, may endanger others. The emotions associated with harboring a contagious agent may cause the patient to feel like an outcast. Discrimination has occurred in housing, jobs, health care, and public assistance, from both fear of contagion and prejudice. Irrational fears and negative responses of the public are a continuing problem confronted daily by patients, families, and advocacy groups.

One of the most disruptive complications of AIDS is its impact on supportive relationships. Whether the family knows about and accepts a patient's homosexuality should be ascertained by the caregiver. The onset of AIDS also may force disclosure of previously disguised drug use in drug-addicted patients, which may weaken family support. The stigma attached to AIDS affects all patients, including children and women.

Patients in the initial crisis stage of AIDS typically have difficulty retaining information due to anxiety and may distort what they are told regarding their illness to deny or otherwise cope with the reality that they have the disease. Contact with support services such as crisis counseling, legal and financial assistance, and psychotherapy should begin as early as possible.[2]

■ Social Adaptation

Patients with AIDS may live in many different social situations: they may live alone, live with a homosexual lover, live with a friend or friends who may be homosexual or heterosexual, or be married to a heterosexual partner. Patients with AIDS may be fully employed, partially employed, or unemployed. The activity level of AIDS patients can vary from being sedentary to very active. Similarly, the hobbies and interests and recreational interests of patients differ.

These facts are pointed out to make the point that AIDS patients are individuals who have a range of personalities and lifestyles, irrespective of their disease. The disease they have is superimposed on their uniqueness as persons. Therefore, how patients with AIDS adapt to their disease socially is also unique to each patient. The clinical course of AIDS imposes certain limitations on their social adaptation. It is important for caregivers to relate to each patient with AIDS as an individual and not anticipate what a patient will or will not do on the basis of their composite experience with AIDS patients as a group. The variable and uneven course of AIDS will, of course, make social, psychological, and physical adaptation to the disease also variable and uneven.

■ Psychological Distress and Psychiatric Disorders

The psychological and psychiatric sequelae of AIDS are modified by factors that characterize the person's previous level of adjustment and social (interpersonal) support. Presence of a personality disorder, as in intravenous drug users, or of a previous major psychiatric disorder is more apt to result in severe psychological symptoms and a maladaptive response to the stresses of illness. The availability of social support is especially crucial because of the need for both physical and social assistance. Both homosexuals and drug users may have to face illness with less support, especially from their estranged families. The drain on friends who accept their lifestyle can be great. In fact, as the illness progresses, the primary support of many patients may be crisis support groups and other patients with HIV. Some common psychological symptoms are listed in Table 15–1.

The major form of psychological distress is preoccupation with illness and with the potential for a rapidly declining course to death. The same issues raised by the diagnosis of cancer and other diseases with high rates of fatal outcomes are raised by AIDS. A normal stress response is seen at diagnosis, characterized by disbelief, numbness, and denial and followed by anger and acute turmoil with disruptive anxiety and depressive symptoms. The anxiety and uncertainty about the disease

TABLE 15–1. COMMON TYPES OF PSYCHOLOGICAL DISTRESS IN AIDS PATIENTS

Anxiety. Uncertainty about disease, its progression and treatment; anxiety about new symptoms; anxiety about prognosis and impending death; hyperventilation, panic attacks.

Depression. Sadness, helplessness, lowered self-esteem, guilt, shame, worthlessness, hopelessness, suicidal thoughts, social withdrawal, expressions of "giving up"; difficulty sleeping, loss of appetite.

Feelings of isolation and reduced social support; rejection by family and others, withdrawal from others. The lack of visitors when hospitalized may confirm these feelings.

Anger at self and others; hostility toward caregivers; refusal to cooperate with caregivers.

Fears about who knows or will know about the illness.

Worry about finances, loss of job, living arrangements, transportation.

Embarrassment about stigma of AIDS; denial of sexual habits.

Denial of drug abuse history.

---

process, clinical course, possible treatment, and outcome continue. Patients are fearful when any new physical symptom develops because it may signal progression of the disease. Hypochondriacal concerns about body function also occur. Anxiety symptoms may take the form of panic attacks, agitation, insomnia, tension, anorexia, and tachycardia.

The symptoms of depression are also prominent. The patient's mood is characterized by sadness, hopelessness, and helplessness. Guilt, low self-esteem, shame, worthlessness, and anticipatory grief are common with social withdrawal and isolation. The idea of suicide if the disease progresses is common in most patients, especially those who have seen friends die of AIDS. Anger directed toward the illness, medical care, discrimination, and public response to the disease is often intense. Expectation of rejection by others, often the result of actual experiences, produces suspiciousness of the motivation of others.

■ Response of Caregivers

A critical factor in quality of care is the attitude and responses of caregivers (all persons providing direct care to patients). Several psychological issues that usually arise separately are combined in the treatment of AIDS in such a way that they create unusually difficult problems. Identification with and sense of personal vulnerability to disease and death are elicited by taking care of young healthy persons who face rapid physical deterioration and death. The fear of contagion was most frightening when the disease was first diagnosed, because guidelines that assured protection from AIDS had not yet been formulated. The large numbers of patients with AIDS in large urban hospitals can cause caregivers to become overtaxed, stressed, fatigued, and fearful of being overwhelmed by the burden of the intensive, complicated care. Negative social attitudes and personal prejudices, especially homophobia, can arise, as can negative attitudes toward drug users and Haitian immigrants.

Considerable information about these issues has been developed by consultation-liaison psychiatry in relation to other diseases and is applicable to AIDS as well. An understanding of caregivers' response to the care of patients with a likely fatal disease comes largely from cancer care. Hospital staff need the opportunity to discuss their feelings about "special" patients with whom identification has occurred. These feelings are usually centered around anticipatory grieving for patients who will die; actual grief with the death of patients; and anger and frustration with the negative responses of others. Caregivers need instruction in how to recognize delirium and account for changes in these patients' ability to adhere to procedures and treatment.

The fear of contagion is best managed by providing up-to-date information about universal precautions. The panic among medical staff, with inappropriate behavior based on irrational fears, has diminished as institutions have promulgated Public Health Service guidelines similar to those for hepatitis B, and provided forums for clarifying misinformation from many sources. Meetings also serve to air concerns about institutional allocation of resources, organization of AIDS services, and burdens experienced by caregivers.

Personal interaction with AIDS patients may elicit otherwise masked attitudes of homophobia and negative views of drug users and patients from other cultures or different lifestyles. Caregivers must be encouraged to explore personal reactions, because it is important that patients feel free to discuss their lifestyle and sexual preference and practices. Ability to openly discuss sexuality is clearly a factor in the relationship between staff and patients that provides emotional support and understanding. The need to discuss sexual precautions and answer questions of lovers and family requires that the staff member feel comfortable in these discussions. The same need applies to drug users. If negative attitudes preclude appropriate interaction, the caregiver should ask to be replaced by another who can openly discuss these issues.

■ Caregiving by Partners of AIDS Patients

Taking care of AIDS patients is a heavy burden, especially if the patient has a partner. Caregiving partners of men with AIDS can differ in five important ways from traditional caregivers. First, caregiving partners of gay men with AIDS are usually male, whereas traditional caregivers are usually wives or adult daughters. Second, people with AIDS and their primary caregivers tend to be young and middle-aged, whereas the traditional caregivers tend to be older. Third, many primary caregivers of men with AIDS are themselves at risk for AIDS or becoming HIV positive, whereas traditional caregivers usually do not have the same disease as the recipient of care. Fourth, in contrast to the relationships of spousal or adult caregivers to their care recipients, which are legally acknowledged and strongly supported by society, the relationships of gay partners are informal and often stigmatized. Fifth, whereas the diseases of traditional care recipients are generally not stigmatized, AIDS is stigmatized and caregiving activities are often hidden from the general community.[3]

Caregivers of HIV-positive men who themselves were HIV positive reported more burden than caregivers who were HIV negative, but the HIV-positive caregivers were more spiritual and sought social support. HIV presents profound challenges to caregiving partners, including adjusting to the recipient's disease progression, having increasing responsibility for decision-making as the disease progresses, responding to unexpected improvement, and managing conflict and fatigue. Caregiving partners of men with AIDS have high levels of dysphoric mood, but also report high morale. Caregivers sustain positive morale by deriving meaning from their caregiving. Health professionals are in a good position to support caregivers and, in turn, help their patients.[3]

■ Long-term Survivors of AIDS

Several cohort studies have documented that a proportion of people who have been infected with HIV for 10 years or more remain not only free of AIDS but also free of symptoms.[4-9] Studies of homosexual and bisexual men have found that about half remain free of AIDS 10 years after initially becoming infected,[4-6,8] and one of these studies, the San Francisco Clinic cohort study, has found that 8 percent of men infected between 10 and 15 years remain clinically normal, with only minor immunologic and hematologic abnormalities. Similarly, studies of people infected through either blood transfusions or antihemophilic factors have shown that a substantial proportion remain free of AIDS, even in the oldest age groups, after prolonged HIV infection. Rutherford[10] projects that 25 percent of people will be free of AIDS 20 years after initial HIV infection and 15 percent will be free of AIDS 25 years after initial infection. A complex web of factors is responsible for survival, including those listed in Table 15–2.

Literature on long-term survivors with AIDS is replete with anecdotal evidence linking survival to (1) a positive attitude toward the illness, (2) participating in health-promoting practices, (3) engaging in spiritual activities, and (4) taking part in AIDS-related activities. A study of 100 HIV-positive patients showed that those who scored higher on Kobasa's Hardiness Scale had a more positive outlook on life, used prayer and meditation, and participated in exercise and special diets.[11]

There are persistent themes of increasing self-care activities after being diagnosed as seropositive, a recognized need to reduce stress and the use of recreational drugs and alcohol, a need to participate actively in health care, and a belief that individuals can positively influence their health through self-care.[12] Solomon and colleagues[13] found that long-term survivors have a sense of personal responsibility for their health and a sense that they can influence health outcomes. They found that their subjects engaged in physical fitness or exercise programs and were able to alter their lifestyles.

Chesney and associates found that a positive mood

TABLE 15–2. CHARACTERISTICS OF LONG-TERM SURVIVORS OF AIDS

- Perceive their treating physician as a collaborator
- Have a sense of personal responsibility for their health
- Have a commitment to life
- Have a sense of meaningfulness and purpose in life
- Find new meaning as a result of AIDS
- Have a prior experience of a life-threatening illness or life event
- Engage in exercise or pursue physical fitness
- Derive useful information from and supportive contact with a person with AIDS
- Are altruistically involved with other AIDS patients
- Accept the reality of the diagnosis
- Have personalized means of active coping and are hopeful
- Alter their lifestyle
- Are assertive and have ability to say "no"
- Show ability to withdraw from taxing involvements and nurture themselves
- Are sensitive to their bodies and physical/psychological needs
- Communicate about their illness and concerns

Adapted from reference 13.

assists HIV-infected individuals in coping with their disease. Indeed, there is evidence to indicate that hopefulness confers health benefits for patients with AIDS, coronary heart disease, and cancer.[14,15]

To compare trends in the length of survival for women and men after diagnosis of AIDS, data were analyzed for 139 women and 7045 men who were reported with AIDS in San Francisco between July 1981 and December 1990. Patients were followed perspectively through mid-May 1991. The median survival for women (11.1 months) was significantly shorter than that for men

(14.6 months). Results suggested that the shorter survival for women may be a result of factors other than gender, possibly including co-factors such as less use of antiretroviral therapy, older age, or other competing health risks.[16]

■ Management Guidelines

The facts outlined previously suggest several guidelines for caregivers to follow. Because psychological, social, psychiatric, and neurologic complications occur frequently, all patients should have early access to social workers (Chapter 13) for planning of physical and financial assistance and referral to local self-help AIDS crisis organizations, as well as psychiatric consultation for monitoring mental status and psychotherapeutic and psychopharmacologic treatment of psychiatric symptoms.

Psychological management requires attention to several key issues. Every health professional should be aware of his or her own possible negative attitudes toward patients with AIDS, fears of caring for the fatally ill, and fears of contagion or prejudices before undertaking patient care. The caregiver should not let these attitudes interfere with care. Health professionals should maintain an active and updated file of information about AIDS, its mode of transmission, and cause and treatment, to provide facts and correct misinformation for other staff, friends, and family. New information emerges so rapidly that a poorly informed caregiver may misinform a patient.

The caregiver must feel comfortable discussing sexual matters with all patients, and know enough about bisexuality and homosexuality to understand the issues and problems as they relate to AIDS transmission. The caregiver should be able to evaluate a patient's mental status and identify altered memory, concentration, orientation, and abstraction, and monitor the patient for cognitive dysfunction at each visit. Otherwise, the caregiver should have a referral resource regularly available to do the monitoring. Because the central nervous system dysfunction associated with encephalopathy and dementia may precede the definitive AIDS diagnosis, its presence must be assessed along with reactive depression and anxiety.

At time of diagnosis, the caregiver must be able to assist the patient in understanding current information about the disease, cause, transmission, available treatment, and sources of care and social support. There must be recognition and discussion of the anxiety and panic associated with fears of progression of the disease, and realistic reassurance given in the context of the situation. Compassionate and sensitive discussion of current treatment and available research protocols must be provided. The range of depressive symptoms (such as sadness, helplessness, hopelessness, and poor self-esteem) should be explored, and questions should be asked about suicidal thoughts and plans. Referrals should be made for support and psychotherapy to deal with loneliness and depression through self-help crisis organizations.

Patients should be encouraged to explore feelings about sexual practices and the sense of guilt that accompanies the knowledge of being a source of contagion to others. Current understanding of precautions for partners, household members, and family, especially "safe sex" with partners, should be discussed, as well as precautions in the use of needles for drug users. Patients should be allowed to express anger toward discrimination, the behavior of others, and stigmatization, and to direct their anger in constructive ways. Help should be offered so they avoid acting in ways that would be self-destructive. Prejudice is likely to interfere with confidentiality and consideration of the patient's emotional well-being.

Fear, uncertainty, and preoccupation with confidentiality are but a few of the many facets of the scientific and societal responses to AIDS. Many deeply troubling issues, particularly the use of the HIV antibody test, tax our abilities to balance the needs of the communities at risk for AIDS and the needs of society as a whole. Sensitivity and respect for the needs of all communities ensure us a responsible and valid solution to these problems. We must avoid, however, the simplistic solutions, such as quarantines, that some propose to protect society.

AIDS causes two types of psychosocial crises, one among patients and the other in the general population; both yield opportunities and pitfalls. Medicine and its allied professions can help marshal intelligent responses to regressive societal forces unleashed by the AIDS dilemma, as well as help patients stave off senses of impending doom and hopelessness and accept the losses imposed on them by the disease.

■ Awareness of Limitations in Caregiving

Health professionals have a strong desire to help others, and look for evidence that their help has been successful in a patient's clinical improvement. Because AIDS has no cure at this time and the clinical course of the disease can change quickly, it is difficult for clinicians to feel a sense of being helpful and experience the satisfaction of seeing a cure. Health professionals' attitudes about their feelings can be sensed by patients, especially AIDS patients, who often look for evidence of their improvement. Health professionals who see primarily AIDS patients may not be aware of the cumulative effects of such a focused practice on themselves. Some health professionals may have to be made aware of their potential or impending burn-out, cynicism, or depression. Health professionals need a support system, too. AIDS is a complex and demanding disease, and caregivers cannot be expected to meet all of the needs of AIDS patients. Perhaps one of the greatest challenges of caregivers is to become aware of their own personal and clinical limitations in caring for AIDS patients.

References

1. Bruhn JG. Counseling persons with a fear of AIDS. *J Cons Dev.* 1989;67:455–457.
2. Bruhn JG. What to say to persons with HIV disease. *South Med J.* 1991;84:1430–1434.
3. Folkman S, Chesney MA, Cooke M, et al. Caregiver burden in HIV-positive and HIV-negative partners of men with AIDS. *J Cons Dev.* 1994;62:746–756.
4. Buchbinder SP, Katz MH, Hessol NA, et al. Long-term HIV-1 infection without immunologic progression. *AIDS.* 1994;8:1123–1128.
5. Hendricks JCM, Medley GF, Van Griensven GJP, et al. The treatment-free incubation period of AIDS in a cohort of homosexual men. *AIDS.* 1993;7:231–239.
6. Lifson AR, Hessol NA, Rutherford GW. Progression and clinical outcome of infection due to human immunodeficiency virus. *Clin Infect Dis.* 1992;14:966–972.
7. Philips AN, Sabin CA, Elford J, et al. Use of CD4 lymphocyte count to predict long-term survival free of AIDS after HIV infection. *BMJ.* 1994;309:309–313.
8. Rutherford GW, Lifson AR, Hessol NA, et al. Course of HIV-1 in a cohort of homosexual and bisexual men: An 11-year follow-up study. *BMJ.* 1990;301:1183–1188.
9. Ward JW, Bush TJ, Perkins HA, et al. The natural history of transfusion-associated HIV infection: Factors influencing progression to disease. *N Engl J Med.* 1989;321:947–952.
10. Rutherford GW. Long-term survival in HIV-1 infection. *BMJ.* 1994;309:283–284. Editorial.
11. Carson VB. Prayer, meditation, exercise, and special diets: Behaviors of the hardy person with HIV/AIDS. *J Assoc Nurs AIDS Care.* 1993;4:18–28.

12. Barroso J. Self-care activities of long-term survivors of acquired immunodeficiency syndrome. *Hol Nurs Pract.* 1995;10:44–53.

13. Solomon GF, Temoshok L, O'Leary A, Zich J. An intensive psychoimmunologic study of long-surviving persons with AIDS: Pilotwork, background studies, hypotheses, and methods. *Ann NY Acad Sci.* 1987;496:647–655.

14. Chesney MA. Psychological distress and health outcomes: The importance of hope. *Ann Behav Med, Int Congress Suppl.* 1996;5039.

15. Chesney MA, Folkman S, Chambers D. Positive affect mediates the link between HIV symptoms and distress, and response to coping intervention. *Ann Behav Med., Int Congress Suppl.* 1996;5040.

16. Lemp GF, Hirozawa AM, Cohen JB, et al. Survival for women and men with AIDS. *J Infect Dis.* 1992;166:74–79.

CHAPTER

Prevention

Barbara Ann Lyons • *Peggy Valentine*

At present, there is no known cure for AIDS, no vaccine available for prevention, and no proven method for eliminating the infectivity of the HIV carrier. For these reasons, great emphasis must be placed on preventing the transmission of HIV.

■ Modes of Transmission

The major modes of transmission for HIV are sexual contact with an infected person and contact with contaminated blood, predominately through the sharing of needles and syringes by injecting drug users. There is no evidence of transmission through casual contact (food, dishes, toilets, or sneezing). Although HIV has been isolated from body fluids and tissues including blood, semen, saliva, tears, breast milk, urine, lymph nodes, brain tissue, cerebrospinal fluid, and bone marrow, only blood and semen harbor moderate to high concentrations of virus and hence are the only body fluids to date that have been epidemiologically linked to transmission.

Because many unknowns still exist regarding HIV infection, it seems prudent to consider all body fluids, tissues, secretions, and excretions from all patients as potentially infectious, particularly if they contain blood. Parenteral or mucous membrane contact with these substances should be avoided. Current universal blood and body fluid precautions state that all body fluids from all patients are to be treated as if infective.

■ Reducing Risk of HIV Transmission

Guidelines have been developed by the Centers for Disease Control and Prevention (CDC) and the Occupational Safety and Health Administration (OSHA) to minimize the risk of exposure to blood and body fluids. Following these guidelines should greatly reduce the transmission of HIV and hepatitis B virus (HBV) to individuals and health care workers.

■ Individual Risk Reduction

For the individual, many methods are recommended to reduce the risk of HIV transmission. Overall, education and gaining correct knowledge concerning the pathophysiology of HIV and its transmission are of the utmost importance, because individuals need to know the facts about the disease and the behaviors that help prevent its spread. Most individuals at risk for HIV infection participate in at least one of several risky behaviors: anal intercourse, sex with multiple partners, injecting drug use (IDU), medical treatment with blood or blood products, or sex with a person who participates in any of the first four mentioned behaviors. Infants are at risk for transmission from their HIV-infected mother while in utero, at delivery, and postpartum.

Sexual contact among homosexuals has been the leading risk factor for acquiring HIV. Risky sex acts include unprotected receptive anal intercourse and oral sex. These types of sex acts may cause local tissue injury, which would be a portal of entry for the virus from the partner's semen. Some homosexuals have multiple sex partners, thereby giving them additional risk. For patients who are homosexual, discussion of their sexual practices is essential. Upon evaluation of the specific practices, protective measures should be discussed. For example, a patient participating in receptive anal intercourse may choose to abstain from the activity. Alternatively, condoms may be used.

Having multiple sexual partners, heterosexual and/or homosexual, is also considered a risky behavior. As the number of people involved increases, so does the risk of one or more of them carrying HIV. Although some people may have had sex with only a few different partners, others may have had sex with hundreds of different people. Prostitutes may not want to inform their clients about their health, and instances of unprotected sex may occur. Prevention of the risk from multiple partners includes patient awareness of the risk involved. The patient may decrease the number of future partners or may choose to use condoms to prevent the spread of the virus.

For injecting drug users, the risk is from blood contact through sharing and/or reuse of hypodermic needles and syringes. IDU is defined as any route in which the skin is broken with a needle, and includes intravenous, intra-arterial, intramuscular, and subdermal routes of injection. Patients who participate in IDU may benefit from a number of preventive measures. Drug rehabilitation is possible for some patients who are motivated to stop their drug use. For patients who cannot or will not cease IDU, safety measures that may help decrease the spread of HIV include not sharing needles, cleaning used syringes and needles with bleach solution, or needle exchange programs. Some patients engage in prostitution to procure drugs and will be at higher risk than from IDU alone.

Even if they do not participate in any risky behaviors themselves, some people may be at risk for acquiring HIV if their sexual partners engage in any risky behaviors. Prevention of HIV in these individuals would include the knowledge of the risks of their sexual partners. For all people with a current or past history of homosexual sexual activity, multiple sexual partners, IDU, and/or blood or blood product treatment, the employment of safer sex techniques with their sexual partners may help prevent the spread of HIV. Sexual abstinence is the only completely safe method to prevent the sexual transmission of HIV. Because this choice is not popular, prevention methods termed safer sex techniques have been outlined. Although the use of safer sex techniques will not prevent the transmission of HIV completely, they do afford some level of protection. A noninclusive list of safer sex techniques includes abstaining from risky sex acts, including anal or vaginal intercourse; the use of a latex condom during risky sex acts; use of the spermicide nonoxinol-9; and the use of massage and touching.

Patients who have been treated with blood or blood product transfusions may be at a higher risk for HIV. Prior to late 1985, the general blood supply was not adequately tested for the presence of HIV antibodies. Additionally, blood clotting factors given to hemophiliacs were also not tested for the presence of HIV. Consequently, many patients requiring blood transfusions or clotting factor administration were inadvertently given HIV. Blood donors are now screened prior to donation for any risk factors for HIV and the blood supply is tested for HIV antibodies; the risk of transmission of HIV is therefore much lower, and was estimated to be between 1 per 40,000 to 150,000 units infused in 1989.[1] Patients who received blood transfusions or blood clotting factors prior to 1985, pending the knowledge of their HIV status, may abstain from sexual contact or employ safer sex techniques. Because a risk remains of HIV transmission from blood transfusion, patients currently receiving blood transfusions may choose the same options. For patients who will need blood transfusion or clotting factors in the future, prevention methods include preoperative autologous blood donation, hemodilution, perioperative blood salvage, and the use of recombinant coagulation factors, recombinant hematopoietic growth factors, and red cell substitutes.[1]

Transmission of HIV to the fetus and newborn is possible, and to some extent preventable. For the known HIV-positive woman, prevention methods may include using contraception to prevent pregnancy and abstaining from breast feeding. Any woman of childbearing age who is sexually active should understand the risk of transmission of HIV to her future children and may want to practice safer sex techniques to keep from becoming infected. As demonstrated in AIDS Clinical Trial Study 076, HIV-infected women can lower the risk of transmission to the newborn through Zidovudine therapy. More details on the prevention of the transmission of HIV from mother to child are found in Chapter 7.

■ Health Care Worker Risk Reduction

For the health care worker (HCW), OSHA guidelines[2] include the use of personal protective equipment (PPE) to decrease the risk from blood or other potentially infectious materials. Gloves, gowns, laboratory coats, face shields or masks, and eye protection are included in PPE. The choice of what PPE is appropriate for each HCW job activity needs to be defined. If a HCW is performing a job task where hand contact with blood or other infectious material is expected, gloves must be worn. For most HCW tasks, single-use gloves are appropriate. These latex gloves are disposed of after one use. If the HCW is allergic to latex, hypoallergic gloves must be provided. Gloving is required for almost all phlebotomy situations. The only exception to the rule is in voluntary blood donation centers, where gloving for phlebotomy is not required. A HCW in a voluntary blood center may choose to use gloves at any time; however, they must use gloves if they have cuts, scratches, or breaks in their skin, while training, or when it is believed that contamination may occur.

For clinical activities where splashes, sprays, splatters, or droplets of potentially infectious material pose a hazard through the eyes, nose, or mouth, face protection should be used. These protection methods include the use of goggles and masks, glasses with solid side shields and masks, or chin-length face shields. These measures would be appropriate for activities including, for example, the use of jet lavage for wound cleansing and tub therapy for debridement of burn wounds. For clinical situations where gross contamination is expected, more extensive coverings such as gowns, aprons, surgical caps/hoods, and shoe covers or boots are needed in addition to gloves and face protection. This level of protection would be needed for clinical activities such as orthopedic surgery or autopsy.

After removal of any PPE, hands must be washed with soap and water as soon as feasible. If access to soap and water is delayed, interim hand-cleansing measures such as use of moist towelettes may be employed, followed by timely appropriate hand washing. Used protective clothing and equipment must be placed in designated containers for storage, decontamination, or disposal.

HCWs with weeping dermatitis or exudative lesions should refrain from all patient contact until the condition resolves. Even though saliva has not been implicated as a source of HIV transmission, limiting the use of mouth-to-mouth resuscitation seems wise. Where emergency resuscitation is predictable, mouthpieces, resuscitation bags (Ambu bags), or other ventilation-assist devices should be available. In the event of a skin or mucous membrane contact with a potentially infectious body fluid, the body area of contact is to be washed with soap and water. In the event of eye contact, copious irrigation with water is recommended. When HCWs experience parenteral exposures, needle sticks, scalpel cuts, or mucous membrane exposure, testing for HIV and hepatitis should be performed (see Chapter 12).

Depending on their specific job requirements, HCWs may be responsible for decontamination of work surface areas or equipment that may involve exposure to blood. Work areas are to be cleaned when (1) surfaces are obviously contaminated; (2) after any spill of blood or other potentially infective body fluid; and (3) at any time the worker leaves a potentially contaminated area, including breaks, meals, or at a shift's end. Each employer is responsible for developing guidelines for decontamination that specify the methods of decontamination used for different surfaces, types of contamination present, and types of procedures done in the area. In addition to commercially available germicides, household bleach (sodium hypochlorite) in a dilution of 1:100 or 1:10 is an effective method depending on the amount of organic material present. Some medical devices may corrode from continual exposure to the 1:10 bleach solution, so that commercial germicides may need to be used. OSHA also recommends that HCWs refrain from eating, drinking, smoking, applying lipstick or lip balm, and handling contact lenses in areas where blood or body fluid exposure is possible.

Prompt disposal of all medical sharps, including needles and scalpels, will minimize stick and cut exposures in HCWs. Containers for disposable and reusable sharps that are puncture resistant and leakproof should be located close by the area where sharps are used. The location of the containers should eliminate the need to set the needle or scalpel on a surface after its use or the sticking of contaminated needles into a mattress of a patient bed or gurney prior to proper disposal. In most clinical situations, recapping, bending, or removal of needles *should not* be performed. These techniques account for the majority of needle sticks and cuts. For testing that requires the needle to be left in place, such as arterial blood gas determination, recapping, bending, or removal of the needle should be performed by a mechanical device or by using the one-hand recapping technique. The use of both hands to recap a needle is to be avoided. The one-hand technique involves use of the needle itself to slip into the needle cap. Pressure on a hard surface may complete the closure. Alternatively, tongs or forceps could be used to place the cap on the needle. Even when performed using an approved method, recapping of needles is limited to those situations when recapping is required.

HCWs are forbidden to handle potentially contaminated broken glass by hand, even if gloves are worn. Glass fragments are to be collected using a brush and dustpan, tongs, or forceps and disposed of in a contaminated sharps container.

Laundry that is contaminated with blood or other potentially infective material should be handled as little as possible and with a minimum of agitation. All soiled linen should be bagged in the area of use and transported to the laundry facility. No sorting or prewashing should be done in patient care areas.

Despite adherence to the principles of universal precautions, certain invasive surgical and dental procedures (cardiothoracic, obstetric/gynecologic, and oral procedures) have been implicated in the transmission of HBV from infected HCWs to patients, and should thus be considered as posing a high risk of exposure.[3] Exposure-prone procedures may also be implicated in the transmission of HIV. Characteristics of such procedures include digital palpation of a needle tip in a body cavity or the simultaneous presence of the HCW's fingers and a needle or other sharp instrument or object in a poorly visualized or highly confined anatomic site.[3] To minimize the risk of HIV or HBV transmission, the CDC recommends the following measures.[3]

- All HCWs should adhere to the universal precautions already mentioned.
- Currently available data provide no basis for recommendations to restrict the practice of HCWs infected with HIV or HBV who perform invasive procedures not identified as posing a high risk of exposure, provided that the infected HCWs practice recommended surgical or dental technique and comply with universal precautions and current recommendations for sterilization/disinfection.
- Exposure-prone procedures should be identified by the medical/surgical/dental organizations and institutions at which the procedures are performed.
- HCWs who perform exposure-prone procedures should know their HIV antibody status. HCWs who perform exposure-prone procedures and who

do not have serologic evidence of immunity to HBV from vaccination or from previous infection should know their HBsAg status and, if that is positive, should also know their HBeAg status.

- HCWs who are infected with HIV or HBV (and are HBeAg positive) should not perform high-risk procedures unless they have sought counsel from an expert review panel and been advised under what circumstances, if any, they may continue to perform these procedures. Such circumstances would include notifying prospective patients of the HCW's seropositivity before they undergo exposure-prone invasive procedures.

- Mandatory testing of HCWs for HIV antibody, HBsAg, or HBeAg is not recommended. The current assessment of the risk that infected HCWs will transmit HIV or HBV to patients during exposure-prone procedures does not support the diversion of resources that would be required to implement mandatory testing programs. Compliance by HCWs with recommendations can be increased through education, training, and appropriate confidentiality safeguards.

The guidelines for HCWs are frequently updated, and it should be noted that clinicians will need to keep informed of any future changes.

■ Prevention in Minority Populations

Minorities continue to be disproportionately represented in the numbers of AIDS cases. Since 1993, African Americans and Hispanics have represented over half of all reported cases of AIDS. A particularly disturbing trend has been noted among young minorities between the ages of

27 to 39 years of age. It is estimated that 1 of every 33 African American men and 1 of every 59 Hispanic men of this age group are HIV infected. For women, 1 of every 100 African American females and 1 of every 200 Hispanic women of the same age group are infected.[4] The HIV seroprevalence rate for Asian Americans, Native Americans, and Pacific islanders remains low; however, Native Americans are rapidly approaching the incidence of AIDS in whites (Fig. 16–1).

There continues to be an overrepresentation of women, children, and heterosexuals with AIDS from these ethnic minority groups. Over 70 percent of women and children, and 79 percent of heterosexuals with AIDS, are African American and Hispanic.[4]

A history of IDU tends to be the major risk factor for the disparity noted in African American and Hispanic populations. Although drug use is prevalent among all race groups,[10] IDU is more highly associated with HIV seroprevalence among these groups. This high-risk behavior, which may or may not be known to a sexual partner, increases the chance of heterosexual and, subsequently, neonatal transmission.[5]

Despite targeted HIV prevention programs, the number of AIDS cases in minority groups continues to escalate. Some members of these groups do not believe the prevention messages and continue to engage in high-risk behavior; others may have more immediate needs of daily survival. Before designing and implementing HIV prevention strategies for minority groups, the provider should consider certain sociocultural issues, which will now be reviewed.

Theories of the Epidemiology of HIV

In some minority communities, there are those who believe that HIV was purposely introduced into the community by the government to control population growth.

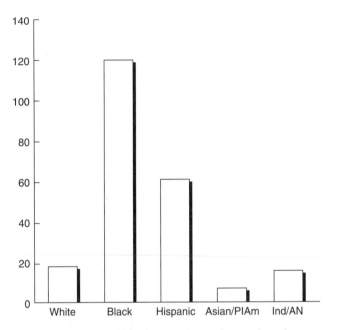

Figure 16–1. AIDS cases and annual rates through December 1995. (adults and adolescents, per 100,000 population.) (*From reference 4.*)

It is believed that the virus was created through genetic engineering to "kill off" undesirable gays and minorities. The theory that AIDS originated in Africa may be interpreted to mean that HIV came from persons of African descent, and that thus they are to be blamed for the disease.[5] Condom promotion is seen by some as population control imposed by the majority so as to decrease the minority population. Others view needle exchange programs as a way to promote drug use in the African American community. These beliefs and perceptions create barriers for HIV prevention programs in that those who believe these theories may not heed government prevention messages.[5–7]

When designing and implementing an HIV prevention program in the African American community, the clinician should first discern what beliefs and perceptions are held. Patients should be encouraged to discuss their feelings and concerns about these issues. Sometimes sharing a story with a philosophical meaning may generate discussion. One story sometimes shared is that of the snake in the house. Should we expend our energy on asking where it came from, or should we rather focus our efforts on getting it out of the house? The provider can also show concern and assist the patient in identifying ways to lower the risk of HIV and other sexually transmitted diseases.

Fear of Homosexuality/Bisexuality

Despite the gay awareness movement of the past two decades, many ethnic minorities do not support the concept of homosexuality and look down on those who are openly gay. Therefore, some minority males choose to remain "closeted" or to engage in bisexual relationships. This lifestyle may be burdensome enough, and the male who is a member of a minority, gay, and afflicted with AIDS may well feel overburdened. Unfortunately, there are few support services in minority communities for gay persons infected with HIV. It is common for African American males to misrepresent their mode of HIV exposure to avoid stigma and maintain support from family and friends.[5,7] The provider may assist the patient through referral to national AIDS minority organizations (see Chapter 20). Some of these organizations provide educational services to the gay community and can provide information on local support groups.

Another issue of importance to the provider is how members of minority groups define homosexuality. For example, Hispanic men may define a homosexual male as the receptive partner in anal intercourse, and the insertive partner may not be considered homosexual.[5] In establishing a common language, it is recommended that providers ask the patient if he has sex with men, with women, or with both.[8]

Bisexuality is an important risk factor to be considered in the Hispanic community, and women partners of bisexual males may be at increased risk for acquiring HIV. In some cases, Hispanic women perceive their relationships as characterized by a power imbalance and thus consider themselves limited in their ability to reduce this risk.[5] In working with women who feel unempowered in their relationships, the provider can recommend various support groups that build self-esteem. The provider can also identify resourcepersons from federal, state, and local governments and community-based organizations to work with the patient.

Disbelief of Prevention Messages

Minority communities have had negative experiences with public health groups in the past, which may cause mistrust of HIV prevention messages today. For example, many remember the Tuskegee Syphilis Study, in which some African American males with syphilis were allowed to progress to an advanced stage of the disease without adequate treatment.[9] This example and others have caused minorities to become mistrustful and to experience a certain amount of discomfort when discussing the impact of HIV/AIDS on their communities. Since the Tuskegee Study, improvements have certainly been made in the research environment to protect human subjects. However, beliefs and perceptions are slow to change—indeed, certain events, however appalling, must remain in our consciousness so that the same mistakes will not be repeated.

The building of trust in patient–provider relationships comes about through a series of interactions and through open and honest communication. One should not always assume that minority providers are best able to relate to minority patients with HIV seropositivity. Minority patients may in fact not be more trusting of minority providers of the same culture; some fear that minority providers are more likely to pass judgment upon them. In any case, it is important to convince the patient that he or she has the provider's support and trust. Sometimes sharing personal information equalizes the balance of power and can help to build a more trusting relationship. This sharing should ideally take place during the first patient–provider interaction.[5]

Poverty

Minorities are disproportionately represented at income levels associated with poverty. They have higher rates of unemployment and lower incomes than white Americans. Most African Americans and Hispanics at risk for HIV are of lower socioeconomic status. These minorities are less likely to seek early treatment for AIDS, tend to seek access to the health care system later in the course of HIV-related illnesses, and die sooner from AIDS than do whites.[5]

Clearly the provider cannot erase poverty and improve access to health care for all; however, he or she can nevertheless exert a positive impact on minority communities by working with their members to promote healthier lifestyles. Minorities often do not know what resources are available outside the community, especially if they do not speak English. The provider can point individuals to local resources that provide free or reduced-fee services. Community forums that involve social service agencies can be arranged to disseminate information on health care services to the public.

Differences in Language and Culture and Their Effect on Communication

In some instances, HIV prevention literature is not communicated effectively to minority populations. HIV prevention programs are further hampered in minority groups because of the presence of diverse communities with culturally specific attitudes and beliefs, including those pertaining to the roles of males and females. For example, in disseminating HIV prevention messages in Native American communities, it is important that the messages be delivered by members of the communities.[5] Similarly, Pacific islanders may not believe or trust messages delivered by individuals from outside their communities. It may therefore be more effective to train outreach workers in these communities to provide HIV education.[5]

Language is a barrier for certain minority groups in gaining access to HIV education because of the variety of languages and dialects among those groups. This is a particular problem in the Asian-American/Pacific islander group and among Hispanic groups. In addition, health care providers may be unable to translate or provide appropriately translated materials. Whenever possible, materials should be written at the appropriate grade level and depict the language, culture, and style of communication of the targeted group.[5,6]

It is also suggested that HIV information specific to women be disseminated. Because minority women face issues involving their cultural roles as spouses and mothers differently from men, separate programs may be needed.

When implementing or participating in HIV prevention programs for minorities, the provider should gain an appreciation of the patient's life experiences, values, and belief systems. This may require a series of visits in the clinical setting and preferably in the domestic environment. Through learning about the individual patient, the provider will have a better understanding of how to disseminate HIV prevention information. Providers should consider the social, cultural, and economic factors that influence HIV prevention in minorities. Providers should also be aware of their own limitations, strengths, and weaknesses and should use all available resources, including local health departments and grantees of the CDC and National Institutes of Health AIDS Education Training Centers.

Prevention Programs That Work

During the past decade, a number of studies have been conducted for HIV prevention. Some of these are relevant for working with minority groups. For example, Jemmott and Jemmott implemented a successful program in reducing high-risk sexual behavior among African American male adolescents in Philadelphia. Through the use of ethnic educational videotapes, role-playing, and other learning activities, participants reported a decrease in frequency of sexual intercourse, fewer sexual partners, and increased condom use.[11]

In working with injection drug users, published works on theories and methods of behavioral interventions provide useful tips in working with this community.[12] Another published work on gay and bisexual African American men demonstrates a model program for HIV risk reduction. Through implementation of weekly group sessions, participants reported a reduced frequency of unprotected anal intercourse. An 18-month follow-up revealed maintenance of behavior change.[13]

Providers should be aware of prevention programs within their communities and promote efforts. An active role can be played through the HIV prevention and community planning process. The CDC issued a guidance document on this process to the 65 state, territorial, and local health departments that receive HIV prevention funds. Participation in the process assures the planning of culturally competent and scientifically sound HIV prevention services that specifically address the unique needs of communities.[14]

References

1. OSHA Instruction CPC 2–2-44C. Enforcement procedures for the occupational exposure to bloodborne pathogens standard, 29 CFR 1910.1030, March 6, 1992.

2. Healthy People 2000. Washington, DC: Public Health Service, 1990.

3. Centers for Disease Control. Recommendations for preventing transmission of human immunodeficiency virus and hepatitis B virus to patients during exposure-prone invasive procedures. *MMWR.* 1991;40:1–9.

4. Centers for Disease Control and Prevention. HIV/ AIDS surveillance report. December 1995;7:17.

5. National Commission on AIDS. The Challenge of HIV/ AIDS in Communities of Color. Washington, DC: 1992.

6. Peterson JL, Marin G. Issues in the prevention of AIDS among black and hispanic men. *Am Psychol.* 1988;43:871–877.

7. Dalton HL. Living with AIDS, 2. *Daedalus.* 1989;118:205–227.

8. Mann J, Tarantola DJM, Netter TW. AIDS in the World. Cambridge, MA: Harvard University Press; 1992.

9. Thomas SB, Quinn SC. The Tuskegee syphilis study, 1932 to 1972: Implications for HIV education and AIDS risk education programs in the black community. *Am J Public Health.* 1991;81:1498–1503.

10. Fullilove MT. Perceptions and misperceptions of race and drug use. *JAMA.* 1993;269:1034. Editorial.

11. Jemmott JB, Jemmott LS, Fong GT. Reductions in HIV risk-associated sexual behaviors among black male adolescents: Effects of an AIDS prevention intervention. *Am J Public Health.* 1992;82:372–377.

12. DiClemente RJ, Peterson JL, eds. Preventing AIDS: Theories and Methods of Behavioral Interventions. New York: Plenum; 1994.

13. Peterson JL. AIDS-related risks and same-sex behaviors among African American men. In: Herek GM, Greene B, eds. AIDS, Identity and Community. Thousand Oaks, CA: Sage Publications; 1995:85–104.
14. Centers for Disease Control and Prevention. HIV Prevention Planning. August 1995.

part V

SUPPORTIVE CARE

CHAPTER

seventeen

Nursing Procedures

Bernadette Montgomerie Canales

The impact of AIDS and HIV disease on the outpatient care setting has been overwhelming and may raise some concern about the adequacy of attention to patient education and risk management. With such a large percentage of patients leaving the hospital setting with vascular access devices and complicated intravenous medication regimens for viral and fungal infections, it is important that the nurse be knowledgeable in all areas of teaching the necessary procedures, and that documentation be provided to patients regarding their role expectations and "troubleshooting" guidelines.

Increasingly patients are being discharged from the hospital setting early in their recovery period. Their home care, which ideally should be managed by a registered nurse, more likely becomes the responsibility of the patient, family, or friends.

■ Outpatient Procedures

Procedures that may be conducted in the outpatient setting that require nursing intervention include indwelling vascular access catheter care, blood transfusions, lumbar punctures, and bone marrow aspiration and biopsies. Primary responsibilities of the nurse should include patient comfort, patient education, and appropriate barrier precautions for the health care worker performing the procedure.

■ Indwelling Vascular Access Catheters

The principal life-threatening complication in any patient who has a vascular catheter is septicemia. In a patient with AIDS, the risk is multiplied many times. Because of repeated infections that result in the need for a future hospitalization to remove the infected Groshong, Hickman, or Port-a-Cath catheter and replace it in the operating room, clinicians have searched for other options. One of these is the Hohn central venous catheter (Figs. 17–1, 17–2). This catheter is introduced percutaneously, and the procedure can be performed at the patient's bedside under local anesthesia (Boxes 17–1 to 17–4). The catheter was designed for short-term use and as a rule should be replaced after 2 or 3 months. Because this is not a "tunneled" catheter, it can easily be removed in the outpatient setting by a trained registered nurse.

Some clinicians who use the Hohn catheter have concluded that dressing changes can be performed less frequently than the usual every 72 hours. With this catheter, patients are required to return to the clinic setting to have a dressing change performed once weekly (Box 17–4). Therefore, patients do not need to worry about doing

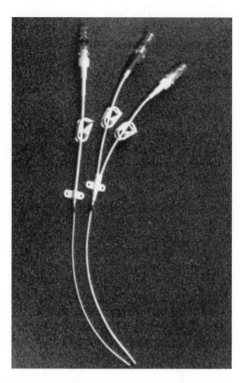

Figure 17–1. Hohn catheters. (*With permission from Bard Access Systems.*)

their own dressing care, and strict controls can be followed regarding the specific care to minimize contamination. In our clinical experience, it has been found that the rate of infection has decreased considerably since we adopted this method of care.

Because Hohn catheters do not have a valve at their proximal end, daily flushing with heparin is necessary. Patients are taught to flush the catheter with 200 units of Hep-lock (100 U/cc) solution using prefilled syringes and

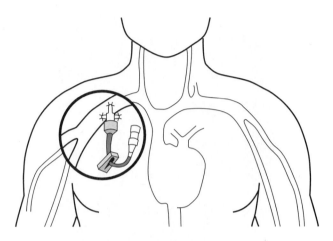

Figure 17–2. Placement of Hohn catheter.

attaching Interlink cannulas, which are plastic tips that pierce the Interlink injection cap without the use of a needle. This has been found to be a helpful safety standard, particularly when dealing with patients who have CMV retinitis and compromised visual acuity. The catheter is also flushed with 10 cc of sodium chloride before and after administration of any intravenous medications using the same Interlink system.

■ Blood Transfusion

Standing orders are often used for blood transfusion procedures (Box 17–5). Despite increasingly accurate crossmatching procedures, transfusion reactions can, and often do, occur. Circulatory overload and hemolytic, allergic, febrile, and pyrogenic reactions can occur in any patient receiving a blood transfusion. In the HIV/AIDS population, who often require frequent transfusion of blood

■ Box 17–1

Patient Instructions for Drug Administration via the Hohn Catheter

Date _____

Name _____

Medication Regimen:

Ganciclovir (DHPG) _____mg in 0.9 percent sodium 100 mL _____daily, 7 days wk

OR

Amphotericin B_____mg in dextrose in water _____ mL daily, 7 days wk

Procedure

Always wipe rubber stoppers with alcohol before inserting needles or cannulas.

1. Assemble materials, prepare yourself and prepare the working surface as instructed.
2. Place ganciclovir/amphotericin B bag on tubing and prime tubing to clear tube of air. Place blue-threaded lock cannula on end of tube.
3. Clean catheter with alcohol. Connect needleless cannula to syringe and flush catheter with 10 mL of 0.9 percent sodium chloride.
4. Connect medication bag and tubing to catheter.

   GANCICLOVIR: Infuse over a 1-hour period (16 drops per minute, 8 drops per 30 seconds, or 4 drops per 15 seconds).

   AMPHOTERICIN B:
   4-hour infusion—Count 5 drops per 15 seconds.
   3-hour infusion—Count 7 drops per 15 seconds.
   2-hour infusion—Count 10 drops per 15 seconds.

■ *Box 17–1 continued*

5. When medication infusion is complete, disconnect the tubing from the catheter.

6. Clean catheter cap (rubber stopper) with alcohol. Flush catheter with 10 mL 0.9 percent sodium chloride.

7. Clean catheter cap with alcohol. Flush catheter with _____ mL Hep-lock solution, 100 units/mL.

8. Discard used syringes and cannulas in sharps container. Place tubing and bags in sealed plastic garbage bag.

9. Store reconstituted ganciclovir in refrigerator prior to use. Ganciclovir is stable for 14 days when stored in refrigerator. Store reconstituted amphotericin B bags in brown paper sack in refrigerator prior to use. It is stable for 14 days.

10. Inspect medication for cloudiness or floating particles before use. Notify clinician and discard if this occurs.

11. Gloves, gowns, and masks are recommended to be used by the person administering the medication.

12. Store all prefilled syringes in refrigerator prior to use.

products, intravenous furosemide (Lasix) is often administered after each unit of blood to lessen the possibility of circulatory overload. As with any patient receiving transfusions, the nurse must exercise care in frequent monitoring of vital signs as well as fluid intake and out-

■ Box 17–2

Patient Instructions on How to Flush (or Rinse) Catheter

It is possible that your catheter tubing could get clogged with a blood clot. To keep this from happening, you will flush your tube with a liquid called heparin. You will be provided with syringes that have been prefilled with the appropriate amount of heparin, and you will need to flush your catheter daily, after each catheter use, and each time the cap is changed.

Supplies you will need
1. Alcohol wipes
2. Prefilled syringe with heparin flush solution (Hep-lock)*
3. "Interlink" needleless cannula
4. Sharps container

Procedure
1. Assemble supplies as above.
2. Wash and dry hands thoroughly. Use soap and water.
3. Remove the cannula from its package and attach it to the syringe without touching the exposed area. Remove any air from the syringe by gently tapping any bubbles to the top, then carefully pushing up on the barrel of the syringe until you see a droplet of liquid on the end of the cannula. Unclamp the catheter.
4. Clean the rubber stopper at the end of the catheter with an alcohol wipe.

> ■ *Box 17–2 continued*
>
> 5. Insert the cannula into the center of the rubber stopper (injection cap) and administer the heparin gently. If no resistance is felt, inject all of the solution slowly. If resistance is felt, DO NOT FORCE—CONTACT YOUR CLINICIAN AS SOON AS POSSIBLE. Reclamp the catheter.
> 6. Dispose of used syringe and cannula in sharps container.
>
> * These instructions should also be followed when flushing with sodium chloride solution before and after medication infusions.

put patterns. Documentation of this as well as any transfusion reaction and treatment should be done.

■ Lumbar Puncture/Bone Marrow Aspiration and Biopsy

The outpatient clinic nurse is often required to assist with these procedures, which require sterile technique and careful patient positioning. The nurse should first ensure that the patient understands the procedure, to ease anxiety and to ensure cooperation. A consent form must be signed indicating that the patient has received adequate explanation of the procedure and its possible advantages and disadvantages. The nurse should check the patient's history for hypersensitivity to the local anesthetic and provide a sedative, as ordered, before the procedure.

Both the health care worker performing the procedure as well as the assistant must wear appropriate pro-

■ **Box 17–3**

Patient Instructions on How to Change Injection Cap

The injection cap (rubber stopper) needs to be changed every 2 weeks. Wash your hands thoroughly before beginning the procedure.

1. Close the slide clamp on your catheter.
2. Peel open the package containing the new injection cap.
3. Hold the catheter in one hand near the cap. With the other hand, twist the cap by turning counterclockwise. Do not remove the rubber stopper from the plastic body.
4. Remove the plastic cover on the bottom of the new cap.
5. Twist the new cap onto the catheter tube.
6. Inject heparin solution as instructed.
7. RECLAMP THE CATHETER.

tective barrier gown, mask, goggles, and sterile gloves. Care should be exercised when handling the instruments and body fluids obtained from the patient. During the procedure, the nurse should be aware of any signs of adverse reaction: elevated pulse rate, pallor, or clammy skin. Bleeding and infection are potentially life-threatening complications that may result from either of these procedures. The nurse should immediately alert the clinician performing the procedure to any significant changes in the patient's condition.

Finally, the nurse is responsible for charting the time,

■ **Box 17–4**

Patient Instructions for
Changing Dressing

The type of dressing used should only need to be changed on a weekly basis. However, if the dressing should become soiled or is just coming off the skin, it should be changed more frequently. Before leaving the hospital, you will be supplied with several dressing kits.

Catheter care kit containing the following supplies
1. Surgeons masks (2)
2. Surgeons gloves (1 pair)
3. Gauze 4×4s (10)
4. Package swabsticks, alcohol (3 sticks)
5. Package swabsticks, povidone-iodine (3 sticks)
6. Gauze 2×2s (2)
7. Gauze 2×2, split (1)
8. Povidone-iodine pad (1)
9. Interlink injection cap (1)
10. Dry swab sticks (3)
11. Skin prep pad (1)
12. Op-site (transparent) dressing 10×14 (1)
    Also: Micropore tape

Procedure
1. Gather all supplies
2. Wash and dry hands thoroughly. Use soap and water.
3. Open Catheter Care kit by touching only the outside of the wrapper. Place on top of a clean dry sheet or towel.
4. Remove masks carefully. Use one for patient, the other for the caregiver.

■ *Box 17–4 continued*

5. Remove old dressing and discard in appropriate manner.
6. Wash hands again.
7. Inspect catheter site carefully. If any redness, swelling, or drainage is noted, or if a suture has become loose, notify your clinician as soon as possible.
8. Carefully remove sterile gloves and put on by:
    (a) Grabbing the turned back cuff of one of the gloves. Pull the glove on your free hand. Be careful not to touch the outside of the glove below the cuff.
    (b) Using the gloved hand, slide the fingers of that hand under the folded cuff of the next glove and pull it on to your hand.
    (c) You can now use either hand to gently arrange your fingers in the gloves. DO NOT TOUCH ANYTHING before you go on to the next steps. (Holding your hands above the level of your waist will help you to remember this.)
9. Open the sterile field containing the rest of the items.
10. Use your nondominant hand to hold the end of the catheter. Your other hand will do most of the work. Use one of the sterile 4 × 4s to prevent contamination of your sterile glove. First, take one of the alcohol swabsticks and clean around the catheter exit site working outward in a widening circle. Repeat this two more times using a new swabstick each time.

    Repeat this procedure using the brown iodine swabsticks.

■ *Box 17–4 continued*

Next, using the brown iodine wipe, clean the tubing from the exit site toward the injection cap.

Using one or more of the sterile 4 × 4s, pat the entire area dry.

11. Take the skin prep pad and wipe the skin around the catheter site, but not immediately surrounding it.

12. Take the 2 × 2 split gauze and place under the catheter hub.

13. Cover this with the other 2 × 2s provided.

14. Apply transparent dressing over this.

15. Secure excess catheter and injection cap to chest with tape.

Person to contact for questions or problems:

_____

date, location, and patient's tolerance of the procedure and any specimens obtained.

■ Trimethoprim/Sulfamethoxazole Desensitization

The use of prophylactic medication regimens will influence a patient's susceptibility to certain infections. Although no regimen is 100 percent effective, and microbial resistance to prophylactic medications is a growing concern, many agents can and do significantly decrease the incidence of certain pulmonary opportunistic infections.[1]

■ **Box 17–5**

Standing Orders for Blood Transfusions

Please check or fill in appropriate response.

1. Allergies: _____
2. Type & cross for _____ units PRBCs
   or
   Type & cross done _____ (date)
3. Pt. to receive transfusion within 24 hours
   _____ Yes _____ No
   may schedule transfusion as convenient
   _____ Yes _____ No
4. Transfuse each unit over 1.5 to 2.0 hours
5. Prior to transfusion premedicate with:
   Tylenol 650 mg PO
   Benadryl 50 mg PO
6. Give Lasix 10 mg SIVP after each unit
   _____ Yes _____ No
   Hold Lasix if BP below _____ or pulse
   above _____
7. May repeat Tylenol 650 mg q 3–4 hours prn for
   temp greater than 101°F.
8. Please obtain CBC posttransfusion
   _____ Yes _____ No
9. For problems, call_____
   Beeper # _____ Phone # _____

The best examples are the use of trimethoprim/sulfamethoxazole (TMP/SMZ, Bactrim or Septra), dapsone, or aerosolized pentamidine for prophylaxis against *Pneumocystis carinii* pneumonia (PCP).[2] TMP/SMZ has efficacy in PCP prevention, and it also provides prophylaxis against a wide range of other pathogens, including the protozoan, *Toxoplasma gondii,* and many bacteria.[3,4]

Many patients are hypersensitive to sulfonamide drugs and are unable to tolerate TMP/SMZ. Some institutions have written protocols (Box 17–6) to desensitize patients to TMP/SMZ, which appear to be quite successful and can be easily performed in the outpatient clinic setting. Essentially, the patient is given a very small dose of TMP/SMZ, by mouth, and observed for a period of time while ever-increasing amounts of drug are slowly introduced. The patient is observed carefully for symptoms of toxicity. Any occurrence of low-grade fevers and/or rash should be treated as they occur (acetaminophen [Tylenol] and/or diphenhydramine [Benadryl] can be given). For fever of greater than 101°F, dyspnea, urticaria, nausea, vomiting, diarrhea, abdominal pain, stomatitis or any other severe reaction, desensitization must be discontinued (refer to Chapter 10 for further discussion on this issue).

■ Cosyntropin Stimulation Test

Patients with AIDS are often prescribed drugs that, among their side effects, alter endocrine function (such as ketoconazole [Nizoral], rifampin [Rifadin], and megestrol acetate [Megace]). The cosyntropin stimulation test is a diagnostic test of adrenocortical function commonly performed in the outpatient clinic area (Box 17–7).

Nursing considerations include observation for allergic reactions: rash, dyspnea, wheezing, or evidence of anaphylaxis. Before administering the test, the nurse should ask the patient if he or she has a history of hypersensitivity to cortosyn; if so, the test is obviously contraindicated.

■ **Box 17-6**

TMP/SMZ Desensitization Schedule

Instructions: Use oral syringes to withdraw TMP/ SMZ for the first 6 doses. Use TMP/SMZ tablets thereafter.

Dispense: 25 mL of TMP/SMZ suspension and 1 double strength TMP/SMZ tablet.

Dosing Schedule

Hour	Dose
initially	0.05 mL
1	0.10 mL
2	1.0 mL
3	2.5 mL
4	5.0 mL
5	10.0 mL
11	1 TMP/SMX DS tablet

Thereafter, prescribe one TMP/SMZ DS tablet orally every day, 7 days a week.

For low-grade fever (< 100.0°F), give 650 mg acetaminophen orally as needed.

For mild rash, give 50 mg diphenhydramine orally every 6 hours as needed.

For urticaria, dyspnea, or fever greater than 101.0°F, discontinue procedure.

■ **Box 17–7**

Cosyntropin Stimulation Test

1. Draw serum cortisol level, label this "pre."
2. Following phlebotomy, administer 0.25 mg of cortosyn IM. Note the time.
3. Exactly 30 minutes later, draw a second serum cortisol and label "post."

■ Vaccines

Because inactivated vaccines pose no additional risk of adverse events and may be beneficial for the HIV-infected individual, they should be considered part of the routine health maintenance for these patients. Specifically, *Haemophilus influenzae* and pneumococcal vaccine should be considered for all HIV-infected individuals.[5] Influenza virus vaccines are ordered annually. These vaccinations should ideally be performed immediately before the flu season (November is a common month for vaccines to be ordered). Nursing considerations should include obtaining a history of allergies, especially to eggs, and general reaction to immunizations. Epinephrine should be made available to treat possible anaphylaxis. Do not give the vaccination to a patient with an acute respiratory infection or any other active infection. Use cautiously in patients with a history of sulfite allergy.

Ensure that the patient understands that the vaccine cannot cause influenza. Fever and myalgias may begin 6 to 12 hours postvaccination but will disappear in 1 to 2 days.

The intramuscular injection should be administered

in the deltoid muscle in adults; for children under 3 years, the anterolateral aspect of the thigh is recommended.

It is thought that the pneumococcal vaccination will protect the patient from infections caused by *Streptococcus pneumoniae* for 5 to 10 years. The pneumococcal vaccine protects against 23 pneumococcal types, accounting for 90 percent of pneumococcal disease. Dosage for adults and children 2 years and older is 0.5 mL IM or SC (not recommended for children under 2 years).

Nursing considerations include obtaining a history of allergies and reaction to immunization. Epinephrine should be available to treat possible anaphylaxis.

The vaccine should be administered in the deltoid or midlateral thigh via intramuscular injection. Simultaneous administration with the influenza vaccine is safe and effective. Adverse reactions include mild fever and soreness at injection site. Severe local reaction can take place when revaccination is administered within 3 years of the initial vaccination.

■ Tuberculin Skin Testing

Tuberculin skin testing should be administered annually (using the patient's birthday as a guide). Using a tuberculin syringe with a 26-g needle, 5 TU (0.1 cc) of PPD is injected intradermally. A wheal (6 to 10 mm in diameter) must form on the skin to indicate that the test was done properly. Nursing considerations include obtaining a history of allergies and reactions to skin tests prior to administration. Epinephrine should be available in case of hypersensitivity.

The skin reaction, if any, should be read within 48 to 72 hours. Indurations of 5 mm or more are considered significant in patients who are HIV positive.

Reactivity to this test may be depressed or suppressed for as long as 4 to 6 weeks in HIV-infected individuals, especially those who have received concurrent or recent immunizations with certain vaccines (such as influenza) or those receiving corticosteroids. If reaction is positive, further testing (chest x-ray, sputum samples) should be done to rule out active tuberculosis.[6]

■ Patient Education

Patients with AIDS and HIV disease present nursing with innumerable challenges and involve all areas of functioning: physical, psychological, economic, and spiritual. Also, because this is a highly publicized disease, patient advocacy is essential to protect patients from unwarranted intrusion into their privacy.

Because this disease most often occurs early in life and is known to be terminal, many patients develop a loss of hope early in the disease process. This loss of hope puts enormous responsibilities on nurses to ensure that the care and support they give is of the highest standards and offers the best possible quality of life.

Much of the fear experienced by patients results from their not knowing what is being done to them. Simple explanations of procedures and nursing care will alleviate this, and will help involve the patient in his or her own care, and so gain cooperation.

References

1. USPHS/IDSA, Prevention of Opportunistic Infections Working Group. Guidelines for the prevention of opportunistic infections in persons infected with human immunodeficiency virus: Disease-specific recommendations. *Clin Infect Dis*. 1995;21(suppl 1): S32–S43.
2. Kovacs JA, Masur H. Prophylaxis for *Pneumocystis carinii* pneumonia in patients infected with the human immunodeficiency virus. *Clin Infect Dis*. 1992;14:1005–1009.

3. Simmonds RJ, Hughes WT, Feinberg J, et al. Preventing *Pneumocystis carinii* pneumonia in persons infected with human immunodeficiency virus. *Clin Infect Dis.* 1995;21 (suppl 1):S44–S48.

4. Hardy WD, Feinberg J, Finkelstein DM: A controlled trial of trimethoprim-sulfamethoxazole or aerosolized pentamidine for secondary prophylaxis of *Pneumocystis carinii* Pneumonia in patients with the acquired immunodeficiency syndrome. AIDS Clinical Trials Group. Protocol 021. *N Engl J Med.* 1992; 327:1842–1848.

5. Broder S, Merigan TC, Bolognesi D. Tropical diseases in the HIV-infected traveler. Textbook of AIDS Medicine. Williams and Wilkins: 1994;317.

6. Moreau D. Nursing 96 Drug Handbook. Springhouse Corporation, PA: 1996:963–964, 972, 1182–1183.

eighteen

Nutrition

Kathryn B. Grayce-Barnes

Deterioration in nutritional status has been shown to have a dramatic effect on immunity, as well as chronic disease.[1,2] The impact of the chronically ill patient's nutritional status has been documented in numerous disease states. Patients with diabetes mellitus, for example, must follow a carefully balanced diet to improve their health state; individuals with renal disease benefit from restriction of protein intake. Persons with bowel disorders, such as Crohn's disease or inflammatory bowel disease, must augment their diets in other ways to prevent exacerbations. Today, the nutritional needs of HIV-infected persons should be similarly examined with particular concern directed toward dietary therapy, nutritional status, and its effect on immunity.

It is important that the provider explore each patient's nutritional status as it relates to their particular disease state. A thorough dietary history should be a part of

Adapted with permission from Nutrition, Immunity, and HIV Disease. *Physician Assistant,* © Springhouse Corporation; August 1995.

every medical history. The practitioner's role should extend to educating and advising patients regarding the range of alternative and complementary therapies— including macrobiotic diets, herbal therapies, aroma therapies, hypnotherapies, and experimental genetic therapies—that are promoted in the HIV-positive community via media and word of mouth. The major goal should be to support the efforts of these chronically ill patients to maintain control of their health care.

■ General Nutrition and Immunity

Dietary composition has been of major interest to the general population, particularly in recent years. In the media and in research sectors, nutritional education has become a major focus. A good diet is defined as intake of proper nutrients needed by the body to maintain optimal health. Research has established that a person's nutritional status plays a key role in quality and length of life.[3] Deficiency of any of the known nutrients decreases the body's ability to fight infection and can result in measurable decline in immune function, particularly in cellular immunity.[2]

Nutrients play varied roles within the body's immune system. Proteins are critical for providing amino acids required for many important structural, motor, metabolic, and hormonal functions. Amino acids are used as "building blocks" for myriad tissue types, enzymes, and neurotransmitters. Lipids play a well-known immunoregulatory role within the body, including maintenance of cell membranes and upkeep of nutrients are essential for lymphocyte function.

Vitamins and minerals are required in varied amounts for metabolism, acting as co-enzymes within the body. Vitamins also act to increase natural killer-cell function, decrease binding of bacteria to epithelial cells, and increase the lymphocyte stimulation response to mitogens. Research has shown that certain vitamin deficiencies are linked to diminished cell-mediated immunity, impaired antibody response, and immune cell proliferation.[4] Our immune system uses minerals to boost neutrophil cells.[2] Our bodies do not synthesize these nutrients, but absorb them from food sources; absorption can be affected by fat intake, total caloric intake, and type of foods ingested.

Nutritional needs change with age, metabolic status, and general wellness. In humans, specific and nonspecific mechanisms work together to achieve a disease-free environment. Aspects of host resistance include physical barriers (skin, mucous membranes), nonspecific mechanisms (complement, interferon, lysozymes, phagocytes), and antigen-specific processes (cell-mediated immunity, immunoglobulins). These defense mechanisms are challenged during infection and act to retard overt infection and to eradicate invasive organisms. Each of these defense mechanisms works optimally with good nutritional status.[5] During times of infection our bodies undergo metabolic changes and our nutritive requirements change to compensate for the increased demand.

As mentioned earlier, decreased immunity and malnutrition have been linked throughout the centuries with increased rates of morbidity, particularly during times of famine and pestilence. Malnutrition caused by misassimilation or poor diet leads to dysfunction of the immune system.[6] This has been substantiated in studies of malnourished patients who were found to have impaired immune responses. The effects of malnutrition on different organ systems are dependent of several factors, including the rate of cell proliferation, the amount and rate of protein synthesis, and the role of individual nutrients in metabolic pathways.[1]

Most of today's research has focused on animals with only one nutritive deficiency, which can lead to misconceptions about nutritional needs. It is now understood that most nutrients require other nutrients in order to be properly used. Therefore, malnutrition should be considered a complex of deficiencies.

■ Nutritional Implications of HIV Disease

The immune response to HIV is strong as with other viral responses; however, in the vast majority of patients, the immune system becomes severely compromised, culminating in AIDS. To date, no prophylactic or therapeutic method has had a substantial impact on the natural course of this viral infection. Intervention is aimed at prolonging life with minimal discomfort or decrease in quality of life.

Several aspects of the HIV illness must be considered when planning prophylaxis or prevention. Although early infection may be clinically asymptomatic, the virus is active and changing homeostasis within the body at a slow rate.[5,7–9] Recent research indicates that HIV infection affects all tissues in the body, resulting in altered body composition and decreased function.[9,10] The main effects include loss of muscle mass, increased metabolic function, and impaired intestinal functioning with consequent loss of body weight. Kotler and associates reported in 1991 that fat metabolism is increased in the presence of increased levels of tumor necrosis factor (TNF) and other cytokines.[10] Increased basal metabolic rate secondary to increased TNF levels and acute sepsis also promote wasting in some patients.

Sharkey and co-workers reported in 1992 that a decrease in CD4 count positively correlated with a decrease in weight, body mass, and arm muscle area.[11] Malnutrition is now thought to be a predictor of survival in HIV disease; moreover, nutritional status influences survival independently of CD4 counts.[12]

■ HIV-Wasting Syndrome

In 1987, the CDC recognized HIV-wasting syndrome as an AIDS-defining illness. The protein wasting is similar to that seen in burn patients. HIV-wasting syndrome is defined as an "involuntary loss of $\geqq$ 10 percent of baseline body weight plus either chronic diarrhea or chronic weakness, and documented fever or condition other than HIV infection that would explain the finding."[13] Between 1987 and 1991, HIV-related wasting was the second most frequent initial AIDS-defining diagnosis.[14]

The deterioration from a good nutritional status to malnutrition is initially subtle, becoming clinically apparent when substantial muscle mass has been lost.[10,15] Death occurs, similarly in starvation, at a point when lean tissue loss is 54 percent of normal. It is generally felt that early intervention is more effective when feeding adjustments are well tolerated.[16] Early wasting can be assessed through several parameters including loss of body weight and decreases in serum potassium and albumin levels. However, body weight can be deceiving when increased interstitial fluid compensates for decreased muscle mass.[17] Thus it is essential to assess all of the risk factors that influence malnutrition, including fever, diarrhea, and acute or chronic infection. This helps eliminate false assumptions when weight loss is in reality a response to reduction in food intake, increased metabolism, malabsorption, or infection.

■ Clinical Assessment of Nutritional Status

An immediate response to HIV infection is change of body composition, and an increase of metabolism, leading to a malnourished state.[10,16] The effects are comparable to those seen in burn patients in that protein wasting occurs, as well as loss of fat and lean body mass.[18] As noted previously, malnutrition has been established as an independent factor that accelerates progression to AIDS.[7] It is critical, therefore, that baseline nutritional status be ascertained, as it becomes a critical factor during subsequent therapy. It may not be necessary to biochemically evaluate nutritional status or assess individual nutrients; however, establishing the usual body weight prior to infection is readily obtainable, useful information. Other clinical risk factors (diarrhea, anorexia, fever) should be assessed in order to determine malnutrition due to intestinal dysfunction or metabolic alteration.[19]

The HIV-positive patient should be counseled properly regarding the importance of a well-balanced diet, regular exercise, safe eating habits, and avoidance of extreme dieting behaviors. Recent literature suggests that doses well in excess of the U.S. Recommended Daily Allowance (RDA) can be crucial in maintaining optimal health in HIV patients. Nutritional supplementation in excess of the RDA has been associated with enhanced immune response.[1,7] Specific nutrients studied include vitamins A, C, D, E, B_6, B_{12}, thiamine (B_1), riboflavin (B_2), folate; the minerals zinc, copper, and selenium; and the amino acid glutathione.[8,14,20–27] Significant deficiencies in vitamins and minerals have been found in asymptomatic seropositive patients, in comparison with HIV-negative controls.[8] These findings indicate that high-dose vitamin/mineral supplementation can be given in many forms, depending on the degree of malnourishment and limitations of the individual patient.

■ Supplementation Therapy

Table 18–1 gives an overview of nutritional components, their sources, and their special uses with HIV patients. The asymptomatic healthy HIV-positive individual may require only a daily dose of a general multivitamin-mineral formula. Formulas that provide 100 percent of the RDA requirements can be taken two to three times a day in conjunction with a well-balanced diet. The clinician should be aware of the vitamin contents of popular over-the-counter supplements. Although vitamin A in the form of beta-carotene may not pose a risk for toxicity, other forms of vitamin A can be toxic in high doses. It should be ascertained that the daily dose of vitamin A in the recommended regimen, including dietary sources, does not exceed the RDA.

Although individual nutrient supplementation can be costly, many patients choose this approach. Adequate counseling should be given regarding the possibilities of toxicity with this option. As mentioned earlier, counseling patients regarding possible interactions between nutritional supplements and drugs is important.[28,29] Interactions can occur between some nutrients and antiretroviral, antiparasitic, antineoplastic, and antibacterial medications.[14] Adequate stores of protein and micronutrients are essential to the efficacy of some drug therapies.[14,28]

Dietary supplementation is available in many forms. If the patient is unable to eat formed foods, liquid supplements are preferred to capsules and tablets. For some patients, powdered supplements that are reconstituted with milk or infant formulas may suffice. Clinicians should be aware that commercial liquid supplementation products are available now that are geared specifically toward the needs of the HIV patient. Care must be taken while choosing which liquid supplementation to use, especially if lactose is poorly tolerated. In general, these products supply

TABLE 18–1. SPECIFIC NUTRIENT SUPPLEMENTATION

Nutrient	Sources	Use in the Body	RDA Dose	Optimal Dose	Interactions/ Effects	Special Hints	HIV Specifics
Vitamin E	Vegetable oils, eggs, nuts and seeds, dark leafy greens, whole grains, legumes, brown rice, wheat germ	Reduces free radicals in the body and blood	12–15 IU/day	Less than 800 IU/day	Doses greater than 800 IU may interfere with coumadin treatment	—	May help to increase time between infection and AIDS
Vitamin C	Citrus, tomatoes, green peppers, spinach, cabbage	Fights bacteria, viruses, and fungi; aids in decreasing stress	60 mg/day	6–20 g/day	Can cause upset stomach, urinary stones, diarrhea in high doses	Spacing total over day reduces risk of side effects	Thought to decrease HIV replication
Beta-carotene (precursor to Vitamin A)	Orange, red, and leafy green vegetables	Fights bacteria and virus; helps thymic and lung function	5000 IU/ day	20,000–50,000 IU/day	Considered nontoxic, whereas vitamin A may be hepatotoxic	Can cause a discoloration of the skin in high doses	Increases WBC count; CD4/8 ratio; percent change of CD4 seen transiently
Co-enzyme Q	Found in health food stores	Improves immune function, heart muscle, thymus, and cell respiration	N/A	30–180 mg/day	Considered nontoxic; total parenteral nutrition may decrease levels	May help people on AZT, decreases fatigue	Decreased levels with progression to AIDS; may increase free radicals
Essential fatty acids	Omega-6 fatty acids in fish oils, canola; gamma linolenic acid in borage and primrose oil	Counters fatigue, helps skin problems	N/A	Up to 7–15 g/day	—	May reduce skin problems, fatigue, and muscle cramping	Help to decrease inflammation, decrease cytokine production

Folic acid/folate	Liver, asparagus, greens	Aids in RBC and WBC formation and Hgb synthesis	180–200 µg/day	400–800 µg/day	Deficiency may occur with Bactrim or pentamidine therapy	Must ingest vitamin B_{12} for proper utilization	—
Vitamin B_6 (pyridoxine)	OTC, most foods; higher amounts in brewer's yeast, eggs, chicken, meat, fish, spinach, wheat germ	Helps in DNA production, red cell proliferation, and protein metabolism	2 mg/day	100 mg/day	—	May be the most important vitamin for HIV persons	—
Vitamin B_{12} or cyanocobalamin	Can be injectable as a sublingual pill or nasally	Helps in anemia, aids in RBC synthesis, may improve brain function	6 µg/day	500 µg/day orally; every 4 weeks by injection	Serum levels may be reduced with Azidothymidine use; megadosing with vitamin C may decrease levels	Most often the deficiency in HIV infection; helps fatigue	—
Multivitamins and minerals	OTC BID-TID	Helps absorption and metabolism	One a day	BID-TID	Consider use of hypoallergenic formulas	Take with meals	May consider liquid formulas for poor PO intake; good primary intervention
Zinc	Seafood, liver, eggs, beef, corn, peas	May aid in skin or taste/smell disorder, improves appetite	12–15 mg/day	25–50 mg/day	Do not use more than 100 mg/day as it may be toxic; works with thymelin hormone	Must use in conjunction with copper for utilization	Increases levels of T-cell production, specifically with IL-2 receptors

TABLE 18-1. (*continued*)

Nutrient	Sources	Use in the Body	RDA Dose	Optimal Dose	Interactions/ Effects	Special Hints	HIV Specifics
N-acetyl-L cysteine (NAC)	OTC	Acts as precursor to glutathione, a critical antioxidant; may be T-cell specific	N/A	90–1800 mg/day	May cause allergic reactions, nausea, vomiting, fevers; interacts with antibiotic treatment; should take 2 hours pre/postdose	Can be very expensive, trade name is Fluimucil, marketed as Mucomyst	Helps increase levels of glutathione
Copper	Seafood, avocados, barley, garlic, nuts, leafy vegetables, OTC	Improves efficacy of zinc	3 mg	3 mg	Too much may cause decreased levels of zinc and vitamin C	Difficult to measure	Decreased in stage I, increased in stage IV HIV disease
Vitamin D	OTC, dairy products, fish, liver oils	Enhances immunity, boosts Ca and P utilization	400 IU	400 IU	Not considered toxic; high doses may cause constipation	Is fat-soluble nutrient	—
Selenium	Seafood, kidney, nuts, brown rice, OTC	An antioxidant, reduces free radicals	200 µg/day	400 µg/day	Greater than 500 µg/day, may be toxic; effects of chronic high doses unknown	Acts with vitamin E	May help to decrease HIV placental transmission; inhibits reverse transcriptase

Thiamine (B₁)	Dried beans, brown rice, poultry, bran, broccoli, grains, OTC	Aids in blood formation, carbohydrate metabolism; needed for intestinal muscle tone	1–1.2 mg/day	50 mg/day	Levels may be decreased by antibiotics, sulfa drugs	Effects energy, necessary for normal GI muscle tone	—
Riboflavin (B₂)	OTC, beans, cheese, milk, poultry, spinach, yogurt	Necessary for RBC, antibody production; aids metabolism	1.2–1.4 mg/day	50 mg/day	Light, ETOH, antibiotics destroy it	With vitamin A maintains mucous membranes	—
Glutathione (an amino acid)	OTC	An antioxidant, reduces free radicals, counters chemotherapy side effects	N/A	N/A	Vitamin E and NAC help to maintain level	Acts as drug detoxifier; not easily absorbed	Decreased levels may exacerbate HIV replication

100 percent of the RDA of vitamins and minerals in addition to extra protein; some contain readily absorbable medium-chain triglycerides, and others are lactose free. In the case of a patient who is unable to swallow, process food in the stomach, or adequately absorb nutrients from the intestine, partial or total enteral or parenteral may be the solution.[30–32]

■ Interventional Nutritional Support

It is the practitioner's responsibility to recognize when a patient's decisions are more detrimental than productive. Although the practitioner should support the patient's efforts to maintain dietary control, the patient must have the ability to recognize when his or her nutritional status is declining. It is imperative to recognize when noninvasive nutritional supplementation is insufficient and a more aggressive system of nutritional delivery is needed.

Enteral and parenteral nutrition systems, in use for decades, are effective means of maintaining the patient with wasting syndrome.[33] The overall goals of invasive nutritional therapies are to support the immune system by maintaining body composition, reversing depletion of fat and lean tissue, and increasing visceral protein levels.[21,32]

Enteral Support

Enteral nutritional support can be provided via nasogastric (NG) tube placement, surgically placed percutaneous endoscopic gastrostomy (PEG) tubes, gastrostomies, or jejunostomies. The type of access should be determined by evaluating the estimated time needed for nutritional intervention. The NG tube is preferred when duration of therapy is estimated at fewer than 6 weeks. A primary concern in enteral nutrition is the danger of aspiration secondary to loss of muscle tone.

Parenteral Support

Parenteral nutrition can be administered by either peripheral or central line placement. The choice is dependent on whether or not the patient is in need of submaintenance therapy or total nutritional support. The infusion formulas used depend upon the individual's overall fluid and nitrogen states.[30–32] Parenteral feeding increases the risk of local infection and sepsis, an important consideration in those immunocompromised by HIV infection. Patients must be watched closely for adverse effects such as reaction to the preparation used and signs of infection.[22] Home care specialists in parenteral support can provide instruction as well as assess improvements in function and nutritional status.

■ Conclusion

Nutrition researchers who conducted early studies of HIV-positive patients were shocked at how little attention was being given to their nutritional status. Many patients were maintained on standard diets without additional nutritional supplementation, despite evidence of wasting, the presence of risk factors for malnutrition, and problems that hindered their ability to ingest necessary nutrients.[23]

It is clear that nutritional support and dietary counseling are increasingly important areas in which quality of life and possibly quantity of life can be enhanced in HIV disease. The most recent studies show that HIV-infected persons are in a hypermetabolic state and, although asymptomatic, can be experiencing deleterious effects secondary to nutritional status.[16] Clinicians can play an important role in encouraging optimal dietary intake with nutritional supplementation, early evaluation by a specialized dietician, and monitoring for initial signs of wasting. Monitoring should continue throughout the disease process, by both clinical information and bloodwork, particularly potassium and albumin levels. With this approach, patients gain the satisfaction of active participation in their care, achieving encouraging short-term results that contribute to patient empowerment.

References

1. Chandra RK. 1990 McCollum award lecture. Nutrition and immunity: Lessons from the past and new insights into the future. *Am J Clin Nutr* 1991;53:1087–1101.
2. Prasad C, Chandra RK. Nutrition and immunity. In: Kotler DP, ed. Gastrointestinal and Nutritional Manifestations in AIDS. New York: Raven; 1991:35–49.
3. Balch JF, Balch PA. Prescription for nutritional healing. New York: Avery; 1990:4–74.
4. Coodley GO, Girard DE. Vitamins and minerals in HIV infection. *J Gen Int Med* 1991; 6:472–479.
5. Beach RS, Cabrejos C, ShorPosner G, et al. Nutritional aspects of early HIV infection. In: Nutrition and Immunology. Canada: ARTS Biomedical Publishers; 1992:241–253.
6. Hellerstein MK. Lean body wasting and therapeutic implications of altered metabolism in AIDS. *HIV.* 1993;3:8–16.
7. Kotler DP. Effect of malnutrition on the progression of AIDS. *HIV.* 1993;3:17–23.
8. Beach RS, Mantero-Atienza E, Shor-Posner G, et al. Specific nutrient abnormalities in asymptomatic HIV-1 infections. *AIDS.* 1992;6:701–708.
9. Kotler DP. Nutrition. *HIV Advisor.* 1992;6:14–15.
10. Kotler DP, Wang J, Pierson RN. Studies of nutritional status in patients with AIDS. In: Kotler DP, ed. Gastrointestinal and Nutritional Manifestations in AIDS. New York: Raven; 1991:231–242.
11. Sharkey SJ, Sharkey KA, Sutherland LR, et al. Nutritional status and food intake in human immunodeficiency virus infection. *J Acquir Immune Defic Syndr.* 1992;7:681–694.
12. Guenter P, Muuraheinan N, Simon G, et al. Relationship

among nutritional status, disease progression, and survival in HIV infection. *J Acquir Immune Defic Syndr.* 1993;6: 1130–1137.

13. Coodley GO, Loveless MO, Merrill TM. The HIV wasting syndrome: A review. *J Acquir Immune Defic Syndr.* 1994;7:681–694.

14. Lands L. Nutritional supplements and HIV infection. *Treatment Issues.* 1992;6:1–6.

15. Grunfeld C, Kotler DP. The wasting syndrome and nutritional support in AIDS. *Semin Gastroint Dis.* 1991;2:1–9.

16. Bell SJ, Mascioli EA, Forse RA, Bistrian BR. Nutrition support and the human immunodeficiency virus (HIV). *Parasitology.* 1993;107:S53–S67.

17. Schwenk A, Buger B, Wessel D, et al. Clinical risk factors for malnutrition in HIV-1-infected patients. *AIDS.* 1993;7: 1213–1219.

18. Mascioli EA. Nutrition and HIV infection. *AIDS Clin Care.* 1993;5:1–5.

19. Coodley GO, Coodley MK, Nelson HD, Loveless MO. Micronutrient concentrations in the HIV wasting syndrome. *AIDS.* 1993;7:1595–1600.

20. Kotler DP, Tierney AR, Ferraro R, et al. Enteral alimentation and repletion of body cell mass in malnourished patients with acquired immunodeficiency syndrome. *Am J Clin Nutr.* 1991;53:149–154.

21. Roederer M, Staal FJT, Ela SW, et al. N-Acetylcysteine: Potential for AIDS therapy. *Pharmacology.* 1993;46:121–129.

22. Schrauzer GN, Sacher J. Selenium in the maintenance and therapy of HIV-infected patients. *J Chem Biol Int.* 1994;91:199–205.

23. Wang Y, Watson RR. Potential therapeutics of vitamin E (tocopheral) in AIDS and HIV. *Drugs.* 1994;48:327–338.

24. Blackburn GL, Bell S. Eutrophia in patients with HIV infection and early AIDS with novel nutrient "cocktail": Is this the first food for special medical purpose? *Nutrition.* 1993;9:554–556.

25. Coodley GO, Nelson HD, Loveless MO, Folk C. Betacarotene in HIV infection. *J Acquir Immune Defic Syndr.* 1993;6:272–276.

26. Segal-Isaacson AE, Rand CJ. Antioxidant supplementation in HIV/AIDS. *Nurse Pract.* 1995;20:8–14.

27. Favier A, Sappey C, Leclerc P, et al. Antioxidant status and lipid peroxidation in patients infected with HIV. *Chem Biol Int.* 1994;91:165–180.

28. Kotler DP, Tierney AR, Culpepper-Morgan JA, et al. Effect of home total parenteral nutrition on body composition in patients with acquired immunodeficiency syndrome. *J Paren Enter Nutr.* 1990;14:454–458.

29. Heymsfield SB, Cuff PA, Kotler DP. AIDS enteral and parenteral nutritional support. In: Kotler DP, ed. Gastrointestinal and Nutritional Manifestations in AIDS. New York: Raven; 1991:243–256.

30. Grunfeld C. Mechanisms of wasting in infection and cancer: An approach to cachexia in AIDS. In: Kotler DP, ed. Gastrointestinal and Nutritional Manifestations in AIDS. New York: Raven; 1991:207–229.

31. Newman CF. Practical dietary recommendations in HIV infection. In: Kotler DP, ed. Gastrointestinal and Nutritional Manifestations in AIDS. New York: Raven; 1991:257–277.

32. Von Roenn JH. Therapeutic options for HIV-associated cachexia. *HIV.* 1993;3:24–29.

33. Chlebowski RT, Grosvenor MB, Bernhard NH, et al. Nutritional status, gastrointestinal dysfunction, and survival in patients with AIDS. *Am J Gastroenterol.* 1989;84:1288–1292.

nineteen
CHAPTER

Rehabilitation

Mary Lou Galantino

Survival and other types of clinical outcomes that characterize HIV disease are important indicators of the effectiveness of the medical care that patients receive. Maximizing function in advanced disease or chronically ill patients can be viewed as secondary prevention. Patient-reported functioning and well-being indicate how they feel about their lives and how they are doing in daily activities. Measurements used to assess patient functioning and well-being by researchers are applicable to health outcome assessment in the clinical setting. Disease- and treatment-specific outcome measurements are more sensitive to disease severity and treatment intervention effects, while generic outcome measurements provide generalizability across diseases or conditions. Specific measurements can provide data about clinically relevant changes, and generic measurements help to indicate the significance of these outcomes in patients' daily lives. Using both types of patient-reported measurements as well as performance-based assessments will provide outcome-based data on HIV patients' functional limitation and disability and help to define relevant rehabilitation protocols for HIV patients.

This chapter describes the various clinical problems often presented to the physical or occupational therapist, and strategies for their intervention. Measurement tools are presented to evaluate outcomes in HIV rehabilitation.

The increasing presence of HIV in all communities, and the chronicity of the disease, warrant early intervention. Although the immune status of the individual may decline over a period of 10 to 15 years, productivity and quality-of-life aspects are important to address. It is possible that certain psychosocial factors could function as co-factors and contribute to the progression of HIV infection. For example, an HIV-positive individual could be exposed to a stressful life event that could have an effect on immune processes relevant to the course of infection.[1]

The effect of stressors on the immune system and treatment of secondary illness has resulted in research on disability in HIV disease.[2] The characterization and description of HIV-related disability is important to underscore in the global management of the epidemic. Data regarding the prevalence, incidence, severity, timing, and assessment of HIV-related physical disability are necessary to develop appropriate rehabilitation interventions.[3] Clinical pathways for rehabilitation may be determined based on clinical findings of functional deficits. Various symptoms presented along the spectrum of HIV disease can be addressed through appropriate assessment and treatment.

Disability assessment and rehabilitation intervention have implications for specific stages of HIV disease, with the intention of maximizing overall function and decreasing the burden of care. The AIDS epidemic has challenged communities to develop and mobilize care networks for persons infected with HIV. A major part of that mobilization has been a push toward community and home-based services.[4] Reliable and valid functional assessment data are necessary to evaluate changes over time in HIV-related disability for patients in the hospital and at home. Epidemiologic data also hold implications for rehabilitation health care workers in terms of expertise in HIV-specific areas and staffing levels.[5] Access to rehabilitation services will need to be considered by public policymakers and financial concerns explored.

Quality-of-life (QOL) measures have been used to quantify patients' perception of their general health status. Three types of QOL measures are general measures, disease-specific measures, and batteries of separate instruments that are scored independently.[6] General QOL measures are designed to be used across different diseases, various groups of patients, and different treatment interventions. The role of disease-specific measures is to assess diagnostic or patient populations with the goal of detecting responsiveness to clinically significant changes. The final type of measure uses a battery that can be put together to assess whatever aspects of QOL need to be measured.

Dimensions of quality of life usually considered relevant for clinical studies include condition-specific symptoms; general health perception; somatic discomfort; physical, social, and role functioning; psychological well-being; and cognitive functioning.[7–9] The QOL measures in HIV-related disability have predominantly focused on clinical drug trials. There are few studies that reflect QOL outcomes with specific rehabilitation intervention in the AIDS population. Most of the reports are case studies and early exercise interventions with HIV-positive individuals.[10,11]

■ Functional Status

AIDS is globally fatal. Before death, it often causes a multitude of medical complications leading to significant physical impairment and functional loss. Symptoms and side effects of various drug interventions are the most specific patient-reported measures of health status. Although such measures may be associated with disease progression, they fail to assess the total impact of a medical condition. Measures that are less specific but assess a broader range of consequences of illness include measures of disability and functional status.[12] For clarity, a distinction should be made between disability and handicap. The former is dysfunction at the personal level while handicap is dysfunction at the role or society level.[9]

Jette[8,9] has further pointed out that health status can be divided into physical manifestations and functional status, of which physical disability is an example. Performance, whether it is physical, mental, emotional, or social, is the key element of functional assessment. In the widely accepted Classification of Human Disablement proposed by the World Health Organization, physical performance translates into disability and physical manifestations into impairment.

Throughout this chapter, functional status refers to a summary evaluation of the individual's manifest importance of various adaptive tasks and activities.[13] The emphasis on performance distinguishes functional status from other aspects of health-related QOL. According to Rapkin and Smith[13] functional status has four important characteristics:

1. It may be described in terms of many different dimensions (such as dependency, pain, fatigue, and global difficulty).
2. It can be assessed in terms of both long- and short-term frames (such as during the past 4 months or past 7 days).
3. It is broad-band (no single dimension can adequately depict an individual's functioning).

4. It encompasses a wide variety of activities, including adaptive tasks, goal attainment activities, and role and social functioning ranging from the most basic (preparing a meal and eating) to the more complex (performing on the job and engaging in social activities).

Various levels of performance and perceptions about functional status may differ between the clinician and HIV-positive individual. This presents a complexity involved in appropriate measurement for the establishment of standards of comparisons relevant for research and planning of long-term care. Functional status assessment is important for creating the fit between individual needs and environmental resources: it can be used to identify when supports are needed, what types of assistance are most appropriate, what demands are excessive, and what opportunities for independence remain unrealized.[14]

■ Types of Quality of Life and Functional Assessment Tools

Modern medicine tends to assess patients more in terms of their morbidity than of their overall health. The emphasis is on anatomic integrity, physiologic and biochemical functioning, and the presence of pathologic lesions. In general practice, patients' problems cover a much wider spectrum than this, and the concept of health needs to include interpersonal and social functioning as well as good physiologic functioning. The impact of HIV infection on quality of life is relative to the stage of the disease, with HIV-infected individuals who are still asymptomatic having much less dimunition in quality of life than patients with AIDS. Table 19–1 summarizes QOL issues for the various stages of HIV disease.

TABLE 19–1. QUALITY-OF-LIFE ISSUES FOR HIV DISEASE STAGES

Stage	CD4+ Categories	Physical Indicators	Moderators of Quality of Life	Quality-of-life Issues
Asymptomatic	≥ 500/μL	May have persistent generalized lymphadenopathy	*Appraisals* Anticipatory grieving, catastrophizing and other cognitive distortions; changed expectations of future; identity and self-esteem issues *Coping* Dealing with present and future uncertainties; at risk for denial, disengagement, substance abuse, risky sex, suicidality; issues of eliciting social support	*Emotional functioning* Depression, anxiety, anger, often increasing at diagnosis and diminishing and recycling as individual confronts realities of living with HIV disease *Role functioning* Often able to work; possible decrements in job mobility and career opportunities; job loss *Social functioning* Fear, isolation, issues of trust in relationships; stigmatization; changes in social support networks due to deaths; relationship and sexual changes; isolation, withdrawal *Physical functioning* Normal but may be altered due to depression or anxiety, may have hypervigilance regarding all physical symptoms *Spiritual functioning* Opportunity to direct attention inward, thus yielding to contemplation of life's meaning, reassessment of spiritual and existential issues
Symptomatic HIV infection	299–499/μL	Emergence of symptoms such as thrush, night sweats, low-grade fevers, oral hairy leukoplakia, peripheral neuropathy; commonly taking antiretroviral drugs and/or PCP prophylaxis	*Appraisals* Anticipatory grieving, catastrophizing and other cognitive distortions; changed expectations of future; identity and self-esteem issues related to threats to occupational and functional abilities *Coping* Dealing with present and future uncertainties; at risk for denial,	*Emotional functioning* Depression, anxiety, anger, often increasing on emergence of symptoms, and then fluctuating with challenges and threats to present and future functioning *Role functioning* Often able to work; may take on new roles as part of HIV support-related network *Social functioning* Changes in social support networks due to deaths; isolation; withdrawal; relationship and sexual changes, stigmatization

				Physical functioning
			disengagement, substance abuse and risky sex	May have reduced energy levels; moderate symptomatology possible cognitive deficits; pain; wasting
				Spiritual functioning
				Anticipatory grieving, sense of relatedness to something greater than the self, unavoidable confrontation with one's own mortality
			Appraisals	Emotional functioning
			Facing chronic illness and death; grieving about current and anticipated losses; catastrophizing and other cognitive distortions; reassessment of spiritual and existential issues	Depression, anxiety, anger may cycle according to fluctuations in disease status and appraisals; relief from uncertainty
				Role functioning
				Diminished capacity for work; role changes—often need care instead of being a caretaker
			Coping	Social functioning
AIDS	< 200/499 µL	Opportunistic infections such as extensive candidiasis, cryptococcal meningitis, Kaposi's sarcoma, tuberculosis, PCP, lymphomas; commonly taking antiretroviral drugs, chemotherapy, antibiotics	Coping strategies may be overwhelmed in dealing with current difficulties such as financial losses, medical costs, treatment and side effects, housing; may lose some traditional coping strategies such as recreational outlets	May have diminished social networks due to lack of mobility, illness, as well as deaths among friends
				Physical functioning
				Self-care difficulties; fatigue; wasting; much time spent in medical care; debilitation from infection and treatments; possible cognitive deficits
				Spiritual functioning
				Essential worth is to provide a framework from which to pose and seek responses to metaphysical questions that are birthed by the presence of a life-threatening disease; integration and transcending of one's biological and psychosocial nature, which gives access to nonphysical realms as prophecy, love, artistic inspiration, completion, and healing actions

Adapted from reference 43.

Clinical trials intend to demonstrate QOL outcomes through specific drug interventions. Various interview styles have collected measures of energy/fatigue; physical, social, role, and cognitive function; depression; health perceptions; and life satisfaction.[15] Others have adapted existing functional scales, such as the Medical Outcomes Survey (MOS) and further include symptom impact, disability, work, functioning, and utilization.[16] Table 19–2 presents examples of patient-assessed generic outcome measurements. Self-report questionnaires (the European Organization for Research and Treatment of Cancer Core Quality of Life Questionnaire) have been evaluated. Box 19–1 summarizes HIV disease-specific measurements. Assessing health-related QOL measures in HIV drug studies and disease progression assists in the planning of health care intervention and patient decisions as demonstrated in the previous sections. However, most available scales are too long and contain items that are not specific to the signs and symptoms found in HIV-positive individuals. The Medical Outcomes Study (MOS) was a 4-year observational study designed to examine the influence of specific characteristics of providers, patients, and health systems on outcomes of care.[17] Adaptations of the MOS applied to the HIV population include short-form (SF)-20,[18] SF-30,[19] SF-36,[20] SF-38 (PARSE—patient-reported status and experience),[21] and the SF-56.[20]

Wu and associates[19] developed the Medical Outcomes Study (MOS)-HIV 30-item form, the first health status instrument specifically for people with HIV/AIDS. Wu and colleagues based the questionnaire on the 20-item MOS short-form general health survey. The modified questionnaire is brief, sensitive to clinically important symptoms or changes, and self-administered, and it distinctly measures dimensions of health that patients might value differently.

An abundance of QOL measures exist, each tapping

TABLE 19–2. EXAMPLES OF PATIENT-ASSESSED GENERIC OUTCOME MEASUREMENTS IN HIV DISEASE STUDIES

Functioning	Well-being	Functioning and Well-being
Karnofsky Performance Scale	Quality of Well-Being Scale (QWB)	Medical Outcomes Survey—Short Form (MOS-SF)
Sickness Impact Profile	Symptom Distress Scale	MOS-SF 30
Instrument ADL (I-ADL)	Present State Examination	MOS-SF 36
Neurobehavioral Function: An ADL Rating Scale		MOS-SF 38
		MOS-SF 56
Katz Activities of Daily Living		Dartmouth COOP Function and Health Status
Functional Independence Measure (FIM)		Measures for Adults
		Quality of Life Instrument

into specific criteria for analysis. Choosing between them is difficult. The optimum QOL instrument is one that taps multiple dimensions of QOL (such as emotional and physical well-being) adequately and allows for integration of these dimensions in an aggregate score. The existing instruments that tend to capture information in one area, may be inadequate in other areas. Health care professionals can make judicious choices based on these assessments, to incorporate various measures throughout clinical care.

■ Rehabilitation Evaluation and Treatment

Physical, occupational, and speech therapists can play a major role in the return to function for an individual who has experienced an opportunistic infection. Various clinical problems often presented to the rehabilitation therapist may include the following.

1. Postural dynamics secondary to weight loss from protein-calorie malnutrition.
2. Past medical history of previous injuries that may exacerbate during HIV disease.
3. Arthrosis secondary to side effects of medication.
4. Myopathies secondary to medication and direct HIV involvement.
5. Peripheral neuropathy secondary to drug toxicity and progression of HIV disease.
6. Neurologic deficits secondary to CNS involvement with resultant neurocognitive changes.
7. Cognitive changes due to CNS opportunistic infections or AIDS dementia complex.

■ Pain Syndromes

Various painful complications may occur at all stages of HIV infection. Pain may also be related to rapid skeletal muscle atrophy, which changes postural alignment and creates sensitive trigger points.[22] Functional ability is compromised, and gait patterns and activities of daily living are altered. Neurotoxic effects of chemotherapy and

HIV itself may produce peripheral neuropathies that are painful and difficult to manage.[23] Pain may also be associated with viral infections, such as herpes zoster.[24] Anxiety and depression may complicate management and require concomitant treatment for effective analgesia.[25,26]

Pain management in HIV first requires an analysis of the many possible causes of discomfort. A comprehensive and interdisciplinary approach is imperative. Multiple-modality intervention can include transcutaneous electrical nerve stimulation (TENS), ultrasound, hydrotherapy, electrical stimulation, laser, microamperage (a low-powered stimulation designed to provide an electrical stimulus without overpowering the action potential due to the presence of voltage-sensitive channels), and biofeedback. Counseling and relaxation techniques may help in some cases. Others may benefit from a behavioral approach to pain management.[27] Deep-breathing exercises, acupressure releases, visualization, soft music, and slow stroking over the primary rami (paraspinal muscle massage) or slow vestibular stimulation, like rhythmic rocking, are effective for promoting parasympathetic dominance. Music and imagery in combination produce significant changes in pain thresholds, heart rate, blood pressure, and respiratory rate.[28,29]

An important aspect of pain management is focusing on posture and body awareness. This emphasis on the body and its alignment may reduce pain associated with the rapid musculoskeletal change observed in many patients. Manual therapy techniques, such as craniosacral, myofascial release or muscle energy techniques, followed by a postural strengthening program, are beneficial.[22]

Peripheral neuropathies are a persistent problem for the patient with HIV. They can be sensory, motor, or both, and may result from demyelination and axon degeneration. The most common type of neuropathy associated with HIV infection is predominantly sensory and affects

10 to 30 percent of patients with AIDS.[30] In a study by Cornblath and co-workers,[31] the most common complaint was plantar pain. Altered sensation, burning in nature, was also noted, and symptoms progressed to involve the entire foot and distal lower extremities. Serial examination showed progressive loss of ankle reflexes. Electrophysiologic studies suggested a length-dependent axonopathy, typical of a dying-back process. Practical application of foot orthotics should be used judiciously. Given the hypersensitive nature of the feet, many patients choose to wear open sandal-type shoes. However, given the area of pain, a careful assessment of appropriate shoe-insert orthotics should be made by the therapist.[32]

Another common problem in these patients is the pain associated with herpes zoster, which may persist long after open lesions subside. Acyclovir, in concert with TENS, appears to help control pain.[24] The placement of TENS electrodes for optimum pain relief in this condition is one electrode at the dorsal skin web between the first and second metacarpals and the other channel electrode at the dermatome of the lesion. An alternative electrode placement may be to simply bracket the shingles.[22]

Polymitosis is the most common HIV related myopathy. This appears as subacute progressive weakness with occasional periods of remission.[33] Drug-induced myopathies may resolve once antiviral medication is discontinued. Physical therapy intervention can focus on decreasing pain through various modalities, joint protection and range-of-motion exercises.

Anxiety-related stress may be another source of pain in the patient with HIV.[25] It should be recognized that the patient's physical complaints are real, even though they may be secondary to emotional stress or anguish. The patient's stress can be managed via biofeedback, manual therapy techniques, and relaxation and visualization exercises. Trigger-point therapy or acupressure may be used for acute or chronic pain by applying deep pressure over painful sites for up to 30 to 60 seconds. Once released, movement of the painful area is encouraged through range of motion. This movement further activates proprioceptors and low-threshold afferents that synapse on the cells in the substantia gelatinosa in the dorsal horn of the spinal cord. Acupressure releases that use several points to regulate a generalized balance and relaxation response will have a calming effect, and therefore, the immune system and self-healing process are more activated.[22]

Energy conservation techniques are important additions for the patient experiencing pain or fatigue. This includes work simplification and strategic planning to perform activities of daily living (ADLs) in an efficacious manner. Architectural barriers may be modified for management of the patient living alone who may be dependent on assistive devices. Occupational therapy services may facilitate these concepts in greater detail.

Physical inactivity is a spontaneous response to stress that may manifest itself as chronic pain; hence, patients should regularly engage in various nonsedentary activities. Because the immune, nervous, and endocrine systems are intimately related, one may speculate that chronic anxiety affects not only pain and the nervous system but also the immune response.[34,35]

■ Neurorehabilitation Strategies

Toxoplasmosis, CNS lymphoma, cerebrovascular accidents associated with HIV, and spinal cord injury from vacuolar myelopathy constitute an array of functional deficits.[31] These CNS insults will present with hemiparesis, paraparesis, and neurocognitive changes. Rehabilitation responses are similar to these same pathologies in noninfected HIV individuals. Although the risk of CNS opportunistic infections is greater, the majority of patients who are HIV positive are not challenged by numerous age-related conditions and can potentially recover more quickly.

■ Exercise

Exercise is beneficial to virtually every type of patient, from both physical and psychological standpoints. However, research into the effects of aerobic and strengthening exercise on the HIV-infected population is limited, making a general exercise protocol a challenge to develop. At the forefront will be the question of whether to exercise patients who have HIV infection, and if so, when and according to what protocol.

Therapists who treat individuals with HIV infection, particularly those who are or who have been symptomatic, may see function and strength vacillate from week to week, as opportunistic infections come and go. Once symptoms arise, they can range from mild fatigue to profound muscle weakness and multiple infections. The immunologic deterioration that follows allows HIV infection to progress further, often resulting in multisystem involvement.

Because of demonstrated links between exercise and stress reduction, endogenous opiates and immunity, similar benefits may be derived from exercise in people infected with HIV. The challenge is determining which members of this population might benefit from exercise and which could have adverse effects.[37–39]

As individuals with HIV/AIDS are living longer and with greater levels of health, the chronicity of the disease warrants community support and long-term care.[40] Various functional and QOL measures can assist in the de-

TABLE 19-3. ASSESSMENT INSTRUMENT OVERVIEW

Instrument	Dimensions	Length	Administration
AIDS Health Assessment Questionnaire (AIDS-HAQ)	Physical function, mental health, cognitive function, social health, energy/fatigue	30 items	Self-administered (5 minutes)
AIDS Specific Functional Assessment (ASFA)	Evaluates the usefulness of an nomothetic approach to functional assessment	Varies	Self-administered, care-provider
Individualized Functional Status Assessment (IFSA)	Patient-generated activities associated with the pursuit of the following goal types: achievement, problem-solving, avoidance prevention, maintenance, disengagement	75 items	Self-administered
Medical Outcomes Study HIV Instrument (MOS-HIV)	Health, pain, physical functioning, role functioning, social functioning, mental health, fatigue, energy, health distress, cognitive functioning, health transition, general QOL	30 items	Self-administered (5 minutes)
HIV Patient-reported Status and Experience (HIV-PARSE)	Physical health, mental health, general health	38 items	Self-administered (5 minutes)
Multidimensional Functional Evaluation of People With HIV	IADLs (4), self-care (8)	12 items	Self-administered
Neuropsychiatric AIDS Rating Scale (NARS)	Assesses patients orientation, memory motor ability, behavioral changes, problem-solving ability, ADL	Varies	Health-care provider
HIV Overview of Problems Evaluation Systems (HOPES)	Global, physical, psychosocial, medical interaction, significant others, sexual	139 items	Self-administered (15 minutes)
HIV-Related Quality-of-Life Questions (HIV-QOL)	Mental health, energy/fatigue, fever, limitations of basic ADL, and intermediate ADL, disability days, all symptoms, sleep symptoms, neurologic symptoms, memory symptoms, pain	30 items	Self-administered (5 minutes)

Name	Description	Items	Administration
HIV Quality Audit Marker (HIV-QAM)	Captures the nurse data-collector's judgment of the status of the patient based on observations, interviews, and record interviews	Varies based on duration of interview	Nurse
HIV Visual Analog Scale	Rates HIV-related symptom severity and general well-being	Varies	Nurse, self-administered
HIV Assessment Tool (HAT)	Physical symptoms related to HIV disease, social/role functioning, psychological well-being, personal attitudes related to well-being	34 items	Self-administered
Multidimensional Quality of Life Questionnaire for Person. With HIV (MQOL-HIV)	Mental health, physical health, physical functioning, social functioning, social support, cognitive functioning, financial status, partner intimacy, sexual functioning, medical care	40 items	Self-administered (10 minutes)

velopment of resources and medical intervention. As survival increases, rehabilitation professionals can anticipate a greater number of referrals for the assessment and management of physical disability in persons with HIV infection.[41] A critical task for health service research is to ensure that HIV health care settings deliver optimum services at reasonable costs. Optimal care requires maximizing autonomous functioning and reducing periods of disability and dependence.[42]

Table 19–3 summarizes the various characteristics of instruments and administration time required for data collection. Overall, the choice for the optimum QOL measure and functional outcome may be a compilation of quantitative and qualitative measures. This would capture additional information that may produce specific themes that would not be elucidated in the standard QOL measurements. A careful selection of these measurements will produce an array of data that will paint a picture of the challenges of living with HIV disease.

There are varied approaches that HIV-positive individuals follow to manage the stressors and chronic nature of the disease. New treatments are embraced by health care practitioners, and individuals are making decisions about the type of intervention and potential alternative approaches they might choose. Their treatment or decisions, and the manner in which they make decisions, can have an impact on how patients adapt to the diagnosis and treatment of HIV and ultimately, how they live with this chronic disease.

References

1. Kemeny ME. Psychoneuroimmunology of HIV infection. In: Zegans LS, Coates TJ, eds. Psychiatric Manifestations of HIV Disease. *Psychiatr Clin North Am.* 1994;17:55–68.
2. O'Dell M. The epidemiology of HIV-related physical disabil-

ity. In: O'Dell M, ed. HIV-related Disability: Assessment and Management. Physical Medicine and Rehabilitation: State of the Art Reviews. Philadelphia: Hanley and Belfus; 1993: S29–S42.

3. Benjamin AE. Perspectives on a continuum of care for persons with HIV illness. *Med Care Rev.* 1989;46:411–437.

4. Salsberry PJ, Nickel JT, O'Connell K, et al. Home health care services for AIDS patients: One community's response. *J Community Health Nurs* 1993;10:39–51.

5. Mukand J, Starkeson EC, Melvin JL. Public policy issues for the rehabilitation of patients with HIV-related disability. In: Mukand J, ed: Rehabilitation for Patients with HIV Disease. New York: McGraw-Hill; 1991:1–20.

6. McSweeney AJ, Creer TL. Health-related quality of life assessment in medical care. *Dis Mon.* 1995;41:1-71. Review.

7. Deyo RA. Measuring functional outcomes in therapeutic trials for chronic disease. *Control Clin Trials.* 1984;12:189.

8. Jette AM. Concepts of health and methodological issues in functional assessment. In: Gresham G, Granger C, eds. Functional Assessment in Rehabilitation Medicine. Baltimore: Williams & Wilkins; 1984:46.

9. Jette A. Physical disablement concepts for physical therapy research and practice. *Physical Therapy.* 1994;74:380–386.

10. Laperriere A, Fletcher NM, Antoni NK, et al. Aerobic exercise training in an AIDS risk group. *Int J Sports Med.* 1991;12(suppl 1):S53–S57.

11. Laperriere A, Ironson G, Antoni WL, et al. Exercise immunology. *Med Sci Sports Ex.* 1994;26:182–190.

12. Cleary PD, Floyd FJ, Weissman J, et al. Health-related quality of life in persons with acquired immune deficiency syndrome. *Med Care.* 1993;31:569–580.

13. Rapkin BD, Smith MY. Assessment of functional status in persons with HIV infection. In: O'Dell M, ed. HIV-related Disability: Assessment and Management. Physical Medicine and Rehabilitation: State of the Art Reviews. Vol 7. Philadelphia: Hanley & Belfus; 1993: S43-72.

14. Lawton MP. Environment and the needs satisfaction of the elderly. In: Carstensen LL, Edelstein BA, eds: Handbook of Clinical Gerontology. New York: Pergamon; 1987:32–42.

15. Revicki DA, Brown RE, Henry DH. Recombinant human ery-thropoietin and health-related quality of life of AIDS patients with anemia. *J Acquir Immune Defic Syndr.* 1994;7:474–484.

16. Bozzette SA, Hays RD, Berry SH, et al. Derivation and prop-erties of a brief health status assessment instrument for use in HIV disease. *J Acquir Immune Defic Syndr Hum Retrovirol.* 1995;8(3):253–265.

17. Tarlov AR, Ware JE, Greenfield S, et al. Medical Outcomes Study: An application of methods for evaluating the results of medical care. *JAMA.* 1989;262:907–913.

18. Watchel T, Piette J, Mor V. Quality of life in persons with hu-man immunodeficiency virus infection: Measurement by the Medical Outcomes Study instrument. *Ann Intern Med.* 1992;116:129–137.

19. Wu AW, Rubin IM, Matthews WC, et al. A health status ques-tionnaire using 30 items from the Medical Outcomes Study: Preliminary validation in persons with early HIV infection. *Med Care.* 1991;29:786–798.

20. Hays RD, Shapiro MF. An overview of generic health-related quality of life measures for HIV research. *Qual Life Res.* 1992;1:91–97.

21. Berry SH, Bozzette SA, Hays R, et al. Measuring health sta-tus in advanced HIV disease: Results from a primary PCP prophylaxis trial. Paper presented at the HIV international conference on AIDS, Florence, Italy, June 1991.

22. Galantino ML, McCormack GL. Pain management. In: Galantino ML, ed: Clinical Assessment and Treatment in HIV. Thorofare, NJ: Slack; 1992:101–114.

23. Galantino ML, Brewer M. Peripheral neuropathies associ-ated with AIDS: A case study in pain management. *Occup Ther Forum.* Valley Forge Press: July 24, 1989, p 11.

24. Galantino ML, Lewis A, Spence D. Physical medicine man-agement of HIV patients. In: Nursing Care of the Person With AIDS/ARC. Rockville, MD: Aspen; 1988.

25. Fields JL, ed. Pain. New York: McGraw-Hill, 1987.

26. Lasange L. Pain and its management. *Hosp Pract (Off Ed).* 1986;21:92.

27. Fordyce WE. Pain and suffering: A reappraisal. *Am Psychol* 1988;43:276.

28. Geden E, Lower M, Beattie S, Beck N. Effects of music and imagery on physiologic and self-report of analogued labor pain. *Nurs Res.* 1989;38:37.

29. Yao JH. Acupuncture, TENS, and accupressure. *Acuther Postgrad Semin.* Libertyville, IL: 1990;1–13.

30. Cornblath DR, McArthur JC. Predominantly sensory neuropathy in patients with AIDS and AIDS-related complex. *Neurology.* 1988;38:794.

31. Cornblath DR, McArthur JC, Kennedy PGE. Inflammatory demyelinating peripheral neuropathies associated with human T-cell lymphotrophic virus type III infection. *Ann Neurol.* 1986;21:23.

32. McDowell D. The patient in the home setting. In: Galantino ML, ed: Clinical Assessment and Treatment in HIV: Rehabilitation of a Chronic Illness, Thorofare, NJ: Slack; 1992: 180–183.

33. Simpson DM, Wolfe DE. Neuromuscular complications of HIV infection and its treatment. *AIDS.* 1991;5:917.

34. Louis W, Doyle A, Anaveker A. Plasma noradrenaline concentrate and blood pressure in essential hypertension, pheochromocytoma, and depression. *Clin Sci.* 1975;48:239.

35. Livnat S, Felten S, Carlson S, et al. Involvement of peripheral and central catecholamine systems in neural immune interactions. *J Neuroimminol.* 1985;10:5.

36. Dalkas MC, Pezeshkpour GH. Neuromuscular diseases associated with human immunodeficiency virus infection. *Ann Neurol.* 1988;23(suppl):S38–S48.

37. Hanson P, Flaherty D. Immunological responses to training in conditional runners. *Clin Sci.* 1981;60:225.

38. Hedefors E, Holm G, Ivansen M, et al. Physiological variation of blood lymphocyte reactivity: T-cell subsets, immunoglobulin production, and mixed lymphocyte reactivity. *Clin Immunol Immunopathol.* 1983;27:9.

39. Targan S, Britcan L, Dorey F. Activation of human NKCC by moderate exercise: Increased frequency of NK cells with enhanced capability of effector-target lytic interactions. *Clin Exp Immunol.* 1981;45:352.

40. Piette JD, Mor V, Fleishman JA. Patterns of survival with AIDS in the United States. *Health Survey Res* 1991;26:75–95.

41. O'Dell MW, Dillon ME. Rehabilitation in adults with human immunodeficiency virus-related diseases. *Am J Phys Med Rehabil.* 1992;71:183–190.

42. Evashwick CJ, Weiss LJ. Managing the Continuum of Care. Rockville, MD: Aspen; 1987.

43. Lutgendorf S, Antoni MK, Schneiderman N, Fletcher MA. Psychosocial counseling to improve quality of life in HIV infection. *Patient Educ Counsel.* 1994;24: 217–235.

twenty

Resources

Cody Patton

HIV and AIDS resources have become an integral part of daily living for those living with HIV and those working in the field. The list of resources included here is only a small sampling of what is available. To begin your own working resource list, contact the National AIDS Hotline and your state or local hotline. Keep track of contacts made at workshops and meetings. Make note of names of services, health care providers, and clinics serving HIV-infected patients. Inform patients that contacts are supportive and available to serve them.

AGENCIES

Academy for Educational Development
1255 23rd Street, NW, Washington, DC 20037
202–884-8855; fax 202–884-8713

AIDS Action Council
2033 M Street, NW, Ste. 802, Washington, DC 20036
202–293-1600

AIDS Clinical Trials
800–874-2572; fax 301–738-6616

American Medical Association
Department of HIV, 515 N State Street, Chicago,
IL 60610
312–464-5460

American Red Cross, HIV/AIDS Education Office
1709 New York Avenue, NW, Ste. 208, Washington,
DC 20006
202–434-4007

**Being Alive/People With HIV/AIDS Action
Coalition**
3626 Sunset Boulevard, Los Angeles, CA 90026
213–667-3262; fax 213–667-2735

Centers for Disease Control and Prevention
1600 Clifton Road, NE MSA24, Atlanta, GA 30333
404–639-0975; fax 404–639-0973

Gay and Lesbian Medical Association
211 Church Street, Ste. C, San Francisco, CA 94114
415–255-4547

Gay Men's Health Crisis
129 West 20th Street, New York, NY 10011
212–807-6664

**The NAMES Project Foundations AIDS Memorial
Quilt**
310 Townsend St., Ste. 310, San Francisco, CA 94107
415–882-5500; fax 415–882-6200

National AIDS Clearinghouse
P.O. Box 6003, Rockville, MD 20850
800–458-5231

National AIDS Hotline
800–342-AIDS (English), 800–344-SIDA (Spanish),
800–243-7889 (TTY/TDD).

National Alliance of State and Territorial AIDS Directors
444 North Capitol Street, NW, Ste. 706, Washington, DC 20001–1512
202–434-8090; fax 202–434-8092

National Association of People with AIDS
1413 K Street, NW, 7th Floor, Washington, DC 20005
202–898-0414; fax 202–898-0435

National Minority AIDS Council
1931 13th Street, NW, Washington, DC 20002
202–483-NMAC; fax 202–483-1153

Pediatric AIDS Foundation
1311 Colorado Avenue, Santa Monica, CA 90404
310–395-9051; fax 310–395-5149

Project Inform
1965 Market Street, Ste. 220, San Francisco, CA 94103
800–822-7422; fax 415–558-0684

DRUG MANUFACTURERS

Abbott
800–328-0255
Clarithromycin/Biaxin, Ritonavir/Norvir

Amgen
800–272-9376
G-CSF/Neupogen

Astra
800–488-3247
Foscarnet/Foscavir

Bristol-Myers Squibb
800–426-7644
d4T/Zerit, ddI/Videx, Megestrol acetate/Megace

Fujisawa
800–366-6323
Aerosolized pentamidine/Nebupent

GlaxoWellcome
800–722-9294
Acyclovir/Zovirax, Atovaquone/Mepron,
AZT/Retrovir, Pyrimethamine/Daraprim,
TMP\SMZ/Septra, 3TC/Epivir

Hoffmann-La Roche
800–285-4484
ddC/Hivid, Ganciclovir/Cytoven, Interferon alpha-
2A/Roferon, Saquinavir/Invirase, TMP\SMZ/
Bactrim

Immunex
800–321-4669
GM-CSF/Luekine

Janssen
800–544-2987
Itraconazole/Sporonox, Ketoconazole/Nizoral

Merck
800–927-8888
Indinavir/Crixivan

Ortho Biotech
800–553-3851
Erythropoetin/Procrit

Pfizer
800–869-9979
Fluconazole/Diflucan, Azithromycin/Zithromax

Pharmacia & Upjohn
800–438–5224
Rifabutin/Mycobutin

Roxane Labs
800–274-8651
Dronabinol/Marinol

Sequus
800–375-1658
Doxorubicin/Doxil

INTERNET RESOURCES

Selected AIDS Resources on the World Wide Web
Comment: Provides a regularly updated list of AIDS and
HIV sites on the World Wide Web. Hyperlink availability
to governmental agencies (eg, CDC, NIH) that provide
HIV-related services.
http://www.tulane.edu/~zeller/aidsres.html

AIDS Treatment Data Network
Comment: Provides information about treatments for
HIV and AIDS.
http://www.aidsnyc.org/network/index.html

AIDS Publications
Comment: Provides listing of timely AIDS treatment
publications.
http://www.critpath.org/pubs.htm

AIDS Treatment News
Comment: AIDS Treatment News reports on experimental
and standard treatments, especially those available now.
http://www.thebody.com/atn/atnpage.html

HIV/AIDS Treatment Related Resources on the Internet
Comment: Provides listing of HIV/AIDS Treatment
Resources.
http://galen.library.ucsf.edu/aidstrials/resources.html

**Index to Project Inform HIV/AIDS Treatment
Information**
Comment: Provides a wide range of HIV/AIDS-related
treatment information with an index of almost 600
individual subject headings.
http://www.projinf.org/offlinc.html

HIV/AIDS Treatment Information Service
Comment: The HIV/AIDS Treatment Information
Service (ATIS) provides information about federally
approved treatment guidelines for HIV and AIDS.
http://hivatis.org/

Alternative Treatments
Comment: Alternative, complementary, and
unconventional approaches to HIV/AIDS treatment are
provided.
http://www.critpath.org/alt.htm

The National AIDS Treatment Advocacy Project
Comment: The National AIDS Treatment Advocacy
Project advocates on treatment and policy issues for
people with HIV and AIDS with drug companies,
governmental officials (including the FDA) and other
treatment and policy advocates.
http://www.aidsnyc.org/natap/

Glossary: Drugs and Treatments
Comment: Provides a glossary of terms commonly
referred to in HIV/AIDS treatment.
http://www.aidsnyc.org/network/drugloss.html

RELIGIOUS ORGANIZATIONS

AIDS Advocacy in African American Churches Project
611 Pennsylvania Ave, SE, Ste. 359, Washington, DC
20003
202–546-8587; fax 202–546-8867

**AIDS Ministry Network—Christian Church (Disciples
of Christ)**
P.O. Box 4188, East Lansing, MI 48826
517–355-9324; fax 517–432-2662

AIDS National Interfaith Network
110 Maryland Avenue, NE, Ste. 504, Washington, DC 20002
202–546-0807; 800–288-9619

Americans for a Sound AIDS/HIV Policy
P.O. Box 17433, Washington, DC 20041
703–471-7350

Brethren Mennonite AIDS Hotline
44 N Queen St., Lancaster, PA 17503
717–394-3380

Christian AIDS Services Alliance
P.O. Box 3612, San Rafael, CA 94912-3612
410–268-3442

Congress of National Black Churches
1225 Eye Street, NW, Ste. 750, Washington, DC 20005-3914
202–371-1091

Lutheran AIDS Network
Holy Cross Lutheran Church, 1165 Seville Drive, Pacifica, CA 94044
415–359-2710

National Catholic AIDS Network
P.O. Box 422984, San Francisco, CA 94142-2984
707–874-3031; fax 707–874-1433

National Episcopal AIDS Coalition
2025 Pennsylvania Ave., NW, Ste. 508, Washington, DC 20006-1813
202–628-6628

Presbyterian AIDS Network
3060A Presbyterian Ctr., 100 Witherspoon St., Louisville, KY 40202-1396
502–569-5794

Seventh-day Adventist Kinship International
P.O. Box 7320, Laguna Niguel, CA 92607
714–248-1299

Southern Baptist Convention
Christian Life Commission, 901 Commerce, Ste. 550,
Nashville, TN 37203
615–244-2495

Union of American Hebrew Congregations/Central Conference of American Rabbis
Joint Committee on AIDS, 75 2nd Ave., Ste. 550,
Needham Heights, MA 02194
617–449-0404; fax 617–449-0419

United Church AIDS/HIV Network
700 Prospect Ave., Cleveland, OH 44115
216–736-3270; fax 216–736-3263

United Methodist HIV/AIDS Ministries Network
475 Riverside Drive, Room 350, New York, NY 10115
212–870-3909; fax 212–749-2641

Unitarian Universalist Association AIDS Resources Network
25 Beacon Street, Boston, MA 02108-2800
617–742-2100; fax 617–523-4123

Universal Fellowship of Metropolitan Community Churches AIDS Ministry
5300 Santa Monica Blvd., Ste. 304, Los Angeles, CA 90029
213–464-5100; fax 213–464-2123

STATE HOTLINES

Alabama	800–228-0469
Alaska	800–478-2437
Arizona	800–342-2437
Arkansas	800–448-8305

California	North	800–367-2437
	South	800–922-2437
Colorado	State	800–252-2437
	Denver	303–333-4336
Connecticut		800–342-2437
Delaware		800–422-0429
District of Columbia		202–332-2437
	Spanish/TDD	202–332-2192
Florida	Business	305–326-8833
	Dade Cnty	305–634-4636
	Non-English	305–326-5148
	Statewide	800–352-2437
	TTY	305–545-5151
Georgia	Statewide	800–551-2728
	Atlanta	404–876-9944
Hawaii	Oahu	800–922-1313
	Other islands	800–321-1555
Idaho		800–833-2437
		202–345-2277
Illinois		800–243-2437
Indiana		800–848-2437
Iowa		800–445-2437
Kansas		800–342-2437
Kentucky		800–654-2437
Louisiana		800–992-4379
Maine		800–851-2437
Maryland	Statewide	800–638-6252
	Teen	301–945-2437
Massachusetts		800–750-2016
Michigan		800–872-2437
Minnesota		800–248-2437
		612–373-2437

Mississippi		800–537-0851
Missouri		800–533-2437
		800–337-2437
		314–516-2761
Montana		800–233-6668
Nebraska		800–782-2437
Nevada		800–842-2437
New Hampshire		800–872-8909
New Jersey		800–624-2377
New Mexico		800–545-2437
New York	Statewide	800–541-2437
	NY City	212–447-8200
	Spanish	800–233-7432
North Carolina		800–342-2437
North Dakota		800–472-2180
Ohio		800–332-2437
Oklahoma		800–535-2437
Oregon		800–777-2437
		503–223-2437
Pennsylvania	Statewide	800–662-6080
	Philadelphia	215–732-2437
Puerto Rico		809–765-1010
Rhode Island		800–235-2331
South Carolina		800–322-2437
South Dakota		800–592-1861
Tennessee		800–525-2437
Texas	Statewide	800–299-2437
	TDD	800–252-8012
	Health Prof.	800–548-4659
Utah		800–366-2437
Vermont		800–882-2437

Virginia		800–533-4138
Virgin Islands		809–773-2437
Washington		800–272-2437
		304–558-2950
West Virginia		800–642-8244
Wisconsin	Statewide	800–334-2437
	Milwaukee	414–273-2437
Wyoming		800–327-3577

INDEX

Other HIV/AIDS Titles
Published by Appleton & Lange

HIV & AIDS: An Interactive Curriculum for Health Sciences

Using all the capabilities of high quality interactive video, sound, and graphics, this program, available in either CD-ROM or interactive videodisc format, covers virtually all aspects of HIV and AIDS.

Macintosh/Windows™/Windows™ 95 compatible
CD-ROM Edition, 4 CD-ROMs, ISBN 0-8385-3780-4, A3780-2
Videodisc Edition, Interactive Videodisc Equipment Required,
ISBN 0-8385-3778-2, A3778-6

AIDS Compact Library

Full text and tables of more than 10,000 AIDS-related articles and 115,000 abstracts and citations from major journals and databases. All on one CD-ROM!

Macintosh/Windows™/Windows™ 95 compatible
ISBN 0-8385-0296-2, A0296-2, (Individual)
ISBN 0-8385-0297-0, A0297-0, (Institution)

AIDS Textbooks on CD-ROM

Textbook of AIDS Medicine, *Pediatric AIDS, 2/e*, and *The Johns Hopkins Hospital Guide to Medical Care of Patients with HIV Infection, 3/e* on one CD-ROM, with full text, tables, and images (some in color).

Macintosh/Windows™/Windows™ 95 compatible
ISBN 0-8385-0177-X, A0177-4 (Individual)
ISBN 0-8385-0298-9, A0298-8, (Institution)

HIV/AIDS Primary Care Handbook

Carmichael et al.

Written by two family physicians and a renowned AIDS specialist, this practical book offers straightforward, concise, and complete guidelines for the ambulatory care of
HIV-infected and AIDS patients.

1994, 228 pp., Spiral, ISBN 0-8385-3557-7, A3557-4

(more on reverse)

CMDT 1997

CURRENT Medical Diagnosis & Treatment 1997

CURRENT Medical Diagnosis & Treatment 1997
Thirty-sixth Edition
a LANGE medical book

Lawrence M. Tierney, Jr., MD
Stephen J. McPhee, MD
Maxine A. Papadakis, MD
all of University of California, San Francisco

The leading annually updated primary care text,
CURRENT Medical Diagnosis & Treatment 1997 is the most
comprehensive, reliable, and timely reference available to
answer common questions in everyday clinical practice.
CMDT 1997 thoroughly covers all aspects of primary care,
including gynecology, obstetrics, urology, dermatology,
psychiatry, neurology, otolaryngology, ophthalmology, and
nutrition.
1997, Paperback, 1587 pp., ISBN 0-8385-1489-8, A1489-2

CMDT 1997 on CD-ROM
A Multimedia Resource for Primary Care

NEW!

Stephen J. McPhee, MD
Maxine A. Papadakis, MD
Lawrence M. Tierney, Jr., MD
all of University of California, San Francisco
Ralph Gonzales, MD
University of Colorado Health Sciences Center, Denver

This **expanded multimedia CD-ROM edition** of the
bestselling **CMDT** contains all the text, tables, and figures of
CMDT 1997, enhanced by color photos, video, and audio, plus
hypertext linking to two popular LANGE pocket guides, and
more!
1997, IBM/MAC Compatible CD-ROM, ISBN 0-8385-1480-4, A1480-1

**To order, or for more information,
visit your local health science bookstore, or
call Appleton & Lange toll free at 1-800-423-1359.**